Indian Women
of Early Mexico

Indian Women
of Early Mexico

Edited by
Susan Schroeder,
Stephanie Wood, and
Robert Haskett

University of Oklahoma Press : Norman and London

This book is published with the generous assistance of
The Kerr Foundation, Inc.

Library of Congress Cataloging-in-Publication Data

Indian women of early Mexico / edited by Susan Schroeder, Stephanie
Wood, and Robert Haskett.
    p. cm.
    Includes bibliographical references and index.
    ISBN 0-8061-2970-0 (alk. paper)
    1. Indian women—Mexico—History—Sources. 2. Indian women—
Mexico—Ethnic identity. 3. Indian women—Mexico—Social conditions.
4. Ethnohistory—Mexico. 5. Mexico—Social life and customs. I. Schroeder,
Susan, 1939– . II. Wood, Stephanie, 1954– . III. Haskett, Robert
Stephen, 1952– .
F1219.3.W6153   1997
305.48'897072—dc21   97-8450
                                                                                        CIP

Text design by Debora Hackworth. Text set in Palatino.

The paper in this book meets the guidelines for permanence and durability
of the Committee on Production Guidelines for Book Longevity of the
Council on Library Resources, Inc. ⊗

1 2 3 4 5 6 7 8 9 10

Contents

Illustrations

Maps

Figures

Tables

Acknowledgments

The editors wish to thank the administrations and staffs of the many archives and repositories in Mexico, the United States, and Europe who have facilitated our research, including Mexico's Archivo General de la Nación, the Archivo Histórico of the Museo Nacional de Antropología e Historia, and the Biblioteca Nacional. We are also grateful for the insights offered by many friends and colleagues as this book developed over the course of the last decade; the perceptive reading and challenging suggestions of the anonymous reviewers of the completed manuscript were particularly valuable. It is fitting as well that along with a number of contributors we acknowledge and express our sincere appreciation for the training and guidance received from James Lockhart. Many of the chapters in this collection are an informed reflection of enduring inspiration from past collaboration. Bill Nelson made sense of the odds and ends of our sketches and produced all our maps with consummate speed and skill. And Wanda Sala, secretary in Loyola's Department of History, in particular warrants recognition for her diligence, patience, and good nature as she typed and retyped the various incarnations of the manuscript over the years. Another dozen trees will be planted in Mexico as compensation, albeit small, for all the paper spent in the production of this work. Finally, we are appreciative of the interest and assiduity of Editor-in-Chief John Drayton and Managing Editor Sarah Nestor at the University of Oklahoma Press, as well as free-lance editor Sheila Berg, who brought this longtime undertaking to fruition.

Indian Women
of Early Mexico

Early Mexico

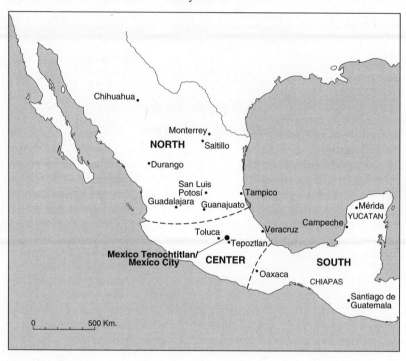

Chihuahua

Monterrey
NORTH Saltillo

Durango

San Luis
Potosí
Guadalajara Guanajuato

Tampico

Mérida
YUCATAN

Campeche

Veracruz

Toluca
Tepoztlan

Mexico Tenochtitlan/
Mexico City CENTER

SOUTH

Oaxaca

CHIAPAS

Santiago de
Guatemala

0   500 Km.

Introduction

Susan Schroeder

This collection of investigations into the histories of Indian women in early Mexico has been brought together to serve several purposes: to abrogate the stereotype of indigenous women as being without history; to furnish complement and counterpoise to other studies of North American Indians and bring to light the voices and recorded histories of Mexican natives; and to exemplify the richness and complexity of the lives of indigenous peoples through scholarly historical analyses.[1] Above all, we seek to reveal native women in the context of their societies, by focusing on life experiences in an evolving cultural continuum representative of several regions of Mexico. Indeed, while ethnicities may vary and roles change, because of the wealth of the sources and the extraordinary advantage of a precedent of native-language record keeping, it is evident that Indian women were not only coprogenitors of their histories but also active participants in influencing the direction those histories would take.

This project began more than a decade ago. In the course of analyzing writings by the seventeenth-century Nahua historian Chimalpahin, I realized that although it was his purpose to exalt the kings of ancient Mexico, much that was unsaid ultimately revealed that women, obviously neither invisible nor silent, as mothers, wives, sisters, and daughters, had almost as much to do with the formation and perpetuation of royalty and rulerdom as did their male counterparts.[2] And some women ruled as full-fledged queens.[3] At the time I first worked on this subject there were few substantive comparative pieces in the historiography based on native-language sources. Intrigued, I began to ask colleagues for information about native women in their research.[4] This tome is the product of those studies.

At least eight of us were students of James Lockhart, whose Monday evening sessions in Nahuatl (and later Yucatec Maya) greatly facilitated our endeavors in ethnohistory and the New Philology.[5] Others represent different scholarly schools and disciplines and thus bring great expertise and balance to the project. Anticipating assertions that only females can write about women and only Indians can write indigenous history,[6] we have sought to be as inclusive as possible, with nearly equal numbers of men and women contributing essays. And we invite all students and colleagues to engage themselves in studying the languages, paleographies, and multivarious cultures of early Mexico. The archives abound![7]

The Histories and the Sources

Few, if any, of the extant indigenous sources were actually written by Indian women, although there is evidence that women participated in the manufacture of pictographic manuscripts during the pre-Hispanic period.[8] Unfortunately, this charge did not carry over to the colonial era. But while women were not necessarily the authors, this in no way diminishes their critical and evident contributions to their societies. Certainly both female and male *huehuetque* (Nahuatl: elders, sages) were historians. Known also as "ancestors," *totahuan tonanhuan* (our fathers our mothers), they were the repositories of wisdom, values, and experience, and together they were essential to each generation's understanding of the past, present, and future. Among the Nahuas of central Mexico, each kingdom or ethnic state (*altepetl*) had its own record keepers (*tlacuiloque*, "writers," "painters") who were responsible for official accounts, essentially pictographic images that prompted oral recitation and often song performances for public edification. Typically ethnocentric, men and women elders imparted what they wanted to be remembered about the social and political marvels of their particular state. The Nahuatl annals that exist today are in many instances transliterations to alphabetic script of the pictographs and oral accounts that were in circulation during the colonial period. Discrepancies in the various collections of annals reflect the micropatriotism and personalism of each altepetl's elders.[9] Once collated and translated, comparisons of altepetl histories will furnish new insights into the wide range of female activities represented, from women as creator-deities or vengeful concubines to their more quotidian roles as mothers, wives, and daughters in their households.[10] While these documents most typically deal with elite women, much information can be extrapolated about women of lower rank. They figure in our more mundane and abundant sources.

We do not intend to limit our discussion to the Nahua women and men of central Mexico. But as a prototype for indigenous history and literacy, the Nahuas serve well. The Mayas and the Mixtecs kept pictographic records too, while most other American Indians relied on oral transmission for their literary traditions. It took a generation or so after the arrival of the Europeans for painter-historian Nahuas under the tutelage of the clergy to make the transition to Roman alphabetic writing. In 1503, even before the Spanish conquest of Mexico, the crown mandated that the natives be taught to read and write and to be good Christians.[11] In truth, there was hardly even a fine line between secular and ecclesiastical pedagogical policies. Moreover, from this time forward the well-defined and often quite complementary gender roles as they were known for the pre-Hispanic era changed, and native women in general experienced a diminishing presence in traditional social spheres. The Church, especially, was instrumental in promulgating ambiguous attitudes, and women became its scapegoats when proselytization efforts were not realized. Throughout the colonial period, even though they were the more fervent churchgoers, in neither educational nor evangelistic programs did Indian women enjoy particular priority.[12] Of course, we cannot speak for all groups, but what is remarkable and especially evident in the essays in this volume is the extraordinary capacity of native women for accommodation, cultural conservatism, and survival in the face of catastrophic change and seemingly insurmountable obstacles.[13]

Colonial Native American Accounts by Spaniards

We are fortunate to have detailed information about Mexico's Indians dating almost from their first contacts with Spaniards (for the role of Indian women, especially that of Malinche, during those initial encounters, see Frances Karttunen's discussion in chapter 14). Letters and chronicles by the conqueror Hernando Cortés are invaluable, as are reports by men in his company.[14] Cortés immediately recognized the riches of North America and its benefits for the Spanish crown and wrote to the king asking for clergy to support his endeavors with Catholic evangelism.

Thousands of women and men were subsequently baptized, but it is likely that theirs was at best a nominal conversion to Catholicism. There was much simulation of Christian ritual as an overlay to traditional religious beliefs. Thus the friars began to collect information about the Indians' ways of doing things in order to eliminate what they viewed as idolatry and other practices that impeded their efforts at proselytization. Here as elsewhere, both women and men were targeted for their roles as religious intermediaries and healers who invoked spirits to restore an individual's, their own, or the community's well-being—all-important, sacred techniques that were passed down through generations along gendered lines.[15] Some Spanish priests compiled native-language vocabularies and grammars to improve their own linguistic skills and facilitate communication with the Indians.[16] Other religious wrote histories in addition to ecclesiastical treatises in native languages for use during Mass, in the confessional, and for catechism.[17] Of great utility were the *huehuetlatolli* (discourses by the elders), which elaborated on social and political protocols of the past and most often were cast in the eloquent high Nahuatl speech forms of both women and men, furnishing examples of rhetoric, dialogue, and interpersonal relations.[18] The friars were quick to make use of the huehuetlatolli, selectively incorporating both the style and the content into Christian sermons for their native congregations (see chapter 2 for Nahuatl-language examples in English translation). Most notable of all the friars' endeavors is the Nahua ethnography by the Franciscan Bernardino de Sahagún, a twelve-volume bilingual compendium of information about Nahua culture.[19] Among all native peoples of the Americas no records are as comprehensive, varied, or sophisticated as those produced under religious auspices in Mexico during the sixteenth century. Subsequently, colonial indigenous literacy took on a life of its own that was realized in a range of genres and lasted until Mexico's independence from Spain.

All friars depended on the Indians as informants, translators, and artists, and occasionally these men are identified by name. Alas, although indigenous women surely figured as importantly as men as subjects in such investigative enterprises, none was listed among the collaborators. Nor did any focus on women alone, in spite of the great numbers of texts produced. Nevertheless, there is abundant evidence in native-language form and content of the important roles that women played in Mesoamerican society.

In one sense the implicit presence of women in texts speaks to gender complementarity, but the topic calls for culling and analysis of these same sources for additional knowledge of perceptions and self-perceptions of women. Note that it is not our wish to portray pre-Hispanic societies as either ideal or static, that is, to assert that change in the Americas can be attributed solely to contacts with Europeans. Rather, we support a processual approach to the subject, with contemporaneous and parallel histories of peoples in Spain and Mexico converging at different levels and at different times with varying outcomes. Most informative is Natalie Zemon Davis's study of the cultural interaction of Iroquois and French women in New France during the seventeenth century, which corroborates her earlier work. As Davis states, "There is always both gain and loss in the process of change."[20]

Colonial Native American Accounts by Indians

As prescribed, the friars established schools for Indian children that turned out to be quite like schools during the Aztec era, with gender roles specific to each corresponding curriculum.[21] Additionally, the Franciscans with considerable enthusiasm established a special *colegio* (secondary school) for the sons of Indian nobility where courses in Latin, rhetoric, philosophy, and theology were also offered. The friars anticipated that graduates would be models of Spanish Christian virtue and assume leadership roles in church and government. As might be expected, boys fared much better than girls in schooling endeavors. While few young native men became seminarians or priests, many did become exemplars of indigenous society in Mexico City and its environs, carrying on the tradition of literacy and leadership as notaries, translators, and government and church officials.

Soon Indian males coupled their writing skills with other Spanish borrowings to further conserve key elements of their culture. There are many examples, produced in native languages or Spanish or both: testaments, petitions, censuses, bills of sale, and *poder* (power of attorney) and *cabildo* (city council) records, to name a few. The agency of women is reflected repeatedly in such documents, as they carried out business transactions, registered protests against transgressions, or hired notaries to record their wills so as to secure their legacies for their heirs.[22] In 1585 an Indian court, the General Indian Court of New Spain, was established to help adjudicate indigenous legal matters.[23] In churches literate Indians took responsibility for all sorts of duties: keeping financial accounts of revenues; marriage, baptismal, and death records; and *cofradía* (confraternity) membership lists and activities. Here too women were active, but while their names appear, they do not sign the documents, putting the mark of a cross instead. We are not certain of their literacy.

Other Indians were hired as copyists of Spanish- and native-language materials, and some even began to generate their own holographic accounts. Again, it was patriotism for their local communities that was the stimulus for these histories, and several were authored by mestizo sons of former nobility who wrote (in Spanish) glorious accounts about their hometowns.[24] The aforementioned historian Chimalpahin was, however, culturally entirely Nahua and of nonelite origin. Writing in the 1620s, he had witnessed devastating changes in his Indian world. He was nevertheless optimistic and wrote in his own language for an Indian readership. He too wrote pridefully about his home region, but he kept to the native style and produced annals of epic proportion about social and political developments that cover close to one thousand years and treat numerous peoples in Mexico. Women as well as men play key roles throughout these valuable records.[25]

Indian Women in the Colonial Era: Education and the Church

The friars' educational programs for Indian girls lasted scarcely a decade.[26] Apparently, family and other social pressures prevailed, for few girls wanted to pattern themselves after their austere, pious teachers, the Spanish *beatas* (lay female religious) recruited as instructors. As with the boys, Indian girls were to assume strict Spanish Christian attributes and, when mature, by their good example train other girls.[27] Just why the friars were so quick to abandon the education of Indian girls and women is not clear. Medieval theologies elicited conflictive attitudes on the part of the clergy, which certainly were a factor. Perceiving women as intrinsically the source of all evil, ecclesiastics necessarily exercised great caution in their dealings with them. But Indian women were also important mediums for instilling Hispanic values in their families, and the friars labored to relegate women's influence and activities to domestic-centered functions exclusively.[28] Already responsible for tending the home fires, their households were conceptualized as living-life centers, a realm of traditional activity poorly understood by men of the cloth.

Not surprisingly, not all women were brought into the fold,[29] and even when they accepted the sacraments many aspects of indigenous culture remained unchanged. Women's resistance, in its various forms, the *ars subtilior*, then, may explain at least in part the absence of any convent in New Spain for Indian nuns until 1724,[30] and it was not until 1753 that a colegio for young native women was established, this time by the Jesuits. Prejudice against them continued, as revealed in a report in 1814 by fray Jacinto López, the nuns' chaplain at their Corpus Christi *"monasterio,"* as he completed his years of tenure at the convent: "There never were nor are there now any intellectuals in Corpus Christi; it is nothing more than a community of simple and holy Indian nuns."[31] (It is possible that the friar might have said the same about Hispanic nuns, just because they were women.) These indigenous women did know Latin, and some definitely knew how to write, as is apparent in their petitions, licenses, and other record books. Of course, most informative would be an inventory of the books, theater pieces, and music scores in Corpus Christi's library.

Convent life for Indians was quite like that of their creole sisters. Their charge was piety and charity, and as religious they followed prescribed routines, which included writing saints' biographies as well as biographies of one another. Pageants, plays, and musical performances were not uncommon within the cloisters.[32] Admittance was determined by *limpieza de sangre* (purity of blood; here, no racial mixture), which kept the convent exclusively for native women (much to the chagrin of creole women). The names of a few Indian nuns have come to us, but their writings remain anonymous.[33] The registers show that novices still took pride in polity and family, listing patronymics and noble affiliations, but these women seem to have relinquished most other indigenous characteristics on taking the veil.[34] We cannot know for certain, however.

Denied the standard opportunities for social mobility and prestige afforded by an education and still enjoyed by Indian men, doubtless native women pursued avenues other than those associated with formal political and church structures to maintain the integrity of their place in colonial society. Archival evidence indicates that many Indian women did not hesitate to resort to legal devices for whatever reasons, even representing their husbands in court (as treated by Susan Kellogg in chapter 5). Others found social outlets and recognition in cofradía activities. Regarding the latter, essentially Church-affiliated lay organizations designed for social welfare, the façade and perhaps the fact were that women eventually took on numerous Church-related duties, which surely pleased the clergy but which were intended to enhance the well-being of indigenous corporate institutions within colonial communities as well.[35] Men, of course, were active too, but the cofradía could serve as a household writ large, through the provision of food, clothing, shelter, medicine, and even mourning and preparation for burials—most of which was women's work anyway.

A good example of Indian women investing much time and energy in such self- and community-serving projects even into the late eighteenth century is a cofradía associated with the church (the Xacalteopan, "straw-topped temple") at the Jesuits' secondary school for Indian boys, the Colegio de San Gregorio, on the *traza* (central district for Spaniards) in Mexico City. Here, in the Congregación de la Buena Muerte (1710–67),[36] both women and men were listed and ranked by office and title similar to positions familiar during the pre-Hispanic era.[37] Most often women outnumbered men, and we have the names and proveniences for the entire officer membership, which at times could be counted in the hundreds. Jesuit (and therefore not parish-based) women's activities included overseeing the health and welfare of their constituents in local neighborhoods as well as recruitment in faraway towns.

Jesuits not uncommonly reconstituted native rituals in their Indian colegios, and at San Gregorio they combined indigenous language, song, instrumental music, dance, and dress with Catholic ceremonies.[38] For this reason it is not surprising that each year dozens of Indian *ichpochtin*, or *doncellas* (maidens, young women), were distinguished with titles and the office of *tlachpanque* (sweepers) for the church's chapel.[39] "Sweeping" (then and even today) in Mexico was a highly charged symbolic, gendered role for females, serving to maintain the equilibrium of the Indian universe (see especially Louise M. Burkhart's discussion of "sweeping" in chapter 1). The girls, in a sense latter-day Aztec temple priestesses, in this instance must have enjoyed a positive association with the priests, for the latter were responsible for establishing the first secondary school for Indian females, the Colegio de Indias Doncellas de Nuestra Señora de Guadalupe, in 1753, located just down the street from San Gregorio. It was no doubt apparent by this time that traditional prerogatives of Indian women seldom interfered with the vital contributions they made to their societies as a whole.

This overview of Mexican sources offers both background and a sampling of the evidence for histories about Indian women. As is well known, the accounts were written by men,[40] some celibate and deliberately biased,[41] and much of the production was in a colonial context.[42] Nonetheless, by their own devices, Indian women, whether alone or collectively, in the city or beyond it, moved in, out of, and across different physical and cultural spheres, making the most of what was new or useful to suit what was appropriate to their circumstances.

At this stage and from the materials at hand, it is evident that the subject of Indian women's history is both vast and complex and that analyses based solely on paradigms of patriarchy with their built-in implications of women as subordinate, oppressed, passive, silent, lost, and so on, will prove incomplete;[43] nor can such constructs be generalized for all situations in early Mexico.

Our purpose is to know better the lives of Indian women, and we have drawn on preconquest precedents whenever possible and sampled ethnic populations from various regions of Mexico and over time. The ideal would be to contextualize all of this information and formulate patterns and generate comparisons among and between both indigenous groups and Hispanic populations. But Hispanic women seldom had experiences that approximated those of their indigenous counterparts (for reasons that become apparent in the following chapters). These investigations about indigenous women are formidable in their own right; interactive and comparative studies, at least for now, are beyond the scope of our design.

In addition, while each author focuses on a particular theme relating to the women being investigated, just how the subject manifests is completely dependent on the sources (or the scarcity thereof). Many topics are being researched for the first time, and an author's conclusions may seem tentative; in some cases, authors' conclusions may even contradict one another. In large part this speaks to the nascent character of studies about native women in early Mexico; but it says even more about the complexity of the field itself. All contributors have probed their sources thoroughly, looking for and finding both continuities and changes in the life experiences of the Indian women they are studying. Some have employed gender studies-related stereotypical terminology, such as equality, patriarchy, and gender complementarity, to accommodate gender-related ideological constructs and to interpret their findings. In these instances, such usages are defined by the authors and elaborated as appropriate to the material. Other authors have found little need for either stereotypical usages or "Western" theoretical models, instead allowing the subject and data to speak for themselves. Surely one of the many appeals of this collection of essays is the variety of approaches to a single scholarly purpose.

Identity, Ethnicity, and Gender Complementarity

For Mexican Indians during the pre-Hispanic era, identity and ethnicity were close to one and the same thing, for membership in an altepetl, *cah* (Yucatec Maya: municipality, or town), *yuhuitayu* (Mixtec: large sociopolitical unit; *yuhui*, "rulerdom"), or some sort of tribal unit determined who one was. And kinship and clan affinities prevailed over geographic location, for a polity or group could move or be conquered and yet the corporation stayed intact as long as traditional lineage and filial structures were operational. Individual Indians had names and tools and wore clothing appropriate to their sex,[44] but clothing designs could also signal membership in a particular polity. Of course, some individuals enjoyed high rank, and there were delineated roles within each unit, but both features were intended to elaborate and enhance one's place in the community, not compromise it.

Thus gender considerations were subordinate to pride of *patria*, and women's (and men's) identity was an aspect of the sociopolitical whole. For this reason, Western definitions of roles and gender per se have little usefulness when interpreting what might be comparable categories for Indians.[45] Even today numerous native women in North America put forth tribal affiliation as the principal criterion for defining themselves;[46] for some, territory is an important part of that concept as well. Supporting this perception is the first female principal chief of the Cherokee Nation Wilma Mankiller's reflection on returning to Oklahoma after many years in exile in California, "To think of myself outside the context of tribe or my family or my community would be very difficult."[47]

In Mexico the ethnopatriotism that was cause for so much history in the first place was eventually attenuated by Spanish political policies. For some time, however, altepetl identity and pride continued with little modification, for the *encomienda* (a grant to collect tribute or the use of labor from a particular indigenous group) and the *doctrina* (an ecclesiastical administrative unit, usually based on an indigenous sociopolitical entity) essentially depended on existing native corporate structures. Distinctions became clouded by the mid-sixteenth century when the crown, for administrative purposes, divided its American colonies into two culturally distinct and politically separate *repúblicas* (republics)—one for Spaniards and one for Indians (blacks, mestizos, mulattoes, and *castas*, or people of mixed race, generally were assigned to the republic of Spaniards).[48] Where once Indians of the Central Basin (and obviously elsewhere in Mexico) identified themselves by their tribes and ethnic states—*timexica* (we Mexica), *tichalca* (we Chalca), *titlatelolca* (we people of Tlatelolco), for example—they were soon, in fact, considered by the Spaniards as apolitical and homogeneous, and indeed some indigenes fashioned themselves thus. Resultant Nahuatl-language usage in their texts—*timacehualtin* (we commoners), *titlaca* (we people)—best describes indigenous self-perceptions, at least at certain levels as time passed.

But while the indigenous ethnic state may have lost ground, ethnicity and identity were realized in local communities where carryovers of political, social, and religious practices from earlier times had more opportunities for expression. Characteristically, the documents reveal that women and men unfailingly identified themselves by personal name (usually a baptismal name along with, at least for a while, an indigenous name or perhaps title) and by their *tlaxilacalli*, or indigenous neighborhood, reflecting an intensification of group commonality at a very local level yet with familiar patterns of differentiation.[49] Depending on the size of the town, one or several cofradías served similar purposes.[50] Yet individual Indian women seldom had official authority in any sphere. Legally, they enjoyed the rights and privileges that Spanish law allowed, and many took advantage of what the court offered so as to defend themselves and their families. For upper-class women, family and wealth and sometimes marriage to a Spaniard determined one's identity.[51] For the majority, however, even though overwhelmed by Spanish values and customs, native language and other cultural criteria continued to set the parameters for the indigenous system. That is not to say that pan-Indianism existed in any form other than an immediate corporate self-consciousness that included both women and men.

Absolute considerations of gender as a feminist construct are better left for a less comprehensive project.[52] Fray Bernardino's cognitive models for Aztec gender roles and "good" and "bad" behaviors, even when informed by Indians, followed medieval perceptions of what the world was like. That it was not a perfect place, neither in Europe nor in America, is readily apparent from the friar's categories as well as the many exceptions to prescriptive behaviors that appear in the sources.

The respective worldviews held by Europeans and Americans

differed radically, yet among the latter, while each tribe or state had its own particular philosophy about its place in the universe, there was generally more of a consensus regarding the holistic and complementary roles of males and females in each group's scheme of things. According to Jay Miller, "Men and women throughout the Americas thought of their lives and work as truly separate and equal (not but equal)."[53] In contrast to European patriarchal structures and paternal attitudes, we do not suppose a Native American *égalité* but rather emphasize the autonomous yet reciprocal nature of indigenous gendered roles.

Gender parallelism among indigenous peoples, however, by no means devolves to arbitrary categories for some roles were symbolic, others very practical. In Mesoamerica, for example, at birth males and females received gendered weapons, that is, power "tool kits," symbolic of what would be necessary for each child's life experiences (boys were given implements for war, girls received weaving swords and brooms).[54] As children and then as adults, their roles remained distinct but complementary as males and females alike waged war in equivalent spheres. Following Inga Clendinnen, "Relationships were revealed not through differentiation, but through permutations and transformations, and spoke more clearly of connection than opposition."[55]

Spanish political and religious institutions inevitably undermined many fundamental indigenous sociopolitical practices and in so doing offset, and in some instances destroyed, the cooperation between women and men. Gendered roles were restructured to follow Hispanic models, and Indian women especially were challenged to preserve order and their place in an often forbidding colonial milieu.

Women's resiliency is exemplified in Steve J. Stern's comparative study of gender relations in three regions of Mexico at the end of the colonial period. Stern's overarching concern is patriarchy with violence, and his focus is criminality among subaltern (however, not ethnic) peoples. Yet in a world of outrageous hardship and violence, he still finds complementarity of men's and women's roles, and even collusion for the advantage of the latter: "For reasons of self-protection and well-being women had to forge a culture of resistance that entangled male authority and pretense in the realm of the conditional."[56] By this time women's repertoires of resistance included fighting fire with fire.

History and Diversity among Indian Women of Mexico

For Mesoamerican women, the home was the universe in microcosm, essentially the nucleus of each tribe or ethnic state. As might be expected, then, aspects of Indian women's households, as society, as polity, as cosmos, are leitmotivs for our essays. And it is by means of analyses of their roles in that context that we come to understand their life experiences by extension. Ideally, real power for women came in the meticulous execution of their gendered assignments, which symbolically transcended the commonplace and ordered their worlds at large. More immediately, women's activities contributed to the preservation of the family unit and afforded transition through generations in spite of the imposition of new and largely unwelcomed institutions, whether indigenous or Hispanic.

Such machinations were perfected long before the arrival of the Spaniards. They were so esteemed that details of rationale and praxis were actually conveyed to the friars. In chapter 1, "Mexica Women on the Home Front: Housework and Religion in Aztec Mexico," Burkhart uses this information to elaborate the critical relationship of "women's work" in the home to the well-being of the community. Sacred and highly personal, women's purposes for cooking, cleaning, companionship, childbearing and childrearing, and religion give new meaning and validation to what might otherwise be considered onerous and mundane chores.

Using similar primary historical data amassed in the course of the sixteenth century, Arthur J. O. Anderson, in chapter 2, "Aztec Wives," treats specifics about gendered roles for husbands and wives in pre-Hispanic times as well as in the early colonial period. Again, the household looms large as the province of Indian women; their duties were so important, in fact, that native tribunals based much of Aztec society's well-being on whether women were carrying out their duties efficaciously. Details of intimacy, fidelity, birthing, and parenting and seemingly eternal obligations to cook, clean, and weave for husband, household, and children are telling of women's great share and of how their activities weighed so significantly in the order of the Aztec world. These sources are doubly charged, reflecting both Indians' and Europeans' views, but Anderson keeps the original Nahuatl (with English translation) for knowledge of the nature and content of indigenous histories.

Taking up the topic of indigenous marriage, Pedro Carrasco, in chapter 3, "Indian-Spanish Marriages in the First Century of the Colony," examines the incidence of such unions and the purposes they served. Class and lucre were key factors but not necessarily the only ones. Occasionally, Spanish men preferred the Indians' lifestyle. But Carrasco also notes that pre-Hispanic practices of donating women for political alliances were not suited to colonial norms, wherein Spanish attitudes of race and class prevailed when it came to marriage. Yet he finds considerable continuity of the native institution of what might be called "bridewealth," with Indian women having their own property and tenaciously hanging on to it. Carrasco largely treats Indian elites, about whom the sources for this subject are the richest, and who continued to enjoy both influence and affluence. His information personalizes the women, telling of names, royal families, Spanish husbands, and children.

Indigenous naming patterns in the colonial period afford immediate information about social and political identity, status, ethnicity, and even the era. In chapter 4, "Gender and Social Identity: Nahua Naming Patterns in Postconquest Central Mexico," Rebecca Horn analyzes the baptismal records from two parishes in Coyoacan, a region on the outskirts of Mexico City. Horn finds clear evidence of Hispanic influence on the indigenous family, not only in the sheer number of baptisms but also in the Spanish given names that were assigned to females and males at the time. However, Indian names and naming patterns typically remained distinct from Spanish ones, especially with the use of second names (whether indigenous or Hispanic), which continued to reflect one's place and role in the local community.

Nonetheless, based on a sample of seventy court cases from Mexico City, in chapter 5, "From Parallel and Equivalent to Separate but Unequal: Tenochca Mexica Women, 1500–1700," Susan Kellogg finds remarkable diminution of Indian women's legal status and influence in their societies over the course of two centuries. Kellogg invests heavily in reconsiderations and elaborations of gendered roles in the household as well as outside it, comparing practices of the pre-Hispanic and colonial eras. Although there was a moment immediately after the conquest when females outnumbered males and thus moved into positions of authority, thereafter it was necessary to adopt new strategies to preserve even traditional space. Kellogg's interest is in evidence of women's litigiousness regarding property settlements, and she finds that Spanish religious and political institutions inevitably had untoward effects when it came to sustained presence and efficacy on the part of native women in the colonial courtroom. Moreover, she postulates that although for some women legal channels were blocked, others did not hesitate to pursue different outlets of resistance and even outright revolt.

In chapter 6, "Activist or Adulteress? The Life and Struggle of Doña Josefa María of Tepoztlan," Robert Haskett challenges speculations regarding diminishing influence in colonial spheres by exemplifying native women's classic capacity for adopting any of several alternative modes to do their part for their communities. Here resistance manifests in doña Josefa's agency, mobility, and aggressiveness in spite of censure and imprisonment. Truly a stalwart character, she makes good use of male allies particularly (and following Stern's findings) but also females to further her cause. Most remarkable, however, for Spaniards and Indians who opposed her politics and methods was the need to resort to pre-Hispanic cognitive, idealized gendered behaviors to identify her real crime.

Stephanie Wood furnishes even closer analysis of the question of women's resistance and cultural continuity through her study of a rich cache of testaments from the Toluca region, west of the colonial capital. In chapter 7, "Matters of Life at Death: Nahuatl Testaments of Rural Women, 1589–1801," Wood too treats the household as focal point, with women's and men's "property" encompassing goods inside the home, such as religious images, and property outside it, such as livestock and agricultural parcels. Gendered considerations of ownership and inheritance are in many instances what might be expected, but these are rural women whose experiences are quite different from their urban counterparts. Wood's sources represent a substantial number of native-language texts that cover an extensive period, and they afford much insight about the effects of men, the countryside, the Spanish, and the centuries on the experiences of even the most humble women.

Moving south to Oaxaca, Ronald Spores, in chapter 8, "Mixteca *Cacicas:* Status, Wealth, and the Political Accommodation of Native Elite Women in Early Colonial Oaxaca," returns the focus to elite women and gender parallelism, but only as a sampling of the great store of available extant data about women of the Mixteca in general. As Spores shows, female elites of both the pre-Hispanic and colonial periods enjoyed extraordinary influence. Spores notes that bilateral kinship reckoning, inheritance patterns, and a tradition fostering positions of high status for both females and males continued even under colonial aegis. He discusses the lives and estates of three *cacicas* (wives of indigenous rulers, and rulers themselves on occasion) and, to preserve their entitlements, the inevitable legal entanglements that were endemic to Indian-Indian and Indian-Spanish relations in the Mixteca. Being single Indian women, their great wealth comes as a surprise, but Spores affirms that this is a key aspect of Mixtec indigenous marriages and family. He adds that the sources furnish even more information about native women that is unique. Clearly, former stereotypes about Mesoamerican culture and conquest must be nullified.

Still in Oaxaca but with a corpus of documents that includes histories of both Mixtec and Zapotec women, in Chapter 9, "Women and Crime in Colonial Oaxaca: Evidence of Complementary Gender Roles in Mixtec and Zapotec Societies," Lisa Mary Sousa examines a mass of criminal records that furnish striking and untypical information about the social and economic experiences of nonelite women in the region. Above all, she finds complementarity between men's and women's roles, in large part an aspect of the community in general but also with much visibility, respect, and individuality of women in particular. Wife beating was not unknown, but women did not hesitate to seek recourse—to protect themselves and their families from abusive husbands and anyone else who threatened.

Moving farther south, to Chiapas, and using yet another form of analysis to interpret Indian women's activities, Kevin Gosner turns to moral economy theories as developed for Africa, Asia, and Europe to interpret gendered participation of Mayas in the Tzeltal Revolt of 1712. In chapter 10, "Women, Rebellion, and the Moral Economy of Maya Peasants in Colonial Mexico," Gosner challenges long-standing impressions of Indian women's worlds being exclusively private

by using a young female Maya's provocative vision of the Virgin
Mary as centerpiece for evidence of women's longtime implicit investment in civil and religious as well as domestic dominions. When
traditional economic hardships are exacerbated by additional exactions, local women take full advantage of their familiar roles as spiritual brokers to rally forces for the community's survival.

In Yucatan, Marta Espejo-Ponce Hunt and Matthew Restall base
their study on both Spanish- and Yucatec Maya-language documents
that afford comparisons and contrasts with urban-based noble and
commoner Maya women as well as with their counterparts in rural
areas. In chapter 11, "Work, Marriage, and Status: Maya Women of
Colonial Yucatan," their focus, like Gosner's, is economic, exemplifying established practices of gender-specific roles and reciprocity
within given patriarchal constraints. Here, however, Hunt and Restall
examine aspects of the division of labor between women and men as
revealed in native wills. Once again, women hold their own and even
"come out on top" when it comes to the business of inheriting, owning, and bequeathing land, tools, livestock, and cloth. Moreover, as
the colonial period progressed, it seems there were greater benefits for
Maya women who remained in their communities. Those who moved
to Spanish cities might profit too, but for Maya women in a colonial
milieu, security, in its most traditional sense, was in the Maya town.

Contrary to the abundant sources for histories about native
women in central, south central, and southeastern New Spain, Susan
M. Deeds has found scant evidence of their experiences in the northern regions, even after many years of research. Focusing on Tarahumara and Tepehuan populations, in chapter 12, "Double Jeopardy:
Indian Women in Jesuit Missions of Nueva Vizcaya," Deeds looks for
indigenous cultural continuities of gendered practice in spite of the
realities of radical cultural change brought by missionization. Where
once survival depended on women's and men's shared duties,
women particularly suffered with the imposition of Spanish Catholic
institutions. Even when self-defense—here husband murder—was
a poor Indian woman's only means to save herself, where under traditional practices there would have been other ways of dealing with
such a man (e.g., move on to a different one), because of her race and
gender she suffered double discrimination and extreme punishment
under colonial patriarchal structures.

Not surprisingly, Leslie S. Offutt finds a similar scarcity of materials about native women in the northeastern reaches of New Spain. Challenged by what she terms "double invisibility," she too looks to the indigenous community as context for information about resistance and change in women's roles. In chapter 13, "Women's Voices from the Frontier: San Esteban de Nueva Tlaxcala in the Late Eighteenth Century," Offutt's interest is in a polity initially established by a colony of Tlaxcalans from central Mexico. Sent to the frontier in the sixteenth century, they were to serve as ideal models of colonial society in the midst of unsettled, aggressive Indians. Their corporate identity would thus serve them well, not only against alien Indians but also against intrusive, usurpative Spaniards. Most remarkable is the ethnopatriotism that unites these "New Tlaxcalans" (and something they surely manipulate to full advantage for continued royal privilege) and is used to invoke social and ethnic barriers against outsiders. Women's roles within this native community are the most restricted of any that we have studied, and one questions if it was the location, the unique circumstances of the ethnic group, exaggerated conditions of race and gender, the late time period, or all four that might have been responsible. However, women do speak up on occasion, with age, marital status, and place in community all factors of their agency.

By design the final chapter is Frances Karttunen's "Rethinking Malinche." Here, Malinche, in a word, represents all women in this volume, for she epitomizes half a millennium (and likely more) of Mexican Indian women's survival strategies. Karttunen traces the social and linguistic significance over the centuries of "Malinche," known also as the Christian doña Marina, the child-woman interpreter-mistress of the sixteenth century, to Mexico's ideological Eve (La Chingada) of today. Yet little known are the extraordinary linguistic skills the woman possessed, to say nothing of her poise and ability to finesse encounters between any number of different groups of Indians and the Spaniards. But Malinche confounds much of what we heretofore postulate for indigenous women—for she knew neither their relationship to the home nor their micropatriotism. Rather, Malinche personifies a complex of resistance attributes—alliance, accommodation, self preservation—that anticipates the consequences.

In "Concluding Remarks," coeditors Stephanie Wood and Robert

Haskett recapitulate these many histories of Mexican Indian women. They find similarities but also variations and some contradictions among women's experiences, as would be expected considering the variety of ethnic populations, the different regions, and the great expanse of time. Thus they caution against premature applications of "Western" constructs for the study of Mexican Indian women and instead emphasize the importance of time and place as they pose new questions to advance our analyses and as considerations for future studies.

Of course, much work remains to be done. By the good example of the fourteen essays in this collection, we expect that Indian women will be the subjects of the research and histories that follow and that, if it is not already, their place in the common ground of Mexican history will be secure.

Central Mexico

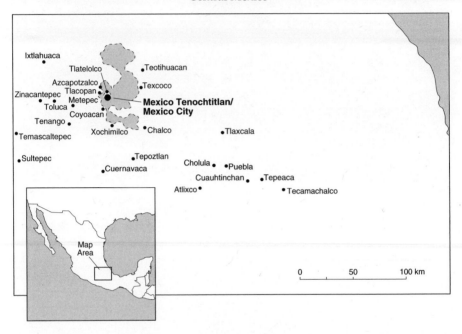

Ixtlahuaca

Tlatelolco   Teotihuacan

Azcapotzalco   Texcoco
Zinacantepec   Tlacopan
   Metepec   **Mexico Tenochtitlan/**
Toluca   **Mexico City**
   Coyoacan
Tenango
     Xochimilco   Chalco   Tlaxcala
Temascaltepec

Sultepec   Tepoztlan
     Cuernavaca   Cholula   Puebla
     Cuauhtinchan   Tepeaca
Atlixco   Tecamachalco

Map Area

0   50   100 km

Mexica Women on the Home Front

Housework and Religion in Aztec Mexico

Louise M. Burkhart

Housewives and Friars

Women in Aztec Mexico occupied a symbolic and social domain that was separate from and complementary to that of men. Although Mexica[1] women were junior to men in status and had limited political authority, to characterize their position in terms of "equality" versus "subordination" is, as Susan Kellogg points out, to impose Western categories that simplify a complex situation and undermine any attempt to understand it on its own terms.[2] In this chapter I examine one aspect of the complex domain of Mexica gender symbolics: the religious significance of domestic occupations that were viewed as "women's work." I consider this topic important for two reasons.

First, discussions of women's roles too often focus on a "public" domain that is presumed both to exist and to be more important than a (presumed) "private" domain. Mexica women worked as marketers, doctors, artisans, priests, and perhaps, occasionally, rulers; hence they were important and had high social status. Alternatively, Mexica women may be viewed as primarily associated with domes-

tic duties; hence they must have been male dominated and of low social status—"just housewives."

But the Mexica had nothing like the "cult of domesticity," with
the corresponding demarcation of the home as a private domain, that
arose along with industrial capitalism in Europe.[3] Nor did they share
the patriarchal household structure long typical of Christian Europe,
with its ideals of male authority and female submissiveness. Just because Mexica women spent much of their time cooking, cleaning,
sewing, and caring for children, duties assigned also to their European counterparts, it cannot be assumed a priori that these activities
were considered in any way trivial or marginal in relation to the male
domain. The significance of women's work and the constitution of
the domestic or household domain are variables that must be examined in relation to their specific cultural and historical contexts.[4]

June Nash argues that Mexica militarism led to a decline in
women's status and in male-female complementarity, since women
had no role corresponding to that of warrior.[5] I suggest that an ideology of male-female complementarity was maintained through an
investment of the home with symbolism of war, not only by means
of metaphor but also via direct ties to the battlefield front. Childbirth
was, as is well known, symbolically militarized: successful delivery
was equated with the taking of a prisoner, and death in childbirth
was equivalent to being captured or killed. However, there were other
parallels between military and domestic contexts, which I will explore below. Most striking is how a man's fate in battle was linked to
actions his wife carried out at home. Domesticated central places and
dangerous peripheral zones were complementary opposites, their
gender signs reversed, which together constituted a whole. Domestic
space was, quite literally, a "home front," and women were its army.[6]

The second reason I consider this topic important has to do with
the dialogue between native people (mostly men) and European men
(mostly priests) out of which the colonial ethnographies and histories, including the sources I use here, emerged. In early colonial Mexico, the identity of the Mexica woman—who she was and what her
proper attributes were—became a contested domain now to be negotiated not simply between women and men but also between indigenous people and Europeans. To approach the Mexica woman by
way of her representation in these texts demands that the motives

and attitudes of the chroniclers be carefully examined; one must also acknowledge that much of that woman's life is unknowable except as a construct of colonial males.

Women's domestic life was a subject about which the early friars had little knowledge and much fear. Large areas were often assigned to a small number of friars unwilling or unable to visit outlying settlements regularly. Native families were obliged to carry their sick and dying to the church to be blessed and shriven by priests who refrained from making house calls. One reason for this avoidance was a fear of women. Friars rarely visited anyone but nobles at home, considering it unseemly to enter the houses of the common people. For a friar to rub elbows with native women in such close and dimly lit quarters might give rise to temptation in his own mind and to suspicion in the minds of others. That this attitude could be carried to extremes is shown by a story told of the Franciscan chronicler Motolinia: he was so devoted to chastity that he reprimanded a fellow friar for having touched the face of a small girl whose mother had carried her to church to be blessed.[7]

Colonial descriptions of household rituals are embedded in a discourse about idolatry and its eradication: as with temple ritual, the point of eliciting these descriptions was to enable priests to evaluate native religious practices, determine what was and was not acceptable, and recognize the latter when they saw it. These categories were not fixed: what seemed harmless or even commendable to one priest might to another reek with the Devil's own stench. Much of the information I use in this chapter was recorded precisely because someone thought it dangerous, idolatrous, and likely to be continuing behind the priests' backs. In the war against Lucifer, the Mexica woman was suspected of consorting with the enemy.

The Mexica woman also appears in colonial texts as an industrious housewife and a mother devoted to the careful upbringing of her children. These representations were useful to the friars both as evidence that the native people were "civilized" (and hence deserved better treatment from colonists) and as a foundation for preaching to women about the proper behavior of Catholic wives and mothers.

Thus in the friars' minds the Mexica woman was split into an evil side and a good side, and the good side was perceived according to European notions of female submissiveness and domestic enterprise. Indigenous discourse that associated women with the home was heard by the friars as descriptions of dutiful housewives, whereas all evidence of the sacred power manipulated by women in that home was read as tricks the Devil played on the weaker sex. I attempt here to merge these two constructs of the native woman into a closer approximation of a whole person.

I will consider the religious significance of the following housekeeping activities: sweeping, the making of offerings, cooking, and textile production.[8] I chose these because, in the ritual orations to young women recorded by the Franciscans Andrés de Olmos[9] and Bernardino de Sahagún[10]—texts representing an idealized view of women as presented to friars by native orators—these activities are invoked to represent proper female behavior. I begin by discussing the Mexica home, this locus of women's power where friars—perhaps quite wisely—feared to tread.

Home, Sweet, Home?

The home, though shared by men and women, was symbolically constructed as female space. A baby girl's umbilical cord was buried *metlatitlan, tlecujlnacazco,* "beside the grinding stone, at the corner of the hearth," since *yn çan cali ynentla,* "only in the house is her place of dwelling"; a boy's was given to warriors to be buried on a battlefield.[11] The respectable elderly woman, in Sahagún's description, receives these epithets: "Heart of the House" (*caliollutl*), which suggests a central, animating force, and "Banked Fire" (*tlacpeoalli*), the fire covered with ashes for the night.[12] Both terms are placed in the mouth of the midwife addressing a baby girl: "You will be the heart of the house, you will go nowhere, you will become a person who goes nowhere. You become the banked fire, the hearthstone. Here our lord plants you, buries you."[13] Although women did carry on activities outside of the house, this symbolic association with the domestic interior appears to have been quite strong. The conventionalized but culturally specific terms in which it is expressed suggest that this is customary usage and not simply an appeal to Sahagún's moral sensibility. Immorality in women was, conversely, associated with a failure to stay home, a tendency to hang about the streets and marketplaces or, worse, to take off on the road of the deer and the rabbit.[14]

The nonelite Mexica woman lived in a *calli*, a house consisting of one or more windowless, four-sided rooms, constructed of adobe or stone with a smokehole in the center of the thatched roof. Doorways opened onto a rectangular courtyard or patio (*ithualli*); arranged around this patio were other calli occupied by her relatives. If the woman was unmarried, an assortment of grandparents, aunts, uncles, and cousins might occupy these other houses. If she was married, these were likely to be her husband's kin; however, in crowded Mexico City, household composition was very fluid and people could determine their living arrangements according to available space and personal choice. The "family" was conceived as a group of people who shared a residential compound—*cemithualtin*, "those of one patio"—rather than as a fixed arrangement of kin.

The residential compound was likely also to include a maize granary (*cuexcomatl*) and a sweathouse (*temazcalli*) as well as a small altar for religious offerings. Surrounding the compound were others belonging to neighborhood units called *tlaxilacalli*, or row of houses, and *calpolli*, or big house. The calpolli functioned as an administrative division for purposes of taxation and military draft, and had its own temple (*calpolco*, "place of the calpolli") and schools.[15]

At the center of the calli lay a hearth bounded by three stones, conceptualized as female deities. Within this hearth a fire smoldered continuously, completely extinguished only for the New Fire Ceremony every fifty-two years. Fire, too, was a god, the "old man god" Huehueteotl, who dwelled at the center of the cosmos just as he dwelled here at the center of the house. So closely were home and hearth identified that when a new house was built, its fire could not be lit from someone else's hearth but had to be drilled anew, in the presence of old men who perhaps represented the elderly fire god; difficulty in kindling this new flame foretold an unhappy life for the inhabitants.[16]

The hearth as a symbol of centrality is, I think, nowhere so elegantly evoked as in a passage from the *Coloquios*, a passage that captures the center/periphery symbolism of home and battlefield as well as the Mexica man's ordained oscillation between them. The text, written in 1564 but set in 1524, represents a Mexica noble explaining to Franciscan friars the noblemen's responsibility for warfare.[17] "We attend to the work of the tail, the wing, so that he takes his heron

standard, his cord jacket, and his digging stick, his tumpline, thus
are left in front of the hearth."[18] "The tail, the wing" is the vassal or
commoner; the standard and jacket are insignia of the warrior; the
digging stick and tumpline represent the common man's agricultural labor. Being a Mexica man meant periodically abandoning
hearth and home and the familiar seasonal round of agriculture for
unknown lands and the dangers of battle. Perhaps that home fire
burning, his tools laid carefully by, was an image the soldier bore in
his mind as he followed his noble lords into war.

Beneath the packed earth floor of the Mexica house lay the pla-
centas of children born therein and the ashes of the family's dead;[19]
the daughters' umbilical cords were, as mentioned, buried by the
hearth. On the floor lay the family's possessions: the grinding stone
(*metlatl*), griddle (*comalli*), and cooking pots; straw mats, seats, and
storage boxes holding extra clothing and the women's spinning and
weaving supplies; the men's weapons and their digging sticks, nets,
or other tools depending on their trade. The broom leaned against the
wall outside.

The house provided a certain amount of protection from dangerous powers. On the five days when the Cihuateteo, or woman
deities, associated with death in childbirth, descended to earth, children had to be confined to the house to protect them from the diseases these failed mothers could inflict on them.[20] Figure 1.1, from
the *Florentine Codex,* depicts a woman sending her children into the
house on One Eagle, one of the days on which the Cihuateteo came
to earth. On the day Four Wind, when the power of sorcerers was
particularly strong, people stuffed their smokeholes with a certain
plant, called "sorcerer sour-fruit thorn," believed to protect the occupants from spells those sorcerers might cast.[21] One could protect
the house from sorcerers on a nightly basis by placing an obsidian
knife in water near the door or in the courtyard.[22] During the *nemontemi,* the dangerously unstructured period of five unnamed days occurring at the end of the 365-day year, *çan calonooaia,* "people would
just lie in their houses."[23]

The home, though, was not a tranquil refuge from the significant currents of cosmos and history but a place where those currents
intersected forcibly with human existence. One could see the Mexica
house as a model of the cosmos, writ small, but perhaps it would be

Fig. 1.1. *Florentine Codex* illustration for "the nineteenth sign; it is called One Eagle." For this day, when the Cihuateteo were said to descend to earth and harm children, a mother is depicted hurrying her offspring into the comparative safety of the house. Fray Bernardino de Sahagún, *Historia general de las cosas de Nueva España, Códice florentino*. Facsimile of the Codex Florentinus of the Biblioteca Medicea Laurenciana, supervised by the Archivo General de la Nación de México, Florence, Italy, 1979, book 4, fol. 62r.

better to see the Mexica cosmos as a house writ large. It was in that smoky interior that the Mexica infant developed its orientation in space and time. It learned that space is quadrilateral and has a central point; it learned the pattern of the day's activities and the calendrical cycles. It learned that order is fragile and temporary: without constant attention and renewal things get old, dirty, and worn out. Lying on its cradleboard by the flickering fire, watching its mother spin and weave, cook and clean, make offerings and pray, the child began to become a Mexica person.

When that child was old enough to venture out into the city, she or he saw that the gods lived in houses too, *teocalli,* or god houses, arranged around quadrilateral patios in the sacred precincts. And outside of the quadripartite city lay the rest of the quadripartite world that had the Mexicas' great temple as its central point. All of this order was fragile. Like the house and its furnishings, that whole world had a tendency to become worn out and dirty if not tended carefully. Just as the housewife had to be constantly vigilant to maintain cleanliness and order, so did the priests in their temples. Much Mexica temple ritual functioned as a kind of cosmic housekeeping: the priests guarded the temple fires, made offerings, prayed, and cleaned; female priests and attendants also spun and wove clothing for the deities and cooked their offerings of food.

Calli was also the third of the twenty named day signs (*tonalli*) in the 260-day ritual calendar (itself an approximation of the human gestation period), and one of the four such signs on which the 365-day year could begin. This sign stands out within the series because it is the only cultural artifact: the other signs denote plants, animals, or other "natural" phenomena such as rain, motion, and death. The analogous place in the Maya calendar is occupied by the sign *akbal,* meaning "darkness," a natural phenomenon but one that is, indeed, characteristic of windowless houses. This dark, enclosed space replicates other, more "natural" enclosures: the womb, the emergence caves of Mesoamerican origin myths. Calli was one of the five day signs associated with the west, the direction of sunset and hence coldness and darkness, and a direction associated, like the house itself, with women. The west was called *cihuatlampa,* "toward the women," and was the dwelling place of the five Cihuateteo, who had as their calendrical names the western day signs with the coefficient of one (One House, One Eagle, One Rain, One Deer, One Monkey). With them dwelled the souls of women who had died in their first childbirth with the fetus still in the womb, unable to emerge from this its original "house."[24]

According to fray Diego Durán's informants, who took their day signs rather literally, persons born on calli were stay-at-home types who obeyed their parents and were afraid to venture abroad in the world.[25] While such a character might be fine for a woman, a "mama's boy" was not likely to get far in militaristic Mexica society. Indeed, years that began on calli were years of ill fortune.[26] Sahagún's astrological consultants recited a litany of nasty traits to be expected of people born on calli: men were raggedy thieves and compulsive gamblers who would die in battle or in sacrifice; women slept too much and did no productive work.[27]

Thus, like other important Mesoamerican religious symbols, calli had multiple and ambivalent associations. It was a symbolic center and thus a place of (relative) order and security. But it was also a womb, a cave linking life and death, earth and netherworld, a dark place unreached by the sun's purifying rays. It might absorb one's initiative, causing one to do nothing but lie around the house all day, unfit for productive labors. It might even conspire with the forces of chaos and death and turn against its inhabitants. Sahagún's informants claimed that the horned owl's hoot could augur such a disaster. If one heard this owl, "perhaps his or her house will disintegrate, the ground will wear away, water will appear here and there, dry leaves will spread about the doorway, the courtyard. The walls will lie about crumbled, will lie about ruined, will lie about in pieces."[28] People would use the property as a latrine and a trash dump. And they would marvel at the fact that a respectable person once had lived there and kept the place clean.

The Power of Brooms

"Attend to the sweeping, the picking up"; "arise quickly . . . , seize the broom, attend to the sweeping"; "take charge of the sweeping, . . . arise in the deep of night."[29] Thus were Mexica women advised, by their mothers, fathers, and in-laws, to begin their day.

For Mexica priests, sweeping was an essential service at the houses of the gods. A priest sweeping a temple precinct is obviously performing a ritual of purification, but must such an act be divorced from its "practical" application in the home before it becomes a ritual? A housewife, rising before dawn to sweep away the night's debris, surely saw herself as an actor in the regeneration of order, dividing day from night and protecting her family from dangerous forces. Housekeeping activities that were highly patterned, surrounded by taboos, and linked to gods and important religious concepts can be considered ritual acts.

In Nahuatl, to sweep is *ichpana*. The more general term for cleansing or purifying is *chipahua*, a term borrowed by the church to express concepts of moral and spiritual purity. The historical linguist Karen Dakin believes that the element *chi-* was once an independent morpheme meaning "straw." Metathesized as *ich-*, this element appears not only in ichpana but also in *ichpochtli*,[30] an irregular word meaning adolescent girl or young woman. This suggests that the act of cleaning a surface with straw was not only an important purificatory act but was also fundamental to the very notion of cleanliness. Sweeping being a frequent activity of young women, for a girl to be called something equivalent to "she of the straw" makes some sense.

Although both men and women could, and did, sweep, in the domestic context the act was more closely associated with females. Baby girls were given small brooms, while baby boys were presented with a small shield and arrows.[31] In the *Codex Mendoza*, the twelve-year-old girl is the child shown sweeping, at her mother's behest; the two males who are shown sweeping elsewhere in the codex are both priests.[32]

Sahagún's catalog of native offerings lists this early morning household sweeping along with such rites as bloodletting and temple sacrifices.[33] The text states that children of both sexes performed this act; the accompanying illustration depicts a family of sweepers. However, in Sahagún's earlier draft of this material, the *Primeros memoriales*, a single sweeper is shown and it is a woman.[34]

Gods as well as mortals swept. Quetzalcoatl, god of wind, swept the roads for the rain gods.[35] He was, it may be noted, a deity of priestly rather than warrior character; sweeping was more properly the province of divine females. Coatlicue conceived Huitzilopochtli, the Mexicas' patron deity, while sweeping.[36] Chimalman was sweeping when she became pregnant with Quetzalcoatl.[37] The closely related deities Tlazolteotl, "Filth Deity," and Toci, "Our Grandmother" (also called Teteo Innan, "Mother of the Gods," and Yaocihuatl, "Enemy Woman"), carried brooms; Toci bore a shield as well.[38]

Figure 1.2 is the depiction of Tlazolteotl a native artist painted for Sahagún. During Toci's festival, Ochpaniztli, "Sweeping the Roads," the roads were indeed swept, as were the houses, baths, and courtyards. Toci was represented by a bundle of straw—as if she were a broom—and mock battles were performed using inverted brooms as weapons instead of swords.[39]

The broom *was* a weapon: it was the housewife's defense against invading dirt and disorder, peripheral forces that, like the enemies of the state, threatened the maintenance of order and centrality. The broom was an object of power, ambivalent because it purified but was itself a carrier of filth. The author of the *Códice carolino*, concerned about persisting "idolatries," wrote that old women left their brooms outside lest the dirt carried by the brooms introduce discord into the house. They called the broom Tlazolteuctli. The author glosses this as "god of anger," but it is clearly a variant name for Tlazolteotl. These women also forbade children to play with the broom. One further "superstition" is noted: a man wishing to seduce a woman could collect the straws that fell from her broom when she swept. Once he had twenty straws (a full "count" in the vigesimal system), he could turn the broom's power against its owner and force her to comply with his desires.[40]

During the nemontemi, the five unnamed days at the end of the year, people especially feared disorder, as, for example, in the form of quarrels, illness, and falls. And they dared not expose themselves to brooms. If a woman wished to clean the dust from her home, she had to blow it away using a fan, turkey feathers, or a mantle.[41]

Susan D. Gillespie has shown how, in Mexica history, women occupied positions of ambiguity and transition, whereas periods of stability were associated with men.[42] This contrast applies to Mexica constructions of gender not only in relation to history. In the cosmic scheme of things, women, with their closer links to the earth and the night, were arbiters of disorder, of creation and disintegration, to a degree that men were not. Women, after all, processed unfinished materials into finished products: foodstuffs into meals, raw fibers into thread and cloth, sexual secretions into babies. A woman with a broom in her hands stood at the intersection of chaos and order: having a certain affinity with the powers that blew dust and debris into her tidy patio, she could also exert control over them and keep them

Fig. 1.2. *Florentine Codex* illustration of Tlazolteotl, described by Sahagún as "the goddess of carnal things, whom they called Tlaçulteotl, she is another Venus." Tlazolteotl is depicted here with her broom and her headdress of spindles and unspun cotton. Fray Bernardino de Sahagún, *Historia general de las cosas de Nueva España, Códice florentino.* Facsimile of the Codex Florentinus of the Biblioteca Medicea Laurenciana, supervised by the Archivo General de la Nación de México, Florence, Italy, 1979, book 1, fol. 11r.

at bay, maintaining the proper balance between her ordered center and the disorderly periphery that threatened to engulf it.

Given these associations, it is not surprising that when men were at war, their wives and other female relations were especially diligent in sweeping. The *Crónica X* annals describe the rituals of warriors' wives. I suspect that illustrations of these rites were incorporated into the pictorial year-count histories as crucial aspects of certain military campaigns. When these pictorial records were transposed into alphabetic script, accounts of the rituals were included in the new narrative versions.

Durán's description of a war with the Huaxtecs tells how the Mexica warriors' wives swept not only at dawn but also at midnight, noon, and sunset: the four corners of the sun's path. Warfare was "solar" business: the war god Huitzilopochtli was identified with the sun; dead warriors went to the sun's home.[43] Would the sun, seeing the woman mark his passage by purifying her home space, reciprocate by granting her husband favors where he labored on the field of battle? As her broom conquered dirt, would his sword conquer enemy soldiers?

Fernando Alvarado Tezozomoc's account of the war between the two Mexica cities Tenochtitlan and Tlatelolco, during which the ruler Axayacatl seized control of Tlatelolco from his brother-in-law Moquihuix, contains the following enigmatic episode. Toward the end of the conflict, in a last-ditch defense of Tlatelolco's temple of Huitzilopochtli, a group of Tlatelolca women came to face the enemy. They exposed their breasts and buttocks; they beat their hands against their abdomens and genitals; they squeezed milk from their breasts; they threw dirt, excrement, and chewed-up tortillas at the Tenochca warriors. They also threw brooms, weaving battens, and warping frames. Axayacatl ordered his soldiers to take the women prisoner without hurting them; his definitive victory was soon established.[44]

The temple, symbolic center of the Tlatelolco city-state and house of the Mexica patron deity, receives its final defense from women who, rather than directly emulate male warriors, instead turn the full force of their womanhood against the invaders. Naked, flaunting their sexual and reproductive anatomy, flinging dirty and disintegrated matter, they embody the power of Tlazolteotl, deity of filth and childbirth. And from the temple steps they throw not darts or spears but brooms. This is woman as arbiter of chaos, putting forth a final defense of centrality and order while at the same time marking the transition of power from one group of males to another. Whether the deeds of these women warriors were expected to deter the enemy or were entirely expressive, or, indeed, whether this episode actually occurred, is unknowable. However, the story is grounded in the role of women as broom-wielding guardians of the home front.

Sahagún records orations ascribed to merchant families on the occasion of an expedition's departure. Older merchants, retired from travel, advise the departing man; he, in turn, encharges them to sweep and clean in his absence.[45] While these words are represented as exchanged among men, that women would carry out much of the actual sweeping may be assumed. The traveler's subsequent words encharge the other men to look out for the welfare of his female relatives while he is away, explaining that "perhaps somewhere our lord will destroy me." Mexica women were not helpless dependents; I take this statement to imply that his fate and theirs are so linked that harm to them at home would provoke a corresponding threat to him on the road. Figure 1.3 is a native artist's representation of a merchant bidding farewell to his home and his female kin.

Friars, even if aware of the ritual character of sweeping, could hardly forbid women to sweep their property. Durán, writing in the late 1570s, suspected that the sweeping of domestic spaces continued to have "idolatrous" significance.[46] However, the practice was easily transferred to Christianity. The Franciscans accepted the sweeping of churches and churchyards as an act of devotion.[47] In the domestic context as well, sweeping seems to have become as vital an act of service to the Christian god and saints as it had been in the pre-Christian context. Stephanie Wood, in an analysis of colonial wills from the Toluca Valley, observes that testators who kept Christian images in their homes often encharged their heirs to sweep around the domestic altars.[48] One man was not satisfied with ordering that his wife and children sweep but also encharged his brothers to yell at them to make sure they did it.[49]

Serving the Gods

A woman's second daily responsibility was to "[attend to] the cleansing of the hands, the rinsing of the faces, the washing of the mouths";

Fig. 1.3. Illustration from "another discourse that the same [elderly merchants] made to those who had already gone far away to trade." Having been exhorted by his elders, the departing merchant expresses concern for the female relatives he leaves behind. Fray Bernardino de Sahagún, *Historia general de las cosas de Nueva España, Códice florentino*. Facsimile of the Codex Florentinus of the Biblioteca Medicea Laurenciana, supervised by the Archivo General de la Nación de México, Florence, Italy, 1979, book 4, fol. 40v.

and, "wash the mouths, especially do not forget the offering of incense."[50] These references to washing are metaphors for the making of offerings to the gods. Daily services to the gods were expected of all Mexicas, but the advice to women suggests that, on the household level, these small reverences were their particular responsibility. The catalog of eighteen offerings to the gods in Sahagún's *Primeros memoriales* depicts women performing the following rites: the laying of of-

ferings (*tlamanaliztli*), the offering of incense in an incense burner
(*tlenamaquiliztli*), the casting of copal incense into a brazier (*copal-
temaliztli*), the ritual eating of earth (*tlalqualiztli*), bloodletting from
the earlobes (*neçoliztli*), and, of course, sweeping.[51] On the day Four
Movement, the day sign of the sun, women and children as well as
men were expected to draw blood from their ears to nourish the
sun.[52]

The *Florentine Codex* description of the morning sweeping describes the subsequent rites: "and when they had swept the first time,
when it was still early in the morning, then they used to make hand-
fuls of offerings, they used to lay them before the Devil [Diablo].
And when they had gone to lay the offerings, then they used to take
their incense burners in order to offer incense."[53] Whoever recorded
this information for Sahagún had learned to refer to the ancestral
deities in demonic terms; he or she was also careful to represent
these acts as occurring in the past.

The daily offerings were made to any images the family might
have in its keeping, and also to the fire. Durán indicates that the fire
god was the focus of many domestic rites: food and drink were offered out of devotion, a desire for health and wealth, or for the benefit of one's children; "a thousand superstitions" were based on the
noises made by the fire and the sparks and smoke it emitted. Durán
was none too confident that such behaviors had ceased.[54] Elsewhere,
Durán describes how appalled he was to find images of saints set up
on household altars with offerings of food, incense, and candles "as
if they were idols."[55] On the fire's calendrical date, One Dog, wealthy
families would have banquets and offer to the fire paper, quail,
pulque, and incense by the basketful; commoners would offer a
poorer quality of incense while the very poor burned aromatic
herbs.[56]

Women whose husbands were at war paid extra attention to the
needs of the gods, using the occasion of the morning offerings to
pray for their men's safety and victory.[57] In a ritual similar to one
performed by warriors themselves, these wives would take out the
femurs of their husbands' former captives, which were kept in the
home and called *malteotl*, "prisoner deity," wrap them in paper, and
hang them from the house beams.[58] Before these relics they would
offer incense and pray for their husbands' safety.[59] Alvarado Tezo-

zomoc places these rites in the calpolco, or neighborhood temple, and includes the additional detail that the women also hung up the absent men's mantles—a way of making the soldier symbolically present at home, in association with relics of his victories.[60] The reverence paid to a man's former captives would, perhaps, lure other enemy soldiers within reach of his weapons.

Beside the Grinding Stone

Once the morning offerings were made, it was time for the woman's next task: "And may you also attend to the water, the grinding stone; and take a firm hold upon, grasp tightly the sauce bowl, the basket"; "look well to the water, the food."[61] Cooking was women's work, ever since the divine Cihuacoatl ground on her grinding stone the dough for human flesh.[62] At the grinding stone, beside the hearth, kneels the thirteen-year-old girl depicted in the Codex Mendoza.[63] According to the Códice carolino, a girl's umbilical cord was buried not just by the hearth but directly beneath the grinding stone.[64] Given the amount of time that women had to spend processing maize into its various consumable forms, it is no wonder that cooking duties were constantly represented to women as their proper work, sacralized by association with the household fire.

Elizabeth M. Brumfiel suggests, based on varying proportions of griddles to cooking pots in archaeological assemblages, that the actual foods women produced varied locally and historically depending on the need for mobility, with griddles prevailing in more urban contexts.[65] In families whose members worked at or close to home, food could be stewed or steamed in pots and eaten at home. However, urban workers engaged in marketing, public works, warfare, and other extrahousehold activities required more portable foods like tortillas and the ground and toasted maize employed as war provisions. Production of the latter foods demanded more intensive labor on the part of women in the home: women's maize processing subsidized the urban economy and imperial expansion.

Although cooking itself was not a ritual, there were various beliefs and rituals associated with it. The following examples are from the appendix to Sahagún's book on omens.[66] This appendix is a catalog of thirty-seven items that, in Sahagún's view, harmed the faith;

priests should preach against them and inquire about them during confession. Almost all occur in the home, and most involve women and children. This attests to the frustration of an elderly priest, his life spent in cloisters and churchyards: women's domestic space has become the church's final frontier.

One of these items is the hearthside burial of the girl's umbilical cord, given the explanatory statement, "She is entirely in charge of water, food; beside the grinding stone she dwells." Perhaps this did not merely "symbolize" a woman's connection to the hearth but was thought actually to tie her to that spot, to draw her irresistibly to the grinding stone. This would account for the practice's inclusion in this list of "superstitions," for it is this sort of "magical" reasoning that Sahagún found particularly offensive.

The hearthstones and the grinding stone had to be treated with caution. In another connection between battlefield and home, men who kicked the hearthstones would suffer numb feet when facing the enemy. Children were told not to lick the grinding stone lest they lose their teeth. If the grinding stone broke while in use, the woman or a member of her household would die.

Maize, like fire, was a god who lived in one's home and had to be accorded due respect. Women warmed the maize with their breath before cooking it, claiming that this way it would not fear the fire's heat. If maize spilled onto the ground, where it was thought to suffer and weep, it had to be gathered up with care. The text here shows an accommodation to Christian discourse, for this careless treatment does not constitute an offense to the maize deity, but rather is to be reported to "our lord," before whom the maize will testify as to its ill treatment, demanding that "this vassal" be punished. Or the result might be famine: an outcome more in tune with a traditional cult of maize than the preceding scenario of accusation and judgment.

Accompanying Sahagún's text on these maize-related practices is the illustration shown in figure 1.4. The painting shows a woman speaking to, or perhaps simply breathing on, the maize as she pours it from a basket into the cooking pot, which rests on the three hearthstones. The artist has placed the scene into a landscape, making it appear to be set outdoors: this is a partial and formulaic adoption of European artistic conventions and should not be read as literally placing an indoor scene in a grassy meadow (the same is true of figure 1.3,

Fig. 1.4. Illustration for "the fourteenth chapter, about the maize." A woman addresses the maize as she pours it into the cooking pot. Fray Bernardino de Sahagún, *Historia general de las cosas de Nueva España, Códice florentino*. Facsimile of the Codex Florentinus of the Biblioteca Medicea Laurenciana, supervised by the Archivo General de la Nación de México, Florence, Italy, 1979, book 5, fol. 16r.

where the merchant's house appears to float above its "landscaped" occupants).

Like the fire, with its "thousand" prognostications that so irked Durán, the maize could convey messages to the housekeeper. If a tortilla became folded over on the griddle, the woman expected the arrival of a guest or the return of her husband; this approaching person was said to have kicked the tortilla.

Certain ritual precautions had to be taken when consuming food. If girls did not sit down to eat, their mothers worried that they would marry far from home—as if the mystical link to their central place, the floor by the fire, would be broken. Cooking is, again, linked to warfare: the cook had to keep her menfolk from dipping food directly into the cooking pot, or they would lose their (future) war captives. Did the tortilla or tamale being dipped represent the prisoner, on whom the man risks losing his grip in the heat of the pot, as in the heat of battle? And she must not eat tamales that stick to the cooking pot, lest a fetus adhere to her womb and she die in childbirth. The tamale:pot::fetus:womb analogy is more obvious than the reasoning behind the captives getting lost in the sauce! However, she could not allow her men to eat these tamales either, or their battle arrows would not shoot. Perhaps they would stick to the men's quivers like the tamale to the pot.

Special foods had to be cooked for many calendrical rituals. Sahagún's account mentions various ceremonial foods used in the temples, presumably cooked by women. For example, on the day One Flint Knife food offerings were brought to Huitzilopochtli from people's houses, including those of the common people.[67] Occasionally, the text refers to ritual uses of food in the home. As part of the Huey Tozoztli ceremonies for the maize gods, women spent the night cooking atolli (maize gruel), which, after sweeping the neighborhood temple, they poured into gourd vessels set about outside, where the hot, steamy mass cooled and thickened in the night air.[68] On the eighth day of Izcalli, a feast called Huauhquiltamalqualiztli, "the eating of tamales made with amaranth greens," was held. In every home these tamales were prepared and shared from household to household. The family then assembled for the meal, but before eating they laid a dish of five of the tamales beside the hearth as an offering to the fire and also gave some to each of the dead family members at their burial places within the house.[69]

A festival called Atamalqualiztli, "the eating of water tamales," was held every eight years. For several days people ate nothing but unseasoned tamales, once a day. This was thought to give the maize a rest from the chile, salt, and other seasonings normally eaten with it.[70]

Special foods were also demanded of the woman whose husband was at war. She would, according to Durán, engage in the midnight cooking of small tortillas, some with corners and others shaped like rolls.[71] She would then grind a little toasted maize (such as was used for warriors' provisions) and place it in a gourd. These foods would be offered at the household altar. Alvarado Tezozomoc's account states that these women would prepare "butterfly tortillas" and toasted maguey worms to offer at various temples; both these foods, as well as toasted maize ground and mixed with water, would be offered in the household rites.[72]

The Spindle Whorl, the Weaving Batten

Once she had swept, made offerings, and fed her family, a woman could turn to another task that defined and constrained her female identity, a task that was *vel ic cioatequitl*, "real women's work,"[73] failure at which meant failure at womanhood itself.[74] "Take charge of the spindle whorl, the weaving batten," the mother told her daughter,[75] and from an early age the girl's hands were trained to turn, first, fiber into thread and, later, thread into cloth. The *Codex Mendoza* depicts girls of three and four being shown how to spin; at age five, the girl works the spindle herself. At fourteen, she weaves on the backstrap loom.[76] Figure 1.5, which depicts the assemblage of a woman's spinning and weaving tools, illustrates a chapter of the *Florentine Codex* dedicated to the training of young noblewomen—a process the text equates with mastery of textile arts.

The midwife who delivered a baby girl presented her with the tools of textile production as well as a blouse and skirt at the bathing and naming ceremony, while a baby boy received weapons, a loincloth, and a mantle.[77] When a man died, his weapons, the femurs of his war captives, and his mantles were cremated with him; a woman took her weaving tools and combs with her into death.[78] The analogy weaving:warfare::women:men is operating here. Similarly, the duty of merchant men to go to distant places could be expressed as "notweaving": parents sending young boys on their first trading expedition would say, "Is he perhaps a woman? Perhaps I will place in his hands a spindle whorl, a weaving batten?"[79]

This identification of tools and garments with gender categories deserves additional comment. The concept of identity was, for the Mexica, a construct based not so much on intrinsic qualities as on attributes and accoutrements. Images were turned into gods by placing on them the appropriate vestments. A human being could, by dressing in a deity's costume, "become" that deity in the ritual context; a man could even become a female deity. At the arrival of Cortés, Moteucçoma sent the accoutrements of an assortment of deities, as if by his choice of garb the mysterious stranger would reveal his identity.[80]

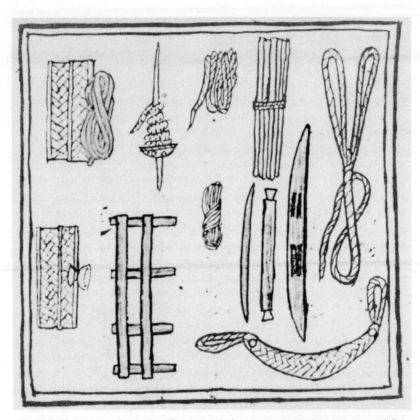

Fig. 1.5. Illustration from the *Florentine Codex* account of "the exercises of the ladies," depicting the tools of spinning and weaving. Fray Bernardino de Sahagún, *Historia general de las cosas de Nueva España, Códice florentino*. Facsimile of the Codex Florentinus of the Biblioteca Medicea Laurenciana, supervised by the Archivo General de la Nación de México, Florence, Italy, 1979, book 8, fol. 31v.

Gender identity, though founded of course on the obvious difference between male and female babies, was, I suggest, similarly embedded in what people wore and carried in their hands. A Mexica, man or woman, was almost never naked, without the garments that marked and helped to constitute his or her identity. That a woman could figuratively be called "a blouse, a skirt" and a man "a loincloth, a mantle" was, thus, a part-for-whole synecdoche rather than a metonym. The ambivalent and sometimes warlike nature of certain female deities was represented by dressing them in loincloths (as in the famous Coyolxauhqui relief from the Mexica Great Temple). Giving a female baby a skirt and a spindle made her a girl, set her on a course toward a womanhood defined more by her garments and her tools than by any more abstract notion of feminine emotions or intellect.

Why spinning and weaving, even more than sweeping or cooking, defined a woman as a woman may be linked to the relative economic importance of these tasks. Whereas she might prepare food only to feed her own household, a woman's textile production not only clothed her family but also involved her in the larger economy. Tribute was paid in cloth; cloth could be used as money in the marketplace.[81] The more cloth a woman produced, the more she and her household prospered. Brumfiel, using archaeological data, suggests that urban women, who spent more time processing maize and could purchase cloth in the marketplace, may have spent less time at this task than their rural counterparts; however, the symbolic association between women and textile production pervaded urban culture as well.[82] Not surprisingly, the gods colluded with the economy to guide women to this labor.[83]

The deities most intimately associated with spinning were the closely related Toci and Tlazolteotl, who wore headdresses made of spindles and unspun cotton (fig. 1.2). These are the same ones who carry brooms: like sweeping, spinning involves an intersection of order and disorder, as masses of fluff and fiber separate and rejoin to form a single smooth line of thread. An analogy may be drawn with the process of gestation, also under the aegis of these deities, which was seen as a consolidation of male and female sexual fluids into the fetus. The spindle, swelling with thread, was compared to a pregnant woman, as in a riddle that asked, "What becomes big with child in only a day?"[84] Thelma Sullivan notes additional sexual symbolism: the insertion of the spindle's wooden shaft into the spindle whorl suggests the act that leads to this "pregnancy."[85]

Eve, whom the colonial Mexica called "our first mother," was also a spinner. After the expulsion from Eden, while Adam learned to work the land, she learned to spin and weave. A native artist's mural

painting in the open chapel at Actopan, Hidalgo, shows this primordial couple engaged in the same sexual division of labor as the native
couples: Eve sits and spins while Adam cultivates.[86]

Weaving and the specialized arts of brocade and embroidery
were the province of Xochiquetzal, a deity represented as younger
and less "earthy" than Toci or Tlazolteotl and apparently associated
with the sexuality of "normal" adult women—Tlazolteotl being the
patron of promiscuous and adulterous women. This is not to say that
Xochiquetzal was sexually restrained: she could, if provoked, play
the seducer, as she does in the story of Yappan.[87] The rhythmic, back-
and-forth motion of weaving, its intertwining of separate threads
into a single web, is, like spinning, an obvious source of sexual innu-
endo, and a deity of weaving might be expected to be sexually active.
That the daughter in the *Codex Mendoza* is not shown weaving until
the age of fourteen may be no accident: the girl has passed through
puberty. This is also the first depiction of the daughter that dresses
her in a skirt and blouse bearing the same designs as those of her
mother.[88]

Weaving was so intimately tied to a woman's sexuality that
women who specialized in ornate brocade and embroidery were assumed (at least by some consultants of Sahagún's) to display a corresponding exuberance in the sexual sphere: "They used to live very
pleasurably, they used to go around having a good time, the embroiderers."[89] Perhaps the income generated from these arts granted
these women such a degree of economic independence that they
could live as they pleased—or cause others to fear that they would.

According to Sahagún's book on the 260-day calendar, women
who were embroiderers and workers of cotton would fast for twenty,
forty, or eighty days culminating in the day Seven Flower, Xochiquetzal's festival.[90] If such a woman broke her fast (which included pro-
hibitions on sex and bathing as well as dietary restrictions), Xochiquetzal would mock her and punish her with infections. It was also
said that such a woman would become sexually intemperate—perhaps as a punishment from Xochiquetzal, perhaps as a direct consequence of her lack of self-control. The text does not indicate whether
ordinary housewives participated in this fasting.

In yet another parallel between the domestic context and the
battlefield, weaving implements could, like brooms, be brandished

as swords: the female deities Cihuacoatl and Ilamatecuhtli wielded weaving battens along with shields.[91] The women warriors of Tlatelolco, in Alvarado Tezozomoc's account cited above, assailed the enemy soldiers with battens and warping frames as well as brooms.[92]

Alvarado Tezozomoc, recounting the rites of women whose men were at war, states that these women went at night to offer food at the temples, "carrying a twisted rope, as thick as a finger, signifying that through the gods their husbands would return victorious, with a great capture of their enemies, and these women carried a weaving shuttle, tzotzopaztli, which was a sign that with swords their husbands and sons would conquer their enemies."[93] These objects, brought from the home and connected with women's textile production, the rope suggesting the umbilical cord as well as spun cordage, were to provoke the desired reaction on the field of battle. House and battlefield were identified, with an inversion of gender, such that a woman's shuttle or batten[94] was ritually translated into a weapon for her son or husband.

The women who died in their first childbirth with the fetus unborn and who rose into the western sky to join the Cihuateteo were called *mocihuaquetzque*, "they who arise as women." After they conveyed the sun from the zenith to the underworld, these dead women would descend to earth and search for "the spindle whorl, the batten, the basket, all the woman's implements"; they would also call on their former husbands to ask for blouses, skirts, and women's tools.[95] Sahagún's text indicates that it was actually "the *tzitzimitl*, the *coleletli*" who used to pull this stunt, appearing to people as if he were one of these women. These are names for malevolent nocturnal deities; by this time these names had become associated with the Devil. What has happened here, as elsewhere in the *Florentine Codex*, is that nocturnal, ghostly apparitions have been subsumed within the demonic identity the friars ascribed to all native deities. Sahagún—or, perhaps, his indigenous assistants—has interpreted the mocihuaquetzque as manifestations of the Devil, "indigenizing" the Christian concept by using the native terms. To older generations of Mexicas, these women were surely numens in their own right and not the Devil in disguise.

Why should these ghosts of nonmothers return in search of spindles? They had been buried in a new skirt and blouse; their tools were, according to the *Códice carolino*, buried with them.[96] Perhaps they sought to compensate for their failure to reproduce through an exaggerated attachment to other signs of womanhood. Or perhaps, being warriors of a sort—like Cihuacoatl, who wielded a shield and batten and with whom they were identified—they sought the female analogues of weapons.

Like the house or patio in which she sat and like the field in which her husband labored, the cloth a woman wove was quadrilateral. In the Quiché Maya *Popol Vuh*, the gods lay out the earth by stretching and folding cords, like a man measuring out his field or a woman preparing the warp for her loom.[97] Did the weaving woman occupy a position of significance in the cosmic scheme?

Cecelia F. Klein sees imagery of thread and cloth pervading Mesoamerican cosmology: the layered cosmic planes are analogous to a folded length of cloth; the underworlds resemble a maze of tangled threads while the upper worlds are ordered like a neatly woven textile.[98] For the Quiché, Barbara Tedlock and Dennis Tedlock note various associations between weaving and other domains, such as agriculture, the growth of forests, the building of houses and shrines, divination, and speech, as well as the solar movements that establish and regulate space and time.[99] Dennis Tedlock suggests further that Mesoamerican calendrical periods should not be seen as wheel-like "cycles"; a model more consistent with native thinking is that of cloth on a loom.[100] The weft travels back and forth in a continuous sequence; designs are repeated at regular intervals but show slight variations from one occurrence to the next. Similarly, episodes of Mesoamerican history do not really repeat themselves but resemble each other, as if woven from the same pattern or template. Klein sees the tree or house pole, around which the weaver looped her backstrap loom, as "the implicit center of the woven cosmos."[101]

As a woman sat there, weaving space and time into a skirt for her daughter or a mantle for her husband, perhaps she was more preoccupied with the children's health or the evening meal than the mysteries of the cosmos. However, that there was something in the act of weaving that replicated ingrained patterns of thought and perception need not be something she contemplated consciously for the act of weaving to be imbued with a sense of rightness, a feeling that things were in their proper place.

If the weaving came out poorly, a woman was likely to experience anxiety. Sahagún's book on people and their virtues and vices includes, in the chapter on nonelite women, descriptions of the weaver, the spinner, and the seamstress.[102] In interpreting the descriptions of "good" and "bad" individuals in this book, it must be kept in mind that this categorization was imposed by the friar to elicit terminology useful for preaching and confessing; for example, a woman might be questioned during confession to see if she did any of these "bad" things. However, some of the terms of abuse applied to poor processors of fiber suggest that such women truly were viewed with alarm. The bad weaver was not only careless and unskilled with her hands; "she damages things, she breaks things, she ominously destroys things, she ominously destroys the surface of things."[103] The first couplet implies immorality and criminality; the second, with its use of *tetzahuitl* (omen, portent, scandal), implies that the woman is some sort of holy terror, an augury of ill fortune. Something is definitely wrong with her: her lumpy, lopsided weaving just may indicate a flaw in the cosmic fabric.

Sahagún's catalog of nasty superstitions includes only one that involves weaving, and the text is difficult to interpret. If a woman's weaving came out crooked, it was said that the *owner* of the garment being woven was a perverse, ungenerous person. A mantle is used to represent the garment in question; the term given is *tilmaoa*, "possessor of the mantle," or, perhaps more accurately, "the one in relation to whom exists the mantle."[104] In his Spanish gloss, Sahagún refers to this person as *aquel para quien era*, "the one for whom [the garment] was."[105] Charles E. Dibble and Arthur J. O. Anderson's translation presents the weaver herself as the guilty party,[106] as does Jacinto de la Serna where he borrows this tidbit from Sahagún.[107] Sahagún's Spanish glosses do occasionally misrepresent what the Nahuatl actually says, but in this case I do not think the friar was careless or confused. It seems odd to me that the weaver should be referred to as the garment's owner rather than its maker. Given the importance of garments and other accoutrements to the construction of a person's identity, it does not seem so peculiar that the character of the intended wearer might affect a garment's construction. Such a belief would, however, strike Sahagún as an illogical super-

stition worth including in his list of devilish absurdities. The idea
that a bad woman would be a bad weaver would not have seemed so
outrageous to him.

Conclusion

The religious orientation of Mexica culture thoroughly permeated the
domestic context, such that the seemingly mundane work of running
a household was imbued with symbolic meanings and hedged about
with rules and omens. Housework was serious, and risky, business.
The home, engendered as female space, was a place of power that, in
its womblike darkness and its centrality, was the opposite of the
bright and distant battlefield where the soldiers of the sun acted out
their own cosmic drama. And yet both stages, house and battlefield,
were intimately and ultimately joined into one, just as woman and
man, in being the two parts of a duality, were, though dressed in different costumes and carrying different props, really one.

To approach Mexica culture with ready-made categories of
"public" and "private" merely distorts the reciprocal images cast by
these mirrored constructions of gender. To judge women's status by
their "public" importance is to miss an essential point: the "public"
hardly existed except as a series of replications and inversions of the
"private," and vice versa. Concepts of home and home life existed,
but these constructs were seen as integrated with the rest of society
and cosmos, subject to the same laws and the same disruptions.

For the friars, the Mexica woman, as both female and native, was
doubly Other. In their minds not only were women, the weaker sex,
more prone than men to demonic temptations, but native people in
general, weak-willed and new to the faith, were easily duped by the
Devil—especially when far removed from the friars' sight. In their
war against Satan, the Mexica residence became a home front of a
different sort. Instead of being in alignment with external space, as a
model for the temple or an inverted complement of the battlefield, to
the friars the home was a private counterspace opposed to the public space of churchyard and town hall, and thus a potential locus of
subversion and resistance. In this way did the friars justify their collusion in the invasive colonial policy of *congregación*, the forced resettlement of native people into large towns and cities.

But how well did the friars know their enemy? Confronted with seemingly contradictory evidence of women's devotion to housework and women's power, they responded by projecting the power onto the Devil and attempting to reconcile the associated behaviors with their own models of female submissiveness and female seclusion. The friars' failure in the field of female education is worth noting here. While their schools for boys flourished, efforts to establish girls' schools floundered from the start. A school staffed by Spanish women recruited by the empress, in which native girls, in Motolinia's approving words, "were taught no more than how to be married women,"[108] survived for only ten years. Its failure was blamed on lack of teachers, but there is no indication that mobs of native girls were clamoring for Spanish-style housewifery. Instead, and in the face of efforts to undermine the consanguineal family system, Mexica women clung to their traditional position within the family, passing their property rights to heirs of their choice and, when necessary, defending themselves in court.[109]

Kellogg demonstrates how colonial civil and ecclesiastical policies had, nevertheless, the long-term effect of separating native culture into public and private domains. Constant emphasis on the individual, the conjugal pair, and the male-headed nuclear family eventually weakened the consanguineal family and its network of kin and neighbors.[110] At the same time, the distinction between "sin" and "crime," enshrined in the structure of Spanish authority, forced a division between a private, moral domain and a public domain of civil life and the law. By the seventeenth century, Kellogg notes, native women were bequeathing property to a narrow range of mostly nuclear-family kin; those who went to court did so as legal minors under male protection rather than as independent plaintiffs. (Also see chap. 5.) The friars' illusion had, to a significant extent, become reality.

The friars' other image, the woman as closet Satanist, was also an inaccurate one. There is no evidence that the average Mexica woman was more resistant to Christianity than the average Mexica man, however well she, or he, understood its precepts. Women participated enthusiastically in what limited roles the Church did make available to them—as neighborhood officials in charge of bringing girls and women to church, as the friars' cooks and tailors, as alms-

givers, as sponsors of masses for dead relatives, as members and
sometimes leaders of religious confraternities, even as cloistered
companions to Spanish and creole nuns.[111] For the colonial Mexica,
there is no convincing evidence of a "household" religion intention-
ally subverting or opposing Christianity—any more than the native
version of Christianity that was practiced openly.[112] A suspicious
priest might see the Devil dance in the sweepings of a woman's
broom, but he knew far more about the Devil than about her.

2

Aztec Wives

Arthur J. O. Anderson

[Utilizing a rich sampling of Nahua colonial accounts to contextualize women in their prescribed roles as upstanding wives and citizens, Arthur J. O. Anderson focuses on the institution of marriage as it was understood in the preconquest era and as it was reformulated by Spanish friars by means of Nahuatl-language Christian treatises. Based on three sources in particular for purposes of comparison, a Nahuatl sermon, a huehuetlatolli *(discourse by Nahua elders), and a Nahua ethnography, overall Anderson finds little change in most indigenous women's lives, however idealized, over the course of the sixteenth century. Nonetheless, his conclusions are yet another reminder of the perils of gender stereotyping, whatever the culture or era. Arthur Anderson died on June 3, 1996.—Eds.]*

In fray Bernardino de Sahagún's *Primeros memoriales*,[1] a rather long passage describes how, every 260 days, on the day Four Reed, four high judges sat in judgment to admonish and castigate all the assembled lords, noblemen, and holders of high and responsible office and, with them, all the women of comparable rank.[2] All feared that they would be accused and found guilty of failing to discharge their duties and that consequently they would be exiled, reduced in rank, or otherwise humiliated, or even killed. As for the women specifically,

cenca neumauhtiloya . . . in çi-
vatl, yn illamatlacatl yn aço y-
tlacavi in içivatequiuh yn
moteneva y malacatl y tzotzopaztli, no iehoatl yc momauh-
tiaya yn aço yn avel tlacazcaltia
yn avel tlacavapava: yn aço
ymichmuchva [sic] yn avel
quipia yn avel quimizcaltia yn
aço otlatlaco yn aço ye momeca-
tia, yn ichpuchtly yn amo
macho:

The matrons and all the old
women were all very much
afraid that perhaps the womanly work, what is called the
spindle whorl, the batten, was
done badly. They were also
afraid that perhaps they had
reared the children badly, that
they had educated the children
badly, that they had not
guarded their daughters well,
had not reared them well. Perhaps a daughter had done
something bad; perhaps she
was living in concubinage with
a man [and] it was not known.

o ca yuhq'n i ynic çenca ne-
mauhtiloya in tetecuti yn pipilti
yn içivava yoan in tequivaque
inçivava, ioan in calqixque inçivava ioan in tequitlatoque inçivava ioan in pipiltin ymich-
puchva ioan tecutli ichpuch
ioan in tequiva ichpuch in
calpixqui ichpuch, in tequitlatoque ymichpuchvan oixquich i
yntla ixco quintecaya, yn
tenonotza yn tecenquixtia
ypampa in cenca nemauhtilo yn
muchi tlacatl quitoa yn itic yn
aço nehvatl noca tlatoloz.

Likewise the wives of the
lords, of the noblemen, and the
wives of the valiant warriors
and the wives of the mayordomos and the wives of the tribute
bosses and the daughters of the
noblemen and the daughters of
the lords and the valiant warriors' daughters, the mayordomos' daughters, the daughters
of the tribute bosses, if they assembled them all before [the
judges], when they admonished
the people, when they grouped
the people, were all therefore
very much afraid. Everyone
said to himself: "Perhaps it is I
who will be accused."

And even though they were later dismissed with an admonition, they were all in fact roundly accused by the first of the four judges. Having thoroughly castigated the men, he turned to the women and said,

nican tonoc yn ticueye in tivipille in ticivatzintli: ça no iuhqui yn avc vel titlacazcaltia in avc vel, titlacavapava, yn tiquizcaltia in ticvapava in muchpuch in tiçivapilli yn tecutli tiçivauh in tequiva tiçivauh in calpixque tiçivauh in tequitlato tiçivauh, in tiquizcaltia in ticvapava in muchpuch yn avcmo ticuitlauiltia in tlacuicuiliztli in tlachpanaliztli in avc vel iquiti in avc tle vel quichiva: Cuix amo itequiuh in xochio in tlapallo yn itonal yn tilmatli, yn itonal maxtlatl yn tlaçotilmatly, yn itech quitlalia yn pilli yn oquichtli. Auh in quauhtli yn oçelotl q'matataca.

Here you are, you with the skirts, you with the shifts, you who are women. In like manner, no longer do you properly rear, no longer do you properly instruct, when you rear, when you instruct your daughters—you noblewomen, you lords' wives, you valiant warriors' wives, you mayordomos' wives, you tribute bosses' wives. When you rear your daughters, when you instruct them, no longer do you urge them to gather up rubbish, to sweep. No longer do they spin well, no longer do they weave well; they do nothing well. Is it not their duty [to make] the flowered, multicolored capes, the breechcloths, the precious capes that the noblemen, the warriors wear, to which they are entitled, for which the eagles, the jaguars toil?

The references to sweeping up rubbish, spinning, weaving, and so on, are traditional references to activities associated with women (see chapter 1 for additional information about such activities). A judge addressing commoners would add the metate, standing for food and drink preparation. One of the Nahua sayings gathered by fray Andrés de Olmos, author of the earliest-known Nahuatl grammar (1547), which he summarized as *Doi muger a alguno para que assienten y biuan en honra* (I give someone a wife, so that they may set-tle down and live honorably), expresses the idea in a series of paired metaphors known as *difrasismos*.

Tepan nicçoa in cueitl, in uipilli; auh tepan nicteca in tço-tçopaztli, in malacatl, in teça-catl: temac noconpiloa in ich-catl, in malacatl, inic onoz in petlatl, in icpalli.	I spread the skirt, the shift for one; and I spread out for one the batten, the spinning whorl. Thus there will be authority and control.[3]

However, spinning and weaving actually were what every woman in the upper levels of society was expected always to do and excel in, judging by the array of weaving-spinning implements listed in the *Primeros memoriales*[4]—cane stalks, various battens, straws, skeins, heddles, various spindle whorls and their baskets, warping frames, divided cords, bandages, and such materials as feathers, the hair of hares and rabbits, and dyes for fine, ornamental, and colored weaving, presumably with cotton. The female commoner was simi-larly equipped, but her gear was simpler and coarser, suitable for maguey fibers, and was augmented by the metate for kitchen duties and tools to extract the juice from the maguey plants and extract and prepare fibers from the leaves for weaving.[5] This equipment is similar to that listed in the *Florentine Codex* as work equipment for women of upper levels of society; to it Sahagún adds, "They make food, they make drink; they do it of their own accord."[6]

Ceremonies immediately after birth foreshadowed all this. Whereas the four little arrows, the bow, the shield, and the umbilical cord that was sent to be buried in the field of battle showed her brother's destination in Aztec society, as much a man's world as ever existed, a girl's spinning whorl, batten, reed basket, skeins, shuttle, cotton, sweeper and broom, and the umbilical cord that was buried near the grinding stone and hearth showed that she "was one who went nowhere; only the house was her abode."[7] Steps were taken early to train children according to approved patterns that within each sex varied somewhat depending on the social status of the fam-ily, standards being stricter and supervision closer for those of the upper and ruling classes.

In general, one can probably accept the information given graphically in the *Codex Mendoza* as accurate enough. Alonso de Zorita must have used some such information, as well as the *huehuetlatolli*, or admonitions of the elders, for the summaries he gives us. While the boy was being brought up to be a warrior or a priest or a merchant or an agriculturist-commoner, girls in the upper levels, he says, at the age of five, began their embroidery-sewing-weaving tasks, were kept busy, were made to keep themselves clean, and were admonished to be discreet in speech, conduct, appearance, and bearing. Supervision was constant, whether the girls remained at home or performed duties at the temple.[8]

Discourses of admonition were addressed to the girls presumably when they were old enough to appreciate them. The father in ruling and upper-class families laid much stress on discretion in behavior, on giving the gods due devotion (keeping vigils, being "diligent with the sweeping"), and also on practical matters. "Look well to the drink, to the food, . . . the art of good drink, the art of good food." "This is the property of—it belongs to—the lords, the rulers." And: "Look well, apply yourself well to the really womanly tasks, the spindle whorl, the weaving stick"; and to feather work, weaving designs, judging colors, and applying them in such work.[9] The mothers, according to Zorita, "charged their daughters with the service of God and the guard of their virtue, and with service and love for their husbands," and admonished them, "See that you live in such manner that you set an example to other wives. . . . [Y]ou must live virtuously."[10]

In more modest levels of society, while the father was advising a married son, in a long admonition, among other things, to "constrain the skirt-owner, the shift-owner to do her work with the spindle whorl, with the batten, with the beverages, with the metate" (*xoconcuitlahuilti in cueye, in huipile, in imalacatequiuh, in itzotzopaztequiuh, in iatequiuh, in imetlatequiuh*) and to look after "the necklaces, the quetzal plumes bred and born of her womb" (*in cozcatl, in quetzalli in oyol in otlacat in ixillan in itozcatlan*),[11] the mother advised her daughter with equally practical admonitions: "Also, put yourself near the beverages, the metate, and really grasp, lift up the sauce bowl, the big basket" (*ma no itlan ximaquiti in atl, in metlatl yhuan huel xictzitzqui, huel xicacocui i molcaxitl, in chiquihuitl*).[12] Furthermore,

in ihquac in aquin ticmonamic-
tiz in quauhtli, in ocelot, ahmo
ixco, ahmo ycpac tinemiz. In
ihquac tleyn michihuallaniz, in
mitztequiuhtiz, in tleyn mitznahuatiz, niman huel tictlacamatiz, ticpaccacaquiz in itlahtol,
ahmo niman ticqualan-
canamiquiz, ahmo niman tix-
tomahuaz, ahmo ticcuepiliz,
ahmo ihuic ticmilacatzaz. Intla
itla yc mitztolinia, ahmo no
oncan tiquilnamiquiz, ahmo yc
ticmoxictiz, yc timotlanectiz
intla ycnotlacatl.

when you marry some eagle [or]
jaguar [warrior], you are not to
walk ahead of [or] over him.
When he asks you something
[or] entrusts something to you,
[or] when he tells you to do
something, you are to obey him
properly, you are to listen pleas-
antly to what he says; you are
not then to receive it angrily,
you are not then to perturb
yourself, you are not to answer
back, you are not to turn your
back on him. If something thus
irks you, neither are you to remind him of it; you are not to
belittle him there because of it,
nor to act selfishly over it if he is
a poor man.

Intla huel moca nemi, ca ye
huel mocuexanco, momamal-
huazco ticmotlaliz, ahmo
yuhquin tehuatl timoquauhpo-
huaz, timocelopohuaz. Ahmo
zan quen ticchihuaz in tlyn [sic]
mitznahuatiz inic ahmo
ticyolitlacoz in Totecuiyo,
yhuan yehuatl inic ahmo
mitztoliniz, zan ihuiyan, zan
yocoxca, tiquilhuiz in tleyn yc
mitztoliniz. Ahmo teixpan,
tenahuac ticpinauhtiz, ca intla
ticpinauhtiz, ca niman yuhquin
tehuatl moyollo, mocuitlaxcol,
in teixpan ticnemitia, in
tichuilana.

If he lives by your bounty,
place him well on your lap, in
your protection, [but] do not
fancy yourself to be like an
eagle [or] jaguar [warrior]. You
are not to do badly what he tells
you to do, lest you offend our
Lord and He afflict you. Softly,
calmly you are to tell him what
afflicts you. You are not to humiliate him before or near others, for if you humiliate him, it
is as if you drag your heart,
your entrails, what you cause to
live, before others.[13]

Zorita evidently knew this admonition, for in his *Brief and Summary Relation of the Lords of New Spain* he provides a digest of part of it for interpretation and indicates the high regard in which some Spaniards held the huehuetlatolli from which it came. The pertinent paragraph follows.

When your parents give you a husband, do not be disrespectful to him; listen to him and obey him, and do cheerfully what you are told. Do not turn your face from him, and if he did you some hurt, do not keep recalling it. And if he supports himself by your industry, do not on that account scorn him, or be peevish or ungracious, for you will offend God and your husband will be angry with you. Tell him meekly what you think should be done. Do not insult him or say offensive words to him in front of strangers or even to him alone; for you will harm yourself thereby, and yours will be the fault.[14]

Such was the expected behavior of mature women, the result, as fray Juan Bautista saw it, writing at the end of the sixteenth century, of training described in a summary statement in his collection of huehuetlatolli. There were, he says,

highly skilled and experienced matrons who educated the young girls with great care and taught and trained them in the understanding and worship of the gods and in other womanly matters, especially in the profession of midwifery and of baptizing the newborn with much ceremony, once when the child was born and again on the most propitious day within the thirteen-day period following its birth. They also trained them in matters concerning marriage, in which the women always were the agents and marriage-makers, and are even today, and in the ways in which they should attend their husbands, not only by giving them support where needful and necessary but even in addition [in serving them] with great discernment and care, perceiving how important a woman's neatness and caring ways are to the tired, weary

man. They also trained them in the knowledge of herbs, both
medicinal and noxious, and in many very special matters
omitted here to avoid prolixity. If present-day Spanish
women were to give such matters even moderate attention,
their houses would be better managed, their children better
taught, and their husbands better treated and less vexed by
the endless, needless expenses which they incur for [their
wives], by which many [men] vex their souls and because
of which they sometimes lose their good name and honor,
and leave many orphans and widows in the poor-house.[15]

One of the means used by the religious to convert the natives
and, in a sense, to restructure native society was the establishment of
schools connected to the churches. Here, fray Gerónimo de Mendieta
tells us,

> Indoctrination and education proceeded on three levels. In
> large settlements, in the school building, the ruling element's
> boys were taught the catechism and reading and writing. In
> the courtyard the commoners' boys were taught the cate-
> chism and then dismissed to assist their elders in their work.
> In small communities—because they were small—boys of
> all social levels were more likely to be indoctrinated and
> taught reading and writing together. The native language
> was used.
>   So much for the boys preparing for a still male-oriented
> society. The girls appear to have been given a more thorough
> and continuous religious education, learning the prayers,
> the Ten Commandments, the Articles of the Faith, the Com-
> mandments of the Church, the Sacraments, and so on,
> grade by grade, group by group, the older girls often teach-
> ing or drilling the younger at their insistence. Matrons es-
> corted and supervised groups of girls, and old men as con-
> stables escorted and guarded them. Though this education
> continued until the girls married, a number of them never
> married but always led chaste and virtuous lives, serving
> as matrons in charge of younger girls, or serving in the

cofradías [socioreligious confraternities, sodalities], in the hospitals, offering spiritual help, and so forth.[16]

What Mendieta writes is interestingly complemented by Sahagún in the prologue to book 10 of his *General History*. Having told that in the early phases of their work the friars had tested native men's fitness to teach and preach, first letting them wear the Franciscan habit but soon finding them "not equal to such a calling,"[17] he then says of the women,

> Since, in the time of idolatry, there were convents for the women who served in the temples and maintained chastity, trials were also made to see if they were capable of being nuns and sisters of the Christian religion and of maintaining constant chastity. And to this end convents and sisterhoods of women were created. And they were instructed in spiritual matters. And many of them knew how to read and write. And those who seemed to us to be well instructed in the Faith, and those who were matrons of good judgment were made Mother Superiors of the others that they might direct them and teach them Christian matters and all good practices.
>
> And certainly, at the beginning, we were of the opinion that the men would be capable as priests and monks, and the women as nuns and sisters. From experience, we learned that, at the time, they were not capable of such perfection. And so the sisterhoods and the convents, which we had planned in the beginning, ceased. Nor do we see even now indications that this can be brought about.[18]

Meanwhile, perhaps the most important element in the education of native children was proceeding according to the ancient, preconquest ways, in the home and by the parents, applying to a greater or lesser extent the corrections metaphorically implied in the following series of difrasismos from Olmos's collection, which he labels *Despertar a algunos con castigo, o corrección* (To awaken people with punishments, or to correct them).

Culutl, tçitçicaztli, uitztli, omitl, cecec atl nictequaqualhtia; yequene tetl, quauitl, mecapalli, tepuztli nictemaca, nictetoctia, in nictequalhtia, inic tetech nicpachoa.

I stimulate one with scorpions, nettles, thorns, [sharpened] bones, and cold water; and also I give one, strengthen one, improve one with stones and sticks, with the head band for carrying burdens, with iron. These I bring upon one.[19]

That some of these stimulants were sometimes applied literally is suggested by illustrations in the *Codex Mendoza*, among various such sources, but mostly the corrections, advice, and admonitions referred to metaphorically above were constantly administered verbally in the form of huehuetlatolli like those quoted earlier. To these the friars and other discerning Spaniards gave great attention; and they saw their value. If they did not consciously adapt and use them in various ways to enhance the propagation of the Faith and to keep their neophytes on the straight and narrow path, the very existence of these huehuetlatolli with so much ancient lore resembling or supporting Christian ideals so continuously drilled into maturing Aztec youngsters provided an impetus of great value to the missionaries. Probably most priests and friars who knew something of Aztec society were well acquainted with the huehuetlatolli.

Sahagún certainly knew them well. He had been associated with fray Andrés de Olmos, and he collected them very successfully himself, as we can see in book 6 of his *General History*. But though Olmos, in his own evangelical writings, adopted much of the florid style highly spiced with literary devices appropriate to the most polished Nahuatl speech—the difrasismo or "coupling of two images to suggest a third meaning," "couplet parallelism as a general feature," and "polynomial repetition with both semantic and poetic force"[20]—Sahagún's works are, in comparison, much plainer, sometimes almost stark, in style. As Charles E. Dibble has phrased it, Sahagún

clearly identifies himself as a purist, ever careful to avoid terms which might serve to perpetuate the concepts of Satan. Perhaps he equated many of the metaphors with the

cantares at the end of Book 2 [of the *General History*], which
he recorded but failed to translate, stating:
    It is a very old custom of our adversary the Devil to
    seek out hiding places for doing his business, in accordance
    to what is in the Gospel, which says: "He who does evil ab-
    hors the light."[21]

What Sahagún valued and used for his religious writings was
the content rather than the style of the huehuetlatolli. For our purposes in dealing with women of early colonial times, I shall refer to
two of his works. One is a sermon on marriage: the relationship to
each other of husband and wife and their obligations. It is from his
collection of sermons dating to about 1540 and revised in 1563; a
copy dated 1588 is used here. The other is his *Manual del christiano*
(1578), of which only a fragment has survived, but what remains
deals with Christian marriage and closely parallels the sermon.[22]
These can be compared in a number of points to certain of the huehuetlatolli gathered by Olmos; with some additions and, no doubt,
emendations, they were eventually published by fray Juan Bautista
in 1600.[23]
    Christian marriage began to be established very soon after the
arrival of missionaries. Mendieta mentions the date 1526 for that of
Hernando Pimentel and others in Texcoco.[24] The date given in the
Codex of 1576 (*Aubin Codex*) for its establishment in Mexico Tenochtitlan is the year 11 House, or 1529. *Nican tzintic ȳ nenamictiliztli*, the
codex comments: Here marriages began.[25] No unusual problems appear to have been noted in the marriages contracted before or after the
conquest by people of lower estate; as a population unable to afford
any form of plural marriage, they were, by and large, monogamous
by necessity. But the powerful and the rich could afford primary and
secondary wives or concubines. Among people of these social levels
it took a decade to begin satisfactorily to make the men monogamous; Mendieta describes the years 1530–40 as being unusually difficult in this respect for the priests.[26] Sahagún thus records his impressions of the matter in book 10 of the *General History*.

    Great were the labors and perplexities we had in the
    beginning marrying those who were baptized and who

had many women, so as to give them those whom the law
requires them to take; for in investigating the relationships
and knowing which was the first, in order to give her to
him, we found ourselves in a labyrinth of great difficulty,
for they lied in saying which was the first, and they committed fraud in order to marry those for whom they had
greater affection. And to know with whom they had performed the ceremony which they practiced when they took
a legitimate wife, it was necessary to review and understand many idolatrous ceremonies and rituals of the time
of their unbelief. And as we knew little of the language,
hardly ever did we gain the insight as we have now learned
it.[27]

But neither the *Manual del christiano* nor the sermon mentions either polygamy or monogamy as such, though both castigate illicit
unions (*nemecatiliztli;* defined in fray Alonso de Molina's *Vocabulario*
as *amancebamiento*).[28] They take monogamy as universally established and concentrate on matrimony in the sense of its being holy
wedlock, *teoyotica nenamictiliztli*, "godly marriage," defined in Molina's
Vocabulario as *casamiēto por la iglesia,* or marriage by or through the
Church.[29] This is, quite naturally, the situation taken for granted, especially in the sermon, whose general theme revolves about well-
ordered marriages, procreation, chastity, virtuous living, chaste
marriage, and marriage as a Sacrament.

For the purpose of considering the similarities between the
propositions brought forth by Sahagún in the sermon and various of
the huehuetlatolli organized by Bautista, we can arrange the sermon's content under four headings: (1) The obligations of the man,
(2) The man's powers, (3) The obligations of the woman, and (4) The
obligations shared by both. This arrangement is more formal than
that of the sermon and more complete than what we find in the
Manual del christiano. In the huehuetlatolli we concentrate on the few
devoted to advice or warnings given by the father to a son and the
mother to a daughter.

1. The man's obligations that are his exclusively center about
support of wife and family.

Monavatil omochiuh in tictemoliz mocivauh itech onequi
yvan in mopilhuan tiquin-
tlaiecoltiz ticnextiz in centli in
etl in chian in chili iuh ca in
teotlatoli.

It became your obligation to
seek for your wife what she requires, and you are to support
your children. You will provide
corn, beans, chía, chili. Such is
the Word of God.

These precepts are paralleled in the huehuetlatolli. The father
thus admonishes his married son,

Ma huel ipan ximapana,
ximotetzilo immotlamatzo-
hualtzin, immoquiltzin,
immonopaltzin. Ma tix-
quatlatziuh, ma titeputztlatziuh;
ma micampa tictlaz immota-
catzin, immocacatzin, immo-
topiltzin. Auh ma ticzozotlauh
immomatzin, immocxitzin, ma
ticnenenec immitzin, immoyol-
lotzin, immacoltzin, immocui-
tlapantzin. ¿Intla yuh ximuchi-
hua, intla xicnenenequi
immitzin, moyollotzin, ach
quen tihcaz, quen tinemiz in te-
tloctzinco, in tenahuactzinco?
¿Auh quen ihcazque, quen ne-
mizque in cozcame, in quetzaltin?
¿Auh quen ihcaz quen nemiz in
cueye, in huipile?

Gird yourself well, exert
yourself for your sustenance,
your vegetables, your prickly
pears. Give no rest to your forehead, to your back. Don't throw
behind you your accumulated
supplies, your carrying frame,
your staff. Give no rest to your
hands, to your feet. Don't submit to the whims of your face,
your heart, your shoulders,
your back. If you do so to
yourself, if you submit to the
whims of your face, your heart,
how will you stand up, how
will you live with people, by
them? And the precious necklaces, the fine plumes, how
will they stand up? How will
they live? And how will she
with the skirt, with the shift
stand up? How will she
live?[30]

And in the huehuetlatolli gathered by Sahagún, the mother-in-law
speaks thus to the young groom at the conclusion of a marriage that
evidently links merchant families.

Ma itlan xonmaquiti in topilli, in cacaxtli, ma mocujtlapan xocontlali in chilçolotl, in iztatapalcatl, in tequixqujtlaltzin, in mjchtlaçultzin: ma xoconmotlatoctili in aoacan, in tepeoacan, a toneoaz, a chichinacaz in moiollotzin in monacaiotzin.

Exert yourself with the staff, the carrying frame. Place the strands of chili, the salt cakes, the nitrous soil, the strings of fish upon your back; travel from city to city. Torment, suffering will afflict your heart, your body.[31]

Both the sermon and the *Manual del christiano* are insistent that the man take care of his wife when she is sick or pregnant, a duty probably not ignored in Aztec society but perhaps relegated to other women in the household or perhaps taken for granted. The huehuetlatolli of fray Juan Bautista are silent or at best laconic and vague.

itechpa xitlachie in cuèye, in huipile, in tleyn iquezpan, iquechtlan ompilcaz; yhuan in tleyn ic tlatotoniaz, yc tlayamaniaz immonextitlantzinco, immotlecuillantzinco.

[L]ook to what [clothing] is to hang from the hips, from the neck of her with the skirt, with the shift, and to what thus is to warm, to give heat by the ashes, by the hearth.[32]

But it is not clear whether warmth is for the wife, the house, or the relatives. The *Manual del christiano* is much more specific, and it may be that it and the sermon contribute something new and better to the marriage relationship.

yn jquac mococoa in ciuatl anoço ie vtztli, yn joqujchhuj monequj ypan tlatoz ynjc paleujloz yn ciuatzintli, ynjc amo tlatequipanoliztica mococolizcujtiz: auh yn jquac omjxiuh yn ciuatzintli monequj malhujloz ynjc amo tlatequjpanoliztica mocaxanjz. Jn iehoanti oqujchti, yn qualli yiollo, cenca qujnmalhuja qujnmocujtlauja yn jnnamjc-

[W]hen the woman is sick or is already pregnant, it is necessary that her husband favor her, so that the "little" woman may be helped, so that she may not become sick through working. And when the "little" woman gives birth, it is necessary that she be well treated so that she may not have a relapse because of working. Those men who are

hoa yn jquac vtzti, anoço yquac mjxihuj.

good of heart treat their spouses very well, take good care of them when they are pregnant or give birth.[33]

In the sermon Sahagún tells the men, "If she is pregnant, you are to seek a hired helper so that she will make the food" (*intla ia otztli tictemoliz in quaquevalli inic ievatl quichivaz tlaqualli*).

2. But the man's obligations also give him certain powers over his wife. He can force obedience. "When your husband speaks to you," Sahagún admonishes the woman, "you are to obey him, you are to honor him, you are to speak to him calmly and quietly even if he scolds you, ill-treats you" (*tictlacamatiz ticmaviztiliz iviyan iocoxca ticnotzaz in manel mitzava mitztolinia*). The *Manual del christiano* gives more details.

yn oqujchtli monequj quizcaliz yn jcivauh: qujcaoaltiz yn aqualli, qujnonotzaz ynic amo iuh qujchioaz yn amo chioalonj yn jiolitlacolocatzi dios. Auh yntlacamo mozcaliznequj, tenonotzaliztica caoaz, atl, cecec, tzitzicaztli qujtoctiz: auh yntlacamo ic mozcaliznequj qujtlatzacujltiz, tel çan tlaixieiecoz.

[I]t is necessary that the man instruct his wife; he is to prevent what is bad; he is to tell her that she is not to do what is illicit, what is offensive to God. And if she does not wish to be instructed, he is to reprimand her verbally; he is to correct her. And if she does not wish thus to be instructed, he is to punish her, though only with moderation.[34]

There is some basis for the above in the huehuetlatolli. The father thus advises a married son,

ma ye oc xoconcuitlahuilti in cueye, in huipile, in imalacatequiuh, in itzotzopaztequiuh, in iatequiuh, in imetlatequiuih yhuan in centetl, in ontetl in cozcatl, in quetzalli in oyol, in otlacat, in ixillan in itozcatlan in cueye, in huipile.

[M]ake the skirt-owner, the shift-owner do her work with the spindle whorl, the batten, her work with the beverages, with the metate, and [with the care of the children] if one, two necklaces, fine plumes have been born, have come into the

world from the womb, from the
breast of the skirt-owner, the
shift-owner.[35]

And the mother advises the daughter, as we have seen, to obey her
husband, to avoid giving offense, and to obey his words cheerfully.
Olmos's summary of this passage from the *Manual del christiano*,
which Bautista includes among his huehuetlatolli, varies slightly but
is explicit.

When you marry and your parents give you a husband, don't be disrespectful to him but on his ordering you
to do something hear him and obey him and do it cheerfully. Do not anger him, do not turn from him. . . . [N]or are
you to do badly what he orders you, because you will commit a sin against God and your husband will punish you.[36]

The sermon also requires that the wife obey the husband's
wishes as to coition, a matter not touched on in the huehuetlatolli,
though probably the woman's acquiescence was taken for granted in
Aztec society. These are Sahagún's words to the women.

amo can [*sic*] ie iyo titlatlacoa in
oc ce oquichtli oticmacac
monacaio ca Oc centlamantli yn
ipā anvetzi in iq̄c mitznequi
monamic tictlacamatiz. . . . Auh
intla ça nen tictlacavaltia. . . .
intla timococova . . . yntla timo-
civacocova yntla mitznequi
monamic xictlacamati inic amo
tlatlacoz . . . no ivan yn iquac ia
totztli intla mitznequi monamic
ximomaca. . . . No ivan yn iquac
ia totztli intla mitznequi monamic xicmomaca.

[N]ot only do you sin if you
have given your body to another man, for in addition you
fall into [sin] when your husband wishes you to obey him
. . . but you falsely abstain. . . .
[I]f you become sick, if you
menstruate, if your husband requires you, obey him so that he
will not sin. . . . Likewise when
you are pregnant, if your husband requires you, give yourself
to him. . . . Likewise when you
are already pregnant, if your
husband requires you, give
yourself to him.

Thus the huehuetlatolli do not invade the intimacy of married couples except as regards a woman's pregnancy. The advice differs from that of the sermon. In book 6 of the *General History* we find the following advice given by the midwife.

in aiamo onmaci piltzintli, in qujn ce, in qujn vme, in qujn ei metztli, ça oc quenman moquazque in jnamjc, injc onmaciz piltzintli. . . . [I]n omacic in ie qualli in ie tomaoa in ijtic otztli, aocmo quenman mahavillacanequiz in oqujchtli aocmo tlalticpac tlamatiz.

[B]efore the baby has attained form, after one, two, [or] three months, her husband should still be accepted, so that the child may attain form. . . . [W]hen what is within the pregnant woman is well formed, when it is enlarged . . . no longer should she at any time take her pleasure with her husband, no longer should she give herself to worldliness.[37]

3. The obligations of the wife are incessant and considerable; and they are confining. The mother warns a young daughter: "Attend only to what pertains to our house and don't go out readily; don't wander in the marketplace, the plaza, the baths, the waters, nor the roads, for it is bad [to do so], because harm and ruin are there."[38] As we have seen above, the rites performed at a girl's birth in preconquest times indicated that she "was one who went nowhere; only the house was her abode." Some of her obligations have been touched on in considering the man's powers and privileges; they are summarized in this statement from Sahagún's sermon: "You are to humble yourself, you are to address him cheerfully, because he governs you" (*çan timocnotecaz ticpacanotzaz yehica ca mopan icac*).

While the husband supports the family, the wife cares for the household. As the sermon expresses it,

monavatil inic tictlacamatiz moquichvi ticchiviliz in atl in tlaqualli ivan in icamisa in itilma in içaravellas iuh ca in teotlatolli.

[Y]our obligation is to obey your husband. You are to make the beverage, the food for him, and his shirt, his cape, his breeches. Such is the Word of God.

In the huehuetlatolli, an admonition from mother to daughter is in
its way explicit: "Put yourself next to the beverage, the metate, and
grasp well, take up firmly the sauce bowl, the big basket" (*ma no itlan
ximaquilti in atl, immetlatl yhuan huel xictzitzqui huel xicacocui i molcaxitl, in chiquihuitl*).[39] And: "Take good care of the spindle whorl, the
batten" (*immalacatl, in tzotzopaztli huel xicmocuitlahui*).[40]

And while the man is responsible for producing and supplying
sustenance and the household goods, "it is the woman's obligation to
put it properly in place" (*in civatl inavatil vel atlaliz*).[41] As the mother-
daughter harangue puts it, "You are to guard well the coffers, the
chests; you are to cover well the vessels, the bowls" (*huel ticpiaz in
toptli, in petlacalli, huel tictzatzaquaz in comitl, in caxitl*). Olmos summarized the situation in his translation of some of the huehuetlatolli
that Bautista published.

> Serve your husband, have his wash-water ready for him,
> and take care to make good bread.
>   And as to the household goods, place them as is fitting
> separately, each thing in its place, and not misplaced just
> anywhere.[42]

Though the sermon requires that the men take good care of their
wives, that they help them when sick or pregnant or when they have
recently given birth, the wives are especially charged with caring for
sick husbands.

in iquac mococova monamic
tictemoliz in patli ivan ticchiviliz in yectli tlaqualli in techi-
cauh vel ticmocuitlaviz ca in
tlaveliloc civatl in iquac mococova y ioquich quicauhtiquiça.

[W]hen your husband is sick
you are to seek medicine for him
and to make proper food for
him, to strengthen one. You are
to take good care of him. For the
evil woman, when her husband
is sick, soon abandons him.

There are no such specific instructions in the huehuetlatolli, but we
may remember that Bautista tells us that a girl's education included
knowledge of both medicinal and noxious herbs.

The sufferings and afflictions of women are part of her lot.

in civatl ca itequiuh ynetoliniliz in iquac otztli in icuac tlacachiva cenca motolinia tlaihiyovia netlamati.

[I]t is the woman's portion to be miserable when she is pregnant; when she bears a child she is much afflicted; she suffers; she is uncomfortable.

These matters are not dwelled on in Bautista's huehuetlatolli, though the *General History* (bk. 6, chaps. 28-30) tells eloquently of the means taken by midwives to mitigate the pain of labor and childbirth, to bring forth the child successfully, and to participate in the rites that made goddesses (Cihuateteo) of the mothers if they died in childbirth.[43] Successful childbirth is described as follows:

In otztli in ie qujmati ijti, in mjtoa: oacico in jmjqujzpan, inic mjxiviznequj: iciuhca caltia, camovia, qujpapaca, vel qujcencaoa: auh njman tlacencaoa, tlachpana in cali: in vncan qujhijoviz cioatzintli, in vncan tlacotiz, tequjtiz, in vncan tlacachioaz.

When the pregnant one already became aware of labor pains, when it was said her moment of death had come to pass, when already she wished to give birth, [the midwives] quickly bathed her, washed her hair with soap, washed her, arrayed her well. And then they arranged, they swept the house where the "little" woman was to suffer, where she was to perform her office, to give birth.

Intla pilli, tlatoanj, anoço mocujltonoa: vme, ey in iticiuh, ytlan onoque, tlatlatolchixque: auh in cenca ie mamana cioatzintli, iciuhca qujtentiuetzi, auh injc qujcivitia in jiehcoliz piltzintli cioapatli tlaquaqualatzalli conjtia in otztzintli.

If she was of noble [family], a ruler's [family], or was wealthy, two, three were her midwives. They remained by her, awaiting her word. And when the "little" woman became much disturbed internally, they quickly placed her in a sweatbath. And to hasten the birth of the baby, they gave the pregnant one cooked *cihuapatli* herb to drink.

Auh in cenca qujhijotia,
conjtia in tlaquatl: ic iciuhca tla-
cati in piltzintli.

And if she suffered much,
they gave her [ground] opos-
sum [tail] to drink, whereupon
the baby was quickly born.[44]

4. Many obligations apply equally to both husband and wife.
One group of these centers about chaste living, mutual love, faith-
fulness, and child rearing.

in tevatl toquichtli in ticivatl
oanquichiuhque Juramento inic
oanmonetoltique in ixpantzinco
Dios in tevatl toquichtli monetol
in tiquixcaviz monamic no ivi in
ticivatl tiquixcaviz in moquichvi
aoccac motech aciz oquichtli. O
inin ca iuh ca in monetol in ixpantzinco Dios ynic vel an-
mopiazque intlacamo anmopia
in amonetol oanmotlaveliltic
ompa aniazque in mictlan.

[Y]ou man, you woman, you
took an oath, thus made a vow
before God. As to you the man:
Your vow was that you would
cleave exclusively to your wife;
similarly you the woman would
cleave exclusively to your husband; never would [another]
man have access to you. Thus
this is your vow before God,
that you would indeed be
chaste. If you do not keep your
vow, woe upon you! You will go
there to the Region of the Dead.

Here the huehuetlatolli are essentially in agreement with the sermon. A father-to-son harangue warns, "Don't anywhere hurt yourself, injure yourself with the skirt, the shift belonging to someone
else" (ma cana tecue tehuipil yn timotzotzon, yc timohuitec).[45] And a
mother warns her daughter; "Don't anywhere give yourself wan-
tonly to another" (ma cana iliviz timotemaca); "do not know two men"
(ma vme oqujchtli mixco, mocpac ma); "never at any time, never ever betray [your husband]; . . . do not commit adultery" (ma nen ica, ma nen
queman ipan tia . . . ma tictlaxin).[46] One remembers, of course, that
Aztec society had been polygynous ever since it had become sedentary, at least in affluent levels of society,[47] and that the young unat-
tached men's sexual mores tended to be lax,[48] rather more so than
young women's, as the friars well knew, for they could use the term
ichpochtli (young maiden) to mean virgin and various forms of the

term to mean female virginity but were at a loss for a term indicating male virginity.[49]

To return to the sermon: "Mutual love is . . . very necessary. If they have been joined in holy wedlock, if they are already there and love each other very much, if they have children, they will be very happy. They will love each other" (*cenca monequi in nenepantlaçotlaliztli intla omonamictique teoiotica in ia cate cènca uel monepantlaçotla intla omopilhuatique cenca pactiiezque motlaçotlazque*). That marriage implies childbearing is not mentioned in Bautista's huehuetlatolli, though it is certainly taken as a matter of course, as we have already been able to see and as it is implied in chapter 4 of Sahagún's *Primeros memoriales*: "Woman; she bears children; she procreates children" (*çiuatl: tlacachioa /mopilhoatia*).[50] Neither is love mentioned in terms obvious to us or perhaps to the religious. However, the huehuetlatolli do record an exchange between newlyweds that is significant.

The Husband

Nonamictzine, tla xicmocaquiti, ma ticcuiz, ma ticanaz in nimitznolhuiliz in zan teonetlazotlaliztica; in ticpaccaceliz in axcan ca otechmocnelili in tlacatl, in teumahuiztli, in tlamache, in yocoxqui, in Ipalnemohuani, ca oyuh tlama iyollotzin, ca otechmolpili.

My companion, listen; grasp, accept what I shall tell you purely with great love. You are to receive it gladly now that the Lord favors us—He Who is holy and worthy of honor, Who possesses tranquillity, the Perfect One, He through Whom one lives, Whose heart has made captives, for He has tied us together.

The Wife

ye nimonacayo, ye nimomio ninochihua. . . . nipomial [i.e., nimopial] niez, notecuiyoquichtli.

I become your flesh, your bones. . . . I shall be what you guard, my lord, my master.[51]

"It is your obligation," the sermon continues, "to sleep together, to eat together; you are to live together; likewise are your goods, your property to be in only one place" (*amonavatil . . . çan çen ancochizque, çan cen antlaq̄zque ancennemizque no yvan in amaxca in amotlatq' can [sic] ceccan yez*).[52] Here the requirements of the sermon may go beyond the admonitions of the huehuetlatolli, though the ancient native lore may have assumed eating, sleeping, and living together to be obvious. Pooling family property may have been an innovation. We have seen that in Aztec society the man accumulates and the woman organizes. What the huehuetlatolli advises and the sermon does not, is that the wife be ready to take over management if the husband is incapable or incapacitated. The mother tells the daughter,

Intla huel moca nemi, ca ye huel mocuexanco, momamalhuazco ticmotlaliz, ahmo yuhquin tehuatl timoquauhpohuaz, timocelopohuaz. . . .	If he lives thanks to you, by our aid, you are to put him under your protection. But you are not therefore to consider yourself an eagle [warrior], you are not to consider yourself a jaguar [warrior]. . . .
. . . In aquin moquichhui, tehuatl tiquilhuiz in quenin ihcaz, in quenin nemiz tlalticpac. Yhuan huel ticmocuitlahuiz in tleyn ihuaz, in tleyn qualoz, in aço mochan in tleyn yc tlatotoniaz, in tleyn ic tlayamaniaz in amonextitlan, in amotlecuillan.	. . . You will tell whoever is your husband how he is to stand up, how he is to live on earth. And you will take care of what is to be drunk, what is to be eaten, or whether in your fireplace, on your hearth, something is thus to be warmed, to be heated.
Yhuan huel ipan titlahtoz in amocuen, in amomil yhuan huel tiquimmocuitlahuiz immotlatequipanocahuan; yhuan huel ticpiaz in toptli, in petlacalli, huel tictzatzaquaz in comitl, in caxitl.	And you are to protect your planted furrows, your fields, and you are to take care of your workers, and you are to guard the coffers, the chests, and cover well the vessels, the bowls.[53]

Olmos simplified all this by paraphrasing thus:

If your husband is silly or a dunce, advise him how to live, and take good care then of the maintenance and all that is necessary in all of your house; you will take care of the lands that you possess and provide for those who work on and guard the property, and cover vessels that contain anything. Don't be careless, and don't wander here and there misguidedly, for thus you will have neither house nor property.[54]

In view of the fact that the Aztec world, after the conquest as well as before, was a man's world, it is interesting, even curious, to note the following statements in the sermon: Man and wife "are equals. . . . They are to obey each other" (*in inamic . . . Monepantlacamatizque*). Somewhat similarly the *Manual del christiano* states, "It is necessary that the man obey his wife regarding coition, because it is his obligation thus to obey her" (*yn oqujchtli, monequj qujtlacamatiz yn icioauh, yn jtechpa yn nenepanoliztli, yehica ca ynaoatil ynjc qujtlacamatiz*).[55] These admonitions appear to be connected with the further statement in the sermon, "You the man already know that your body is someone else's goods, goods belonging to your wife" (*in tevatl toquichtli ya ticmati in monacaio ca teaxca iaxca in monamic*); "Likewise you the woman" (*ca no ivi in ticivatl*). This point is also prominently made in the *Apendiz de la postilla* (Appendix to the Apostle), quoting Saint Paul.

in ciuatl in teuiutica omo-namjcti, in jnacaio ca amo iaxca, ca iaxca in oqujchtli . . . çan no iuh . . . in oqujchtli teuiutica omonamjcti, in jnacaio amo iaxca, ca yaxca yn iciuauh.	[W]hen a woman is married in holy wedlock, her body is not her property; it is the man's property. . . . Likewise the man married in holy wedlock: his body is not his property; it is his wife's property.[56]

Such propositions, of course, do not occur in the huehuetlatolli.

Fulfillment of religious obligations is in one way or another constantly urged in the sermon. Reference to the Word of God is frequent; so is the admonition to confess transgressions. The man is told, "You are to love your wife's soul, you are to desire for her that our Lord may have mercy on her soul" (*amonavatil in toquichtli tictlaçotlaz in ianima mocivauh ticnequiliz in ma quimotlaoculili in tote° ianima*). "And you the woman, you are to love your husband's soul; you are to treat it well" (*auh in tevatl ticivatl in ianima monamic tictlaçotlaz ticmalhuiz*). So similarly in Bautista's huehuetlatolli, where one sees a good deal of influencing by the friars. A father tells his son,

in canin ixpan tiquizaz in ixiptlatzin in Totecuiyo ahnozo itlazohuan, ahnozo Cruz huel ticmahuiztiliz; ixpan timopachoz ahnozo timotlancuacoloz. Auh intla huel yehuatl in Totecuiyo Iesuxpo in inacayotzin (in ihtic moyetztica in Sancto Sacramento) ixpantzinco tiquizaz, tlapana-huiya inic ticmotlatlauhtiliz in ica muchi moyollo, ca moteouh, ca motlahtocatzin, ca motema-quixticatzin, ca motlazotatzin in ihtic moyetztica in Sancto Sacra-mento. Yhuan huel ticmahuiz-tiliz in itocatzin in Totecuiyo Jesu Christo. Yhuan in ilhuitzin huel ipan timocencahuaz.

Yhuan tiquintlahpaloz in i-tlachihual in campa cate in ah-nozo cana tiquinnamiquiz . . . in teoyotica teyacanque, in tepach-ohuanime in padreme.

[W]herever you pass in front of the image of our Lord, or His beloved, or the cross, you will greatly honor it; you will bow be-fore it or bend your knee; and much more so if you pass in front of the body itself of our Lord Jesus Christ (which is in the Holy Sacrament). Thus you will pray to Him with all your heart, for He is your God, for He is your Lord, for He is your Redeemer, for He is your revered Father Who is in the holy Sacrament. And you will greatly honor the name of our Lord, Jesus Christ, and on His feast day you will array yourself very well.

And you will greet His sons, wherever they may be or wherever you may meet them . . . the guides in holy matters, those who rule, the Fathers.[57]

No such exhortation passes from mother to daughter in the hue-huetlatolli. There are other indications, however, that follow rather closely the preconquest pattern. Here, first, is some of what a ruler said to his daughter.

Izcatqui in motequjuh in tic-
chioaz: in ceiooal, in cemjlhuitl
xitlateumati, mjiecpa ivictzinco
xelcicivi in iooalli, in ehecatl: xic-
tlaitlanili, xicnotza, xictzatzili,
ivictzinco ximaçoa: oc cenca in
movetzian, in mocochian. . . .
xicnotza, xictzatzili in tlacatl, in
totecuio: in iehoatzin in iooalli,
in ehecatl, ca mahaviltitzinoa in
iooaltica mitzcaquiz: auh vncan
mitzicnoittaz, vncan mitzmacaz
in tlein molhvil momaceoal.

Here is your task, which you are
to do: Be devout night and day.
Sigh many times unto the Night,
the Wind. Plead with, speak to,
cry out to him, stretch out your
arms to him, especially at your
reclining place, at your sleeping
place. . . . Speak to, cry out to the
master, our lord, to Him of the
Night, the Wind, for he rejoices
to hear you by night, and thus
he will show compassion to you,
he will give you what are your
deserts, your merit.[58]

A salutation by one aristocratic woman to another follows a similar
pattern.

Noconetzin, nocihua-
piltzin, ma ximehuititie, at
oncan in, in cuelachitzinca, in
cemilhuitzintli in timotlacotilia,
in timotequitilia in itloctzinco,
in inahuactzinco in Totecuiyo,
Ipalnamohuani, in Dios. In tic-
motlachpanilia, in ticmo-
tlacuicuililia. In cuelachitzinca,
in cemilhuitzintli in ticochitle-
hua, in titemictlamati in ipal-
tzinco in chane, in cale, imma-
coche, in tepotze. Azo vmpa
yauh immochoquitzin, immi-
xayotzin, immelcicihuitzin,
immotlaocoyalitzin inic telcici-
hui,inic titlaocoya in ixpantzinco in Totecuiyo, in Tloque,
in Nahuaque.

My child, my lady, raise
yourself up; perhaps here for a
little time, a day, you exert
yourself, you work beside, near
our Lord, Him through Whom
there is life, God. Sweep for
Him, clean up for Him. For a
little time, one day, you rise
quickly from sleep, you are informed in your dream thanks
to Him, to the master of the
home, of the house, to Him
Who has the neck, the back [to
carry and support you]. Perhaps your weeping, your tears,
your sighs, your affliction go
there, for you sigh, you afflict
yourself before our Lord, master of what is near, what is
nigh.[59]

The sermon's final admonition is also one for which there is good basis in the huehuetlatolli. Speaking of parents' obligations to their children, Sahagún says,

in iquac ie vevein niman an-quitemolizque in innamicvan ynic mopiazque yvan anquim-ixtlamachtizque ynic quimixi-machizque t° ya ixq'ch	[W]hen your children are grown, then you are to seek their spouses for them, so that they will be chaste; and you will make them prudent so that they will know our Lord. This is all.

If properly brought up, the parents themselves had thus been married off. According to Sahagún's huehuetlatolli in book 6 of the *General History*, the father said of his maturing son,

Motolinia injn totelpuch: ma cana ticcihoatlanjcan, ma cana itla qujchiuh: ma cana cueitl, vipilli tepan ca, ma cana tepan ia: ca ie iuhquj ca omacic	This poor youth of ours: Let us seek a woman for him lest he somewhere do something. He may somewhere meet a woman; he may commit adultery. For it is his nature; he has matured.[60]

And they entrusted the search to a professional matchmaker, who proceeded according to the ancient customs, which in this respect were still observed at the end of the sixteenth century. For this was the elders' business. The father told his unmarried son,

Intla cueitl, huipilli itlan ticalaquiznequiz, titechilhuiz in timonahuan, in timotahuan; ahmo zan ticmotlaliliz, ahmo zan ticmitalhuiz, ca tinane, ca titahua, ca titquihua, timamalo.	If you wish to go in by the skirt, by the shift, you are to tell us, your mothers, your fathers. You alone are not to propose it, you alone are not to speak, for you have a mother, you have a father; for you are [still] one who is taken, one who is carried.[61]

In other words (as Olmos interpreted it), "If you wish to marry, first inform us of it, and don't dare do it without us."[62]

It will have been evident that most of the data presented here are provided by men. A great deal of it is, in fact, about men, since much of the information about the lot of women is significant only if compared to the lot of men. So from more than one point of view we have seen a man's world. So it was in preconquest times, and in this respect postconquest times were not significantly different. *Plus ça change, plus c'est la même chose.* For improving the material lot of women was of little interest to either the exploiters of the conquered or, for a different set of reasons, to the friars, their often unwilling companions. At least such appears to have been the case in early colonial times.

But there were exceptional cases. Various kinds of specialists existed, about whose doings and methods not much is known. Some of the most interesting ones were classed as sorcerers and sorceresses. Unlike the men, who tended to deal in rather sinister activities, the women tended to be healers. The *Primeros memoriales* lists some—the one who diagnosed by casting kernels of corn (*tlaolli q'tepevia*), or by looking at one's reflection in the water (*atlan teittaya*), or by observing the way cords fell (*mecatlapouhqui*); or who cured by removing an object from one (*tetlacuicuiliqui*) or sucking it out of one (*techichinani*), or by using various techniques (*tepatiani*).[63] Even the *ticitl* (a generic term for physician or midwife) was sometimes considered a sorceress in colonial times.

There were successful women in commercial life. Here is one described in book 4 of Sahagún's *General History* in terms suitable to marketplace activities.

cenca mocuiltonoa, itla uel mailiz, vel muchioaz in jtiamjc, vallanecujliz, vel motlacâtiz, qujhimatiz, qujtlâtlamachiz in jtiamjc, in jtlaca.	[S]he would become very rich. She would produce well, make her wares well, and bargain astutely. She would be of good birth, and would arrange and distribute her merchandise and her people.[64]

Another is of a higher social level, perhaps that of the successful warrior.

mocuiltonoz, motlacamatiz, ioan oqujchnacaio, chicaoac, oqujchtlamatiz, moqujchpoaz, oqujcheoaz, teoqujchtlamachti iez: ioan much inemac vellatoz, motlatoljmatiz, vel tenotzaz, vellatoltecpanaz, yieieian, icacatian, in qujtlaliz tlatolli, vel ixe, ioolo, mozcalianj iez. Etª.

[S]he would become rich and wealthy; courageous, strong; reckoned as a man, and hardy. She would give honor as a man. And [among] her gifts, she would speak well, be eloquent, give good counsel, and arrange her conversation and manner of speaking well in her home. She would be observant, of good memory, discreet, and so on.[65]

The works of a few women have survived in the poetry they composed—almost universally a man's accomplishment in the Nahua world. One was named Macuilxochitzin; she was a daughter of Tlacaelel, powerful in state affairs, a sort of king maker, just before the midpoint of the fifteenth century, in the time of Itzcoatl, the first Moteucçoma, and Axayacatl, and she composed poetry fitting to those warlike times.[66] There may have been more such poets than we know of through existing records. A short poem follows, unusual because of its intimate quality, by an unknown composer, surely a woman to judge by the direct address word *nonantzin*, which would be *nonantzine* if a man spoke. It is of unknown date but probably ancient.

Nonantzin ihcuac nimiquiz mitlecuilpan xinechtoca; ihcuac tiaz titlaxcalchihuaz ompa nopampa xichoca. Ihcuac tla acah mitztlatlaniz: ¿Nonantzin, tleca tichoca? xiquilhuiz ca xoxohui in cahuitl ihuan in nechochoctia ica cecenca popoca.

My little mother, when I die inter me by your hearthside. When you go to make tortillas weep there on my account. And whenever someone asks you: My little mother, wherefore do you weep? You'll tell him: For the wood is green and it makes me weep with so much smoke.[67]

And there were some women who ruled men in this man's world of the Aztecs and their neighbors. We do not find any in Aztec history, though in book 10 of Sahagún's *General History*, a *tlatocacioatl* (woman sovereign) is described: "a woman-ruler, governor, leader— a provider, an administrator" (*cioatlatoani, tepachoani, teiacanani, tetlataluiani, tlanaoatiani*); she is "a provider of good conditions, a corrector, a punisher, a chastiser, a reprimander" who is "heeded, obeyed," who "creates order, establishes rules" (*tlauelmamanitiani, atl cecec, tzitzicaztli quitecani, quitlaçani, tealcececaui, tetzitzicazui, caco, nepechtequililo,tlatecpana, naoatillalia*)[68]—all attributes of a good male ruler. Where woman rulers are portrayed in action, however, is in various of the *relaciones* (annals, accounts) of Chimalpahin, who gives examples of two women "who succeeded to tlatocayotl [rulership] in Amaquemecan, bore the royal titles, exercised the full powers of the office, and passed it on to their descendants." Of the second of his examples, Tlacocihuatzin, an early fifteenth-century ruler of Tlailotlacan Teohuacan, Chimalpahin says, among other things, that she

otlahtocatico yn oteyacanaco yn otlapachoco yn oc no ypan tlateotoquiliztli y tlacatecollonotzaliztli. . . . teohua teuhctli mochiuh, Mexico y macoc tlahtocayotl, chiuhcnauhxihuitl yn tlahtocat

ruled, led, and governed when it was still in the time of idolatry and devil worship. . . . [She] became *teohua teuhctli* and was given the rulership in Mexico Tenochtitlan. She ruled . . . for nine years.[69]

"Chimalpahin makes a point of saying that both these female rulers were greatly feared and had full powers of justice, including the power to make judgments of life and death over their subjects," though it should be noted that he also suggests that the second one may have been regent rather than ruler, governing under the direction of her husband.[70]

It would be tempting to classify another group of women, the *ahuianime*, or pleasure girls, sometimes labeled courtesans or harlots, as exceptions or at least misfits. Actually, they were an accepted segment of Nahua society, as long as they obeyed the rules, valuable as companions of young warriors or warriors-to-be, or of certain persons to be sacrificed, and as important participants in the many song-dance rituals. They are given a bad name by the chroniclers or by the men who informed them, who defined an *ahuiani* as "an evil woman who finds pleasure in her body, who sells her body" (*cioatlaueliloc, inacaio mauiltiani, nacanamacac*),[71] though she certainly was no prostitute as we define the term. There must have been misfits and individuals who violated the Aztecs' sumptuary laws in all levels of the society, of whom nothing has been reported; but here is an early sixteenth-century example named Tiacapan, who was of such high rank that she could not escape notice.

yn ohueix̄ nimā ye mahauiltia. achto conā yn ipiltzin Neçahualpiltzintli ytoca Neçahualquentzin/oxxihuitl yn ichan catcah, auh yn ocontlatzilhui. nimā ye conana tocpacxochitzin çe xihuitl yhuā tlahcoxihuitl yn ichan catcah in ocōtlatzilhui, nimā ye conana in tzotzotlacatzin oxxihuitl yn ichan̄ catcah yn ocontlatzilhui. nimā ye conana ȳ cohuanacochtzin ye otztitiuh quin ōpa ȳ mixihuito ychan cohuanacochtzin. oncā tlacatque ȳ Don hernando yhuiyantzin, yhuā Don pedro çihuateotl. hacā oquichhua catca yn innantzin ça mahuiltiaya.

[W]hen she grew up, she then lived a life of pleasure. First a son of Nezahualpiltzintli named Nezahualquentzin took her. She remained in his home two years, but she disliked him. Then Tocpacxochitzin took her; for a year and a half she was in his home. She disliked him. Then Tzotzotlacatzin took her. She was in his home for two years. She disliked him. Then Cohuanacochtzin took her. She went pregnant [and] there gave birth in Cohuanacochtzin's home. Thence were born don Hernando Ihuiyantzin and don Pedro Cihuateotl. Not few were their mother's husbands; she was just living a life of pleasure.[72]

Of course, this is a man's report; it is directed to *Joan de pomar que dios quarde en Tescuco*. Still, she truly was exceptional.

In fact, nothing in the position of Aztec wives had altered much throughout all the strife, upsets, and changes during the sixteenth century. "The good maiden is yet a virgin, mature, clean, unblem-

ished, pious, pure of heart, benign, chaste, candid, well disposed."
"The mature woman is respected, revered, dignified—a woman of
the home. She works; she never rests." She is "resolute, firm of heart,
constant, vigorous, resolute; persevering, . . . long-suffering; she ac-
cepts reprimands calmly—endures things like a man. . . . She goes in
humility."[73] So wrote Sahagún's informants toward the end of the
sixteenth century.

　　Plus ça change, plus c'est la même chose.

3

Indian-Spanish Marriages
in the First Century of the Colony

Pedro Carrasco

Early colonial Mexican society was based, essentially, on a clear distinction between Spaniards and Indians. The subordinate position of the latter is obvious in a great variety of relationships—economic, political, and social—including sexual relations between members of the two groups. Questions of culture contact and race mixture (*mestizaje*) have been discussed by various authors (e.g., Richard Konetzke, Magnus Mörner, Claudio Esteva), but with an emphasis on mestizaje resulting from relationships that were largely a matter of informal unions and concubinage, topics that are marginal to our subject.

In spite of the separateness of the Indian and Spanish communities within the totality of colonial society, legal marriages between members of the two ethnic groups did occur, and an examination of such marriages should add to our understanding of the colonial situation as a whole. Of principal concern is the social condition of the parties to these unions and the ways in which such marriages affected their reputations and the possibilities for improving their situations in the social hierarchy.

I shall not attempt here a complete and systematic discussion of interethnic marriages. This chapter is based on material I happened upon while looking for information on pre-Hispanic social organization and its continuation into the colonial period. Certainly, there are more data on the subject available in the archives; however, I believe the examples presented here are sufficient to define the different types of marriages according to the social conditions of the parties concerned.

My data are largely anecdotal and do not lend themselves to quantification. There is a document, however, that is worth summarizing here, since it furnishes quantitative information on the marital status of Spanish *vecinos* (residents) of Puebla in 1534, little more than a decade after the conquest.[1] There were a total of 81 vecinos, 35 of them conquistadors and 46 of them later arrivals. The conquerors are further classified into 22 married to Spanish women, 7 married to native women (*mujeres de la tierra*), one of them listed as a widower and 6 as single. Of those who were not conquistadors, 19 had Spanish wives, one of whom is listed as a widow. Another 4 had wives in Spain and had sent for them. Of the rest, 13 were married to Indian women and 10 were single. Thus, of a total of 65 married men (one a widower), 20 had married Indian women, a proportion of 30.7 percent. Of the 29 married conquistadors, 7 (including the one widower), or 24.1 percent, had married Indian women. Of the 36 married men who were not conquerors, 13, or 36.1 percent, had married Indian women.

There was, therefore, a higher proportion of later arrivals married to Indian women than of conquistadors. This difference might be related to the fact that the conquerors had been in New Spain longer and had more time to bring their wives from Spain, but it is also probable that their higher status gave them an advantage in competing for Spanish wives in the first decade or two after the conquest, when there were few Spanish women in the colony. In any case, the proportion of Spanish men marrying Indian women was higher than the estimates given by Magnus Mörner for Spanish America as a whole.[2]

The indigenous society over which the Spanish took control was highly stratified, with complex marriage customs that continued to play a role in determining the sexual and matrimonial relations between the two ethnic groups (see chapter 2). As for marriage customs brought by the Spanish, although I have not studied them in detail, I believe they can be summarized as based on a preference for marriage between individuals of the same social stratum, on the subordination of women, and on a code of sexual morality different for men and women. As an old saying has it, *casar y compadrar, cada cual con su igual*.[3] The man married a woman of his own class who had to be a virgin and would give him legitimate heirs. Since the woman brought a dowry to the marriage, its value, if sufficient, compensated for any difference there might be in social standing. Occasional sexual liaisons outside marriage, or concubinage, usually took place with women of a lower social condition.

In the Antilles, concubinage with native women was a frequent practice, but the preferred form of matrimony was to a Spanish woman. Formal marriages with Indian women did occur, but they were in a minority; there are some instances of Spaniards who came to New Spain from the Antilles already married to Indian women.[4]

Early on it was learned that in certain cases marriage with Indian women could be useful as another way of maintaining dominance over the indigenous people. In 1516 Cardinal Francisco Jiménez de Cisneros advised the Hieronymite friars sent to govern the Indies that it would be advantageous for Spaniards to marry the daughters of *caciques* (Arawak: indigenous rulers) who had no male descendants, so that within a short time the heirs to the land and the authority of the caciques would be Spanish.[5]

In pre-Spanish Mexico, as in Spain, the predominant form of marriage was between individuals of the same social class. The two principal social strata were nobles (*pipiltin*) and commoners (*macehualtin*), or *macehuales*, as the Nahuatl word entered Spanish. Among the nobility polygyny was customary, and within this practice there were different types of unions. For women of high rank marriage was arranged by a formal petition and celebrated in a public ceremony. A woman of a lower social level was taken as a secondary wife in what Spanish writers described as concubinage.

Polygyny made it possible for members of the ruling class to maintain simultaneously a number of matrimonial alliances with differing political implications. There were two clearly established ways of doing this. In one, the ruler of highest rank, as, for instance, the king of Tetzcoco, would give his daughters in marriage to the lower-level kings of the fourteen subkingdoms (such as Teotihuacan) who were directly subject to him. The Tetzcoca princess would bring land as a dowry and would become the mother of the heir to her husband's position. This type of marriage regulated relations between the ruling lineages of the Acolhuacan polities and the dominant lineage of Tetzcoco.

In the other type of marriage lords of the highest rank would take as wives women of high but lesser rank. For example, the rulers of Tenochtitlan took as wives princesses of subject cities, and a son of such a union became the next ruler of his mother's city of origin. Or a Tenochca prince would be installed as ruler of a conquered kingdom and would marry a princess of that place. In both of these subtypes of marriage a prince of the Tenochca ruling dynasty would be brought into another realm to establish a kinship relation with the local dynasty through marriage to a princess of that lineage. The subordinate kingdom thus acquired members of the predominant lineage who were, through the female line, descendants of the local dynasty.

The women who entered into these royal marriages were accompanied by female relations and servants who also became members of the ruler's household as secondary wives or concubines, except for those he might present to some of his relatives and subjects. The donation of women as a way of establishing and maintaining political relations was customary in ancient Mexico.[6]

As we examine the marriages that took place in the early colonial period between members of the two ethnicities, it is immediately evident that there were very few marriages between Indian men and Spanish women. There were several reasons for this: the subordinate position of the indigenous population as a whole as a conquered people; the reluctance, within the Spanish system, to give a woman in marriage to a man of a lower class; and the scarcity of Spanish women, especially in the early years of the colony.

Therefore, in the few known cases of this type of marriage, the men were of the highest social level. Several members of the Tenochca nobility married Spanish women: don Martín Neçahualtecolotzin, a son of Moteucçoma;[7] don Hernando de Tapia, a son of don Andrés de Tapia Motelchiuhtzin;[8] and don Diego Luis Moteucçoma, a son of don Pedro Tlacahuepantzin and thus a grandson of the emperor. Don Martín accompanied Hernando Cortés on his first return to Spain, in 1528, and married a Spanish woman. He returned to New

Spain with his wife but was killed by poison soon after their arrival. Don Martín's widow was taken to Mexico City and then "disappears from history."[9] Don Diego Luis also went to Spain and married a Spanish woman, but he remained in Spain and began the line of the counts of Montezuma [sic].[10]

There is also some information on indigenous leaders from other places who married Spanish women, as, for example, don Antonio Cortés of Tacuba,[11] and a cacique of Tecamachalco.[12] In Michoacan, three descendants of the Cazonci (the indigenous ruler) married Spanish women: don Francisco Tariacuri, don Pablo Huitzimengari, and don Constantino Huitzimengari.[13]

Almost nothing is known about the Spanish women who entered into these marriages. From the point of view of the indigenous nobility, the practice of marrying women of the conquering group may perhaps have been seen as similar to the pre-Hispanic custom of the rulers taking wives from the superordinate lineage, but it never became formalized as a well-defined policy of matrimonial alliances.

The situation of a group of high-ranking Indians who were in Spain in 1533 comes closest to the kind of treatment that would have indicated recognition of these elite representatives as equivalent or similar to the Castilian nobility, but they met with the rejection of such a policy by the crown. A proposal in support of the Indians was submitted by the Council of the Indies (Consejo de las Indias) to His Majesty.

> From New Spain the president and judges have sent five Indians, one a son of Motezuma [sic] who had come at other times to kiss Your Majesty's hands, and other *principales* [Indian nobles], because it seemed to them that they were persons who it did not seem advisable should be at present there. They have been here for five or six months, they have been given what was necessary and because it does not seem advisable that they should return to that land at the present time and they are here at Your Majesty's expense, it seems to the Council that in the meantime they should be doing something that would serve Your Majesty; especially Motezuma's son [could serve as] *contino de casa* [a position at court], and two in the Horse Guard and two in the Foot

Guard; and it would be well thought of there because it would appear that it pleases you to make use of them in your household and court. Your Majesty will order in this matter whatever [Your Majesty] pleases.[14]

The royal decision was given in a marginal note that instructed the Council to do as they saw fit; but the request as to the positions in the Guard was denied.[15]

The Mexica nobles were thus not admitted to His Majesty's service as the Council recommended. Although eventually they all returned to New Spain, it is clear that they were kept in Spain because the royal government did not want them to be in the colony at that time. Similarly, don Diego Luis de Montezuma and his descendants were obliged to remain in Spain, and it was not for well over a century, until 1696, that a count of Montezuma went to New Spain as viceroy.

Marriages between Spanish men and Indian women were much more frequent, and the resulting situations differed according to the rank of the individuals concerned. As we have seen, in the Antilles there had already been a declared policy that Spaniards should marry heiresses of the local caciques. In New Spain, rather than succession to the position of cacique, the indigenous princesses' dowries, consisting of large tracts of land, were clearly the prime factor in their marriages to Spaniards.

Several daughters of indigenous rulers married Spaniards; the best-known example is that of two of the daughters of Moteucçoma. Doña Isabel married her father's heir apparent and his two succeeding rulers—Atlixcatl, Cuitlahuac, and Cuauhtemoc[16]—all of whom died in the course of the Spanish conquest. Subsequently, after a short time as mistress of Hernando Cortés, she was granted, under special conditions, the *encomienda* (a grant of Indians for tribute) of Tacuba and then married three conquistadors successively. The first, Alonso de Grado, an hidalgo, had a varied career during the conquest but on the whole prospered, and it was Cortés who arranged his marriage to doña Isabel. Grado died not long after this marriage, and the princess subsequently married Pedro Gallego, with whom she had a son called don Juan de Andrada Montezuma, ancestor of the Andradas. Finally, doña Isabel married Juan Cano, *encomendero* (recipient of the right to collect tribute from a select group of Indians) of Macuilxochitl, who held various official positions.[17] Doña Leonor de Montezuma married the conqueror Cristóbal de Valderrama; she was the widow of another conquistador, Juan Páez, when she married Valderrama. The latter was given the encomienda of Ecatepec. Their daughter, doña Leonor Valderrama de Montezuma, married a Spaniard, don Diego Sotelo; on her father's death the Indian town of Ecatepec passed into the hands of her husband.[18]

Of the royal house of Tetzcoco, doña Ana, a daughter of King Neçahualpilli, married the conqueror Juan de Cuéllar, bringing as her dowry several places in Acolhuacan.[19] A daughter of don Pedro, governor of Tetzcoco (probably don Pedro Coanacochtzin), married Juan Freyle, who came to New Spain a few years after Cortés and participated in the conquest of Nueva Galicia.[20] He held certain public offices and served for a time as interpreter for the Real Audiencia.[21]

Doña Inés Tiacapan, a daughter of the ruler of Tenayuca, who had been living with her cousin don Pedro Tlacahuepantzin, was not able to obtain the dispensation necessary for marrying him; she then married the Irishman Rodrigo Ires.[22] Doña Francisca Verdugo Ixtlilxochitl, heiress of the ruler of Teotihuacan and granddaughter of King Ixtlilxochitl of Tetzcoco, married the Spaniard Juan Grande, a descendant of one of the pilots of Christopher Columbus and also of a conqueror. This marriage prospered, and their descendants married Spaniards, who were, for the most part, government officials. They were the grandparents of the famous mestizo historian don Fernando de Alva Ixtlilxochitl.[23]

The daughters of the local rulers of various towns near the colonial capital also married Spaniards: doña Agata María, the daughter of don Tomás de San Martín Quetzalmaçatzin of Chalco;[24] doña Cristina, the daughter of the ruler of Tihuacan [sic] and doña Ana, the daughter of the Tenochca king Cuitlahuac;[25] doña Magdalena de Mendoza, a daughter of don Baltasar de Mendoza Itzcuauhtzin of Tlatelolco;[26] and doña María Jacinta Cortés Chimalpopoca, a granddaughter of the ruler of Tacuba.[27] Outside the Valley of Mexico, Spaniards married the daughters of caciques in Teutila, Oxitipan, and Michoacan.[28]

A very different case is that of the famous Malintzin, or doña Marina (see also chapter 14). The position she achieved in postconquest New Spain was through her own intelligence, courage, and loyalty to the Spaniards during extremely dangerous and difficult times. One of twenty women presented to Cortés by the leaders of Tabasco on the gulf coast, doña Marina soon became indispensable to him as an interpreter and intermediary between the various indigenous groups they encountered. Cortés, who had a Spanish wife already, gave her to Alonso Hernández Portocarrero, a cousin of the count of Medellín; after his return to Spain, doña Marina remained with Cortés. Doña Marina accompanied Cortés on the expedition to las Hibueras and along the way was formally married to one of his captains, Juan Jaramillo, who in 1533 was granted the encomienda of Xilotepec.[29]

The donation of women by the rulers of Tlaxcala to the newly arrived Spaniards is well known. According to Diego Muñoz Camargo, the rulers first presented them with three hundred female slaves, but later, "seeing that some of these slave women got along well with the Spaniards, the *principales* (noblemen) themselves gave their own daughters so that, if by chance any should become pregnant, the descendants of such valiant and daring men would remain among them."[30] After referring to doña Luisa Xicotencatl, the daughter of one of the four rulers of Tlaxcala who was given to Pedro de Alvarado, Muñoz Camargo says that among the indigenous people, "the rulers took absolutely whichever woman they wanted, and they were given to them as men of power. And, following this usage, many daughters of the rulers were given to the Spaniards, so that they would leave descendants there, in case they should go away from this land."[31]

Little is known, however, about the individual unions of these Tlaxcalan princesses with Spaniards. Alva Ixtlilxochitl identified five of the princesses, who were probably the same young women given to the Spaniards named by Bernal Díaz del Castillo.[32] With the exception of doña Luisa Xicotencatl, they perished in the disastrous flight from Tenochtitlan.[33] Under the circumstances it is not likely that any formal marriages took place.

A case that is frequently cited is that of the aforementioned doña Luisa Xicotencatl, given to Pedro de Alvarado. They formed a lasting relationship from which originated the best-known descendants of this conquistador. However, he did not actually marry until later—a Castilian woman, doña Francisca de la Cueva, and after her death, her sister, doña Beatríz. Doña Leonor, the daughter of don Pedro and doña Luisa Xicotencatl, was more fortunate than her mother. She married don Pedro Portocarrero and, afterward, don Francisco de la Cueva. Both men were officers with Alvarado in the conquest of Guatemala. Portocarrero was connected with the family of the counts of Medellín; de la Cueva, a cousin of the duke of Alburquerque, became captain general of Guatemala after the death of Alvarado.[34]

Doña Elvira Toznenitzin, daughter of don Alonso Quauhtimotzin, a principal of Topoyanco, first had two illegitimate children with Jerónimo de Aguilar and later married the conquistador Gregorio de Ribas.[35] Another Tlaxcalan who was the daughter of a principal married the interpreter Antonio Ortiz, about whom more will be said later.

In the Archivo de Indias there are documents of a lawsuit, from 1559 to 1560, over the encomienda of Cuauhtinchan that provide considerable information about the marriage of another Tlaxcalan, a daughter of Calmecahua, who was baptized with the name of Angelina and married a conqueror, Juan Pérez de Arteaga. He had been granted half of Cuauhtinchan,[36] was a resident of Puebla, and was described by Bernal Díaz as a rich man.[37] He also served as an interpreter.[38] In his testament Pérez de Arteaga declared that he and Angelina had been legally married: "I was married and received the nuptial benediction legitimately according to the order of the Holy Mother Church of Rome to Angelina Pérez de Arteaga, daughter of one of the principales of the four cabeceras [head towns] of Tascala [sic], she being a maiden."[39]

Their eldest son was Juan Pérez de Arteaga el Mozo (the Younger), to whom he left the encomienda. After Angelina died, Juan Pérez de Arteaga el Viejo (the Elder) married a Spanish woman, Catalina de Santa Cruz, with whom he had another son, Alonso. After her husband's death, doña Catalina litigated against Juan Pérez the Younger and asked that the encomienda be given to her son Alonso, then a minor. The questionnaire she submitted for the suit stated that "the said Angelina served the said Juan Pérez now deceased, who had her in his possession as a servant and concubine and not as a wife, [and] the said Juan Pérez de Arteaga who litigates was the son of the said Angelina; he had no certain father nor do they know whose son he was, only that he was under the authority of the said Angelina who served the said Juan Pérez now deceased."[40]

According to the questionnaire and witnesses for Juan Pérez the Younger, however, Juan Pérez the Elder had married Angelina thirty-six years before, that is, in 1523, when "she was a girl of about twelve or thirteen years of age, a maiden and judged to be such by her behavior and reputation, and the legitimate daughter of Calmecahua, a ruler and Indian principal of one of the four cabeceras of the province of Tascala."[41]

Juan Pérez the Younger declared as follows: "I was naturally begotten by the said Juan Pérez de Arteaga; and although I was born before my said father had legally married my said mother, in consideration [of the fact] that at the time that she bore me he could have married her [since] she was a maiden and of noble ancestry, by marrying her I became as legitimate as though she had borne me afterwards."[42]

One witness, Cristóbal Martín de Leyve, a conquistador, declared that he along with other persons had witnessed the marriage of Juan Pérez de Arteaga the Elder and Angelina Pérez in the city of Mexico, the marriage being performed by Juan Díaz, a priest who had come with Cortés. Later, after Angelina had given birth to Juan Pérez de Arteaga the Younger, they moved to Puebla, where this same witness was present when they received the nuptial benediction in the monastery of Santo Domingo and subsequently saw them living together as husband and wife.[43] In regard to Angelina, he added that it was "public knowledge and widely known that she was the daughter of a principal of the four cabeceras of the city of Tascala and as such this witness saw that Indians from the said province of Tascala came to serve her as a daughter of the principal."[44]

The witnesses for Juan el Mozo included two Indian women, one called Leonor, who said she had been the wife of Rodrigo de Resino, a Spaniard who was a resident there; the other, Francisca Ruiz, a native of Guatemala, now a widow, who had been the wife of Pedro Gallardo, a conquistador. The first declared that she was present at the marriage of Juan Pérez de Arteaga and Angelina, by Juan Díaz (who had baptized this witness). Both Leonor and Cristóbal Martín de Leyve state that Juan Pérez de Arteaga the Younger was born after the marriage ceremony, although he himself stated that he was born before the marriage.[45]

Viceroy don Luis de Velasco decided in favor of Juan Pérez. Alonso appealed to His Majesty and the Council of the Indies. In Seville I did not see any information on the final disposition of the case. However, in 1564, Cuauhtinchan was mentioned as the encomienda of Juan Pérez de Arteaga.[46]

As the sixteenth century progressed, marriages of Spanish men and Indian heiresses seem to have been frequent. Indian nobles in colonial times held entailed estates. As in Spanish usage, these estates were transmitted through males by primogeniture, but in the absence of sons, a daughter succeeded. Nonentailed property was inherited by the widow and by sons and daughters.

According to a royal order dated April 16, 1585, the caciques of Tlaxcala reported

that in that province many Spaniards have married women who were the widows of caciques and other rich natives who have left property, houses, and other estates which [although] belonging to the children of the first husbands the said Spaniards whom they [the widows] marry spend, take, and diminish it and sue to have it left to their children, in which there is great disorder and much harm to their republic, entreating me to order that as soon as the said widows marry the said Spaniards or any other person, since the property of the first husband is entailed they should be put under guardianship, with which will be restored much property of orphans who are now dispossessed and poor because their estates have been usurped in this way.[47]

The royal order instructed the president and judges to take notice and see that justice was done.

In two recent publications on Tepeaca, Hildeberto Martínez documents an interesting example of how the Spanish acquired land through marriage to Indian noblewomen.[48] In the second half of the sixteenth century, doña María de la Cruz, a descendant of one of the leading noble families of Tepeaca, inherited a house, tracts of land, and farmhands. Around 1568 she married an equally noble Indian principal, don Francisco de Guzmán, with whom she had a son, don Sebastián.[49] Don Francisco died in about 1578; don Sebastián died intestate in 1598 at the age of twenty-two.[50] From the two men doña María inherited all the property, workers, land, and other things pertaining to the *cacicazgo* (indigenous estate) of the late don Francisco de Guzmán.[51]

In her will, written in 1602, doña María declared that while she was a widow and not subject to matrimony, she had two natural children, one called Pedro de la Cruz and the other Juan, a young boy.[52] The name of the father was not given. In 1622 Pedro de la Cruz said in his will that he was "the natural son of doña María de la Cruz, an Indian, cacica and principal, formerly a native of the said city of Tepeaca, who is now deceased, to whom he was born when the above was single and he never knew who his father was."[53]

Later, doña María married a Spaniard named Alvaro Pérez de Navia, who would help her to defend her properties. Doña María declared in her testament that one Pedro Alonso Cortés, a resident of Puebla, had appropriated much of the land of the cacicazgo that she had inherited from her son, saying that his wife had the right to these properties; and she, doña Maria, had not been able to hold the properties free from risk "because the aforesaid had always been a very powerful man in this province and she [was] poor and a woman with no one to help her, until now that she had married the said Alvaro Pérez, her husband, who had begun to pursue the said lawsuit."[54]

That is, through her marriage to Alvaro Pérez de Navia, doña María acquired a Spanish husband to help her in her lawsuits with another Spaniard, Pedro Alonso Cortés, also married to an Indian noblewoman, doña Isabel de Espina. Doña Isabel was the cousin of several Indian caciques of Tepeaca with the surname Guzmán, who had made her a gift of land on the boundaries of Nopaluca.[55] She must have been of the lineage of the Guzmáns, and for this reason Pedro Alonso Cortés argued that his wife had a right to the lands of the cacicazgo of the Guzmáns, which doña María de la Cruz also claimed. This was, in effect, a family quarrel, with each woman relying on a Spanish husband to protect her interests.[56]

Doña María de la Cruz named as her heirs her two natural sons and her husband, Alvaro Pérez. She increased the latter's portion and named him as guardian of her sons as well as executor together with her brother, Clemente de la Cruz.[57] When doña María's widower, Alvaro Pérez de Navia, drew up his will in 1615, he declared that he was still carrying on lawsuits about his wife's land with several persons, among them Pedro Alonso Cortés and his heirs.[58] Similarly the testament of don Pedro de la Cruz in 1616 refers to the lawsuit with Pedro Alonso Cortés and others.[59]

The Spaniards not only acquired land for themselves when they married Indian women. In some cases they lived in the wife's hometown and their behavior led them to be accused of creating problems by their interference in local government. In 1582 the viceroy ordered the *corregidor* (Spanish official in charge of a district) of Cholula to investigate and carry out justice in a case that the governor and principales of the city had reported to him.

> In the said city lives and resides Diego García Villavicencio, a Spaniard married to an Indian woman related to the natives who hold public office and responsibilities, who in this way had managed to enter into their municipal councils and assemblies and to be present at the elections that they hold, and to carry on lawsuits and to incite them to carry on these suits, creating factions and causing unrest and quarrels between one group and another, in such a way that as a consequence unjust lawsuits have been carried on and quarrels stirred up and from this have resulted many troubles harmful and notably damaging to the people of the said city; moreover, having been put in charge of taking the said natives to the labor draft for the fields in the Valley of Atrisco where they were to report, and having delivered the number of workers that they are obliged to provide, he sells some of them to his own advantage to persons who pay him for them and use them for various purposes, for [kinds of] work which should not be allowed.[60]

I have another, earlier example of this kind of situation from the Cuicatec region of Oaxaca. In 1543, Andrés de Tapia, encomendero of Tepeucila, was engaged in a suit with the royal attorney concerning ill treatment, excessive tribute demands, and despoilment of the

Indians.[61] The Indians presented a painting of jewels that Tapia had taken. He asserted that these were things they had paid him before the tribute assessment had been made. Tapia said further that the Indians had ordered the painting to be copied, having been induced to do so by a Spaniard named Melchor Rodríguez, who was married to an Indian woman in the town. Tapia presented various Indian witnesses who made declarations as to the character of Melchor Rodríguez. One of them described Rodríguez as follows:

> a man of bad conscience and deceitful and as such he is held to be and is so degraded that he eats with the Indians on the floor like an Indian, and once I saw a Spanish *bachiller* [one who holds a university degree] arrest him because he found him dancing with the Indians, and it is public knowledge that he has eaten grasshoppers and played *batey* [an indigenous ball game] with his buttocks and arm with the Indians, and for this among them he is considered to be of little worth and very vile and debased.[62]

Other witnesses made similar accusations as to his character and behavior, emphasizing his associating with Indians and eating their food.[63] In short, numerous witnesses, some of whom were Indian principales, affirmed that they considered Melchor Rodríguez to be no better than a macehual.

Several of the *nahuatlatos*, or Indian-language interpreters, were either mestizos or Spaniards married to Indian women. In 1578, of six interpreters employed by the Real Audiencia, five were mestizos.[64] I have no data indicating whether they were the children of legal marriages.

Another interpreter, the aforementioned Juan Grande, had married doña Francisca, cacica of Teotihuacan. Juan Grande seems to have had a good reputation; he was in fact described as being very well known during the later years of the sixteenth century.[65] The case of the interpreter named Antonio Ortiz was quite different.

Ortiz's Indian wife, named Isabel, was a native of Tlaxcala, the daughter of a principal. She had first been married to a conquistador, Melchor de Villacorta, who had held Indians in encomienda.[66] In 1546 during the *visita* (an official tour of inspection) of Tello de Sandoval, among the objections made by Licenciado Tejada concerning the actions of her second husband, Antonio Ortiz, during this process were accusations of bribes, thefts, suborning witnesses, and selling free men as slaves. As for his character and his not very private life, it was said,

> While married to a woman of this land he publicly kept as mistresses many Indian and mestiza women, he was a great drunkard, gambler, blasphemer, very deceitful and of little truth, and a man who held honor in little esteem. His social relations were with Indians and among Indians, whom he commonly deceived. He was such a bad Christian that he seldom entered the church and of such a deteriorated conscience that for whatever was given or promised to him or for whatever advantage might come his way or ill will he might have against someone, he would perjure himself and swear the opposite of the truth. . . . [H]e was and is so evil and of such depraved and evil customs and vices that he lived more like a pagan than a Christian. He was so shameless and considered honor of so little worth that he exposed himself publicly on many different occasions and before many people; in particular, many times while playing cards he was seen drunk, acting crazily and stark naked.[67]

In the machinations of Antonio Ortiz against Licenciado Tejada two other nahuatlatos participated, against whom the lawyer also made accusations. Of Francisco Triana, it was claimed, "He is a Morisco, the slave son of Moriscos, and thus he like his parents slaves of the Marquis of Tarifa and recently converted. . . . Although he was and is married in Castile, he has for sixteen years had sexual relations with many Indian women, living more in accordance with the law of Mohammed than as a Christian."[68] He was accused of being drunk, of vomiting what he has drunk, and of exposing his private parts. He was also said to spend most of his time with Indians, eating with them on the floor and taking part in their dances.[69] Similar things were said about the other interpreter, Marcos Romero, a cousin of Francisco Triana.

To conclude, from the examples given here it is clear that the Indians' rank within the indigenous social stratification was of decisive importance in marriages between Indians and Spaniards. Very few Indian men married Spanish women; of those who did, all were of the highest social level, members of the royal families of the three kingdoms of the Aztec Empire and of the royal lineage of Michoacan. Only don Hernando de Tapia, faithful servant to the Spaniards, was not of a royal lineage.

Marriages between Indian noblewomen and Spaniards were much more frequent. Some of the women were members of the royal lineages of Tenochtitlan or Tetzcoco, but others came from less important kingdoms. The search for an Indian heiress seemed to have been a conscious policy as a means of acquiring landed estates, although we also find doña Maria de la Cruz who by marrying a Spaniard found a protector to defend her properties.

In all these marriages both the men and the women who married Spaniards must have come from among the most Hispanicized sectors of the indigenous community. Their high rank within indigenous society and their wealth inclined them toward acculturation and assimilation with the dominant class in the colony, and it was customary for their descendants also to marry Spaniards.

The marriages and subsequent lives of Spaniards of a lower social condition, as the nahuatlato Antonio Ortiz and Melchor Rodríguez of Tepeucila seem to have been, are more problematic. The data above come from lawsuits in which the opposing party tried to discredit them, and are not entirely trustworthy. What is most apparent is that adoption of indigenous culture and living among Indians were used as evidence of a low social level.

Within these norms there is a great variety of situations, but it is not easy to evaluate the different factors that play a role, given the scarcity of information on the individuals and the circumstances of their marriages. Indian women of high rank seem to have had no difficulty finding a Spanish husband, but we have only occasional glimpses of their lives after marriage. We know, for example, of the two Indian women married to Spaniards who were friends of Angelina, the Tlaxcalan wife of Juan Pérez de Arteaga. Their testimonies suggest they may have formed a circle of friends; perhaps they were excluded from a social relationship with Spanish women. And it is clear that Pedro de Alvarado did not wish to marry Luisa Xicotencatl, in spite of her status as a Tlaxcalan princess, postponing marriage until he could acquire a Spanish wife.

When the rulers of Tlaxcala presented noblewomen to the Spanish invaders, they were acting in accordance with the forms of donation of women and matrimonial alliances customary in the Nahua kingdoms. Their motivation in wishing to acquire descendants of the Spaniards as members of their own group recalls the manner in which the Tenochca installed Acamapichtli as king, giving him women with whom he would engender the Mexica nobility. But the Tlaxcalans must have soon realized that pre-Hispanic matrimonial practices did not necessarily produce the same desired results in colonial times. The marriages just considered can be better understood in terms of the norms of Spanish society, based on class differences and reinforced by the distinctions between Spaniards and Indians. The kind of life that would indicate an inferior moral and social level could include the adoption of indigenous customs and living among and socializing with Indian commoners (the macehuales). Straightforward evaluations of racial differences are seldom found in the documents, although they must have existed. Social stratification based on the distribution of power and wealth and the concomitant classist mentality associated with it explain the basic motives for interethnic marriages during the first century of the colony.

4

Gender and Social Identity

Nahua Naming Patterns
in Postconquest Central Mexico

Rebecca Horn

Naming patterns among the Nahuas of colonial central Mexico present various challenges to the ethnohistorian. Most Nahua women carried such names as María Juana—simply two common given names and no surname. Without considerable contextual material the investigator is unable to tell them apart. Standing out in the archival records, in contrast, is an elite woman named doña Leonor de Guzmán. With her rare title of nobility, a less common given name, and a Spanish surname, this individual can be tracked with more certainty through the records, resulting, for example, in a tendency to focus on the noblewoman to the neglect of the women commoners.[1] For all that naming patterns obscure our knowledge of Nahua women, however, they can also tell us a great deal. In general, names both individuate, that is, "designate unique individuals," and differentiate, that is, "discriminate social categories,"[2] including ethnicity, social rank, gender, and kinship. The absence of a title of nobility, an unusual given name, and an impressive Spanish surname is as much an indication of social rank, for example, as is their presence.

This study concerns Nahua naming patterns in early seventeenth-century central Mexico as a window on the social status of

Nahua women. It is based largely on baptismal records from the province of Coyoacan, located just southwest of Mexico City. An important pre-Hispanic regional state (altepetl), Coyoacan experienced significant Spanish settlement in the early postconquest period because of its proximity to the capital, its fertile soils, and its abundant sources of fresh water.[3] Change occurred more quickly in communities located near Mexico City than in regions more remote from the capital; patterns established for Coyoacan have widespread relevance throughout the Valley of Mexico. By the early seventeenth century, postconquest Nahua naming patterns were well established although constantly being refashioned with the ongoing transformation of rural Nahua society.

Because they record the names of large numbers of individuals—both male and female—from all levels of society, baptismal records are an especially valuable source on Nahua naming patterns. Samples of hundreds of names from one time and place can highlight naming patterns difficult to discern in scattered records from various periods. My discussion of Nahua naming patterns is based on the earliest extant baptismal records from two Coyoacan parishes.[4] I have compiled and analyzed the names of all the children and all the mothers and fathers recorded in the parish of San Jacinto Tenantitlan (San Angel) for the years 1619–29 and in the parish of San Juan Bautista for the years 1638–46.[5] Additional information has been gleaned from a wide variety of other documents in both Spanish and Nahuatl.

The baptismal registers are succinct, providing only the names of the individuals involved and their relationships to one another. Each entry typically includes the date of baptism, the given name of the baptized child, the given name and frequently the "second" name of the child's parents and godparents,[6] and the name of the officiating priest; on occasion the parents' hometown and ethnicity are also mentioned. Presumably, all of the various participants involved in the ritual of baptism had an opportunity to influence the naming of the child. Officiating priests probably provided more guidance in the immediate postconquest years, when Nahuas were not yet well acquainted with Spanish names; over time parents and possibly godparents probably had more of a say.

In postconquest central Mexico, the first names of Nahua men *and* women were drawn from a limited range of possibilities chosen from the names of Christian saints. The second names of men, however, were quite distinctive, reflecting their participation in the public sphere, where such names were often acquired. These second names served to locate a man as a member of a ruling family, as a member of a family of scribes, or as part of the larger group who held public office. Except for the names of the wives of high nobles and rulers, such as doña Leonor de Guzmán, women typically carried less distinctive second names than men and remained invisible as individuals in the realm of politics and the public domain.

Preconquest Naming Patterns

Understanding the transformation of Nahua naming patterns after the conquest is hindered by the fact that preconquest naming practices are not well understood. Single names seem to have been the rule for the bulk of the population, with nothing resembling the European-style family surname.[7] In a naming ritual typically held three days after birth, Nahua infants received a calendrical name, Ce Mazatl (One Deer), or Ome Tochtli (Two Rabbit), for example, chosen from among the most auspicious day signs close to the date of birth. Noncalendrical names are also common, although the circumstances under which an individual acquired one or whether it entirely displaced the initial calendrical name is not known. Whereas male names were quite diverse and personal, often being descriptive of an individual's characteristics or attributes, female names were far more stereotypical. Moreover, the most common female names— Tiacapan (Eldest or Firstborn), Tlaco (Middle), Teiuc (Younger), Xoco (Youngest), or Moçel (Only)—were "gender-specific"; they were not typically used for men. These names located a woman by reference to birth order but hardly distinguished her from other women. Thus, as expressed in naming, kinship largely defined a woman's identity, not surprising in a society that dedicated infant boys as warriors and infant girls as wives in the naming ritual of the newborn.[8]

Whereas distinctions between male and female naming in the preconquest period were pronounced, those based on social rank were less so. Some noblewomen did carry names typical of men, and some noblemen did take on titles of office as a kind of second name,

but beyond this nobles shared naming practices with the bulk of
Nahua commoners: male names were typically more diverse and
colorful than were female names. Moreover, neither commoners nor
nobles carried anything resembling a "family" name, a reflection of
Nahua kinship principles. The one exception to the lack of reference
to family was in certain royal dynasties in which the same names
were used in succeeding generations, "thus associating a set of
names with a specific dynasty and rulership."[9]

Postconquest Naming Patterns
First Names

After the conquest Nahuatl-language names gradually fell by the
wayside and were replaced with the names of Catholic saints typical
of Spaniards and indicative of Christian baptism. A tally of the given
names of both female and male children baptized in the parishes of
San Jacinto Tenantitlan and San Juan Bautista in the early seventeenth
century and the given names of their parents demonstrates that
Nahua women and men drew their names largely from among those
used by contemporary Spaniards.[10] María, Juana, Francisca, and Ana
were the four most common female names, with María and Juana pre-
dominating. Among the males, Juan, Miguel, Domingo, and Francisco
were the four most common given names, Juan being the most popular by far (see table 4.1).[11] These findings closely parallel studies of
Nahua naming patterns in other areas of sixteenth- and seventeenth-
century central Mexico: Nahua women were most commonly named
María, Ana, and Juana; and Nahua men, Juan, Miguel, and Pedro.[12]
    A few popular names predominated among both Nahua men
and women in early seventeenth-century Coyoacan, with no substantial difference in the diversity of male and female names apparent.[13] The more or less equal diversity of male and female names reflects the fact that—in contrast to the noncalendrical names of the
preconquest period—the given names of Nahua men and women in
the postconquest period were not divided into "two nearly exclusive
sets on the basis of sex."[14] Among the Nahuas most women's names
were feminized versions of the names of male saints; the popularity
of these gender-equivalent names thus reflects less originality in the
range of name choice for females.[15] The popularity of male saints un-

Table 4.1
Twenty Most Common Female and Male Names
in Two Coyoacan Parishes, Early Seventeenth Century*

	Females			Males	
Name	Number	Percentage	Name	Number	Percentage
1. María	438	20	Juan	692	31
2. Juana	303	14	Miguel	143	6
3. Francisca	118	5	Domingo	112	5
4. Ana	114	5	Francisco	106	5
5. Isabel	76	3	Nicolás	96	4
6. Dominga	74	3	Diego	85	4
7. Magdalena	71	3	Pedro	79	4
8. Agustina	70	3	Baltasar	58	3
9. Pascuala	66	3	Josef	54	2
10. Ursula	65	3	Agustín	53	2
	1,395	64		1,478	68
11. Gerónima	60	3	Melchor	51	2
12. Sebastiana	57	3	Gaspar	47	2
13. Petronilla	56	3	Mateo	42	2
14. Catalina	52	2	Sebastián	42	2
15. Mariana	48	2	Gerónimo	41	2
16. Melchora	47	2	Pascual	40	2
17. Angelina	46	2	Jacinto	37	2
18. Nicolasa	44	2	Felipe	34	2
19. Josefa	36	2	Andrés	34	2
20. Lucía	32	1	Tomás	34	2
	1,873	86		1,880	86
Total number of cases	2,189		Total number of cases	2,189	

Sources: GSU microfilm rolls 291-094, vol. 2; 237-889, vol. 1.
*Percentages rounded off.

doubtedly reflects the tendency of Spanish clergy to promote them; and the use of feminized versions of those names reflects the shortage of recognized female saints.[16]

Parish priests surely encouraged Nahuas to adopt the Spanish practice of naming a child for the saint associated with his or her date of birth or baptism. Nahuas may have been inclined to use the Catholic ritual calendar in naming as it parallels the preconquest practice of calendrical names in that date of birth was crucial to name choice; we know that naming a child for a household saint or for the saint's day on which the child was born or baptized was characteristic of patterns among Nahuas in eighteenth-century Mexico.[17] Although the practice of naming after a household saint cannot be ascertained from the early seventeenth-century Coyoacan baptismal records, the registers do demonstrate that, with the exception of the most popular names, the date of birth or baptism was a common basis for assigning Nahua children names.[18]

Many studies of child-naming practices in Western Europe and the United States between the sixteenth and nineteenth centuries consider name sharing among kin and what it suggests about the nature of kinship in a given population.[19] As one scholar has put it, "Because the name places a child in relationship to others, the specification of which kin shared names helps to define the linkages and boundaries of kinship."[20] The naming of children after family members other than parents, that is, after grandparents, uncles, aunts, and godparents (often family members), reflects the importance of kinship ties (both lineal and lateral) beyond the nuclear family, often including bilateral familial ties.[21] The narrowing of name sharing among kin by the nineteenth century, as argued by one scholar, reflects the emergence of the modern, or nuclear, family.[22]

The extent to which Nahua children of colonial central Mexico were named after near or extended kin is difficult to determine, in large part because the lack of family names among the bulk of the population precludes the reconstruction of Nahua families (except among the nobility). Scattered evidence does suggest that name sharing between children and their same-gender parents and grandparents was not unknown. During the initial naming ritual for babies in the preconquest period, for example, the midwife bathed the baby boy: "And then they there gave him a name, they there gave him his earthly name. Perhaps they would give him the name of his grandfather; it would enhance his lot."[23] And the early postconquest censuses from the Morelos region demonstrate that while siblings did not commonly carry the same baptismal name, mothers and fathers and their same-gender children often did.[24] The dominance of birth-order names among women suggests that female members of a nuclear or extended family would have frequently shared names, while the greater variety and often idiosyncratic nature of male names suggests that name sharing may have been less common among males. The sample of Coyoacan baptismal records studied here points to a weak preference for naming children after parents of the same gender, as do scattered testaments and other notarial documents from sixteenth- and early seventeenth-century Coyoacan.[25] This suggests that naming children after same-gender parents was practiced in early seventeenth-century Coyoacan, although the overwhelming dominance of the name María among females and the name Juan among males suggests that name sharing in many cases was less a reflection of "the boundaries and linkages of kinship" than the general preference for a few very popular names.

The dominance of the small number of popular names among the Nahuas of early seventeenth-century Coyoacan suggests that certain names gained popularity among both Nahuas and local Spanish clerics. The names Juana and Juan obviously reflect the patron saint of the local sociopolitical unit, San Juan Bautista. Similarly, the popularity of the given names Dominga, the sixth most common female name, and Domingo, the third most common male name in early seventeenth-century Coyoacan, undoubtedly reflects the fact that Coyoacan was within the doctrinal domain of the Dominican order. Naming after ward or jurisdictional affiliation was a common practice throughout colonial central Mexico, conspicuous in late sixteenth-century Culhuacan and in the late seventeenth-century and eighteenth-century Toluca Valley.[26] One suspects that naming after resident religious orders was also a common practice, Francisca and Francisco and Agustina and Agustín being especially popular names in Franciscan and Augustinian areas much as Dominga and Domingo were in Dominican Coyoacan.[27] Francisca and Francisco and Agustina and Agustín were also popular in early seventeenth-century Coyoacan, however, and comparative studies are needed to establish to what extent certain names were popular throughout colonial central Mexico or reflected regional differences.[28]

The popularity of María, Juana, and Juan in early seventeenth-century Coyoacan, therefore, reflected both indigenous and Spanish influences. Nahuas may have preferred the names Juana and Juan and Dominga and Domingo as an expression of micropatriotism, clerics doubtless encouraging their use in recognition of the local jurisdiction and resident religious order. The popularity of the name María reflects an incipient but modest Marian devotion in the region, the spread of which was most likely encouraged by resident clerics. But it was far from the vigorous, more familiar Marian cults evident among Spaniards in the next century.[29]

Second Names

Given names based on Christian saints became widespread among central Mexican Nahuas by the 1550s following the initial wave of mass baptisms during the first generation of colonial rule. Although in many documents Nahuas continue to be referred to by a single given name, others attest to the use of second names, both indigenous and Spanish. How and when Nahuas acquired such second names is not clear. Perhaps officiating clerics did not know and hence did not record second names, or perhaps these names were acquired after baptism at some later important moment in the individual's life.[30] The latter is suggested by the early seventeenth-century Coyoacan baptismal registers: they rarely mention more than one name for a baptized child, yet the parents typically were identified by a first and second name. In view of this, much of the following discussion on the second names carried by Coyoacan Nahuas in the early seventeenth century draws on an analysis of parents' names in the baptismal records, supplemented by scattered references in other documents. If the registers are any indication, the patterns of acquisition of additional names had changed by the mid-eighteenth century. Many entries in Coyoacan baptismal registers at that time record two names for baptized children, resembling the Spanish practice of giving both a forename and a surname at baptism.[31]

Much more diverse than given names, second names ranged from the Nahuatl-language names characteristic of the preconquest period to names drawn from Spaniards and Spanish tradition. Second given names, the full names of saints, names based on Catholic devotions, Spanish surnames and partronymics, and most directly the Spanish honorific titles of don and doña came to mark social distinctions among Nahuas. Although noblewomen partially crosscut this pattern, second names nonetheless exhibit a pronounced gender differentiation: Nahua women did not typically carry the "high-status" names characteristic of men. The transition from Nahuatl-language names of the preconquest period to the variety of postconquest second names was gradual and undoubtedly varied from region to region.

Nahuatl-language names were not immediately displaced by Spanish ones in colonial central Mexico; rather, they were often retained and served as a second name. The Morelos census material dating from around 1540 constitutes the earliest postconquest record of large numbers of Nahua names; in it individual household members were often identified by both their Christian baptismal name and a Nahuatl name called *macehualtoca,* or commoner name, although it is not entirely clear which was the primary form of address.[32] The pattern of a Spanish given name and a Nahuatl-language second name is evident until the late sixteenth century and is attested throughout central Mexico.[33]

In sixteenth-century Coyoacan indigenous names are found almost exclusively among males, undoubtedly reflecting the greater variety of male names in the preconquest period. Juana Quauhtzontecontzin (Blockhead; literally, "Wood-Head"), mentioned as the late grandmother of a San Jacinto resident selling land in 1608, is a rare and humorous example of a Nahua woman who carried an indigenous second name.[34] Another woman, doña María Xalatlauhco, who claimed to be a member of the Coyoacan ruling family, was identified, not by such a personal characteristic, but by the name of the town in the Valley of Toluca where she had married the local ruler and continued to reside.[35] And only two of the mothers of children baptized in the two parishes in early seventeenth-century Coyoacan (of a total of 1,473) carried Nahuatl-language second names—in both cases, Xochitl (Flower). Even the birth-order names typical of females in the preconquest period and common in neighboring Culhuacan are rarely attested after the mid-sixteenth century in Coyoacan. During an investigation of tribute abuses in the early 1550s, several of the (relatively few) women to testify were identified by a Spanish given name and a second, Nahuatl birth-order name, suggesting that they were still common at that time.[36] But the only example dating after the mid-sixteenth century is a Juana Xoco (Youngest) who sold a parcel of land in 1572 and claimed to be a citizen of Xocoyoc, literally, "At the Place of the Youngest Child."[37]

In contrast, examples of Nahuatl-language second names among males in sixteenth-century Coyoacan are numerous and diverse. Second names that had been prominent preconquest titles are evident both among the highest ranks of the Coyoacan ruling class, including those who carried the honorific title don, and among the lower ranks of the nobility.[38] Less prominent males also retained Nahuatl-language names, often of animals typical of preconquest calendrical names or names descriptive of an individual's personal attributes, occupation, ethnicity, or place of origin.[39]

In Coyoacan, Nahuatl-language second names are evident through the late sixteenth century, more or less paralleling trends elsewhere in central Mexico.[40] The infrequent use of indigenous second names by the early seventeenth century in the region of Coyoacan is demonstrated by the sample of baptized children in which only 4 of the parents (2 fathers and 2 mothers) of a total of 1,473 had such names. Except for a few prominent dynastic names, especially Moteucçoma, indigenous names fell into general disuse regionwide by the second quarter of the seventeenth century, when the second names of Nahuas were mostly drawn from those of Spaniards.[41]

The most common second name of Nahuas throughout the colonial period was simply another baptismal (given) name, for example, María Juana or Juan Diego (see table 4.2).[42] This type of second name was apparently derived from the religious names taken by mendicant friars, the most common of which was a saint's name, as in "de San Pedro," added to an individual friar's own baptismal name. Among Nahuas the full saint's name typical of friars was apparently contracted, dropping the "de San" element and leaving only the given name.[43] By the end of the sixteenth century, then, the names of Nahua commoners typically consisted of two elements, both of which were Spanish given names.[44] Double given names typically varied among the different members of a family in sixteenth- and early seventeenth-century Coyoacan.[45]

In view of the dominant Nahua choices of first names (Juan, Juana, and María), one might expect (after taking account of those double names that combined Juana and María) that the second element of such pairs would draw from a larger pool of names, since the most popular ones in many cases had already been used. To judge from the baptismal records of Coyoacan, this was in fact the case. The range of the parents' second given names was more diverse, including many relatively unusual ones—Elena, Clara, and Beatríz for the

Table 4.2
Twenty Most Common Second Names of Mothers and Fathers
in Two Coyoacan Parishes, Early Seventeenth Century*

Mothers			Fathers		
Name	Number	Percentage	Name	Number	Percentage
1. María	288	20	Juan	73	5
2. Juana	135	9	de la Cruz	70	5
3. Francisca	76	5	Diego	57	4
4. Gerónima	73	5	Francisco	56	4
5. Ana	49	3	Bautista	51	3
6. de la Cruz	43	3	Jacinto	48	3
7. Magdalena	41	3	Juárez	48	3
8. Ursula	36	2	Miguel	44	3
9. Pascuala	27	2	Nicolás	40	3
10. Catalina	20	1	Martín	37	3
	788	53		524	36
11. Luisa	20	1	Gaspar	36	2
12. Isabel	19	1	Domingo	29	2
13. Agustina	19	1	Hernández	27	2
14. Angelina	18	1	de Santiago	24	2
15. Verónica	15	1	Melchor	23	2
16. Paula	10	1	Ramos	22	1
17. Elena	9	1	Mateo	21	1
18. Lucía	8	1	Gerónimo	21	1
19. Melchora	8	1	Jacobo	18	1
20. Bautista	8	1	Agustín	17	1
	922	63		762	52
Total number			Total number		
of cases	1,473		of cases	1,473	

Sources: GSU microfilm rolls 291-094, vol. 2; 237-889, vol. 1.
*Percentages rounded off.

females and Julián and Benito for the males—with none of these examples appearing among the twenty most common names. Furthermore, with the exception of the name María, a more even distribution
among the pool of names characterized the second given name of the
parents of Nahua children baptized in the two Coyoacan parishes of
San Jacinto Tenantitlan and San Juan Bautista than among the pool
of first names of children and parents already discussed.[46]

Another group of names distinct from the double first names typical of Nahua commoners and indicative of a higher stratum in Nahua society were mendicant names that had retained the "de San" element or others taken from famous friars.[47] The formulation Juan de Gante, an appellation borne by a Nahua from Coyoacan, is surely associated with the famous fray Pedro de Gante, one of the first three Franciscan friars to arrive in New Spain.[48] Other Nahuas carried the name of a particular saint rather than the more generic María or Ana, as in the case of the prominent Nahua noblewoman from sixteenth-century Coyoacan, doña Catalina de Sena.[49] John the Baptist was perhaps the most common saint's name among Nahuas; in early seventeenth-century Coyoacan the gender-equivalent names Juana and Juan Bautista were especially popular, an obvious homage to the local patron saint.[50]

Other than Juana and Juan Bautista, saints' names appear relatively infrequently among the parents of children baptized in the parishes of San Jacinto Tenantitlan and San Juan Bautista in the early seventeenth century. And in some cases the use of a saint's name (with the de San/ta element retained) as a second name may not have represented a true second name at all but rather may simply have identified the person with a place, referring to the patron saint of an individual's hometown or district. Verónica de Santa María Magdalena, the mother of a child baptized in the parish of San Jacinto Tenantitlan, was probably from the town Santa María Magdalena Atlitic, located within the parish. And another mother, Dominga de San Nicolás, was in all likelihood from San Nicolás Totolapan, another important town in the parish.[51] Moreover, many Nahuas may have been identified by a single given name in most circumstances, using the name of a home district or town only when away from it, a common feature of naming patterns when surnames are not yet permanently fixed.[52]

Nahua names with two elements might also be drawn from Catholic lore and doctrine, including, among others, de la Cruz, de los Angeles, de los Reyes, and Domingo Ramos (a play on Domingo de Ramos or Palm Sunday). Excluding second given names, the most popular second name recorded in the early seventeenth-century baptismal records—among both mothers and fathers—was de la Cruz, reflecting a Christcentric devotion. This name is, however, the exception to the otherwise pronounced difference in the frequency of devotional second names among men and women. Both Santiago and (Domingo) Ramos were quite common among the fathers in early seventeenth-century Coyoacan but were rarely used among women.[53] Nahua women, for their part, at times carried second names that referred to various representations of the Virgin Mary, although far less frequently than other devotional names carried by men. Although not as common as they would become a century later, names such as de la Concepción, de la Visitación, and de la Asunción were found among mothers of children baptized in early seventeenth-century Coyoacan.[54]

Spanish surnames, too, were adopted by Nahuas in colonial central Mexico, in many cases drawn from a prominent Spaniard who served as baptismal sponsor. In the sixteenth century many indigenous rulers took or were given the names of famous conquerors, *encomenderos* (recipients of the right to collect tribute from a select group of Indians), clerics, and viceroys. Hernando Cortés, for example, sponsored so many Nahua rulers that Cortés became one of the most common noble names in sixteenth-century central Mexico.[55] Thus, in the Coyoacan region (which formed part of Cortés's Marquesado grant), a don Luis Cortés was active in municipal affairs in the mid-sixteenth century,[56] and seven fathers of children baptized in the two Coyoacan parishes in the early seventeenth century had Cortés as a second name. Nahuas also drew their names from Spaniards active in a particular region—the encomendero's staff, or resident clerics and estate owners. Coyoacan offers abundant examples. Juan Altamirano, the father of a Nahua selling land in 1612, was the namesake of Juan Alonso Altamirano, the *corregidor* (highest Spanish provincial official) of Coyoacan between 1595 and 1596.[57] The surname de León is repeatedly attested among Coyoacan Nahuas, undoubtedly derived from the mid-sixteenth-century Spanish official Luis León Romano, who served in the region, and a prominent local Spanish landowning family that shared the same surname.[58] And Baltasar Téllez, who together with his widowed mother sold a piece of land in San Jacinto to a Spaniard in 1591, was the namesake of a member of a prominent local Spanish landowning family that acquired substantial holdings in the area.[59]

Local Spanish professionals might also serve as the source of surnames for local Nahuas, in some cases for individuals who shared the same occupation. A striking example from Coyoacan is the Spanish notary Alonso de Suero who wrote the (Spanish) text accompanying the "Códice de Coyoacan," believed to be the *pintura*, or painting, associated with the investigation of tribute abuses carried out in the region in the early 1550s. Alonso de Suero apparently accounts for the number of Nahua notaries over several generations who carried the same surname.[60] Spanish names may not have been those of specific individuals or families at all but may have been recognized more generally by Nahuas as being prestigious within the Spanish context and used for that reason. A case in point may be the indigenous Coyoacan ruling family, which adopted the Spanish surname Guzmán and used it into the eighteenth century.[61] While no specific individual or family with the surname Guzmán emerges from the local Spanish context, the nearby capital offered possibilities, the most obvious being Nuño de Guzmán, the notorious president of the Second Audiencia.

Spanish patronymics were also adopted as second names by the Nahuas of colonial central Mexico. These names were probably drawn from the humble Spaniards present in the largely indigenous countryside as traders, farmers, or employees of encomenderos. In some cases they may have been given to Nahuas by the officiating priest at baptism, undoubtedly the case with the regionwide use of the surname Juárez in Coyoacan; over time the name became "almost as characteristically 'Indian' as Santiago or a double first name."[62] Juárez was by far the most popular patronymic among fathers of Nahua children baptized in the parishes of San Jacinto Tenantitlan and San Juan Bautista, but others, including Hernández, Sánchez, Ramírez, Pérez, and Jiménez, were evident as well. Although names taken from prominent Spanish families are the more readily documented, there were undoubtedly many humble Hispanics resident in Coyoacan from whom Nahuas may have acquired such names.[63]

In the sixteenth and seventeenth centuries, Nahuas with Spanish patronymics as second names represented an upper stratum of indigenous society similar to those who bore the various types of religious names (excluding double given names). Many with Spanish patronymics also carried the Spanish honorific titles *don* and *doña*, indicative of their higher social rank. These titles were originally granted by Spaniards to indigenous rulers in recognition of their rank. The Nahuas, already accustomed to titles of political office, quickly adopted Spanish honorific titles but used them in novel ways. Among the few elite Spaniards who claimed the right to be called don, the title was acquired at birth and held for life. Among Nahuas, the pattern was apparently more diverse. In some instances, individuals held the title by right of birth, much as with Spanish practice, but others assumed the title on attaining high municipal office, and still others used the title only when holding specific positions.[64] In the sixteenth century the title doña was widely held by Spanish noblewomen, much more frequently than don was held by Spanish noblemen. The opposite seems to have been the case among Nahuas, apparently because indigenous noblewomen did not hold municipal office or head lordly houses.[65]

In Coyoacan males carrying religious names and Spanish patronymics, along with other more prestigious Spanish surnames and often honorific titles, held important municipal offices, paralleling trends found in studies of municipal government in colonial Tlaxcala and Morelos.[66] A small corps of officers drawn from the indigenous nobility typically rotated among different offices on Nahua town councils in colonial central Mexico. Municipal officeholders often moved from lower to higher office, although there were exceptions: a governor, for example, might return to occupy the lower position of *alcalde* (judge) or *regidor* (councilman). Name changes frequently accompanied the acquisition of higher office, often including the adoption of the honorific title don.[67] In Coyoacan, a Baltasar who served as regidor in the 1540s later became known as Baltasar de León, after which he also adopted don as he continued to hold municipal office throughout the 1550s.[68] This pattern of a name change accompanying the acquisition of municipal office undoubtedly drew on preconquest precedents in which rulers acquired additional names at critical junctures in life—accession to the throne, victory in battle, the taking of a captive.[69]

Although evidence of such progressive name changes is not abundant among Coyoacan officeholders, naming patterns discerned from baptismal records indicate an unequivocal difference between the frequency of religious names and Spanish patronymics among Nahua men who held municipal office and—more to the

point here—among Nahua women who did not. In the early seventeenth century mothers of children baptized in the parishes of San
Jacinto Tenantitlan and San Juan Bautista had significantly fewer religious names and Spanish patronymics than did fathers, a difference
illustrative of the infrequency with which Nahua wives and husbands carried the same second name.[70] The striking difference between the frequency with which women and men carried Spanish
patronymics suggests that there were fewer avenues by which women
might distinguish themselves and earn higher-recognition names.

Nahua women from Coyoacan who did carry Spanish patronymics or religious names as second names were undoubtedly of high
noble status, as was the case in late sixteenth-century Culhuacan.[71]
The relative infrequency of these names among Nahua women in
contrast to Nahua men, however, has important implications for the
way in which the social status of Nahua women was defined. Although double first names are typical of Nahua commoners, such
names among women do not always indicate low social status, as
is suggested by evidence from other communities of central Mexico.
In late sixteenth-century Culhuacan, for example, two given names
"seem to have been a marker of slightly higher status among women,
a step above use of a birth-order name."[72] Nonetheless, although
ranked higher than women with birth-order names, most women
with double first names were still of relatively low status. Some
clearly were not, however; several women with double first names in
the Culhuacan study carried the honorific title doña. And significantly, some women of high status clearly did not carry "high-status"
names. Unlike their male relatives, the women were not afforded the
opportunity to participate in the activities, such as municipal office-
holding, by which those names were acquired.[73] Rather, the status of
women was derived from the men associated with them, husbands
or sometimes fathers. This is clearly illustrated in the witness lists of
testaments from late sixteenth-century Culhuacan, where women
are often identified by addition of their husband's name, whereas the
converse is not true.[74]

Those prominent Nahua women who at birth acquired high-
recognition names such as Spanish surnames and patronymics did
so because these, more than most other second names, had probably
become linked to specific families and were passed on from genera-

tion to generation presumably to males and females alike.[75] This is the case with the indigenous Coyoacan ruling family that for generations carried the Spanish surname Guzmán; the heir to the actual title *tlatoani*, or the indigenous rulership, was indeed named don Juan de Guzmán in succeeding generations.[76] Even female members of the family, including doña Leonor de Guzmán, mentioned previously, carried the surname. Spanish surnames were passed from generation to generation in other Nahua families as well. In some central Mexican areas, notarial skills, another prestigious occupation closed to indigenous women, were passed on within noble families from father to son. Surnames were also passed from generation to generation among Coyoacan notarial families in the sixteenth century: the Galicias, Felicianos, and Sueros each produced at least two notaries, and presumably the women of these families carried the surname as well.[77]

Conclusion

In the aftermath of the Spanish conquest the Nahuas of central Mexico adopted Spanish names along with Christian baptism. Within decades, given names typical of Spaniards and drawn from the names of Christian saints had become widespread among Nahuas. By the early seventeenth century, naming among both Nahua men and Nahua women was characterized by the dominance of a small number of saints' names, with a few being especially popular. Parents as well as officiating priests apparently influenced name choice; patterns indicate a strong preference for naming after the local patron saint, the saint's day associated with the child's birth, and (less pronounced) the same-gender parent. The diversity of names carried by males and females was essentially the same, reflecting the fact that most women's names were feminized versions of the names of male saints.

In striking contrast to first names, Nahua second names were distinctly different from Spanish ones and were strong indicators of both social rank and gender. Differentiation by social rank is evident in the contrast between the double first names typical of commoners and the diverse second names typical of nobles, including Nahuatl-language names, the (full) names of saints, devotional names, and

Spanish surnames and patronymics. Furthermore, the Spanish surnames carried by nobles were passed within families, whereas the
double given names of Nahua commoners were not typically passed
on to succeeding generations.

Gender differentiation was pronounced. Consonant with preconquest naming patterns, males carried more varied second names
than did females. Nahuatl-language names, devotional names, but
especially Spanish surnames and patronymics were much less frequent among women than among men. These differences in naming
patterns reflected the different roles accorded men and women.
While men often acquired more prestigious names over the course of
their lives for their attainment of office or for other publicly recognized accomplishments, women were restricted from such activities.
Their public status was derived from the men associated with them,
husbands or sometimes fathers.

The distinctive naming patterns of Nahua men and women
make it nearly impossible to trace a woman commoner through various documents or across generations. It is precisely for this reason
that understanding the naming patterns themselves is so crucial:
they not only provide important clues to general features of postconquest Nahua life—changing lists of popular names as an expression of religious devotions, for example—but also offer a window on
the collective lives of women commoners, whose very names make
them difficult to trace as individuals.

From Parallel and Equivalent to Separate but Unequal

Tenochca Mexica Women, 1500–1700

Susan Kellogg

I heard it said by an old Indian woman, who they brought to me for [her] knowledge of religion, because she had been a priestess, that they also had a Festival of Resurrection and of the Nativity and Corpus Christi, like us and at the same time as us, and she pointed out to me other important festivals like we celebrate. I said to her: "Evil old woman, the devil knew so well how to arrange and sow his evil herbs and to mix them with grain, so that you did not finish learning the truth."
—Durán, *Historia de las indias de Nueva España e islas de la Tierra Firme*[1]

During the early colonial period, Tenochca Mexica women participated in legal and social processes to a degree whose only parallel in Latin America is with Inca and Andean women and which was often largely unrecognized by Spanish chroniclers of the time.[2] Mexica women's active involvement in litigation was rooted partly in pre-Hispanic patterns of parallel and complementary gender relations. This pattern of gender relations gave women certain property rights and positions of authority (such as priestess, as shown in the above-

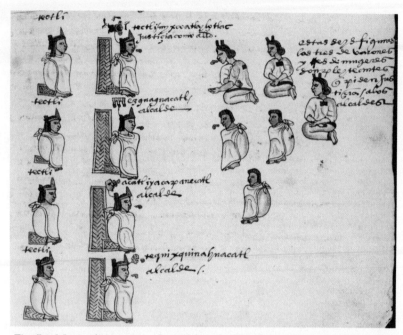

Fig. 5.1. Mexica litigants, male and female. This figure, from the *Codex Mendoza*, illustrates both women's jural adulthood and gender parallelism in the pre-Hispanic jural realm. MS. Arch. Selden A.1, fol. 68r. Courtesy of The Bodleian Library, Oxford University.

cited passage) and endowed them with "jural adulthood"[3] even as they were simultaneously blocked from participation in the highest-prestige activities in their society.[4] (See fig. 5.1.) Women's legal activities also partly rested on the demographic upheavals of the sixteenth century that unbalanced sex ratios and helped to generate numerous property disputes. By the seventeenth century, however, the legal status of Mexica women declined as new notions of separate but unequal spheres developed among the indigenous populations of the Valley of Mexico. Yet even after the seventeenth century—when women had clearly lost the relatively strong position they held during the immediate postconquest era—they continued to challenge the colonial state through legal and extralegal means.

The aim of this chapter is to trace the changing legal and social status(es) of Mexica women, especially nonelite women, from the late pre-Hispanic period to the beginning of the eighteenth century. While their overall status did decline, I will show that this decline was complex. Evaluating their status in any particular period is complicated because it was a product of so many different factors—material, social, and ideological. Thus, while the concept of gender parallelism has proven useful in helping to understand the organization of gender roles in pre-Columbian civilizations,[5] the concept may need some refining when applied to the Mexica to explicate how both gender complementarity and gender differentiation across a variety of social and material realms structured women's experiences and lives in the late precolonial and early colonial periods. While I concentrate on Mexica women in Tenochtitlan/Mexico City (hence the use of the term "Tenochca Mexica"), much of what I have to say is relevant to the experience of Nahuatl-speaking peoples across the Valley of Mexico.

Gender Relations during the Late Pre-Hispanic Period

Gender roles and relations in late pre-Hispanic Tenochtitlan were compounded of both complementary and hierarchical relations, though the former outweighed the latter. The complementary aspects of gender relations expressed themselves in a variety of ways, including genealogy and kinship, labor and work, and politics and religion. Complementary gender relations were frequently expressed through parallel structures of thought, language, and action in which males and females were conceived of and played different yet parallel and equally necessary roles.

Mexica gender parallelism had its roots both in Nahua forms of culture, thought, and ideology and in Nahua kinship ideology and structure. The former prominently featured dualities and complementaries that sometimes emphasized contrast and opposition and sometimes merged the contrasts into a unity. The kinship system was rooted in a cognatic descent system that structured both the conceptualization of and social groupings organized by kin and family members.[6] As I have argued elsewhere, cognatic descent systems are those in which genealogically based claims and rights to kin group membership, property, or positions of authority are rooted in the establishment of an individual's place in a line of descendants in which men and women are considered to be genealogically and structurally equivalent.[7] The Mexica cognatic descent system was based in part on the recognition that both the mother and the father contributed fluids—again, equally necessary—that formed a fetus. Babies were said to be constituted by the biological substances of their mothers and fathers and the "blood, color, and essence" of their parents.[8] Cognatic descent units, perhaps referred to generally by the Nahuatl term *tlacamecayotl*, in which descendants traced membership back four to five generations helped to structure households, marriages, and neighborhood groupings through which property ownership, work relations, ritual practices, and political activities all took place.

Thus, for example, under the Mexica cognatic system of descent both women and men could acquire property through inheritance. Describing the customary ways that property was divided in central Mexico, Motolinia[9] stated that while

> the will was not the custom in this land . . . they left the houses and estates to their children, and the eldest, if he were male, possessed it, and was in charge of his brothers and sisters, as the father did in his life. The siblings growing and marrying, the older brother divided with them according to what he had; and if the children were to marry, the siblings themselves entered in the estates and did with their nephews as I have said the older brother did with the other property.[10]

Early colonial Tenochca wills indicate that Mexica men and women held roughly equivalent inheritance rights in three distinct categories of property: houses, land, and movable items.[11] Male *and* female siblings inherited property owned by their fathers and mothers. Sarah Cline has observed that "women's control of property does not appear to have been a postconquest innovation."[12] Their ownership and control appears to have arisen primarily out of their inheritance rights as daughters and sisters. In the precolonial period, however, women's ability to activate their inheritance rights to land may have been constrained by the tendency of the eldest male in a sibling group to act as a guardian for the group and by scarcity of land as a resource.[13] Nevertheless, even though women's rights to land may often have remained residual, those residual rights could be passed on to children and other relatives and descendants.[14]

In the late pre-Hispanic period, women's access to property—whether gained through dowry or inheritance—allowed them to function somewhat autonomously of their husbands. For example, the property that women brought into marriage was kept separate from that brought to the marriage by men,[15] and the Mexica distinguished between those household goods that belonged to men and those that belonged to women.[16] Women also had access to space within domestic house structures, probably with sleeping and work areas separate from men's.[17] As we will see below, women's access to property during the pre-Hispanic period was reinforced by immediate postconquest social conditions and these property rights partly underlay their legal status and jural independence in the early colonial period.

Just as women had independent access to property during the pre-Hispanic period, so their productive activities were organized somewhat apart from their husbands' control both within and beyond the household. Their extrahousehold labor is particularly interesting because it was a source of economic independence for women and was overseen by "female administrators" (who will be described further below). Women performed many essential productive tasks within or for households, including cooking, cleaning (which had both sanitary and religious implications), caring for children, marketing, spinning, weaving, and carrying out the daily round of household rituals. Women also performed a variety of activities outside the household, in palaces, temples, markets, schools, and craftsworkers' organizations. Women served as priestesses, teachers, merchants, healers and midwives, professional spinners, weavers, and embroiderers.[18] Thus women—like men—provided labor necessary to sustain their households and to fulfill their households' labor, tribute, and ceremonial obligations.

Because of their property rights and labor contributions, adult Mexica women were considered to be autonomous and not the dependents of men. The day sign discussions in book 4 of the *Florentine Codex* are quite revealing in this regard. In the description of the very

first day sign, Ce Cipactli, "One Crocodile," fray Bernardino de Sahagún's informants suggested that women as well as men had the capacity to merit or earn the good fortunes due them for being born on
this day. Noble or commoner men would be rulers or brave warriors;
a woman would prosper and be able to feed others.

> She would have food and drink available. She would have
> food for others to eat; she would invite others to feast. She
> would be respectful. She would be visited by others; she
> would revive and refresh the spirits and bodies of those
> who lived in misery on earth. . . . [O]f her fatigue and effort,
> nothing would be in vain. Successful would be her dealings
> around the marketplace, in the place of business; it was as
> if it would sprinkle, shower, and rain her wares upon her.[19]

But men and women also equally shared the capacity to destroy the
good fortune by neglecting their responsibilities. Women born under
the fourth sign, Ce Xochitl, "One Flower," were said to be skilled embroiderers. But this sign was described as "indifferent," and thus in
order for a woman to be skilled in embroidery, she had to do penances, fast, and draw blood. If she did not perform her penances, she
would harm her sign and thereby merit "complete poverty and misery."[20] She would then fall into poverty and would sell herself into
prostitution.

Not only were women viewed as economically autonomous, but
they could pass on the fruits of their economic hard work and good
fortune to their children as shown by the discussion of the ninth sign,
Ce Coatl, "One Serpent," which was a special sign for merchants.
For example, women merchants born on this day were thought to be
particularly successful: "She would be quite rich, she would be a
good provider; she would be well-born. She would look to and guard
the services and the property of our lord. She would be a guardian
and administrator. Much would she gather, collect, save, and justly
distribute among her children."[21] Thus women—like men—were
viewed as responsible for their own economic well-being and could
contribute to the economic well-being of their descendants.

Women's labor was highly valued by the Mexica. One of the associations with "good women," especially good commoner women,

throughout the *Florentine Codex* is with labor and hard work. The good mother, for example, is described as constantly working,[22] as are the "middle-aged" woman and the "mature" woman.[23] Noblewomen also could be described as hardworking. One such description of the *cihuatecuhtli* (noblewoman) states that not only does she work hard, use resources carefully and well, but she also "governs" and "leads."[24] Thus women's productivity was cited as a reason that men were reluctant to abandon polygamy during the early colonial period.[25] Women's labor was also likely valued in this very war-oriented society because women—whether noble or commoner—often had to manage households and productive activities in the absence of men. The rituals women performed when their husbands went to war suggest that these were intended to aid men's success and that husbands were absent frequently since women were to use the bones of prisoners previously captured by their husbands in earlier campaigns as ritual objects.[26] Surely, large numbers of men were absent for long periods due to frequent warfare and the expansion of the empire of the Triple Alliance.[27] At the same time, across the Valley of Mexico populations were increasing, as was population density.[28] Not only were women bearing and caring for these children, large amounts of their time must have been spent in extrahousehold, "productive" (as opposed to "reproductive") labor for households and crafts groups that had to both feed their own members and meet the increasing demands of palaces and temples.

One way women might have met all the demands placed on them was to buy prepared or semiprepared food, called *tianquiztlaqualli,* in the marketplace. An enormous number of cooked foods, many of which were meat or fowl with a variety of seasonings, were available in the marketplace.[29] Even when men went off to war, the food supplies appear to have been provided primarily through the markets and not by the women of individual households.[30]

Some of women's productive tasks were overseen by female "administrators." In the marketplace, women were not only vendors, they were administrators (*tianquizpan tlaiacanque*) as well. The responsibilities of these administrators were to make certain that the prices of goods sold were fair, to make war provisions, and to assign tribute. Both men and women were appointed to these positions.[31] But market supervisory positions were not the only ones held by women.

The term "tlaiacanque"[32] recurs in another context in the *Floren-tine Codex*, suggesting that it could also be used for women who held administrative authority in the *cuicacalli*, or song houses, which were part of the royal palace or attached to major temples, according to fray Diego Durán.[33] During the month of *Huey tecuilhuitl* (Great feast of the lords), couples living in concubinage (*nemecatiliztli*) were brought for judgment before the cuicacalli. A man would be punished by having his possessions taken, and he was beaten, burned, and expelled from the cuicacalli. Sahagún's informants then explained that the "mistress(es) of women" (*cihuatetiachcahuan*) expelled the woman. "Nevermore was she to sing and dance with the others; nevermore was she to hold others by the hand. Thus the girls' matrons [*ich-pochtlaiacanqui*] established; thus they resolved."[34] *Ichpochtlaiacanqui* means administrator or director of young women, and in conjunction with the term "cihuatetiachcahuan" it is reminiscent of the paired terms *tiachcauan* (older brothers) and *telpochtlatoque* (leaders of youths) used for the male teachers in the *telpochcalli*, or school for commoner youths.

The existence of parallel structuring of male and female *barrio* (neighborhood) leadership roles is further suggested by Durán in his chapter on the "schools of dance" (his term for the cuicacalli in his volume on rites and ceremonies): "In order to collect and bring these young men to teach them [to dance], there were old men, assigned and chosen only for that office, in all the barrios, who were called *teanque*, which means 'men who go to collect young men.' In order to collect the young women there were old Indian women, appointed by all the barrios, who were called *cihuatepixque*, which means 'women guards' or 'mistresses.'"[35] Early colonial legal documents for both Tenochtitlan and Culhuacan indicate that women were included among the *tepixque* (generally referred to as "cihuatepixque," or women guards) and *tlaxilacalle* (referred to as "cihuatlaxilacalle," or woman ward [elders]).[36] This parallel structuring did not include higher levels of administration or governance, where positions were held by men. Women were also excluded from warfare and the warrior hierarchy.

Yet even at the highest levels of the state and governance there was a linguistic gender parallel made. The ruler of the Tenochca Mexica was referred to as the *tlatoani* and his second-in-command and closest adviser was called the *cihuacoatl* (woman serpent). "Cihuacoatl" was also the name of a female deity who was associated with the "rain-moisture-agricultural fertility" complex of deities identified by H. B. Nicholson.[37] The cihuacoatl as political persona would not replace a tlatoani who died (i.e., he was not a successor), but he could substitute for him at ceremonial occasions. Angel María Garibay K. believed that the use of the term "cihuacoatl" embodied the representation of a "female principal" at this highest level of government.[38] The tlatoani himself was spoken of in a way that suggests that he carried male and female qualities or at least paternal and maternal responsibilities. Thus he was frequently described metaphorically as the parent, as the *father and mother*, of his people.[39]

Gender parallelism as an organizing theme can also be discerned in the religious realm. The major deities of sustenance, dedicated to maize (Xilonen, Iztac Cinteotl, Chicomecoatl), salt (Huixtocihuatl), and maguey (Mayahuel) were all female as was one of the water deities, Chalchiuhtlicue, the wife of Tlaloc, the other major water deity. Other female gods, Toci and Cihuacoatl, represented earth and fire. All of these deities were worshiped during the eighteen monthly calendrical ceremonies, and some were also worshiped in their own temples.[40]

Temples had individual male and female priests called *tla-macazque* and *cihuatlamacazque*, respectively. *Tlamacazque* generally was used for lower-status priests, and *quacuiltin* was used for higher-status priests. The cihuatlamacazque lived in temples and helped carry out calendric rituals. Infant girls were offered by their parents to the *calmecac*, the school for elite youths, to become priestesses, though relatively few women remained as such for their whole lives, in contrast to male priests.[41] Women in religious service were trained by priestesses who oversaw their education and well-being.[42] Males held the highest-status priestly positions and carried out human sacrifice, but women helped prepare sacrificial victims.[43] Betty Ann Brown has argued, however, that women priestesses are depicted in the *Primeros memoriales* as sacrificing a female victim during the month of Ochpaniztli, "Sweeping the Road."[44]

The *cihuaquacuiltin* were higher-status, older priestesses. The holder of one particular title, the Iztaccihuatl cihuaquacuilli, watched over those women who swept and kept the fire at Toci's temple, Atenchicalcan. The *Florentine Codex* suggests that this was a position of some authority. "And any who made supplications [to the goddess] spoke to the Iztac ciuaquacuilli. This one determined all that was done here at [the Temple of] Atenchicalcan."[45]

We should not neglect the other roles played by women in education and life-cycle rituals. The *ichpochtiachcauh* (leader or mistress of young women) in the telpochcalli was in charge of young girls.[46] The *cihuateopixqui*, a female religious functionary, taught dancing to girls in the cuicacalli as already described. And a midwife not only delivered babies but also officiated during the ceremonies conducted after a child was born.[47] In these ceremonies, the midwife helped the baby to be born and led the ceremony in which she cut and gave the umbilical cord of a boy to warriors to bury on a battlefield[48] or buried the girl baby's umbilical cord within the house by the hearth.[49]

Women also played key ceremonial and strategic roles at marriage. Several older women, called *cihuatlanque*, negotiated a marriage once the bride had been selected by the groom's family.[50] Their role in the marriage was symbolized during the wedding ceremony when they tied the shirt of the groom to the skirt of the bride after the bride and groom had been presented gifts by their respective mothers-in-law. The matchmakers then placed the couple in a chamber and, according to Sahagún's informants, "put them to bed."[51]

Thus, during the late pre-Hispanic period, indigenous society was characterized by a significant degree of gender parallelism in language and social structure that both reflected and signaled the complementarity of the male and female realms. But gender parallelism did not connote complete gender equality; particularly in the realms of politics and religion, gender parallelism was compatible and existed with a degree of hierarchy. Males always held the highest-status positions of authority in these realms. This was also true of merchants and crafts guilds.

Likewise, in the symbolic realm, women could be thought of in negative ways. Female mythicohistorical figures, collectively referred to as "women of discord" by Susan D. Gillespie, were associated with historical periods of great political change.[52] Cowardice or defeat in warfare was also symbolically associated with women, female attributes, or the material items women used for production.[53] But women could also engage in highly inflammatory and warlike behavior, as when Tlatelolca women taunted Tenochca forces during the siege of Tlatelolco by exposing their nude bodies, expressing breast milk, and sprinkling it on the Tenochca Mexica warriors. Likewise, female deities could impart powerfully negative images even when associated with basic values of Mexica culture.[54] Across these realms of politics, warfare, and religion, we find that symbolic concepts of women often connoted female power. While a certain degree of sexual antagonism may be read into some of these examples,[55] they do not express notions of women as weak, dependent, or polluting.[56] The powerful drive in Mexica thought and culture to unite complementary yet opposed forces was expressed through gender symbols and structured everyday life and social arrangements.

In the everyday realm of life, responsibilities and ceremonies were structured so that men and women had semiseparate activities and organizations. The organization of production, politics, and religious practices ensured that women had access to positions of authority. While women did not serve in the very highest levels of political administration or governance and were excluded from the warrior hierarchy, women, like men, held administrative authority in markets, temples and houses of song, and neighborhoods. The imposition of Spanish colonial rule, however, was accompanied by an eventual and marked decline in the status of Mexica women. In the early colonial period, women's access to positions of authority eventually decreased and the older division between male and female realms, semiseparable and autonomous, gave way to a new division between public and private realms with a consequent lowering of the formal status of women.

The Conquest and Its Aftermath for Mexica Women

The gender complementarity that played such a crucial role in the conceptual and social structures of the Tenochca Mexica did not fare well over time in the postconquest era. But the new shape of gender relations did not emerge immediately because its emergence depended on the development of a colonial cultural system, one that was quite different from that of the pre-Hispanic era. The emergence of this new system took from fifty to seventy-five years in the Valley of Mexico region and was based, in part, on new, more hierarchical notions and definitions of gender roles and relations. Ironically, in the intervening period, from about the 1530s to the 1580s, women's status—particularly in urban areas—was enhanced in certain ways. It was enhanced for two reasons. First, the postconquest demographic imbalance in sex ratios in which women outnumbered men meant that women were succeeding to positions of authority within households, kin groups, and political units at higher rates than previously.[57] Second, the introduction of a law code and legal system that proved to be highly malleable reinforced women's autonomy in the short run.

Law was a major colonizing tool brought by the Spaniards to the Americas. Neither Spanish law codes nor those formulated in the colonies, such as the *Recopilación de leyes de los reynos de las Indias*, dealt specifically with Indian women, but Spanish law codes, especially the *Siete Partidas* and the *Leyes de Toro*, did elaborate the legal rights of Spanish women. We would be wise to remember that we cannot simply read women's status off these codes. Law codes and actual behavior or practices are not one and the same, but they do offer us some parameters for analyzing women's property rights and activities, though, in terms of everyday life, these applied most often to elite women. Still, legal compilations offer clues about women's status beyond the realms of law and property and provide an index by which to measure some of the beliefs and attitudes brought by male colonists.[58]

Scholarship on Spanish women's property rights suggests that in both Spain and its colonies, women had access to and control over property. Dowry and inheritance were the major means of women's access. Dowries legally belonged to women, and their permission was needed to sell or otherwise alienate them.[59] While husbands could use dowries' earnings as they wished, women could recover their dowries on the event of their husbands' death or if they were granted an ecclesiastical divorce. When the wife died before her husband, the dowry either was be divided among her children or, if she had no children, was returned to her parents.[60] Laws concerned with dowry and inheritance suggest that legal limits were placed on the patriarchal authority of fathers and husbands under Spanish law.

These legal limits are also demonstrated by Spanish bilateral inheritance laws. According to the *Leyes de Toro*, the spouse and children were the preferred heirs whose claims had to be satisfied before those of parents, siblings, or others.[61] While testators were free to leave one-fifth to one-third of their estates to spouses or children through a *mejora* (a special bequest to an heir), the inheritance rights of both male and female children were safeguarded. But Asunción Lavrin and Edith Couturier also show convincingly that "wom[e]n in practical terms [had] an economic edge over the potential rights of the children."[62] None of these property rights can be used to argue that men and women were equal under the law. In fact, women's inequality was explicitly written into Spanish law codes.

Women were expressly prohibited from formal participation in the political and religious affairs of Spanish society. They could not be judges, lawyers, or priests, nor could they hold political office or vote. Yet women did have legally sanctioned access to a broad range of activities: they could serve as guardians for children or grandchildren, and they could speak for elderly relatives in court if husbands or other appropriate male relatives were not available. They could conduct or partake of a broad set of legally defined economic activities, including buying, selling, renting, or inheriting property.[63] "They could lend and borrow money, act as administrators of estates, and form business partnerships. They could initiate litigation, be their own advocates in court, and appear as witnesses (except in wills)."[64]

Spanish women's legal rights balanced restriction and protection but did so in the context of a patriarchal society in which law fundamentally supported the power and authority of fathers and husbands. Single children, whether male or female, remained under the father's authority unless they were explicitly emancipated. Fathers were given primary authority over key aspects of their children's lives, including their educations, legal affairs, and property transactions.[65] While in New Spain, women often served as executors of their husbands' wills and guardians for their children, husbands legally and practically did have great control over their wives' property and transactions.[66] But while the husband's permission was necessary in order for his wife to undertake legal activities, the reverse was not the case. Nonetheless, we shall see that in the case of Indian women, these codified conditions for women's legal activities were not always met, and it is to a description of *their* legal activities that I now turn.

When the Spanish crown encouraged New Spain's aboriginal population to use its legal authorities and institutions for dispute settlement, it unwittingly provided an arena for the expression and negotiation of complex conflicts among both real people and cultural themes of gender, class, and ethnicity. The legal arena was one in which women were particularly present—almost as if they were compensating for their loss of power and authority in other realms of their lives. The rapid disappearance of the institutions in which women had held power—such as temples, calmecac, or cuicacalli—suggests that the contexts in which women could exercise authority were declining. The whole notion of parallel institutional structures for men and women likely suffered with the loss of the religious, political, and economic institutions and forms of organization that both supported and expressed this parallelism. Even when institutions survived, such as markets, the formal roles of women in positions of authority began to disappear. For example, control of the large markets in Mexico City passed from Mexica to Spanish hands after the 1530s as Spanish *alguaciles* (constables), always male, took over the duties of the tianquizpan tlaiacanque.[67]

Yet women's legal participation did attract comment from sixteenth-century Spanish jurists. One Spanish judicial official with extensive experience in central Mexico during the sixteenth century wrote,

> When some Indian has a dispute, though the Indian may be very important, able, and skilled, he will not appear before the court without bringing his wife with him, and they inform and speak that which by reason of the lawsuit it is necessary to say, and the husbands are very timid and quiet; and if the court asks something that it wishes to know, the husband responds: "here is my wife who knows it"; and in such manner it has happened to me upon asking one Indian or indeed many, "what is your name?" and before the husband responds, his wife says it; and thus in all other things; thus they are, men who have submitted to the will of the woman.[68]

Indigenous women's legal participation in property cases concerning native residents of Mexico City is striking during the sixteenth century.

The courts were a gendered arena in which women explicitly could play no role beyond that of litigant or witness. Nonetheless, women did play a significant role in litigation heard in colonial New Spain's legal system during the sixteenth century. I want to explore two issues in relation to Mexica women's legal participation during this period: what was the range of that participation, and how did their participation change over the course of the early colonial period?

During the sixteenth century, women and men initiated litigation at about equal rates; this holds true for defending in litigation as well.[69] As compared to men, however, women testified at far lower rates.[70] The range of transactions in which women participated was broad: they made wills, served as witnesses for wills (for both female and male testators, though female witnesses did so more often for female testators), bought, sold, and inherited property, and acted as legal guardians for children and grandchildren when fathers or parents were not available. There were gender differences in some legal transactions, however. First, Mexica women appeared much more often than men as guardians for minor children. Second, Mexica men had more ways to claim access to or transfer property. In addition to buying, selling, and inheriting property, which women also did, though at lower rates than men, men received property through dowry or grants, or they rented property, especially houses. Women did not participate in any of these latter kinds of transactions. A third gender difference is that women much more often claimed access to or rights over property as a result of inheriting it. Men claimed inheritance about as often as they claimed other means of transfer (including sale, dowry, or *mercedes*, "grants," usually of land) as the basis for their rights.[71] Women frequently made wills to attempt to control the disposition of their wordly goods, movable and immovable. During the sixteenth century, more Tenochca women's wills were submitted to bolster legal cases than were men's.[72]

One area where there appears to have been greater continuity than change in women's roles, especially for commoner women, was production and work. Mexica women's access to higher-status forms of production probably decreased as indigenous control over elite crafts declined over the course of the colonial period,[73] but women continued extrafamilial forms of production and employment throughout the colonial period. Early on, women in agricultural areas gave "specified amounts of cotton cloth" in tribute.[74] In urban areas, they continued to work in the marketplaces[75] and provided various types of personal service.[76] They also worked in crafts, textile production, and tobacco processing.[77] The censuses of both 1753 and 1811 showed that Indian women in Mexico City exhibited high labor force participation rates. Indian and *casta* (racially mixed) women were far more likely than Spanish women to be employed. Almost half of all Indian women, 46 percent, listed an occupation in 1811. Domestic service and food preparation were the common sources of employment, though Indian women worked in markets and at other kinds of work as well.[78]

At the same time that women were making a significant contribution to production and playing an important role in the lawsuits protecting Indian property holdings and placing limits on the ability of the Spanish state to exploit Indian properties, they were losing their political and religious positions of power and authority. They were also being subjected to a religious ideology that laid new and great stress on their honor and purity. Mexica goddesses, depicted by images rich in associations with fertility, power, and sexual symbolism,[79] had little in common with Catholic images of Mary and other saints.[80] Mary was repeatedly depicted as pure of body and soul and as a perpetual virgin.[81]

While the early priests encouraged celibacy and virginity for both young men and women, Mexica religious texts of the early colonial period suggest that virginity was being specifically associated with women and female deities.[82] This ideology helped to define a domestic domain to which women were to be limited in both a physical and a social sense. One text states that girls should follow the example of Mary: "Do not go about passing by people, do not go about from house to house. Do not linger in the marketplace, do not sit here and there among people, do not stand in the road, do not address men, do not smile at people."[83] In another text in which Sahagún contrasted Saint Clare with the activities and ways of life of Mexica noblewomen, he stressed how plain, simple, and virtuous Saint Clare was. The noblewomen, in contrast, are "continually going out, they follow the roads about, they pass out among the houses, they go around in front of people in the marketplace, thus do the women make people desire them. They wish to be seen. *But Saint Clare just enclosed herself.*"[84]

Of course, Mexica women could hardly enclose themselves completely because of the need on the part of both their families and the colonial economy for their labor; but an ideology of purity and enclosure *was* being preached to Mexica men and women which further undermined women's ability to hold formal positions of authority. This new and restrictive ideology was to have its greatest effect on Mexica society and culture after 1585 and particularly during the seventeenth century when new, specifically colonial, forms of Indian culture, society, and social practices emerged.

Indian Women in Mexico City in the Seventeenth Century

By the seventeenth century, the status of Mexica women had visibly declined. In the legal realm, Indian women were far less likely to initiate property litigation than in the sixteenth century. While women continued to serve as witnesses for wills or property sales, they no longer appeared as legal guardians of minor children in lawsuits. Wills made by women were rarely presented by men or women to bolster ownership claims as they had been in the sixteenth century. In the economic realm, the rates at which women bought, sold, or inherited property were much lower than in the sixteenth century. Thus women's independent access to property became more limited.

Two developments account for women's declining status. First, and most important, by the seventeenth century, the legal identity of women had become increasingly intertwined with that of their husbands. Seventeenth-century legal records reveal that husbands were generally the driving force behind lawsuits undertaken by their wives, even in cases where the property had been inherited by the wife. Of the eighteen cases dating from the seventeenth century, only two include litigants who were female without males playing the major roles. When males did speak for women in lawsuits, most often they were husbands, but brothers occasionally did, as did a nephew in one case.[85] An excellent example of the increased tendency for women to be treated as legal minors can be found in the Archivo

General de la Nación.[86] In this case, Diego Nunciales and his wife, Marta María, residents of the barrio of Santa Lucía in Santiago Tlatelolco, sued Francisco Pablo and his wife, Beatríz Francisca, residents of the barrio of Tezcatzongo in Santa María la Redonda. The suit was over a plot of land (*suerte*) measuring 100 by 20 *brazas* (1 braza = 1.67 meters) in the community of Santo Tomas Petlachiuhcan. Diego and Marta claimed that she had inherited the property from her father, Jusepe Ximénez, who they said had bought it in 1542. Francisco and Beatríz claimed that Beatríz had inherited this same land from her paternal grandmother, Juana Xoco, who had herself received it from don Diego de Mendoza, who was reported to have stolen it from Juana Xoco's father, Chimalteuhtzin. On each side, then, it was the woman who claimed ownership, although all documents from the case itself listed either the husband and wife with the husband's name first or only the husband's name. By the seventeenth century, men were increasingly serving as intermediaries between women and legal and political realms.

The second source of women's declining status lies in the ultimate disappearance by the seventeenth century of many of the Mexica social institutions in which women held formal power and authority as earlier noted. By the seventeenth century, the pre-Hispanic system of gender parallelism was breaking down. The religious, political, and economic organizations that had given tangible expression to gender complementarity and parallelism had been weakened and transformed, and an ideology emphasizing the patriarchal authority of husbands and fathers, tied to beliefs that stressed the need for women's sexual purity and honor, was expressed clearly and repeatedly by both religious and legal institutions.[87]

To state that indigenous women's status was declining is not, of course, to claim that Mexica women wholly lacked a voice in political, religious, or economic affairs. A few clues suggest that Mexica women continued to play some role in political organization. Women continued to serve as witnesses in property litigation and often in wills. Their participation may imply that women held some institutionalized position(s) through which they were called on as witnesses. Male witnesses in wills and legal cases were often low-level barrio officials; perhaps some of these women represent the female equivalent.

Indian women may also have been at the center of counterhegemonic activities expressing opposition to both male domination and
the domination of the colonial state. Native female ritual specialists
were treated by Spanish and casta women as having special medical
and ritual knowledge.[88] This special knowledge was used by women
of other ethnic groups for sexual witchcraft intended obliquely to
counter male domination.[89] Indigenous women also used these
practices within their own communities[90] and they continued to
serve as matchmakers in defiance of Church policy.[91] Ruth Behar
has argued that women's ritual practices were an expression of a limited power, one circumscribed by male domination and women's
consequent ability to exercise power only in the private domain.[92]
While the fall in women's status is clear, symbolized most sharply by
women's decline from jural adults to jural minors and by the restrictive ideology that drew sharp boundaries between male public, political, and economic activities and female private and domestic activities, they were able to draw on their domestic roles in overtly
political contexts.

Women were frequent participants in and even, on occasion,
leaders of colonial rebellions. William B. Taylor has written,

> Militiamen called in by the Spanish authorities were likely
> to encounter nasty mobs of hundreds of women brandish-
> ing spears and kitchen knives or cradling rocks in their
> skirts, and young children and old people carrying or
> throwing whatever they could manage, as well as better-
> armed groups of adult men. "The whole community" and
> "multitudes" of armed villagers of all ages are descriptions
> constantly repeated in the reports and testimony. The place
> of women is especially striking. Perhaps because men were
> more often traveling outside the community or working
> fields several miles from town, more women than men usu-
> ally took part. In at least one-fourth of the cases, women led
> the attacks and were visibly aggressive, insulting, and re-
> bellious in their behavior toward outside authorities.[93]

Similar events took place in Mexico City as well. Accounts of the
Mexico City uprising of 1692 speak of Indian women starting this ac-

tion. Letters describing the unfolding of the uprising suggest that Indians plotted to simulate the trampling and death of an elderly woman to foment further rebellion. These accounts also suggest that one of the sites attacked early in the second day of the uprising was the viceroy's wife's balcony at the royal palace.[94] Indigenous women in the colonial period, including those of Mexico City, thus had a long history of confronting both men and the colonial state.

Conclusion

I have traced the changing social and legal statuses of Mexica women from the late pre-Hispanic period through the beginning of the eighteenth century. While it is clear that their status declined, especially in the legal realm, this decline was complex, partly because Mexica women of different classes did not have identical experiences during any of the periods described here and partly because gender was itself influenced by other realms of colonial life. Especially important were emerging concepts of race and religion, along with changing power relations between Indians and other groups in colonial society.

While gender parallelism structured many aspects of pre-Hispanic Mexica life, such parallelism could never be complete because of the multiple, complex, even contradictory meanings attached to gender as a scheme for social organization. Mexica conceptions of gender provided a construct that shaped men's, women's, and children's daily lives and acted as a symbol of both equivalence and hierarchy. While the Inca transformed the parallel gender structures of non-Inca Andean peoples, the Mexica embraced all the contradictions inherent in ideas of parallelism *and* hierarchy and separation *and* merging that gender as a set of structures, practices, and symbols provided. The imposition of colonial rule had a powerful influence on women's experiences and gender as an organizing principle among the Mexica.[95] Many of the complex Mexica concepts of gender did not survive this transition, and women's activities and lives became more circumscribed and controlled. Yet they still held enough power and authority to play significant roles in Indian protests and uprisings against colonial rule throughout central Mexico. Gender parallelism and hierarchy embodied elements of both complementarity and differentiation. What changed in central Mexico between the late pre-Hispanic period and the beginning of the eighteenth century was the balance between these elements and the contexts in which women, especially nonelite women, could operate.

6

Activist or Adulteress?

The Life and Struggle
of Doña Josefa María of Tepoztlan

Robert Haskett

On July 23, 1712, the *receptor*[1] don Francisco Capellón y Espinosa and six constables made their way to an aging two-story house crammed behind an *obraje* (textile workshop) in the Monserrate district of Mexico City. The viceroy had instructed them to find and arrest a Nahua woman named Josefa María and an indigenous man named Miguel Francisco, both from Tepoztlan in the Cuernavaca region, who were accused of living together "in unchaste friendship." What little light was left in the summer sky was too weak to penetrate the narrow street as the Spaniards drew near their destination at about 9:00 P.M. Having picked out the appropriate doorway in the twilight, the officers unceremoniously burst into the house, where they discovered the naked Josefa and Miguel sleeping together on a rude bed under a single white blanket. The pair leaped up in alarm but were quickly apprehended and forced to dress themselves. When questioned by an interpreter who had accompanied the arresting party, Josefa admitted that the man, whom she called Miguel de Santiago, was not her husband but added that they slept together because there was just one blanket in the house. Continuing to speak for both, she claimed they were in Mexico City because of some litigation connected with the internal affairs of Tepoztlan. But an upstairs neighbor named Matias Francisco, who had been attracted by the noise, eagerly told the receptor that the two were indeed "living in sin" and had been jailed in the past for this crime by the *alcalde mayor* (chief magistrate) of Cuernavaca. Having heard and seen enough, Capellón marched Josefa and Miguel off to jail.[2]

It seemed to be just another sordid case of human fallibility, and this was certainly the line followed by the colonial bureaucracy. But there was really quite a bit more involved here than adultery. What the Spaniards were reluctant to admit was that Josefa, whose real name was doña Josefa María Francisca, a widowed *cacica* (ruling-class noblewoman) of Tepoztlan, located in what is now the state of Morelos, was an aggressive political activist. Along with don Miguel Francisco, a former *alcalde* (town officer), she was one of the leaders of a faction among Tepoztlan's ruling elite bent on the achievement of two goals: ending the town's obligation to send tribute workers to the mines of Taxco and removing a tyrannical governor named don Nicolás Cortés and his cohorts from municipal office. It was don Nicolás, in an effort to discredit his enemies, who had brought doña Josefa's alleged affair to the attention of the authorities in the first place. Those officials, who seemed reluctant to admit that an indigenous woman could wield any political influence, were quite willing to concentrate on the "corrupting allures" of her sex.

Modern scholars have hardly explored in any detail the possibility that Nahua women of colonial Mexico could have an overt political role, or, in other words, have some direct influence in the operation of indigenous town government. Only a few tantalizingly brief remarks about politically active native women have appeared in print. In the colonial presence of Nahua women as witnesses for testaments or as litigants, Susan Kellogg hears echoes of a precontact ideology of "gender parallelism" that allowed women—especially elite and near-elite women—to carry out overtly political functions. Both Alvis Dunn and Irene Silverblatt have suggested that during the colonial era native women could carry out overt political acts during relatively brief periods of stress. Steve J. Stern has found that indigenous women of late colonial central Mexico—including women of Tepoztlan—participated in the "public political space," most visibly in "ad hoc politics associated with emergencies" such as localized rioting.[3]

Even so, the theme of colonial political activism, and more specifically, sustained, long-term political activism, among indigenous women remains to be elaborated. As in the case of colonial Hispanic women, other aspects of indigenous women's lives have received far more scholarly attention. As a concentration on the activities of "great women" such as Sor Juana Inés de la Cruz, La Malinche, and Isabel Moteucçoma has expanded to embrace the careful analysis of the lives of "ordinary" women of various social stations and ethnicities, we are discovering that their stories do not always conform to the "archetype" of the submissive, powerless being of social legend. Non-Hispanic women, especially those of the lower classes, could be found in a variety of occupations and as heads of households. Coupled with an ability to own and manage businesses and landholdings, their tendency to appear in court as litigants has gained a certain notoriety, above all when inheritance or property was at stake.[4] Recent studies tend to agree, however, that sooner or later the prominence of women in litigation and as property owners faded, leaving them more subordinate to men than ever before.[5]

Doña Josefa, though illiterate and unable to speak Spanish, did have real, long-term political power in eighteenth-century Tepoztlan. She was a respected ally and a feared opponent. It is true that hers is only one well-documented story, but there is every indication that she was not alone, for it is clear that other indigenous women of the Cuernavaca region engaged in distinctly political activities. In a colonial society that stereotypically considered women inferior to men and therefore barred them from public life, how had doña Josefa and these other women achieved their influence? Were indigenous males less uncomfortable with political activism by indigenous women than their Spanish contemporaries? Were there traditions in either Iberian or indigenous culture—such as an ideology of gender parallelism similar to that identified by Kellogg—that allowed women to exercise some sort of political role?

Women's Hidden Political Role

Like their contemporaries elsewhere in New Spain, Cuernavaca's Nahua women acted as market vendors, manufactured and sold pulque, textiles, and other goods, and owned property in their own right. Female members of the elite, such as a seventeenth-century unmarried cacica of Yecapixtla named doña Inés Cortés, sometimes held large agricultural or livestock estates.[6] The jurisdiction's indigenous women went to court to protect their properties, no matter how humble or extensive; in 1694 the Cuernavacan cacica doña Felipa de Haro Bravo and two of her daughters successfully defended her dowry, bride gift, and other property from confiscation when her husband, the governor don Antonio de Hinojosa, was convicted of tribute fraud.[7]

Indeed, women were held accountable for their husbands' crimes and debts. It was not uncommon for local indigenous or Spanish authorities to jail the wife of an absent miscreant or tribute debtor. For instance, a 1607 roster of criminals in the Cuernavaca jail speaks of "Francisca Tiacapan of Quechollapa, whose spouse took some white pulque from Miguel Quauhtli, also of Quechollapa," and of the doubly unfortunate Angelina Coxcahua of Tetecala, whose spouse, "a fiscal [lay assistant to the priest], did not come back [from the mines of Taxco]."[8] Vigorously facing life's misfortunes, the region's indigenous women had petitions written on their behalf to complain of the unjust arrest or mistreatment of their husbands by others, or of their own abuse, and sometimes rape, at the hands of indigenous men, Spanish civilians, civil officers, and even friars and priests.[9] And when crises loomed, the region's indigenous women typically were prominent participants in tumultos, or localized uprisings designed to protect the town, its people, or its landholdings from some external threat.

All of this could be interpreted as conforming to the overwhelmingly "domestic" picture of native women. As litigants and even as rioters they can be seen as engaging in the defense of home, hearth, and their own and their families' integrity. But the objectives of rioting were often as much political in nature as otherwise, and there may have been more to some of these other activities than meets the eye. Though its complete veracity might be questioned, the text of a local history, written in Nahuatl, from Cuernavaca mentions that along with male elites, illamatque, or elder women, witnessed land boundary verifications. When more traditional kinds of sources are scrutinized, this document's implication that a tradition of feminine political influence existed in the area is bolstered by evidence that wives and other relatives of indigenous *gobernadores* (leaders of town councils) acted as the political allies of male members of the ruling elite. In 1568, doña María Cortés, widow of Cuernavaca's conquest era *tlatoani* (ruler), don Hernando Cortés, joined forces with the town's council to force a Cortés family-owned sugar estate to pay wages to tribute laborers. Wives and sisters of a seventeenth-century governor of Xiuhtepec acted with members of the male ruling group to obtain recognition of corporate landownership, and the widow of an alcalde of Achichipico was prominent among those calling for the removal of a corrupt governor. In the adjacent Toluca Valley, the widow of a governor made an ultimately unsuccessful attempt to be allowed to complete her husband's term of office.[10]

Finally, it emerges that some petitions and some court cases involving women from a broader social spectrum had political undertones. The early 1630s were a time of internal turmoil for Cuernavaca, as the council and other prominent indigenous citizens fought the Taxco mine *repartimiento* (tribute labor obligation) and other forms of involuntary servitude, attempted to have an objectionable friar removed from the Franciscan monastery, and splintered into factions over the thorny question of legitimacy and succession in the governorship. All three struggles were interrelated (e.g., the friar was meddling in the election at the same time he was conniving with civil authorities to deliver repartimiento workers at any cost), and all three affected and brought direct action from a group of Cuernavaca's women.

In two revealing Nahuatl petitions received by the chief administrator of the semiautonomous Cortés estate, the Marquesado del Valle, a local notary recorded the complaints of a group of eleven women.[11] They asserted that an unnamed friar (in other documents we find he was the Franciscan fray Nicolás de Origuen) was mistreating them and their husbands. A grasping taskmaster, he forced young girls and boys to carry sand and stone for some repairs to the monastery. The ill-tempered religious beat three sick people, a man and two women, when they had the misfortune to come to him for some paternal comfort. The friar was not only violent, he was perverse as well. The women begged, "Do not let the maidens be instructed at the church anymore, because nothing good comes from it, for he [the friar] fornicates with them." The sly cleric also connived with local Spaniards to gain from the absence of husbands forced to travel to the mines of Taxco. When the men were gone, the friar "deposited" their spouses in the homes of various Spaniards and the local alcalde mayor, where "all of us spun every day and all through the night. . . . At times on Sunday and feast days all of us spin . . . [and] he doesn't feed us." The women also objected to the heavy-handed activities of a church *topile* (officer) and of a fiscal, whom they claimed was an ineligible Spaniard; they requested that since "there are nobles [*pipiltin*], let one of them become fiscal." Times were tense, too, because mulatto, mestizo, and black thieves "break the doors, they destroy them; they carry away all the turkeys, the chickens, the maize, chili, squash seeds, and cotton mantles." Concluding that all this upheaval was driving people away and endangering the steady delivery of tribute, the women requested that the friar and his topile be removed.

It might be said that in speaking of their personal misfortunes, these women were merely trying to protect themselves and their families from the disruptive effects of the Taxco repartimiento, the abusive friar, and the local crime problem. But there is a distinctly political dimension to their actions as well. By stressing the disruptive nature of the corrupt friar's machinations, these women hoped to have him ejected from the *villa*'s (a Spanish urban designation) monastery and from their lives. By relating the consequences of their husbands' absence because of the repartimiento, they sought to bring that burdensome obligation to an end. These goals were shared by a faction within the cabildo for which the friar was a sworn and meddlesome enemy. In fact, these two petitions, as well as later testimony taken from some of the same women, were presented as evidence in the larger court case undertaken by the cabildo members. The female litigants were active allies of the male officers; each group was pursuing the same design in a contest in which the personal and the political were inseparably joined.

Doña Josefa's Political Career

Doña Josefa María Francisca of Tepoztlan is an almost larger-than-life example of a politically active indigenous woman. According to a male witness, doña Josefa had spent her whole life in litigation, that it was in fact her only *oficio* (occupation).[12] Her first real appearance in the surviving record, however, came in 1705 during a protracted suit centered around the hated Taxco mine repartimiento and the wrongdoing of the Tepoztecan governor, don Nicolás Cortés. This was undoubtedly not the first time that the thirty-eight-year-old doña Josefa had been active in the political life of the town, since a former *regidor* (city councilman) stated that she "ase los tlatoles y capitanea para el pleito" (makes the speeches and leads in pursuing the litigation). In other words, she was already being recognized by friend and foe alike as an important leader of one of Tepoztlan's major political factions, accused even of personally heading an effort to collect illegal fees from the people to finance the litigation.[13]

Doña Josefa and several members of the local officer group were unsuccessful in 1705, primarily because their opponents were numerous and had the sympathy of local Spanish officials. But her faction spent twenty more years trying to end Tepoztlan's obligation to send tribute workers to Taxco and to shatter the rule of those who supported the levy, including don Nicolás Cortés and the powerful governing-class Rojas family. The Taxco levy was generally hated because it not only took men away from their homes and families for weeks at a time but was dangerous as well. Aside from the rigors of travel over bad roads, repartimiento workers were usually employed carrying heavy bags of ore out of the shafts or in stirring mercury-laced mud as part of the refining process. Injuries and mercury poisoning killed many and left others debilitated for life.

So it was in 1711 and 1712 that doña Josefa was again prominent among those continuing the fight against don Nicolás Cortés, a "loyal ally" of Spanish interests whose repeated and illegal reelection to the governorship was routinely approved by the colonial bureaucracy. Doña Josefa was by now firmly ensconced in Mexico City, having fled there sometime earlier after escaping from Cuernavaca's jail where she had been held for tribute indebtedness and adultery.[14] It was in 1712, of course, that don Nicolás successfully used the "fact" that doña Josefa and the married don Miguel Francisco were illicit lovers to have the pair arrested. Both they and several other cohorts who were apprehended at about the same time steadfastly maintained their innocence, stressing the legality of their struggle to end the iniquitous situation facing their town (and not coincidentally keeping their faction from controlling the council apparatus). For a time it seemed that doña Josefa would be "deposited" (jailed) in a *recogimiento,* or house of correction for women, and in fact this was a common fate of accused adulteresses.[15] But at the end of six months, doña Josefa and don Miguel were sentenced to time already served and released with an admonishment to live peacefully and chastely in the future.

But doña Josefa did not live "peacefully," and if her detractors are to be believed, she did not abide in chastity either. In 1713, this self-styled "poor widow" brought suit against the Spanish receptor Capellón, accusing him of stealing 130 pesos from her Mexico City lodgings at the time of her arrest and of later confiscating three yokes of oxen and a mule to cover legal costs. Capellón was eventually ordered to return the money and livestock, but no record exists that this was actually done. She was not long out of the public eye; in 1720 and again in 1724, doña Josefa was one of the leaders of a faction fighting the reelection of don Nicolás de Rojas, political heir of don Nicolás Cortés (who had been murdered some years before), and, inevitably, against the continuation of the Taxco mine repartimiento.[16]

Tensions surrounding the repartimiento and the rule of don Nicolás de Rojas came to a head in the summer of 1725 when he jailed a levy of workers scheduled to go to Taxco.[17] He had been facing renewed resistance to the repartimiento since May, at which time doña Josefa and don Miguel Francisco were once more the ringleaders of the opposition. Charged with inciting the commoners to evade their tribute obligations, don Miguel and five other male *cabecillas* (leaders) of the antirepartimiento faction, but not doña Josefa, had been arrested. But when a local Spanish *teniente* (lieutenant to the alcalde mayor) tried to escort the group from Tepoztlan to the jail at Cuernavaca, his party was attacked by a large number of indigenous women and children who, pelting the Spaniards with rocks and curses, were able to free two of the prisoners.

So, on August 15, the governor don Nicolás thought he was justified in jailing a group of repartimiento workers on the eve of their departure for Taxco. This was too much for the beleaguered townspeople, who that night rose in a *tumulto,* attacked Tepoztlan's jail, and freed the workers (along with a small number of petty criminals and tribute debtors). Witnesses claimed that the majority of the rioters had been women, among them the spouses of the prisoners and some of the prominent opposition leaders. Rock-toting women were said to have been the most prominent besiegers of their own town officers and the local Spaniards in Tepoztlan's monastery and were among those who heaped verbal abuse on a friar who attempted to quell the rioters with peaceful words.[18]

The rioters faded away by the end of the second day, their goals apparently reached, and in the aftermath local Marquesado officers typically arrested a few men but no women. The August tumulto seemed to have been the kind of spontaneous outbreak of violence remarked elsewhere by William B. Taylor.[19] But in early September, and again later in the month, when don Nicolás de Rojas and Spanish officials twice more tried to force tributaries to go to Taxco, there was renewed rioting, again with women most in evidence. There are very strong indications that in these two outbreaks the violence was being orchestrated by a small number of people, and it is not surprising to find that doña Josefa and don Miguel Francisco were the alleged conductors. Among those arrested in the aftermath was Angelina María, the supposedly wronged wife of don Miguel Francisco. She was identified as the leader of the female rioters, at one point directing a group of one hundred women who broke into the sacristy of the monastery and stole some holy ornaments and vestments.[20] The goods, it was said, were taken to Mexico City to doña Josefa's residence in the Monserrate district, to be sold to pay for more litigation.

Showing surprising loyalty for a woman whose husband had been carrying on a notorious affair for over thirty years, Angelina denied don Miguel's or her own guilt. Yet she was the only woman to be punished for her role, initially being sentenced to a year of obraje labor followed by six months of work at an *hospital de indios* ("Indian" hospital), a sentence that was commuted in 1726 by the Audiencia to the year of imprisonment she had already endured. The sentences of the arrested men, who were threatened with a year of labor in an *hacienda de minas* (refinery) in Taxco, were similarly commuted at the same time. Doña Josefa, who seems to have coordinated events in Tepoztlan from her self-imposed exile in the Valley of Mexico, could not be located. Her supporters claimed that she was ill in a place called San Juan de Dios and had nothing to do with the tumultos. The whole truth was never discovered, nor was doña Josefa

ever again named as an active political figure in Tepoztlan. Perhaps
doña Josefa, who in 1725 would have been around sixty-three years
old, died of a biological enemy that no amount of litigation could
defeat.

Activist or Adulteress?

Spanish officials charged with the enforcement of the Taxco repartimiento and the collection of tribute, who viewed cooperative intermediaries such as the governors don Nicolás Cortés and don Nicolás
de Rojas in a favorable light, were very hostile to those who went
against their aims, especially if they were uncooperative Nahuas.
Heirs to almost two hundred years of experience dealing with political disputes involving indigenous men, colonial administrators and
judges of the early eighteenth century generally categorized indigenous male adversaries as corrupt and irreligious troublemakers, un-
reliable drunkards, or persons who were too inept to hold office on an
indigenous town council. When deciding guilt or innocence, though,
the Spanish emphasis was less on moral or social shortcomings than
on pragmatic concerns, such as the extent to which some financial
malfeasance connected with tribute collection had occurred. The
punishment meted out to alleged wrongdoers, if any, was further
mitigated by the connections of the accused among influential
Spaniards and, secondarily, prominent indigenous elites.

Colonial officials were less sure in their reactions when faced
with the obvious involvement of indigenous women in cabildo affairs. They were not unaware that indigenous women had a good deal
of influence in community matters, and officials and travelers sometimes remarked on the outspokenness of native women, even when
their husbands were present.[21] It is true that Spain had a powerful
female monarch in Isabel of Castile and that women of the high aristocracy had at one time been able to inherit lordships of towns. Local
female property owners had attended town assemblies. But except
for the queen, by the eve of the invasion of the Americas whatever
political power women nobles wielded was largely ceremonial in nature, and town assemblies had long since been dominated by men.[22]
By the early 1700s, the feminine exercise of overt political power
went against the cultural values of the colonial authorities, espe-

cially if it was being exercised by a mere Nahua and in opposition to Spanish interests.

Because she was acting with men, doña Josefa was tarred with the same brush that was routinely used to discredit political miscreants. Like her male counterparts, she found that in a subtle effort to discredit the faction, Spanish notaries routinely robbed all of its members of their marks of social distinction by omitting the titles "don" and "doña" from their names. Typically, the whole faction, doña Josefa included, were in 1712 defamed by the alcalde mayor, don Tomás Pérez de la Penilla, as "in the majority seditious and riotous agitators." Spanish officials and clerics emphasized that all of the faction's members failed to pay their tribute and to attend church, and in 1712 had tried to convince the people to stop repair work on Tepoztlan's monastery church, damaged in an earthquake in August 1711.[23] A later Spanish officer excoriated don Miguel Francisco and doña Josefa for being "professional rebels" and for causing the ruin of Tepoztlan.[24]

The faction's indigenous enemies responded in a similar manner, adding details that touched more directly on the internal affairs of Tepoztlan, its government, and its people. In the great dispute of 1725, adherents of the governor don Nicolás de Rojas accused the faction of circulating an inflammatory Nahuatl document that urged Tepoztlan's indigenous citizens to resist the Taxco repartimiento and even charged them with the murder of the governor don Nicolás Cortés![25] The illegitimacy of the faction's leaders was stressed not only by omitting their noble titles from written records but also by labeling some of them as vagabonds and "outside agitators" who held no municipal office and by calling them "a bunch of troublemaking commoners." These were serious personal faults in an era when the legitimacy of one's noble lineage, spurious as it might actually have been, was becoming an ever more important criterion for admission to the active ruling groups of towns such as Tepoztlan.

When doña Josefa was treated as an individual, however, the nature of the crimes attributed to her was different from those ascribed to her male colleagues. Spanish and allied indigenous officers alike spoke of her tenacity and aggressiveness and emphasized her sexual deviance. Above all, they highlighted her alleged adulterous affair with don Miguel Francisco, which by 1725 was said to have gone on for at least thirty years, beginning while her husband, Gregorio Francisco, had still been alive. Far from placing most of the blame on don Miguel Francisco, witnesses asserted that the aggressive doña Josefa had corrupted him. Judges were treated to descriptions of the pair being discovered at five in the morning drunkenly cavorting in a carnal embrace. Nahua witnesses alleged that the pair failed to attend church because of their "evil friendship" and that they had begun their endless litigation in the first place only to save themselves from punishment for their sexual misdeeds. Doña Josefa was called a "depraved" woman acting only to further her lover's career. She was "the worst of the accused," the "most seditious of those who insist on unrest." She led wives to "work against their husbands" and was even an unfit mother. According to her own son, who was not a member of his mother's faction, she had threatened to put him in an obraje if he refused to go along with the effort to bring an end to the Taxco repartimiento. At the close of the 1712 adultery case, a Spanish fiscal attached to the Audiencia summed it all up when he said that doña Josefa was "a discredit to her sex."[26]

In Spanish society from at least the twelfth century, one of the main ways a woman was discredited was to call her sexual conduct into question, and charges that an erring woman was an adulterer were common; much later, Spanish lay and religious authorities continued to regard sexual deviance as "dangerous to the social order."[27] In colonial New Spain, punishments for female adulterers are reported to have been harsher than those for men.[28] This double standard was clearly in operation in doña Josefa's case. Not only was don Miguel Francisco excused from much of the blame because doña Josefa had supposedly led him on, her longtime adversary don Nicolás de Rojas escaped any censure or punishment despite the fact that he was repeatedly accused of publicly keeping a mistress in Tepoztlan, a plebeian woman who made and sold the alcoholic beverage called *tepache* in her home.[29] This was a far cry from the direct action taken when an indigenous woman who had become too active in politics was arrested and tried for a similar offense.

Even without her reputed sexual promiscuity, doña Josefa's forceful involvement in her community's political affairs and her alleged failures as a mother were enough to win her censure. Other women who left the "normal" bounds of feminine behavior but who were not accused of sexual crimes, such as Angelina María and those involved in the riots of the summer and fall of 1725, were treated to similar forms of character assassination. Witnesses emphasized their aggressiveness, their violent use of rocks, and their tendency to employ shockingly foul language to intimidate. For instance, a Spanish *maestre de escuela* (schoolteacher) claimed that during the course of the rioting a group of indigenous women came to his home and taunted his wife with foul and abusive language. A Spanish resident named doña Francisca de la Bera y Zapata reported that native women, speaking in loud voices, cried that they were going to burn down the schoolteacher's house as well as the houses of all the other *gente de razón* (Spaniards) in Tepoztlan. The "violent tempered" wife of one of the men being sent to Taxco was said to have attacked and to have torn out a hank of hair from the head of an indigenous *alguacil* (constable) who had been sent to get him.[30]

All of these women violated Spanish gender ideology about the proper comportment of women. At least on a utopian plane, it was totally unacceptable for women, above all noblewomen, to be unchaste, aggressive, violent, stubborn, and overly proud. It is true that women could be active in a relatively wide variety of commercial and even managerial activities and that widows generally had more freedom of action than married women. But their distinct status in relation to men of the same social class was never forgotten. Enshrined in a series of manuals and instruction books written mainly by ecclesiastics, noblewomen, especially, were to be virginal, pious, shy, and obsequious. They were to be skilled administrators of the household and conspicuous in the accomplishment of charitable work.[31] The extent to which Spanish women of any class conformed to these ideals is being questioned, but when confronted with the actions of someone like doña Josefa these notions were certainly in the minds of colonial officials and others inculcated with such values.

Among the latter, presumably, were members of Tepoztlan's indigenous ruling group. But they reacted against the activism of some of Tepoztlan's women from more than just a Hispanic perspective. It is quite possible that older, precontact Nahua traditions still made themselves felt, especially elements that were not dissimilar to the social teachings of the conquerors. Recent insights into what is being seen as gender parallelism among the Nahua (including those offered by several contributors to this volume) notwithstanding, and though one must be somewhat skeptical of the possibly Spanish Catholic-influenced information provided to the sixteenth-century ethnographer fray Bernardino de Sahagún by his elite male informants, it is clear that the precontact Nahua had an elaborate gender ideology that included specific ideal traits for both women and men of various types and social levels. The *Florentine Codex* preserves very detailed expectations for women, including noblewomen. "Good" noblewomen were not surprisingly those who were dignified, honorable, and modest. A good noblewoman was a protective person, "one who loves, who guards people," a tender person who was "humble, appreciative, . . . irreproachable, faultless."[32]

Clearly, as far as her colonial indigenous enemies were concerned, doña Josefa was none of these things. Many of the *Florentine Codex*'s descriptions of the "bad noblewoman" read surprisingly like the later anti-doña Josefa rhetoric emanating from members of Tepoztlan's ruling group. To them, this aggressive, troublemaking adulteress who led men into ruin and caused revolt among the people would have more easily fit the conquest era images of the "bad noblewoman" who was "violent, furious, savage, revolting, . . . irresponsible, irritable, excitable." She "incites riots, she arouses fear, implants fear, spreads fear, . . . she impels fight, causes havoc among people." Just like doña Josefa, a bad noblewoman "introduces one into error," she is "a spreader of hatred, . . . arrogant, unchaste, lewd, debauched, . . . a perverted woman."[33] And like the more generalized "evil woman" of the *Florentine Codex*, doña Josefa would have been seen as a "carnal woman . . . who finds pleasure in her body. . . . Wheresoever she seduces . . . she brings him to ruin. The scandalous woman is an adulteress."[34]

The fact remains that in spite of such traditions, regardless of all the crimes and moral vices attributed to doña Josefa, some members of the indigenous ruling group were not opposed to her political activities. She was, after all, accepted as an ally and leader by a faction composed primarily of male members of the town's indigenous elite. She did not owe her influence to her extramarital affair with don Miguel Francisco but rather to her own ability. A male ally spoke of her in admiring terms in 1712, stating that the cacica "through her solicitude and hard work has induced the people to gather together the money necessary to pay for the divine cult of the church and for the costs of litigation."[35] Why were these indigenous attitudes different from those of the Spaniards and their indigenous allies in Tepoztlan, who honored the gender ideology of the conquerors, at least in the breach?

Perhaps the key lies ultimately in the different traditions of Nahua and Spaniard. An increasing volume of work looking beyond the narrow confines of the conquest era is showing that indigenous ways were not completely obliterated by the vicissitudes of colonialism and that many persisted, if in a modified form, for a very long time. If the *Florentine Codex* is to be trusted, pre-Hispanic Nahua culture may not have been entirely closed to the political activities of elite women. It is true that when the training of elite women is described, only domestic skills such as weaving and preparing food are emphasized.[36] This same sort of "domestic" orientation is quite evident in chronicles such as those written by the Texcoco mestizo noble Juan Bautista Pomar and in composite histories composed by such Spaniards as José de Acosta, fray Toribio de Benavente (Motolinia), and Francisco Javier Clavijero. The so-called Bancroft Dialogues, a *huehuetlatolli,* or Nahuatl-language socialization manual containing a good deal of information about social conventions of apparent preconquest origin, refers to husbands as the "heads and trunks" of wives and lists the kinds of things all women, including noblewomen, were expected to learn: "The girls were taught all the different things women do: sweeping, sprinkling, preparing food, making beverages, grinding [maize], preparing tortillas, making tamales, all the different things customarily done among women; also [the art of] the spindle and the weaver's reed and various kinds of embroidery; also dyeing, how rabbit down or rabbit fur was dyed different colors."[37]

Using this kind of source, some modern researchers have concluded that though elite women could have a ceremonial role in religion, they were completely excluded from public office and other political activities and had rights inferior to those of noblemen.[38] Miguel León-Portilla believes that although there is some evidence that women could act as professional notaries, their "supreme mission" was to bring men into the world.[39]

But other scholars of the precontact era are asserting that elite women had more centrality in the political scheme of the central Mexican state.[40] Susan D. Gillespie, while not identifying any truly independent governing capacity for Mexica noblewomen, clearly establishes their crucial role in dynastic succession and political legitimacy. Silvia Garza Tarazona de González believes that the portrayal of Coyolxauhqui at the head of the "400 rabbits" is symbolic of a leadership role for women, and she reminds us that one of the four leaders of the wandering Mexica was a woman named Chimalma. She also cites *Relaciones geográficas* from Justlahuaca, Mistepeque, Ayusuchiquilazala, Xicayan and Putla, Zacatepeque, Oaxaca, Chiapas, Veracruz, the central plateau of Mexico, and the Huasteca as indicating that women assumed the role of governors or leaders and states that these sources show that the practice may have been more widespread. Finally, she refers to a recently discovered relief in Mexico City showing a female ruler of Culhuacan, garbed for war, being vanquished by Tezcatlipoca, perhaps standing for the conquest of Culhuacan by the Mexica under Moteucçoma Ilhuicamina.[41] Pedro Carrasco mentions two "queens," including Atotoztli, daughter of Moteucçoma Ilhuicamina, who briefly succeeded her father, and records a line from a *probanza* (petition) of doña Isabel Moteucçoma, daughter of the second Moteucçoma, which stated that "if there were no males who were close relations and most worthy, females could succeed to the rulership."[42] Susan Kellogg believes that Mexica women may have had some kind of judicial role, such as that of "marketplace directors," enjoyed a measure of authority in craft guilds, in the *cuicalli*, or house of song, as priestesses in temples, and as *cihuatepixque*, or female ward heads, and may have had a measure of power at even higher political levels. Kellogg believes, as well, that the Nahua tendency to describe rulers as the "fathers and mothers" of the people meant that "both the male and female aspects of parenting were deemed necessary for adequate leadership." In the Cuernavaca region, including Tepoztlan, the description of male town leaders as "fathers and mothers" continued well into the colonial era.[43]

Direct evidence of this propensity to link political authority (in real and symbolic terms) to both genders can be found in some of the standard postconquest native-language accounts. The Bancroft Dialogues, in a section containing conventions of discourse surrounding the marriage of a ruler, contains language that implies some kind of political role for rulers' spouses. Speaking of the awaited arrival of a newly wed female consort, the text has the ruler say, "Let me quickly hear word from them how a party will come to bring the lady our sister to come to govern her city and occupy [her? its?] throne, where it will come to fruition that she will console me, and her [little] brothers-in-law and sisters [sisters-in-law] and her vassals will be looking up to her."[44]

Moreover, there are some suggestive phrases in the *Florentine Codex*'s description of "good" noblewomen that allude to some kind of acceptable leadership or political role. Apparently unaware that they seemed to be contradicting themselves, the elite male informants told the friar that as well as being modest, chaste, and humble, it was acceptable for "good" noblewomen to be "vigorous, . . . fierce, stern." Aside from their role as exemplars, "good" elite women were characterized as "valiant, having valor, bravery, courage." Even more to the point, and using many of the same terms applied to male rulers, a worthy elite woman "governs, leads, provides for one, arranges well, administers peacefully. . . . The noblewoman [is] a woman ruler [*cioatlatoani*], governor, leader. . . . The good woman ruler [is] a provider of good conditions, a corrector, a punisher, a chastiser, a reprimander. She is heeded, obeyed; she creates order; she establishes rules."[45]

Had doña Josefa's enemies been familiar with the *Codex*, they would have argued that she may have tried to govern, but she did not "provide good conditions" or "create order." Yet here is a rationale, however submerged in a much larger array of "traditional" feminine roles and attributes, for some sort of precontact female political power.

Conclusion

Doña Josefa, other women active in the resistance to the Taxco repartimiento and in seventeenth-century Cuernavacan efforts to rid themselves of a troublesome priest, and indigenous wives who spoke forthrightly in public, even in the presence of husbands, may well have been heirs to similar traditions. Yet in the precontact era, there seem to have been many strictures facing politically active women.

Postconquest indigenous women of New Spain, such as doña Josefa, were caught in a double bind in their relation to the colonial state. They were considered fundamentally subordinate by Spaniards because they were not only "Indians" but female as well. No matter that doña Josefa was a cacica, it was simply not acceptable for her to become involved directly in governmental affairs in opposition to her overlord's interests. Rather than legitimize her political role by prosecuting her in the same way as politically active indigenous males, they chose to attack her honor and femininity by emphasizing her supposed failures as a woman.

A more ambivalent attitude was present among Tepoztlan's indigenous ruling group. Some of the Tepoztecan elite, adherents of what may have been an alternative gender ideology that held open the possibility for elite women's political participation, welcomed the able leadership of the astute doña Josefa. But others, by now heavily influenced by Spanish ideals of femininity, saw in doña Josefa's alleged leadership in the tumultos, her supposed violent and forceful nature, and her purported sexual promiscuity an unacceptable challenge to the colonial status quo. They were unwilling to admit that an indigenous noblewoman could have a legitimate political role, especially if such a denial would further their own partisan goals. So they labeled her a common, aggressive, morally corrupt woman, an unfit mother, and one who worked to set wife against husband and so destroy the very fiber of family life. Even the conquest era informants of Sahagún, as well as the recorders of huehuetlatolli, who already may have been feeling the weight of Spanish social teachings and gender ideology, had nearly obscured in a plethora of "domestic" rhetoric the possibility that a Nahua noblewoman could enjoy some sort of political influence.

Still, in Tepoztlan, in Cuernavaca, and elsewhere, there was a possibility for indigenous women to participate in the political life of their communities, a product of precontact tradition and the pressured atmosphere of the colonial era. Under Spanish rule, communities such as Tepoztlan were faced with mounting threats to their physical survival when a distant government could decree that a significant percentage of the local male population had to be absent every week from their families and fields to participate in the repartimiento and when corrupt indigenous officers who nonetheless abetted Spanish interests were maintained in power through the influence of local Spanish officials and clergy. Firmly rooted in older traditions, the ability of doña Josefa and other similar women to rise to political action seems to have occurred in a partial vacuum of male legitimacy, when traditional heads of household were missing and when elites who had "sold out" to the Spanish held official sway.[46]

The extent to which doña Josefa's larger-than-life leadership role was an aberration remains to be tested by studies of other times and places. One thing is very clear. Doña Josefa may have been an adulteress, but she was above all else an activist struggling against the twin burdens of restrictive gender and racial ideologies to be heard.

7

Matters of Life at Death

Nahuatl Testaments of Rural Women, 1589–1801

Stephanie Wood

Feeling an unavoidable summons to the heavens, Ignacia Cristina of Calimaya called the bilingual church assistant to her deathbed to record her final will and testament in her native language, Nahuatl. Ignacia Cristina, one of many victims of a plague sweeping the Toluca Valley in the late 1750s and early 1760s, claimed to have no worldly possessions. She promised an eighth of a peso "for Jerusalem" and asked that her husband arrange for the burial of her body and a mass for her soul. For this extremely modest estate, the church assistant apparently waived the requirement of a formal executor and witnesses for the will. Sadly, either the husband could not raise the fee for her mass or he, too, soon succumbed to the epidemic, for a note appended to Ignacia Cristina's testament states that no priest performed the mass.[1]

Countless indigenous men and women met a similar fate in the periodic epidemics that ravaged the American continents and islands after unknown European diseases came ashore with the unwitting conquerors and settlers. The vast majority of the stricken did not have the chance to put their humble requests in writing. For historians trying to reconstruct the lives of those who faced the chal-

lenges of conquest, the indigenous testaments that are being uncovered in the archives are welcome, historically significant sources.

For example, S. L. Cline's analysis of a rich cache of sixty-five
sixteenth-century Nahuatl wills has already illuminated previously
undetectable patterns of sociocultural continuity and change.[2] One
of Cline's most significant contributions is her demonstration of the
importance of gender, combined with social class and wealth, as a
force shaping the postconquest roles and conditions of the indigenous people. Native men and women experienced Hispanic influence in different ways. Cline notes how indigenous men were more
likely to adopt Spanish clothing and how access to political power,
many occupations, literacy in Nahuatl, and the use of esteemed
Spanish names remained virtually closed to indigenous women. She
also reminds us, however, that indigenous women "were not pawns
without property . . . [but] received wealth in the form of land and
houses by inheritance and dowry and asserted their claims to property through the Spanish judicial system." They also had access to
greater intimacy (such as through marriage) with Spaniards—something that could affect the nature and rate of culture change.[3]

To extend Cline's recovery of the complexities of indigenous
women's experiences over a longer period, I have gathered another
108 Nahuatl testaments from hamlets and towns of the highland Valley of Toluca, just west of the Basin of Mexico. These 59 women's wills
and 49 men's wills, most of them embedded in the records of inheritance disputes housed today in Mexico City's Archivo General de la
Nación, date from 1589 to 1801 (the majority, however, are from the
eighteenth century).[4] The Toluca region testaments allow us to continue tracking concrete developments in the daily lives of native people confronting new social, economic, and political systems and the
intruding Hispanic culture. The object here is to probe the Toluca testaments for the lesser-known activities of rural indigenous women
in particular, employing the men's wills primarily for comparative
purposes.

Rural indigenous women represent a demographically significant sector of highland colonial society. They were a crucial ingredient in family and community survival. Yet their experiences—as relevant as men's for comprehending the complex processes of life in
the colonial indigenous world—are very little studied. This is partly

owing to the difficulty of locating relevant source materials, such as the wills presented here. But it may also be attributed to modern stereotypes of rural native women as unimportant, church-dependent, domestic drudges who are dominated by the men in their lives and have no political influence and no important economic activities. Many surprises lie in store for those who subscribe to this view, even if we cannot argue that the complete opposite was true. A great many rural women lived quiet lives with few incidents that would bring them to the historian's attention, yet they faced daily struggles that made of colonial life an intricate, richly textured tapestry. What individual women did and believed surely holds telling clues to the evolution of more general functional and ideological trends as cultural contact escalated over time. There were social and cultural dynamics inside the home, neighborhood, and community that we are only just beginning to uncover.

Native Women of Toluca

The occasion of paying someone to draw up a testament provided individuals with a chance to reflect on their accomplishments in life, often punctuated with personally momentous events like marriage and birth, and to survey accumulated possessions. Wills gave individual women a rare chance to record their voices for posterity, providing retrospective glimpses of life at death. One surprise for many observers will be that rural indigenous women even left testaments.[5] Granted, we have located fewer testaments for humble married women than we have for those who enjoyed some degree of independence, wealth, or status. Forty-two (71%) of the fifty-nine women in this Toluca group appear to have been widows, although they rarely indicate their marital status directly. Furthermore, sixteen (27%) of the fifty-nine had social or economic prominence. Six bore the sparingly applied title of nobility for women, "doña." Among the other ten were women who had relatives or spouses within the titled indigenous nobility. Some of these, as well as a few others, had accumulated considerable property, at least when compared to the destitute Ignacia Cristina.[6] Although a number of penniless and married women also found the opportunity, elite women and widows apparently had more freedom and a greater need to put their testaments in order. Furthermore, competitors would find the properties of these latter women more desirable and would take them to court, indirectly ensuring the survival of their testaments in litigation records.

The range of wealth and status that separated testatrices is one of the remarkable features of these rare sources and deals another blow to dated notions of an undifferentiated mass of "peasants" and to the rapidly waning idea of a common experience for all indigenous women. Despite sharing certain obvious cultural and biological commonalities, native women were equally separated by socioeconomic distinctions. For example, the penniless Ignacia Cristina stands in sharp contrast to Francisca María, an indigenous woman of the same general vicinity who died in the same epidemic. Francisca was the granddaughter of a titled indigenous noble and the wife of a native man with a somewhat rare Spanish surname (suggesting some measure of status). In contrast to Ignacia's lack of a single witness, two native dons and a gathering of indigenous church and town officials served as witnesses for Francisca. As one testimony to her wealth, Francisca bequeathed nine saints' images, on the high end of the scale of the average number of precious icons a family might own. She also possessed, apparently independent of her husband, two houses, each with its adjoining lot (called *solar* in Spanish, or *xolal* in Nahuatl), two unremarkable pieces of land inherited from her grandmother, and four large parcels passed down from her illustrious grandfather. The sum total of these properties was significant; they could be sown with twenty-three *almudes* and three *cuartillos* (the equivalent of about twenty-nine gallons) of seed, twenty times the holdings of the poorer testators.[7]

Land and Labor

In this fertile agricultural region, known for supplying maize to the capital for centuries, land was the crucial ingredient in production. Land possession, particularly by the mid- to late colonial period, not only meant survival; it was also a vehicle to wealth and power. Hence the ownership of land by women had a bearing on their status in society. Cline finds that indigenous women of late sixteenth-century Culhuacan held "the same types of property and in approximately the same amounts" as indigenous men.[8] She suspects that this was partly owing to the abundance of land following epidemics and suggests that as the native population recuperated in the seventeenth and eighteenth centuries and competition increased over this precious resource, women may have become excluded from inheriting land.[9]

Although the Toluca Valley is slightly more removed from the heart of Spanish settlement in Mexico City than is Culhuacan, the struggle for land there was played out along much the same lines as the colony matured. For this reason, the Toluca Valley provides an excellent testing ground for Cline's hypothesis about women's inheritance and ownership of land. Competition between individuals and communities and between indigenous people and Spaniards was certainly running high by the end of the seventeenth century, about the same time indigenous wills and inheritance disputes become abundant.[10]

Indeed, indigenous male testators from the Toluca Valley mentioned sons more often than daughters as heirs in their wills. Nineteen bequeathed to sons only or to sons and other heirs who were not their children. Only five singled out daughters in the same way. Sixteen remembered offspring of both genders.[11] Sources are unavailable to compare actual family size and numbers of living children of each gender with the numbers of offspring that were included in the wills, but one suspects that male children would not have been that much more numerous than female and that the choice to single out sons was the operating factor.

The same pattern of favoring sons is seen in women's wills. Twenty of their testaments designate sons but not daughters, twelve designate daughters only, and just seven include both. The slightly greater number of women's wills that mention daughters but not sons may be a carryover from pre-Hispanic traditions. In early colonial Mexico City at any rate, according to Susan Kellogg, indigenous "women left land primarily to daughters and grandsons."[12] The gradual shift toward favoring sons may reflect growing influence from Spanish culture and the colonial legal system that allowed for entail (although it was relatively rare in Mexico), in addition to increasing pressures on resources. Men, too, had possibly shifted in the same direction over time, for men in early colonial Mexico City had usually left land to "wives, brothers, and daughters, though sisters and sons were left significant amounts."[13]

In the aggregate, while females did not inherit as frequently as males, they were truly plentiful among the heirs of both testators and testatrices. Quantifying the amounts of land given to each gender might be more telling, but because land measures were frequently omitted in the testaments, this is impossible to do with any exactitude. However, a smattering of notes made about heirs who inherited larger or a greater number of parcels does again point toward the slight preference shown male heirs despite a general adherence to the practice of partible inheritance, or the fairly even distribution of properties to all legitimate offspring.[14]

In addition to slight gender imbalances in the transmission of property from one generation to the next, there is a notable tendency for husbands to leave relatively little to their wives. Ten testators who completely ignored their wives may have been widowers. Six testators known to have living spouses left their wives the family home (one wife also specifically got the solar, and two wives got other small parcels) with the stipulation that they raise the children or grandchildren there.[15] Another wife inherited some land, but she was required to use it to serve a saint.[16] Only four wives came into small inheritances without stipulation.[17]

Husbands may have felt that their wives did not require land because the children would care for them as long as they lived. Two testators specifically entrusted their wives' welfare to their sons.[18] In addition, when husbands left land to minor children, perhaps they were assuming the wives would oversee production on the land until the children came of age. Two women's wills of the 1760s contain examples of trusteeships over land that was left to them but was earmarked eventually to go to other heirs.[19] In early colonial Mexico City, Kellogg finds women had only "use rights" to patrimonial land and houses, which usually went with more extensive rights to children and siblings. Although classifications for "bought" and "inherited" land that were so important in the sixteenth century had diminished by the eighteenth century, perhaps indigenous concepts governing the transmission of inherited land still affected the continuing pattern of usufruct for spouses.[20]

Wives might not have been left much by their husbands for another reason. They may have had agricultural parcels that were already considered their own, perhaps inherited from parents or presented as a kind of dowry to their husbands but considered something that would automatically stay with them on their husbands' death. For the latter case, unfortunately, certain evidence of dowries is lacking in these testaments. There is not a single example in these wills of the term *cihuatlalli* (woman's land, possibly dowry lands) that Cline found in sixteenth-century Culhuacan. Asunción Lavrin and Edith Couturier may be correct in suggesting that the granting of dowries remained an alien practice, particularly for indigenous rural women of humble means.[21]

Evidence for married women's retention of properties inherited from prior generations is also somewhat murky. About half (six of eleven) of the married women with living spouses appear to be landless, for they bequeathed no property or goods at all. They seem primarily concerned to express their wishes about masses for their souls.[22] The other half mentioned only small parcels. One had some livestock and another a few small *magueyes* (century plants). It is not clear whether these properties were held separately from husbands, but they could have been. The husband of the woman with the livestock died the same year and left a separate testament, which would suggest that they each had their own properties to dispose.[23]

The parcels that daughters, nieces, granddaughters, sisters, and the like, inherited might conceivably have been maintained through marriage and beyond, despite their being somewhat shadowy in testaments. Perhaps, again, the women had usufruct rights and therefore were not always inclined to list such parcels in wills as though they were private properties. Widowed testatrices sometimes mentioned houses or parcels inherited from parents and grandparents. Land from mothers is the single most recurring type among those mentioned. The five examples of this underscore the fact that daughters did inherit and that they were slightly more likely to inherit from their mothers, as noted above.[24]

How widows added to the possibly small inheritances they received from deceased parents and grandparents, siblings, and former husbands is something the wills do not clarify. But the widows represented in these testaments, along with some of the other female testators, did own sometimes significant amounts of real estate and other goods, although not as much as the male testators. Table 7.1 compares the numbers of parcels bequeathed by women testators to

Table 7.1
References to Various Kinds of Property
(percentages making reference of total number of each gender)
Toluca Region, 1589–1801

	Testatrices	Testators
Domestic Property		
Solares (house land)	61	57
Houses	51	71
Specific rooms	8	6
Furniture/chests	5	2
Clothing/linens	3	4
Cooking/weaving items	5	0
Cultivated Fields		
0 parcels	20	2
1 parcel	22	14
2 parcels	25	20
3–5 parcels	17	16
6–9 parcels	10	41
10–16 parcels	0	6
Farm Improvements		
European livestock	10	14
Indigenous poultry	2	0
Cuexcomatl (indigenous silos)	5	10
Metl/magueyes (century plants)	36	15
Capulin (native cherry trees)	0	2

those bequeathed by men. While 61 percent of the testatrices possessed solares (usually land adjoining houses), only 51 percent mentioned houses. Testators may have been taking the houses for granted in those wills mentioning only solares. Thus it is conceivable that regardless of which sex was reporting, the figures for both houses and solares appear to be lower than they actually were.

Since these were predominantly farming people with enough property to render making wills worthwhile, there were few who failed to mention agricultural parcels; among those who did not bequeath such property, twelve women (20% of that group) overshadowed the sole male (2% of his group). Most of the testatrices who did have some additional land had only one or two plots, and a smaller although still significant number had up to five. Among the men, ownership of from one to five properties was very common, too. But

Table 7.2
References to Indigenous and Spanish Land Terms
(percentage making reference of all landowners of each gender)
Toluca Region, 1589–1801

	Testatrices	Testators
Indigenous Terms for Parcels		
Tlalli (cultivated field)	36	75
Milli (cultivated field)	30	44
Indigenous Measures for Land and Groups of Magueyes		
Quahuitl (rod)	28	29
Cuemitl (ridge or row)	13	23
Pantli (maguey row)	6	6
Tlaxelolli (measure of seed)	0	2
Spanish Measures for Land		
Almud (4 quarts of seed)	43	40
Vara ("yard" of 33 inches)	6	13
Fanega (48 quarts of seed)	2	10
Yunta ("yoke" of oxen)	2	2
Cuartillo (2 quarts of seed)	2	6
Cuartilla (8 quarts of seed)	0	2
Spanish Terms for Parcels		
Pedazo (parcel)	6	19

then there is a significant bulge in the ranks of those with six to nine parcels (41%), and it was only men who held as many as ten to sixteen parcels each, the latter being the largest amount possessed by a single individual in this group. In contrast, no woman had more than nine parcels of any description.

The indigenous terms for these parcels and the Spanish and indigenous terms for units of measure are given in table 7.2. Additional research into the exact meaning of the former may shed light on possible inequalities that escape notice with a simple accounting of numbers of parcels. For example, while women had about equal numbers of *tlalli* and *milli* (agricultural parcels, the contextual distinction not being entirely clear), men were much more likely to possess tlalli. It may be that a tlalli was larger or of greater fertility than a milli.

Further complicating efforts to compare the value of parcels held by men and women, testaments frequently omit description of land quality. Physical measurement of the properties in question is inconsistently included as well, but those measures that do appear give a vague sense of the size of certain plots. Testators would simply describe a piece of land as a certain number of rods, or rows, or a certain number of seed measures (which could be planted rather than expected in the yield). Unfortunately, we are uncertain about the length of the rod and the length and width of a row, making the ultimate quantification of land areas impossible.

As concerns Spanish and indigenous terms for measures, some variation appears in the way men and women used certain terms. While approximately the same proportion of women as men referred to the indigenous *quahuitl*, a rod or stick of undetermined length, a somewhat greater proportion of men than women counted their lots by the Spanish *surco*, an agricultural row, somewhat akin to a furrow but emphasizing the raised land rather than a plow cut or groove.[25]

Both sexes were equally familiar with and preferred the Spanish *almud* (equal to four quarts of seed), often rendered *almo* in Nahuatl, over any indigenous measure.[26] Parcels measured by the almud ranged from one-half to eleven of these units in size, but the vast majority, or thirty-three plots held by nine men and two women, were three almudes in extent. What is more, there are several examples of six- or nine-almud parcels being divided in halves and thirds, respectively, perhaps breaking them back down into their original three-almud components.

While the ubiquity of the almud measure and its being counted in threes may suggest a forsaking of native units and original vigesimal divisions, the three-almud parcels may actually disguise a common indigenous measure. When testamentary analysis has accumulated enough equivalencies between European and indigenous measures, it may be found that three almudes worked out to some frequently recurring, symmetrical number of quahuitl, or rods. For instance, one will indicates that sixty quahuitl was four almudes, and two others point to ten quahuitl per almud. (Variations in soil fertility or in the regionally specific size of the measures may account for the differences.)[27]

Observing subtle variations in the use of terminology by men and women is a fruitful method for examining the nuances in relationships between gender roles and culture change. There are several minor indicators that native men were more familiar with or comfortable using imported Hispanic terminology and technology. For example, men more frequently used the Spanish loanword *pedazo* (parcel) and European measures such as *fanega* (48 quarts) and *vara* (33-inch yard), as shown in table 7.2.[28] They exhibited a greater likelihood to count cultivated rows as surcos. They were also somewhat more likely to be raising European livestock, as shown in table 7.1.

What accounts for these differences? Diverging degrees of exposure to the new culture is a more compelling explanation than some "female" reluctance to accept foreign ways. Urban indigenous women of Peru have been found to be quicker than were men to adopt European customs, yet here we see indications of an opposite force at play.[29] In urban settings indigenous women had greater access (as domestic workers, concubines, and wives) to the private side of Spanish life and, through retail activities, for example, could acquire economic, technical, and legal information. In rural areas, in contrast, indigenous men went in larger numbers to work on estates, where they became more familiar with agricultural tools, measures, products, and the language of the trade, while women remained more in the indigenous communities or performed domestic work in the estate households.[30]

Women's significant though lesser role in stock raising argues against cultural conservatism on their part; they were not reluctant to take on the care of European animals. Men's greater role in stock raising may also have had an economic dimension, in that stock required capital to which men might have had greater access, related to their more dominant role in landownership and management and their greater ability to earn wages on estates.[31] Possibly also adopted with the raising of European stock was the attitude that it was primarily the work of men, although the numbers do not yet sustain the full acceptance of such a gender bias in the indigenous world.

In fact, we have yet to identify clear-cut divisions of labor between the sexes in agricultural pursuits. Women owned agricultural parcels. Testators specifically asked women to work certain parcels, for instance, to provide for the celebration of a saint. Women also made occasional references in their testaments to tending fields.[32] Additionally, women seem to have dominated in raising magueyes (called *metl* in Nahuatl). Thirty-six percent of testatrices, compared to 15 percent of male testators, bequeathed the century plants in their wills (see table 7.1).

Some observers may hasten to emphasize women's role as principally a domestic one, deemphasizing their contributions to agriculture. Women do bequeath the only cooking and weaving items (grinding stones and yarn balls) in the testaments.[33] Additionally, testatrices make the only two references to kitchens.[34] Returning to the issue of century plants, women routinely raised them on solares, near the home. But magueyes also served as informal fencing for distant parcels, and in many wills we see evidence of organized cultivation exceeding the concept of the kitchen garden.[35] Magueyes planted in six or eight rows recur; one woman had sixty plants under her care.[36] Further, women may have had primary responsibility for producing and selling pulque, the alcoholic drink derived from these cacti.[37] A distinction between work inside and outside the home falls short of accurately describing indigenous women's occupations in the rural areas of Toluca (see also Lisa Sousa's description of Mixtec and Zapotec women in chapter 9).

The Sacred

Just as women participated actively in various agricultural and pastoral pursuits, men entered energetically into the realm of worship practices in the home. Both men and women maintained and passed on religious imagery of Christ, Mary, Joseph, and other favorite saints—objects of devotion for the whole family. These "images" might be small oil paintings on wood, prints, or, less frequently, carved wooden or stone statuettes, known in Spanish as *imagenes de bulto*, or images in the round. Very occasionally, by this late date, religious items such as *lienzos* (paintings on canvas) and crucifixes take their place among the icons maintained in some special place in the indigenous home.[38] Three testators and three testatrices mention having oratories or sanctuaries in their homes; others probably had small altars or tables where their images were kept.[39]

Men were actually more likely to mention images in their wills than were women (63% of the former as opposed to 47% of the latter). Of course, in both cases it is unclear which sex actually had the primary duty of maintaining these images in the home. They may have fallen under the care of the family as a whole. Very often, the numbers of these objects left by any one individual are not spelled out, but when they are, the range that emerges for men is from one to twelve and for women, one to sixteen. Wealth as much as piety may have affected the numbers of images maintained, for one-third of both the men and the women who bequeathed religious objects were among the socially or economically prominent in their communities.

Just as men, in general, were more likely to mention images in their wills, these objects were bequeathed to male relatives more often than to female relatives. Here, gender plays a more definite role. Testators and testatrices alike typically entrusted their images to sons and only secondarily to daughters. But wives make up the next most notable group to receive the precious paintings and statuettes. Many testators spoke of their house, their images, and their solar all in the same clause, frequently leaving the three components as a unit, intact for the benefit of one or more family members and to celebrate the particular saints.[40]

Looking for gender difference in culture changes associated with the reshaping of religion after conquest, one might expect to find, as with agriculture, that those who had greater contact with Spaniards were quicker to exhibit the influence of new ways. Since rural indigenous men were more geographically mobile, going between their communities and Spanish estates or visiting urban centers where Spaniards were concentrated, producing a greater likelihood for them to adopt, for example, Spanish dress earlier, were they more likely to embrace the Catholic faith more quickly?[41] Or did indigenous women actually have greater contact with the Catholic church?

Parish churches penetrated the hearts of most pueblos in the Toluca region by the eighteenth century, facilitating women's access to the intrusive faith. The more mobile men, in contrast, may have been less able to attend mass regularly. Charles Gibson relays an observation from 1556 that native men "were less concerned with church attendance than women."[42] Whether this was true, widespread, and lasting is a question in search of an answer, but we do *not* see a more eager embrace of Christianity by indigenous women in these late colonial testaments.[43]

The maintenance of the native family's cult of the saints may have had an indigenous precursor. Although possibly referring to neighborhood chapels rather than private oratories, the *Junta eclesiástica* of 1539 expressed some concern about "a survival of polytheism in the multitude of little chapels erected by the Indians, 'just like those they had once had for their particular gods.'"[44] The provisioning of home altars with flowers and incense and the sweeping of the floor below saints' images corresponded to rituals associated with idols in pre-Hispanic times, according to fray Diego Durán and other early colonial chroniclers.[45] The late colonial sexual division of labor in this regard also echoed the somewhat stronger role for men but a significant one for women in serving the temples and gods in these ways.[46]

The modest numerical superiority of men's owning and inheriting religious images honored in indigenous homes may have had one other minor dimension. Although the Virgin Mary was the most popular figure celebrated on home altars, the array of male saints was much larger than that of females, and individuals often had a very personal connection with the saints they served. In a separate study of many of these same Nahuatl testaments, I have found twenty-four examples wherein family members shared the name of and had a special devotion to a saint venerated in the home. The number of male saints represented by three or more images in those testaments amounted to eleven, while only three female saints had the same representation. The greater involvement of men in the cult of saints probably explains the wider range of male saints' images adored in the homes, but it could also be that men's greater attachment was at least partly owing to some sense of brotherhood with the panoply of male near-divinities.[47]

While one might tend to think of María and José as the quintessential names for indigenous men and women, reflecting the adopted importance of Mary and Joseph in their religious life and some perceived lack of imagination, the selection and distribution of saints' names not only took on increased complexity over time but also reflected a continuing difference in status for men and women. A comparison between the Culhuacan testaments and these from the Toluca region helps to elaborate such changes and continuities (see also Rebecca Horn's discussion of naming patterns in chapter 4).

By the start of the Toluca run (1589), completely gone were the humble Nahuatl birth-order names such as Tiacapan (firstborn), Tlaco (middle child), Xoco (youngest).[48] At the same time the prevalence of two Spanish given names for women, generally connoting low social status, increased greatly. Forty-nine of the Toluca women had such names, as we saw above in the examples of Ignacia Cristina and Francisca María.

A much wider spectrum had superseded the repetitious recurrence of María, Juana, and Ana of the sixteenth century, however. In this group of fifty-nine testatrices, only nine bore the first name María.[49] The Toluca group also includes only five Juanas and one Ana. Illustrating the growing diversity, forty-five unique given names are represented among the Toluca testatrices, thirty-one of them serving as first names, with a somewhat smaller, at times overlapping range of twenty-three second names.

The use of Spanish patronymics, so common today, had not yet made many inroads into the indigenous communities of the late colonial period. Where it had, the practice tended to be restricted to elite families and especially to male elites. Only five women in the Toluca group had a first name followed by a Spanish surname, in this case the common de la Cruz, and three others had the fairly rare last names Subersa, Setina, and Cortés.[50] Cortés was the patronymic surname of the indigenous "señor de Toluca" and his descendants, including this noblewoman testatrix. Her full name was doña Ana Cortés Acaxochi; she was the only one of the testatrices to use a pre-Hispanic name. She was also the only one of the Toluca group to have her will recorded in the sixteenth century.[51]

Parents had become much more imaginative in the naming of daughters, yet they still favored saints' names and drew from a slightly narrower range of names for their daughters than they did when naming their sons. The forty-nine male testators from the Toluca region had forty-two different first and second given names. Spanish patronymics, although often humble, are also much more prevalent among the indigenous men, as noted above. Eight of them carried the name de la Cruz, a very popular appellation among families in the Calimaya area. Also seen are Torres, Ramos, García, Alcantara, de los Reyes, and de los Angeles. Whereas 83 percent of the native testatrices had two given names, the same could be said of only 45 percent of the males.

Concluding Remarks

As the colonial period progressed and competition over resources heightened, had the relatively greater importance accorded to men in sixteenth-century indigenous society increased significantly in various aspects of daily life? Such an increase is not clearly evident with regard to naming patterns. Women may even have gained a little ground, with more comparable (though still skewed) numbers of both groups coming to bear simply two given names, and a greater variety of them. But while the details had changed in the later colonial era, naming practices continued to show a slightly greater effort to accord status to males and somewhat more conservatism in the selection of names for females.[52]

As we have seen, there is more evidence of an increased role for men in landholding, but the data are still limited. Only a very careful comparison of types of land and numbers of parcels brings to light the inequality between the sexes in the late period. Although Cline found "approximately the same" kinds and amounts of land owned by men and women in the sixteenth century, this might have to be quantified more specifically before we can measure the degree of change that had occurred over time. The stunning point here is that in many categories in tables 7.1 and 7.2, comparing Toluca women's and men's properties, near-parities arise.

Since widows figure so prominently in this group of women, Deborah Kanter's recent finding of "widows' extreme vulnerability as landholders" in the late colonial Toluca Valley is intriguing. Basing her assessment on only sixteen cases, Kanter argues that as land competition became intense in the densely settled Tenango del Valle area in the eighteenth century, the families of widows' late husbands preyed on their inheritances. While indigenous town councils "passively sat on the sidelines . . . Spanish judges . . . firmly supported the widow and her children and ordered república officers to see that the woman received a fair share from her in-laws."[53] It is unclear what the net result was in the aggregate, but the threat Kanter identifies was surely a significant one, and it seems to have increased dramatically after independence. By the late nineteenth century, she claims, "female land tenure hardly existed."[54]

If, as the wills in my study indicate, widows made up the largest

number of independent landowning women in the indigenous communities, it makes sense that as population increased and resources
became ever scarcer their holdings would come to be viewed with
jealousy. But while an increasing preference for male control of land
at the expense of women might be an expected result, the Tolucan testaments demonstrate that the degree of inequality was not actually as
stark as Kanter's study suggests or as Cline's predicted. It is true that
ownership and inheritance patterns detected in the present study do
seem to point to a progressively lesser role for women in landholding
as compared to men. But their position was still very significant on
the eve of independence. The women represented in the testaments
often owned, bequeathed, and inherited significant amounts of land
and movable property. They were also highly active in maguey cultivation and probably the pulque trade, a vital economic venture
that may have taken many Toluca Valley women to Mexico City in
the eighteenth century. Furthermore, women were vociferous in
their defense of corporate landholdings, frequently filling the ranks
of rural demonstrations and riots—an indication of their vested interest in this precious resource so crucial to community survival.[55]

Despite the mobility and exposure that such activities as pulque
distribution and rioting over land may have given women, it is still
presumed that indigenous men had comparatively greater contact
with Spaniards in rural areas, particularly as occasional laborers on
private estates but also as representatives of the municipality in most
dealings with colonial officers. This interchange, in turn, may account for the continuing tendency for native men in rural areas to be
quicker to adopt (or adapt) Hispanic ways. This is seen, for example,
in men's somewhat more noticeable use of Spanish terms for land
and measures and the raising of European livestock. A slightly more
limited access for women to the cult of the saints in indigenous
homes (and possibly in the public arena, too) may be owing in part
to a continuing sexual division in worship practices that reach back
to pre-Hispanic times.

Testaments—and particularly those in the native languages—
provide some precious clues for illuminating the private side of life in
the indigenous world, including kinship patterns, as well as material
and spiritual culture. But we await research in other internal records,
such as bills of sale, rental documents, acts of possession, and birth

and marriage documents, to elaborate such topics.[56] As we can round out the picture of daily life for indigenous people, we will then move more profitably toward comparisons with other regions of Mesoamerica and with Hispanic women's experiences and gain greater insights into the nature of the broader colonial world.

South Central Mexico

Acatlan

Teotitlan

Petlacingo

Chila

Tequixtepec

Papalo

Usila

Huajuapan

Tonala

Coixtlahuaca

Tamazulapan

Silacayoapan

Teposcolula

Yanhuitlan

Nochixtlan

Tecomaxtlahuaca

Villa Alta

Achiutla

Tilantongo

Jaltepec

Tabaa

Tlaxiaco

Etla

Yalalag

Antequera/Oaxaca

Putla

Chalcatongo

Cuilapan

Coyotepec

Macuilxochitl

Zaachila

Tlacolula

Tlacochahuaya

Mitla

Yolotepec

Zimatlan

Ocotlan

Zacatepec

Ayoquesco

Amuzgos

Pinotepa

Jamiltepec

Tututepec

0   50 km

Map Area

8

Mixteca *Cacicas*

Status, Wealth, and the Political Accommodation
of Native Elite Women in Early Colonial Oaxaca

Ronald Spores

When the Spaniards arrived in Oaxaca in the 1520s they found in place a native political system controlled by a hereditary elite and articulated by marital and voluntary alliance and military conquest. The Mixtec system consisted of a constellation of small states, or *cacicazgos*, extending from southern Puebla to the Pacific coast and from the Valley of Oaxaca west to Guerrero. Bilateral kinship reckoning, rules of inheritance, and requirements of status group endogamy had channeled power and property through royal status women and men throughout the Mixteca since A.D. 1000. Although much of the area came under the political-tributary control of the Culhua Mexica in the early sixteenth century, there was virtually no interference by the Aztecs in native political, social, and economic institutions, and there was a high level of independence in the Mixtec system of government.[1]

As the Spanish established control over Oaxaca, they not only tolerated the preexisting political system but also reinforced the authority of the traditional rulers and incorporated them into their plan of acculturation, economic exploitation, religious conversion, and implementation of the system of social welfare and conflict res-

olution.[2] Native lords, called *caciques* by the Spaniards, remained in
political power positions in their communities, and the rights and
privileges of the rulers and their families were reinforced and protected both in theory and in practice. Although males occupied official positions of authority as governors of native communities,
women were recognized as legitimate *cacicas* (indigenous noblewomen), held great wealth in land, houses, livestock, and movable
property of all kinds, were entitled to specific services from the population of the communities making up their cacicazgos, and functioned as regional entrepreneurs.

During the sixteenth century, the vast majority of communities
in the Mixteca fell into one or another of at least fifty cacicazgos.[3]
Ruling caste couples, widows, widowers, and orphaned children
assisted by guardians held legal titles to power, property, and privilege in these polities. Women and men succeeded to title through inheritance by direct descent from a line of royal caste ancestors, by ab-
dication of preceeding rulers, and by marriage. Women, in effect,
became consorts of their cacique husbands when they married. Likewise, when cacicas married men from other communities, the women
were recognized as the true and legitimate holders of their own
señoríos (Spanish-language equivalent of *cacicazgo*), and their husbands were entitled to privileges only by virtue of their relationship
to their wives. Legitimate offspring of cacicas inherited title, or titles,
held by their mothers as well as those of their fathers.

Among the prominent sixteenth-century cacicas in the Mixteca
were Cauaco (One Flower) and María Cocuahu (Two House) of Yanhuitlan; Francisca de Mendoza of Tilantongo; Inés Rojas and María
de Saavedra of Achiutla and Tlaxiaco; Inés de Osorio and Catalina de
Peralta of Teposcolula; Ychique Yatonatle Suchi (Catalina de Zárate),
Juana de Santa María, María de Osorio, and María de Guzmán of
Tejupan; Juana de Rojas of Tlacotepec; Ana de la Cueva of Tecomas-
tlahuaca; and doña Ana de Sosa of Tututepec.[4] Mixteca cacicas were
involved in frequent lawsuits to protect their rights and privileges. It
is through these lawsuits and through the special awards, grants,
permits, and protections granted by crown officials that we know a
great deal about Mixteca cacicas—their status and role, the privileges to which they were entitled, and their political and economic
circumstances.

All cacicas who inherited titles in their own right were recognized by the natives, the crown government, and the Church. They had the highest social status and were the wealthiest individuals in their domains. Their pensions from the *sobras de tributos* (community funds derived from tribute) ranged from about 50 silver pesos to 400 pesos per year. They were exempted from tribute payment. Economically more important than their allowances and exemptions from tribute, however, was their right to services by Indians in their fields and households.

Cacicas owned the best houses in the principal towns of their cacicazgos and possessed the most fertile irrigable lands, orchards, grazing lands, saltworks, mineral deposits, large herds of sheep and goats, as well as horses, cattle, mules, and burros. Rarely, and only in the principal centers like Yanhuitlan or Teposcolula, did anyone, Spaniard or Indian, possess greater wealth or prestige than they. None lived a more sumptuous life. They wore the finest clothes, had abundant jewelry, furniture, and works of art, and were carried on palanquins when on extended journeys. The natives provided them with tribute and personal services in their houses and fields. Cacicas gave lavishly to the church, and, in return, they sat in places of honor at mass and in fiestas and were buried in the nave of the principal church of their cacicazgos. In every way the cacicas stood at the pinnacle of native society and occupied a position at least comparable to high-status Spaniards, even *encomenderos* (individuals with a grant to collect tribute or the labor of a given group of Indians) or a Dominican prior. Mixteca cacica status equaled or exceeded that of the *ladina-mestiza* (racially mixed, Hispanicized) daughters and granddaughters of Moteucçoma, such as Isabel de Moteucçoma, who held *encomiendas* (grants of Indians for tribute or labor) in the Mixteca.[5]

The "golden age" of the Mixteca cacica was the period from about 1550 to 1620. Strong native traditions and a favorable set of Spanish laws and institutions, including those put in place by the Dominicans, reinforced the status and power of the traditional native rulers. After the middle 1600s, patterns of direct lineal succession were weakened by failure to produce children, by death of direct successors, or through usurpation. Population increases that followed the disastrous declines of the sixteenth and early seventeenth century also placed demands on lands by native populations. Especially desirable, of course, were the highly productive lands that had traditionally been held by the native lords. Spanish courts and administrators, however, continued to recognize the institution of the Spanish *mayorazgo,* or "cacicazgo" as it applied to the caste of Mixtec *señores naturales* (indigenous nobles), and insisted on legal demonstration of direct lineal succession and right to title throughout the colonial period.

Ultimately, the role, power, position, and wealth of the Mixteca cacicas eroded, particularly after the mid-eighteenth century. But there was variation in the pattern, and in many instances we see a very strong persistence of the cacicazgo until independence in 1819–21. Cacicas continued to occupy positions of importance well into the mid-nineteenth century, particularly in the Huajuapan-Acatlan area of northern Oaxaca, southern Puebla, and their property and financial holdings formed the basis for family estates that persisted into the twentieth century.[6] For purposes of illustration, it is useful to examine a few cases in more detail. Three exemplars of sixteenth-century "cacicadom" in the Mixteca were Ana de Sosa of Tututepec, Catalina de Peralta of Teposcolula, and María de Saavedra of Tlaxiaco-Achiutla.

Sixteenth-Century Cacicas
Ana de Sosa of Tututepec

Tututepec, on the Pacific coast of Oaxaca, was the seat of a pre-Hispanic conquest state that dominated the region from the Isthmus of Tehuantepec to the borderlands between Oaxaca and the present state of Guerrero.[7] It was the scene of fierce battles between the Mixtecs and the Spanish forces under Pedro de Alvarado in 1522 and was recognized by natives and Spaniards alike as one of the richest, most productive areas of Mesoamerica. Following the death of the señor natural of Tututepec, the title fell to a son who took the name Pedro de Alvarado. The cacica was Ana de Sosa, who, on the death of Pedro, around 1550, became cacica of the province of Tututepec. She was confirmed or reconfirmed as cacica in 1554, in 1559, and again in 1561 and occupied that position, and effectively asserted her authority and defended her entitlements through the courts, until the son of Pedro and Ana, Melchor de Alvarado, succeeded to the title in about 1570.[8]

Ana de Sosa had vast holdings. She possessed 12 *estancias* (communities where she held land and was entitled to tribute and personal services), 31 *huertas* (groves) of cacao, great stretches of farming and grazing lands, highly productive saltworks, *lagunas* (lagoons) rich in fish, game, and shellfish, and numerous houses, including the *tecpan,* or palace complex, in Tututepec. She also held valuable movable property in the form of gold, silver, jade, coral, and turquoise jewelry and necklaces, precious bird plumage, vast quantities of cotton *huipiles* (blouses) and skirts and other textiles, livestock, and stores of products from her fields, saltworks, lagunas, and huertas. Her holdings on the Oaxaca coast clearly exceeded those of don Tristán de Luna y Arellano, the powerful Spanish encomendero and the largest landowner in the region in the middle to late sixteenth century. Only the estate of Hernando Cortés in the Valley of Oaxaca and in Tehuantepec would have exceeded that of Ana de Sosa.

Melchor de Alvarado, Ana's son, succeeded to the cacicazgo of Tututepec in 1570. He, like Ana, successfully defended his title against usurpation by Alonso de Mendoza, *hijo bastardo* (bastard son) of Pedro de Alvarado, and was reconfirmed as cacique in 1580, 1582, and 1588. In 1601, Isabel de Alvarado, granddaughter of Ana de Sosa, was confirmed by the viceroy and Audiencia of New Spain as cacica of Tututepec and Juquila.[9]

Ana de Sosa was undoubtedly the wealthiest and most powerful woman, native or Spaniard, in southern New Spain in the mid-sixteenth century. Were it not for a few legal and administrative documents in the National Archives in Mexico, we would know nothing of her or her life. Had she been cacique, rather than cacica, and had she been Azteca, instead of Mixteca, she would be much better known to history.

Catalina de Peralta of Teposcolula

Catalina de Peralta succeeded to the royal title at Teposcolula in 1569.[10] She acquired the cacicazgo after a long court battle with Felipe de Austria of the ruling family of Tilantongo. Felipe was the widower of the daughter of the deceased cacique of Teposcolula and claimed further that when the cacique line at Teposcolula was terminated, as occurred when the cacique Pedro de Osorio died on July 2, 1566, without living children, the title would fall to a son of the cacique of Tilantongo. Catalina, however, was able to substantiate her claim to the title as the daughter of Pedro de Osorio's sister and the cacique caste relative nearest her uncle. She further reinforced her claim by demonstrating that she was the granddaughter of the pre-Hispanic rulers of Teposcolula, Lord Tecpateutl (Tecpantecuhtli) and Lady Ozomasuchitl. In 1568, then, don Felipe de Austria was forced to relinquish title to the rightful heir, doña Catalina.

Teposcolula was the Spanish administrative capital of the Mixteca, and an important cacicazgo both before and after the Spanish conquest. The legally declared value of the goods (*bienes*), houses, jewels, lands, and orchards was "*seis mil pesos de oro de minas y mucho más*" (six thousand pesos of gold and much more), an enormous sum for the sixteenth century.[11] Among the properties that Catalina inherited were five dwellings, including the sumptuous caciques' palace built for Pedro de Osorio's son, Felipe de Osorio, prior to the latter's death, and all properties located in the central, or tecpan, section of Teposcolula. Catalina received twenty parcels of the most highly productive river-bottom land in the Teposcolula Valley, the most productive salt mine in the central Mixteca, and two large orchards of apples, pears, peaches, and oranges. Substantial returns were realized through rental of these properties to Spaniards, to wealthier natives, and to the Dominican and Jesuit orders of the Mixteca, Oaxaca, and Puebla. She also acquired large quantities of jewelry (much of it of pre-Hispanic origin), fine textiles, silverware, furniture, and huipiles, skirts, and other clothing by way of inheritance and acquisition.[12] Although she was forced into extensive litigation, she successfully defended her title to Teposcolula until her death. As happened frequently in the sixteenth-century Mixteca, however, Catalina suffered a fate similar to her predecessor at Teposcolula. She died childless, and her title reverted to a cacique-class cousin at the end of the sixteenth century.

María de Saavedra of Tlaxiaco

In 1573, a youthful María de Saavedra succeeded to the cacicazgos of Achiutla and Tlaxiaco, two of the largest and wealthiest native patrimonies in the Mixteca. She received title at the death of her father, don Felipe de Saavedra, who inherited Tlaxiaco from his grandfather, Cuzcaquautli (Jewel-Eagle), and his father, Francisco de Maldonado.[13] Proper succession in the royal lineage was of utmost importance to Mixtec cacique families, and Felipe had directed in his will of November 15, 1573, that his daughter should marry the son of his sister, doña Isabel de Rojas of the cacique family of Tlaxiaco-Achiutla. This propitious marriage would constitute a firm alliance and ensure legitimate succession and control by members of the ruling lineage.

In addition to numerous lands, houses, and entitlements to lifelong tribute and services from the subject populations of her cacicazgos, doña María also inherited movable property from don Felipe.[14] Included in the inventory of goods were 54 silver *flores*, 18 spoons, pitchers, 11 necklaces, incensors, a *chasuble*, a *diascaste*, 18 "toothpicks," miscellaneous items of silver and beaded jewelry, religious images, capes, books, decorated *cocos*, 3 magnets, large quantities of textiles, trunks, a large herd of sheep, 3 pack mules, and even a silver pick "with which I cleaned my ears," and a pair of eyeglasses. As with all Mixteca cacicas, she also received vast quantities of huipiles and skirts, most of them lavishly decorated with woven designs, *tochimite* (rabbit fur), and bird plumage.

In real property, María inherited the extensive lands of the cacicazgo of Tlaxiaco, which included many huertas of fruit trees, nine large *milpas* (fields) located in the most productive lands of the region, and unspecified stretches of grazing and resource-producing and collecting lands. This was clearly the largest and most valuable configuration of real estate owned by any individual in the province of Tlaxiaco in the middle to late sixteenth century. She held enough property in 1581 that she was able to donate and sell some of her more valuable lands to the Dominican monastery of Tlaxiaco.[15]

In 1587, María de Saavedra, in compliance with her father's instructions, was married to Francisco de Guzmán, son of the cacique of Yanhuitlan, Gabriel de Guzmán, and doña Isabel de Rojas of Tlaxiaco-Achiutla.[16] As previously mentioned, doña Isabel was María's patrilateral aunt, meaning that the marriage was between first cousins, a common practice among members of the endogamous Mixtec cacique caste in colonial as well as pre-hispanic times. In celebration of María's marriage, the natives of Tlaxiaco were ordered to spin 40 *fardos* (large bundles) of cotton cloth and to provide numerous other services.[17] Witnesses stated, however, that doña María was "one of the greatest cacicas of this Nueva España, and the natives of this said pueblo are obliged to provide not only forty fardos of cotton but much more because there are nearly 2,500 [tribute-paying] Indians." Viceroy Villamanrique was persuaded that "the said doña María is the greatest cacica that there is in all of this Misteca [*sic*]." On May 11, 1587, he ordered that all services be provided and affirmed that "it has always been customary among them in that province that when the children of *los señores* [the nobles] married, the natives aided the recently married couple with cotton yarn and clothing and other things."

In 1717, doña Manuela Pimentel y Guzmán, the cacica of Tlaxiaco and Achiutla at that time, presented a petition to the viceregal government stating that

> Francisco de Gusmán and doña María de Saabedra, caciques of Achiutla and Tlaxiaco, died without children, and they were succeeded by their legitimate heir don Baltasar de Velasco, and upon his death it passed to his son and heir don Francisco Pimentel y Gusmán, my father, who by provision of his will left me the said cacicazgo of Achiutla and Tlaxiaco.[18]

The direct line of señores naturales of Tlaxiaco came to an end with the death of María in the mid-1590s.

Although the lineage of María de Saavedra failed because of lack of offspring, the titles to Achiutla and Tlaxiaco were passed in an orderly and legal fashion to an *heredero transversal* (collateral heir), Baltasar de Velasco, or so it appeared. One hundred years after María's death, doña Manuela Pimentel y Guzmán was widely recognized as cacica of Tlaxiaco, Achiutla, and other señoríos, but the documentary record indicates that subsequent to years of litigation, the lands of María's cacicazgo passed into the hands of the community of Tlaxiaco. The *cabildo*, or town council, of Tlaxiaco claimed that María had no legitimate heirs and that although she died intestate, she stipulated before her death that her holdings should go to the community.[19] Ultimately, Tlaxiaco's claims were affirmed by the Real Audiencia.

Other Cacicas and Other Times

Not all cacicazgos were of the size and importance of Tlaxiaco, Yanhuitlan, Teposcolula, or Achiutla. Juana de Rojas was a member of the family ruling the small cacicazgo of Tlacotepec located in the central Mixteca.[20] She was married to Jerónimo de Rojas, cacique of Ocotepec, and went to reside there with her husband.

Following the death of doña María López, cacica of Tlacotepec, in 1593, a nephew, Juan de Guzmán y Velasco, cacique of Tlatlaltepec, assumed title to Tlacotepec. Although he had been named as successor in doña María's final testament, doña Juana de Rojas and her husband entered into litigation against don Juan and claimed usurpation of title. They proved that Juana was more directly related to María and to Juana's cacique grandparents, don Pedro and doña María Hernández, than was Juan de Guzmán. Their allegations were substantiated, and they were awarded title to the Tlacotepec cacicazgo. While the case was being litigated, doña Juana's husband died, and she became sole possessor of Ocotepec and Tlacotepec, two relatively small but important cacicazgos. As a result, she was entitled to receive tribute and services from both of her holdings as well as being placed in possession of houses and many parcels of land in Ocotepec and Tlacotepec.

The cacicazgo of Ocotepec remained important throughout the colonial period. In the late eighteenth and early nineteenth century, doña Pascuala Feliciana de Rojas, a descendant of doña Juana de Rojas and don Jerónimo de Rojas, was the wealthy and well-known *muy ladina* (very Hispanicized) cacica of Santo Tomás Ocotepec, Santa Cruz Nundaco, and several other communities in the Mixteca Alta and Baja.[21] As the colonial period continued, there were increasing challenges to the privileges and rights to cacicazgos. These challenges came from the cacica's own communities, neighboring communities, or other caciques, from the Dominicans, and from Spaniards, mestizos, and individual Indians. Doña Pascuala was challenged at various times by her own community, by the adjoining community of Cuquila, and by the cacica of Cuquila. Despite invasions of her properties and numerous legal suits, she remained in possession of enormous quantities of land, which were customarily rented to well-to-do Spaniards or Indians or to communities for agriculture and grazing. Some land was lost, but most of her claims were substantiated, and her heirs continued in possession of her lands well into the postrevolutionary period.

Discussion

The several cases cited above are representative of consistently recurring patterns in the Mixteca during the colonial period. Cacicazgos varied in size and composition, and some cacicas were much more wealthy, prestigious, and influential than others. The rules of succession and the cacica lifestyle, however, were the same everywhere. All of the cacicas of the Mixteca were, after all, members of the same endogamous caste, and all were related through marriage and kinship. Whether at Acatlan, Huajuapan, Zapotitlan, or Tequistepec in the north, Tonala, Silacayoapan, or Tecomaxtlahuaca in the west, Tututepec on the Pacific Coast, or Tilantongo, Yanhuitlan, Coixtlahuaca, Tejupan, Teposcolula, or Tlaxiaco in the central Mixteca, each cacicazgo had its ruling couple and family.

The cacicazgo system brought social, political, and ethnic cohesion to the region more effectively than any other native or Spanish institution. Cacicas provided an essential link in the system of marital alliance that existed in the Mixteca from at least A.D. 1000 until the end of the colonial period. Until the 1800s they were recognized by the supporting common class and Spanish courts, administrators, and clergy and continued to enjoy high status and wealth and to receive special privileges and services.

Two views are frequently expressed by students of colonial native society. One view is that native Mesoamericans were defeated by the Spaniards and existed thereafter as a dominated, subjugated, and seamless underclass with little or no power over their own lives or their relationships with the colonials. A second view is that colonial native women were dominated by and subservient to men and that they played an insignificant role in social life beyond the family level, or in the economic and political life of the region. According to these views, natives were without power, prestige, or wealth. They were simply helpless victims of the Spanish in their program of conquest and exploitation. Likewise, women are hardly visible at all in modern depictions of native colonial life.

Insofar as the Mixteca is concerned, the image of the downtrodden native masses simply does not conform to social reality. Indians played an active role in the colonial culture that was forming around them. They were not passive nonactors in a great power game controlled by the Spaniards. But there was never significant organized resistance, or a concerted effort by natives to resist or overthrow Spanish control.[22] That occurred only in the early nineteenth century and as a result of the agitation and leadership provided by disgruntled *criollos* (American-born Spaniards) and mestizos. The natives played their own game of adaptation and accommodation, and except for their understandable failure to adjust to an unintended biological extermination from European diseases, the strategy worked quite well. They survived in their towns and villages, and they managed to retain much of their traditional way of life, or they devised an acceptable mix of European and native cultures. This does not mean that all Indians were social equals. They were part of a stratified colonial-indigenous social system in which some Indians ranked above other Indians, some Spaniards ranked above other Spaniards, and Indians ranked both below and above Spaniards. Most ranked at the lower end of the social hierarchy, but clearly not all.

The second myth that should be refuted is that native women were somehow inferior and subservient to male counterparts. As demonstrated by Ana de Sosa, Catalina Peralta, María Saavedra, and Juana de Rojas, this is simply not the case with Mixteca cacicas. They were equal in rank to their brothers and husbands and succeeded to titles in their own right. They held wealth and property and were regarded with great deference by natives and Spaniards alike. Cacicas were active and influential in the social, economic, and political life of western Oaxaca and played an important role in the formation of colonial Mixtec society.

Lengthy perusal of hundreds of documents pertaining to all classes of colonial Mixtec women, poor natives as well as cacicas, reveals clearly that they held, manipulated, bought, and sold property, ran businesses, even committed crimes and received punishment equivalent to that given to men.[23] In physical encounters with men, it was often the woman who prevailed, and with respect to the courts and administrative system, women frequently brought claims or were involved in civil lawsuits from the mid-sixteenth century until the end of the colonial period. The differences are that they were involved in economic and legal/criminal matters less often than men, and they did not hold formal political offices or act as *mayordomos* (property and fiscal overseers).

Conclusion

Studies of native society in colonial Oaxaca have been biased in two ways: (1) they have focused primarily on the elite (caciques and *principales,* or nobles); and (2) they have been concerned overwhelmingly with the activities of males. Women have remained sequestered "between the lines" of the focused studies of Zapotecs and Mixtecs, the most "visible" of colonial societies, and in the edited collections of studies of agriculture and agrarian matters, ideology, government, economy, migration, and ethnicity. Women, as well as children and the laboring/tributary class, are most likely to appear in the more statistically oriented studies, such as those dealing with demographics, settlement, or social class. Seldom, however, do they appear individually, descriptively, or as active participants in the life and history of the region. These are traditional biases reflecting (a) the nature of colonial documentation and (b) the implicit male-oriented biases of researchers, whether male or female. It is customary and perhaps easier to proceed in this fashion, but it is readily apparent that this is an inadequate, inaccurate, and misleading approach to the study of colonial culture in Oaxaca or elsewhere in Mexico.

If one cares to focus on native women in the colonial period, it is clear that the documentation does exist, and it reveals quite convincingly that women did play active, important, even influential roles in indigenous and Euro-Indian society. First, this is reflected most convincingly in the activities of aristocratic women in native society as economic actors, especially in the Mixteca and in the Valley of Oaxaca, and as critical figures in the planning and maintenance of formal religious activities and institutions throughout the region. These, of course, are women coming from the highest-status group in indigenous Oaxaca. This is not only a reflection of documentary bias favoring the aristocracy, but it is also an indication of the fact that it was primarily aristocratic women who were involved in such matters.

The activities and interests of women of all socioeconomic statuses and classes were reflected in their participation in civil and criminal matters handled through the Spanish courts and administrative institutions and through ecclesiastical offices. Such repositories as the Archivo General de la Nación, Archivo General del Estado de Oaxaca, Archivo Regional de la Mixteca, Tlaxiaco, and Archivo del Poder Judicial del Estado de Oaxaca contain hundreds of suits, complaints, petitions, and awards involving native women of all classes. This means that although researchers continue to emphasize the aristocracy in colonial times, we may perceive the activities of commoners as well as aristocrats as they perform quite discernible roles in the colonial cultural arena. If we are to understand colonial life in Oaxaca, it is not only desirable that we do so—it is mandatory.

9

Women and Crime in Colonial Oaxaca

Evidence of Complementary Gender Roles in Mixtec and Zapotec Societies

Lisa Mary Sousa

In August 1630, Juana de San Francisco notified the Mixtec officials of Teposcolula that her husband had beaten her with a stick and had whacked her on the head with a butcher's knife.[1] Speaking on her own behalf, Juana explained that a certain Sebastián had stopped at her house to ask if she had any *pulque* (an indigenous fermented alcoholic beverage) for sale. As they stood in the patio talking, Juana realized that her husband, Juan Francisco, a church singer, was approaching. She ordered Sebastián to hide from her jealous husband in the steam bath. Sebastián scurried across the patio, leaving his hat behind in the commotion. When Juana's husband entered and discovered the hat, he cruelly beat her. She pleaded with him to spare her life, and the pulque customer fled.

Juana de San Francisco was one of many indigenous women who sought justice from native and Spanish authorities during the colonial era. In criminal records from the Mixtec region of western Oaxaca and the Zapotec area of eastern Oaxaca, now preserved in the Archivo de Poder Judicial de Oaxaca, native women, regardless of class, prominently appear as plaintiffs, defendants, and witnesses. As plaintiffs they initiated suits over personal and property crimes. As defendants they attempted to explain the actions of which they justly or unjustly had been accused. And as witnesses women furnished detailed and sometimes expert testimony about the events and persons in question. Thus these records provide a window onto women's interpersonal, household, and community relationships, roles, and responsibilities.

Although court proceedings contain valuable details for assessing women's status, they have been relatively little researched (however, see Susan Deeds's and Susan Kellogg's informative studies of native women of other ethnic groups and their involvement in the colonial legal system in this volume). In *The Mixtecs in Ancient and Colonial Times*, Ronald Spores describes the Teposcolula court in the Mixteca Alta and the types of cases prosecuted. William B. Taylor, in *Drinking, Homicide, and Rebellion in Colonial Mexican Villages*, statistically analyzes eighteenth-century criminal records from the Mixteca Alta and central Mexico to establish patterns of social behavior. Both of these works combine information about women, but neither specifically addresses gender ideology and women's roles. No previous studies of Zapotec women have utilized colonial criminal records from the Villa Alta.[2]

This chapter provides an overview of native women's participation in the criminal court from 1570 to 1750 and analyzes colonial criminal records from the Teposcolula and Villa Alta collections to show that concepts of complementarity shaped Mixtec and Zapotec gender roles, respectively. A review of the criminal records and sixteenth-century ethnographic sources reveals striking similarities between the Mixtec and Zapotec regions and, therefore, supports an interpretation of a generally common gender ideology of complementarity, although regional variations and idiosyncrasies undoubtedly existed.

The Concept of Complementarity

Women's frequent use of the courts and the testimony preserved in criminal records reveal the complementary nature of indigenous social organization. The concept of complementarity recognized the contribution of both male and female as necessary to create the whole and, thus, accorded both men and women important relationships and responsibilities in the household and the community. Although a gendered division of labor was maintained, indigenous communities and households were not divided into "public" and "private" spheres, whereby men exercised a role in the community and women were relegated to the home. Rather, Mesoamerican households were loosely organized social units whose members were obligated to each other and the community through shared responsibility; these "families" were not well-defined nuclear units of blood relatives headed by a patriarch. In Mixtec and Zapotec regions, community membership served as the basis for indigenous women's identity, rather than their relationship with a male authority figure (husband or father). Although complementarity did not guarantee full equality, women exercised broader social, economic, and political roles in this context than in a patriarchal system.[3]

Mixtec and Zapotec cosmologies reveal a gendered view of the universe and of life-sustaining relations underscoring the centrality of the concept of complementarity. Both societies conceive of the universe as composed of two parts: a female earth and a male sky. Rain symbolizes sexual exchange in the center that fertilizes and produces life on earth.[4] Preconquest and sixteenth-century codices, which provide important clues to indigenous ideology, also contain evidence of the complementary nature of Mixtec gender relations. In codices, the Mixtecs represented their sociopolitical unit, the *yuhuitayu,* with a glyph of a man and woman, the ruling couple, seated on a woven reed mat facing each other.[5] The mat in Mesoamerican iconography symbolizes authority; since mats served as beds, they also connote the ruling couple's intimacy and, by extension, lineage. The depiction of both the male and the female rulers highlights the Mixtec tradition of tracing dynastic rulership through both the maternal and paternal lines.[6] Thus both female and male elements were necessary to symbolize Mixtec social, economic, and political life in the yuhuitayu glyph. In fact, women appear to have ruled more frequently in the Mixteca than in Nahua central Mexico; apparently, royal status outweighed gender in considerations of succession to yuhuitayu rulership.[7]

The codices also portray women's involvement in the religious life of the community. Illustrations in the codices of priestesses as well as priests reveal the complementary nature of gender roles in

Mixtec religion and social ideology. The depiction of offerings of tortillas and pulque in the codices also suggests women's participation in Mixtec religion as producers of sacred and symbolic food. Even further, criminal records from the Mixtec and Zapotec regions illustrate how the ideological concept of complementarity was played out in daily gender relations.

Women in the Court

Criminal cases contain a great deal of information about quotidian male and female interaction. Normally, a plaintiff (or plaintiffs) filed charges with native officials who presided on the *cabildo* (Spanish-style municipal council staffed entirely by indigenous males in native communities). Both the plaintiff and the defendant presented three witnesses. Cabildo members would judge minor cases themselves and report serious or violent crimes to a Spanish official. In towns where a Spanish official resided, or when the plaintiff feared bias from indigenous officials, he or she might notify the *alcalde mayor* (the chief Spanish administrator and judge of a district that included several indigenous communities) directly. A notary would then take statements from the plaintiff, the accused, and their witnesses, through an interpreter. Sometimes two interpreters were employed, as when María Ortiz, María Ocelosuchil, and doña Marta de los Angeles complained that they had been trampled in the market by a runaway horse; their case was conducted through Tomás Gerónimo, interpreter in Chocho and Nahuatl, and Gabriel García, who translated from Nahuatl to Spanish.[8] The alcalde mayor would decide the case after reviewing the written evidence. Women's frequent participation in the courts, where all of the officials were men and proceedings were lengthy and complex, belies a passive and naive role.

Criminal records, like most indigenous documents, reflect a tradition of legitimizing one's business before the community.[9] Rich with personal statements, such records reveal the importance people vested in their community's opinion about them. Pedro de Caravantes explained that he murdered his wife, María Montiel, because she had disgraced him by committing adultery with Domingo de la Cruz.[10] Similarly, Diego Conquihui asked town officials to sentence his wife to a public beating in the plaza on market day for having committed adultery.[11] Like indigenous men, women used the court to settle their disputes before the community; women also testified as witnesses and defendants in court.

In colonial courts, both women and men were first referred to by name, and then as an *yndio/a natural* (Indian man or Indian woman) of a certain pueblo. Sometimes marital status, community office, occupation, and age also were provided. Although women often were defined by their relationship to men and referred to as "María, wife of Gaspar," for example, men also might be introduced in reference to their spouses in the records. At any rate, these references are inconsistent. For example, in one case Cecilia López is named with no mention of her marital status.[12] In a related case, however, she is identified as Pedro López's wife.[13] Ultimately, community membership was the core of native identity for both men and women.[14] References to the *macehuales e yndias* (tribute-paying commoners and Indian women) or *yndios e yndias* (Indian men and Indian women) in petitions initiating cases against indigenous or Spanish officials for tribute abuses further illustrate the community's recognition of its male and female members. Such complaints frequently addressed the increased burden on women due to excessive demands for cloth and personal service in officials' homes.[15]

The virtual absence of belittling or condescending language to describe women further negates an inferior secondary role. Indigenous plaintiffs, defendants, and witnesses rarely described women as helpless, naive, or dependent. Indigenous testimony seldom implied that adult women lacked experience or relied on male protectors. The rare appearance of such language is telling, however; in 1632, María López attempted to justify her adulterous affair with Agustín de Barros by stating that as a "weak woman and with little understanding" she consented to go with him to a nearby field.[16] Indeed, María may have been naive for she was only fourteen years old. The rare use of self-deprecating language by several citizens of the Zapotec town of Lachirio in 1716 also is illuminating; confessing to manufacturing *aguardiente* (a distilled alcoholic beverage), María Catalina explained that "as a woman and a stupid person [*tonta*] she did not know what she was doing."[17] Significantly, three of the ten men who were accused in the same case also justified their activities by stating that they were "tonto." Clearly, it was not their biological makeup that made them stupid but the fact that they were caught. They were not, of course, too stupid to know that they stood a better chance of acquittal by employing an excuse that might appeal to Spanish officials.

Other examples of patronizing language comes from Spanish witnesses, and even then only in rare cases. When Gerónimo de Arevalo, a Spaniard, testified against Sebastián Gómez for the attempted murder of his wife, Magdalena Gaitán, he stated that she had been "a good Indian and Christian who served her husband."[18] Another time, Juana de Mendoza's and Magdalena Alvarado's Spanish lawyer requested their release from prison explaining paradoxically that as "weak and inexperienced" women they had been tricked into promoting rebellion in the community.[19] Incidentally, Taylor also noted the near-absence of gender-specific language used in insults, finding only one reference to an indigenous man making a macho insult in eighteenth-century Teposcolula records. By comparison, in central Mexico, where Hispanic influence was more prominent, he found that indigenous men were responsible for twenty-one of thirty-five macho insults.[20]

Whether as plaintiffs, witnesses, or defendants, women spoke for themselves in the courts; only under rare circumstances, for example, if a woman was on the verge of death, did her husband, parent(s) or other relative represent her. In murder cases the parents of the female victim jointly brought the case to the officials. Furthermore, female defendants were never put in their husbands' custody. Women's sentences, like men's, included imprisonment, fines, and public whipping. Men's and women's community-based identity and their enthusiasm for settling disputes in a "public" forum clearly show that Mesoamerican societies did not follow the patriarchal tradition of male heads of household publicly representing the family. Rather, men and women shared many of the same privileges and similar status as members of their community despite, and perhaps because of, their distinct responsibilities.

Women as Plaintiffs

As plaintiffs, women brought charges against indigenous men, indigenous women, and Spaniards for a variety of reasons, including wife beating, assault and battery, homicide, adultery, robbery, and abuse of power. By filing suits, women spurned subordinate status in household, community, and Spanish-Indian relations. Furthermore, women participated in a dialogue concerning native conceptions of morality and justice by initiating criminal suits.

In the majority of complaints brought by women, they accused their husbands of adultery and battery. Women often complained that their husbands had pushed, beaten, or whipped them. In more extreme cases, men attacked their wives with clubs, rocks, knives, or machetes. In a wife-beating case from the Mixteca Alta, María de Aguilar told officials that her husband, Melchor, had beaten her with a stick. She explained that he had instructed her to rise early on the day of the beating to prepare food for the guests staying at their home.[21] Accordingly, she got up at four o'clock in the morning and walked to her godmother's house to ask for help grinding corn for tortillas and preparing *atole* (a thick, indigenous beverage made with water, ground corn, and spices). María's godmother sent her daughter, María Cunquaa, to assist her. In the meantime, however, Melchor had arisen and realized that his wife was not there. When he saw that she was not in the kitchen, he asked her sister, Lucía, where she had gone. Lucía thought she might be at the basin in the public plaza washing the corn kernels she would grind for tortillas. But Melchor did not find her there either, and he grew suspicious that she was committing adultery with Andrés, a mulatto. Although Melchor found María in the kitchen when he returned, he proceeded to beat her in a jealous rage.

Court cases of wife beating show that women had recourse when their husbands acted violently. A woman's ability to make a claim against her husband undermined his attempt to control her absolutely. Moreover, local officials, who pursued the case, and community members, who served as witnesses, reaffirmed her status as a valued member of the society and condemned her husband's abusive behavior.[22]

Occasionally, women complained that they were victims of violence inflicted by other women. When Andrea Hernández accused her husband of adultery and named Cecilia López as the "other woman," Cecilia countersued and accused Andrea of battery.[23] Cecilia claimed that Andrea and five other women entered her house and beat her up, pulling her hair and tearing her *huipil* (a loose-fitting, tuniclike garment typically worn by indigenous women). Further complicating matters, Cecilia claimed that she was two months pregnant and that she had miscarried because of the beating.

Women also brought criminal cases against outsiders. Juana López appeared before Mixtec officials and filed charges of battery against Juan Enríquez, a Spanish merchant.[24] While she was at the market selling hay, Juana argued with Enríquez over the price. He pushed her, knocking her to the ground, but she jumped back up and they continued to fight. When he shoved her a second time, she fell and gashed her head. Witnesses confirmed her claim that she had been seriously injured and testified that she bled profusely. In the final judgment, the alcalde mayor fined Enríquez eight pesos, five of which went to Juana. In another case against a Spaniard, María Martín, a Mixtec, accused her Spanish priest of abusing his power, claiming that he had imprisoned her under false pretenses so he could steal the horse that she inherited from her husband.[25] Although the Spanish defendants enjoyed a higher status than their accusers, in neither of these cases did an appointed male act on the woman's behalf. Clearly, women were not afraid of challenging secular or religious Spaniards, regardless of their power in the community.

Women also filed cases on their children's behalf. In 1603, Catalina Saquaz, a native of Coixtlahuaca, notified the court that her nine-year-old daughter, Juana Sayo, had died after being raped by fifteen-year-old Diego Cunqo.[26] Since Diego was a minor, he was put in custody of a local Spaniard. Despite the gravity of the crime, Catalina never asked a male relative to present her case to the authorities.[27]

In 1596, Francisca Hernández and her husband, Joaquín Gaitán, also appeared on their daughter's behalf to file criminal charges of attempted murder against their son-in-law, Sebastián Gómez.[28] He confessed to having poisoned his wife (i.e., their daughter), Magdalena Gaitán, who was then eight months pregnant. Magdalena suffered a violent miscarriage and awaited certain death, dehydrated and delirious. At each step in the proceedings, the records refer to both Joaquín and Francisca as the plaintiffs. Regardless of gender or the relationship between plaintiff and defendant, Mixtec ideology obviously allowed women to speak directly for themselves and their children.

Like their Mixtec counterparts, Zapotec women filed criminal complaints of adultery, battery, and wife beating. Both Mixtec and

Zapotec women also petitioned the court when they were robbed. In 1729, two widows reported that their house in the Zapotec town of Solaga had been robbed while they were at a festival in Tabaa.[29] María de Gregoria lost eighty pesos and Catalina de Santiago lost forty, money that they had saved from renting out their mules and oxen.

Women also challenged indigenous authorities by directly approaching the alcalde mayor when they suspected unfair treatment at the community level. In 1704, María Gutiérrez complained to the alcalde mayor that one night at around ten o'clock, the governor and an alcalde came to her house and pounded on the door ordering her to open up.[30] She refused because she was concerned about the safety of her young daughters. When María denied them entry, they set the house on fire, forcing her and her children to flee. The Zapotec officials confessed to arson and tried to justify their intimidation tactics by implying that her husband was a master of idolatry. Significantly, her husband never testified or petitioned in the case. Nevertheless, the Spanish judge ordered them to pay for the lost house and belongings. In another instance, Catalina de Arebado feared bias on the part of indigenous officials when she accused the governor's brother of robbing her house.[31] Unhappy with their initial handling of the case, she eventually reported it to the alcalde mayor. During the course of the investigation, the Zapotec governor and alcalde perjured themselves and were eventually reprimanded and imprisoned for obstructing justice.

As plaintiffs, Mixtec and Zapotec women were able to make the ideal of complementary roles a reality and to bring into balance relations with their husbands, other community members, indigenous officials, and even Spaniards. Women's participation in the court system as witnesses and defendants further complements their roles as plaintiffs. These roles and the subtle evidence left in the course of testimony about daily life illustrate women's shared privileges and responsibilities that engendered strong bonds at both the household and the community levels.

Women as Witnesses

Whether men or women brought the case, women frequently reported what they had seen or heard to the court, and they occasionally testified as expert witnesses.[32] In the Mixteca Alta, male witnesses outnumbered their female counterparts at a ratio of approximately three to two; in part, this might be explained by the frequent testimony of local officials (always male) who intervened in disputes, verified injuries, and examined homicide victims.[33]

It should be noted that, in contrast, Zapotec women rarely appear as witnesses in similar records from the Villa Alta.[34] In part, this observation can be explained by the fact that the alcalde mayor resided in the Spanish settlement of Villa Alta, which was at some distance from many of the Zapotec towns of the jurisdiction.[35] Nevertheless, as male witnesses recount events they often explain how women had told them what they had seen or heard. Although Zapotec women appear less in the official Spanish records, frequent references to them appearing before native officials suggest that Zapotec women shared a similar social and legal status as Mixtec women did within the community.

The aforementioned cases against Sebastián Gómez for attempted murder and Andrea Hernández for battery provide examples of the role of female witnesses. In the case against Sebastián Gómez, the alcalde mayor ordered Ana de Luna, a female healer and midwife, to testify.[36] As an expert witness, she related how she had discovered a poisonous substance in the beverage that Sebastián had given his wife; and then she described her attempts to heal the dying woman. Similarly, the alcalde mayor ordered María García, a midwife, to examine Cecilia.[37] She concluded that Cecilia had not been pregnant but that she simply had menstrual bleeding. Her testimony provided crucial evidence, because if Cecilia had miscarried, her case against Andrea Hernández would have been far more serious. More frequently, women reported what they had seen or heard in the market, on the road, in a field, or in the household complex and generally commented on the character of the plaintiff and defendant.

Women as Defendants

Mixtec and Zapotec women appear in the criminal records as defendants as well as plaintiffs and witnesses. Women were accused of crimes ranging from adultery to drunkenness to inciting rebellion. Only rarely were women tried for attempted murder or homicide.

In a typical case against a woman for being rebellious, Mixtec officials of Teposcolula charged Juana de Mendoza with disobeying the *alcaldes* (judges) and *regidores* (councilmen), inciting rebellion, selling pulque, and committing adultery with a married man.[38] The officials complained that they were no longer able to convince people to go to church or collect tribute because Juana encouraged them to disobey.[39] In defending herself, Juana explained that she had only tried to convince some of the women not to obey because of an increase in tribute that created hardship for them. Traditionally, all of the women in the community were divided into groups of four with each group being responsible for weaving one *manta* (a length of cloth) to pay tribute for the festival of their patron saint.[40] But the officials had increased the amount that year, ordering that groups of three women produce a manta, instead of the usual four.

In fact, charges against women for inciting rebellion were not rare. In his statistical analysis of eighteenth-century criminal records from Teposcolula, Taylor found that "in at least one-fourth of the cases, women led the attacks and were visibly more aggressive, insulting, and rebellious in their behavior toward outside authorities."[41] Indigenous people revolted when they felt that outsiders threatened the community's integrity. Uprisings were usually directly related to increases in tribute, new laws, and complaints about local Spanish officials.[42]

Women's participation in local rebellions reveals women's relations with the community. Although officials collected tribute through a male household representative, women also had a direct stake in tribute assessment and the community's survival. The fact that widows paid half the usual tribute amount attests to women's equal contribution to the total payment. As tributaries, women worked in *caciques'* (indigenous rulers') and Spaniards' homes, wove textiles, ground corn, and prepared tortillas. Even when women were at home weaving, they were still tied to the community as producers of valuable tribute items. Woven goods were (and still are) lucrative trade commodities.

Other cases from the Zapotec region further illustrate women's active participation in traditional community rituals. On Christmas Day, 1716, an indigenous official of Analco notified the Spanish alcalde mayor that all of the people of Lachirio were drunk on *tepache de caña* and *tepache de plátanos* (fermented alcoholic beverages made with cane and bananas, respectively).[43] When the alcalde mayor's representative went out to investigate, he found only one person in the entire village who was sober—an indigenous alcalde who had stayed home from the celebration to tend to his wife, who had just given birth. The Spanish official proceeded to arrest thirteen people, ten men and three women. The prisoners admitted that some people in the community owned *trapiches* (mills), which they kept hidden in a gully from Spanish officials, who had forced them to stop making tepache in the past. One of the accused, María Catalina, stated that "in the town making tepache was a custom of all the natives, men and women, for all of their celebrations."[44] Juana María, another defendant, explained that "all the natives make it in different trapiches, which they have in the gullies, because it is an ancient custom to make it in the town for all holidays."[45]

The statements by Juana de Mendoza, María Catalina, and Juana María reveal women's participation in the struggle to maintain indigenous values and relationships and to subvert Spanish pressure to change. Their activities and attitudes can be more fully understood within a discussion of Mesoamerican social organization and gender roles.

Social Organization and Evidence of Complementary Roles

Women's participation in the courts and the evidence provided through testimony illustrate the dynamics of native household and community organization. Kinship was loosely defined in indigenous society and, therefore, was not focused on a clear male or female authority (see also Ronald Spores's discussion of female cacicas in chapter 8).[46] Relevant terminology from several Mesoamerican societies points to the lack of anything comparable to the hierarchical family of blood-related members that serves as the foundation of patriarchal society. No Mixtec or Zapotec linguistic term connotes the European sense of "family."[47] Instead, Mixtec and Zapotec refer to the people who live in a household complex.

As shown in the criminal records, community membership served as the basis of any man's or woman's identity. This is still evident in contemporary indigenous societies, where women wear regional-specific clothing that clearly associates them with their pueblos. The fact that women brought criminal suits without the approval or representation of a male authority figure further highlights the absence of a patriarchal tradition in which a woman's identity is shaped by her relationship with a patriarchal figure, either her husband or her father.

A careful analysis of indigenous labor patterns and household organization reveals the lack of distinction between "public and private spheres."[48] Men did work outside the home, as carpenters, painters, and agricultural laborers; they engaged in long-distance trade; and some held political office. Women were largely responsible for household duties, including cooking and weaving. However, within the indigenous community, traditional female tasks were not carried out in a "private" setting. Even household duties such as laundry and cooking required women to leave the confines of the patio. Women laundered clothes in rivers and, as we saw in María Aguilar's case, washed their food in the town plaza. In addition, women like Juana de Mendoza and Juana de San Francisco not infrequently operated small businesses such as taverns and inns out of their homes, thereby changing the nature of the home from a "private" to a "public" place. Other women rented their horses, mules, and oxen from their homes to local men. Certain tribute-specific duties like weaving also gave the home a "public" aspect.

Some female responsibilities required women to leave the home altogether. As midwives and healers, women traveled through the community to serve their patients. Women also ran the indigenous markets, selling everything from cotton and clothing to food and animal fodder, as in the case of Juana López. They sometimes traveled to distant markets, as did María Pérez and Ana Pérez, sisters who went from Achiutla to Teposcolula to sell cotton mantas.[49] Although women did not hold civil political offices, they did control community resources and to a large extent the local economy through their participation in the markets.

Indigenous landholding patterns also required geographic mobility. Although men were primarily responsible for planting, women also tended and harvested plants and trees. Juana María, on trial for making and drinking tepache, alludes to the gendered division of agricultural labor when she explains that as "a poor widow and as a single woman she did not have cane or the means to sow it. [Instead] she cut some plantains to make a little beverage to celebrate Christmas." Evidence from the same trial illustrates the complementary nature of male and female labor within the household; in the course of his confession, Bartolomé Manzano told Spanish officials that "in his pueblo, those who could sowed cane which their women sold in the plaza."[50]

On a practical level, women's work complemented men's and was necessary to the survival of the community and household. Some aspects of women's work also held symbolic importance. Women produced items such as pulque and tortillas that were offered in indigenous rituals to the earth to reconfirm the sacred covenant between humans and the earth that ensured life and fertility.[51] These foods were also exchanged in social settings to create bonds within the indigenous community. Women's weavings offered through tribute further strengthened the social fabric that bound the indigenous community together by reinforcing ties between the indigenous nobility and the tribute-paying commoners.

Criminal records evidence women's various economic activities, showing that women were neither isolated from the community nor economically dependent on men. Women maintained their own finances separate from their husbands' accounts; this may explain why a woman could directly challenge her husband in criminal court and withstand his imprisonment or forced labor sentence in a convent or an *obraje* (factorylike shop that came to be known for its dismal conditions).

Incidental details in the records illustrate women's participation in the cash economy. When doña Marta de los Angeles complained to local officials in Coixtlahuaca in 1577 that she and two other women had been trampled by a horse in the market, she testified that in the jumble she had lost two huipiles and five gold pesos.[52] This would have been a significant amount for any indigenous person at that time. Zapotec women also left evidence of their financial standing when they reported robberies to local officials. In 1729, María Gregoria and Catalina de Santiago lost eighty and forty pesos, respectively, when their house was robbed.[53]

Throughout the colonial period Mixtec and Zapotec women frequently appeared in the criminal courts. Perhaps due to weaker and slower penetration of Spanish culture, gender relations do not appear to have changed as dramatically as in central Mexico.[54] Criminal records from throughout the period contain significant information about women's activities and their relationships. We can better understand native women's participation in resistance movements, their activities in the local economy, and the formation of their social relationships and identity by carefully reading and analyzing criminal cases. Future research will benefit from the use of varied sources containing different types of information that can help us more fully appreciate the complexity of native women's experiences and strategies in early Mexico.

Conclusion

Although criminal records portray women as socially, economically, and politically (at least subversively) active, they also reveal men's efforts to dominate their wives. In the case against Juan de San Francisco, he defended his wife beating on the grounds that he had ordered her not to sell pulque after dark. Similarly, Melchor de Aguilar, who also was tried for battery, stated that he had instructed his wife to rise early to cook for their guests. In both cases, the husbands lost their tempers when their wives did not precisely carry out their orders. Husbands (but not necessarily wives) apparently felt that they could punish their wives. Miguel Jiménez beat his wife when he caught her having an affair with her cousin; but he used the criminal system to file formal charges against her lover.[55] Taylor shows that during the eighteenth century, 18 percent of all homicide victims in the Mixteca Alta were female, usually the wife or lover of their murderer.[56] Although rare, complaints of rape further attest to violence against women.[57]

Nevertheless, the stories of Mixtec and Zapotec women now contained in the criminal records destroy the stereotype of absolute male domination in economic, social, and political spheres and highlight the complexity of indigenous women's experiences in colonial Mexico.[58] While firm conclusions about the status of women in Mesoamerican societies require further interdisciplinary research, let us learn from the stories of Juana de San Francisco and María de Aguilar who prosecuted their spouses for violent abuse.[59] Let us remember Juana López and María Martín who confronted Spaniards for abuse of power, and Juana de Mendoza who challenged a tribute increase that placed a greater burden on women specifically. By examining their experiences within a framework of complementarity, we can see that indigenous women were afforded a greater social and economic role in their communities than ever possible in a patriarchal society.

Southeastern Mexico

Map Area

Dzemul
Dzidzantun
Mérida/
Tiho
Ixil
Motul
Tekanto
Cacalchen
Dzibikak
Samahil
Bolon/Bolompoyche
Ebtun
Valladolid/Saci
Sotuta
Tabi
Yaxcaba
Tixmeuac
Tetzal

Campeche

Tila
Palenque
Hueytiupan
Tumbala
Yajalon
Chilon
Ocosingo
Guaquitepec
Cancuc
Chamula
Oxchuc
Tuxtla
Huistan
Ciudad Real
Zinacantan

0   50   100 km

Women, Rebellion, and the Moral Economy of Maya Peasants in Colonial Mexico

Kevin Gosner

The Virgin spoke to her with these words, "María, you are my daughter."
She responded, "Yes, Señora, you are my mother."
The Virgin continued, saying, "Daughter, make a cross on this place and mark the earth. It is my will that a shrine be made here for me to live with you."
She appeared as a woman, very pretty and white.
—Agustín López (father of María López)[1]

La indizuela and the Virgin

In the summer of 1712, a young Maya woman's ecstatic vision of the Virgin Mary captured the imagination of native peoples throughout the southern province of Chiapas, in New Spain. Encouraged by her stepmother, María López had told her story to her neighbors in Cancuc, and news of the miracle spread quickly to Tzeltal and Tzotzil villages nearby. Some greeted her account with skepticism, but she won over the *alcaldes* (town magistrates) and *regidores* (city councilmen) on the village council. They organized a work party to construct a small chapel at the site of the miracle, and María took up residence there. In a hidden sanctuary within the structure, the *indizuela* (diminutive for "Indian girl"), as Spanish texts often called her, began to carry on regular conversations with the Blessed Mother, and outside the threshold, she began to preach to ever-increasing numbers of pilgrims.

Cancuc's curate, a Dominican named Simón de Lara, was none too happy about the celebrated events that were visited on his parish. Fray Simón was particularly disappointed in María's father, Agustín López, for López served him as sacristan in the church and was widely respected in the town. The priest brought father and daughter to the churchyard, denounced the miracle as the Devil's work, and whipped them both soundly for perpetrating such a fraud. María tearfully refused to recant, and when confronted with angry protests from his parishioners, a fearful de Lara fled temporarily to the neighboring village of Tenango.Through late June and July, the preaching of this thirteen-year-old Maya woman attracted more and more followers from indigenous towns throughout the highlands. Continued Spanish attempts to suppress the cult only aroused greater interest among the curious and provoked greater militancy among the faithful. The arrest of the *justicias* (local officials) in Cancuc who had lent their support to María and threats from fray Simón that the chapel would be torched by the militia if the *cancuqueros* (residents of Cancuc) persisted in worshiping there prompted Agustín López to organize a clandestine political apparatus and prepare to defend the cult with the force of arms. The decisive break came in the first week in August, when the town officials imprisoned in the capital escaped and returned to Cancuc and when the provincial bishop announced the start of a pastoral inspection tour that would inevitably impose new burdens. From the shrine center, María López called the Mayas to war: "Jesús, María, and Joseph. Señores alcaldes: I, the Virgin of the Rosary, command you to come to the pueblo of Cancuc. Bring all the silver from your church, and the ornaments and bells, with all the *cajas* [local treasuries] and drums, and all the books and money of the *cofradías* [confraternities], because now there is neither God nor King. Come at once, because those who do not come will be punished. Y a Dios. Ciudad Real de Cancuc. La Virgen Santissima María de la Cruz."[2]

The convocation sparked one of the largest and most prolonged

Indian rebellions in the history of New Spain, and earned María López (more commonly known as María de la Candelaria) enduring notoriety.[3] She remains one of the very few individual indigenous women of the period, from anywhere in New Spain, whose name is widely recognized among historians.

Though surrounded, and sheltered, by a web of male *mayordomos* (administrators, head men), *vicarios* (vicars), and *capitanes* (captains), who made most of the key political and strategic decisions that shaped the rebellion, María López played a unique, essential, and very public role until the bitter end of the uprising, when Cancuc was overrun by Spanish forces on November 21, 1712. A charismatic provocateur, her adept public performances sustained the spirit of the rebel faithful, made tangible the leadership's claims to a higher moral authority, and enabled them to extract hard sacrifices from their followers. Yet her performances defied Maya (and Spanish) norms that excluded women from formal participation in public positions of civil authority.

This seeming contradiction invites questions about the social and cultural contexts that, on the one hand, lent legitimacy to María López's actions and, on the other, shaped the contributions that Maya women more generally may have made to political discourses at the time of the rebellion. Of the two issues, the first is perhaps less problematic. Though historically Church officials often reacted with skepticism or even outright hostility to news of an apparition, the efficacy of these miracles was an accepted, indeed celebrated, part of Catholic teaching.[4] In colonial Chiapas, for example, stories of Marian visitations were included in Dominican sermons devoted to the Ave María and the recitation of the Rosary.[5] Mayas themselves believed in the omnipresence of spiritual beings in the temporal world, who were revealed in dreams, in religious ceremonies that induced visions, and in response to prayers and gift giving. Moreover, individuals were paired at birth in relationships of interdependence with supernatural guardians known as *naguales*, whose power (or weakness) was manifested in the relative good fortune, respect, or authority that men and women accrued throughout their lives.[6] And finally, the Mesoamerican tradition of the *hombre-dios*, or man-god, offered the model of extraordinarily pious and powerful figures who became so closely identified with a sacred force that they achieved divinity themselves.[7] Together, these two rich traditions provided a cultural context that made María López's claims credible in the eyes of her community and enabled her to exercise the kind of individual power and authority that in normal times was entirely forbidden to women. This chapter, however, will look beyond the exceptional experience of one woman and attempt to cast María's actions in a broader interpretative framework that recognizes the contributions of ordinary Maya women to public life and links the particular social and economic experiences of these women to the causes of the rebellion.

Gender and the Construction of a Moral Economy

The Tzeltal Revolt took place during the decline of Habsburg rule in Central America, a decline marked by a prolonged economic depression, the erosion of royal authority, and bitter jurisdictional disputes among Spanish officials. For Indian communities, these conditions brought heavier tax burdens, more onerous labor obligations, and greater interference with local self-government. In a larger study of the rebellion, I have characterized the impact of these changes as an assault on the Maya moral economy.[8]

This interpretative framework derives from the work of E. P. Thompson and James C. Scott.[9] In an essay on food riots in eighteenth-century England, Thompson linked the material causes of popular unrest to the cultural norms and moral assumptions that infused political discourses within communities and also between local peoples and government authorities. These riots marked a period in the formation of the British state when, as the industrial revolution advanced, government was abandoning paternalist codes of conduct toward the poor, codes that included the regulation of grain markets. Scott took a similar approach in a book on rural rebellions and the impact of colonialism on peasants in twentieth-century Burma and Vietnam. In *The Moral Economy of the Peasant*, he wrote, "How, then, can we understand the moral passion that is so obviously an integral part of the peasant revolts we have described? How can we grasp the peasant's sense of social justice? We can begin, I believe, with two moral principles that seem firmly embedded in both the social patterns and injunctions of peasant life: the *norm of reciprocity* and the *right to subsistence*."[10]

A rich ethnographic literature suggests that principles of reciprocity are rooted in the social life of families and kin groups and then extrapolated and reconfigured at higher levels of the social order.[11] Among peasants, discourses about subsistence also originate in family life, for households and related kin provide the labor that secures food. Because of their roles in the social reproduction of their families, we recognize that peasant women wield influence in the so-called private, domestic spheres of hearth, water hole, and even field.[12] However, scholars have disagreed about the extent to which they exercise power in public domains, where moral principles also are articulated and contested.

Early debates on this issue were largely carried on at the level of abstract theory, and included explorations of the universal subordination of women as well as critiques of colonial state formation and the impact of Western capitalism on "traditional" modes of production.[13] Much of this literature posited that as states became more centralized and production less kinship based, the status of women has invariably declined, and the gap between private and public domains has widened. Subsequent critiques of this premise offered case studies that challenged the paradigm, including work by Irene Silverblatt and Susan Kellogg on gender parallelism in non-Western state systems like Tawantinsuyu in the Andes and Tenochtitlan in central Mexico.[14] Others have argued convincingly that dichotomies such as private/public or informal/formal are rooted in Eurocentric models of social processes and are categories that a priori relegate women's activities to subordinate spheres.[15] As a result, scholars like Jane Fishburne Collier, Sylvia Junko Yanagisako, and John Comaroff have urged transcending these dichotomies by focusing on "social wholes," by (in Comaroff's words) "historical, structural, and cultural analysis of the interconnections between domestic arrangements, relations of gender and class, and systems of production and exchange."[16]

The prominent historian of Spanish America, Steve J. Stern, has attempted just this in a controversial new book, *The Secret History of Gender*. Stern introduces his study as, in part, an inquiry into the "interplay and convergences between gendered understandings and organization of authority at the household and community levels of society and popular understandings and experiences of legitimate and illegitimate authority in general."[17]

This perspective invites us to look for ways in which Maya women may have bridged private and public spheres to contribute to negotiations of a moral economy. First, however, features of the public domain that played a role in this process must be identified. In formal terms, Maya civic life was organized around the activities of four sets of offices: the municipal council, or *cabildo;* the parish positions of *fiscal* (lay assistant to the priest), *maestro de coro* (choirmaster), and sacristan; the cofradías and *alféreces* (sponsors of religious rites; standard-bearers); and the hierarchy of village shamans.[18] All, in one way or another, mediated economic and political relations with Spanish authorities. In turn, these relations were based on principles of limited reciprocity in which the crown recognized (with the exception of the shamans, of course) the legitimacy of local indigenous elites and extended them certain privileges. In return, officeholders did their best to assure order and stability in local villages and organized the payment of tribute and church fees to provincial governors and the clergy. Local support for these officeholders rested on their success in shielding villagers from demands for labor or encroachments on land that jeopardized the security of subsistence. As will be discussed below, they also were required to fulfill a variety of ceremonial obligations that embodied Maya notions of reciprocity between humankind and the supernatural and kept the Maya cosmos in relative balance.

The activities of *brujos* or *nagualistas* (witches, spiritual mediators), as they were called, were obviously different from those of other public figures. Nonetheless, they also were an important element in how Mayas constructed a moral economy. Shamans enabled Maya men and women to fulfill individual and familial ceremonial obligations. They also functioned as agents of social control and as protectors of the norms of reciprocity when recruited to perform acts of "black magic" to avenge breaches of those norms. Female shamans arguably have been the only enduring figures in Maya public life devoted to the particular interests of Maya women.[19] Presumably, then as now, they were especially sought out by women who confronted problems in courtship and marriage or faced a difficult pregnancy and labor.

Of the four sets of public offices, women were eligible to occupy positions of authority only in the latter two. While the few surviving records of colonial cofradías in Chiapas confirm that most sodalities were led by male mayordomos, there were exceptions.[20] In Yajalón, a Tzeltal community that was among the most militant in 1712, the Cofradía of Our Lady of the Rosary named eight "madres" each year to serve alongside the male *prioste* (head officeholder) and his four mayordomos.[21] More notably, the Cofradía of Jesús Nazareno in Yajalón named only female officers, eight madres.[22] Unfortunately, documentation has not been found which shows the extent of formal female participation in cofradías of the period elsewhere in the highlands. However, James Lockhart's study of the Cofradía of the Most Holy Sacrament in seventeenth-century Tula (central Mexico) suggests that such participation may not have been as uncommon in New Spain as once thought. This question deserves real attention, for as Lynn Stephen has shown for modern-day Oaxaca, the opportunity to serve in the cofradías has enabled contemporary peasant women to have a significant impact on community politics, an impact that has diminished as the confraternities have declined.[23] Finally, that women were counted among Maya shamans is documented by Bishop Francisco Núñez de la Vega as well as by reports of ceremonies performed by *brujas* (female witches) during the rebellion.[24]

More central to the theme of this chapter are the ways in which women contributed to public life alongside the formal male-dominated office structures. Though women themselves were forbidden to hold offices in town and parish administration, the men who did were dependent on the economic and social support of their female kin. Marriage marked adult status, but more importantly, wives and daughters enabled civil and religious officeholders to fulfill the ceremonial obligations on which their legitimacy depended. Highly ritualized feasts, food exchanges, and gift giving were essential elements of Maya public culture, as they still are. Recruitment to office was accompanied by bouts of ceremonial drinking and meal taking; Holy Week and saint's day activities were marked by community banquets called *convites;* and, whether in the churches or at hidden mountain shrines, prayers to supernatural benefactors nearly always included symbolic or tangible offerings of food and drink.[25] All of these rituals contributed to the construction of male power, but all were incomplete without the participation of women.

These ritual food exchanges were the central metaphor of the

Maya moral economy.[26] They symbolically linked the private world of hearth and home to the public domain of kinship and community. They unambiguously embodied social imperatives of reciprocity and also concretely linked those principles to the Maya peasant's preoccupation with provisioning food and assuring the collective security of subsistence. Finally, these rites made Maya women instrumental to the construction of public values, even though the rituals themselves put men at center stage and relegated wives and daughters to auxiliary roles on the sidelines.

On the eve of the Tzeltal Revolt, these ceremonial practices were threatened. Poor economic conditions made it increasingly difficult to bear their expense, and royal authorities worried that their high cost left mayordomos bankrupt. In 1690, a royal judge, Joseph de Escals, condemned the feasts and drinking bouts and sought to ban cofradía celebrations altogether.[27] The ban, however, was never enforced. At the same time, Church authorities took steps to regulate cofradía accounts more carefully, and in the process exposed them to visiting bishops looking for new sources of revenue. The pastoral inspection by Bishop Alvarez de Toledo in 1709 depleted cofradía funds by half all across the highlands.[28]

Spanish attacks on the structures that maintained public ceremony struck at the heart of Maya community culture and undermined the contributions of women to that culture. The rebel cult founded by María López held the promise of revitalizing these practices and assuring that principles of reciprocity, together with other dimensions of the Maya moral economy, would be upheld and respected.

Women's Labor in the Tribute Economy

The rebels who rallied to the indizuela's cause came from twenty-one Maya communities in the central and eastern regions of the highlands, the poorest districts in the province.[29] Almost all the pueblos were located in *tierra fría*, or cold country. Here, ecological conditions limited agricultural yields, and distance from the royal highway and the relative absence of Spanish landholdings limited opportunities to supplement subsistence with income from trade and wages from hacienda labor. For the *tzeltales, tzotziles,* and *choles* who lived in these upland valleys, their poverty made the impact of Spanish economic demands especially onerous. At the end of the seventeenth century, with the provincial economy mired in a prolonged depression, those demands were escalating.

During the waning years of Habsburg rule, civil and Church authorities throughout Central America worked to tighten administrative controls within their jurisdictions. In Chiapas, after several decades of neglect, the *alcaldes mayores* (chief magistrates) instituted yearly censuses of Indian tributaries and standardized tribute rates. A series of bishops reformed parish organization to assure more regular visits by the clergy and reconstituted village cofradías to assure that the Mayas would shoulder much of the costs of the reforms. Though these changes further eroded the security of subsistence, by the early eighteenth century they had become routine. In "normal" years, Mayas in the highlands found ways to accommodate them, and in years of plague, locust infestations, or other calamities, colonial authorities usually reconciled themselves to losing revenue until the crisis passed. Other levies, however, were never accepted as routine by Mayas, and these regularly sparked bitter protests because they could not always be anticipated and were difficult for local officials to manage.

One such practice was the failure of regional governors and provincial bishops to pay for the food and labor they required during their periodic visits, a failure that violated royal policy.[30] Another was the *repartimiento de mercancías,* the system of coerced trade whereby alcaldes mayores compelled Mayas to purchase goods at rates well above the recognized fair price, or, conversely, to sell Maya goods at far below their accepted market value.[31] Though a widespread and common practice throughout the colonies, it, too, violated the letter of Spanish law.

Both practices weighed especially heavily on the shoulders of Maya women. The Spanish clergymen and civil authorities who imposed on the hospitality of rural villagers took it for granted that local *indias* (Maya women) would cook and provide other domestic services during their stay. The chickens and eggs these unwelcome guests consumed also were the products of female labor. On occasion, indigenous women must have been subjected to sexual harassment and rape as well.

Maya women figured in the forced exchanges of the repartimientos de mercancías as weavers of cotton cloth (*mantas*) and spinners of thread. In the Tzeltal and Tzotzil towns whose people fought alongside the Cancuc rebels, these products dominated the illicit trade, and here the system seems to have been organized primarily to step up textile production and cheat Mayas out of fair prices. Just what impact these demands had on women's contributions to subsistence cannot be documented, but they must have imposed on time devoted to cultivating vegetable gardens and raising chickens. They also deprived at least some Mayas of opportunities to sell their cloth for cash or barter in Ciudad Real.[32]

As the following testimony reveals, the confiscatory trade in cotton cloth shaped Tzeltal idioms of poverty in the early eighteenth century. María Lopéz's father, Agustín, used these words to describe his own circumstances and those of other rebel leaders: "In this time and occasion they were poor: myself and the others could scarcely put our hands on a single manta."[33] In all the testimony generated by the Tzeltal Revolt, this is the closest any individual Maya came to an explicit commentary on the expropriation of women's labor, but it is eloquent in its simplicity.

However, one of the reprisals brought by rebels against local Spaniards also spoke dramatically, if obliquely, to the abuse of women. In August 1712, twenty-six Spanish, mestizo, and mulatto women were similarly taken at Ocosingo and brought as captives to Cancuc.[34] Their male kin had fled the town, expecting that an advancing rebel army would spare the women and children they left behind, as Mayas had done earlier when Chilón was invaded. This time the rebels reacted with a vengeance; the children were massacred. The women were tormented, taken to Cancuc, and then forcibly "married" to rebel men in the parish church.

Juana Bárbara Gutiérrez, a thirty-year-old mestiza, survived the ordeal to tell this story:

> When Indians from different pueblos entered [Ocosingo], they beat her and, tying her up, imprisoned her in the town jail with the other women. They took her to Cancuc and then entered the new shrine. They made her pray before the images of Nuestra Señora del Rosario, San Juan Evangelista, and San Antonio that were on the altar. They asked for the

rosary around her neck and placed it on a silver cross that was on the altar, and when they returned it, it was a flower taken from the pile at the foot of the cross. Threatening to beat her, they made her listen to masses that the Indians said, sermons that they preached, and processions that they made. One night, at two or three o'clock, the Indian called the vicario de San Pedro entered her lodging and told her that that day she would have to marry an Indian from Yajalón. She resisted, because of the reverence that she had for the Blessed Sacrament and to spare her husband the hurt. They commanded her to undress and tied her to a chair and gave her many lashes. Finding that she lacked the strength to endure the beating and afraid of being killed, she gave her word to marry.[35]

Perhaps fifteen to twenty other captive women were similarly compelled to yield. They seem to have been put to work in the households of the men they were paired with, but whether these "marriages" included sexual exploitation is uncertain. Gutiérrez's account suggests they likely were. Several were murdered in the last days of the revolt, as royal forces advanced on Cancuc.

The testimony of those who survived was solicited by a religious tribunal representing the Holy Office of the Inquisition called to ascertain whether they had fallen into idolatry and heresy while in captivity. The whole proceeding seems to have been highly coded, with a wide range of issues left unexplored, probably in an effort to protect the women's reputations from further damage. Though individual rebels implicated in their murders were held for trial, none of the Mayas who took these women into their households was charged for the abuses they may have committed.

Since other rebel actions revealed a conscious effort to invert the dominant-subservient relationship of Spaniards and Mayas, this whole episode can be read as Maya retribution for the exploitation of their own wives and daughters. How indigenous women may have felt about these marriages can only be imagined. Some may have approached the captives with sympathy and pity; others undoubtedly treated them with the same anger and vengefulness as did their male kin.

Spanish authorities themselves would tacitly acknowledge that the abuse of indigenous women's labor contributed to the outbreak of the rebellion. Included in legislation issued after the pacification was an order that forbade all Spanish travelers, including civil and Church officials, from demanding food and other domestic services when moving about the countryside.[36]

Conclusion

Elsewhere in southern Mexico, abusive repartimientos and illicit trading in cotton textiles also have been linked to indigenous rebellions. Brian R. Hamnett, for example, reported a "Oaxaqueño jacquerie" that began in Tehuantepec in March 1660 and spread west into the Valley of Oaxaca and the Mixteca Alta later the following year.[37] William B. Taylor has suggested that women were conspicuously active in these events, a phenomenon that Margaret A. Villanueva, in particular, has tied to the exploitation of weaving.[38] According to Taylor, "Militiamen called in by Spanish authorities were likely to encounter hundreds of women brandishing spears and kitchen knives or cradling rocks in their skirts."[39] In fact, he argues that fully one-fourth of the 142 cases in Oaxaca and central Mexico he studied for *Drinking, Homicide, and Rebellion* were led by women.

In Chiapas, the notorious riot in Tuxtla in 1693 fits this pattern.[40] A mob angered by the indigenous governor's complicity in the alcalde mayor's repartimientos stoned to death the governor, don Pablo Hernández, and the alcalde mayor himself, Manuel de Maisterra, as well as another royal official, Nicolás de Trejo. Women were prominent in the mob and were among those held for trial afterward.

However, women's participation in the Tzeltal Revolt does not fit the pattern. Taylor's cases, and the incident in Tuxtla, were for the most part small, localized, relatively disorganized acts of violence in the marketplaces and church plazas of rural towns. By contrast, the Tzeltal Revolt was a real war, fought army against army in the style of the wars of conquest, and included skirmishes along the mule paths and trails of the mountains as well as pitched sieges on the outskirts of Maya pueblos. Women likely helped to build the barricades and trenches constructed to hinder Spanish militiamen, but neither Spanish records nor Maya testimony suggest that they comprised a significant portion of the actual rebel fighting force—with the following exceptions. During the last stages of the pacification, as Chamula's parish priest, fray Joseph Monroy, roamed the countryside near San Pedro Chenaló, rumors reached him of a *capitana* (female captain), a former mayordoma at the shrine, leading a rebel band in hiding.[41] Reports from the field indicate that she was actually captured, but she was never identified by name and no further record of her has been found. The only other women singled out for their connection to the rebel army were four brujas brought to Guaguitepeque as the captain general Nicolás Vásquez vainly tried to regroup his troops.[42] They performed ceremonies to enlist supernatural aid but dispersed after five days when they failed.

The economic and social forces that shaped women's activism in the small urban riots that Taylor describes also seem to have been significantly different from those in Chiapas, even though the textile trade and repartimientos de mercancías were important in both regions. In Oaxaca and central Mexico, towns were growing in the period he writes about, and their commercial links to the agricultural hinterland were becoming more complex as wage labor and market participation intensified among indigenous peoples. These developments were altering modes of production associated with an earlier tribute-dependent economy and, presumably, changing gender divisions of labor in rural villages, though this last point has not really been studied. By contrast, the economy of Chiapas was depressed and undercommercialized at the start of the eighteenth century, and here the repartimientos de mercancías cut off Maya women from the few opportunities in commercial markets that existed, leaving more customary modes of production pressured but intact.

These contrasts draw attention to the question of linking women's political participation to their place in household and community systems of production and commerce. In the Oaxaca cases, the collective character of political action among indigenous women may reflect the impact of economic changes that were pulling them away from more customary forms of household and kinship-based labor. In other words, as the regional economy became more commercialized (as more women became sellers in local markets), their consciousness may have been shaped by early experiences of class as well as of gender and ethnicity. Taylor, it should be said, did not hazard such a theory. He simply suggested that "perhaps because men were more often traveling outside the community or working fields several miles from town, more women than men usually took part."[43] However, his comment serves as a reminder that changes in production that altered men's work also could affect patterns of women's political action.

By contrast, in the early eighteenth century, highland Chiapas lacked local markets of similar scale and offered few opportunities for women in commerce, except in the marketplace of Ciudad Real. Though women worked collectively within families and kin groups, they lacked the opportunities for work outside the household that were available to peasant women in other regions. These conditions, then, may have discouraged political action of the kind described by Taylor, or of the kind that took place during the riot in Tuxtla, where local markets among the Zoque were similar to those in Oaxaca.

To explore these apparent contrasts fully, much more work remains to be done on the relationship in both regions between modes of production, market systems, and household structure, on the one hand, and patterns of women's political action and the gendered construction of political discourses, on the other. Such research promises to illuminate the diversity of women's experiences under colonial rule and guard against tempting generalizations that hide that diversity.

11

Work, Marriage, and Status

Maya Women of Colonial Yucatan

Marta Espejo-Ponce Hunt and Matthew Restall

Southeast of central Mexico lies the lowland limestone peninsula of Yucatan. Although the area is one of marginal soil fertility, no surface water, and yearly cycles of dryness, its large and sophisticated indigenous population attracted Spanish settlers, who by 1547 had pacified the Maya and occupied their major centers. The realities of food and tribute production, having always determined the economic relationship of men and women to each other, to their community, and to the larger Maya world, now also dictated the pattern for the establishment of colonial Yucatan. Although the political decentralization of the Maya had hindered their subjugation, the Spaniards found a unit of sociopolitical organization—the *cah*, or Maya municipality—that, like the *altepetl* of the Nahuas of central Mexico, greatly facilitated the profitable imposition of colonial rule.[1]

Before and after the conquest the position of Maya women was largely decided by their role in Yucatan's economy. Indigenous men continued to be responsible for raising the staple crop and for hunting; indigenous women continued to care for their households, to raise domestic animals, to tend their gardens of fruits and vegetables, and to weave the all-important cotton cloth that dressed young and old, poor and rich, and was used in trade. It was this cotton cloth, the single most important item of early colonial trade, that soon became the staple of Maya tribute.[2]

Although Maya men labored to contribute their share of corn to feed the colonists, it was on women producers that the *encomienda* (grant of the right to receive labor or tribute from an indigenous polity) system fell heaviest.[3] In addition, both men and women would contribute their personal labor working in households, building new roads and towns, and transporting goods throughout the peninsula. But when construction work was completed and beasts of burden were introduced to travel the roads, women were still working in households either as periodic labor or on a permanent basis. Thus for most of the colonial period, women were the domestic servants, the concubines, and the main providers of the major cash item of trade. The position of women seems doubly onerous when one considers that the conquest appears only to have exacerbated the unequal status of women in a society that already favored male over female with respect to political authority, family structure, and, to a far lesser extent, inheritance practices.

In a letter of 1589 to the governor of Yucatan, the cah of Tetzal apologized for prior complaints made by the community against their priest, dismissing such protests as *canxectzil y[etel] ch'upulchi,* "tale-telling and women's gossip." The interpreter general's accompanying translation glosses the phrase as *algunos chismes de yndios,* "some Indian gossip."[4] The impression this gives of colonial Yucatec society, that it was structured along racist and sexist lines, is supported by a cursory glance through the archival evidence of the times. Women's names are absent from the lists of the political officers of the Maya *cabildos* (municipal councils), bodies that were themselves subordinated to the Spanish authorities. Female Maya testators disclose less wealth in their wills than their male counterparts, who in turn appear sadly impoverished beside the colonists, whose wills often include many pages of inventory.[5] The singular dependency of the Spanish population of Yucatan on their Maya hosts can make the case for an indigenous population (and women in particular) overburdened with tribute payments, personal service, *obvenciones* (tithes) to the clergy, community taxes, and forced *repartimientos* (labor drafts).[6] Institutional sources of documentation further support a historical perspective that is pessimistic in its assessment of colonial society.

A more complex picture is revealed by delving deeper into the source material, usually farther from Spanish influence; here, just as the indigenous communities are seen actively pursuing their own agendas within (and even oblivious to) the larger colonial context, so too are Maya women witnessed participating actively (even independently) within these communities. The reality of cultural persistence in Yucatan includes Maya women inheriting and bequeathing property, actively participating in interfamily politics, and fulfilling a vital and central socioeconomic role. To offset the above anecdote from Tetzal, we might turn to a significantly late colonial example of the potential difference between Spanish and Maya attitudes toward women: a Maya-language petition of 1804 names eight men and ten women of one indigenous family as owners of a tract of land; the Spanish translation names only the men.[7]

Maya women not only played a crucial role in the preservation of Maya culture, but they acted as key links to Spanish culture. Indigenous women learned Spanish ways, but they also taught their ways and language to many a Spaniard. If Mérida was labeled a *mestizo* (racially mixed) society by the people of Campeche in the latter part of the nineteenth century,[8] it was because the Maya women of Yucatan had been successful in incorporating much of what was theirs into Spanish society. Yucatan by the national period boasted of more than three hundred thousand people who spoke Maya.[9]

The local sources (including close to two thousand extant documents in the native language), the notarial archives, and the parish records tell a story of survival, of compromise, of creative opportunism, and of the manipulation and circumvention of rules and regulations.[10] The indigenous women of Yucatan appear in such records in expected activities typical of their gender and culture, but in situations that illustrate their ability to mitigate the rules of the colonial circumstance. These two approaches to history (the institutional and the biographical-social) are by no means mutually exclusive. The legal and institutional perspective is the point of departure for a description of whole segments of society. Local records, however, provide insight into the functioning of the system and also illuminate those sectors of society—among which indigenous groups *and* women figure prominently—ignored by traditional histories.

The following pages, then, converge on postconquest Maya women from two perspectives, one based on Spanish-language documentation that provides biographical vignettes of indigenous women among Spaniards, the other based on Maya-language records that open a window onto indigenous community society. In both cases Maya women appear as economic agents able to act independently albeit within certain social confines. This chapter thus advances the argument that some Maya women (despite being burdened with particular severity by Spanish colonial demands) seemed to find opportunities for mobility in that gray area between Spanish society in the heart of Mérida and Maya society in the *cahob* (plural of *cah*). Most Maya women, however, remained in an indigenous environment that was largely unaffected in structure by colonial rule. Some examples in the Spanish sources show evidence of indigenous women adapting to a postconquest urban environment. However, inheritance patterns and other information contained in Maya-language wills reveal elements of continuity as well as adaptation; such material is rich enough to enable us to begin reconstructing the daily working life of the Maya woman.[11]

Indigenous Women in the Spanish Community
The Nobility

When the Spaniards arrived in Yucatan, there were no great cities of the size and importance of Tenochtitlan, Texcoco, Azcapotzalco, and others in central Mexico, and thus there were no outstanding urban centers on which to impose the Spanish capital. The great Maya city-states of Chichen Itza, Tulum, Mayapan, and others were reduced in size or abandoned when the Spaniards first set foot on the peninsula. Consequently, there were no dynasties in Yucatan of the stature of the Moteucçoma family and the Mexica nobility, the *cacique* (gubernatorial) class of the Maya being dispersed throughout the various city-states of the peninsula.[12] Nor was there the shortage of women prevalent in central Mexico in 1521, as the Spaniards did not consolidate their position in Yucatan until 1542 to 1547, by which time all the older Spanish men were married, while the younger men soon married the daughters of their elders. As a result, the conquerors and first settlers of Yucatan were an exclusive group almost from the start, concentrating their activities in the Spanish city of Mérida and marrying among themselves.

Some indigenous women married *encomenderos* (encomienda holders) of Yucatan, but they were not native Maya. Two of these women were relations of Moteucçoma, young girls barely twelve years old who accompanied Beatríz de Herrera, wife of Montejo the Elder, when the latter couple entered Yucatan after 1546.[13] Both women married conquistadors of Yucatan. One of Moteucçoma's relations, doña Leonor de la Encarnación, became the wife of Francisco Bérrio. She inherited the encomienda on his death and retired to the newly founded convent of the Concepcionistas in Mérida. The rent from the encomienda became her dowry, and the income helped the nuns for many years.[14] To retain the encomienda, so that it would not be reassigned after she entered the convent, Bérrio's widow remained unprofessed until her death in 1618.[15] The second relation to Moteucçoma, doña Mencia de Moteucçoma, married Cristóbal Lucero. Her progeny endured in upper-class ranks in Mérida, Campeche, and Valladolid for three centuries: her descendants were the family of the Arguelles y Aranda.[16] There is notice of another indigenous woman, Sabina, from central Mexico, a companion to Diego Briceño, a conqueror of Yucatan, who became his second wife. She seems to have been a commoner. Her descendants, if there were any, did not retain title or privileges to the encomienda, which was inherited by Briceño's son by his Spanish wife.[17]

Later on, particularly in the first part of the seventeenth century, some noble Maya women did make alliances with Spaniards, but these men were usually a notch down the ladder in social prestige compared to the conquistadors and first settlers.[18] The marriages were mutually advantageous in that the dowry of a wealthy Indian woman often made it possible for an impoverished Spanish newcomer to enter trade or buy position (see also Pedro Carrasco's discussion of Indian-Spanish marriages in chapter 3). For the woman and her family, the marriage meant entrance into the Spanish world and often into the Spanish power structure. Of particular notice is the marriage of a female member of the Rodríguez family from Dzidzantun, who had taken the name of the conqueror and encomendero

Juan Rodríguez de Sosa. Her husband, the son of a merchant, received enough dowry to purchase a *regimiento* (the office or jurisdiction of the *regidor,* or councilman) in Mérida and eventually lay claim to an encomienda. The father and brother of the bride moved to Mérida, purchased a fledgling *estancia* (private landholding), and were interim *alcaldes* (municipal judges) in the city several times before 1648. In the late seventeenth century one Rodríguez was still functioning in Mérida as a merchant.[19] A similar story is that of doña Inés de Viana, whose family also adopted a Spanish name. She was of the nobility of Motul, just northeast of Mérida in the Ceh Pech district. Her dowry was one of the largest recorded in the early seventeenth century, 1,500 pesos, and it enabled her husband to succeed in trade and to purchase property.[20] Another seventeenth-century marriage was that of María Chaueb and Captain Juan Rodríguez de la Vega. She surely brought him an important dowry, because he figured prominently in the city and their son, Captain Antonio Rodríguez de la Vega, appeared frequently as a merchant in the notarial documents of the late seventeenth century.[21]

Commoners

As may be expected, *macehual* (commoner) women were the most numerous in the city and towns.[22] Through the colonial period large numbers of indigenous women were rotated into the city for personal service—grinders of flour, weavers, wet nurses, and maids—for short periods of one, two, or three weeks at a time. Many stayed on as long-term servants. Eventually, some became independent city dwellers in their own right. It was an advantage to the women to leave the village permanently (they would then be excused from tribute) and an advantage to the Spanish *vecinos* (residents) to have permanent servants who could be relied on to stay indefinitely and be incorporated into their households. Through the local records and in wills, it is possible to discern in time the increasing status of indigenous women in the urban environment.

In 1688, Atanasia de la Cruz, a woman servant, was given some property when her employers left Mérida for Mexico City. Her daughter, Angela de Ulibarri, was apparently fathered by one of the merchant Ulibarris, and although they provided for her and seemed to have cared for her welfare, they did not take the child with them when they left Yucatan. The girl was endowed with a house and lot, and a priest, Bachiller Nicolás Gregorio Carrión, was entrusted with her education. We also know that the priest, on his death, provided amply for Angela. In this case, the daughter of this indigenous woman was then in a position to make a good marriage and to advance further in city society. In a similar situation were Juana Domínguez and her sister, children of Catalina Chable, who were left a city lot and some cash in the will of the merchant Captain Francisco Domínguez, whose adopted and/or illegitimate daughters they presumably were. In the same will Domínguez also provided for another Maya girl, said to be the daughter of a couple who had served him. The girl was to be given a house and lot on reaching majority age. In other words, he had provided all of these young women with a dowry and the chance of a relatively good marriage.[23]

By the second half of the seventeenth century in Yucatan, indigenous women acted as fully capable personae before the law. Neither they nor their Spanish sisters were in fact legally capable, but custom allowed for considerable latitude. Maya women bought and sold property in their own right and were bequeathed property by Spaniards either because of genuine affection or because the latter felt obligated to do so after years of having been served in various capacities. Angelina de la Raya, called "India ladina vecina de Mérida" (Hispanicized Indian resident of Mérida) in the records, sold property next to the church in the *barrio* (suburb) of Santa Ana, one of the indigenous communities, or cahob, immediately surrounding the *traza* (core layout) of Mérida. She was said to have obtained the property through her own efforts. Viviana Hau and her two daughters were provided for in the will of Joseph Fernández Palomino, a storekeeper and petty merchant. She had attended the store for many years while he scoured the countryside buying and selling. Ignacio and Casilda, the children of María Pat, a Maya woman, were given a lot and house to live in by Bachiller Juan de Palma Machuca, because their mother had been a faithful servant and housekeeper. Magdalena Piste was provided for in the will of doña María Bohorques. She was the daughter of the "grandmother" Juliana Piste, who was said to have nursed and helped rear doña María's youngest child, Cristóbal. Similarly, doña Melchora Pacheco left money to her indigenous servant, who looked after her during a prolonged illness. And doña Mencia de Vellorin and doña Thomasa del Granado Baeza left city lots with houses on them, as well as money, for their women servants Andrea Etch and Antonia Tzuc. We learn that the Maya women could alienate the property if they so pleased, because the Spanish women also requested in their wills that they not do so.[24]

Indigenous Women in the Maya Communities

In the Maya communities of rural Yucatan, the impression given by local documentary sources is that by the seventeenth century indigenous women were enjoying a position parallel, although not equal, to the status of Spanish women. As the Spanish presence increased in the *cabeceras* (regional head communities) near the Spanish centers, Maya women availed themselves of whatever opportunities for advancement were there, and their experiences echoed the situation in Mérida and other towns. In the more remote areas, where Spaniards and Hispanicized Indians were seldom seen, Maya women functioned in a strictly indigenous environment. Even here, however, they fully participated in the exchange and bequeathing of property and, through marriage, engaged in the practice of interfamily alliance and the acquisition of land without purchase. Furthermore, the division of labor by gender provided women with a role no less important or dignified than that of their male kin.

Mérida's Indigenous Suburbs and Cabeceras Near Mérida

The five original communities of Tihó, the Maya settlement on which Mérida was founded, survived through the colonial period as suburbs of the Spanish capital. The Spaniards referred to these communities as barrios—indeed, their central plazas were and still are only blocks away from Mérida's own *zócalo* (central square)—but the Maya, despite this proximity to the seat of the colony, continued to call them cahob. And in most respects they were just like the cahob of the Maya countryside, complete with a cabildo of Maya officers. Notarial records for Mérida's suburbs survive in Spanish from the late seventeenth century on, and in Maya from the turn of the eighteenth century on.[25] By this time they had lost their Maya names and were known simply as La Mejorada (the Maya invariably dropped the "La"), San Cristóbal, San Sebastián, Santiago, and Santa Ana (or, more commonly, Santana). Toward the end of the colonial period other documentary evidence of increasing Hispanicization is revealed: more and more Spaniards appear as purchasers of property; growing numbers of Indians have Spanish patronyms; bills of sale start to become notarized in Spanish.

Women feature as an integral part of this pattern of change. On record as property owners, vendors, and purchasers in these communities were Spanish women, Maya women, and women who appear to be indigenous with Spanish patronyms—no doubt reflecting the process of *mestizaje* (racial mixing) that must have been thriving here. In Mejorada in 1770, Josepha Chan bought a house plot, with well and orchard, for ten pesos from her elder brother, Manuel; in 1782, Simona Chan sold a plot in Santiago to Sergeant Carlos Pinto, whose new neighbors included Sebastiana "Pacheca" and "Yliponsia Solisa"; and the following year in San Cristóbal "teudora" Pérez sold a thirty-peso inherited plot that bordered on property owned by her kinswoman "yliponsa" Pérez.[26] Only one of the Pérez women is identified as a *besino*, meaning a Spaniard; the Pacheco and Solís women of Santiago were most likely not considered Spaniards.

This close contact between the two ethnicities was not necessarily typical of late colonial Yucatan. In the colony as a whole indigenous families with Spanish surnames are less apparent after 1650. There seems to have been a greater separation between the city and the countryside with respect to social interaction between Spaniard and Maya. Noble indigenous women were no longer in a position to intermarry with Spaniards. The number of Spanish women in Mérida, Campeche, and Valladolid had increased, and ambitious newcomers had no trouble finding a wife. If the conquest of Yucatan was too late for indigenous women to become the wives of conquerors and first settlers, after the mid-seventeenth century the availability of Spanish women of encomendero and merchant families preempted alliances such as those related earlier in this chapter. There was also the wealth factor. The records do not show the cacique class as especially wealthy, save in terms relative to the average Maya macehual, although the Spaniards in the city and towns did not seem much better off. Gone were the days of 1,500-peso dowries for both indigenous and Spanish women. This worked against previous opportunities for upward mobility among the Maya nobility. Noble-women after 1650 are seen in the cahob rather than in the Spanish-dominated cities and towns, and they functioned in the Spanish world through commerce or by intermarriage with Hispanicized in-dividuals, not Spaniards.

The will of doña María Cristina Chuel, drafted in Mérida in 1692, stated that she was the daughter of don Francisco Chuel and doña Catalina Pat of Dzibikak. She stated further that she had married a nobleman of the cabecera of Samahil, that she was a resident of that community, and that she had no children from her first or subsequent marriages. She had inherited property from her father and also from her first husband, but because it included land, she had given the land to an uncle to tend for her. Just when she decided to place cattle on the land, she did not reveal, but the placing of cattle was done by *acordada*, that is, with formal permission from the authorities to create an *estancia de ganado mayor* (cattle ranch). She had married in Samahil a second time, a *mulato pardo* (mulatto) in the employ of some Span-iard, and after his death she had moved to Mérida. There she had married a petty merchant who had been doing business in Samahil, a Hispanicized person who lived in the city and had a Spanish sur-name. Most probably doña Cristina had met this individual, Manuel de Flores Jorge, when he went to Samahil on business. We suspect that he was not a merchant or a person of status because none of his relatives or friends, who witnessed doña Cristina's will, could sign their names. At the time the will was drawn, this third husband had also died, and doña Cristina's considerable wealth (the estancia, bee-hives, houses, furniture, town lots, gold jewelry, carved statues of saints, silk embroidered *huipiles*, or indigenous dresses) was left to an uncle and to her "entenado" (stepson, or adopted child), a mestizo who was either the child of the third husband or someone doña Cristina had adopted. The land in particular had been willed to the uncle, returning the property to the male line of the Chuel or Pat families in Dzibikak.[27]

Commoner women in the cabeceras were another story. Their activities were normally of a more traditional nature and centered in their cah and its immediate environs. However, they could also be-come involved with Spaniards or Hispanicized individuals in petty commerce, and some formed irregular alliances with them, having children and carrying on business activities for them in the cahob. Marriage in these cases was rare, but the alliances provided the women with some form of status and economic advancement for themselves and their progeny.

The will of Antonio Paredes, read into the notarial records in Mérida, was drawn up in the cabecera of Yaxcaba and was witnessed in Maya by the *escribano* (notary) of that cah. In it Paredes stated that he had been traveling the area of Yaxcaba-Sotuta for many years and that during those years he lived on and off with an Indian woman who attended to business matters for him during his absences. He wished to recognize four daughters, whom he named individually, and to leave to them the bulk of his estate in four equal parts. The girls were to remain with their mother after his death, and she was to administer their belongings until they were of marriageable age. The will spelled out in great detail what Antonio Paredes was leaving to this Maya woman and to each child: monies owed to him by various caciques along the road from Mérida to Valladolid, sheep, horses, beehives, corn, a house and four city plots in Mérida, a house and village plot in Yaxcaba. He did not seem to feel the need to marry the Maya woman even at the time of his death, but he left her most of the cash, the debts owed to him by certain caciques, and two city plots in Mérida. In this case a commoner indigenous woman, through an irregular alliance, had furthered her status in both Maya and Spanish societies and had become the owner of real property and other wealth in the capital city.[28]

Similar to the preceding story, but probably more common, was the situation of Luisa Na, a Maya woman from Dzemul, a cah in the northern coastal district. She was legally married to the mestizo petty merchant (*tratante*) Joseph de Escobar, and had four girls by him. When he took ill in Mérida, where he had been on business, he had his will drawn up by the local escribano. Through this document we know that he was a reasonably successful tratante. He had already endowed one of his daughters with 150 pesos in silver, on her marriage to his business partner, Tomás Palomo. The other three girls were minors and were to inherit the bulk of his estate on their majority. However, his wife was to raise the girls and administer their property, and she benefited from an extensive list of goods owed to him that amounted to several hundred pesos in silver and other merchandise such as cotton, salt, canoes used in trade, and beasts of burden.[29]

The Cahob

In the interior, at a distance from Mérida and its port of Campeche, Maya society was less subject to influence from everyday Spanish activity. By getting away from the core area where Spanish influence was the strongest and by moving beyond the Spanish-language sources that have been the traditional basis of Yucatan's historiography and analyzing the abundant but largely untouched notarial material in Maya, we can acquire some insight into the status of women in Maya society.

It seems unlikely that the role of women in postconquest cah society represented a significant change from pre-columbian female status. There is possible evidence of a matrilineal descent system equal to the patrilineal in the Maya term for noble, *almehen*, which includes both the word for a woman's child (*al*) and that for a man's son (*mehen*), similar to the Spanish term *hidalgo;* the pre-hispanic naming system also gave equal importance to the female line as represented in the matrilineal *nal* (maternal) name—which was replaced after the conquest by a non-lineal Christian name. The operation of matrilineal descent does not seem to be fundamentally different from colonial era inheritance patterns; the evidence of hieroglyphic texts, to the degree that they can currently be read, indicates that female participation in society and politics was active but circumscribed by gender-specific roles—just as it was after the conquest.[30]

Moreover, there is colonial era evidence that the primary social unit of the Maya, the family, was a patriarchy. Maya society contained a structure of representation, whereby the *batab* (the cah governor, called a cacique by the Spaniards) represented the officers beneath him and by extension the people of the community. When a Maya document begins *ten cen batab,* "I who am *batab*," it is thereby defined as a cah document. Likewise the head of a family represented its members—the collective use of the pronominal first-person singular among the Maya today has been well documented.[31]

Patriarchal representation functioned not only in speech and in official action but also legally—in terms of land tenure. Although women are recorded as buying, owning, and selling land, as well as inheriting and bequeathing it in wills, a woman is never described as the owner of a *col* or *kax* (field or forest) when descriptive reference is being made to that land by a neighbor. For example, a Maya testator from Ixil locates a plot of kax by naming its neighbors: "Francisco Canul to the south, Manuel Cutz to the east," and so forth.[32] Just as Francisco Canul is not physically to the south—unless he happens to be working his plot—neither is he the sole owner of the kax; he represents it, linguistically and perhaps legally, in his role as patriarchal representor of his family. Land description by the colonial era Maya was notably indigenous in style and technique, so it seems likely that its patriarchal implications were not a postconquest innovation.[33]

The same can be said of the pursuit of official cabildo politics in the colonial cah, many aspects of which were Spanish in form but also conformed to traditional indigenous practice, including the exclusion of women from office. Women had no role in the cabildo, or within the local religious hierarchy, and were thus illiterate, as only access to the offices of escribano and *maestro* (teacher) afforded literacy.[34]

Having said this, it is clear that Maya women played a key sociopolitical role in the workings of marriage alliances among the indigenous nobility. After the conquest the power an individual could exercise within Maya society was determined not only by one's record of political office but also by a collusion of other factors that included individual and family wealth as well as one's connection to traditionally powerful families.

Pasquala Matu is an example of a well-off and well-connected Maya woman in colonial Yucatan. She was one of the wealthiest women in Ixil at the time of her death in 1766, when she left behind some land, two wells, and some forty items of clothing.[35] The Matu were one of the dozen most important patronym groups in Ixil at this time.[36] A Juan Matu served as an executor the year following Pasquala's death and in 1768 was the senior regidor on the cabildo. To be an executor of a will was not to hold office, but only men of importance (usually noblemen) were chosen. Pasquala's executors included don Andrés Pech; the Pech were the preconquest dynastic rulers of the area.[37] Pasquala's husband, Sebastián Yam, was also an executor the year his wife died. The Yam family was represented on the cabildo too: by 1777 they had an alcalde and a regidor, and ten years later two more Yam in the same posts. A third family made up the triple alliance that would have been part of Pasquala Matu's support network: the family of her mother, Luisa Coba. The Coba were a powerful Ixil patronym group, attaining the number two office of *teniente* (lieutenant) on the 1766 cabildo, filling alcalde and regidor posts other years, and revealing considerable landed wealth in the testamentary record. Two of Pasquala's four sons married women named Coba. Because it was strictly taboo in Maya society to marry someone of the same patronym, this was as close as one could get to keeping it in the family.

Through the will of Pasquala's cousin-in-law, Matheo Matu, who died the previous year, we can extend this network even further. Pasquala's third son married a Couoh—not an unimportant connection either—and we find that cousin-in-law Matheo's mother was also a Couoh. If these four families (Matu, Yam, Coba, and Couoh) were a marital alliance group, they had cabildo representation every year from 1765 to 1769, the five years covered by Ixil's extant testaments. (See figs. 11.1 and 11.2.) The wills show other marriages within these four families, as well as incidences of adjacent landholdings. Of course, there are a limited number of Maya patronyms, and alliances were not so tight as to make every marriage a strategic or political one. Yet there is a clear pattern in Ixil revealing several alliance groupings, above which were the Pech, who seem to be allied to almost everyone.[38]

There is evidence of a similar process at work in seventeenth-century Cacalchen, a cah also within the old province of Ceh Pech. To judge by a run of thirty-four wills from 1646 to 1679, two of the wealthiest families in the cah were the Couoh and the Uitz.[39] The two patronyms in the corpus that are instantly recognizable as old ruling dynasties are Pech and Cocom. In the will of Cecilia Couoh we find that these four names come together. Cecilia's sister is married to a Pech; she herself is married to a Cocom. Of her two daughters, one is married to a Uitz. The other daughter is married to an Yuiti; although no Yuiti testaments have survived, the patronym appears among the lists of cabildo officers and executors along with Couoh, Uitz, Pech, and Cocom. Not only is Cecilia a vital part of the family alliance, but her individual wealth—which included twenty bee-

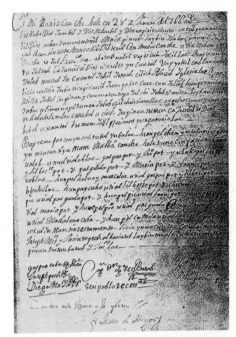

Fig. 11.1. Will of María
Canche, written by Pablo
Tec, notary of Ixil, 1766.
TI: 12, fol. 7r. Colección
Carrillo y Ancona,
Mérida, Yucatan.

hives, two pieces of land, and a horse—indicates that she was no
pawn of a male-dominated network, but an active participant in her
own right.

By looking further at the evidence of Maya-language testaments,
in particular by analyzing inheritance patterns, we gain some insight into the socioeconomic role played by all Maya women, wealthy
and poor alike. Perhaps the primary defining feature of gender roles
in cah society was the division of labor. The evidence from the cah of
Ixil suggests that men were more likely to work away from the *solar*,
or house plot, tending the *milpa* (land under cultivation) or cutting
the kax, whereas women tended to work within the confines of the
solar. This is demonstrated in a number of ways by data drawn from
some two hundred eighteenth-century wills from Ixil and Tekanto,
cahob in the Ceh Pech region, and from Ebtun, a Maya community
outside Valladolid.[40]

First, women were twice as likely to bequeath a solar as they

Fig. 11.2. Will of Luisa Tec, written by Marcos Poot, notary of Ixil, 1767. *TI:* 56, fol. 27v. Colección Carrillo y Ancona, Mérida, Yucatan.

were a parcel of kax, whereas men were marginally more likely to leave kax to their heirs. Because recipients of both solars and kax were just as likely to be male as female—or, most likely, a mixed-gender sibling combination—the implication is that during the course of a lifetime land gravitated into the hands of the gender that worked it. In other words, if the sons and daughters of a testator all jointly received a solar and a parcel of kax, for their wills to adopt a typical pattern the kax must in time be considered the sons', and the solar the daughters'. One way in which this might work is via marriage, with a woman's kax interests passing into her husband's hands and a man's solar share passing into his wife's control. What is significant, then, is not so much that there were patrilineal tendencies in the inheritance of workable land outside the solar but that women were undoubtedly a part of that land tenure system. Indeed, in Ebtun men and women displayed no land preference to either sex.[41]

Second, most of the flora and fauna willed in Ixil were situated on the solar. Although the men appear to have the edge in terms of ownership of orchards, trees, and vegetable gardens, note that every single bequest of such property by male testators went to a wife, daughter, or both. Likewise the majority of bequests of beehives, which would have been located at the back of the solar as they are today, went to wives and daughters. The others went to sons—who would eventually, if not already, have their own wives and daughters to tend to the family's apicultural interests. In Tekanto, too, there was a decidedly matrilineal bias to beehive inheritance. In Ebtun, however, there was no gender preference shown in the bequeathing of hives and related equipment. Perhaps this was because the primary economic activity on the solar was apiculture, apparently to the complete exclusion of arboriculture and the virtual exclusion of cattle raising, thus producing greater male participation.

Of the many variations of livestock, only two—pigs and chickens—would not leave the solar (with their owners at least) save for the purpose of being sold. Significantly, the only mention of these creatures occurs in wills by women. As for other types of livestock, the female ownership record is poor: few women in Ixil owned horses or mules, and fewer still owned cattle (none in Ixil and Ebtun wills). It is tempting to conclude that these animals were therefore the preserve of men. But when we look at bequest patterns, we see that horses and mules were almost twice as likely to go to female heirs (more than twice if we include wife-with-children) than to males, and with cattle the odds were even. Livestock was presumably seen as an effective means of support for a widow.[42] Still, by the time these women drew up their wills, the animals were in male hands. In other words, horses and cattle *were* ultimately a male preserve. Once in female hands, cattle were consumed during the owner's lifetime, and horses were passed on by daughters to their husbands (no doubt often as dowries) and hired out by widows before being left to mostly male family members.

Third, if we accept that, as a general rule, only men labored in the field and forest, we would expect to find only men owning the appropriate tools and such tools to be ubiquitous among the wills of such peasant farmers. Sure enough, not a single tool is mentioned by any of Ixil's or Ebtun's female testators. And about half the male testators have at least one of five tools, the common ones being a machete and ax. Moreover, when it comes to men bequeathing tools, they are left to sons, only being given to daughters when no male heirs are mentioned. The single exception to this is the case of Pasqual Huchim,[43] who is unusual in that he appears to be very young. He leaves three small children in the care of his parents; he has debts, he has no solar of his own, and his two daughters are presumably still unmarried. Pasqual's will provisions are thus consistent with the primary inheritance pattern of the postconquest Maya, that of *cetil*, or the even distribution of property to all heirs, for his meager goods are bequeathed as equally as possible—a bed to his wife, a blanket to his son, a machete to one daughter, and an ax to the other. He may also have been concerned to provide each daughter with a male object of value to bring into marriage.

The fourth way in which division of labor by gender is shown in wills from Maya communities is the evidence of cloth and clothing. Ixil women bequest proportionately four times as many such items as do men. One woman, the aforementioned Pasquala Matu, is particularly wealthy in this respect, listing forty items of cloth and clothing in her will. Her pool of heirs, five men and five women, was only slightly larger than average, so there can be no doubt that Pasquala was a businesswoman, manufacturing and/or trading in clothing— especially as she dies with eleven complete male outfits (eleven shirts and eleven trousers) and five complete female outfits (five huipiles and five slips). Similarly, Felipa Couoh of Ebtun leaves behind four clothing items as well as two large pieces of cloth and six smaller ones.[44] No doubt much of the weaving done by Maya women was to fulfill tax quotas, as it was on the shoulders of the women that the *manta* (tribute blanket) burden fell, but there is no record of tribute products including Maya apparel.

Of all cloth and clothing items bequeathed by men in Ixil, eight-tenths are male items such as shirts, trousers, and cloaks. Only a few items of female clothing are willed by men, and these under particular circumstances. Bernardino Cot, a father whose wife has died, wills a dress and a slip, which he describes as being *canan* (guarded or looked after). He leaves the clothing in the care of his daughter-in-law, to be passed on to her daughter, as requested in the will of Bernardino Cot's late wife.[45] In other words, special circumstances aside, men own and leave to their sons male items of cloth and clothing. Women, however, own and leave a wide range of such goods pertaining to both sexes. This implies that women are not only responsible for washing clothes (one female testator from Ixil leaves a washing bowl), but also for making them, a suggestion strengthened by the fact that two items that appear in women's wills—yarn and lengths of cloth—are not mentioned in men's. Unfortunately, there is no mention in Maya documents of weaving equipment, as there is in the Nahuatl wills from Culhuacan.[46]

The overall gender balance of inheritance patterns for male donors in Ixil is roughly level. Sons do benefit more than daughters (by 30% to 18% of all recipients), but if we divide recipients strictly by sex, adding wives to the scale (21%), women come out on top. This compares tidily with equivalent data from the wills of Tekanto: sons constitute 29 percent of all recipients, daughters 20 percent, but wives come in with 11 percent to tip the scales back. In Tekanto there was a tendency to bypass daughters in favor of grandchildren, of both sexes in even proportions, thereby roughly maintaining the gender balance.[47] A specific example from Cacalchen illustrates well the gender-balance pattern: Alonso Couoh left behind fifty beehives, of which he willed twenty-five to his son, twenty to his wife, and five to his daughter.[48] The figures for Ixil's female donors correlate closely with those from Tekanto. Women tend to favor female kin, although in Ixil this is largely because a high proportion of female movables consists of women's clothing. Then if husbands are added to sons, the gender balance is approximately restored: this is true for all of the cahob studied.

There is one other aspect of the division of labor that is unrelated to inheritance patterns: reproductive (as opposed to productive) relations. Only women could bear and nurse children, and as women worked in or near the home, responsibility for preteens must have also been theirs. By computing the numbers of children mentioned by testators and using samples from different decades, we derive a statistical suggestion that from the mid-seventeenth century to the end of the colonial period the number of surviving Maya children more than doubled to 4.2 per testator.[49] We have no information on infant mortality, but this figure obviously represents a minimum number, and, by extension, much work for the Maya mother.

A key aspect of the female role presented by the evidence above has been her relationship to her husband. Via her husband she is connected to the primary social unit of Maya society, the family, and from there to the power politics of the primary sociopolitical and geographical unit of that society, the cah. The implication is twofold, first, that a woman depended on her husband, and second, that without the institution of marriage, a woman's position was severely weakened. This was not necessarily the case, as this chapter has shown, and as the following example illustrates. A testator of Cacalchen, Ana Xul, in using her will to draw up an accounting of her finances, recorded for posterity the fact that she was functioning as a regional bank; at the time of her death in 1678 she had at least a dozen debtors from at least three cahob, and she left behind a small fortune in cloth and clothing. Ana was married, but this was clearly *her* business.[50]

As for women without husbands, widows do not seem to have been economically disadvantaged, and unmarried women received property more or less evenly with their brothers, property that could be used to support them should they not get married. Nor was a woman necessarily disadvantaged by an extramarital relationship with a man. Pedro Mis of Ixil provides in his will for a woman and her child, both of whom he claims to have adopted. It is clear that the woman is his mistress: Pedro Mis's wife is still alive, and the mistress's child has his mother's name; there is no question of charity, as the woman was a Pech; and the use of "adoption" to cover extramarital relationships occurred likewise among the Nahuas of central Mexico. Pedro Mis's wife is his chief beneficiary, but he leaves his mistress a solar and the bulk of his estate goes to his illegitimate—and only—son. Another Ixil testator, Juan de la Cruz Coba, fails to mention his father's name, as was the custom in that cah, and bears his mother's patronym. If he was illegitimate, it is significant that his will shows him to be a wealthy man by Ixil standards, with some of that wealth inherited from his mother.[51]

One advantage that community women had over Maya women who had moved into the fringes of Spanish society was the protection of the cah cabildo. This body did not record on paper its adjudications of local disputes, but some notes written by Ebtun's senior officer in 1824 imply that in Maya society the private mistreatment of women was considered a public concern, and unacceptable moreover. In that year Ignacio Camal was jailed for twenty-four hours "for beating his wife while he was drunk," and Buenaventura Cutis was thrown in jail on two separate occasions for wife abuse and for beating a second woman.[52]

The Maya concepts of community and representation meant that the individual Maya enjoyed access to the opportunities of the colonial legal system via the authority that his or her cah cabildo had within that system. This included the benefits of some of the documents already discussed, such as wills and bills of sale. But it also allowed for the presentation of petitions and grievances—without prejudice to gender. Thus the cabildo could come to the rescue of the women of the cah as a whole. In 1589, for example, Tixmeuac complained that their priest had been refusing to confess women unless they "give themselves to him . . . and recompense him sinfully."[53] Or the community officers might defend individuals. For example, the 1811 cabildo of Ebtun drew up a notarized complaint on behalf of Valentina Un, whose daughter had suffered an injury to her arm at the hands of doña Rafaela Rosado when in the kitchen of don Pedro Canton.[54] In the colonial environment Valentina's daughter was endangered, but her connection to the Maya world gave her recourse via the cah authorities to—ironically—Spanish law.

A final anecdote from the archives is instructional. "As for my daughter, Agustina Yam," saya Marta Mis in her will of 1769, "I've left her nothing, because she does nothing on my account, as my lord the Batab and the magistrates well know; she has no shame, that one!"[55] Marta is an independently wealthy woman, but her chastising of her daughter implies an expectation of, perhaps even a need for, gender solidarity, and in the end she must turn to the all-male officers of the cabildo to legitimize her complaint.

Conclusion

Women could and did gain and maintain status in colonial Maya society, but that status was in many ways defined and delineated by gender. Assigned specific roles, women were denied equal opportunity or access to certain areas of social, economic, and political activity. Yet being female was not necessarily a handicap. Women were illiterate, but so were all but two or three men in each Maya municipality or cah. Women were denied political office, but most offices were a pecuniary disadvantage. One's fate in Maya society was more likely to be predetermined by the patronym and economic level into which one was born than by one's gender. That is not to say that gender differentiation guaranteed equality, but neither did it necessarily amount to exploitation, and among a people whose survival depended on an unstable climatic environment, it was at least a source of social stability.

The information presented above on the labor of Maya women implies that life was all hard work—raising children and animals, tending the house plot, weaving cloth—and that this work was aggravated by the demands of colonial rule, especially in an area where cloth products were not replaced by pecuniary tribute as in central Mexico. Yet if Maya women in many ways suffered a double disadvantage in colonial Yucatan, the documentary record portrays them not as victims but rather as survivors. As a scholar of postconquest Nahua society has pointed out, "the conquest opened up new opportunities for Indian women."[56] Creatively, often opportunistically, Maya women pursued upward mobility into the ranks of Spanish society, establishing marital or illicit liaisons with colonists. They also purchased property and acquired for their children the material rewards of decades of domestic service.

Within their own communities Maya women likewise sought to improve their lot through hard work and the skilled management of property and business—from weaving to beekeeping to banking— and through the manipulation of interfamily politics. It has been suggested that indigenous female access to land tenure, inheritance, and exchange may have been broadened in central Mexico by postconquest demographic decline; whether or not this was true in Yucatan, Maya women clearly enjoyed such access even in the late eighteenth century at a time of population growth.[57] In short, the Maya woman of Yucatan was not a passive object of male action but an active participant—an actress in her own right—in the social drama of Maya life.

Northern Mexico

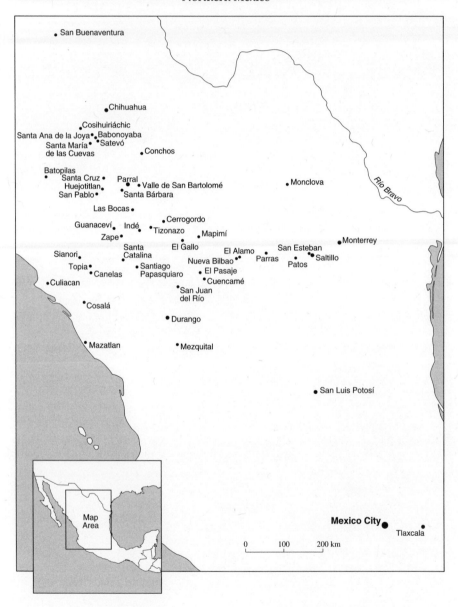

San Buenaventura

Chihuahua

Cosihuiriáchic

Santa Ana de la Joya • Babonoyaba
Santa María • Satevó
de las Cuevas

Conchos

Batopilas
Santa Cruz • Parral
Huejotitlan • • • Valle de San Bartolomé
San Pablo • Santa Bárbara

Monclova

Río Bravo

Las Bocas •

Cerrogordo

Guanaceví • Indé
Zape • Tizonazo
Mapimí

Monterrey

Sianori •
Santa
Catalina
El Gallo
El Alamo
San Esteban

Topia •
Nueva Bilbao • Parras
Saltillo
Canelas
Santiago
Papasquiaro
El Pasaje
Patos

Culiacan •
Cuencamé

San Juan
del Río

Cosalá •

Durango

Mazatlan •
Mezquital

San Luis Potosí

Map
Area

Mexico City •
Tlaxcala

0   100   200 km

12

Double Jeopardy

Indian Women in Jesuit Missions of Nueva Vizcaya

Susan M. Deeds

Everyone knows that the Tarahumaras are an uncivilized class of people; even those who are Christian are ignorant of most of the dogmas of our religion. Therefore they have absolutely no knowledge or understanding of the gravity of their crimes, or of the penalties for them. . . . [In this case] she was just this ignorant not only because of her race but also because she is a woman.[1]

The above passage from the proceedings of a late colonial criminal case of husband murder in Chihuahua is one of the very few direct references to the behavior of Indian women that I have encountered in many years of archival research on the transformations wrought by Spanish intrusion among five Indian groups—Acaxees, Xiximes, Conchos, Tepehuanes, and eastern Tarahumaras—in the seventeenth and eighteenth centuries. Their territories in the Sierra Madre Occidental of northern Durango, southern Chihuahua, and eastern Sinaloa became part of the New Spanish province of Nueva Vizcaya. If trying to recover any Indian voice has been problematic in the case of these nonliterate peoples represented almost totally by outsiders in the written record, then finding the voices of native women has been especially difficult.[2] The following (1) summarizes a sparse documentary record concerning native women in Nueva Vizcaya and (2) analyzes in depth a single case (but one with possibly broad implications) that reveals a good deal about the ways in which Indian women were perceived by the dominant society and suggests strategies for examining the differential impact of colonization on women and men.

Elsewhere I have looked at the effects of Spanish colonialism on indigenous organization of production, labor, land tenure, and demography.[3] I have also examined Indian responses to the impositions of the Jesuit mission system—which ranged from catastrophic population decline to rebellion and to subtler forms of accommodation and resistance.[4] Of the five groups mentioned above, the Acaxees, Xiximes, and Conchos disappeared altogether by the end of the colonial period. Outcomes across and even within groups varied considerably, but the efforts by subordinated peoples to retain certain elements of autochthonous culture were universal.[5] Women, as well as men, were active agents in the perpetuation of shared cultural memories and religious values. Counterhegemonic codes (although constantly evolving and transforming) have been crucial to the survival of Tepehuanes and Tarahumaras.[6] What clues will help us to understand how men and women contributed to the persistence of values and habits that were contrary to Spanish norms? One avenue of inquiry is to look at gender roles in ritual activities; another is to examine the ways in which colonization affected household organization and the sexual division of labor. In pursuing these questions, one must carefully probe the archival record. Although colonial officials steeped in patriarchal and hierarchical values—and especially Jesuits proscribed in their intercourse (in a societal as well as a sexual context) with women—were not inclined to say much at all about them, Indian women do appear in judicial records, population counts, parish records, and reports of economic activities, where they survive. Keeping in mind the trap of dichotomizing formal/informal or public/private spheres,[7] what can gendered labor systems tell us about the construction of indigenous communities and cultural reproduction?

To answer that question—and to understand the effect of missionization on gender roles—one would have to know first what the sexual division of labor looked like in these societies before contact. Scholars disagree about the nature of sociopolitical organization in these groups before the late sixteenth century. The debate centers on population densities. Some revisionists argue that denser, more stratified agricultural and trading societies were common in the Mexican northwest on the eve of contact. Therefore, they say, the conventional view propounded by Edward Spicer and others which asserts that these were *ranchería* societies—dispersed, egalitarian, and heavily dependent on hunting and gathering to supplement a more haphazard agriculture—only applies to the aftermath of disorienting socioeconomic transformations induced by catastrophic effects of Old World diseases that preceded sustained contact by Europeans themselves.[8] Although the revisionist view may have some merit in the case of Acaxees, Xiximes, and Tepehuanes, the Tarahumaras probably conformed closely to Spicer's description. In either case, women would have been involved in agricultural tasks, but perhaps to a greater degree in the ranchería societies where hunting and gathering were at least as important as agriculture.

Regardless of the merits of this controversy about the late fifteenth and early sixteenth century, it is possible to sketch a composite picture of the division of labor in Sierra Madre groups by the late sixteenth century when Spaniards began sustained penetration into these territories. There was considerable complementarity in productive activities. Both men and women cultivated corn, beans, and squash; gathered mescal and other plants; and transported goods and belongings between shifting ranchería locations. Men exclusively were hunters, and, given the frequency of intertribal warfare, they were also warriors and raiders. Women were responsible for food preservation, preparation, and distribution; weaving; pottery making; and child rearing.[9] Females and males inherited equally from both mother and father. Kinship was reckoned bilaterally, and polygyny was practiced, although it was most common among wealthier males. Marriage partnerships were not immutable. For example, since Tarahumara males and females who were not kin could not interact, partners did not have the opportunity to get to know one another before marriage. Therefore, it was not uncommon for people to marry several times before finding a suitable partner.[10] Abortion was also practiced.[11]

Ritual roles are more difficult to ascertain. Although there is evidence of female shamans, most ritual specialists seem to have been men and the office hereditary. Women were active participants in the ceremonies preceding and following warfare. According to Jesuit accounts of Xixime warfare, for example, young women were central to martial ritual. During battle, a young virgin would fast in a cave. A defeat of her group's warriors signified her lack of virtue, and she was banished. But in victory, the returning warriors presented her with the head of one of their victims. After whispering endearments to this symbolic husband, she led other women in celebratory dancing with this and other severed heads, a prelude to ritual feasting on the victims' bodies.[12] Other communal rituals, which also involved the participation of both sexes, focused on ensuring balance and harmony in the universe and material survival through warfare and agriculture. In the case of the Tarahumaras, the consumption of fermented mescal and maize beer (*tesgüino*) in celebrations that included ritual dancing also occurred around communal projects, including clearing, planting, harvesting, and construction.[13] The prominence of warfare seems to have conferred more privileged status on men who accumulated prestige based on military prowess and bravery, and women seem increasingly to have been the objects of raids by enemy groups in the late prehistoric period.[14] Does this practice signify that women were highly valued for their potential productive and reproductive capacity, or that they were simply the objects of exploitation for these purposes? Was this a long-standing practice, or the early result of the particularly high mortality of women and infants in epidemics? One could ask many more questions in trying to assess the degree to which these societies were stratified by gender before contact. There is little doubt that a gender hierarchy existed in political and ritual functions. At the same time, the contributions of women to the economic maintenance and reproduction of the household and community were highly valued.

In what ways were these gendered patterns affected by Spanish colonization? The most obvious changes were effected by several features of the Jesuit mission regime: the curtailment of intertribal warfare, the introduction of livestock, the intensification of agriculture, forced settlement (*reducción*) in villages with a hierarchy of male officials, and the insistence on monogamy. Spanish imperialism deemed the latter two introductions crucial to controlling colonial subjects and delegated the regulation of sexual, conjugal, and domestic life to the clergy. The attempted imposition of Spanish cultural norms and Christian religious values met a range of responses that varied across time, place, and gender.

The reorganization of production had direct consequences for the sexual division of labor. The intensification of agriculture near mission villages and the introduction of livestock, especially sheep, tended to move agricultural labor toward a primarily male sphere while the time-consuming task of herding became the preserve of women and children.[15] Men hunted and primarily women gathered, although these activities became circumscribed as the non-Indian population increasingly encroached on wilderness areas (monte). Forced draft labor (repartimiento) took men away from mission villages to work rotations in Spanish mines and haciendas. Sometimes their wives accompanied them, but often women stayed behind to tend their fields (milpas).[16] Colonial demands often necessitated a practical flexibility in the allocation of tasks. Women continued to perform the household chores related to food preparation and cloth making. In fact, their involvement in certain productive activities expanded—particularly in providing personal domestic service to Spaniards and in textile making.

While women's work probably increased overall as a result of these changes, their participation in Spanish-sanctioned ritual activities and community decision making was minimal. Males were appointed to perform religious duties as catechists, sacristans, and overseers of other areas of church affairs. The Jesuit-imposed hierarchy of village officials (governors, lieutenants, and various enforcers of new rules) excluded women and permitted some males to benefit disproportionately from missionary gift giving as well as from petty trading. These male officials also had greater access to mission resources.[17] The new political regime provided a means for males to acquire distinction, perhaps counterbalancing the loss of warfare as an avenue to prestige, and it had the potential to disrupt traditional pressures toward equalization of distribution. The dependence of nuclear families on missionary gift giving as well as their obligations to mission agriculture subverted indigenous systems of labor reciprocity. Although both men and women succumbed to European-introduced diseases, women of childbearing age, along with children, were at particularly high risk during epidemics.[18]

The degree to which native men were influenced by the Jesuits' depreciation of women is not clear, but there are indications that they valued women's productive activity highly. At the same time, Indian men seemed to accept readily the notion of women's obedience to their husbands or at least their presumed timidity or shyness. That this belief had precontact antecedents is reinforced by the following statement attributed by Jesuits to some Tarahumaras who refused conversion. Taunting male compatriots who refused to join them in rebellion against the Spaniards, the rebels reportedly asked them "if the Spaniards were their husbands."[19] Indian men protested the abuse of their women by Spanish conquerors and settlers, especially rape.[20] Contemporary observations by Jesuits noted the infrequency with which Tarahumaras used corporal punishment to correct misdeeds: social control was imposed mainly through public sermons by elders. Yet the missionaries also observed that violence and adultery were most likely to take place during drinking parties.[21] Furthermore, the precontact pattern of raiding for women does not suggest that Indian women had enjoyed an environment that was secure or free from rape and physical abuse. Did such mistreatment increase or abate as Spaniards tried to impose their will? One can speculate that the Spanish example, whereby Spanish men not only escaped punishment for abusing Indian women but also were allowed to act with considerable impunity in using force to control their own women, did not serve to ameliorate conditions for indigenous women.[22]

How did Tepehuan and Tarahumara women respond to the changes wrought by contact? Were female strategies different from male strategies in dealing with cultural upheaval? Let me mention some patterns that emerge—at the risk of totalizing the experiences of very diverse Indian women. Both Tepehuanes and Tarahumaras revolted against Spanish rule within a generation of its imposition. I have treated these first-generation revolts elsewhere as millenarian responses to the cataclysmic changes induced by disease and the Spanish demands for labor.[23] Although there is evidence that the rationale for these revolts (by the Tepehuanes in 1616 and the Tarahumaras at midcentury and in the 1690s) came from precontact ritual specialists, a few of whom were women, and that women participated in the preparation and hoarding of supplies before the revolts, in no case were women the publicly visible proponents or leaders. This contrasts with studies of later village revolts in Mexico where women played more instrumental roles (see also Robert Haskett's discussion of female activists in chapter 6).[24] After these first-generation rebellions failed to expel the Spanish invaders, Tepehuanes and Tarahumaras sought other options. Many fled to remote, inaccessible areas in the Sierra Madre Occidental where the Spaniards had little incentive to pursue them.[25] Those who could not exercise this option (or did not choose to) resorted to subtler combinations of resistance and accommodation to the colonial system. We are all familiar with the kinds of tactics that have been described as weapons of the weak: foot-dragging, dissimulation, feigned ignorance, pilfering, and clandestine ritual celebrations.[26] When it came to evasive tactics, women had some advantages. For one thing, their infrequent contact with Jesuit priests could be justified within the context of Spanish and Catholic morality, which prescribed that women should remain as much as possible within the protected environment of the house and away from the dangers of the outside world (and their own latent sexuality). There is a parallel in contemporary Tarahumara society in which women are strictly enjoined against interacting with outsiders.[27] Also, as primary caregivers to children, they had high potential for transmitting counterhegemonic ideologies across generations.

Missionaries complained that few women confessed and stepped up their efforts to concentrate on converting children (often by boarding them away from parents in the missions).[28] At least in the early years of missionization, women were more likely to present obstacles to conversion than to serve as cultural brokers. The Christian practice of confession was a problem for Indians everywhere, but the emphasis on disclosing sexual sins tended to further discourage female confession.[29] This is related to women's active participation in the ritual drinking and dancing (tesgüinadas) that continued in spaces away from the missions. Jesuits tried with varying degrees of success to put an end to these "demonically inspired lascivious and drunken spectacles" that promoted "indolence, incest, and idolatry."[30] They harshly condemned women's participation in such activities as shamefully wanton and lewd. This is, of course, a common theme in European writings about colonial women that use sexual images as metaphors in justifying policies of segregation and exclusion.[31] In eroticizing the cultural differences of the other, Spaniards constructed a superior moral space for themselves.

In general terms, Spanish colonial society held that all women were weaker than men in moral terms and less resistant to temptation. Yet female virtue was central to the Spanish concept of male honor since a man could be dishonored by the public disclosure of the sexual activities of a sister or wife. Therefore, women were deemed to need special protection and especially seclusion to protect their virtue.[32] This restriction of social space theoretically applied to all women regardless of gender or class, but in practice it was mainly and deliberately applied to Spanish women, thus buttressing a racial hierarchy in which otherness could be explained in terms of sexual aberration and perversion. Persuading Spanish men that Indian and mixed-race women were lacking in morality and worthiness was crucial to maintaining a race-based social hierarchy. The colonizers' value system, of course, was far from the consciousness of many Tepehuan and Tarahumara women who took advantage of the opportunity afforded by autochthonous celebrations—which used overt sexual symbolism in fertility rites—to reinforce communal values and to exercise sexual freedom.

The Christian imposition of monogamy was resisted by both men and women; it was often cited as a primary motivation for revolt.[33] Principal Indian males especially objected to the loss of productivity that resulted from having only one wife because it lowered their status. Furthermore, the higher incidence of female mortality argued for taking more than one wife.[34] But Christian marriage also had potentially negative effects for women. For one thing, it meant that women who did not marry faced greater social and economic uncertainty. More serious, it may have contributed to a higher incidence of violence against women by their spouses.

In general, and throughout New Spain, the Catholic church promoted a politics of marriage that rested on the inviolability of the husband's authority and his role as a provider. By extension, a wife's lack of obedience and humility deserved punishment and even justified violence (presumed to be edifying). And adultery merited severe punishment only if it was committed by the wife. The Church also took on the role of mediator in cases of domestic dissension and violence. The typical consequence for male misbehavior through adulterous relationships or physical abuse of wives (*dando mala vida*) was an admonition from the local priest to change his conduct. Resort to the judicial system rarely produced results, and women often stayed in abusive relationships.[35] Conjugal violence was also related to alcohol, whose consumption patterns had broadened beyond ceremonial uses in the colonial context. How were women to protect themselves from aggravated assaults? The precontact practice of simply changing partners was no longer an option that could be practiced openly. Nor was Catholic divorce or annulment a practical possibility for Indian women. As the lesson was poetically expressed by Spain's renowned sixteenth-century writer, Miguel de Cervantes, "Better the worst relationship than the best divorce."[36] Nor would the Church sanction the return of the wife to her parents' household. In this situation, as the colonial period wore on, colonial Mexican women not uncommonly resorted to witchcraft.

In fact, witchcraft and magic came to be commonly associated with sexuality and marriage in colonial Mexico. As a means to deal with errant and abusive men, it was practiced not only by Indians but also by *casta* (mixed-race) and even Spanish women. The most common form involved the ensorcelling of food, but the incantations to and symbols of supernatural power often related to indigenous beliefs and spiritual healing practices.[37] I have seen only a few cases for the Tarahumara area, but they indicate that Indian women (and men) became involved with non-Indians in non-Christian rituals designed not only for curing but also to curb abusive behavior. By the middle of the colonial period, these cases betray the evolution of a popular magical religious culture, which was syncretic in nature and transcended class and caste lines,[38] to mitigate the abuses of domestic violence.

If we are to judge by the archival judicial record, much more rarely did women in colonial Mexico—Indian or non-Indian—initiate or perpetrate violent action in domestic disputes. In the very few cases uncovered by historians in which wives murdered their husbands, they did so by poison.[39] That is why the case highlighted by the opening quote is so noteworthy. In the early morning hours of December 29, 1806, María Gertrudis Ysidora de Medina, a Tarahumara Indian woman from the village of Santa Ana de la Joya, bashed in her husband's head.[40] Was this incident so anomalous that there is no value in its retelling? At the very least, the case assembled by officials against her conveys salient Spanish views about Tarahumara women. But can an isolated, seemingly deviant event also tell us something about Tarahumara women's responses to Spanish attempts to Christianize and "civilize" them?[41] The reader will have to judge from the following reconstruction, based on the judicial record of the case itself and documents that describe the socioeconomic milieu of the community in which it occurred.

La Joya was a *visita* (mission station) of the Jesuit mission of San Francisco Javier de Satevó, founded in the 1640s at the easternmost edge of Tarahumara country. Located in the foothills of the Sierras along the Río San Pedro about sixty miles south of the city of Chihuahua, the mission district flourished economically in its early years and at its peak boasted several thousand head of cattle and sheep that were raised for sale in regional markets.[42] Nonetheless, the expanding landholdings and livestock of Valerio Cortés del Rey along the San Pedro, later to become part of his *mayorazgo* (entail), portended difficult times for the future, as the Indians realized when they took their complaints over damaged milpas to two governors of Nueva Vizcaya in the 1660s.[43] Following a subsistence crisis and the destructive epidemics of measles and smallpox in the 1690s, the mission declined in numbers of Indians and economic productivity. Subsequently, the silver bonanzas near Chihuahua in the first decade of the eighteenth century increased the demand for mining labor in the nearby missions of Satevó and La Joya.[44] Through the eighteenth century, epidemics and encroachments on mission lands by neighboring Spanish ranchers further impoverished the mission.[45] Population fluctuated in accordance with migrations in and out of the villages, but flight became increasingly common, and labor drafts continued to commandeer those who remained in the villages. Recurrent contact between baptized and non-Christian Tarahumaras frustrated missionaries, who complained of the lack of progress in conversion. Although some mission residents were bilingual by the early eighteenth century, the Jesuits reported in 1725 that those women who did confess would only do so in their native tongue.[46]

By midcentury, demographic and economic transformations in

the region coalesced with increasing official criticism of the Jesuits throughout New Spain and with their plans for expansion into Alta California, to convince the order to turn over its Nueva Vizcayan mission field to the bishop of Durango. When the secularization process was finalized in 1753, only about two hundred people remained in La Joya. Most of those were absent from the village for much of the year, working for paltry wages (usually paid in kind) in the mines or providing repartimiento service on haciendas. Others eked out an existence, harvesting meager fields of corn and beans and foraging for wild foods. Only a handful of villagers owned any sheep or cows. The departing Jesuit missionary doubted that the Indians could support the new parish, noting that they had never contributed more than a few squash, tamales, or ears of corn to the mission's upkeep.[47]

The priest of the new parish of Satevó quickly concurred and moved to appropriate mission lands for himself. After opining that his parishioners were insufficiently prepared to celebrate the Eucharist despite the long Jesuit tutelage, he also determined that it was best to avoid celebrating religious feast days because of the "idolatrous" celebrations that accompanied them. Especially chagrined to learn of La Joya's poverty, he made little effort to offer Mass there.[48] The number of Indian residents declined to fifty in 1787, and the non-Indian population surrounding the village outnumbered the Indian villagers.[49] As a result of the expanding non-Indian population, the area surrounding Satevó and Babonoyaba was detached from Chihuahua in 1793 to become a separate administrative district (*subdelegación*).[50] In spite of Apache raids and modest silver output, the Chihuahua region was characterized by demographic growth and the expansion of landholding and latifundia in the late eighteenth century.[51]

By 1800, La Joya still had its quota of elected Indian officials, but power was shifting to the demographically dominant Spanish and mestizo residents whose number included the local schoolteacher and small farmers (*rancheros* and *labradores*) to whom the Tarahumaras were leasing and losing lands. The outsiders were supported by officials in Chihuahua who inveighed against the lack of stability in Tarahumara settlements, complaining that the Indians too easily moved from hacienda to hacienda and from mining camp to mining camp, working for short periods without paying off their debts. In the

view of religious and secular authorities, these shiftless natives were
not interested in earning their subsistence but rather sought to flee
civilized, Christian life (*vida política y cristiana*) in order to enjoy total
license by "having many women and getting drunk."[52] Another
manifestation of Spaniards' concern over their lack of control is evident in the frequent accusations (sometimes founded and sometimes
not) of Tarahumara raiding, either on their own or in league with
Apaches, which not uncommonly resulted in their imprisonment and
execution.[53] Resisting official attempts to ensure a secure supply of
mining labor and to impose social control over them, many eastern
Tarahumaras and other intraregional migrants mixed with immigrant muleteers, itinerant vendors, miners, and artisans, forging new
social networks often around amusements such as dancing, drinking, and cockfighting.[54]

    In La Joya, Indians and non-Indians coexisted amid changing so-
cial and economic conditions, but they were clearly differentiated as
opposites in Spanish discourse. In this heterogeneous ethnic and cultural milieu, Tarahumara communal solidarity was severely eroded
and access to productive resources more circumscribed. These problems were exacerbated by drought conditions and food scarcity in
the middle of the first decade of the nineteenth century.

    The gory details of the murder of Mariano Burero, like his wife a
Tarahumara Indian and known for his excessive indulgence in drinking and gambling, spread like wildfire through the small village. José
Cervantes, the lieutenant governor of La Joya, was making his rounds
to collect payments (in agricultural products) for the parish priest
who resided in Satevó. When no one responded at Burero's home, he
looked around and found Ysidora behind the house. Cervantes
pressed her for the whereabouts of her husband three times, and she
finally responded that he was inside but that he was dead and she
had killed him. She begged Cervantes not to report the crime for the
sake of her children.[55]

    It was time to call for help. Cervantes related what had happened
to the pueblo's governor, Francisco Medina, who happened to be Ysidora's father and who ordered Cervantes to return to Burero's home
with the local constable and four neighbors. On entering, they discovered Mariano's body. His skull had been crushed, and a large rock,
presumably the murder weapon, lay nearby. Ysidora was nowhere in

sight, so the constable sent Cervantes off to look for her. He discovered her heading out a mile or two from the village and took her back for questioning by the local justice. Perhaps realizing for the first time the seriousness of her predicament, she attempted to blame the murder on Cervantes but quickly recanted.

Two days after the murder, the thirty-year-old prisoner testified that she had killed her husband after he returned home in the early morning hours, dead drunk from tesgüino. As soon as he passed out on his bed, she took a huge rock and dropped it on his head, killing him instantly. When asked her motive, she answered that her husband had always treated her badly (*siempre le dió mala vida*) as everyone in the village knew. On this particular occasion, before going out to carouse, her husband had bound her hands and feet and left her tied up all night in freezing temperatures, freeing her only when he came home at sunrise. The *subdelegado* (district official) asked why she had resorted to murder, thus demonstrating her "lack of piety," instead of presenting a formal complaint to the authorities. She replied that she was sorry for what she had done but at the time had not been thinking clearly, as she was nearly numb with cold and blinded by rage.

Testimony was also taken from five local citizens—all male and non-Indian. Although the general consensus was that Mariano was something of a drunk and a wastrel given to gambling, none of these witnesses admitted to having firsthand knowledge that he mistreated his wife. One of them, the schoolteacher, had once heard from Ysidora's mother that Mariano had injured her daughter's arm. At a hearing held in March after the court had appointed a prosecutor and counsel for the accused, only two other witnesses were called to testify. Neither the prosecutor, Juan Antonio Borunda, nor the defender, Domingo Tarango, was literate or trained in law; still they were the "best that could be found in this jurisdiction of miserably poor cultivators and herders." Ysidora's father and governor of the pueblo, Francisco Medina, one of only two Indian witnesses in the whole proceeding, testified that his daughter had brought a complaint against her husband in June of the previous year. Mariano had beaten her with a mesquite club, injuring her so severely that she had taken refuge in her father's house to recover. After three months, Mariano took her home and resumed his beatings. Medina stated that his son-in-law had been a ne'er-do-well gambler and drunk who could not even feed his family. He, Medina, had assumed the role of provider.

José Ribera, the former governor of La Joya, provided further testimony. Also a local healer, he had attended Ysidora in her father's house after her arm had been severely injured by her husband. He added that when he was governor, the accused had presented a complaint charging that her husband was having an affair with another woman in the village. Ribera characterized her actions as that of a jealous woman but reported that he had fulfilled his obligations by admonishing Mariano to stop his philandering.

It would seem as though the case was building against Mariano. In fact, the defender's first tack was to emphasize that Ysidora had acted in self-defense after a repeated pattern of abuse. He attributed her failure to report the beatings to fear of Mariano's retribution, which could be deadly. Tarango also cited Mariano's failure to provide for his family, one of the main tenets of Catholic marriage. Not so, countered the prosecutor, who suggested it was quite likely that Ysidora had been misbehaving and committing adultery just like most of the other Indian women of these villages. More probably Mariano had tied her up because she insisted on going to the party. Everyone knew, he added, that the women could rival the men in their capacity for drunkenness. What else could one expect from an ignorant Indian—especially an Indian who was also a woman?

The prosecutor argued that there was no corroboration for the allegations by Ysidora and her father that she had been abused. Why hadn't the governor disciplined Mariano for these acts? Furthermore, Borunda was convinced that she had committed a heinous crime, one that had been premeditated and that deserved the punishment prescribed by Spanish medieval law in cases of parricide. She should receive two hundred lashes and then be thrown into the river inside a bag into which a viper, a dog, a cock, and a monkey had also been placed.[56]

In the face of the prosecution's call for the death penalty, the unschooled defense attorney moved to change his strategy, perhaps because he realized that the self-defense argument was not supported in the law. Ysidora was indeed uneducated and stupid, he argued, but as a simple Indian, she should be treated as a minor by the court. In their rudimentary state, Indians were naturally incapable of understanding malice. Indian women, involved in their domestic chores, were even more innocent and naive. And they were more susceptible to "malignant inner forces" that compelled them to carry out acts of violence—in a state of temporary insanity invoked by demons.[57] In sum, even the defense attorney portrayed Ysidora as miserable and ignorant, condemned both by race and by gender.

A number of procedural concerns delayed the subdelegado's decision; finally, in August 1808, he ruled that neither the status of a minor nor insanity could be applied in this case. Citing the need to have justice served in a public and exemplary manner, he called for the death penalty and sent the judgment on to the *audiencia* (high court) of Guadalajara for confirmation. There the process stalled once again as trained lawyers appointed to study her case and defend her argued that extenuating circumstances justified a royal pardon. That argument was ultimately rejected, but final confirmation of the death sentence did not take place until early 1811. By this time, Ysidora had been incarcerated for over four years in two jails that the defenders described as "human slaughterhouses."[58] Bureaucratic delays and the independence insurrection were responsible for continued inaction, but finally in 1812 the high court ruled to apply leniency in the case due to extenuating circumstances. Citing the lack of premeditation and the neophytic condition of Tarahumara Indians—especially females—in matters of judgment and reason, the audiencia issued a five-year prison sentence.

Added to the five years she had already served, Ysidora Medina's sentence totaled more than ten years—a long incarceration by colonial standards. In Mexico, the most common penalties for homicide were labor service, fines, and corporal punishment. When jail sentences were imposed, they generally did not exceed five or six years. Capital punishment was relatively infrequent.[59] Several scholars of the criminal justice system in the Spanish colonies have commented on the fairness and leniency of legal proceedings. Many have detected impartiality in applying the law across racial lines as well as a tendency to consider extenuating factors (such as lack of premeditation, passion, and drunkenness) in sentencing. It is noteworthy that none of these studies has statistically considered gender difference in punishments. Yet in her study of eighteenth-century Chihuahua, Cheryl Martin reports severe judgments against women who deviated from the norms of female submission and argues that although in this frontier area social boundaries tended to be negotiable in terms of race and class, this was not true in the case of gender, where Spanish patriarchal values could not easily be contested.[60] In the case of Ysidora, lack of premeditation and limited powers of reason were specified as the extenuating circumstances rather than her physical and mental condition at the time of the murder.

What are we to make of this case? From it we learn very little about Ysidora Medina herself. We have no information about her children—how many there were, their ages, or who cared for them. Ironically, we know more about the dead person—the victim Mariano—than about the living defendant and witnesses. And what we do know—that his life was dissipated by drunkenness and gaming—does not evoke much compassion for his demise. Why did Ysidora even admit to the crime? What were the material conditions of her life? Why didn't her father, the governor of the pueblo, have more influence to protect her? Here we have a crime of passion rendered in abstract legal formulas that expunge vitality: the life of the community is imperceptible; Ysidora's fears for herself and for her children are only hinted at; her father's feelings do not surface in the matter-of-fact testimony. Emotion is overwhelmed by will—the will of the state to impose its order—leaving little place for empathy or affection.

Can we look between the lines or spot incidental remarks to fill in the gaps? What is missing? The most obvious omission is testimony that might have revealed more about the conditions of her marriage. The authorities called on witnesses to corroborate or contradict the allegations of mistreatment. How were these individuals selected? Why were there no female witnesses or anyone who had more intimate knowledge of her life? Did this have to do with the fact that Tarahumara women rarely interacted with outsiders? The only sympathetic witness was her father, a member of her own ethnic group. The former Indian governor, although substantiating that she had been injured, chose to emphasize her jealousy over Mariano's dalliances rather than her afflictions, thus implying that she might have provoked (and therefore deserved) his anger. Male voices are in virtually complete control of the scene, promoting a patriarchal order that crosses racial lines. (The one dissident voice is muted by consanguineal ties.)

This did not mean that there was equality among men in this community whose indigenous core had been decimated. As the non-Indian residents acquired land, native resources contracted and Tarahumara networks of labor reciprocity deteriorated. The traditional ceremonial practice of consuming tesgüino at times of cooperative work effort had given way to nightly gatherings at the local watering hole, occasions solely dedicated to drinking, gambling, and carousing. In the changing milieu, colonial officials persisted in their efforts to extract resources through a variety of taxes. As we have seen, even in a time of drought and scarcity, the parish priest did not desist in collecting his pound of flesh from all heads of households in La Joya. This was a village of farmers and ranchers with smallholdings, a community in transition from its indigenous bases but not yet engulfed by the growing tendency to latifundia. While economic stratification moved slowly, it favored mestizos and Spaniards who did not have to provide tribute and labor service. The power of the Indian governorship was obviously diminished.

It is tempting to speculate about how the particular situation of Ysidora and Mariano may have related to the loss of indigenous structures and networks of support. Yet any attempt to fit the particular circumstances of this case into a larger societal context can only be suggestive. In general, the way the case was argued conforms to other studies of the colonial period in demonstrating a tendency for officials and elites to attribute "uncontrollable" behaviors to *calidad*, or racial status.[61] In this view, poverty and misery were inherent conditions of base birth and not the results of a hierarchical and inequitable colonial system. The persistent Spanish evocation of this belief served to perpetuate a race-based hierarchy. In this schema, Indian men stood far down the ladder, but a gender ethic that considered all women to be naturally lacking in moral fiber and potentially unruly dictated an even lower status for Indian women. In a dominant society that conceived female sexuality as being in need of vigilant regulation to preserve racial purity and Spanish control, judgments were particularly harsh in regard to Indian women whose different cultural practices were construed as perverted and depraved. This was perhaps even more true in volatile frontier conditions that engendered a patriarchal order struggling to maintain clear social boundaries and obsessed with protecting itself from female trespass.

But strictures on Indian women did not emanate solely from their colonial oppressors. In this case, an Indian spouse, although relatively powerless in the society, was potentially lethal within the family, buttressed as he was by Spanish and Catholic patriarchal law and practices. The status and respect for their productive contributions enjoyed by Indian women before Spanish colonial rule were overshadowed and eroded in the more acculturated communities by the Church's insistence on female subservience. Even worse, Indian women's alleged promiscuity and lascivious nature nourished the fantasies of European males and justified the violence of Indian men.

In this case, the Jesuits' imposition of monogamous unions grounded in wives' submission to husbands provided the context and rationale for Mariano to literally tie Ysidora to her "proper place."[62] Furthermore, his excessive consumption of alcohol—beyond ceremonial usage—and his failure to provide for his family may be linked to the gradual breakdown of Tarahumara identity and cooperative labor efforts. In the late eighteenth century, the old mission villages of the eastern Tarahumara were overpowered by growing numbers of mixed-race and Spanish outsiders. In an atmosphere of double jeopardy—both ethnic and gendered—Ysidora's rage might be viewed as a state of cultural illness. Was there no antidote to her powerlessness? For a fleeting and dazed moment, she must have thought she had found it. The relief turned out to be just as ephemeral as her resistance.

Women's Voices from the Frontier

San Esteban de Nueva Tlaxcala
in the Late Eighteenth Century

Leslie S. Offutt

It takes a keen eye to ferret out materials that illuminate the lives of women in centuries past; the scarcity of sources in which women figure is a handicap under which scholars have labored for decades. Indian women are, if anything, even less visible than European women in the record, doubly handicapped by gender and by race; when they do appear, most frequently they are spoken about or spoken for, rarely allowed their own voices. It is far easier to sketch the general outlines of the development of the community in which they operated; and indeed, in this examination of indigenous women in San Esteban de Nueva Tlaxcala, on the northeastern frontier, an understanding of the development of the pueblo itself is essential, for women's actions were inextricably linked to that history. The conditions under which this Indian town was forged and tested during its existence led it to cling to traditions of resistance and defense, creating a heritage that continued to shape the responses of its residents two centuries after the town's foundation. Women no less than men knew the history of San Esteban and integrated that legacy of struggle against abuses into their own efforts to rectify perceived injustices against themselves and their families. As San Esteban the pueblo had reacted against encroachments from neighboring Spaniards, so too San Esteban women responded by recalling the heritage of resistance on which their community was based. The personal aspect of the struggle to define and defend corporate integrity is what brings San Esteban women into focus.

San Esteban de Nueva Tlaxcala, one of a number of colonies established beginning in the late sixteenth century far to the north of the Nahua heartland, was a manifestation of efforts of the time to find better ways of defending the northern reaches of New Spain against the marauding groups collectively known as Chichimecas.[1] The northern frontier had been ravaged for decades by incursions by the nomadic groups, and Saltillo, founded in the 1570s as a livestock-raising outpost supplying the silver mines of Zacatecas and Cuencamé, was on the verge of abandonment by the early 1590s, desperate for whatever aid the crown could dispatch.[2] The colonization scheme effected under the direction of Viceroy don Luis de Velasco was designed to counter the threat of Indian raids by providing models of sedentary Indian agriculturalists that the nomadic groups might be induced to emulate. The crown's choice of the central Mexican province of Tlaxcala was a logical one. Allied with the Spanish as early as 1519, Tlaxcala had proven its merits in earlier colonizing ventures in southern Mexico in the 1520s; thus the Spanish call for colonists later in the century was not without precedent. And by the early 1590s, a declining economy in Tlaxcala led many to seriously consider the crown's invitation. Seventy-one couples and their families and an additional sixteen men settled at San Esteban de Nueva Tlaxcala by October 1591; these nearly two hundred fifty Tlaxcalans were welcomed to the region by fewer than sixty Spaniards.[3] To offset the hardships incurred by their uprooting and resettlement in a hostile environment, the Tlaxcalans who agreed to participate as colonists negotiated a most favorable arrangement with the Spanish crown. Among the privileges secured was the recognition of the nobility (*hidalguía*) of the colonists, exemption from tribute and personal service, the grant of an independent corporate existence, and physical separation from the Spanish.[4]

The latter two points became especially critical for the residents of San Esteban de Nueva Tlaxcala over the course of its long and uneasy coexistence with Saltillo. Saltillo enjoyed no authority over the residents of San Esteban, although the two communities were separated only by an irrigation canal leading from the main spring on the hill overlooking Saltillo. With its *protector de indios* (defender of the Indians) appointed by the viceroy and its independent *cabildo*, or municipal council, answerable in the judicial realm directly to the royal Audiencia in Mexico City, San Esteban appeared, in theory at least, to enjoy an enviable independence from outside interests.

Theory and practice diverged, however. San Esteban confronted repeated efforts by Saltillo residents, often backed by Saltillo's cabildo, to chip away at the integrity of the indigenous community. In the eighteenth century alone, royal officials authorized three separate boundary surveys, each in response to conflicting claims on the part of the two cabildos.[5] Moreover, evidence suggests that the Hispanic residents of Saltillo and its surrounding ranchos and haciendas often attempted to co-opt the labor and services of San Esteban residents.[6]

In response, San Esteban developed a tradition of corporate defense over the course of its independent existence (the pueblo was finally absorbed by Saltillo in the late 1820s), a tradition that itself drew on Tlaxcala's unique accommodation to the Spanish presence in central Mexico. Tlaxcalan assistance had been essential to the Spanish success against the Aztecs in 1520–21, and over the course of the sixteenth century the Tlaxcalan cabildo had secured a number of concessions from the crown in recognition of the province's contribution to the conquest of the Aztec Empire. The Tlaxcalan colonists who made their way north in 1591, like their ancestors before them, were imbued with a sense of their own strength and an awareness of how far and how forcefully they might push against encroachment on their privileges and practices. Tlaxcala's own independence from local Spanish control, the maintenance of its corporate integrity—indeed, its florescence in the mid-sixteenth century—constituted the heritage on which San Esteban continued to draw in its own experiences with Hispanic Saltillo. Whether in successfully challenging Hispanic efforts to encroach on the land of the Indian town or in the continued use of Nahuatl in both the private and public realms as late as the last decades of the eighteenth century, San Esteban residents considered the maintenance of their separate cultural identity essential to the survival of their independence within the surrounding Hispanic world.[7]

This study examines that sense of integrity as it was embodied in two distinct areas. The first is the struggle toward a definition of what constituted a community member, where the question of ethnicity was central. What defined a Tlaxcalan from San Esteban? What constraints did she or he operate within? How essential was maintenance of a specific standard of identity? The second area involves the actual defense of the rights of an individual *as a citizen of San Esteban.* How did one define one's personal concerns in light of the privileges granted San Esteban residents? Could one bring those rights to bear in defense of one's family or personal interests, interests that might in another context be considered opposed to those of the larger community? Did civil status (as wife, mother, or widow) affect the seriousness with which women's complaints were received?

One might expect the struggles to have been defined and waged exclusively by the leading men of the town, those who were politically active and in regular contact with local and regional political authorities; no matter what the ethnic or racial group being investigated, Latin American women rarely emerge from the wings onto the political stage. Indeed, in the matter of determining community membership, the concerns of the women involved did appear to be secondary to the greater community interests. Women seem to have been allowed only indirect influence in the resolution of the problem that their actions brought to the fore. In determining ethnic or racial identity, the role of woman as childbearer was of paramount importance, but while her actions in that realm, specifically as it concerned exogamous unions, might have precipitated a response that helps us to understand the definition of community operative some two centuries ago, nonetheless her role was more passive than active. In the second area, where the question was one of defining one's individual rights as a member of the corporation, San Esteban women spoke more loudly and were more actively engaged in efforts to defend personal and community interests. While certainly not dominant in the historical record of San Esteban, women were not completely hidden from sight. As Susan Kellogg found for Aztec women of the early colonial years, Indian women enjoyed a juridical identity and participated in the Hispanic legal system to validate traditional claims to property.[8] Although none of the San Esteban cases investigated here is concerned with property rights, nonetheless Kellogg's identification of Indian women's legal rights permits us to understand how San Esteban women were able to move from the private to the public sphere. In that public arena, where traditionally women played a far less critical role, their participation in the debate was an essential element in helping to define community concerns, even while their focus was on more modest personal goals.

This study looks at the last decades of the colonial period, roughly 1780–1810.[9] Even at this late date, from which far more materials have survived in the archives than from earlier periods, cases involving women are far from numerous in the documentation. San Esteban women suffered under the handicap of double invisibility—as Indians and as women—in a medium—court documents, censuses, land sale records—where elite members of the Hispanic sector predominated. Only fourteen cases involving San Esteban women survive in Saltillo's municipal archive for the thirty-year period in question. Of those, I have selected six for their richness of detail and ability to illuminate certain concerns of the women involved and of the larger community. Despite the limited number (and cases involving San Esteban men are not much more frequently encountered), these cases provide an invaluable window on female roles, behaviors, and expectations in this Indian town at the turn of the nineteenth century.

Individual Identity and the Larger Community

The emphasis on identifying San Esteban in relation to the outside as a distinct, integral entity was reflected in the ethnic and racial consciousness of its residents and in their efforts to maintain the "purity" of the community in keeping with the privileges secured from the crown in 1591. In some respects the ethnic purity of the community was a fiction. José Cuello notes that the Indian town had absorbed numerous band Indians during the course of the seventeenth century, although by the eighteenth century this seems to have been forgotten and the town considered itself historically unadulterated Tlaxcalan.[10] Believing itself (and believed by outsiders to be) ethnically pure, corporate integrity would be compromised by allowing any outsider to marry into the community; the fear of *desigualdad de sangre*, or impurity of blood, was as much a concern in late eighteenth-century San Esteban as it was in the Spanish colonial world.

Women represented the chink in the armor of San Esteban's ethnic and racial exclusivity. It was they who bore the next generation, they who were charged with inculcating cultural values in their children. As childbearers and teachers they assured continuity between the homogeneous past and the uncertain future; the community's continued integrity rested on their fulfillment of their responsibilities. Paradoxically, while women, through their reproductive function, held great power, the patriarchal structure of society hindered their ability to act independently. Respectable native women, as did their Hispanic counterparts, suffered restraint of choices, whether concerning work, mobility, or marriage partners; only if they were willing to challenge the limits of socially acceptable behavior could they hope to break through these constraints.[11]

Two cases from the 1790s vividly illustrate the importance placed on ethnic purity in defining group integrity. In both cases the issue was an unequal marriage in which union with an outsider threatened to weaken the community; the non-Indian (or impure) spouse represented the wedge that other outsiders might use to divide and ultimately destroy the community itself. In both cases the fathers spoke at length about their opposition to the proposed marriages, citing numerous reasons for their opposition but coming ultimately to the argument that the intended spouses were unequal, an inequality based solely on an ethnic criterion. Of all the many reasons why fathers would go to court to block their children's marriages, here was the reason that most reveals the thinking of the community as it defined itself in relation to the Hispanic world.

The first case found don José Joaquín Ramos, a Tlaxcalan from San Esteban, appealing to the judge of the first instance (*alcalde de primer voto*) in San Esteban on behalf of his son in the alleged abduction of a young woman. Ramos argued that his son, Juan Calistro, had taken María Josefa Bueno to nearby Monterrey simply to attend a festival; now her father was demanding that he marry her, implying that the younger Ramos had deflowered her on the promise of marriage. In response, Ramos argued that María Josefa had begged his son to take her to Monterrey; he acknowledged only his son's stupidity in failing to recognize the woman's designs, not his culpability as her seducer. Indeed, Ramos painted María Josefa as a whore, accusing her of having had illicit relations with his nephew and with her own brother prior to her overtures to his son. But not until Ramos came to argue his final two points was the central issue in his protest revealed. María Josefa Bueno was not from San Esteban, nor was she even Indian. Ramos argued forcefully that customarily no Tlaxcalan chose a spouse from Saltillo, especially one from a *mala casta*, or inferior ethnicity, without facing immediate disinheritance and expulsion from the pueblo. Further, he argued that Tlaxcalans should be protected and shielded from efforts such as those of María Josefa's father to force a marriage on a resident of San Esteban, on the grounds of the town's historical privileges and its citizens' reputations as nobles. To allow the marriage of his son and a *casta* (racially mixed) woman from Saltillo, he asserted, would fly in the face of the privileges granted the Tlaxcalans by the crown two centuries earlier.[12]

While not directly involving San Esteban women, this case lays bare the essential role of women in maintaining the social order carefully negotiated by the town's founders. This father clearly feared what desigualdad de sangre implied for San Esteban. From a private matter between two presumably consenting individuals, the issue had grown to involve the nature of the community itself, its rights, its privileges, its ability to discipline those who challenged its norms. The culprit who brought this into focus was the woman—in this case an outsider, a mala casta whose effort to marry this errant son of San Esteban represented to the father the point of a knife aimed at the heart of the community itself. Woman, through her reproductive function, through her sexuality, threatened to compromise the corporate identity that San Esteban had struggled to establish and maintain. Note the references not only to community tradition (a child of the pueblo did not marry outside the pueblo without incurring banishment) but to royal privilege as well (San Esteban was to be protected from such violation by virtue of the concessions secured in the sixteenth century). Don José Joaquín Ramos drew on both community tradition and viceregal guarantees to focus attention on the inviolability of standards designed to protect San Esteban from the outside world. Note as well the larger question of status operative here; though most San Esteban residents who appeared in the records of the late eighteenth century had abandoned the honorific title "don," this irate defender of traditions retained that indicator of high status, a vestige of the privileges of nobility granted to the original settlers in 1591. For familial and community reasons, Ramos must struggle against the possible contamination by casta blood that would result from the marriage of his son to María Josefa Bueno. Regardless of the woman's character (unfortunately, nothing is known beyond Ramos's accusation that she had been sexually promiscuous; the record contains no defense of her reputation, either by her family or by witnesses called on her behalf), what loomed largest in this case was the necessity of protecting the pueblo from racial contamination. Only marriage to a Tlaxcalan woman from San Esteban would do; only through such an association could the integrity of the community be upheld.

The dearth of evidence to the contrary suggests that most San Esteban women did marry within the community. Only deviant cases made their way to the courts, but those that did may illustrate in an indirect fashion the essential function of Indian women in preserving corporate integrity. Another case from the 1790s brings home this point. In this instance José Manuel Quiterio had taken Juana Jacoba from the home of her father, don José Hernández, San Esteban's first *alcalde* (judge), and delivered her to the custody of the local parish priest, hoping through his action to persuade her father to agree to their marriage. Hernández was incensed; he raged against the circumstances of his daughter's abduction, refused them permission to marry, and demanded the return of his daughter. The critical issue, he said, was that José Manuel was not the equal of his daughter;[13] the Saltillo cabildo, to which the matter was referred, verified this assertion through the testimony of three elderly witnesses from San Esteban who had known the parents and grandparents of the young suitor. Here it was not a matter of one or the other being an outsider; both were San Esteban residents, and both were considered generally to be Tlaxcalans. But careful inquiry brought to light that José Manuel's grandmother had been a *coyota*—a mixed-blood—a heritage that tainted him as well. Although he had been considered Tlaxcalan, as had his parents and three of his grandparents, the desigualdad de sangre associated with his coyota grandmother haunted him and made him an inappropriate suitor.[14]

The insistence on ethnic purity that emerges in Hernández's suit suggests its overriding importance in defining membership in the community; although to this point José Manuel had been considered and accepted by San Esteban as one of its own, when it came to mingling his blood with one whose bloodlines were pure, this father and community leader drew the line. Were the record to have ended there, Juana Jacoba, the young woman at the heart of this dispute, would have emerged in the historical record as little more than a cipher, a pawn between two contending forces, father and suitor.

But the case did not end there. Though able to marshal three witnesses to attest to the impurity of the suitor's bloodlines, and insisting that the main motive for his pursuit of the case was the matter of the inequality between the two, not the bad conduct of the suitor in abducting his daughter,[15] five days later Hernández relented. Appearing before the Saltillo council he stated that José Manuel had humbled himself before him sufficiently to persuade Hernández to accept him as his son-in-law, and the cabildo ordered this information sent along to the parish priest so that nuptials could be arranged.

What could have taken place in the intervening few days to cause don José Hernández to reverse himself so completely? The wounded pride of this leading citizen motivated his initial response. He argued that this vicious man who had pursued his daughter was unable to bear the costs of marriage; further, his daughter's abduction had disgraced both her and her family. In this context, the suitor's ethnic inferiority could easily be invoked in an effort at least partially to redeem the family's reputation by preventing the marriage. But the argument of impurity of blood as an impediment to marriage appears ultimately to give way in this case to more pressing concerns. Don José spoke of the travails his daughter had undergone, perhaps an oblique reference to her loss of virginity.[16] Interestingly, the parish priest in whose custody the daughter had been placed was not called as a witness, nor, of course, was she; those who were most familiar with the circumstances of the woman's abduction, or who could most clearly speak of her concerns, were kept voiceless in this proceeding. But the complete turnaround in Hernández's position suggests that family honor became an issue, and ultimately that honor was best safeguarded (or restored) by viewing the elopement as a fait accompli and accepting a marriage on the couple's terms. At a certain point, families were forced to concede that the shame of a dishonored daughter more seriously compromised their reputation than an interethnic marriage.

If this is indeed what transpired in the case of Juana Jacoba and José Manuel Quiterio, our impression must be of a woman willing to take a public position regarding her choice of a spouse. There is nothing in the record to suggest that she fought off her abductor, or that she was misled by a lover who sought to seduce and then abandon her. That she was lodged by her abductor in the house of San Esteban's curate indicates that her suitor not only was conscious of her safety, but he was also hopeful that the priest, as a moral leader in the community, might by harboring her indicate his implicit support of the union. Far from a fallen woman seduced by someone with no intention of honoring her later, Juana Jacoba appears to have actively conspired in this elopement, to have risked her honor on the assumption that the honor of the family was of greater concern to her father and worth restoring through the only means available, with an end to forcing her father's hand to grant his approval of her marriage. Here the inequality of bloodlines was less important than restoring the honor of the family. Finally, that José Manuel had been considered to this point a San Esteban Tlaxcalan (one had to go back to his coyota grandmother to find the root of the inequality, and then it was only fuzzily remembered by the witnesses) must have smoothed the acceptance of this young man as a son-in-law.

The above cases allow us to hear only by reference the voices of the women whose involvement was central to the issue of community identity. They were offstage, spoken of in the third person, more shadows than people. In the first case, that of the casta temptress attempting to seduce her Tlaxcalan paramour (or so the documentation portrays it), and in the second, where the honor of a pure Tlaxcalan woman had perhaps been compromised, we see examples of women who were in a very real sense at the mercy of the men around them. Fathers ranted about them, arguing that for the sake of community integrity and family honor marriages should not take place between these unequal spouses; father or male community leader possessed the authority to dictate whether marriages were to take place to rectify these presumed injustices. On that level these women might be thought of as passive. But one might more compellingly argue that on another level these might be considered women who actively worked toward a certain goal: in the case of the alleged temptress, a legitimate marriage after her freewheeling life (if the assertions of the father of her intended groom are to be believed); in the case of our Tlaxcalan maiden, a marriage with the man of her choice. Through the use of their bodies they could threaten, or could maintain, the integrity of the community. But their control was limited; while they challenged the social expectations of late eighteenth-century society regarding honor and virtue, it was not they who ultimately decided their fate. That was left to the symbol of corporate authority (the cabildo or the subdelegate) to which these cases were submitted. These were not "noisy women," women whose voices were raised in the public arena in pursuit of their wishes or on behalf of their families.

Women as Defenders of Community Integrity

Certain women in late eighteenth-century San Esteban did take more aggressive steps into the public realm, seeking redress of grievances and through that process challenging the strictures under which women normally operated. The conditions that prompted these women to come forward in each case touched quite directly on their private lives: they came to court after suffering a personal loss of some sort, moved by pain or humiliation to protest. Their public stance suggests a broader familiarity with social constraints as well as a willingness to push against those limits.

Stepping from the shadows carried risks, to be sure, as the case of Lorenza Matiana de Luna attests. This San Esteban resident came before the local representative of the regional royal magistrate (*teniente de alcalde mayor*) don Juan Manuel del Campillo in June 1790 to charge that the governor and first alcalde of the pueblo had beaten her when she dared to request her brother-in-law's release from the local jail. They had also called her a whore and then proceeded to whip her brother-in-law, her husband (who was also imprisoned), and another prisoner. In response to Campillo's request for witnesses, four men came forward to support Lorenza Matiana and to assert that the officials were drunk when they whipped the prisoners. The San Esteban politicos did not deny that they had beaten the prisoners; indeed, they argued that the three had been disobedient and the punishment was deserved, although they admitted to Campillo that a second beating given to two of the prisoners was somewhat irregular. They claimed not to have beaten the men after Campillo had ordered them to desist. Finally, they asserted that Lorenza Matiana had instigated the trouble.[17] Unwilling to admit fault, making no mention of the drunkenness that four witnesses had testified to, they turned the attack against the woman who had brought the complaint, accusing her of stirring up trouble for them. Campillo refused to act in this case, instead sending it on to the provincial governor with no comment. The final resolution of the case is not known.

In a similar case María Nepomucena de Lara came before the local interim military commander in February 1790 to charge that several militiamen had accosted her husband, José de la Cruz, a San Esteban carpenter, after a bullfight, inflicting such great harm that he lay near death. Describing herself as his poor young wife now charged with raising their family,[18] María Nepomucena portrayed herself and her husband as innocent victims. They had been walking home in the vicinity of a bullfight when her husband became involved in the altercation that very nearly took his life. She filed suit in hope that at the very least the perpetrators would be required to bear the cost of her husband's medical care and possible funeral expenses. But the testimony of those she accused challenged her account, with the consensus being that there was so much confusion in the general melee that it was impossible to determine who had beaten her spouse. The notary of Saltillo's council was dispatched two weeks after the attack to interview the victim, who had miraculously survived his serious head wounds, but those wounds had left the unfortunate carpenter unable to speak or to reason clearly or even to understand how he had come to his present state. It was clear that in all likelihood he would not work again and that his wife would be unable to pay for the care rendered by the local doctor.

The various accounts all seemed ultimately to point to Sergeant Juan Antonio del Pilar, another San Esteban resident, as the perpetrator. He admitted in his own testimony that, resisting being tied up for his participation in the initial stages of the brawl (he insisted he was provoked by the carpenter), he began beating about with his sword. While Pilar swore that he did not know whether he struck the carpenter, others testified that only he and de la Cruz were armed with swords and that they had been at the center of the brawl from its beginnings. Adding to the appearance of guilt was the fact that he had already once escaped from jail, only to be returned the following day. No record of the final disposition of the case survives, but one can surely surmise that, whatever the fate of Juan Antonio del Pilar, María Nepomucena de Lara, left with a disabled husband and a family, and with no visible means of support, would bear a heavy burden for years to come.[19]

What had these women gained by coming forward to challenge the status quo? More clearly in the first than in the second, the "noisy woman" became an object of public censure; despite Lorenza Matiana's clear indictment of San Esteban's local politicos for mistreating both her and her imprisoned relatives and despite witnesses who corroborated her account of beatings and libelous statements, there were those who refused to accept or acknowledge the possible veracity of this woman's accusations. She was a poorly informed troublemaker, interfering in areas where convention dictated she should not tread.

María Nepomucena's charges were ultimately no more seriously heeded. Although they did give rise to an investigation, with numerous witnesses to the brawl in which her husband was so severely injured, her story of their having been accosted while innocently walking home was discredited. Granting that her account to the authorities might have been colored by the dire straits in which she now found herself, those straits themselves might have been sufficient to draw from the presiding judge, or from the attending physician, some sympathetic response to this woman now left to care for her family without the assistance of her husband. Nothing of the sort appears in the record; while several men involved in the altercation were released from prison after they pleaded an inability to provide adequately for their families, no provision was made to care for María Nepomucena and her family. In these two cases, it is difficult to see what at all was gained by their daring to move from the shadows into the public arena and voice their concerns.

While the risks of confronting authorities in defense of one's family could be great, there were partial victories as well. The archives contain two cases from the turn of the nineteenth century in which a mother's concern for her son's welfare drew her into the public realm to argue the case in the local courts. The widow María Juana Bernarda dictated a letter to Saltillo's first alcalde in 1799 on behalf of her son, a shoemaker who had been imprisoned for assault against a clerk in a store owned by one of the most influential residents of

Saltillo, the senior municipal councillor (*regidor alférez real*) don José Miguel Lobo Guerrero. She argued that her son had been provoked into attacking the clerk, and now feared that he would be mistreated in jail. In the ensuing investigation, the accounts of those involved differed dramatically. The shoemaker claimed that the clerk had begun to argue and call him names when he commented that the shoe leather he was examining in the shop was expensive. The clerk asserted that while they had discussed the price of leather, the assault came later; the Indian had left and then returned with a knife to stab him. The judge dropped charges against the Indian shoemaker but assessed a fine of 25 pesos to pay the surgeon who treated the wounded clerk. The mother's defense of her son's interests resulted in his liberation.[20]

    In another case that reveals more of the unsavory side of daily life in San Esteban, the widow María Magdalena petitioned the sub-delegate on behalf of her son, José de Jesús, who had been imprisoned by the local Indian governor and fined for the crime of living in concubinage. María Magdalena charged that the imprisonment and fine were unjustified; her son strayed because of drunkenness, which impeded his self-control. At the very least she wanted him freed from jail, but more important was her demand that the fine of four pesos be reduced to two pesos and the two-peso overpayment be returned to her, because as residents of San Esteban they were exempt from crown taxes.[21] She argued that everyone knew that the cabildo and commissioners conspired to get poor San Esteban residents drunk and then assessed fines or required them to provide personal service, and she demanded that the subdelegate investigate this abuse and bring it to a halt. As scathing as this indictment was, no action was taken to reprimand the San Esteban cabildo that allegedly perpetuated this abuse against the common citizens of the pueblo. The outcome of the case was that her son *was* released from jail, but he was required to pay the four-peso fine, which was then used to buy lime to make cement to rebuild a wall. He was further forbidden to have contact with those who had led him into concubinage in the first place, under threat of fifty lashes and other penalties unspecified in the court's decision.[22]

    These two cases suggest something of the nature of San Esteban women's worldview, their awareness of the context in which they operated, and the possibilities open to them if they pushed the limits of social acceptance. In the first case, in which the shoemaker had assaulted a bullying clerk, while the resolution did not indicate specifically that the Spanish clerk provoked the attack, the fact that the shoemaker was freed suggests that his mother, in making her claims, had reason to believe that justice was on her side and that she might prevail over the original judgment that had mandated the imprisonment of her son. To have challenged a representative of a leading Saltillo family by questioning the version of the circumstances that painted her son as the aggressor, *and to have won his release*, suggests the tremendous confidence the widow María Juana Bernarda felt in the rightness of her cause; the assessment of a 25-peso fine does nothing to diminish her accomplishment. Her action and her success, though some might label it partial, suggest that San Esteban residents did in some instances understand quite clearly the system under which they operated, and could work within that system to achieve resolutions that benefited them at the expense of the Hispanic residents of the adjoining town.

Similar conclusions may be drawn from the example of María Magdalena, who went to such lengths to free her dissolute son from jail. Perhaps it was difficult for her, perhaps even distasteful, to defend one who had so blatantly flouted community conventions by maintaining a concubine; surely the presiding judge had no qualms about pointing out his "public sins and adulteries." But the larger issue to this San Esteban widow was corporate privilege, the right of exemption from taxation that formed an integral part of the pueblo's identity. Her son's imprisonment for his public sins provided the opportunity to remind the subdelegate, and the Indian governor as well, of the inviolability of those privileges. That the fine was simply redefined in such a way as to allow it to be viewed as a contribution (forced though it was) toward public works, the purchase of lime for concrete for the improvement of an existing wall, should not detract from the impact of María Magdalena's accomplishment: she forced the local political authorities to confront the fact of the long-standing privileges that defined San Esteban's relation to the outside world and to acknowledge, at least implicitly, the validity of her argument that these perquisites were not to be tampered with.

But the question still remains what it was about these latter two cases that proved so compelling that the authorities would accept the legitimacy of the assumptions on which these women operated; after all, is not the earlier image of the young woman left with an incapacitated husband and a family to feed at least as poignant as the picture of a mother defending her wayward son? Here it appears two issues are relevant—age and civil status. Unlike the earlier plaintiffs, both young married women defending their husbands who by virtue of their imprisonment or incapacity could not defend themselves, these latter two women were mothers of adult children, mature members of San Esteban society who by virtue of their age were worthy of greater attention and respect, even deference, than their younger sisters. Second, these women were widows, operating within a society where only widowhood freed women from the restraints on their public actions exercised first by fathers and later by spouses. The death of a spouse in the Hispanic world could be liberating, allowing a woman for the first time to manage her own financial and personal affairs unquestioned. One might expect that these San Esteban women, operating in a world that despite the theoretical independence of the two towns had been penetrated by Spanish culture and values, might also have gained greater independence through their widowhood.[23]

Conclusion

One might come away from the preceding discussion struck by the distinct roles exemplified by the two types of cases treated above: in the first, at the most basic level, the woman appears as object (despite what seems to be Juana Jacoba's active conspiring in her abduction), as being essential to the definition of community by virtue of her reproductive abilities but ultimately acted on rather than acting under her own volition; in the second, the woman steps from the shadows and finds her voice to rail against those who would injure her family or challenge her (and her community's) privileges. But is this contrast between powerlessness and strength, between passive and active, so clear? Are the two responses as diametrically opposed as they first appear? Perhaps a better way of viewing these differing responses is to consider the context from which these examples emerge. The overriding issue in all these cases is what constitutes the community itself. How, after all, does San Esteban define itself, if not through the actions of its residents? Where else are we to find the voice of the corporation, if not in the voices of its citizens? What most concerns these people is continuity and survival. On the one hand, women's actions had to be controlled, because through their particular vulnerability as women, as bearers of the next generation of Tlaxcaltecans, community integrity required their protection. In these cases women who were acting outside the norm were adopting a radical stance; they threatened the community through their rebelliousness. On the other hand, women taking the stage to defend their family interests were in microcosm what the larger corporation did every time the San Esteban cabildo came before the Saltillo cabildo, or appealed to the various protectors, subdelegates, governors, and other assorted authorities to argue for the recognition of its rights to land and water and to clearly defined and inviolable boundaries between the pueblo and the Hispanic town. San Esteban had abundant examples of how to protest, how to challenge; its residents knew the rights that had been granted the pueblo at its creation and knew further how to play up the deep-seated interests in the maintenance of those rights as they put forth their own personal agendas. Interestingly, it was these activist women who moved outside the traditional role who ultimately might be classified as conservative elements in society. While they breached community standards through their public actions, those actions were pursued precisely with the goal of restoring their families, with the added aim of restoring corporate rights as well. Noisy or quiet, San Esteban women were central actors in the drama of cultural contact and struggle for community integrity that played itself out not only in the more heavily indigenous heartland but on the distant frontier as well.

Key sites critical to the alliance of doña Marina and Hernando Cortés

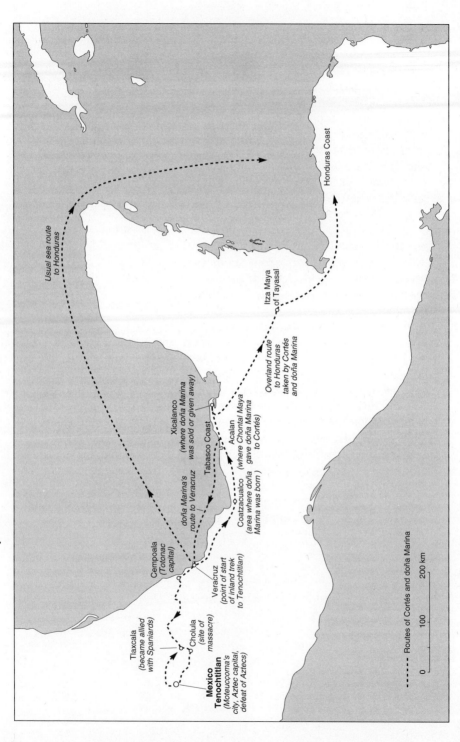

Usual sea route to Honduras

Honduras Coast

Itza Maya of Tayasal

Overland route to Honduras taken by Cortés and doña Marina

Xicalanco (where doña Marina was sold or given away)

doña Marina's route to Veracruz

Tabasco Coast

Acalan (where Chontal Maya gave doña Marina to Cortés)

Coatzacualco (area where doña Marina was born)

Cempoala (Totonac capital)

Veracruz (point of start of inland trek to Tenochtitlan)

Tlaxcala (became allied with Spaniards)

Cholula (site of massacre)

Mexico Tenochtitlan (Moteuccoma's city, Aztec capital, defeat of Aztecs)

------ Routes of Cortés and doña Marina

0   100   200 km

14

Rethinking Malinche

Frances Karttunen

Marina/Malintzin/Malinche. There was no one remotely like her then, nor has there been since in the semimillennial history of the Americas after Columbus. Pocahontas and Sacajawea run distant seconds. Like these other women, she is now enclosed within an edifice of myth, a construction all the more fantastic and obscuring because it has had more centuries to develop and because many different groups have an investment in it. While the myth of Sacajawea was erected almost entirely by the American women's suffrage movement of the late nineteenth and early twentieth century, the idea of Malinche has different resonances for Europeans and for Mexicans, for Latin American men and for feminists, for Mesoamerican Indians and for mestizos, for Mexican nationalists, historians, sociologists, writers, and artists. Her myth is pervasive within Mexico and beyond its edges, but, understandably in light of how long ago the events of the conquest took place, it is much embroidered. It is time to set aside the accretion of colonial and postcolonial ideas about her that are, from our point of view, old (although not nearly old enough to be credible) and to try to think about her anew.

Her name, like her person, was handed back and forth and invested with multiple significances. When she was given to Hernando Cortés and his party in 1519, she received the baptismal name of Marina. Nahuatl speakers, who recognized no distinction between r and l, thereafter addressed her reverentially as Malin-tzin. The Spaniards in turn heard Malintzin as Malinche, a name that in the course of Mexican history has become synonymous with selling out to foreigners. Yet to the old conqueror Bernal Díaz del Castillo, who made her the heroine of his account of the conquest of Mexico, she was always "doña Marina," the respectful Spanish doña being the very equivalent of the Nahuatl honorific -tzin.

The Nahuas' Malintzin

Indigenous Mexico has represented Malintzin in myriad ways. She appears in pictorial documents and maps from the sixteenth century on. In 1552 the Indian city of Tlaxcala, which had allied itself with Cortés against the Aztecs, commissioned a painted record (lienzo) of the events of the conquest, and she figures again and again in its eighty-eight scenes, versions of which have proliferated like fragments of the True Cross (fig. 14.1).[1]

What appears to be the oldest surviving piece is not a lienzo at all but four scenes painted on native paper and heavily annotated in Nahuatl. Both the handwriting and the style of personal and place-name glyphs indicate that this version dates from the mid to late sixteenth century. Two scenes are of the meeting of Cortés and the lords of Tlaxcala on the road outside the city. One is of Cortés parleying with the lord Xīcohtēncatl in his palace, and one is of Xīcohtēncatl and the other Tlaxcalan lords presenting their daughters to Cortés and his soldiers in a sign of their alliance with the Spaniards against Moteucçoma and the Triple Alliance of Mexico Tenochtitlan, Texcoco, and Tlacopan. Marina (so labeled) mediates each scene.[2]

It was Nahua colleagues of fray Bernardino de Sahagún who wrote and illustrated the Florentine Codex, a grand project undertaken in the third quarter of the sixteenth century. Book 12 tells of the conquest of Mexico in parallel columns of Nahuatl and Spanish, and already in the frontispiece there Malintzin is, interpreting on the beach even as the Spaniards unload their crates, firearms, and livestock. She appears in half a dozen more illustrations within the text, and book

Fig. 14.1. Doña Marina interprets for Hernando Cortés in the palace of the Tlaxcalan lord Xicoténcatl. From the mid-sixteenth-century anonymous Lienzo de Tlaxcala Manuscript. Nettie Lee Benson Latin American Collection. The General Libraries, the University of Texas at Austin. Photograph by George Holmes.

12 ends with her interpreting for Cortés as he addresses the defeated rulers of the Triple Alliance.

Dramatically, she is a central character in folk theatricals that have survived to the present. At some point after evangelization was under way, pageants were devised in which Malintzin and "the Captain" (Cortés) are the agents of the triumph of Christianity, and these enactments live on both in indigenous languages and in Spanish as the Dance of the Conquest. In some versions of the *danza de la conquista*, Malintzin dispenses with the Captain altogether, and in other versions, a single actor with a double-faced mask plays both Malintzin and Cortés.[3]

This is no new thing, for Bernal Díaz tells us that Nahuatl speakers addressed Cortés himself as "Malinche." To Díaz, this was simply ellipsis for "Marina's Captain," since Cortés and his inter-

preter were always together when negotiations were conducted.[4] Yet
if we consider the long Mesoamerican tradition of two-headed and
two-faced figures and the Aztec tradition of *ixiptlayotl*, "representation," there may be more to this matter of Cortés being "Malinche."
In Aztec religious practice chosen human beings served as temporary embodiments of deities, providing them with a conduit through
which to speak and act in the world inhabited by humans. At the end
of their service some of these stand-ins would be flayed, and priests
would dress in their skins in order to speak and act through them in
yet another way. Perhaps the Aztecs and their neighbors perceived
the Nahuatl-speaking woman as the *ixiptla*, "representative," of something behind both her and Cortés, the mouthpiece of some poorly
understood and mysterious "Malinche" making itself manifest for
the first time in Cemanahuac (the Nahuas' own name for their
world), where no Malinche had ever been known before.

Much has been made of the notion that the indigenes initially
perceived the European men as gods. So far as I know, nothing has
been made of the possibility that their interpreter was perceived as
the *ixiptla* of a supernatural force. Yet it might help us to understand
her remarkable nerve in situations of sheer terror. For the Spaniards,
the most horrific fate imaginable was to be taken captive by the
Aztecs and sacrificed before their pyramid-top temples (as some of
them in fact were). For a person from within Mesoamerican culture
acting out the sort of mediating role doña Marina had assumed, the
final trip up the pyramid steps to the waiting sacrificial knife was inevitable and not without honor. The good *ixiptla* had to live each day
for itself, performing his or her role to perfection.

Ixiptla refers to both one's "representative" and one's "likeness";
xayacatl is both "visage" and "mask." Collectors of Mexican dance
paraphernalia catalog scores of Malintzin masks. Many are red.
Many bear lizards and snakes on cheek and brow, creatures associated with rain. Some are lovely, and some are hideous. Some are militant: as a participant in the conquest Malintzin may wear an ostrich-
plumed European helmet or stare out from the open beak of an Aztec
eagle-warrior's headdress. Perhaps the most striking indigenous
representation of her, and certainly a very common one among the
dance masks, is as a pink-cheeked, blue-eyed European woman,
perhaps with devil's horns or a ruff of butterfly wings or both.[5] In

one drama she weaves among the dancers threatening them with a snake, as one by one they fall to the ground, her victims.[6] Here Malintzin merges with the intimidating Mesoamerican deity Coatlicue (Her Skirt Is Snakes) and the biblical Eve.

Indians of Mexico's central highlands associate her not only with deficiency of pigment and with reptiles but also with mountains. For people who live today in the states of Tlaxcala and Puebla, the volcano from which the rains descend on their valley is Malinche. In the Nahua communities within the Valley of Mexico, Malintzin stories are told about the snowy volcano Iztaccihuatl, "White Woman," that looks so much like a sleeping woman. In these stories she is provider and protector rather than traitor, a presence whose resolute slumber guards agricultural folk just as the neighboring volcano Popocatepetl guards her, a theme that has made its way onto hundreds of thousands of Mexican calendars and velvet paintings.[7]

According to Bernal Díaz, in 1526, after Cortés had taken her off to be his interpreter among the Mayas, rumors flew among the Spanish residents of Mexico City that doña Marina had died and been revealed in the night burning with Cortés in hell-fire.[8] But they were reported back alive soon after. That was a false alarm, but in time she became firmly associated with la Llorona, the wailing woman who haunts Mexican nights grieving for her children and leading unwary men to their deaths. At the very beginning of book 12 of the *Florentine Codex* a wailing woman appears as an omen of the coming destruction of Aztec Tenochtitlan.[9] The identification of the inconsolable and dangerous Llorona with Malintzin/Malinche came sometime later and continues to this day in Mexico among Indians and non-Indians alike.[10]

Sixteenth-century indigenous representations of Malintzin portray her not as evil or immoral but as powerful. Her garments are elegant, her hair coiled in the distinctive horns of the proper Nahua matron, her demeanor serious. The Nahua writers of the *Florentine Codex* do not fail to accord her name the honorific -tzin every time they mention her, while they only occasionally write "Motecuçomatzin" [sic], especially after the point in their narrative when Cortés and his party occupy Moteucçoma's city. Later Cuauhtemoc enters their account and shares with Marina the courtesy of consistent, unfailing -tzin. Thus it is clear that neither resistance to the

Spaniards nor ultimate surrender deprived an individual of honor in the eyes of Sahagún's assistants; both "Quauhtemoctzin" and "Malintzin" are spoken of with deferential respect, and "Motecuçoma" is not, a subtle matter of Nahuatl morphology that does not survive translation into English or Spanish.

The Construction of Malinche

According to Bernal Díaz's account of the conquest, doña Marina was beautiful and intelligent, capable and loyal, admired and well liked by the men whose lives were on the line in the conflict. He credits her with repeatedly saving them all from disaster. Cortés himself is almost silent about the woman who not only interpreted for him but also bore him a son whom he named Martín after his father. But his men and their children and grandchildren corroborated Bernal Diaz's testimony.[11] At the very end of the sixteenth century, in a *probanza* (petition) seeking a reward in recognition of her father's services, Isabel Pérez de Arteaga assembled the testimony of witnesses that her father had attached himself to doña Marina and been the first Spaniard to learn to speak Nahuatl. The witnesses agreed among themselves that Juan Pérez de Arteaga, like his leader Cortés, was also called "Malinche," a statement in accord with what Bernal Díaz had also written far away in Guatemala.[12] Not least among the individuals who raised probanzas elaborating doña Marina's role in the conquest were her own daughter by Juan Jaramillo and her grandson, the son of don Martín Cortés.

So it was that among creoles, much as in the Dance of the Conquest, she was celebrated for her crucial aid in defeating all who opposed Cortés and for bringing Christianity to the heathen. Bernal Díaz places in her mouth a speech in which she asserts that she considers herself fortunate to be a Christian and saved from the worship of idols and moreover to have had the honor of bearing a son for Cortés and to be married to Juan Jaramillo.[13]

But this comfortable tradition of doña Marina as cheerful philanthropist was not to last. Elizabeth Salas has exactly pinpointed the sea change: "Her status as a great *conquistadora* declined at exactly the same time that the Mexicans threw out the Spaniards in 1821."[14]

The casting of great bells traditionally requires some human blood, and so it seems to be in the forging of national identity. A scapegoat was needed for three centuries of colonial rule, and one was easily found in doña Marina, who was sexualized as the Indian woman who could not get enough of the white man.[15]

In a wink she was demoted from crucial interpreter and counselor to lover and wily mistress of Cortés, traitor to her race, mother of mestizos. To this day it seems that hardly any writer, male or female, can describe her in any terms but sexual. Patricia de Fuentes identifies her as "Cortés's mistress and the mother of his bastard son," and Frans Blom refers to her as "a tender morsel."[16] In her book on doña Marina, Hilde Krueger writes, "For these young Indian women, so animal-like in their approach to sex, the idea of chastity or virginity had no meaning at all."[17] It is a relief that Peter Gerhard describes doña Marina simply as "the interpreter and early companion of Cortés."[18] In contrast, in his influential *Labyrinth of Solitude*, Octavio Paz styles her the original "chingada" and the Mexican nation as "hijos de la chingada."[19]

This preoccupation is now well into its second century. Already in 1845 in a contribution to a Yucatecan literary journal, V. Calero portrayed her as an ambitious woman more "ardent, passionate, impetuous" than wise who had to be tutored by the Spaniard Jerónimo de Aguilar and rescued from errors resulting from the "defects of her basic education." According to Calero, Cortés fell captive to the charms of this woman "in the morning of her life," and it was her enchantment rather than any action on his part that "resulted" in their son, don Martín.[20]

After the revolution, at the height of the Mexican mural movement in 1926, José Clemente Orozco painted Cortés and Malinche naked together, the corpses of Indians beneath their feet, he reaching across her in a gesture of negation, she voluptuous, low of brow and dull of eye, a veritable Neanderthal (fig. 14.2). Today in the calendar art and velvet paintings of Mexico, she has been trivialized into a swooning scantily clad blond bombshell, half Barbie doll, half Anita Ekberg.

In *La interminable conquista de Mexico*, the cartoonist Rius could think of nothing else to do with Malinche than to make her into the

Fig. 14.2. Hernando Cortés and Malinche. Close-up from the mural by José Clemente Orozco, in the stairwell at the Antiguo Colegio de San Ildefonso, Mexico City, 1926. Photograph by Stephanie Wood.

doxie whose success depended on being able to speak three languages and "kiss in three more."[21] Again in *500 años. Fregados pero cristianos,* published for the Columbian quincentenary year, Rius describes her as one of "20 estupendas mozas" and already able on first meeting to speak Spanish as well as two local languages. Despite Cortés's existing matrimonial ties, leers Rius, "it might be suspected that this Marina was something more than a bilingual secretary, since she subsequently gave señor don Hernán two children. And when he tired of Marina, he lent her to Hdez-Portocarrero and then made her marry Juan Jaramillo in 1524."[22] These popular comic-book treatments of the conquest are aimed at exposing to a mass audience the abuse of Mexico's indigenous peoples. As distressing as their bungled history is the sheer misogyny in what passes for social satire.

Searching for the Person within the Myth

Most of what we think we know about doña Marina we owe to Bernal Díaz del Castillo. Cortés in his letters to Spain mentions her just twice, once as "my interpreter, who is an Indian woman" and once by name as "Marina, who traveled always in my company after she had been given me as a present with twenty other women."[23] His biographer, López de Gómara, devotes a paragraph or so to her history and the discovery by Cortés of her multilingualism. He says that Cortés "offered her more than her liberty" if she would be his interpreter and secretary. He concludes, "This Marina and her companions were the first Christians to be baptized in all New Spain, and she and Aguilar were the only trustworthy interpreters between our men and those of the country." Christian though she had become, López de Gómara refers to her in the very next sentence as "the slave girl."[24]

For a fuller story we must turn to Bernal Díaz, but with caution. Despite its convincing tone and detail, his account of the conquest has come in for its share of debunking. In particular, we should take with a grain of salt the speech he attributes to doña Marina in which she expresses her heartfelt satisfaction with her situation and says she would not exchange her place for a realm all her own.[25] Since her words were supposedly addressed to her kin, they would have been uttered in Nahuatl, so how could Bernal Díaz know for certain what she had said? Verbally facile as he claimed she was, she might have said something quite different to her relatives and then given an altered translation pleasing to Spanish sensibilities. Or Bernal Díaz may have composed the speech himself decades later in the course of writing a good story in which doña Marina figured as the heroine. Or, then again, it might be an accurate report of her sincere sentiments. We cannot know.

López de Gómara says she was born into a noble Nahua family in the community of Oluta; Bernal Díaz says it was Painala.[26] In any case, it was near Coatzacualco in the transitional area between Nahua central Mexico and Maya Yucatan. Andrés de Tapia and Francisco López de Gómara state that as a child she was stolen by merchants and sold into the Maya area.[27] Bernal Díaz weaves a more dramatic story of her being handed over secretly by her mother and stepfather to people of Xicalanco so as to clear the inheritance of her younger half-brother. In this story, too, she changed hands again and ended up in the Chontal Maya area at the base of the Yucatan peninsula, where she was given to Cortés in a group of twenty women.[28]

There can be no doubt that her childhood experiences made her bilingual, an unusual condition for a woman of noble lineage, for such women lived extremely circumscribed and sheltered lives.[29] She was able to communicate with Jerónimo de Aguilar, who had been marooned in Yucatan for many years and had learned Maya through a total immersion experience comparable to her own. And she spoke her native language with central Mexican Nahuatl speakers, including Moteucçoma himself.

There are two pieces of evidence that her linguistic accomplishment extended well beyond simple survival bilingualism. First, dialect differences apparently troubled her little. Although she had learned Maya among the Chontales and Aguilar had learned among the Yucatec Mayas, she was able to work with him from the first. Later, she interpreted between Cortés and the Itza Maya ruler Canek in the heart of the Peten district, although Itza Maya is treated by some Mayanists as a separate language from Chontal and Yucatec Maya.[30] Moreover, although she came from the Tabasco region, far from the central highlands of Mexico, she was able to converse with Moteucçoma's emissaries on the Veracruz coast. Then she interpreted negotiations with the Tlaxcalans, whose Nahuatl was and still is distinct in a number of ways from the Nahuatl of the Valley of Mexico. As the conquest closed in on Moteucçoma and the Triple Alliance, she interpreted in the valley itself, in Tenochtitlan, and in the other cities surrounding Lake Texcoco. And some years after that, she had no difficulty with the Nahuatl of communities far off in Honduras. According to López de Gómara, "The messengers were very glad to talk with Marina, because their language and that of the Mexicans were not very different, except in pronunciation."[31] Yet it is exactly these differences in pronunciation that more often than not lead Nahuatl speakers to claim that their regional dialects are mutually unintelligible.

Apparently doña Marina had an unusual ability to screen out superficial differences that many find daunting and to attend to deeper commonalities. But the second piece of evidence of her linguistic versatility has to do with something she had to learn. Namely, she was able to understand a certain register of Nahuatl known as *tecpil-lahtōlli*, "lordly speech."

Lordly speech is a style of speaking, the only style that would be used in the presence of Motēucçōma, the greatest lord of all. A speaker of mundane Nahuatl would be as helpless in dealing with it as someone ignorant of the rules of Pig Latin would be in trying to understand and speak the apparent gibberish that results from just a pair of reversal rules applied to English.[32] In tecpillahtōlli indirection and reversal are all-pervasive. Elaborate courtesy requires that one say the opposite of what one means, and one adorns one's nouns and verbs with prefixes and suffixes until they resemble grammatical equivalents of the churrigueresque columns of eighteenth-century Mexican churches.[33] Native intuition cannot help with this; one must be schooled in it. That doña Marina could communicate with Motēucçōma's representatives, negotiate with the lords of Tlaxcala, investigate a plot in Cholula, and ultimately interpret between Cortés and Motēucçōma himself supports the claims of Bernal Díaz, López de Gómara, and others that she had been born and raised within a Nahua noble family before people began to hand her around as a piece of disposable property.

Her ability to acquire languages did not stop with Maya. Doña Marina and Aguilar worked together as an interpreting team through the fall of Tenochtitlan, but by the time Cortés launched his expedition to Honduras, Aguilar was out of the picture, and doña Marina was functioning as a trilingual interpreter, translating directly between Spanish and Nahuatl in central Mexico and Honduras and between Spanish and Maya in Acalan and the Peten. The Nahua historian don Fernando de Alva Īxtlīlxōchitl claims that she learned Spanish in a "few days," which is surely an exaggeration, but there can be no doubt that her dependence on Aguilar was short-lived.[34]

Her unique gifts were as yet unrecognized, however, when the Chontal Mayas gave her as part of a package to the Spaniards. The twenty women, together with male slaves, ornaments, and other material goods, were a bribe to Cortés to get him to move on, to leave the Maya area and go prey on Motēucçōma. Resorting to euphemism, Calero says the women were given to Cortés "para hacer tortillas."[35] Once in Spanish hands, the women were summarily baptized and distributed to provide the men with sexual services. This juxtaposition of a Christian sacrament with rape is jarring to our sensibilities, but the sixteenth-century Spaniards, Bernal Díaz included, were quite frank about it.

A piece of myth is that prior to this experience, doña Marina's indigenous name had been "Malinalli Tenepal." We owe the "Tenepal" to the Nahua historian Chimalpahin, who added a marginal note to his copy of López de Gómara that her full name was Marina or Malintzin Tenepal, Marina/Malintzin being her Christian name and Tenepal her lineage name.[36] "Tenepal" may be a construction developed in hindsight. Tēneh means "that which possesses an edge or lip," and according to the sixteenth-century lexicographer fray Alonso de Molina the metaphor tēneh tlahtōleh, "one who possesses a lip, one who possesses speech," refers to one who speaks vociferously. The postposition -pal adds the sense of "by means of." Hence "Tenepal" would be a close equivalent of la lengua, the Spanish sobriquet for doña Marina.

The idea that Aguilar (the only one who could have done so) engaged the group of women in conversation in Maya prior to their baptism, learned that the calendrical name of one had in a previous life been malīnalli (grass, a Nahuatl day sign that would have been meaningless to him), and chose "Marina" for her as a close approximation is profoundly unlikely, although that story has been accepted as gospel since the nineteenth century.[37] In the aftermath of combat, with hostile Chontal Mayas doing all they could to deflect the Spaniards from their shore, there was hardly time to get acquainted. As soon as the sacrament had been bestowed, Cortés divvied up the women, and Marina fell to one of his lieutenants, Alonso Hernández de Puertocarrero. It was only later, on another shore, that Cortés discovered her unique usefulness and reclaimed her for himself.

The Spaniards' first encounter with Nahuatl was on the coast of what they named Veracruz. Aguilar, who had served the party well in Yucatan and Tabasco, was suddenly faced with an unfamiliar language. It was then that Marina was observed speaking with the most recently encountered indigenes. Since she, and she alone, could translate for Aguilar, who could then translate for Cortés, she was transformed on the spot from Puertocarrero's drudge to Cortés's pearl without price.[38]

The men who had asked doña Marina in Nahuatl to identify the leader of the Spanish forces were emissaries of Moteucçoma, sent by him to the coast to investigate the strange beings who had arrived from across the sea. They brought with them painters to make a record for their ruler, and so it was that Cortés and doña Marina sat for their first portrait not long after they met and perhaps only hours after Cortés had taken her back from Puertocarrero. Word went inland to Moteucçoma that the Spaniards were on their way to his city with a Nahuatl-speaking woman called Malintzin.[39]

The Gulf of Mexico coast was not then, nor is it now, a mainly Nahuatl-speaking area. The first mainlanders Cortés and his men encountered on their home turf were Totonacs, whose language was equally unfamiliar to Aguilar and doña Marina. But doña Marina had the presence of mind to ask for Nahuatl interpreters, who were readily available, since the Totonacs, like so many Mesoamerican peoples, were tribute payers to Moteucçoma. Here the chain of interpretation grew attenuated to the point that it is a wonder any communication was accomplished at all. Cortés spoke in Spanish to Aguilar, who translated his words into Maya for doña Marina. She in turn translated from Maya to Nahuatl. The local interpreters then translated from Nahuatl to Totonac. The process was then reversed for conveying information back to Cortés.[40]

Among the Totonacs, the Tlaxcalans, and the Cholulans, doña Marina was set the task of assisting Cortés in playing people off against each other, misleading them to keep his potential enemies off-balance and acquiring allies through a mix of sweet talk and intimidation. The duplicity was mutual, and, according to Bernal Díaz, it was in part through doña Marina's perceptiveness that the Spaniards avoided traps laid for them as they relentlessly pressed on to the interior in search of Moteucçoma.

The characterization of her as Malinche the traitoress turns on just such circumstances. López de Gómara, Bernal Díaz, and Cortés himself all concur that the Cholulans planned to entrap the Spaniards within the walls of their city and slaughter them but that a noblewoman of Cholula revealed the plot to doña Marina and urged her to flee from the Spaniards to the protection of the noblewoman and her family. According to Bernal Díaz, the woman offered immediate marriage to one of her sons. Doña Marina, both sources say, pretended to go along with the scheme in order to learn more details and then informed Cortés. Bernal Díaz adds that doña Marina had also through bribery and astute questioning learned of the plot from two Cholulan priests. Cortés then seized the initiative and with the assistance of his Tlaxcalan allies slaughtered the Cholulans in their own plazas and temple precincts and sent Moteucçoma's agents back to their ruler with a message of bloody intimidation.[41]

Again we must beware of taking these men at their word. The story of the Cholulans' intended treachery serves the Spanish case well, and the implication of Moteucçoma in the affair serves to justify the way Cortés made an example of Cholula. But while we may question whether the plot was real or invented by Cortés, there is no doubt that a terrible slaughter befell the city, and blood would seem to be on doña Marina's hands.

Yet we must ask whether, if she were indeed invited to change sides, doña Marina had any reason to trust the Cholulans. She was not one of them. Perhaps the woman who urged her to save herself was deceiving her to separate Cortés from his interpreter. Or if the woman was sincere in her proposal to make doña Marina her daughter-in-law, for doña Marina that would have meant being handed on to yet another strange man.

It does not appear to me that a question of ethnic loyalty can legitimately be raised here. At this time in Mesoamerica the indigenes had no sense of themselves as "Indians" united in a common cause against Europeans. They identified themselves as Mexihcah, Tlaxcaltecah, Chololtecah, and so on. As she was none of these, how could Malintzin be a traitor to all or any of them? By all reports, she saw her best hope of survival in Cortés and served him unwaveringly. Rather than the embodiment of treachery, her consistency could be viewed as an exercise in total loyalty. The problem for Mexican national identity after Independence was that the object of her loyalty had been a conquistador.

From Cholula Cortés and his party continued up over the saddle between the volcanoes Iztaccihuatl and Popocatepetl, from whence lay revealed the floor of the Valley of Mexico with its great lakes and shoreside cities. They headed directly for the city that lay out in the lake, connected to its edges by causeways. All his efforts to divert them having failed, Moteucçoma finally came forth from his city (as the Tlaxcalan lords had done) to meet Cortés on the road.

According to the Nahua writers of the *Florentine Codex*, Moteŭc-çoma addressed Cortés and his interpreters in flawlessly honorific speech, drawing on all the devices of polite rhetoric, all the metaphors of stewardship and hospitality. They represent Cortés's reply, transmitted through Malintzin, as utterly plain and devoid of honorific markers.[42] Then, according to the writers, the Spaniards touched Moteŭcçoma (for this they use two paired Nahuatl verbs) and examined him freely with their eyes (another two verbs).[43] For Moteŭc-çoma, a ruler in whose presence his subjects never raised their eyes from the ground, this was unimaginable. But no physical blow could have fallen as hard as the handful of Nahuatl sentences the writers say came from Cortés through Malintzin.

We can no more trust the speech Sahagún's assistants place in her mouth than the one Bernal Díaz did, but we can certainly appreciate the enormity of the situation. The Mesoamerican societies she knew, Nahua and Maya, observed elaborate rules of behavior, and by word and deed she was implicated in heart-stopping violations. Nor was this initial meeting the most challenging of her interpreting chores. Once within the city, Cortés used his interpreting team to demand that a chapel to the Virgin Mary be set up on top of the city's main pyramid, and it also fell to doña Marina to advise Moteŭcçoma that he was being taken into custody, a prisoner of his unwelcome guests.

From the time Moteŭcçoma was forced to reside among the Spaniards, Cortés and his lieutenants spent a great deal of time whiling away the hours with him. They learned to play one of the Mesoamerican games of chance, Moteŭcçoma's treasures passing back and forth among them. Once, to demonstrate their easy superiority over his subjects' war canoes, they built and rigged sailboats and took their royal prisoner out skimming over the expanses of Lake Texcoco.[44] During all these hours of contact, a Spanish boy who served Cortés as a page was absorbing Nahuatl and became a second conduit of information exchange between the Spaniards and Moteŭcçoma. Bernal Díaz relates that he made use of the boy, Orteguilla, to importune Moteŭcçoma for "a very pretty Indian woman," and indeed Moteŭcçoma responded by giving him a noblewoman with a dowry.[45] She was baptized doña Francisca, and we do not hear of her again.

The more Orteguilla came to understand Nahuatl, the more alarmed he became, according to Bernal Díaz. Present but ignored at discussions between Moteucçoma and other lords from the Valley of Mexico, he knew enough to know that he did not understand what was going on. At his call, Cortés brought doña Marina and Jerónimo de Aguilar, to whom Moteucçoma issued a warning that the Spaniards should withdraw immediately if they valued their lives. According to the account, Orteguilla—having come to share doña Marina's direct knowledge of their situation—was reduced to helpless tears, in dramatic contrast to doña Marina's steadiness.[46]

During this uncertain time, Bernal Díaz also tells us that Moteucçoma proposed a marriage alliance by offering one of his daughters as wife to Cortés (see also Pedro Carrasco's discussion of bride donation for political alliance in chapter 3). Cortés, we are told, explained that he could not enter into marriage with the girl since as a Christian he was permitted but one wife and he already had one. But he accepted the girl into his safekeeping.[47] Various sources seem to show that Cortés in fact took three of Moteucçoma's daughters into his keeping. They were baptized Isabel, María, and Marina, and Isabel bore Cortés a daughter.[48] By López de Gómara's reckoning, by the end of his life Cortés had fathered four children by his (second) Spanish wife, one by a Spanish woman to whom he was not married, his son Martín by doña Marina, and three daughters by three different Indian mothers.[49] One of those mothers was Moteucçoma's daughter. His sexual activities, we see, were not confined to doña Marina, much less to his marital bed.

The situation of the Spanish party within Tenochtitlan was precarious and grew more so over time. Cortés had to leave his forces there under his next-in-command, Pedro de Alvarado, in order to deal with the challenge of a new group of Spaniards who had arrived on the coast, and by the time he had settled the matter and returned with reinforcements, Alvarado—later notorious for his brutal conquest of the peoples of Guatemala—had committed slaughter within Moteucçoma's city that echoed the Cholula massacre in ferocity but had none of the prior action's strategic value. On the contrary, it undermined what little authority the Spaniards commanded by virtue of holding the person of Moteucçoma. As the situation deteriorated, Moteucçoma was killed. There are conflicting accounts of how it happened: Spanish sources claim he was struck by a stone thrown by one of his own subjects; indigenous sources say he met his death at Spanish hands.[50] Then insecurity turned to rout as the Spaniards attempted to flee the city under cover of night and rain.

According to Bernal Díaz, doña Luisa, daughter of the Tlaxcalan lord Xicohtēncatl (who on baptism had been given to Pedro de Alvarado), and doña Marina were placed under the protection of thirty soldiers, who were also responsible for a group of valuable hostages. The attempted withdrawal was immediately discovered, and in the dark and wet a ferocious attack descended on Spaniards, prisoners, allies, and horses. When the survivors regrouped at a safe distance from Tenochtitlan, they found that doña Marina and doña Luisa had escaped with their lives, as had some of Xicohtēncatl's sons. But doña Elvira, daughter of the Tlaxcalan lord Māxīxcatzin, had perished together with some of the sons and daughters of Moteucçoma.[51] Doña Isabel was not among her dead siblings, however. She survived the conquest and three Spanish husbands to eventually die in 1551 (see also Pedro Carrasco's treatment of doña Isabel in chapter 3).[52]

Now began the siege of Tenochtitlan. Cortés attacked over water with ships and artillery, while smallpox raged within its walls. The city that had enchanted the Spaniards with its beauty and orderliness was ravaged and reduced to stinking rubble. From time to time the Spaniards demanded capitulation in exchange for an end to the destruction. A witness testifying in court proceedings years later related that during the siege a Spanish soldier who had learned to speak Nahuatl was interpreting, but the Aztecs insisted on having doña Marina instead, and Cortés had to send soldiers by boat to the city of Texcoco to fetch her before the negotiations could go forward.[53]

By high summer 1521, Tenochtitlan no longer existed. Its last ruler, Cuāuhtemōc, gave himself up to Cortés, who immediately began through doña Marina and Aguilar the same sort of flattery and expressions of affection that he had previously laid on Moteucçoma. The end would come out the same. After an extended period of captivity Cuāuhtemōc would die, and there would be conflicting accounts of his death as well.

Only now, after two years of sexual use in Spanish hands, was doña Marina pregnant. Having been in the thick of armed conflict and having avoided death by sacrifice, drowning, and smallpox,

doña Marina gave birth to Cortés's son. Young Martín would remain his potential heir, for a long time. At age six he would accompany his father to Spain. His father would successfully petition for
his legitimation, the boy would become a knight of Santiago, and
eventually, according to Cortés family history, he would die fighting
Moors in the War of Granada. But the birth of a half-brother, also
Martín, deprived him of the marquisate he would otherwise have
inherited.[54]

In what circumstances doña Marina lived between the summer
of 1521 and the autumn of 1524, who attended her through her pregnancy and assisted at the birth of her son, we do not know. Cortés at
this time was involved in domestic difficulties. His wife, whose existence he had invoked to block a marriage alliance between himself
and Moteucçoma, came from Cuba and took up residence with her
husband in his new palace at Coyoacan, south of the massive construction site where Tenochtitlan was being rebuilt as Mexico City.
She arrived in August 1522. Before the year was out, she was dead
and Cortés was under suspicion of choking the life out of her with
her own necklace, although charges were not brought against him
until seven years later. By then doña Marina was dead too.

In the autumn of 1524, when little Martín was just beginning to
walk and talk, much too soon for him to form a lasting memory of
his mother, Cortés called on her to interpret on an overland trek to
Honduras. The child was left in the care of one of Cortes's kinsmen,
and the expedition began. At the very beginning of it, doña Marina
was married to his lieutenant, Juan de Jaramillo. In a tantalizing vi-
gnette, López de Gómara remarks that Jaramillo was drunk at his
wedding and Cortés was criticized for letting the union take place,
since he and doña Marina had children [sic] together.[55] It is after this
that Bernal Díaz has doña Marina make her statement to her relatives in Tabasco about her satisfaction with her good fortune to be
Christian, the mother of Cortes's son, and the legitimate wife of
Jaramillo.

Then it was off with horses and pigs, musicians and jugglers,
trunks and firearms into a rain forest world amenable only to canoes
and blowguns. Men and animals wallowed and drowned or perished
of hunger. The royal hostage Cuāuhtemōc, who had been brought
along, was put to death for unclear reasons. According to her grand-

son, whose probanza sought to maximize her contribution to the conquest, doña Marina had uncovered a plot against the Spaniards by Cuāuhtemōc and his fellows. The Chontal Mayas claimed credit for the discovery by their leader, Paxbolonacha of Acalan. Bernal Díaz says two Aztec hostages came forward to warn Cortés, while López de Gómara, repeating Cortes's own account, says the plot was revealed by a note written on paper in hieroglyphs.[56] In view of all this conflicting testimony, we cannot be sure doña Marina denounced Cuāuhtemōc, but she undoubtedly interpreted at his summary examination and trial, and Bernal Díaz states that she assisted the Franciscan friars in confessing him before his execution. Cuāuhtemōc, the chronicler says, at the last spoke bitterly to Cortés of the degradation to which he had been brought.[57] For his words to reach Cortés, doña Marina would have had to translate and deliver them.

When the expedition reached the ruler Canek in his fastness of Tayasal, the Maya lord advised Cortés through doña Marina that they should make straight for the coast and continue their travel by sea, but Cortés persisted in traveling overland. By the time the survivors of his folly reached their goal in Honduras, they found that the punitive mission they were on had long since been made pointless by the death of the rebel Cortés was after.

At great loss of life, nothing much had been accomplished. But doña Marina, whose powers of survival had again carried her through while others expired on every side, was pregnant again, and on or soon after the sea trip back to Veracruz she gave birth to Jaramillo's daughter, who was baptized María. It is the testimony of doña María, given more than twenty years later, that tells us what little there is left of her mother's story.

Doña Marina did not long survive the birth of her second child. Within the year, Jaramillo remarried. This time his wife was a Spanish lady, and doña María grew up a mestiza stepchild in a Spanish household. When her mother had been married to Jaramillo, Cortés had endowed the marriage with the encomienda of Xīlōtepec. Some twenty years after doña Marina's death, nearly as many years after his remarriage, Jaramillo died and left doña Marina's dowry not to their daughter but to his Spanish wife. This outrage touched off a lawsuit that simmered for years until the sides agreed to split the inheritance and give up the litigation.[58]

Conclusion

There is nothing more to doña Marina's personal story. Within ten years of falling into the hands of the Spaniards she was dead. She had survived longer than many Indian women and men during that fatal decade, and like so very many women who lived and died anonymously or nearly so she gave birth to mestizo children. She did not have a chance to be with her children, and they were deprived of any memory of her. Contrary to the romantic stories, she did not go to Spain, was not presented at court, did not have a palace in Chapultepec, was not alive in the 1530s. She was not the only Indian woman impregnated by Cortés, and surely he was not her love slave. It seems to me that their relationship was pragmatic in the extreme. They needed each other to survive, but all the power lay with Cortés.

When she was given to him, she may have been very young, truly in the morning of her life as Calero put it. Clearly she was not barren, since she eventually bore two children, yet there was a significant lapse before she became pregnant for the first time (a convenient one in terms of her night-and-day interpreting duties). If adolescence seems incompatible with her accomplishments as counselor and negotiator, one need only consider the case of Eva, a young woman of the Khoikhoi, who played a similar role in mediating between the indigenous peoples of the Cape of Good Hope and the Dutch in the seventeenth century. Bilingual by virtue of being taken as a child into the household of the Dutch governor, she served as his adviser and interpreter in settling a war between the Khoikhoi and the Europeans and thereafter went into seclusion, apparently on the occasion of her first menses.[59] Fecundity, when it finally arrived, was her undoing and led to her abandonment by both the governor's family and her Khoikhoi relatives. Sacajawea, too, was an adolescent when she walked across the continent with Lewis and Clark. She and her co-wife had been acquired while still children by the expedition's Canadian French interpreter, Toussaint Charbonneau, a man with a taste for very young Indian women. All these competent, cheerful, enduring young interpreters can be viewed as child survivors of chronic sexual assault.

To reiterate, doña Marina's inevitable fate was rape, not the making of tortillas. She had absolutely no choice about whether she would be sexually used, and very little control over by whom. When she was given to Cortés she had no one to turn to, nowhere to flee, no one to betray. She was not Aztec, not Maya, not "Indian." For some time already she had been nobody's woman and had nothing to lose. That made her dangerous, but it says nothing about her morality.

With no hope of escape from a group of men, in the face of inevitable rape, doña Marina managed to do what today's women's survival books advise. Exploiting her only asset, her multilingualism, she succeeded in attaching herself to what primatologists would call the alpha male (Cortés), who would not willingly share her with the others. (When he did relinquish her to Jaramillo, it was with a legitimate wedding and an income.) She worked hard at making herself one of the men, ever ready day or night to serve, always helpful and outgoing. Bernal Díaz characterized her as cheerful and "without embarrassment."[60] For a woman in her situation, any other strategy would have been suicidal.

Today in Mexican popular imagination her reputation has fallen victim to the blame-the-(sexual)-survivor syndrome. Like many a woman who has so suffered, her own character has come into question, her survival become distasteful, her collusion with her rapists reprehensible.[61] In many ways, her fate resembles that of Patty Hearst, a less gifted young woman who fell into the hands of minor league terrorists, was sexually brutalized, survived, and ended up in prison.

But if we are in the blame-the-victim business, there is another place to look. What put doña Marina into the hands of strangers before Cortés ever came on the scene? In book 12 of the *Florentine Codex* she is represented as haranguing the citizens of Tenochtitlan from a rooftop.[62] Throughout his account, Bernal Díaz praises her cleverness and ability to manipulate people through her talk. This is a far cry from the ideal described by Alonso de Zorita.

> Many daughters of rulers never left home until the day of their wedding. . . . A ruler's daughter went about in the company of many elderly women, and she walked so modestly that she never raised her eyes from the ground. . . . She never spoke in the temple, save to say the prayers she had been taught; she must not speak while eating, but must

keep absolute silence. . . . The maidens could not go out to
the gardens without guards. If they took a single step out
the door, they were harshly punished, especially if they had
reached the age of ten or twelve.[63]

Is it possible that by the time she reached the age of ten or twelve
this particular noble daughter had proven herself constitutionally
unfit for such a life? And lest her vociferous *tēntli*, her lengua that
would not be quiet, bring shame and ruin on them all, her harsh punishment had been what Bernal Díaz describes, to be secretly given
away by her own family and mourned as though dead? We cannot
but speculate.

Doña Marina's invaluable multilingualism distinguished her
from the other women who fell into the hands of Cortés and his men.
She was not branded on the forehead, gambled for, fought over. She
survived to be made the legitimate and dowried wife of a conqueror,
and her name, in all its forms, has survived four and a half centuries.
Without her services the European conquest of Mexico would inevitably have come, but not as soon and perhaps not to Cortés. Yet in
another sense, her fate was like the other women's. She was caught
up in an adventure the likes of which the world has not seen again.
She was impregnated by two different men and contributed children
to the first generation of mainland mestizos. Before middle age her
life was over.

This is no love story, no tale of blind ambition and racial be-
trayal, no morality play. It is the record of a gifted woman in impossible circumstances carving out survival one day at a time.

Concluding Remarks

Stephanie Wood and Robert Haskett

Testing theoretical concepts of gender—ideologies, roles, and relationships—was not our first concern in compiling these essays. Yet
the work of our contributors necessarily has touched on a number of
key issues surrounding the ideals and realities of relationships between women and men of various classes ethnicities, times, and
places. Moreover, by its very existence this volume raises two fundamental questions: Why study women in general? Why study indigenous women of colonial Mexico in particular?[1]

Leaving aside the second inquiry for the moment, it can be said
that as far as women of Latin America are concerned, a growing volume of work is actively expanding the horizons of what has traditionally been regarded as "history." By incorporating the experiences of a once-ignored segment of humankind, who have made up
roughly half of the population throughout time, scholars have made
it clear that the study of women does more than simply recover additional historical data to add balance to our knowledge of the past.
The more we discover about the historical experiences of women, the
more challenges arise to customary thinking about the structuring of
human societies and the ways in which those societies function. Un-

suspected relevance is being found in lesser-known forms of economic and political activity carried out by women. Previously hidden or disguised avenues to power and social status are being unmasked. Religious belief and practices are being reevaluated as potential sources of influence for women, even though leverage was usually differentially distributed between them and men.[2]

Even as women's history has gained the attention of scholars of Latin America, most of what we have learned concerns elite white women, who are more immediately accessible in the historical records.[3] The quincentenary of the first Columbian voyage, which led to a quickening interest in the meaning of the "encounter" and European invasion, resulted in works that in the majority gave indigenous women a passing glance. Only in recent times have the scattered, pioneering efforts of investigators to uncover the dimensions of indigenous women's lives begun to coalesce into an identifiable body of scholarly literature, sometimes highlighting them as actors on a broader societal stage, sometimes placing them more narrowly within their own cultural framework.[4]

Why study indigenous women of colonial Mexico in particular? Indigenous women continued to make up a large portion of the colonial population in places like New Spain. Demographic density had been considerable prior to contact, a fact that probably aided its physical recuperation after devastating diseases had so shockingly reduced it in the sixteenth century. During the long period of Spanish overlordship, surviving indigenous women were often crucial agents of cultural continuity and change, acting consciously and unconsciously along with men to forge new, colonial indigenous societies. Some of these native women made personal liaisons with Spanish men; others worked for them on a regular or rotational basis; still others, particularly those living in rural communities on the periphery of European settlement, may for centuries have had little contact with the newcomers.

What these women made of their own lives, of their relationships with indigenous men, with outsiders, and with the Spanish ecclesiastical and civil hierarchies forms an inseparable and critical part of "colonial history." Their preservation of an authentically "indigenous" lifestyle—sometimes actively, sometimes passively—is thought to have been facilitated in those areas where the Spanish presence was light and does not seem to have determined crucial features of everyday life. Indigenous society may have remained sufficiently separate over a number of generations to allow the indigenous cultural milieu to have been the dominant one, especially in rural women's lives. Among our authors, Marta Espejo-Ponce Hunt and Matthew Restall suggest indigenous communities had their "own agendas within (and even oblivious to) the larger colonial context," apparently especially so in the *cahob*, or rural communities of the interior. Inga Clendinnen has noted how the "Spanish presence . . . little . . . touched so many of the routines of the lives of women."[5]

But by expanding on the work of these pioneering scholars, the work of some of our contributors, such as Susan Deeds, strongly suggests that even women living in communities away from colonial heartlands felt the presence of the new imperial domination in ways that, once discovered, can reveal new dimensions of the colonial experience and legacy.[6] Conversely, other authors find that women living cheek by jowl with the Hispanic other in the center of the colony preserved unexpectedly durable indigenous traits. And while we will never know for certain, and acknowledging the risks of projecting back in time, our investigations into the experiences of indigenous women of New Spain may well provide us with important clues that could unravel some of the mysteries of the precontact period.

In fact, the analyses presented in some of the essays in this volume do indeed stretch across the traditionally recognized historical eras of pre- and postconquest. The subject matter of many of the ethnohistorical sources used by the authors here transcends and even obscures the conventional temporal break symbolized by the European invasion, a situation that in some cases makes obtaining a reliable understanding of "purely" native constructs problematical. Arthur J. O. Anderson's essay is representative of such studies. It straddles the line dividing preconquest from conquest, examining oral traditions that were recorded after Spanish arrival but that largely treat the pre-Columbian era. His discussion focuses on materials rich in fascinating detail but marked to some extent by the hand of European religious whose intention was to influence indigenous lifestyles. Providing further complications for analysis, these sources often present prescriptive gender ideology, with native men dictating model conduct and idealized descriptions of institutions such as marriage. Nahua social doctrine emerges sounding either heavily influenced by Christianity or remarkably and coincidentally like it, as we see, for instance, in the admonition, obey your husband.

This is not to say that the customary division of historical time and space lacks any value for those of us seeking to understand better how societies and cultures are changed through contact and colonization. Its preservation as an interpretive tool forces all of us to confront the impact of European conquest and colonization on indigenous gender relations, among other social and cultural concerns.

A number of recurring themes that have emerged in women's history are applicable to the spatial and temporal frame of this anthology. The gaps in our knowledge are many, but in these studies we endeavor to fill in a few of those gaps, even if by treading on new ground we are bound occasionally to trip and stumble. Control over sexuality and reproduction, the nature of domestic relations (marriage, dowry, polygyny, divorce, widowhood, etc.), the division of labor in family maintenance (inside and outside the home), education, and the possible formation of gender-based solidarity due to same-sex groupings and networking represent some of the many subjects that, given sufficient sources, scholars such as those represented here are beginning to (or would like to be able to) examine.[7]

In Search of Mesoamerican Gender Relations

Scholarly interest in the roles and status of women of so-called non-Western cultures such as those of precontact Mesoamerica has been inspired, in part, by the hope that the oppression of women is not a human universal, that we may find examples of gender-equal societies somewhere in human history.[8] Increasingly, in studies of gender ideology and gender roles in the precontact era, however, investigators are coming to the conclusion that the "Western" feminist dream of "equality" has muddied our views of other cultures and periods. Irene Silverblatt argues, for instance, that we must "transcend our heritage's determinisms" of such things as "gender configurations." Louise Burkhart, one of the contributors to the present volume, has questioned the applicability of concepts such as equality/subordination, public/private domain, and the supposed triviality of managing the household.[9] For this reason, a number of alternative interpretations that include concepts of reciprocity, parallelism, or complementarity—constructs that accord women's roles more importance than "Western" cultures did or do—are being adopted.

The basic idea behind all of these concepts is that gender ideologies in some precontact societies defined the roles carried out by women and men as being roughly balanced, rather than asymmetrical; for example, Silverblatt has identified what she defines as gender complementarity in pre-Inca society. Similar ideas have been developed by Mesoamericanists. Susan Kellogg argues here and elsewhere for the existence among the Aztecs of what she calls gender parallelism: the figuring of descent through both female and male lines, partible inheritance, the existence of "parallel" hierarchies of priests, with women serving important female deities while men attended to male deities, and the existence of both female and male marketplace judges.[10] Anderson finds mutual obligations between spouses and shared responsibilities toward children, not to mention examples of women poets and rulers. Robert Haskett suggests that elite Nahua women may have carried out what could be defined as parallel, independent political roles, a supposition supported by Susan D. Gillespie's conclusions about the importance of Aztec "queens" in the legitimation of dynastic succession.[11] Among the Maya, Rosemary Joyce has identified images of what she defines as gender complementarity in stone sculpture, ceramics, and figurines.[12]

Yet there continues to be a good deal of debate over the exact meaning, even the accuracy, of these newer analytical concepts. Our own contributors Espejo-Ponce Hunt and Restall, using colonial evidence that they characterize as "notably indigenous in style and technique," have found more inequality than interdependence in precontact Yucatan.[13] It is possible that colonial era derogatory remarks uncovered by these authors indicate a disdain for women; in one instance the people of Tetzal recanted some complaints against a Catholic priest by belittling them as "tale-telling and women's gossip." One might see this same apparent equation of women with weakness and negativity among the Mexica, who taunted reluctant warriors as "women." Purépecha elite of Michoacan would question their indigenous opponents' strength and bravery in conquest battles by comparing them to women: "They are lightweights! Are they strong men? No, they are women!"[14]

Yet readers should remember Lisa Mary Sousa's discussion of insults and give heed to Louise Burkhart's observation in this volume that such remarks may not be demeaning women and feminity but only questioning the fitness of males. Haskett's article includes evidence of a "parallel" situation, in which the femininity of the politically active doña Josefa María was questioned by describing her actions as being overly masculine. In other words, such remarks may actually provide indirect evidence for something like an ideology of parallelism, in which certain traits are associated with masculinity, others with femininity, without necessarily impugning the role of one or the other.

It is quite likely that cultural and social variables and differences in time and space—as well as limitations of the known source base and scholarly bias—are behind some of this analytical dissonance. Aside from keeping these factors in mind, we need to use terminology as precisely as possible, delineating, for instance, the subtle differences between complementarity and parallelism and their manifestations in different temporal and cultural contexts. We need continually to ask whether gender ideology, the often prescriptive ideals of behavior, exactly reflected the reality of gender roles? And following the warnings of Clendinnen, we should avoid sentimentalizing a lost world of "social and sexual harmony."[15]

However much studies (including many in the present volume) of women and gender in the precontact Americas might disagree, even those who speak of such things as gender parallelism also recognize that neither gender ideologies nor the concrete daily activities of women and men were ever constructed in neat, unchanging, and symmetrical kinds of relationships. Both Silverblatt and Kellogg have cautioned that neither complementarity nor parallelism should be considered the same thing as "equality." Among the Mexica, for instance, there is little evidence that women had access to the most prestigious priestly posts.[16] Gillespie's "queens" rarely seem to have exercised direct temporal political power, generally the province of men. Working from postconquest sources, often those left by Spanish male ecclesiastics, Clendinnen argues for less clear-cut gender relations among the preconquest Maya. She presents evidence for both inequality and mutuality and in some areas finds gender interdependence, hypothesizing that Yucatec Maya women were "separate and subordinate" but not necessarily "segregated and subjugated."[17]

So it must be stressed that women's roles and situations in Mesoamerica and elsewhere were rarely static culturally, socially, geographically, or temporally. Ideal prescriptions for those same roles and situations (of both individuals and groups) often existed in sharp contrast to the realities of human imperfection, although both are revealing of societal values.[18] We must bear in mind the crucial distinctions that marked the lives of women living in sedentary, imperial societies such as the Mexica as opposed to those living in sedentary but nonimperial societies such as the Mayas. Women (as well as men) living in semisedentary and nonsedentary societies undoubtedly faced even more radically different realities.[19]

The vastly different political, economic, social, and cultural organizational structures affecting people's lives had a significant bearing on women's roles and status. Social hierarchy and ethnic diversity, most pronounced in sedentary imperial societies, meant that class and ethnic differences could have cut through gender unity. Since life and culture during the precontact era was dynamic rather than unchanging, woman's place in any one grouping (indeed, even the sociocultural nature of the group itself) was subject to change over time. To cite just one type of evolving political situation, the organized militarism of imperial societies such as the Mexica, which emphasized the primacy of male deities associated with war and the successful male warrior as a social ideal, directly affected gender roles and relationships in both Mesoamerica and the Andes. The complementarity or parallelism of women's and men's roles gave way to increasing gender hierarchy on both temporal and symbolic planes, often contemporaneous with and seemingly affected by activities of expansionist states.[20]

Burkhart's work suggests that there may have been shifts in gender ideology to compensate for this rise of militarism that at least slowed the erosion of parallelism. Elaborating and revising some earlier treatments of male-female complementarity, she finds a complement for men's warrior role and its incumbent status in the symbolism of war that the Mexica invested in the home, a primary symbolic battlefield for women.

Surviving Conquest and Colonialism

The same issues raised by studies of women of the precontact era are applicable to the postconquest period. Added to them, of course, are questions touching on the effects of invasion and the attempted imposition of Spanish social and gender ideologies on indigenous societies. Here it can be asked if the study of gender can offer any special insights for understanding the consequences of conquest?

Based on the work of the authors contributing to the present volume, as well as on other studies of indigenous women and colonialism, the answer to this basic question would have to be "yes." Of course, there has been and continues to be debate as to exactly what befell native women after the Spanish arrival. Returning to the idea of gender parallelism or complementarity, for instance, Silverblatt sees the acceleration of Inca period tendencies for Andean women of every social level to become more subordinate once Spanish rule and gender ideology was introduced.[21] Only those willing to flee to the high *puna* (altiplano), and especially those who practiced shamanism, enjoyed some modicum of self-determination.[22] However, Restall has argued that while colonial Yucatec Maya women seem to have operated in an essentially partriarchal environment, they were not passive victims of rape and other forms of abuse and moreover enjoyed real economic importance as producers of goods destined for the tribute system.[23]

Once again, differences in time, space, class, and the like may well underlie the variegated sociocultural landscape inhabited by colonial indigenous women. So it is not surprising that other studies, including many by the authors in this volume, would contend that while colonial indigenous women were certainly subordinate in many ways, they were not abjectly powerless to control at least certain aspects of their own lives. For the colonial Mixtecs and Zapotecs of Oaxaca, Sousa finds evidence for the durability of gender complementarity well into the colonial period, in many ways impervious to the presumed spread of European-style patriarchy. Similarly, Stephanie Wood has found little evidence for a profound breakdown of gender complementarity, or at least a markedly increased victimization of indigenous women, in late colonial Toluca.[24] Just as Burkhart finds that precontact Mexica women and their society devised ways to compensate for male-dominated militarism, women living in the colonial era can be found engaging in what Kellogg describes as "counterhegemonic activities." This was not just true of the center, but also in "frontier" areas such as Nueva Vizcaya, where Susan Deeds finds evidence for the practice of witchcraft among indigenous women to counter domestic violence.

For central Mexico, the most spectacular of these counterhegemonic activities was women's prominent participation in rural indigenous riots and demonstrations of the late colonial period. If Robert Haskett's study of Tepoztlan is any indication, participation in these events crossed class lines, though in this particular case leadership seems to have been taken by women of the local elite.[25] His study suggests that the ability of postconquest indigenous women to achieve political legitimacy may have had precontact roots. Burkhart lends support to this view when she recalls Alvarado Tezozomoc's description of women defending Huitzilopochtli's temple. Whatever traditions allowed women to exercise power and authority before 1519, the dislocations and cultural alterations that occurred after this date may actually have enhanced the political legitimacy of at least some indigenous women. It can be posited that women could and did act when traditional male elites allowed themselves to be too thoroughly co-opted by the Spaniards. In the countryside of central Mexico later in the colonial era, the added stress on families and communities represented by Spanish tribute exactions and mounting external pressure on farmland, water, woods, and pasture may have led women spontaneously to rise along with men to defend them. These were issues touching on the defense of local autonomy and the security of subsistence, issues that would have affected women at least as profoundly as men. In Tepoztlan, for example, women whose men were forced to work miles away in Taxco would have been harder pressed to keep their families together as well as fulfill their obligations to the colonial state and Catholic church. In response they, like men, were willing to contest the right of outsiders to endanger their survival. The fact that women took a leading role in this and other similar disturbances of the eighteenth century suggests that some form of sociopolitical gender parallelism continued after 1519.[26]

The option of violence was just one aspect (and perhaps not even the most important one) in what is emerging as a dialogue in which colonial indigenous women negotiated their status and roles in life. The work of Kellogg, Haskett, Wood, Sousa, and Leslie S. Offutt, for example, portrays women as active, sometimes eager, seekers of redress for themselves, their families, and their communities in the Spanish courts. Evidence for such a dialogue can be found, as well, in rather unexpected places. For Coyoacan, in the Valley of Mexico, Rebecca Horn has examined the ways in which Nahua women's social identities (as illustrated in naming patterns and access to titles of nobility) were negotiated in the colonial context. In research encompassing a broad range of age and class distinctions, examining naming patterns for rich and poor, young and old, looking for gender differentiation, she finds among given names for females and males of the early seventeenth century that women tended to have as wide a variety as men. Only in second or surnames did women have a less varied repertoire than men, though both groups had by now adopted Spanish appellations. At the same time, women's names as well as men's continued to reflect social rank. Wood finds essentially the same patterns in colonial rural Toluca. If variety of naming was linked in some way to gender status, then it would seem as if women were subordinate in some ways. Yet the fact that they had taken Spanish names, and that elite women marked themselves off from commoners, in part, with more elaborate names and titles suggests that they enjoyed a status approaching that of elite men and decidedly above that of either commoner men or women. Perhaps the history of naming patterns suggests that indigenous people lost (or gained) status under Spanish rule, but in different aspects of their lives and at different paces depending on their sex as well as on their social rank.

How active a role women played in the selection of names (as opposed to husbands and fathers or even Catholic priests) remains to be seen. A more fundamental ability of women to control or at least participate in their marital choices is one of the most basic issues related to "colonized" women and is addressed by several of the authors here. Frances Karttunen provides a refreshing look at the quintessential cultural mediator, Malinche, a woman who seems to have made personal choices of self-preservation that have often been pictured as betraying cultural loyalties. Of noble Nahua birth, this woman of many names has been described in numerous roles, as a Maya-speaking slave, then a "present" to Spanish invaders, a baptized Christian, a slave to and rape victim of the Spaniards, an interpreter and mistress to Cortés, an enemy to Nahua resisters of the Spanish conquest, a wife to a conquering lieutenant, and a bearer of mixed-heritage children. Karttunen, skillfully sorting through the many historical perspectives and judiciously treating the politically colored portraits, the myths, and the most reliable primary accounts, finds not a traitor but a woman who negotiated her own survival by creatively capitalizing on what could have been disastrous circumstances.

Strategic marital alliances were a key element in Malinche's negotiations, a tactic used in a similar way by other Mesoamerican women and their families. Pedro Carrasco's discussion of indigenous-Spanish marriages shows that such cross-ethnic unions (in contrast to concubinage) were more numerous than has regularly been thought. The wealth, prestige, and influence over the larger, highly stratified Nahua community that elite women enjoyed and the possibilities in marriage for strategic alliances made them attractive to Spanish settlers. Native players manipulated such Spanish desires and shared with them schemes for strengthening wealth and influence. They additionally hoped to produce more valiant offspring, sons and daughters better able to thrive in the new world of colonialism. Like Malinche, many of the indigenous women involved in these matches may have been able to exercise a certain amount of choice. But Carrasco also identifies a practice rooted in indigenous culture, what the Spanish defined as "the donation of women," the dispersal of women by men to other men for social or political ends, suggesting that in marriage choice paternal figures (indigenous and otherwise) had the most power—even if younger men were also the pawns of some of these arrangements made by elders. Just as Nahua lords had sought to cement political alliances by "donating" women of their families to other powerful lords (this is undoubtedly what was behind the "gift" of Malinche to Cortés), so too did colonial Nahua men seek to ally themselves with powerful local Spaniards by "donating" their daughters in marriage.

Can similar patterns be found away from the center? In Yucatan, while liaisons between elite Maya women and seventeenth-century Spanish settlers did not quite rank with earlier Moteucçoma-*encomendero* (recipient of the right to collect tribute from a number of indigenous families or communities) alliances, Espejo-Ponce Hunt and Restall show that Europeans of lesser means sought to bolster their own status and wealth through marriage to noble, propertied indigenous women. As far as Oaxaca is concerned, Ronald Spores underlines, too, how indigenous elites, including elite women, could rank higher than some Spaniards. Both case studies provide some relief from the stereotype of the elite Spanish male taking the humble indigenous woman as concubine. Spores's discussion of *cacicas* (elite indigenous women) also underlines the significance of social status recognized both in the native and Spanish worlds for determining very different lifestyles for women of New Spain. After reading his description of three exemplary individuals, one should be able to dispense once and for all with the image of all indigenous women as poor, downtrodden peasants.[27]

In fact, the work of a number of our authors indicates that indigenous women could often maintain, perhaps even increase, their economic power after the conquest. Kellogg's analysis of indigenous women of Mexico City shows them to have been very important in marketing, food preparation, and domestic service. In the sixteenth century they held what seems to have been a large amount of property and to have been willing to go to court to protect that property.[28] While Kellogg suggests that Mexica women were less likely to own property and litigate about it in the seventeenth century, Wood's study of testaments from the adjacent Toluca Valley indicates that women continued to control significant amounts of land to the eve of independence. In Toluca, as in Mexico City and elsewhere, women seem to have been centrally important in small-scale commerce, in this case especially in the production and sale of pulque.

If further research maintains a distinction in property-holding patterns for women living in Mexico City as opposed to the Toluca Valley, the difference may hinge on the relative size and aggressiveness of their nonindigenous populations. And while the economic experiences of women of the colonial capital and of Toluca indicate that indigenous women were rarely reduced to a homogenous group of impoverished peasants, they do point to the preservation of a system of social stratification that not surprisingly gave elite women a better chance to marry well, own and control significant amounts of property, and avoid various kinds of manual labor; women who worked outside of the home in Mexico City, in Toluca, and in Yucatan's administrative capital of Mérida were invariably of humble social origins.

In fact, urban-rural distinctions seem to have played a role in the preservation of a socially complex indigenous world. It could be argued that the economic variety and dense populations of the colonial cities gave commoner indigenous women many more opportunities than their rural counterparts. The indigenous women who married into prosperous Spanish encomendero or landowning families like those discussed by Carrasco, Spores, and Espejo-Ponce Hunt and Restall, transforming themselves into urban women if they were not such already, were the most privileged. In this these scholars echo the findings of Elinor Burkett in her study of indigenous women of the postconquest Andes. Burkett asserts that the intimacy of many urban indigenous women with Spaniards gave them freedom and advantages that indigenous men did not have. Demography certainly helped to provide opportunities for alliances with colonial power holders, as it may well have in Yucatan, because away from Lima indigenous women often outnumbered both indigenous men and Spanish women.[29] The fate of humble women who lived in or migrated to the cities may not have been as positive in terms of cultural and ethnic survival. Kellogg has found significant shifts during the seventeenth century in the lives of the indigenous women of Mexico City, and Juan Javier Pescador believes that women who migrated from the countryside to that same capital crossed "borders of occupation, social class, and . . . ethnic identity. Outside their villages, Indian women soon found that being Indian entitled them to little."[30]

The picture we have been able to fashion of conditions in the countryside is not yet as sharply focused, in part because poorer, more dependent, and less socially prominent rural women can slip through the cracks of the documentary record. Social stratification did persist in the countryside, as evidenced by the sociopolitical prominence of Tepoztlan's doña Josefa María and the relatively well-to-do elite women of Oaxaca and Yucatan. The lot of commoner women in the countryside is less certain, or perhaps just less uniform. In Tepoztlan, female relatives of male tributaries faced increased socioeconomic burdens because of the demands of such things as the Taxco mine *repartimiento* (labor draft). This same kind of situation seems to have existed in the Andes, where Burkett stresses the increased hardships imposed by Spanish labor practices on Andean women.[31]

But just as one comfortably concludes that a solid rural-urban dichotomy has been established, other data shatter any such scholarly complacency. Relatively humble indigenous women of Toluca held and controlled property in their own right. Sousa reminds us how rural women were very active in local markets, having a major impact on the local economy and controlling community resources. In Yucatan, Espejo-Ponce Hunt and Restall find that Maya women living in their traditional communities not only enjoyed the protection of the local indigenous town council (true in the center as well), but many seem to have been able to maintain or increase an economic role in the form of property management, weaving, or beekeeping. Here these two authors agree with Clendinnen, who has noted elsewhere that the colonial economic system seems to have allowed Yucatec Maya women to expand their roles.[32]

At the same time, the lives of indigenous women of the "frontiers" may have departed significantly from various patterns suggested for the inhabitants of central Mexico, Oaxaca, and Yucatan with the advent and evolution of Spanish rule. Within the Tlaxcalan immigrant community of late colonial Saltillo, Offutt has found a great concern to protect the group's cultural purity. Yet in certain circumstances this community, surrounded as it was by Spaniards and people of mixed heritage, far from the sedentary indigenous heartland, could not avoid the formation of cross-cultural marital alliances. The Tlaxcalans of Saltillo, at least, had cultural roots in the sedentary Nahua heartland. To a certain extent Offutt's late colonial cases parallel earlier conditions uncovered by the other contributors. The women of San Esteban de Nueva Tlaxcala, like their counterparts in Mexico City or Mérida, participated actively in the economic life of their community.

Up to a point this last feature was probably true among peoples with less sedentary traditions, too. But it should be noted that Deeds finds evidence in Nueva Vizcaya that the complementarity of gender roles gave way to growing distinctions between indigenous men and women. Although the Tarahumaras and others attempted to preserve their own form of cultural integrity by violently resisting Jesuit attempts to impose monogamy and other aspects of Catholic Iberian culture, by the end of the colonial era patriarchal patterns emerged, leading to the erosion of women's status. Aside from nearly two hundred years of social indoctrination at the hands of Jesuit and secular priests, contributing factors seem to have included severe demographic dislocation as well as exaggerated land loss driven by the numerical ascendancy of nonindigenous society.[33]

New Directions

Neither this book nor the individual articles contained in it pretend to be exhaustive. It remains to be seen, for example, if non- or semi-sedentary women living near Saltillo and the Tlaxcalan enclave of San Esteban followed the same life patterns and faced the same gender relations as their sedentary sisters. And despite the anxiety of the citizens of San Esteban to maintain their ethnic purity, one cannot help wondering if some of the "Tlaxcalan" women and men inhabiting the community were actually acculturated "Chichimeca," and what, if any, process of cultural exchange had taken place between the differing indigenous ethnicities that might have affected the patterning of women's lives.[34]

In the end, the evidence herein is tentative, raising as many if not more questions as it answers. It is probably premature to make too many hard and fast conclusions about similarities and differences among the distinct cultures—the Mexicas of the imperial center, the broader Nahua world, the Mixtecs and Zapotecs of Oaxaca, the Mayas of Chiapas and Yucatan, the Tarahumaras, and the Tlaxcalan enclave of Saltillo in the north—taken in by our sample. We must continue to look for the ways in which such things as race, ethnicity, social class, and temporal evolution made a difference in the shaping of gender ideologies and in the actual playing out of gender roles.[35] We must strive to avoid making value judgments based on our own cultural experiences, neither ascribing to others our own situations nor creating in them a cultural other.[36] We should always remember that when assessing how women and men thought and acted, difference does not necessarily mean devaluation. And it remains for future studies to extract broad social theory from a synthesis of these and other works that are focused on specific times and places and that have addressed different concepts and facets regarding gender.

It is not too early, however, to pose numerous questions for intensive investigation. Is it possible that patterns of equality or subordination between the sexes bear some relationship with the degrees of sedentaryness and the process of imperial expansion of the native states? What are the full implications of gender distinctions found in the urban areas among women removed from the traditional indigenous world versus those found among women who remained in those communities? Did indigenous women living on Spanish estates in the countryside experience yet different situations? In what ways did social class, place of residence (urban vs. rural, ethnic urban enclave vs. mixed Hispanic-indigenous communities, center vs. fringe), and ethnicity affect the trajectory of a shift from gender complementarity to gender inequality? Will further study support the contention that those women who were more likely to link up with conquerors (such as urban women) were especially well placed for cultural exchange? Conversely, did urban women face exposure to greater levels of discrimination, abuse, and the erosion of indigenous-style gender relations?[37] Will the stereotype of rural women's greater cultural conservatism hold up?

Another recurring theme in the essays as in the more general literature on indigenous women is the role indigenous women played as cultural mediators.[38] Can the study of indigenous gender ideologies, roles, and relations both before and after the conquest in fact be used as a tool of analysis to highlight the significance of differing degrees and differing types of cross-cultural contact? If so, we cannot ignore the implications of this kind of contact between Spanish, *casta* (racially mixed), and African women (as well as men) with Mexica, Nahua, Mixtec, or Maya women (and men). Beyond cultural exchange, how did race mixture affect gender power relations and connections between indigenous peoples and European and African newcomers? Finally, we should search for differences and similarities between the status and roles of indigenous women and those of mixed, African, or European heritage as well as relative female-male relations within a single ethnic or racial group.[39] For instance, Della M. Flusche and Eugene H. Korth have stressed, in examining indigenous women of colonial Chile, how "contrasts that characterized" the lives of nonwhite women are more apparent than any commonality of experience.[40]

Foreign concepts of public and private spheres and their interplay with gender roles and ideology might have less relevance for early New Spain than a consideration of the sometimes competing, sometimes complementary distinction between individual and community.[41] In her article, Offutt reveals cases that do indeed appear to divide between individual interests and corporate interests. As she shows, for some individuals cross-cultural unions held an attractiveness, yet for others there was an overriding concern to preserve and protect the indigenous purity of the community. Some of these same considerations must have underlain the actions of women who intermarried with Spaniards, chose to live among non-Indians in places such as Mérida, or elected to follow their sociopolitical fortunes in a community such as Tepoztlan.

There are undoubtedly many other innovative ways to approach the issues raised by the study of women, and of indigenous women in particular, that have not occurred to us. Though she does not develop the theme to any degree, Clendinnen has suggested an intriguing mechanism for comparing gender status. In a recent article, she observes how Yucatec Maya men's clothing over the Spanish colonial period was "reduced to the new simplicity of unadorned shirts and loose trousers" while "women's dress remained highly expressive, as did their modes of decoration and presentation of self."[42] Martha Few, examining the lives of women of seventeenth-century Santiago de Guatemala, urges us to "link religion, along with gender, race, and class," as we analyze such things as resistance and the creation of "an identity for themselves as women within colonial partriarchal structures."[43] Perhaps a particularly focused analysis of some of the sources investigated by our authors, such as testaments and estate inventories, can be employed to test the apparently gender-specific cultural implications of these findings.[44]

Summary Observations

The discussion that has been emerging from the recent literature on women and gender and from our own contributors, especially, cautions us about applying "Western" constructs, about ignoring cultural relativism, and about remembering the importance of time and place (history). Despite such cautions it is possible to make some tentative conclusions based on the work of our authors. Full equality for indigenous women in early Mexico remained elusive over the entire span of time taken in by this anthology. Some measure of mutuality, parallelism, or complementarity existed between indigenous women and men across Mesoamerica both before and after Europeans came on the scene, with regional and temporal variations. However, there is also evidence for women's subordination in certain of life's arenas both before and after contact. Spanish patriarchal social relations and cultural values most likely had an impact on indigenous culture, but with tempo and degree affected by human geography and factors that take into account distinctions between individuals and communities, plus ethnicity and social class.

But women were rarely passive victims. They worked hard, used whatever overt or hidden avenues to power were available, participated in many activities that would have been alien or prohibited to European women, litigated their causes in the courts, and negotiated (with indigenous men and with the colonizers) their own personal positions and those of their progeny to carve out the best possible present and future they could given their circumstances.

Notes

Introduction

1. Although doubtless egregious to some, for want of any other term quite so specific, the term "Indian" appears in the title of this collection and is intrinsic to the narratives of many of the essays contained herein. Whenever possible, of course, the name of a particular ethnic or linguistic group is employed; in other instances, especially for the collective or a more general identification of our subjects (and following the precedent established by the University of Oklahoma Press), "American Indian" or "Indian" is used (and note that this same form is used by several of the American Indian scholars referred to in this chapter and the sources, e.g., Paula Gunn Allen, Rayna Green, and Wilma Mankiller). Following any dictionary definition but especially the *Oxford English Dictionary*, the alternative terms "native" and "indigenous" refer to *anyone* born in a given geographic region, and hence neither is exclusively appropriate to the purpose and content of this anthology.

2. For just one example of similar machinations in medieval Europe, see Jenny M. Jochens, "The Politics of Reproduction," *American Historical Review* 92:2 (1987): 327–49.

3. Numerous scholars deny that indigenous women held actual offices of rulership, preferring instead to define *cacica* (Arawak: feminine form

for *cacique*, "head man," "ruler") as wife of a cacique. Nahuatl terminology lends itself more explicitly to the role of a female ruler, that is, *cihuatlatoani*, literally, "woman ruler," i.e., "queen." For additional discussion on the role of Mesoamerican women and rulership, see Susan D. Gillespie, *The Aztec Kings: The Construction of Rulership in Mexica History* (Tucson: University of Arizona Press, 1989), passim; Susan Schroeder, *Chimalpahin and the Kingdoms of Chalco* (Tucson: University of Arizona Press, 1991), 183–85; Lisa Mary Sousa, "Women and Crime in Colonial Oaxaca: Evidence of Complementary Gender Roles in Mixtec and Zapotec Societies," chap. 9, this volume; Ronald Spores, "Mixteca *Cacicas*: Status, Wealth, and the Political Accommodation of Native Elite Women in Early Colonial Oaxaca," chap. 8, this volume; and Kevin Terraciano, "Ñudzahui History: Mixtec Writing and Culture in Colonial Oaxaca" (Ph.D. diss., University of California, Los Angeles, 1994), 274–96. Also see Valerie Shirer Mathes, "A New Look at the Role of Women in Indian Society," *American Indian Quarterly* 2:2 (1975): 131–39.

4. The article was subsequently published as "The Noblewomen of Chalco," *Estudios de Cultura Náhuatl* 22 (1992): 45–86. In 1989, Stephanie Wood and Robert Haskett joined me as coeditors.

5. See especially James Lockhart, *Nahuas and Spaniards: Postconquest Mexican History and Philology*, Nahuatl Studies Series, no. 3 (Stanford and Los Angeles: Stanford University Press and UCLA Latin American Center, 1991), and *The Nahuas after the Conquest: A Social and Cultural History of the Indians of Central Mexico, Sixteenth through Eighteenth Centuries* (Stanford: Stanford University Press, 1992), 7, 375.

6. Patricia Seed, book review, *Hispanic American Historical Review* 70:4 (1990): 688–89, reiterates these two questions regarding the role of men in recording and interpreting women's experience and the popular notion of a universal absence of a "subaltern" voice (following Gayatari Spivak). The primary sources by and about indigenous Mexicans speak loud and clear answers to both speculations.

7. For a dated yet informative overview of such documents, see Howard F. Cline, ed., *Guide to Ethnohistorical Sources*, vols. 14 and 15 of *Handbook of Middle American Indians*, gen. ed. Robert Wauchope (Austin: University of Texas Press, 1975). There are, of course, numerous studies about colonial Mexico that are important for context and that treat Indian women. See, e.g., Ana María Atondo Rodríguez, *El amor venal y la condición femenina en el México colonial* (México: Instituto Nacional de Antropología e Historia, 1992); Pilar Gonzalbo Aizpuru, *Las mujeres de la Nueva España: Educación y vida cotidiana* (México: El Colegio de México, 1987); Asunción Lavrin, ed., *Latin American Women: Historical Perspectives* (Westport, Conn.: Greenwood Press, 1978); Asunción Lavrin, "*Lo femenino:* Women in Colonial Historical

Sources," in *Coded Encounters: Writing, Gender, and Ethnicity in Colonial Latin America*, ed. Francisco Javier Cevallos-Candau, Jeffrey A. Cole, Nina M. Scott, and Nicomedes Suárez-Araúz (Amherst: University of Massachusetts Press, 1994), 153–76; Josefina Muriel, *Los recogimientos de las mujeres* (México: Universidad Nacional Autónoma de México, 1974), *Cultura femenina novohispana* (México: Universidad Nacional Autónoma de México, 1994), and *La sociedad novohispana y sus colegios de niñas*, vol. 1 (México: Universidad Nacional Autónoma de México, 1995); María J. Rodríguez-Shadow and Robert Shadow, "Las mujeres aztecas y las españolas en los siglos XVI y XVII. Análisis comparativo de la literatura social," *Colonial Latin American Historical Review* 5:1 (1996): 21–46; Patricia Seed, *To Love, Honor, and Obey in Colonial Mexico: Conflicts over Marriage Choice, 1574–1821* (Stanford: Stanford University Press, 1988); and Marcela Tostado Gutiérrez, *El álbum de la mujer. Antología ilustrada de las mexicanas*, vol. 2: *Época colonial*. (México: Instituto Nacional de Antropología e Historia, 1991).

8. See, e.g., don Domingo de San Antón Muñón Chimalpahin Quauhtlehuanitzin (hereafter, Chimalpahin), *Society and Politics in Mexico Tenochtitlan, Tlatelolco, Texcoco, Culhuacan, and Other Nahua Altepetl in Central Mexico*, ed. and trans. Arthur J. O. Anderson and Susan Schroeder, vols. 1 and 2 of *Codex Chimalpahin*, gen. ed. Susan Schroeder (Norman: University of Oklahoma Press, 1997); and Miguel León-Portilla's comment in support of female authorship, as cited in Muriel, *Cultura femenina novohispana*, 12. Yet compare Inga Clendinnen's "We hear no Mexica women's voices at all," in her *Aztecs: An Interpretation* (Cambridge: Cambridge University Press, 1991), 154.

9. For specific information regarding the important roles held by elderly women, see Frances Karttunen and James Lockhart, ed. and trans., *The Art of Nahuatl Speech: The Bancroft Dialogues*, Nahuatl Studies Series, no. 2 (Los Angeles: UCLA Latin American Center, Pubs., 1987), 144–45, 148–61.

10. Archaeology is another important methodology for additional data on women's experiences. See, especially, Elizabeth M. Brumfiel, "Weaving and Cooking: Women's Production in Aztec Mexico," in *Engendering Archaeology: Women and Prehistory*, ed. Joan M. Gero and Margaret W. Conkey (Cambridge, Mass.: Basil Blackwell, 1991), 224–51. Brumfiel's quote from Jacques Soustelle underscores our findings: "The Mexican woman . . . had a great deal to do" (p. 246).

11. Robert D. Wood, *"Teach Them Good Customs"* (Culver City, Calif.: Labyrinthos, 1986).

12. This was not a policy specifically against Indians. See Lavrin, *Latin American Women*, 25, who finds that no educational texts for women (in general) were published during the colonial period.

13. For a classic study on this subject, see Margaret Mead, *The Changing Culture of an Indian Tribe* (New York: AMS Press, [1932] 1969). In his "Life on the Edge," *New York Review of Books* 41:7 (April 7, 1994): 3–4, Clifford Geertz succinctly notes, regarding new trends and findings in studying indigenous peoples, "Instead of the romance of loss, we have the pragmatics of struggle."

14. In English translation some examples are Anthony Pagden, ed. and trans., *Hernán Cortés: Letters from Mexico* (New Haven: Yale University Press, 1986); Lesley Byrd Simpson, ed. and trans., *Cortés: The Life of the Conqueror by His Secretary, Francisco López de Gómara* (Berkeley: University of California Press, 1964); Genero García, ed., *Bernal Díaz del Castillo: The Discovery and Conquest of Mexico* trans. A. P. Maudslay (New York: Farrar, Straus, and Giroux, 1970); and Patricia de Fuentes, ed. and trans., *The Conquistadors: First-Person Accounts of the Conquest of Mexico,* (New York: Orion Press, 1963). And consult individual chapters for references to key works both inside and beyond central Mexico.

15. Most familiar are fray Andrés de Olmos, *Tratado de hechicerías y sortilegios, 1553,* ed. Georges Baudot (México: Universidad Nacional Autónoma de México, [1553] 1990); and Hernando Ruiz de Alarcón, *Treatise on the Heathen Superstitions that Today Live among the Indians Native to this New Spain, 1629,* ed. J. Richard Andrews and Ross Hassig (Norman: University of Oklahoma Press, [1629] 1984).

16. Fray Alonso de Molina, *Vocabulario en lengua castellana y mexicana y mexicana y castellana* (México: Editorial Porrúa, [1571] 1970); and for the seventeenth century, Horacio Carochi, *Arte de la lengua mexicana* (México: Universidad Nacional Autónoma de México, [1645] 1983).

17. Fray Diego Durán, *The History of the Indies of New Spain,* ed. and trans. Doris Heyden (Norman: University of Oklahoma Press, 1994); fray Toribio de Benavente o Motolinia, *Motolinia's History of the Indians of New Spain,* ed. and trans. Elizabeth Andros Foster (Westport, Conn.: Greenwood Press, 1973); fray Alonso de Molina, *Confesionario mayor en la lengua mexicana y castellana* (México: Universidad Nacional Autónoma de México, [1569] 1984); fray Pedro de Gante, *Doctrina cristiana en lengua mexicana* (México: Centro de Estudios Históricos Fray Bernardino de Sahagún, [1553] 1981); and fray Bernardino de Sahagún, *Psalmodia Christiana (Christian Psalmody),* trans. Arthur J. O. Anderson (Salt Lake City: University of Utah Press, 1993), and *Adiciones, apéndice a la postilla y ejercicio cotidiano,* trans. Arthur J. O. Anderson (México: Universidad Nacional Autónoma de México, 1993). For the *Exercicio quotidiano* in English translation, see Chimalpahin, "Society and Politics in Mexico Tenochtitlan . . . ," vol. 2.

18. Karttunen and Lockhart, *The Art of Nahuatl Speech;* fray Juan

Bautista, *Huehuetlatolli* (México, 1600); fray Andrés de Olmos, *Grammaire de la langue nahuatl ou mexicaine*, ed. Rémi Siméon (Paris: Imprimerie Nationale, 1875); and fray Bernardino de Sahagún, *Florentine Codex: General History of the Things of New Spain*, vol. 6: *Rhetoric and Moral Philosophy*, ed. and trans. Arthur J. O. Anderson and Charles E. Dibble (Santa Fe and Salt Lake City: School of American Research and University of Utah Press, 1969).

19. Fray Bernardino de Sahagún, *Florentine Codex*, 12 vols. For a synthetic treatment of Mesoamerican women based largely on those texts, see Anna-Britta Hellbom, "The Life and Role of Women in Aztec Culture," *Cultures* 8:3 (1982): 55–65, and also María J. Rodríguez-Shadow, *La mujer azteca* (México: Universidad Autónoma del Estado de México, 1991). For assorted additional studies on Indian women in early Mexico, see *Ethnohistory, Special Issue: Women, Power, and Resistance in Colonial Mesoamerica*, ed. Kevin Gosner and Deborah E. Kanter, 42:2 (Fall 1995).

20. Cited in Mary Beth Rose, ed., *Women in the Middle Ages and the Renaissance: Literary and Historical Perspectives* (New York: Syracuse University Press, 1986), xvii; and Natalie Zemon Davis, "Iroquois Women, European Women," in *Women, "Race," and Writing in the Early Modern Period*, ed. Margo Hendricks and Patricia Parker (London: Routledge, 1994), 243–58, 350–61.

21. Muriel, *La sociedad novohispana*, 23–36, 53–55, 73–93. See also Pilar Gonzalbo Aizpuru, *Historia de la educación en la época colonial. El mundo indígena* (México: El Colegio de México, 1990); Alfredo López Austin, *La educación de los antiguos nahuas*, 2 vols. (México: SEP, 1985); and Tomás Zepeda, *La educación pública en la Nueva España en el siglo XVI* (México: Editorial Progreso, 1972).

22. For primary texts and secondary studies based on a variety of literary genres, see especially S. L. Cline, ed. and trans., *The Book of Tributes: Early Sixteenth-Century Nahuatl Censuses from Morelos*, Nahuatl Studies Series, no. 4 (Los Angeles: UCLA Latin American Center, 1993); S. L. Cline and Miguel León-Portilla, eds., *The Testaments of Culhuacan*, Nahuatl Studies Series, no. 1 (Los Angeles: UCLA Latin American Center, 1984); Robert Haskett, *Indigenous Rulers: An Ethnohistory of Town Government in Colonial Cuernavaca* (Albuquerque: University of New Mexico Press, 1991); Rebecca Horn, *Postconquest Coyoacan: Nahua-Spanish Relations in Central Mexico, 1519–1650* (Stanford: Stanford University Press, 1997); James Lockhart, *Nahuas and Spaniards;* James Lockhart, ed. and trans., *We People Here: Nahuatl Accounts of the Conquest of Mexico*, Reportorium Columbianum Series, gen. ed. Geoffrey Symcox (Berkeley: University of California Press, 1993); James Lockhart, Frances Berdan, and Arthur J. O. Anderson, eds. and trans., *The Tlaxcalan Actas: A Compendium of the Records of the Cabildo of Tlaxcala (1545–1627)* (Salt Lake City: University of Utah Press, 1986); and Matthew Restall, *Life and*

Death in a Maya Community: The Ixil Testaments of the 1760s (Lancaster, Calif.: Labyrinthos, 1995).

23. Woodrow Borah, *Justice by Insurance: The General Indian Court of Colonial Mexico and the Legal Aides of the Half-Real* (Berkeley: University of California Press, 1983).

24. Two such examples are Fernando de Alva Ixtlilxochitl, *Obras históricas*, 2 vols., ed. Edmundo O'Gorman (México: Universidad Nacional Autónoma de México, 1975–77); and Fernando Alvarado Tezozomoc, *Crónica mexicáyotl*, trans. Adrián León (México: Universidad Nacional Autónoma de México, 1949), and *Crónica mexicana*, ed. Manuel Orozco y Berra (México: Editorial Porrúa, [1878] 1975).

25. For the collected Nahuatl and Spanish writings of Chimalpahin in English translation, see *Codex Chimalpahin*, 6 vols., gen ed. Susan Schroeder (Norman: University of Oklahoma Press, 1997).

26. Muriel, *La sociedad novohispana*, 53–74.

27. Ibid., 84–86.

28. Similarly, in New France the Jesuits expected that female Indian converts, using their influence on their families, would facilitate the establishment of new Christian villages. See Carol Devens, *Countering Colonization: Native American Women and Great Lakes Missions, 1630–1900* (Berkeley: University of California Press, 1992), 20.

29. There are several excellent studies treating different forms of Indian women's resistance: Devens, *Countering Colonization*, 21–3, 29–30; for northern Mexico, Ruth Behar, "The Visions of a Guachichil Witch in 1599: A Window on the Subjugation of Mexico's Hunter-Gatherers," *Ethnohistory* 34:2 (Spring 1987): 115–38; for colonial New Mexico, Ramón A. Gutiérrez, "A Gendered History of the Conquest of America: A View from New Mexico," in *Gender Rhetorics: Postures on Dominance and Submission in History*, ed. Richard C. Trexler (Binghamton, N.Y.: Medieval and Renaissance Texts and Studies, 1994), 47–63; and for Peru, Irene Silverblatt, *Moon, Sun, and Witches: Gender Ideologies and Class in Inca and Colonial Peru* (Princeton: Princeton University Press, 1987).

30. Ann Miriam Gallagher, "The Indian Nuns of Mexico City's *Monasterio* of Corpus Christi, 1724–1821," in *Latin American Women*, ed. Asunción Lavrin, 150–72.

31. Gallagher, "The Indian Nuns," 164.

32. For an excellent study of the "female subculture" in convents in early modern Europe, see Elissa Weaver, "Spiritual Fun: A Study of Sixteenth-Century Tuscan Convent Theater," in *Women in the Middle Ages*, ed. Mary Beth Rose, 173–205. And see Muriel, *Cultura femenina novohispana*, 313–471.

33. In sixteenth-century Italy, in spite of their prolific contributions, "among the nuns only the saints have been remembered." Cited in Mary Beth Rose, "Introduction," in *Women in the Middle Ages*, ed. Mary Beth Rose, xxiii. Muriel, however, lists the names of numerous Indian and creole nuns; *Cultura femenina novohispana*, 44–120.

34. Lavrin, "Introduction," in *Latin American Women*, ed. Asunción Lavrin, 14, suggests that these Indian nuns developed a "new set of values and behavior catering to the Spanish society and borrowing from it at the same time, but still maintaining its own identity. An Indian nunnery meant the complete adoption of the conqueror's religion."

35. The situation for Indian women in early Mexico is often overly generalized, indicating a static, exclusive society, which is a direct contradiction to the evidence presented in this volume. For such a study, see Laura A. Lewis, "The 'Weakness' of Women and the Feminization of the Indian in Colonial Mexico," *Colonial Latin American Review* 5:1 (1996): 73–94. For important studies on cofradías, see Asunción Lavrin, "Mundo en contraste. Cofradías rurales y urbanas en México a fines del siglo XVIII," in *La iglesia en la economía de América latina siglos XVI al XIX*, ed. A. J. Bauer (México: Instituto Nacional de Antropología e Historia, 1986), 235–76; Nancy M. Farriss, *Maya Society under Colonial Rule: The Collective Enterprise of Survival* (Princeton: Princeton University Press, 1984); William B. Taylor, *Drinking, Homicide, and Rebellion in Colonial Mexican Villages* (Stanford: Stanford University Press, 1979), 19, 52, 118; and Lockhart, *Nahuas after the Conquest*, especially 218–29.

36. See Susan Schroeder, "Nahuas and the *Bona Mors* at the Colegio de San Gregorio." Paper presented at the XVII International Congress of the History of Religions, Mexico City, August 1995.

37. See Schroeder, *Chimalpahin and the Kingdoms of Chalco*, 154–97.

38. The accounts by the Jesuit Andrés Pérez de Ribas are informative: *Historia de los triunfos de nuestra santa fe entre gentes las más bárbaras*, 3 vols. (México: Siglo Veintiuno Editores, [1645] 1992); and see John Bierhorst, trans., *Cantares mexicanos: Songs of the Aztecs* (Stanford: Stanford University Press, 1985), 88–90, for a description from Pérez de Ribas about a ceremony at the Colegio de San Gregorio, and also p. 96, where he cites Cervantes de Salazar's discussion of Indian women's dancing activities.

39. Congregación de la Buena Muerte MS., Instituto Nacional de Antropología e Historia, Archivo Histórico, Mexico City, Col. Ant., Colegio de San Gregorio, v. 119.

40. Not uncommonly, even standard secondary studies tend to obfuscate any consideration of women's possible roles. See Sharisse D. McCafferty and Geoffrey G. McCafferty, "Engendering Tomb 7 at Monte Albán: Respinning an Old Yarn," *Current Anthropology* 32:2 (1994): 143–66.

41. Clendinnen, *Aztecs*, 154, and Lavrin, *Latin American Women*, 24–29, for example.

42. Even with such variety and abundance, all texts, whether in Spanish or in indigenous languages, require critical evaluation not only for their content but also for their authorship, the circumstances of their production, and the nature of the text itself. Little is known of individual indigenous authors, even notaries, much less the situations by which they came to possess literary skills as professionals.

43. Joan Kelly's pioneering call, in her *Women, History, and Theory: The Essays of Joan Kelly* (Chicago: University of Chicago Press, 1984), to "restore women to history and to restore our history to women," based on her negative findings of women's experiences in Renaissance Italy as understood through theoretical perspectives of patriarchy has since been modified substantially by means of an expanded, interdisciplinary intellectually inclusive focus. See Rose, "Introduction," in *Women in the Middle Ages*, ed. Mary Beth Rose, xiii–xv.

44. For some studies regarding cross-dressing and berdaches, see Bierhorst, *Cantares mexicanos*, 496; Clendinnen, *Aztecs*, 167–71; Raymond E. Hauser, "The *Berdache* and the Illinois Indian Tribe during the Last Half of the Seventeenth Century," *Ethnohistory* 37:1 (1990): 45–65; Cecelia F. Klein, "Fighting with Femininity: Gender and War in Aztec Mexico," *Estudios de Cultura Náhuatl* 24 (1994): 219–53; and Richard C. Trexler, *Sex and Conquest: Gendered Violence, Political Order, and the European Conquest of the Americas* (Ithaca: Cornell University Press, 1995), passim.

45. See Rayna Green's most informative introduction to *Native American Women: A Contextual Bibliography*, ed. Rayna Green (Bloomington: Indiana University Press, 1983), 1–17; Gretchen M. Bataille and Kathleen M. Sands, eds., *American Indian Women: A Guide to Research* (New York: Garland Press, 1991); and, for informative essays relating to gender and power among native peoples in the United States, see Laura F. Klein and Lillian A. Ackerman, eds., *Women and Power in Native North America* (Norman: University of Oklahoma Press, 1995). Also, for Peru and the highly structured roles there, see Kimberly Gauderman, "Father Fiction: The Construction of Gender in England, Spain, and the Andes," *UCLA Historical Journal, Special Issue: Indigenous Writing in the Spanish Indies* 12 (1992): 122–51.

46. James A. Clifton, *Being and Becoming Indian: Biographical Studies of North American Frontiers* (Chicago: Dorsey Press, 1989), x, xiii; Devens, *Countering Colonization*, 13, where the tribal unit is the primary concern, yet gendered roles figure importantly in determining how to preserve it; and see Paula Gunn Allen, *The Sacred Hoop: Recovering the Feminine in American Indian Traditions* (Boston: Beacon Press, 1986), 43–44, 56, who states that "an

American Indian woman is primarily defined by her tribal identity." For a study about a Mexican Indian woman's identity as such in the twentieth century, see Judith Friedlander, "Doña Zeferina Barreto: Biographical Sketch of an Indian Woman from the State of Morelos," in *Women in the Mexican Countryside, 1850–1990,* ed. Heather Fowler-Salamini and Mary Kay Vaughan (Tucson: University of Arizona Press, 1994), 125–39.

47. Wilma Mankiller, "One Woman's 'Trail of Tears' Ends, with Honor, Back Home," *New York Times,* November 4, 1994; and see Wilma Mankiller and Michael Wallis, *Mankiller, a Chief and Her People: An Autobiography by the Principal Chief of the Cherokee Nation* (New York: St. Martin's Press, 1993). For the importance of tribal identity among indigenous women in U.S. cities, see the native author Jennie R. Joe, "Gender and Culture: American Indian Women in Urban Societies," in *Violence, Resistance, and Survival in the Americas,* ed. William B. Taylor and Franklin Pease G.Y. (Washington, D.C.: Smithsonian Institution Press, 1994), 249–65.

48. R. Douglas Cope, *The Limits of Racial Domination: Plebeian Society in Colonial Mexico City, 1660–1720* (Madison: University of Wisconsin Press, 1994), 3; James Lockhart, Introduction, in *Provinces of Early Mexico: Variants of Spanish American Regional Evolution,* ed. Ida Altman and James Lockhart (Los Angeles: UCLA Latin American Center, 1976), 11–28; and see Magnus Mörner, *La corona española y los foraneos en los pueblos de indios de América* (Stockholm: Almquist and Wiksell, 1970), for a careful explication of the royal legislation that contributed to the delineation of the two groups.

49. See Charles Gibson, *The Aztecs under Spanish Rule: A History of the Indians of the Valley of Mexico, 1519–1810* (Stanford: Stanford University Press, 1964), 166–93; and Lockhart, *The Nahuas after the Conquest,* 14–58, 94–140.

50. Lavrin, *Latin American Women,* 30.

51. See Sylvia Van Kirk, *Many Tender Ties: Women in Fur-Trade Society, 1670–1870* (Norman: University of Oklahoma Press, 1983), 6, 8, 25–27, for examples of native women of western Canada who actively sought European husbands, anticipating a life of enhanced material and physical comforts. For these women, marriage defined their position. See Seed, *To Love, Honor, and Obey,* 17–19, for Spanish influence on colonial marriages. Yet marriage could work both ways: see Elinor C. Burkett, "Indian Women and White Society: The Case of Sixteenth-Century Peru," 106–07, in *Latin American Women,* ed. Asunción Lavrin, regarding conquerors in Peru and the benefits for themselves and their children on marrying an Indian woman of high rank; and Gibson, *Aztecs under Spanish Rule,* 124–25, discusses an Indian woman of considerable wealth and influence in colonial Mexico.

52. For feminist history, see, e.g., Kelly, *Women, History, and Theory,* and Silverblatt, *Moon, Sun, and Witches.* Robert Darnton suggests two phases

for recent feminist history, one empirical and triumphalist and the other theoretical and expansionist, and sees a place and future for an even "broader and more ambitious history" for women even with "contemporary codes of womanhood"; "Cherchez la Femme," *New York Review of Books* 42:13 (1995): 22–24. See as well Rolena Adorno's caveat regarding the limitations of trendy literary jargon and sweeping generalizations on effective scholarship, "Reconsidering Colonial Discourse for Sixteenth- and Seventeenth-Century Spanish America," *Latin American Research Review* 28:3 (1993): 135–45.

53. Here "equal" is not defined as an aspect of the Western politicized concept of power. Jay Miller, "Society in 1492," in *America in 1492: Selected Lectures from the Quincentenary Program*, ed. Frederick E. Hoxie (Chicago: D'Arcy McNickle Center for the History of the American Indian, Newberry Library, no. 15, 1992), 160; and "A Kinship of Spirit," in *America in 1492: The World of the Indian Peoples Before the Arrival of Columbus*, ed. Alvin M. Josephy, Jr. (New York: Alfred A. Knopf, 1992), 305–37. See also Mona Etienne and Eleanor Leacock, "Introduction," in *Women and Colonization: Anthropological Perspectives*, ed. Mona Etienne and Eleanor Leacock (New York: Praeger, 1980), 9–12; and Deven's discussion of "vital symmetry," in *Countering Colonization*, 13.

54. See Clendinnen, *Aztecs*, 173, 174–209. Two useful and informative anthologies for gender studies about indigenous women are Virginia E. Miller, ed., *The Role of Gender in Precolumbian Art and Architecture* (Boston: University Press of America, 1988); and Gero and Conkey, *Engendering Archaeology*.

55. Clendinnen, *Aztecs*, 168–72, 206–07.

56. Steve J. Stern, *The Secret History of Gender: Women, Men, and Power in Late Colonial Mexico* (Chapel Hill: University of North Carolina Press, 1995), 301.

Chapter 1. Mexica Women on the Home Front

A Spanish translation of this article has been published in *Mesoamérica* 23 (June 1992): 23–54 (translation by Chris Lutz). I wish to thank Robert Haskett, Susan Kellogg, Susan Schroeder, Michael Smith, and Stephanie Wood for their comments and suggestions.

1. This ethnic marker designates the Nahuatl-speaking group that inhabited Tenochtitlan and Tlatelolco, the two island settlements that comprised Mexico and became the center of Mexico City. The Mexicas were the dominant power within the Aztec Empire. Because of linguistic and cultural similarities, compounded by immigration and intermarriage, little distin-

guished the residents of Tenochtitlan and Tlatelolco from other Nahua groups of the Basin of Mexico and nearby regions.

2. Susan Kellogg, "Cognatic Kinship and Religion: Women in Aztec Society," in *Smoke and Mist: Mesoamerican Studies in Memory of Thelma D. Sullivan,* ed. J. Kathryn Josserand and Karen Dakin (Oxford: British Archaeological Reports Press, 1988), 2:676. Scholars who have focused explicitly on the issue of male dominance include June Nash, "The Aztecs and the Ideology of Male Dominance," *Signs* 4:2 (1978): 349–62, and "Aztec Women: The Transition from Status to Class in Empire and Colony," in *Women and Colonization: Anthropological Perspectives,* ed. Mona Etienne and Eleanor Leacock (New York: Praeger, 1980), 134–48; María J. Rodríguez-Shadow, *La mujer azteca* (México: Universidad Autónoma del Estado de México, 1991); Colin M. MacLachlan, "The Eagle and the Serpent: Male over Female in Tenochtitlan," *Proceedings of the Pacific Coast Council on Latin American Studies* 5 (1976): 45–56; and Sharisse D. McCafferty and Geoffrey G. McCafferty, "Powerful Women and the Myth of Male Dominance in Aztec Society," *Archaeological Review from Cambridge* 7 (1988): 45–59. Not surprisingly, they find in colonial and secondary sources evidence to support their positions—whether they see women as subordinated (Nash, MacLachlan-Shadow) or as relatively equal (McCafferty and McCafferty).

3. John Comaroff and Jean Comaroff, *Ethnography and the Historical Imagination* (Boulder, Colo.: Westview Press, 1992), 266.

4. Ibid., 267.

5. Nash, "The Aztecs," 356–59.

6. Cecelia F. Klein, "Fighting with Femininity: Gender and War in Aztec Mexico," *Estudios de Cultura Náhuatl* 24 (1994): 219–53, discusses the image of the woman warrior in Aztec iconography and mythology. She also makes a number of observations regarding links between female tools and domestic work and the male domain of warfare.

7. Fray Gerónimo de Mendieta, *Historia eclesiástica indiana,* ed. Joaquín García Icazbalceta (México: Editorial Porrúa, 1980), 619. Not all friars were immune to such "temptations," especially in later years. By the late sixteenth and early seventeenth century, some friars working as parish priests were being accused of sexually abusing native women (Robert Haskett, pers. com.). See also Robert Haskett, "'Not a Pastor, But a Wolf': Indigenous-Clergy Relations in Early Cuernavaca and Taxco," *The Americas* 50:3 (1994): 318–22.

8. I do not attempt to analyze here other rituals that occurred in the home but only at crucial life-cycle junctures such as birth and marriage, and which were under the direction of outside specialists (matchmakers, midwives, curers, diviners) rather than the housewife herself. On pregnancy

and childbirth, see Thelma D. Sullivan, "Pregnancy, Childbirth, and the Deification of the Women Who Died in Childbirth," *Estudios de Cultura Náhuatl*
6 (1966): 63–95, and " 'O Precious Necklace, O Quetzal Feather!' Aztec Pregnancy and Childbirth Orations," *Alcheringa/Ethnopoetics* 4 (1980): 38–56; Luis
Alberto Vargas G. and Eduardo Matos M., "El embarazo y el parto en el México prehispánico," *Anales de Antropología* 10 (1973): 297–310. Several chapters
of book 6 of the *Florentine Codex* are devoted to marriage, pregnancy, and
childbirth. The other principal source on the wedding ceremony is folio 61
of the *Codex Mendoza*, ed. Frances F. Berdan and Patricia Rieff Anawalt
(Berkeley: University of California Press, 1992). On women's participation in
temple ceremony (as well as other aspects of civic life), see especially the sahaguntine and Durán texts and also Betty Ann Brown, "Seen but Not Heard:
Women in Aztec Ritual—The Sahagún Texts," in *Text and Image in Pre-Columbian Art: Essays on the Interrelationship of the Verbal and Visual Arts*, ed.
Janet Catherine Berlo (Oxford: British Archaeological Reports Press, 1983),
119–53; Anna-Britta Hellbom, *La participación cultural de las mujeres indias y
mestizas en el México precortesano y postrevolucionario* (Stockholm: Ethnographical Museum, 1967); Kellogg, "Cognatic Kinship"; and McCafferty
and McCafferty, "Powerful Women."

    9. Fray Juan Bautista, *Huehuehtlahtolli*, ed. Miguel León-Portilla,
trans. Librado Silva Galeana (México: Comisión Nacional Conmemorativa
del V Centenario del Encuentro de Dos Mundos, 1988).

    10. Fray Bernardino de Sahagún, *Florentine Codex: General History of
the Things of New Spain*, ed. and trans. Arthur J. O. Anderson and Charles E.
Dibble (Santa Fe and Salt Lake City: School of American Research and University of Utah Press, 1950–82), bk. 6.

    11. Sahagún, *Florentine Codex*, 4:3–4, 5:186, 6:171; Angel María
Garibay K., ed., "Códice carolino. Manuscrito anónimo del siglo XVI," *Estudios de Cultura Náhuatl* 7 (1967): 48. All translations from Nahuatl texts are
my own. For most quotations from the *Florentine Codex* I do not provide the
Nahuatl text, since it is available in the Dibble and Anderson edition.

    12. Sahagún, *Florentine Codex*, 10:11.

    13. Ibid., 6:172.

    14. Louise M. Burkhart, "Moral Deviance in Sixteenth-Century
Nahua and Christian Thought: The Rabbit and the Deer," *Journal of Latin
American Lore* 12 (1986): 107–39.

    15. Susan Kellogg, "Kinship and Social Organization in Early Colo-
nial Tenochtitlan: An Essay in Ethnohistorical Analysis and Methodology,"
in *Ethnohistory, vol. 4 of Supplement to the Handbook of Middle American Indians*,
ed. Ronald Spores (Austin: University of Texas Press, 1986), 103–21, "Cognatic Kinship and Religion," and "The Social Organization of Households

among the Tenochca Mexica Before and After Conquest," in *Prehispanic Domestic Units in Western Mesoamerica: Studies of the Household, Compound, and Residence,* ed. Robert S. Santley and Kenneth G. Hirth (Boca Raton, Fla.: CRC Press, 1993), 207–24, has extensively analyzed kinship organization and residential patterns for sixteenth-century Mexico City; my brief description of the Mexica household is based largely on her work. The exact difference between the tlaxilacalli and calpolli remains, like many details of the operation of these units in territorial and social terms, obscure. See also James Lockhart, *The Nahuas after the Conquest: A Social and Cultural History of the Indians of Central Mexico, Sixteenth through Eighteenth Centuries* (Stanford: Stanford University Press, 1992). Most written and pictorial sources represent the calli as one-roomed; however, Michael E. Smith, *Archaeological Research at Aztec-Period Rural Sites in Morelos, Mexico,* vol. 1: *Excavations and Architecture,* University of Pittsburgh Memoirs in Latin American Archaeology, no. 4 (Pittsburgh, 1992), 305–09, describes archaeological remains of multiroomed houses in nonelite urban contexts.

    16. Sahagún, *Florentine Codex,* 5:194.

    17. Fray Bernardino de Sahagún, *Coloquios y doctrina cristiana,* ed. and trans. Miguel León-Portilla (México: Universidad Nacional Autónoma de México, 1986), 140. The Nahuatl text is as follows:

titocuitlauja yn itequiuh yn cuitlapilli yn atlapalli,
inic concui yn iatztauh yn imecaxicol,
auh in ivic yn imecapal,
inic ontlalilo in tlecuilixquac

León-Portilla, *Coloquios,* 141, interprets *tlecuilixquac,* literally, "on the forehead of the hearth," as referring to the placement of the tumpline on the *man's* forehead. Hence he reads the four objects as a series and misses the essential contrast between the first pair and the second pair, as well as the allusion to the hearth.

    18. Men left their digging sticks in front of the hearth, literally, "on its forehead" (*tlecuilixquac*), while women are represented as dwelling beside the hearth (*tlecuiltitlan*) or at the corner—literally, at the ear—of the hearth (*tlecuilnacazco*). That these locatives refer to fixed locations, different parts of the house reserved for men's and women's tools and activities, is possible, but at present I have no further evidence.

    19. Sahagún, *Florentine Codex,* 6:169, 3:45.

    20. Ibid., 4:41, 81, 107.

    21. Ibid., 45.

    22. Ibid., 5:192.

23. Ibid., 2:171.
24. The burial rites for such a woman required that her body be removed from the house through a hole opened in the back wall; Garibay,
"Códice carolino," 46. Leaving through the door would replicate the vaginal
delivery she had been unable to accomplish; in apparent recognition of her
own blocked exit, her family broke a wall out in order to remove her from
the house/womb.
25. Fray Diego Durán, *Historia de las indias de Nueva España e islas de
Tierra Firme,* ed. Angel María Garibay K. (México: Editorial Porrúa, [1570–
79] 1967), 1:229.
26. Ibid., 1:223.
27. Sahagún, *Florentine Codex,* 4:93–94.
28. Ibid., 5:161.
29. Bautista, *Huehuehtlahtolli,* 312, and Sahagún, *Florentine Codex,*
6:95, 131. The text in Bautista reads: *itlan ximaquilti in tlachpanaliztli in
tlacuicuiliztli.*
30. Karen Dakin, pers. com.
31. Sahagún, *Florentine Codex,* 4:3–4; Mendieta, *Historia eclesiástica,*
267.
32. Berdan and Anawalt, *Codex Mendoza,* 3:60r, 62r, 63r.
33. Sahagún, *Florentine Codex,* 2:199.
34. Fray Bernardino de Sahagún, *Primeros memoriales* (Norman: University of Oklahoma Press, 1993), 255v. Brown, "Seen but Not Heard," points
out various contexts in which women's actions depicted in the illustrations
for the *Primeros memoriales* are not mentioned in the accompanying text; in
the *Florentine Codex* women's ritual roles are even more obscured.
35. Sahagún, *Florentine Codex,* 1:9.
36. Ibid., 3:2.
37. Mendieta, *Historia eclesiástica,* 82–83.
38. I base this on their representations in the sahaguntine texts; fray
Bernardino de Sahagún, *Códice florentino* (México: Secretaría de Gobernación,
1979), 1:10v, 11r; Sahagún, *Primeros memoriales,* 263r; the Durán illustrations,
Historia, 1: *lámina* 24; and the *Codex Magliabechiano,* by Elizabeth Hill Boone
and Zelia Nuttall (Berkeley: University of California Press, 1983), fol. 27r.
39. Durán, *Historia,* 1:144–49; Sahagún, *Florentine Codex,* 2:112; and
Doris Heyden, "Las escobas y las batallas fingidas de la Fiesta de Ochpaniztli,"
in *Religión en Mesoamérica,* ed. Jaime Litvak King and Noemí Castillo Tejero
(México: Sociedad Mexicana de Antropología, 1972), 205–11. Toci was, in
Mexica mythologized history, identified with the Culhua princess Yaocihuatl, "Enemy Woman," who was sacrificed to Huitzilopochtli—much to her
father's distress. Betty Ann Brown, "Ochpaniztli in Historical Perspective,"

in *Ritual Human Sacrifice in Mesoamerica*, ed. Elizabeth H. Boone (Washington, D.C.: Dumbarton Oaks, 1984), 195–210, interprets the Ochpaniztli rites as a commemoration of that event and the ensuing war with Culhuacan. For more on the mythological significance of Yaocihuatl and the Culhuacan conflict, see Susan D. Gillespie, *The Aztec Kings: The Construction of Rulership in Mexica History* (Tucson: University of Arizona Press, 1989).

40. Garibay, "Códice carolino," 36–37.

41. Sahagún, *Florentine Codex*, 2:171.

42. Gillespie, *Aztec Kings*.

43. Durán, *Historia*, 2:164–65.

44. Fernando Alvarado Tezozomoc, *Crónica mexicana*, ed. Manuel Orozco y Berra (México: Editorial Porrúa, [1898] 1975), 392. Durán's version of this episode mentions the naked women expressing milk and beating their bellies but does not state that they threw anything; Durán, *Historia*, 2:263. Klein, "Fighting with Femininity," who discusses this episode at length, notes that these sources reflect the perspective of victorious Tenochtitlan, while a Tlatelolcan source described by Barlow depicts the women fighting like male soldiers (p. 224). She sees in these women symbolism of the "archetypal conquered women"; the household implements they throw "must be understood as magical weapons, womanly counterparts to the darts and spears hurled by men" (pp. 227, 238).

45. Sahagún, *Florentine Codex*, 4:66.

46. Durán, *Historia*, 1:65, 149.

47. Mendieta, *Historia eclesiástica*, 419, 429.

48. Stephanie Wood, "Adopted Saints: Christian Images in Nahua Testaments of Late Colonial Toluca," *The Americas* 47:3 (January 1991): 282–83.

49. Ibid., 283. I also discuss sweeping in Burkhart, *The Slippery Earth: Nahua-Christian Moral Dialogue in Sixteenth-Century Mexico* (Tucson: University of Arizona, 1989), 117–24. See this work also for further treatment of the symbolism of filth and purification. My conception of the order/chaos dialectic running through Nahua religious thinking, including the place of women within the overall symbolic scheme, owes much to the work of Alfredo López Austin, *Cuerpo humano e ideología. Las concepciones de los antiguos nahuas*, 2 vols. (México: Universidad Nacional Autónoma de México, Instituto de Investigaciones Antropológicas, 1980).

50. Bautista, *Huehuehtlahtolli*, 312; Sahagún, *Florentine Codex*, 6:95. The text from Bautista reads: *[itlan ximaquilti] in tematequiliztli in teixamiliztli in tecamapaquiliztli.*

51. Sahagún, *Primeros memoriales*, 254v-255v.

52. Sahagún, *Florentine Codex*, 4:6–7.

53. Ibid., 2:199.

54. Durán, *Historia*, 1:169–70.

55. Ibid., 1:147–48.

56. Sahagún, *Florentine Codex*, 4:87–88. Although I am omitting an analysis of birth rituals from this discussion, the importance of the fire in that context should be noted. See, e.g., Sahagún, *Florentine Codex*, 6:111; Jacinto de la Serna, "Manual de ministros para conocer y extirpar las idolatrías de los indios," in *Tratado de las idolatrías, supersticiones, dioses, ritos, hechicerías y otras costumbres gentílicas de las razas aborígenes de México*, ed. Francisco del Paso y Troncoso (México: Librería Navarro, 1953), 1:77; and Ponce de León, in Angel María Garibay K., *Teogonía e historia de los mexicanos. Tres opúsculos del siglo XVI* (México: Editorial Porrúa, 1979), 123–24.

57. Durán, *Historia*, 2:358.

58. Sahagún, *Florentine Codex*, 2:60.

59. Durán, *Historia*, 2:165.

60. Alvarado Tezozomoc, *Crónica mexicana*, 539–40.

61. Bautista, *Huehuehtlahtolli*, 312; Sahagún, *Florentine Codex*, 6:95. The text from Bautista reads: *ximaquilti in atl im metlatl, yhuan huel xictzitzqui huel xicacocui im molcaxitl in chiquihuitl*.

62. As told in the *Leyenda de los Soles*, where the dough is comprised of bone and blood; John Bierhorst, ed. and trans., *History and Mythology of the Aztecs: The Codex Chimalpopoca* (Tucson: University of Arizona Press, 1992), 146. In the Quiché Maya *Popol Vuh*, Xmucane grinds white and yellow corn into human flesh, adding grease from her hands to provide fat; Dennis Tedlock, ed. and trans., *Popol Vuh* (New York: Simon and Schuster, 1985), 163–64.

63. Berdan and Anawalt, *Codex Mendoza*, 3:60r.

64. Garibay, "Códice carolino," 48.

65. Elizabeth M. Brumfiel, "Weaving and Cooking: Women's Production in Aztec Mexico," in *Engendering Archaeology: Women and Prehistory*, ed. Joan M. Gero and Margaret W. Conkey (Cambridge, Mass.: Basil Blackwell, 1991), 224–51.

66. Sahagún, *Florentine Codex*, 5:183–96.

67. Ibid., 4:77–78.

68. Ibid., 2:61–62.

69. Ibid., 167.

70. Ibid., 175–76.

71. Durán, *Historia*, 2:164–65.

72. Alvarado Tezozomoc, *Crónica mexicana*, 311, 540.

73. Sahagún, *Florentine Codex*, 6:96.

74. For a discussion of links between female gender identity and textile arts, see Sharisse D. McCafferty and Geoffrey G. McCafferty, "Spinning and Weaving as Female Gender Identity in Post-Classic Mexico," in *Textile*

Traditions of Mesoamerica and the Andes: An Anthology, ed. Margot Blum Schevill, Janet Catherine Berlo, and Edward B. Dwyer (New York: Garland Press, 1991), 19–44.

75. Bautista, *Huehuehtlahtolli*, 314: *im malacatl in tzotzopaztli, uel xicmocuitlahui*.

76. Berdan and Anawalt, *Codex Mendoza*, 3:58r, 60r.

77. Sahagún, *Florentine Codex*, 6:201, 205.

78. Ibid., 3:43.

79. Ibid., 9:14. Mexica historical chronicles contain a number of episodes in which men's valor was denied or mocked by dressing them in women's garments or giving them cotton to spin. Nash, "Aztecs," 356, sees this sort of thing as evidence that "the tools and raw materials used by women became a metaphor for subordination and humility." To demean a man's prowess by implying that he is "womanly" does not, however, necessarily imply an insult to women, but merely indicates that he is an unfit male. Conversely, female deities who dressed in loincloths were dangerous and ambivalent, not models to which human women were to aspire. See also Klein, "Fighting with Femininity."

80. Sahagún, *Florentine Codex*, 12:11–13.

81. Frances F. Berdan, "Cotton in Aztec Mexico: Production, Distribution and Uses," *Mexican Studies/Estudios Mexicanos* 3 (1987): 235–62.

82. Brumfiel, "Weaving and Cooking," 236.

83. On the economics of textile production, see especially Berdan, "Cotton in Aztec Mexico," and Brumfiel, "Weaving and Cooking." On the garments themselves, their construction and their uses, see Patricia Rieff Anawalt, *Indian Clothing Before Cortés: Mesoamerican Costumes from the Codices* (Norman: University of Oklahoma Press, 1981).

84. Sahagún, *Florentine Codex*, 6:239.

85. Thelma D. Sullivan, "Tlazolteotl-Ixcuina: The Great Spinner and Weaver," in *The Art and Iconography of Late Post-Classic Central Mexico*, ed. Elizabeth H. Boone (Washington, D.C.: Dumbarton Oaks, 1982), 14.

86. I am not familiar with any native Mexican texts or images that represent the Virgin Mary as spinning or weaving, although such do exist in European tradition.

87. Hernando Ruiz de Alarcón, *Aztec Sorcerers in Seventeenth-Century Mexico: The Treatise on Superstitions by Hernando Ruiz de Alarcón*, ed. and trans. Michael D. Coe and Gordon Whittaker (Albany: State University of New York, Institute for Mesoamerican Studies, 1982), 293–95.

88. Berdan and Anawalt, *Codex Mendoza*, 3:60r.

89. Sahagún, *Florentine Codex*, 4:7.

90. Ibid.

91. On Cihuacoatl, see, e.g., her depictions in the *Primeros memoriales*, the *Florentine Codex*, and the *Codex Magliabechiano*; the accompanying text in the *Florentine Codex* says "she has a turquoise batten," *xiuhtzotzopace:* Sahagún, *Primeros memoriales*, 264r; *Florentine Codex*, 11; Boone and Nuttall, *Codex Magliabechiano*, 33r. The *Codex Borbonicus* depicts Moteucçoma dressed as Huitzilopochtli, accompanied by his second-in-command, the Cihuacoatl, dressed like this deity and carrying a batten; *Códice Borbónico*, ed. Francisco del Paso y Troncoso, facsimile of 1898 Florence edition (México: Siglo Veintiuno, 1979), 23. (In the *Borbonicus*, the accompanying Spanish gloss labels this figure *papa mayor*, "great priest"; however, a high priest would have been dressed like Quetzalcoatl, not Cihuacoatl.) Ilamatecuhtli is represented carrying a batten in the *Florentine Codex* for her festival of Tititl; Sahagún, *Florentine Codex*, 2:155.

92. Alvarado Tezozomoc, *Crónica mexicana*, 392.

93. Ibid., 311.

94. Alvarado Tezozomoc, who was a native speaker of Nahuatl, equates this term with a shuttle, *lanzadera de tejer,* but Molina glosses it as *palo ancho como cuchilla con que tupen y aprietan la tela quese texe;* fray Alonso de Molina, *Vocabulario en lengua castellana y mexicana y mexicana y castellana* (México: Editorial Porrúa, [1571] 1970), fol. 154r—that is, a batten used to push down the weft to tighten the weave. I have been following Molina's usage; however, it is possible that the same word could have also been used for a shuttle. Molina's Spanish-to-Nahuatl section glosses *lançadera de texedor* as *pacyo acaltontli,* "weft little-reed," but the Nahuatl-to-Spanish has no corresponding entry (nor have I found this term in the descriptions of weaving in the *Florentine Codex*). In the description of the Tlatelolca women, Alvarado Tezozomoc defines *tzotzopaztli tzatzaztli* rather ambiguously as *tejederas y urdideras* [sic], "weavers and warpers"; *Crónica mexicana*, 392. *Tzatzaztli*, which I have glossed as "warping frame," is not in the dictionaries.

95. Sahagún, *Florentine Codex*, 6:163; Sullivan, "Pregnancy, Childbirth," 90–91.

96. Garibay, "Códice carolino," 47.

97. Barbara Tedlock and Dennis Tedlock, "Text and Textile: Language and Technology in the Arts of the Quiché Maya," *Journal of Anthropological Research* 41 (1985): 127–28; Dennis Tedlock, *Popol Vuh*, 72, 243–44.

98. Cecelia F. Klein, "Woven Heaven, Tangled Earth: A Weaver's Paradigm of the Mesoamerican Cosmos," in *Ethnoastronomy and Archaeoastronomy in the American Tropics*, ed. Anthony F. Aveni and Gary Urton (New York: Annals of the New York Academy of Sciences, 1982), 385: 1–35.

99. Tedlock and Tedlock, "Text and Textile."

100. Dennis Tedlock, paper presented at "Re-creating the New

World Contact: Indigenous Languages and Literatures of Latin America,"
NEH Summer Institute, University of Texas at Austin, July 10, 1989.
    101. Klein, "Woven Heaven," 21.
    102. Sahagún, *Florentine Codex*, 10:51–52. I use these descriptions,
from chapter 14, since they apply to commoner women. Chapter 10 also describes the tailor, spinner, and weaver but refers to people who make their
living at these trades rather than to housewives; in the accompanying illustrations, the tailor and the spinner are men (the latter uses a spinning wheel)
and the weaver, though a woman with a backstrap loom, is depicted within
a much more "Europeanized" setting than her counterpart in chapter 14.
    103. Ibid., 10:52.
    104. The Mexica not having a full-fledged notion of private prop-
erty, "to have" being expressed rather as "to keep" or "to guard," the latter
gloss, though clumsy, is perhaps closer to the native idea. Here I follow a
suggestion by Michel Launey, "Contribuciones recíprocas entre la lingüística general y la cultura náhuatl," paper presented at the Instituto de Investigaciones Antropológicas, Universidad Nacional Autónoma de México,
August 6, 1984, for interpreting this grammatical construction.
    105. Sahagún, *Códice florentino*, 5:21r.
    106. Sahagún, *Florentine Codex*, 5:192.
    107. Serna, "Manual de Ministros," 1:216–17.
    108. Fray Toribio de Benavente Motolinia, *Historia de los indios de la
Nueva España*, ed. Edmundo O'Gorman (México: Editorial Porrúa, 1979), 182.
    109. S. L. Cline, *Colonial Culhuacan, 1580–1600: A Social History of an
Aztec Town* (Albuquerque: University of New Mexico Press, 1986); and
Susan Kellogg, "Aztec Women in Early Colonial Courts: Structure and Strategy in a Legal Context," in *Five Centuries of Law and Politics in Central Mexico*,
ed. Ronald Spores and Ross Hassig, Vanderbilt University Publications in
Anthropology, no. 30, (Nashville, 1984), 25–38, "Kinship and Social Organization," and *Law and the Transformation of Aztec Culture, 1500–1700* (Norman: University of Oklahoma Press, 1995).
    110. Susan Kellogg, "Hegemony out of Conquest: The First Two
Centuries of Spanish Rule in Central Mexico," *Radical History Review* 53
(1992): 27–46.
    111. These examples of women's participation in Catholic custom
are taken from Cline's analysis of late sixteenth-century Nahuatl wills from
Culhuacan, in *Colonial Culhuacan;* and from the chronicles of the Franciscans
Motolinia, *Historia de los indios*, and Mendieta, *Historia eclesiástica*.
    112. Native constructions of Christianity differed in fundamental
and important ways from orthodox Christian doctrine. The friars had limited
understanding of the extent to which their messages were transformed in

translation and appropriated by native interpreters. Rather than an "idols behind altars" split mentality or a syncretic mixing, I see a creative reworking of
Christianity into a native mode. See, e.g., Louise M. Burkhart, *Holy Wednesday:
A Nahua Drama from Early Colonial Mexico* (Philadelphia: University of Pennsylvania Press, 1996); "The Amanuenses Have Appropriated the Text: Interpreting a Nahuatl Song of Santiago," in *On the Translation of Native American
Literatures*, ed. Brian Swann (Washington, D.C.: Smithsonian Institution Press,
1992), 339–55; and "Flowery Heaven: The Aesthetic of Paradise in Nahuatl
Devotional Literature," *Res: Anthropology and Aesthetics* 21 (1992): 88–109.

Chapter 2. Aztec Wives

1. Fray Bernardino de Sahagún, *The Primeros memoriales, of fray
Bernardino de Sahagún*, trans. Thelma D. Sullivan, ed. H. B. Nicholson,
Arthur J. O. Anderson, Charles E. Dibble, Eloise Quiñones Keber, and
Wayne Ruwet (Norman: University of Oklahoma Press, 1997), chap. 3, §15.
2. There is no exact parallel to this ceremony in the *Florentine Codex*,
though the judgment ceremony described in fray Bernardino de Sahagún,
Florentine Codex: General History of the Things of New Spain, ed. and trans.
Arthur J. O. Anderson and Charles E. Dibble (Santa Fe and Salt Lake City:
School of American Research and University of Utah Press, 1950–82), 4:91,
which took place every 260 days on the day One Dog, may have been somewhat similar. Another judgment ceremony is told of in Sahagún, *Florentine
Codex*, 2:106, but it is associated with the month of Huey Tecuilhuitl rather
than the ritual calendar.
3. Fray Andrés de Olmos, *Grammaire de la langue nahuatl ou mexicaine*, ed. Rémi Siméon (Paris: Imprimerie Nationale, 1875), 218.
4. Sahagún, *Primeros memoriales*, chap. 3, §8 (first part).
5. Ibid. (second part).
6. Sahagún, *Florentine Codex*, 8:49.
7. Ibid., 4:3–4; 5:186; 6:201.
8. Alonso de Zorita, *Life and Labor in Ancient Mexico: The Brief and
Summary Relation of the Lords of New Spain*, ed. and trans. Benjamin Keen
(New Brunswick: Rutgers University Press, 1963), 136–37.
9. Sahagún, *Florentine Codex*, 6:95–96.
10. Zorita, *Life and Labor*, 147–48.
11. Fray Juan Bautista, *Huehuetlatolli. Que contiene las pláticas que los
padres y madres hicieron a sus hijos, y los Señores a sus uasallos, todas llenas de doctrina moral y política*, ed. Miguel León-Portilla, trans. Librado Silva Galeana
(México: Comisión Nacional Conmemorativo del V Centenario del Encuentro de Dos Mundos, 1988), 357–58. Facsimile of the original 1600 edition.

12. Bautista, *Huehuetlatolli*, 313–14.
13. Ibid., 321–23.
14. Zorita, *Life and Labor*, 150.
15. Bautista, *Huehuetlatolli*, prologue (unpaginated).
16. Fray Gerónomo de Mendieta, *Historia eclesiástica indiana*, ed. Joaquín García Icazbalceta (México: Editorial Porrúa, 1980), 418–21.
17. Sahagún, *Florentine Codex*, prelim. vol., 76.
18. Ibid., 78.
19. Olmos, *Grammaire*, 213.
20. Munro S. Edmonson, Introduction, in *Sixteenth-Century Mexico: The Work of Sahagún*, ed. Munro S. Edmonson (Albuquerque: University of New Mexico Press, 1974), 12.
21. Charles E. Dibble, "The Nahuatlization of Christianity," in *Sixteenth-Century Mexico*, ed. Munro Edmonson, 231–32.
22. Fray Bernardino de Sahagún, "*Sermones en mexicano*," vol. 2, MS. 1482, Biblioteca Nacional de México (1588), and fray Bernardino de Sahagún, *Manual del christiano*, MS. Mexicaine 402, Bibliothèque Nationale, Paris (1578). I am indebted to Barry David Sell, University of California, Los Angeles, for a copy of the sermon, and to Wayne Ruwet, of Powell Library of the same university, for a copy of the *Manual del christiano*, which had been lost to scholars for many years but which Ruwet recently rediscovered.
23. Bautista, *Huehuetlatolli* (1988).
24. Mendieta, *Historia eclesiástica*, 296–97. There may have been an earlier one, for which he gives no date.
25. *Historia de la nación mexicana: Códice de 1576*, ed. and trans. Charles E. Dibble (Madrid: Ediciones José Porrúa Turanzas, 1963). Facsimile of the *Codex of 1576*.
26. Mendieta, *Historia eclesiástica*, 300–06.
27. Sahagún, *Florentine Codex*, preliminary vol., 79.
28. Fray Alonso de Molina, *Vocabulario en lengua castellana y mexicana y mexicana y castellana*, ed. and intro. Miguel León-Portilla (México: Editorial Porrúa, [1571] 1970), (Spanish-Nahuatl), 9r.
29. Ibid. (Nahuatl-Spanish), 100v.
30. Bautista, *Huehuetlatolli*, 355–57.
31. Sahagún, *Florentine Codex*, 6:133.
32. Bautista, *Huehuetlatolli*, 358–59.
33. Sahagún, *Manual del christiano*, 13v.
34. Ibid., 12r.
35. Bautista, *Huehuetlatolli*, 356–57.
36. Ibid. (facsimile), 90r.
37. Sahagún, *Florentine Codex*, 6:156.

38. Bautista, *Huehuetlatolli* (facsimile), 89v.

39. Ibid., 312–13.

40. Ibid., 314–15.

41. Read *vellatlaliz* (*vel tlatlaliz*).

42. Bautista, *Huehuetlatolli* (facsimile), 87v.

43. Sahagún, *Florentine Codex*, 6:159–67.

44. Ibid., 167.

45. Bautista, *Huehuetlatolli*, 304–05.

46. Sahagún, *Florentine Codex*, 6:102.

47. Brigitta Leander, *Herencia cultural del mundo náhuatl a través de la lengua*, SepSetentas 35 (México: Secretaría de Educación Pública, 1972), 30.

48. Sahagún, *Florentine Codex*, rev. ed., 3:57, 59, 66.

49. See Molina, *Vocabulario* (Nahuatl), 32v (*ichpochotl*, etc.), and (Spanish), 117v (*virgen o donzella*, etc.).

50. Sahagún, *Primeros memoriales*, chap. 2, ¶2.

51. Bautista, *Huehuetlatolli*, 368–69.

52. In Sahagún, *Manual del christiano*, 13r, it is stated, "Their possessions are to be [owned] jointly" (*ceiez yn jntlatquj*).

53. Bautista, *Huehuetlatolli*, 320–23.

54. Ibid. (facsimile), 90v.

55. Sahagún, *Manual del christiano*, 12v.

56. Fray Bernardino de Sahagún, *Apendiz de la postilla*, MS. 1486, Ayer Collection, Newberry Library, Chicago (1579), 5th Admonition, near the end (no fol.).

57. Bautista, *Huehuetlatolli*, 278–79.

58. Sahagún, *Florentine Codex*, 6:95.

59. Bautista, *Huehuetlatolli*, 396–97.

60. Sahagún, *Florentine Codex*, 6:127.

61. Bautista, *Huehuetlatolli*, 294–95.

62. Ibid. (facsimile), 79v.

63. Sahagún, *Primeros memoriales*, chap. 3, §12.

64. Sahagún, *Florentine Codex*, 4:74.

65. Ibid., 79.

66. Miguel León-Portilla, *Trece poetas del mundo azteca* (México: Universidad Nacional Autónoma de México, Instituto de Investigaciones Históricas, 1967), 155–62.

67. Leander, *Herencia cultural*, 63–64.

68. Sahagún, *Florentine Codex*, 10:46.

69. Susan Schroeder, *Chimalpahin and the Kingdoms of Chalco* (Tucson: University of Arizona Press, 1991), 183–85.

70. Ibid., 185.

71. Sahagún, *Florentine Codex*, 10:55.
72. Chimalpahin's version of Alvarado Tezozomoc's text can be found in don Domingo de San Antón Muñón Chimalpahin Quauhtlehuanitzin, *Society and Politics in Mexico Tenochtitlan, Tlatelolco, Texcoco, Culhuacan, and Other Nahua Altepetl in Central Mexico*, vol. 1, ed. and trans. Arthur J. O. Anderson and Susan Schroeder, in *Codex Chimalpahin: Collected Works*, 6 vols., gen. ed. Susan Schroeder (Norman: University of Oklahoma Press, 1997), 26–177.
73. Sahagún, *Florentine Codex*, 10:12, 46, 51.

Chapter 3. Indian-Spanish Marriages in the First Century of the Colony

This chapter began as a paper prepared for the symposium "La Historia de las Mentalidades," held in Mexico City in November 1986. It has been published in its original form in *Familia y poder en Nueva España. Memoria del Tercer Simposio de Historia de las Mentalidades* (México: Instituto Nacional de Antropología e Historia, Colección Científica 228, 1991), 11–21; and with minor changes in *Cincuenta años de historia en México*, ed. Alicia Hernández Chávez and Manuel Miño Grijalva (México: El Colegio de México, 1991), 1:103–18. The Spanish version of this chapter has been translated, with some minor changes and additions, by Hazel G. Carrasco. I have also added material on the population of Puebla in 1534. Since the original version of this chapter was presented, a number of recent publications have treated related subjects. Some, such as Pilar Gonzalbo Aizpuru's *Las mujeres de la Nueva España. Educación y vida cotidiana* (México: El Colegio de México, 1987), and Elizabeth Kuznesof's "Raza, clase y matrimonio en la Nueva España. Estado actual del debate," in *Familias novohispanas. Siglos XVI al XIX*, ed. Pilar Gonzalbo Aizpuru (México: El Colegio de México, 1991), 373–88, have, as does Magnus Mörner's *Race Mixture in the History of Latin America* (Boston: Little, Brown, 1967), a broader perspective on the whole question of interethnic unions than does this short essay. However, none of these studies provides data that would modify the major points of this chapter.
1. Francisco del Paso y Troncoso, *Epistolario de Nueva España* (México: Editorial Porrúa, 1939–42), 3:137–44 (hereafter, *ENE*).
2. Mörner, *Race Mixture*, 26, 35–39, 65–67.
3. Gonzalo Correas, *Vocabulario de refranes* (Madrid: Revista de Archivos, Bibliotecas y Museos, 1924), 109.
4. Mörner, *Race Mixture*, 26.
5. Ibid., 37.
6. See Pedro Carrasco, "Royal Marriages in Ancient Mexico," in *Explorations in Ethnohistory: Indians of Central Mexico in the Sixteenth Century*, ed.

354 Notes to Pages 90–93

H. R. Harvey and Hanns J. Premm (Albuquerque: University of New Mexico Press, 1984), 41–81.

7. Fernando Alvarado Tezozomoc, *Crónica mexicayotl*, trans. Adrián León (México: Universidad Nacional Autónoma de México, 1949), 151.

8. Rafael García Granados, *Diccionario biográfico de historia antigua de México* (México: Universidad Nacional Autónoma de México, 1952–53), 3:202.

9. Howard F. Cline, "Hernando Cortés and the Aztec Indians in Spain," *Quarterly Journal of the Library of Congress* 26 (1969): 87.

10. Alvarado Tezozomoc, *Crónica mexicayotl*, 152.

11. Guillermo S. Fernández de Recas, *Cacicazgos y nobiliario indígena de la Nueva España*, Instituto Bibliográfico Mexicano, no. 5 (México: Biblioteca Nacional de México, 1961), 25.

12. Archivo General de Indias, Seville (hereafter, AGI), Justicia 1013, no. 1.

13. Delfina E. López Sarrelangue, *La nobleza indígena de Pátzcuaro en la época virreinal* (México: Universidad Nacional Autónoma de México, 1965), 171, 186, 218.

14. The Spanish text is as follows:

De la Nueva España enviaron el presidente e oidores cinco indios, uno hijo de Motezuma que otras veces había venido a besar las manos de V.M. y otros principales, porque les pareció que eran personas que no convenía que al presente estuviesen allá. Ha cinco o seis meses que están aquí, háseles dado lo necesario y porque no parece que conviene al presente que vuelvan a aquella tierra y están aquí a costa de V.M. parece al consejo que entre tanto, se pusiesen en alguna cosa que sirviesen a V.M.: especialmente al hijo de Motezuma contino de casa y los dos en la guarda de caballo y los dos en la guarda de pie; y sonará bien allá porque parezca que en su casa y corte se huelga de servir de ellos. V.M. mandará en ello lo que fuere servido. (AGI Indiferente 737, Consultas originales del Consejo y Cámara de Indias, Madrid, 24 julio 1533)

15. Ibid.

16. Carrasco, "Royal Marriages," 62.

17. Amada López de Meneses, "Tecuichpotzin, hija de Moctezuma (¿1510–1550)," *Revista de Indias* 9 (1948): 472, 473, 476; Fernando de Alva Ixtlilxochitl, *Obras históricas*, ed. Edmundo O'Gorman (México: Universidad Nacional Autónoma de México, 1975–77), 2:178; Victor M. Alvarez, *Diccionario de conquistadores* (México: Instituto Nacional de Antropología e Historia, 1975), 1:#440, #194.

18. Alvarado Tezozomoc, *Crónica mexicayotl*, 154; Alvarez, *Diccionario*, 2:1067.

19. Bernal Díaz del Castillo, *Historia verdadera de la conquista de la Nueva España* (México: Editorial Porrúa, 1955), 2:337–38; AGI, México 203, Ramo 2, no. 15.

20. Francisco A. de Icaza, *Diccionario autobiográfico de conquistadores y pobladores de Nueva España* (Madrid, 1923), 2:142.

21. Alvarez, *Diccionario,* 1:#355.

22. Alvarado Tezozomoc, *Crónica mexicayotl,* 134, 138; Icaza, *Diccionario autobiográfico,* 2:106.

23. Guido Münch G., *El cacicazgo de San Juan Teotihuacan durante la colonia* (México: Instituto Nacional de Antropología e Historia, 1976), 20, 25; but see Alvarado Tezozomoc, *Crónica mexicayotl,* 161.

24. Don Domingo de San Antón Muñón Chimalpahin Quauhtlehuanitzin, *Annales,* trans. Rémi Simeón (Paris, 1889), 220.

25. Alvarado Tezozomoc, *Crónica mexicayotl,* 161.

26. Ibid., 173–74.

27. Fernández de Recas, *Cacicazgos y nobiliario,* 25.

28. Icaza, *Diccionario autobiográfico,* 2:77–78, 124, 210; López Sarrelangue, *La nobleza indígena,* 189–205.

29. Díaz del Castillo, *Historia verdadera,* 54, 57; Rafael García Granados, *Diccionario biográfico de historia antigua,* #4651; Peter Gerhard, *Geografía histórica de la Nueva España, 1519–1821* (México: Universidad Nacional Autónoma de México, 1986), 393.

30. viendo que algunas de estas esclavas se hallaban bien con los españoles, los propios principales daban sus hijas propias porque, si acaso algunas se empreñasen, quedasen entre ellos generaciones de hombres tan valientes y esforzados. Diego Muñoz Camargo, "Descripción de la ciudad y provincia de Tlaxcala," in *Relaciones geográficas del siglo XVI. Tlaxcala,* ed. René Acuña (México: Universidad Nacional Autónoma de México, 1984), 1:238.

31. los señores absolutamente tomaban la mujer que querían, y se las daban como a hombres poderosos. Y, por esta orden, se dieron muchas hijas de señores a los españoles, para que quedase de ellos casta y generación, por si se fuesen de la tierra. Ibid.

32. Alva Ixtlilxochitl, *Obras históricas,* 2:214.

33. Díaz del Castillo, *Historia verdadera,* 1:225, 399, 404.

34. Adrián Recinos, *Pedro de Alvarado. Conquistador de México y Guatemala* (México: Fondo de Cultura Económica, 1952), 222–24; Alvarez, *Diccionario,* 1:#286, 2:#861; Díaz del Castillo, *Historia verdadera,* 1:225.

35. George R. Conway, *La noche triste, documentos. Segura de la frontera en la Nueva España, año de MDXX* (México: Antigua Librería Robredo, de José Porrúa e Hijos, 1943), 94.

36. Icaza, *Diccionario autobiográfico,* 1:29.

37. Díaz del Castillo, *Historia verdadera*, 2:348.

38. Manuel Orozco y Berra, *Los conquistadores de México* (México: Pedro Robredo, 1938), 50.

39. fui casado e velado legítimamente según orden de la Santa Madre Iglesia de Roma con Angelina Pérez de Arteaga hija de uno de los principales de las cuatro cabeceras de Tascala siendo ella doncella. AGI Justicia 162 Ramo 3, fol. 12r–v.

40. la dicha Angelina india sirvió al dicho Juan Pérez ya difunto, la cual tuvo en posesión de sirviente e manceba e no de mujer, [y que] el dicho Juan Pérez de Arteaga que litiga fue hijo de la dicha Angelina, no tuvo cierto padre ni saben cúyo hijo fue, más de estar en poder de la dicha Angelina que servía al dicho Juan Pérez ya difunto. Ibid., 32r.

41. era moza de edad de hasta doce o trece años, doncella y en tal hábito y reputación tenida e hija legítima de Calmecahua señor e indio principal de una de las cuatro cabeceras de la provincia de Tascala. Ibid., 15v.

42. fui hijo naturalmente engendrado por el dicho Juan Pérez de Arteaga; e que fuera nacido antes que el dicho mi padre legítimamente se casase con la dicha mi madre, atento que al tiempo que ella me hubo pudiera casarse con ella que era doncella y de noble generación, casándose quedaba tan legítimo como si después me hubiera. Ibid., 44r.

43. The Spanish text is as follows:

después que se fueron de Coyoacan a México, el dicho Juan Pérez de Arteaga el Viejo tenía en su casa a la dicha Angelina Pérez india con la cual vido este testigo que se desposó por palabras de presente en la dicha ciudad de México estando este testigo presente e otras personas de que no tiene memoria y los desposó Juan Díaz clérigo que vino con el Marqués del Valle e después de esto vido este testigo estar preñada la dicha Angelina Pérez e después la vio parida del dicho Juan Pérez de Arteaga el Mozo después de lo cual vio este testigo que el dicho Juan Pérez de Arteaga y la dicha Angelina Pérez su esposa vinieron a vivir a esta ciudad de los Angeles en la cual vio este testigo que se velaron en el monasterio de Santo Domingo de esta ciudad y esta testigo como amigo suyo se halló a las velaciones y después los vio estar juntos haciendo vida maridable como marido y mujer. (Ibid., 45v)

44. público y notorio ser hija de un principal de las cuatro cabeceras de la ciudad de Tascala y como a tal vio este testigo que la venían a servir indios de la dicha provincia de Tascala como a hija del principal. Ibid., 46r.

45. Ibid., 55r, 57v.

46. *ENE*, 10:26.

47. The Spanish text is as follows:

que en aquella provincia se han casado muchos españoles con mujeres que han enviudado de caciques y otros naturales ricos que han dejado bienes, casas y otras heredades que perteneciendo a los hijos de los primeros maridos los dichos españoles con quien se casan se lo gastan quitan y disminuyen y pleitean para dejarlo a sus hijos en que hay gran desorden y en mucho daño de su república suplicándome mandase que luego que las dichas viudas casasen con los dichos españoles u otra cualesquier persona siendo de mayorazgo los bienes del primer marido se pongan en tutela con lo cual se restituirán muchos bienes de huérfanos que están desposeidos y pobres por tenerles de esta manera usurpadas sus haciendas. (AGI México 1091, Libro C2, fol. 129v–130r)

48. Hildeberto Martínez, *Tepeaca en el siglo XVI* (México: La Casa Chata, 1984), 62–63; and *Colección de documentos coloniales de Tepeaca* (México: Instituto Nacional de Antropología e Historia, 1984), passim.

49. Martínez, *Colección*, 544–45.

50. Ibid., 534, 538–39; Martínez, *Tepeaca*, 197 n. 85.

51. Martínez, *Colección*, 550.

52. Ibid., 552.

53. hijo natural de doña María de la Cruz, india cacica y principal natural que fue de la dicha ciudad de Tepeaca que es ya difunta, de la cual nació siendo la susodicha soltera y que no supo quién fue su padre. Martínez, *Colección*, 586.

54. por haber sido el susodicho siempre hombre muy poderso en esta provincia y ella pobre y mujer e no haber tenido quien le ayude hasta agora que se casó con el dicho Alvaro Pérez su marido que ha comenzado a seguir la dicha causa. Ibid., 551.

55. The donors included doña María de la Cruz herself, as the widow of don Francisco de Guzmán; Cristobal Xuárez, together with his wife, doña Luisa de Guzmán; and don José de Guzmán. Martínez, *Tepeaca*, 202 n. 128.

56. The name Espina suggests a connection with Pedro de Espina, a vecino of Puebla, who held parcels of land adjacent to those of doña Isabel de Guzmán and who was the executor of the testament of the latter. Martínez, *Colección*, 534–35. Both Pedro de Espina and Pedro Alonso Cortés were witnesses to don Sebastián's formal act of taking possession of his property. Ibid., 514–18. Pedro Alonso Cortés also had business of another sort with the Indians of Tepeaca. In 1603 he loaned the governor and principales 1,700 gold pesos so that they could pay the royal tribute. Ibid., 400–06.

57. Ibid., 552–53.

58. Ibid., 581.

59. Ibid., 587.
60. The Spanish text is as follows:

en la dicha ciudad vive y reside Diego García Villavicencio, español casado
con una india emparentada con los naturales que ejercen los oficios y cargos
de república, el cual por esta vía tiene y ha tomado mano de entrar en sus cabildos y ayuntamientos y asistir en las elecciones que se hacen y tratan y
seguir pleitos, incitarles a seguirlos y sustentarlos, haciendo parcialidades y
causando desasosiego y revueltas entre los unos y los otros, de suerte que por
su orden se han seguido causas injustas y movido revueltas y resultado de ello
muchos inconvenientes en daño y perjuicio notable del común de la dicha ciudad; de más de que, encargado de llevar los dichos naturales al repartimiento
de los panes del Valle de Atrisco donde deben acudir, y entregado del
número que están obligados a dar, vende para su interés particular algunos
de ellos a personas que se los pagan y ocupan en diversos efectos, trabajos a
que no se debe dar lugar. (Archivo General de la Nación, México [hereafter,
AGN], Indios 2, exp. 177. Published by B. B. Simons in *Tlalocan* 4 [1964]: 298)

I have modernized the spelling and punctuation.
61. AGI Justicia 198, no. 7.
62. Hombre de mala conciencia e mentiroso y por tal es tenido y es
tan apocado que come con los indios en el suelo como indio y una vez vido
que lo prendió un español bachiller porque lo halló bailando haciendo mi-
tote con los indios e que es público que ha comido cigarrones y jugado al
batey con las nalgas y con el brazo con los indios e que por esto es tenido
entre ellos en poca cosa e muy ruin e apocado. Ibid.
63. lo tiene por hombre de poca conciencia y es apocado porque....
[O]yó decir que le habían visto comer cigarrones e otras bellaquerías e le
vido jugar a la pelota que se dice el batey y con los codos y que por esto lo
tiene por tal como dicho tiene. Ibid.
64. The five mestizos were Martín Gómez, the son of a conquistador,
Juan de Leyva, Díego de León, Pedro López de Barahona, and Rodrigo
Gutiérrez, recently deceased. AGN Hospital de Jesús 290, 1476v.
65. Münch, *El cacicazgo*, 20, 25.
66. Icaza, *Diccionario autobiográfico*, 2:157.
67. The Spanish text is as follows:

siendo casado con mujer de la tierra estaba públicamente amancebado con
muchas indias y mestizas, era gran borracho, jugador, blasfemo, muy mentiroso y de poca verdad e hombre que estimaba en poco la honra. Su trato y
conversación era con indios y entre indios a los cuales comunmente en-

gañaba. Era tan mal cristiano que pocas veces entraba en la iglesia y de tan rota conciencia que por cualquiera cosa que le fuese dada o prometida o por cualquier interés que se atravesase o mala voluntad que contra alguno tuviese se perjuraba y juraba en contra de la verdad. . . . [E]ra y es tan vicioso y de tan depravadas y malas costumbres y vicios que vivía más como gentil que como cristiano. Era tan desvergonzado y tenía en tan poco la honra que muchas e diversas veces públicamente e ante muchas personas hacía plaza de sus vergüenzas; especialmente, jugando al triunfo viéronle muchas veces borracho fuera de juicio y desnudo en carnes. (AGI Justicia 260, fol. 21r–v)

68. es morisco, esclavo hijo de moriscos e ansí él como sus padres esclavos del marqués de Tarifa y nuevamente convertidos. . . . Estando como estaba y está casado en Castilla, ha dieciséis años que está amancebado con muchas indias viviendo más a la ley de Mahoma que como cristiano. Ibid.

69. Ibid., 21v.

Chapter 4. Gender and Social Identity

This article is based on a paper presented at the Pacific Coast Branch of the American Historical Association in August 1989 in Portland, Oregon. I would like to thank Susan Kellogg for her comments on the original paper in Portland as well as the editors of this volume and Eric Hinderaker for comments on a later version.

1. See, for example, Pedro Carrasco, "Royal Marriages in Ancient Mexico," in *Explorations in Ethnohistory: Indians of Central Mexico in the Sixteenth Century*, ed. H. R. Harvey and Hanns J. Prem (Albuquerque: University of New Mexico Press, 1984), 41–81; Charles Gibson, *The Aztecs under Spanish Rule: A History of the Indians of the Valley of Mexico, 1519–1810* (Stanford: Stanford University Press, 1964); Robert Haskett, *Indigenous Rulers: An Ethnohistory of Town Government in Colonial Cuernavaca* (Albuquerque: University of New Mexico, 1991); Susan Schroeder, *Chimalpahin and the Kingdoms of Chalco* (Tucson: University of Arizona Press, 1991).

2. Anthropologists have moved away from this dual definition of naming, especially evident in a growing ethnographic literature on the symbolic meaning of nicknames. The ethnographic context necessary to assess such meanings—the shifting use of names in different social settings or at various times in an individual's life—is, however, largely lacking for pre- and postconquest central Mexico. Criminal records, which often include elaborate testimony with descriptions of individuals, including their aliases, might prove useful, at least for the late colonial period when they are relatively abundant. I would like to thank Sonya Lipsett-Rivera for pointing this out to

me. Also see the examples of nicknames among *castas* (persons of mixed race) in R. Douglas Cope, *The Limits of Racial Domination: Plebeian Society in Colonial Mexico City, 1660–1720* (Madison: University of Wisconsin Press, 1994), 32, 97, 58–59, 114. For various discussions of nicknames, see Stanley H. Brandes, "The Structural and Demographic Implications of Nicknames in Navanogal, Spain," *American Ethnologist* 2:1 (1975): 139–48; George A. Collier and Victoria R. Bricker, "Nicknames and Social Structure in Zinacantan," *American Anthropologist* 72:2 (1970): 289–302; Richard Price and Sally Price, "Saramaka Onomastics: An Afro-American Naming System," *Ethnology* 11:4 (1972): 341–67; and Renato Rosaldo, "Ilongot Naming: The Play of Associations," in *Naming Systems*, ed. Elisabeth Tooker, *Proceedings of the American Ethnological Society* (1980) (1984): 11–24. The quote is from Rosaldo, "Ilongot Naming," 22.

3. See Rebecca Horn, *Postconquest Coyoacan: Nahua-Spanish Relations in Central Mexico, 1519–1650* (Stanford: Stanford University Press, 1997).

4. For a history of Coyoacan parishes in the sixteenth and seventeenth centuries, see Horn, *Postconquest Coyoacan*, chap. 1. Coyoacan remained under Dominican auspices until it was secularized in the mid-eighteenth century; Gibson, *The Aztecs under Spanish Rule*, 106. For extant registers, see David J. Robinson, *Research Inventory of the Mexican Collection of Colonial Parish Registers*, no. 6 of Finding Aids to the Microfilmed Manuscript Collection of the Genealogical Society of Utah, ed. Roger M. Haigh (Salt Lake City: University of Utah Press, 1980), 32, 36–37.

5. The sample includes 626 baptismal entries (291 girls and 335 boys) from the parish of San Jacinto Tenantitlan, dating from 1619 to 1629, and 847 entries (425 girls and 422 boys) from the parish of San Juan Bautista, dating from 1638 to 1646. See Genealogical Society of Utah (hereafter, GSU) microfilm rolls 291–094, vol. 2, and 237–889, vol. 1.

6. Throughout this discussion I use the term "second name" for the various kinds of names (including Spanish surnames) Nahuas carried in addition to first (given) names. I use this term rather than "family name" or "surname" to maintain a distinction between indigenous and Spanish concepts of naming. Nahuas often carried more than one name, but, unlike Spanish family names, Nahua second names were not typically passed on from one generation to the next.

7. Much of the current research on surnames worldwide concerns surnames as biological markers, that is, the relationship between surname distribution and genetic inheritance. For a sample of this research, see the special issue of *Human Biology*, entitled "Surnames as Markers of Inbreeding and Migration," 55:2 (1983). The study of surnames as biological markers, however, presumes a naming system in which "offspring regularly take the surname of one parent" (p. 341). This approach is therefore inapplicable to

the Nahuas of colonial central Mexico, who did not typically pass on surnames within families.

8. For Nahua naming practices, see Inga Clendinnen, *The Aztecs:
An Interpretation* (Cambridge: Cambridge University Press, 1991), 56–57,
112–13, 153–54; James Lockhart, *The Nahuas after the Conquest: A Social and
Cultural History of the Indians of Central Mexico, Sixteenth through Eighteenth
Centuries* (Stanford: Stanford University Press, 1992), 117–30; and S. L. Cline,
Colonial Culhuacan, 1580–1600: A Social History of an Aztec Town (Albu-
querque: University of New Mexico Press, 1986), 117–22. Lockhart, *The
Nahuas after the Conquest*, 119, makes the point about the gender-specific na-
ture of women's names. For a recent review of pan-Mesoamerican naming
practices among nobles, including Nahuas, see Joyce Marcus, *Mesoamerican
Writing Systems: Propaganda, Myth, and History in Four Ancient Civilizations*
(Princeton: Princeton University Press, 1992), 191–221. For a description of
the naming rituals, see fray Bernardino de Sahagún, *Florentine Codex: General
History of the Things of New Spain*, ed. and trans. Arthur J. O. Anderson and
Charles E. Dibble (Santa Fe and Salt Lake City: School of American Research
and University of Utah Press, 1969), bk. 6, chaps. 30–38.

9. Lockhart, *The Nahuas After the Conquest*, 118. On Nahua kinship,
see Lockhart, *The Nahuas*, 59 ff; Susan Kellogg, "Kinship and Social Organization in Early Colonial Tenochtitlan," in *Supplement to the Handbook of Middle American Indians, vol. 4: Ethnohistory*, ed. Ronald Spores (Austin: University of Texas Press, 1986), 103–21; and idem, "Cognatic Kinship and Religion:
Women in Aztec Society," in *Smoke and Mist: Mesoamerican Studies in Memory
of Thelma D. Sullivan*, ed. J. Kathryn Josserand and Karen Dakin (Oxford:
British Archaeological Reports Press, 1988), 2:666–81. The lack of family
names among Nahuas stands in sharp contrast to the patronymics used
among the Maya. See Marcus, *Mesoamerican Writing Systems*, 211–20; and
Ralph L. Roys, "Personal Names of the Maya of Yucatan," *Contributions to
American Anthropology and History* 6: 31–48.

10. Nonetheless, despite their use of Spanish names, Nahuas did not
duplicate Spanish naming practices; that is, the pools of given names used
by the two groups were not identical. According to James Lockhart, Nahuas
of central New Spain are known to have carried certain saints' names such
as Pablo, Tomás, and Ambrosio, which were rare or unknown among sixteenth-century Spaniards; Lockhart, *The Nahuas*, 119. Of these three examples, only Tomás appears among the twenty most common male names in
the baptismal records of early seventeenth-century Coyoacan. Pablo was apparently used much less frequently, appearing in the Coyoacan sample only
nine times (of a total of 2,230). Ambrosio never appears among the names of
baptized boys and their fathers in early seventeenth-century Coyoacan, al-

though it was not entirely unknown in the region; a prominent late six-teenth-century Coyoacan notary was named Ambrosio Rafael (Bancroft Library [hereafter, BL] MS. 84/116m, fol. 361r, dated 1596), as was the notary, Diego Ambrosio, active at least in the year 1631, Archivo General de la Nación (hereafter, AGN), Hospital de Jesús, legajo 318, exp. 14, fol. 69r.

11. Juan accounts for a striking 31 percent of the male names in the sample. Among the females, the name Juana accounts for 14 percent, and María is consistently the most popular female name, at 20 percent of the sample from the two parishes. By the eighteenth century María was also a common name among males, although less common than among females. See William B. Taylor, "The Virgin of Guadalupe in New Spain: An Inquiry into the Social History of Marian Devotion," *American Ethnologist* 14:1 (February 1987): 16–17.

12. Cline, *Colonial Culhuacan*, 117; Lockhart, *The Nahuas*, 119.

13. The ten most popular given names accounted for 64 percent of the females in the parishes of San Jacinto Tenantitlan and San Juan Bautista and for 68 percent of the males. Even more striking, the twenty most popular names account for 86 percent of the names of females and 86 percent of the names of males. The variety of given names is approximately the same between females and males in the early seventeenth-century Coyoacan baptismal records, totaling fifty-nine names for females and fifty-three names for males.

14. See Daniel Scott Smith, "Child-Naming Practices, Kinship Ties, and Change in Family Attitudes in Hingham, Massachusetts, 1641 to 1880," *Journal of Social History* 18 (1985): 544. Smith indicates that gender-equivalent names were rare among the English, a child-naming practice retained by some populations in the United States in the colonial and national periods. Susan Kellogg argues that a transition from gender-specific to gender-equivalent names was one indicator of indigenous women's declining status in the postconquest period. See Susan Kellogg, *Law and the Transformation of Aztec Culture, 1500–1700* (Norman: University of Oklahoma Press, 1995), 116.

15. Among the early seventeenth-century baptismal records of Coyoacan, gender-equivalent names include the following, with an asterisk indicating that the name is among the twenty most common female and male names: Agustina*, Agustín*; Andrea, Andrés*; Antonia, Antonio; Bernardina, Bernardo; Blasina, Blas; Damiana, Damián; Dominga*, Domingo*; Feliciana, Feliciano; Felipa, Felipe*; Francisca*, Francisco*; Gerónima*, Gerónimo*; Gregoria, Gregorio; Jacinta, Jacinto*; Jacoba, Jacobo; Josefa*, Josef*; Juana*, Juan*; Juliana, Julián; Lorenza, Lorenzo; Manuela, Manuel; Martina, Martín; Melchora*, Melchor*; Micaela, Miguel; Nicolasa*, Nicolás*; Pascuala*, Pascual*; Paula, Pablo; Sebastiana*, Sebastián*; Serafina, Serafín; Tomasa, Tomás*.

16. David Herlihy discusses the popularity of feminized saints' names as a reflection of the shortage of recognized female saints in fifteenth-century Tuscany. See Herlihy, "Tuscan Names, 1200–1530," *Renaissance Quarterly* 41:4 (1988): 574. Stephanie Wood discusses the dominance of male saints worshiped in Nahua homes in the late eighteenth-century Valley of Toluca. See Wood, "Adopted Saints: Christian Images in Nahua Testaments of Late Colonial Toluca," *The Americas* 47:3 (1991): 278.

17. Taylor, "The Virgin of Guadalupe," 17; and Wood, "Adopted Saints," 278–80.

18. Naming after a saint's day is evident in regard to the following saints: Andrés, Agustín, Baltasar, Bartolomé, Bernabé, Blas, Catalina, Domingo, Francisco, Gerónimo, Jacinto, Josef, Lorenzo, Lucas, Lucía, Magdalena, Marcos, Mateo, Matías, Melchor, Miguel, Nicolás, Pedro, Sebastián, Simón, Teresa, Tomás, and Ursula.

19. Herbert G. Gutman, *The Black Family in Slavery and Freedom, 1750–1925* (New York: Pantheon, 1976); David W. Dumas, "The Naming of Children in New England, 1780–1850," *New England Historical and Genealogical Register* 132 (1978): 196–210; Jacques Dupaquier, "Naming-Practices, Godparenthood, and Kinship in the Vexin, 1540–1900," *Journal of Family History* 6:2 (1981): 135–55; Cheryll Ann Cody, "Naming, Kinship, and Estate Dispersal: Notes on Slave Family Life on a South Carolina Plantation, 1786 to 1833," *William and Mary Quarterly* 39:1 (1982): 192–211; Daniel Scott Smith, "Child-Naming Practices as Cultural and Familial Indicators," *Local Population Studies* 32 (Spring 1984): 17–27; and idem, "Child-Naming Practices, Kinship Ties, and Change in Family Attitudes"; Edward H. Tebbenhoff, "Tacit Rules and Hidden Family Structures: Naming Practices and Godparentage in Schenectady, New York, 1680–1800," *Journal of Social History* 18 (1985): 567–85.

20. Smith, "Child-Naming Practices, Kinship Ties, and Change in Family Attitudes," 542.

21. Tebbenhoff, "Tacit Rules and Hidden Family Structures"; Cody, "Naming, Kinship, and Estate Dispersal"; Gutman, *The Black Family in Slavery and Freedom.*

22. Smith, "Child-Naming Practices as Cultural and Familial Indicators"; and idem, "Child-Naming Practices, Kinship Ties, and Change in Family Attitudes."

23. Sahagún, *Florentine Codex,* bk. 6, chap. 38, 203–04.

24. S. L. Cline, "The Spiritual Conquest Reexamined: Baptism and Christian Marriage in Early Sixteenth-Century Mexico," *Hispanic American Historical Review* 73:3 (1993): 470–71.

25. Among the 716 girls baptized in the two parishes, 48 (7%) had the same given name as their mother, almost half of whom shared the name

María. Among the 757 boys baptized, 109 (14%) carried their father's name, almost half of whom shared the name Juan.

26. Cline, *Colonial Culhuacan*, 119; and Wood, "Adopted Saints," 278.

27. The name Domingo was especially prominent in the Morelos community of Yautepec, which was a Dominican jurisdiction. See Cline, "The Spiritual Conquest Reexamined," 472.

28. The dominance of a few popular names was not unique to the Nahuas of colonial central Mexico. Child-naming patterns among populations in Western Europe and the United States in the seventeenth century were also characterized by the dominance of a few popular names, with the list varying among different groups, reflecting different cultural values. Many studies of naming practices are concerned with the cultural values conveyed by the choice of names, in particular as reflected in changing lists of popular names over time. Name choice reflects not only kinship practices but also religious sentiment, as shown, for example, in the changing use of biblical names over time. By the nineteenth century the number of names given to children in Western societies had expanded, perhaps reflecting changing notions about the individuality of children. See Smith, "Child-Naming Practices as Cultural and Familial Indicators"; and idem, "Child-Naming Practices, Kinship Ties, and Change in Family Attitudes"; Dupaquier, "Naming Practices, Godparenthood, and Kinship in the Vexin." It would be of great interest to students of cultural change to understand the narrowing or expansion of name choice and alterations in the list of popular names for various regions of central Mexico over the course of the colonial period.

29. Taylor, "The Virgin of Guadalupe," 16.

30. A study of naming patterns in late seventeenth-century Mexico City finds that surnames were not important among castas until an individual reached adulthood, most likely at the time of marriage. See Cope, *The Limits of Racial Domination*, 58–66.

31. See GSU microfilm roll 291–097, parish of San Juan Bautista, 1732–51.

32. Cline, "The Spiritual Conquest Reexamined," 471.

33. The practice of using a Spanish given name and a second indigenous name is apparent in other parts of Spanish America. See, for example, the discussion of Guaraní naming patterns by Christina Bolke Turner and Brian Turner, "The Role of Mestizaje of Surnames in Paraguay in the Creation of a Distinct New World Ethnicity," *Ethnohistory* 41:1 (1993): 139–65, esp. p. 142.

34. AGN Bienes Nacionales (hereafter, BN), vol. 1453, exp. 12, fol. 184r. In combined form, in writing, there is no way to tell the difference between *quahuitl* (wood) and *quauhtli* (eagle). Thus Quauhtzontecontzin might

be Eagle-Head, which would, alas, spoil the humor. Nonetheless, compounds with *quahuitl* are much more common.

35. Horn, *Postconquest Coyoacan*, chaps. 2 and 5.

36. See Pedro Carrasco and Jesús Monjarás-Ruiz, eds., *Colección de documentos sobre Coyoacan* (México: Instituto Nacional de Antropología e Historia, 1978), 1:20, 23–24; for Culhuacan, see Cline, *Colonial Culhuacan*, 118–19.

37. BL 84/116m, fol. 349r.

38. Don Pablo Çacancatl, whose second name was a preconquest title, was an important nobleman closely related to the Coyoacan ruling family and active in municipal affairs in the 1520s; Horn, *Postconquest Coyoacan*, chap. 2. Don Pedro Tlillancalqui, mentioned as the father of a land seller in 1568, also carried the honorific don and a prominent preconquest title as a second name; BL 84/116m, fol. 76r. Others who carried preconquest titles as second names but without the honorific don included Juan Tlailotlac, among the earliest documented town officials; Bartolomé Atempanecatl, who served on the Coyoacan *cabildo* (city council) in the mid-sixteenth century; Juan Tecpanecatl, who served as a witness to a land sale in 1573; and Martín Huecamecatl, mentioned in 1579 as the late father of a land seller (Horn, *Postconquest Coyoacan*, chap. 2; and BL 84/116m, fols. 51r, 64r). In a land sale dated 1577, Huecamecatl, citizen of Tenantitlan, is mentioned as a neighboring landowner (see fol. 70r).

39. The grandfather of a Nahua selling a piece of land in 1586 was Yopicatl, an ethnic name, for example, and Miguel Xiutecatl's second name identifies him as a "Person from Xiuhtlan," BL 84/116m, fol. 52r and 361r, 1596. Another example of a name that refers to place of origin is Çiltecatl, "Person of Çilli"; see BL 84/116m, fol. 52r, dated 1586. Gerónimo Tetzotzonque, "Mason," literally, "Stone Pounder," who served as a witness to a land sale in 1567, was identified by craft, as was Rafael Quauhxinqui, "Carpenter," who witnessed a land sale in 1587; see BL 84/116m, fol. 69r, and AGN BN, legajo 1453, exp. 12, fol. 185v. Another later example is Pedro Tetzontzonqui, who served as a witness to a land sale in 1610, AGN BN, vol. 1453, exp. 12, fol. 184. And during a land investigation of 1554, Martín Quauhtli, "Eagle," Francisco Cihuaihuinti, "Woman-Crazy," Francisco Xico, "Bee," Martín Xochitl, "Flower," Juan Icnoyotl, "Misery," Miguel Opoch, "Left-Hand," and Alonso Mimich, "Fish," were mentioned as working various pieces of land. The translations of the names from 1554 are taken from Arthur J. O. Anderson, Frances Berdan, and James Lockhart, eds. and trans., *Beyond the Codices* (Berkeley: University of California Press, 1976), 84–85.

Many other scattered examples confirm the common use of Nahuatl-language second names among males in sixteenth-century Coyoacan. They include descriptive names: Pedro Chapolmetztli, "Grasshopper-Legs," literally, "Thigh of a Grasshopper," Juan Huehuetzin, "Old-Man," Hernando Ix-popoyotl, "Blind Person," Miguel Tepehui, "Scatterbrain"(?), literally, "Scatter"; animal names: Pedro Quauhtli, "Eagle," Juan Quauhtli, "Eagle," Miguel Epcohuatl, "Skunk," Antón Totoquan, "Bird"; and other miscellaneous names: Juan Chinan, "Fence," Juan Tezcatl, "Mirror," Francisco Tlacatl, "Person." See BL 84/116m, fols. 48r, 59r, 60r, 61r, 64r, 74r, 80r, 350v, 353r, and 361r, and AGN BN, legajo 1453, exp. 12, fol. 184r. The dates for these references range from 1566 to 1596, except for Hernando Ixpopoyotl, which is an example of a relatively late attestation of a Nahuatl-language name, dated 1610. For earlier postconquest references to Nahuatl-language names among males, see the many examples in Carrasco and Monjarás-Ruiz, *Colecciones*, vol. 1, dating from the early 1550s.

40. For the declining use of Nahuatl names, see Lockhart, *The Nahuas after the Conquest*, 127, 222, 225.

41. In the late colonial period there was apparently a resurgence of indigenous second names, especially among prominent Indians, Haskett, *Indigenous Rulers*, 158, 198; and Lockhart, *The Nahuas*, 130. See John K. Chance, "The Urban Indian in Colonial Oaxaca," *American Ethnologist* 3:4 (1976): 620. Chance reports the use of indigenous names among urban Indians in eighteenth-century Oaxaca, individuals often being "identified by their Spanish names and surnames followed by an indigenous name, or *sobrenombre*." These sobrenombres may have been used to indicate ethnic divisions.

42. David LaFrance and G. P. C. Thomson report that well into the twentieth century the Indians of the Sierra Norte de Puebla generally had only Christian names; see LaFrance and Thomson, "Juan Francisco Lucas: Patriarch of the Sierra Norte de Puebla," in *The Human Tradition in Latin America: The Twentieth Century*, ed. William H. Beezley and Judith Ewell (Wilmington, Del.: Scholarly Resources, 1987), 2.

43. It is unclear whether or not the same process occurred with the feminine form "de Santa." See Lockhart, *The Nahuas*, 122.

44. The adoption of an European given name as an Indian surname was not unique to the Indians of central Mexico. Ethnographers have distinguished four types of surnames among the Cree-Ojibwa Indians of Weagamow Lake, Ontario, Canada, in the nineteenth century (they had only unitary individual names before contact with the English). The four types of surnames are an English given name, an English surname, an Indian name, and a translation of an Indian name. See Edward S. Rogers and Mary Black Rogers, "Method for Reconstructing Patterns of Change: Surname Adoption by the Weagamow Ojibwa, 1870–1950," *Ethnohistory* 25:4 (1978): 327.

45. At times a child might carry the exact name of the same-gender parent. In 1579 the widow María Magdalena sold a piece of land; the trans-

action was confirmed by her son-in-law and daughter, who was also named María Magdalena; BL 84/116m, fol. 54r. In another land transaction in 1610, a father and son were both named Rafael Mateo; AGN BN, legajo 1453, exp. 12, fol. 193v.

46. María, as popular as a second name among the mothers of children baptized in the two parishes as it was as a first name among mothers and daughters, accounted for 20 percent (in comparison to 20 percent who had María as a first name). Juana constituted the second name of mothers in 9 percent of the cases (in contrast to 14 percent of mothers and daughters from the two parishes who had Juana as a first name). Juan was still a top choice, but no more common than the other top five names. In contrast to 31 percent of fathers and sons who had Juan as a first name, fathers with Juan as a second name constituted only 5 percent of the total in the two parishes. The dominance of the three names Juan, Juana, and María is even more striking when one looks at first and second names together. In the two early seventeenth-century Coyoacan parishes, 23 percent of the mothers had the name Juana and 42 percent had the name María as either a first or a second name. Seven percent combined the two names; in view of the popularity of María as a first name, it is not surprising to find that among the 7 percent, a larger number of women were named Juana María (74 cases) than María Juana (32 cases). Among the men, 42 percent of the fathers had Juan as either a first or a second name.

47. Lockhart, *The Nahuas after the Conquest*, 122–23.

48. GSU microfilm roll 237–889, vol. 1, March 3, 1620.

49. Anderson, Berdan, and Lockhart, *Beyond the Codices*, 54.

50. There were several males named Juan Bautista who appear in late sixteenth-century Culhuacan testaments, suggesting that this name may have been generally popular among Nahuas throughout colonial central Mexico. See Cline, *Colonial Culhuacan*, 120.

51. GSU microfilm roll 237–889, vol. 1, September 6, 1623, and June 23, 1628.

52. In medieval Europe "place-name surnames were most often used away from the place of the name." See Bernice A. Kaplan and Gabriel W. Lasker, "The Present Distribution of Some English Surnames Derived from Place Names," *Human Biology* 55:2 (1983): 243–50. In "Tacit Rules and Hidden Family Structures," Tebbenhoff discusses a variety of naming customs used among the immigrants to New Netherland in the colonial United States in the seventeenth century before surnames were permanently fixed. Among them were patronymics and "descriptive names derived from the individual's village, farmstead, occupation, or personal characteristics" (see pp. 568–69).

53. Lockhart, *The Nahuas after the Conquest*, 123, states that the surname Santiago "continued for the whole colonial period to have implica-

tions of relatively high position" while Domingo Ramos "carried no special implications of rank."

54. De la Concepción, de la Visitación, and de la Asunción are each found twice (in a total of 1,473) among the mothers of children baptized in the two Coyoacan parishes in the early seventeenth century. For the frequent occurrence of second names that refer to various representations of the Virgin Mary in early eighteenth-century Coyoacan, see GSU microfilm rolls 291–097, parish of San Juan Bautista, 1732–51; 291–098, parish of San Juan Bautista, 1751–83; 237–890, vol. 9, parish of San Jacinto Tenantitlan, 1714–25. For religious names among castas in late seventeenth-century Mexico City, see Cope, *The Limits of Racial Domination*, 61–63.

55. Lockhart, *The Nahuas after the Conquest*, 123.

56. Horn, *Postconquest Coyoacan*, chap. 2.

57. AGN BN, legajo 1453, exp. 12, fol. 181r. In the mid-sixteenth century Licenciado Juan Gutiérrez Altamirano, a relation of Cortés, was also involved in the administration of Coyoacan.

58. See, for example, Ana and Antonia de León, the children of a Nahua woman who sold a piece of land in 1591, BL 84/116m, fol. 354v; Domingo de León, mentioned as a neighboring landowner in a land sale dated 1596, BL 84/116m, fol. 361r; and the Coyoacan notary Juan de León, who was active at least in 1587, AGN BN, legajo 1453, exp. 12, fol. 185v.

59. In this case the connection between the seller and the Téllez family is quite direct; two of the witnesses to the land sale were Spaniards with the Téllez surname, BL 84/116m, fol. 357r.

60. See Horn, *Postconquest Coyoacan*, chaps. 2 and 4; and Miguel León-Portilla, "Códice de Coyoacan. Nómina de tributos, siglo XVI," *Estudios de Cultura Náhuatl* 9 (1971): 57–74.

61. Gibson, *The Aztecs*, 157–58; and Horn, *Postconquest Coyoacan*, chap. 2.

62. Lockhart, *The Nahuas after the Conquest*, 124.

63. For a discussion of Spanish surnames among castas in late seventeenth-century Mexico City, see Cope, *The Limits of Racial Domination*, 61–66.

64. Haskett, *Indigenous Rulers*, 135–41; and Lockhart, *The Nahuas after the Conquest*, 126.

65. Lockhart, *The Nahuas after the Conquest*, 126.

66. The regidores of the Coyoacan town council in 1552, who were probably typical, included don Luis de San Pedro, Juan de San Lázaro, Pedro de Paz, Toribio Silvestre, Miguel de la Cruz, and don Martín de Paz. And almost all the alcaldes serving on the Coyoacan town council between the mid-sixteenth and the mid-seventeenth century carried religious names, Spanish patronymics, or surnames. In 1630, for example, Coyoacan alcaldes

included Baltasar Núñez, Baltasar and Francisco Ramírez, Juan Cortés, Antonio de Luna, Juan Carlos, and Francisco Juan, Horn, *Postconquest Coyoacan*, chap. 2. For Tlaxcala, see James Lockhart, Frances Berdan, and Arthur J. O. Anderson, eds. and trans., *The Tlaxcalan Actas: A Compendium of the Records of the Cabildo of Tlaxcala (1545–1627)* (Salt Lake City: University of Utah Press, 1986); for Morelos, see Haskett, *Indigenous Rulers*.

67. Name change with the acquisition of office has been demonstrated in regions as diverse as Tlaxcala in central Mexico (Lockhart, Berdan, and Anderson, *The Tlaxcalan Actas*, 22) and the Audiencia of Quito (Karen Vieira Powers, *Andean Journeys: Migration, Ethnogenesis, and the State in Colonial Quito* [Albuquerque: University of New Mexico Press, 1995], 140, 153–54, 159). The latter examples of name change are not linked explicitly to the acquisition of office but rather are related to more general measures of social mobility, including landownership.

68. See BL 84/116m, fol. 44r; and Horn, *Postconquest Coyoacan*, chap. 2.

69. Marcus, *Mesoamerican Writing Systems*, 192. Marcus points out that we know Nahua nobles almost entirely by secondary names rather than by the calendrical names received at birth.

70. Of the religious names, only de la Cruz and Bautista appear among the twenty most common second names of mothers, while de la Cruz, Bautista, Ramos, and Santiago appear among the top twenty names of fathers. The relatively limited number of female second names is even more striking in regard to Spanish patronymics. Only 4 of the 847 mothers of children baptized in the parish of San Juan Bautista and 1 of the 626 mothers in the parish of San Jacinto Tenantitlan carried a Spanish patronymic as a second name; in all cases the name was Ramírez (although it is not known whether this name was drawn from a local Spanish family). Of the fathers, 56 (7%) of the 847 in San Juan Bautista and 92 (15%) of the 626 in San Jacinto Tenantitlan carried patronymics. In contrast to the mothers, four patronymics, Juárez, Hernández, Jiménez, and Pérez, were included among the twenty most common second names of fathers.

71. Cline, *Colonial Culhuacan*, 121.

72. Ibid., 120.

73. As argued in regard to naming patterns among Chinese women of the Hong Kong New Territories: "The lives of men are punctuated by the acquisition of new names, new roles, new responsibilities and new privileges; women's lives, in comparison, remain indistinct and indeterminate." See Rubie S. Watson, "The Named and the Nameless: Gender and Person in Chinese Society," *American Ethnologist* 13:4 (1986): 619.

74. Cline, *Colonial Culhuacan*, 30.

75. Over time, however, the tendency to carry names within families

may have gained currency even among Nahuas who did not carry the more prestigious Spanish surnames. A striking instance of shared second given names are three brothers, Fabián, Baltasar, and Gabriel, each of whom carried the second name Leonardo, as did their father, Juan Leonardo. As Juan Leonardo's father was called Yopicatl, mentioned above as an example of an indigenous ethnic name, the transformation of names in this family reflects broader trends in sixteenth-century central Mexico. See BL 84/116m, fol. 52r, dated 1586.

76. Horn, *Postconquest Coyoacan*, chap. 2.

77. Ibid.

Chapter 5. From Parallel and Equivalent to Separate but Unequal

Many thanks to Steven Mintz, Louise Burkhart, Victoria Pasley, Cristina Rivera-Garza, and the editors of this volume for helpful comments and suggestions. I also gratefully acknowledge the financial support of the Doherty Foundation, the Bunting Institute, the National Endowment for the Humanities, and the John Carter Brown Library.
    1. This passage reads in Spanish:

yo oí decir a una india vieja, que me la trujeron por sabia en la ley, que debía de haber sido sacerdotiza, que tambien ellos tenían Pascua de Resurección y de Natividad, como nosotros y en el mesmo tiempo que nosotros y Corpus Cristi, y señalóme otras fiestas principales que nosotros celebramos. Yo le respondí: "Mala vieja, el diablo que tan bien supo ordenar y sembrar su cizaña y revolverla con el trigo, para que no acabásedes de conocer la verdad." (1:5:244–45)

    2. Irene Silverblatt, *Moon, Sun, and Witches: Gender Ideologies and Class in Inca and Colonial Peru* (Princeton: Princeton University Press, 1987); Elinor C. Burkett, "Indian Women and White Society: The Case of Sixteenth-Century Peru," in *Latin American Women: Historical Perspectives,* ed. Asunción Lavrin (Westport, Conn.: Greenwood Press, 1978), 101–28; Frank Salomon, "Indian Women of Early Colonial Quito as Seen through Their Testaments," *The Americas,* 44:3 (January 1988): 325–41; and Ann Zulawski, "Social Differentiation, Gender, and Ethnicity: Urban Indian Women in Colonial Bolivia, 1640–1725," *Latin American Research Review* 25:2 (1990): 93–114.

    3. I define "jural adulthood" as the capacity to take social and legal responsibility for one's self as an *adult,* even if the concept of adult personhood is thoroughly "genderized" as it was among the Mexica; that is, the adult woman was treated as one kind of human being, whereas the adult

man was another. Those societies in which women were treated as jural adults differ from those in which they were treated as jural minors under the protection, socially and legally, of men (whether these men were fathers, brothers, or husbands). I draw in a general way here on feminist anthropological literature that examines how women are defined as persons in a variety of societies. This literature is summarized in Henrietta Moore, *Feminism and Anthropology* (Minneapolis: University of Minnesota Press, 1988), 38–41.

4. For recent discussions of the roles, status, and experiences of pre-Hispanic Mexica women, see Inga Clendinnen, *Aztecs: An Interpretation* (Cambridge: Cambridge University Press, 1991), chaps. 6–8; María J. Rodríguez-Shadow, *La mujer azteca* (México: Universidad Autónoma del Estado de México, 1991); María de Jesús Rodriguez, "Enfoque y perspectivas de los estudios sobre la condición femenina en el México antiguo," *Mesoamérica* 19 (June 1990): 1–11; Elizabeth M. Brumfiel, "Weaving and Cooking: Women's Production in Aztec Mexico," in *Engendering Archaeology: Women and Prehistory,* ed. Joan M. Gero and Margaret W. Conkey (Cambridge, Mass.: Basil Blackwell, 1991), 224–51; S. L. Cline, *Colonial Culhuacan, 1580–1600: A Social History of an Aztec Town* (Albuquerque: University of New Mexico Press, 1986), chap. 7; Susan Kellogg, "Aztec Women in Early Colonial Courts: Structure and Strategy in a Legal Context," in *Five Centuries of Law and Politics in Central Mexico,* ed. Ronald Spores and Ross Hassig, Vanderbilt University Publications in Anthropology, no. 30 (Nashville, 1984), 25–38; Susan Kellogg, "Cognatic Kinship and Religion: Women in Aztec Society," in *Smoke and Mist: Mesoamerican Studies in Memory of Thelma D. Sullivan,* ed. J. Kathryn Josserand and Karen Dakin (Oxford: British Archaeological Reports Press, 1988), 2:666–81; Colin M. MacLachlan, "The Eagle and the Serpent: Male over Female in Tenochtitlan," *Proceedings of the Pacific Coast Council of Latin American Studies* 5 (1976): 45–56; Sharisse D. McCafferty and Geoffrey G. McCafferty, "Powerful Women and the Myth of Male Dominance in Aztec Society," *Archaeological Review from Cambridge* 7 (1988): 45–59; and June Nash, "The Aztecs and the Ideology of Male Dominance," *Signs* 4:2 (Winter 1978): 349–62.

5. For a discussion of gender parallelism, see Silverblatt, *Moon, Sun, and Witches,* chap. 3. Also see Kellogg, "Cognatic Kinship and Religion," 673–76; and Clendinnen, *Aztecs,* 170.

6. On Nahua forms of thought and culture, see Louise M. Burkhart, *The Slippery Earth: Nahua-Christian Moral Dialogue in Sixteenth-Century Mexico* (Tucson: University of Arizona Press, 1989); Miguel León-Portilla, *Aztec Thought and Culture: A Study of the Ancient Nahuatl Mind* (Norman: University of Oklahoma Press, 1963); Alfredo López Austin, *Cuerpo humano e ideología. Las concepciones de los antiguos nahuas,* 2 vols. (México: Universidad

Nacional Autónoma de México, 1980); and H. B. Nicholson, "Religion in Pre-Hispanic Central Mexico," in *Handbook of Middle American Indians*, gen. ed. Robert Wauchope, vol. 10: *Archaeology of Northern Mesoamerica*, pt. 1, ed. Gordon F. Ekholm and Ignacio Bernal (Austin: University of Texas Press, 1975), 395–446. Recent treatments of Mexica kinship patterns include Edward Calnek, "The Sahagún Texts as a Source of Sociological Information," in *Sixteenth-Century Mexico: The Work of Sahagún*, ed. Munro S. Edmonson (Albuquerque: University of New Mexico Press, 1974), 195–200; Edward Calnek, "Kinship, Settlement Patterns, and Domestic Groups in Tenochtitlán" (unpublished MS); Pedro Carrasco, "Social Organization of Ancient Mexico," in *Handbook of Middle American Indians*, gen. ed. Robert Wauchope, 10: 349–75; and Susan Kellogg, "Kinship and Social Organization in Early Colonial Tenochtitlan: An Essay in Ethnohistorical Analysis and Methodology," in *Ethnohistory*, vol. 4 of *Supplement to the Handbook of Middle American Indians*, ed. Ronald Spores (Austin: University of Texas Press, 1986), 103–21. For a different interpretation, one that deemphasizes descent, see Jerome Offner, *Law and Politics in Aztec Texcoco* (Cambridge: Cambridge University Press, 1983), 163–213; and James Lockhart, *The Nahuas after the Conquest: A Social and Cultural History of the Indians of Central Mexico, Sixteenth through Eighteenth Centuries* (Stanford: Stanford University Press, 1992), chap. 3.

	7. Kellogg, "Kinship and Social Organization," 105–06. On cognatic forms of kinship organization, see Roger Keesing, *Kin Groups and Social Structure* (New York: Holt, Rinehart, and Winston, 1975), 91–96; and George Murdock, "Cognatic Forms of Social Organization," in *Social Structure in Southeast Asia*, ed. George Murdock (New York: Viking Fund Publications in Anthropology and Wenner-Gren Foundation for Anthropological Research, 1960), 1–15.

	8. "In timezio, in tintlapallo, in timoxijo. . . ." Fray Bernardino de Sahagún, *Florentine Codex: General History of the Things of New Spain*, ed. and trans. Arthur J. O. Anderson and Charles E. Dibble (Santa Fe and Salt Lake City: School of American Research and University of Utah Press, 1950–82), 6:32:175; 40:216. (Note that citations to the *Florentine Codex* and other major chronicles include the "book," chapter, and page numbers.)

	9. In the first section of this chapter, I rely heavily on three of the early religious chroniclers of New Spain, the Franciscans Toribio de Benavente (or "Motolinia") and Bernardino de Sahagún and the Dominican Diego Durán. Each was fluent in Nahuatl, and each had extensive experience in the Valley of Mexico. Sahagún's work, particularly the *Florentine Codex*, is of special importance because of the depth of his linguistic competence and his use of a group of elite male elders as informants. Sahagún's informants' memories were no doubt clouded by the passing of time and traumas. And

the information they provided reflected both their gender and their social position as well as Sahagún's own interests. Yet their texts are a linguistically and culturally rich corpus offering unique insights into Nahua culture.
    10. This passage reads in Spanish:

el cual testamento no se acostumbraba en esta tierra, sino que dejaban las casas y heredades a sus hijos, y el mayor, si era hombre, lo poseía, y tenía cuidado de sus hermanos y hermanas, como lo tenía el padre en su vida. Yendo los hermanos creciendo y casándose, el hermano mayor partía con ellos, según tenía; y si los hijos eran por casar, entraban en las heredades los mismos hermanos, y hacían con sus sobrinos, como he dicho que hacía el hermano mayor, de la otra hacienda.

Fray Toribio de Benavente o Motolinia, *Memoriales o libro de las cosas de la Nueva España y de los naturales de ella*, ed. Edmundo O'Gorman (México: Universidad Nacional Autónoma de México, 1971 [ca. 1536–43]), chap. 40:134–35.
    11. Susan Kellogg, "Social Organization in Early Colonial Tenochtitlán-Tlatelolco: An Ethnohistorical Study." (Ph.D. diss., University of Rochester, 1980), chap. 3; Susan Kellogg, "Aztec Inheritance in Sixteenth-Century Mexico City: Colonial Patterns, Prehispanic Influences," *Ethnohistory* 33:3 (Summer 1986): 315–24; and Cline, *Colonial Culhuacan*, 65–77.
    12. Cline, *Colonial Culhuacan*, 84.
    13. Ibid., 116.
    14. This pattern is suggested by the will of Hernando de Tapia, Archivo General de la Nación, ramo Tierras (hereafter, AGNT with legajo and expediente numbers) 37–2, 1576:fols. 78v–94r, and the litigation over part of de Tapia's estate by his niece, doña Bárbara Marta, 46–4, 1581. For more information on primary archival sources used in this chapter, see note 71.
    15. Durán, *Historia de las indias de Nueva España*, 1:5:57.
    16. Sahagún, *Florentine Codex*, 7:12:31.
    17. Juan Baptista Pomar, "Relación de Texcoco," in *Nueva colección de documentos para la historia de México*, ed. J. García Icazbalceta (México: Imprenta de Francisco Díaz de León, [1582] 1891), 3:68 (p. ref. for 1891 ed.).
    18. The single most useful ethnohistorical source on Mexica women's labor is the *Florentine Codex*. This material is ably summarized by Anna-Britta Hellbom, *La participación cultural de las mujeres indias y mestizas en el México precortesano y postrevolucionario* (Stockholm: Ethnographical Museum, 1967), 126–45.
    19. oniez in qujz, in qujquaz, tetlaqualtiz, tecoanotzaz, tetlacamatiz, ipan calacoaz, qujtechieltiz in atl, in tlaqualli: ypal ihiiocujoaz, ypal ceviz in jiollo, in jnacaio, in tlaihiiovitinemj tlalticpac . . . muchi onieoatiz, in tlein

maailia, atle nenquijçaz, in içiaviz, yn jtlapaliviz, atle nenvetziz, vel moti-
tianqujz in tianquiznaoac, in nentlamachoian: iuhqujn pipixaviz, ipan tepe-
viz, ipan tzetzeliviz in jtiamjc. Sahagún, *Florentine Codex*, 4:1:2.
    20. "çan moch icnoiotl, netoliniliztli." Ibid., 4:7:25.
    21. [auh intla cioatl,] vel motlacamatiz, vel motlaiecoltiz, vel motla-
catiz, qujttaz, qujpiaz in jteicneliliz, in jcococauh totecujo, tlaçaloanj, tlapa-
choanj iez, vel qujntlaçalhujz, qujntlapachilhujz, qujntetzontiz, qujntlatla-
machiz in jpilhoan. Ibid., 4:15:59.
    22. Ibid., 10:1:2.
    23. "iolloco cioatl," "omacic cioatl." Ibid., 10:3:11, 12.
    24. "tlapacho, tepachoa." Ibid., 10:13:46.
    25. Motolinia, *Historia de los indios de la Nueva España* (Madrid: His-
toria 16, 1985 [ca. 1536–43]), pt. 2, chap. 7:174.
    26. Durán, *Historia de las indias de la Nueva España*, 2:19:164–65. Also
see Louise Burkhart's chapter in this volume as well as Brumfiel, "Weaving
and Cooking," 226, 234–36, 239–43.
    27. For a useful discussion of the interrelationship between warfare
and social organization among late pre-Hispanic Nahuatl-speaking peoples,
see Ross Hassig, *Aztec Warfare: Imperial Expansion and Political Control* (Norman: University of Oklahoma Press, 1988), esp. chaps. 2–4. On the issue of
the relationship between frequent husbands' absences and women's work,
the analogy to the matrilineal Iroquois leaps out. Anthony Wallace shows
that the frequent absences of Iroquois husbands and fathers reinforced
women's economic autonomy and political roles; *The Death and Rebirth of the
Seneca* (New York: Knopf, 1969), 28–30. Also see Diane Rothenberg, "The
Mothers of the Nation: Seneca Resistance to Quaker Intervention," in
Women and Colonization: Anthropological Perspectives, ed. Mona Etienne and
Eleanor Leacock (New York: Praeger, 1980), 63–87.
    28. William T. Sanders, Jeffrey R. Parsons, and Robert S. Santley, *The
Basin of Mexico: Ecological Process in the Evolution of a Civilization* (New York:
Academic Press, 1979), 184–86.
    29. Sahagún's informants provided a long list of cooked foods eaten
by nobles which came from the market, in *Florentine Codex*, 8:13:37–38.
Cortés also describes how both fresh, or raw, *and* prepared foods were available. Hernando Cortés, *Cartas de relación de la conquista de Méjico* (Madrid: Espasa-Calpe, [1519–26] 1932), 1:99–100.
    30. Sahagún, *Florentine Codex*, 8:19:69.
    31. Ibid., 67–69.
    32. The term "tlayacanqui" is related to the verb *yacana*, which
means "to guide another or govern a *pueblo*," as well as to the *tlayacati*, which
refers to being first or in front; fray Alonso de Molina, *Vocabulario en lengua*

castellana y mexicana y mexicana y castellana, ed. and intro. Miguel León-Portilla (México: Editorial Porrúa, [1571] 1970), pt. 2, fols. 30r, 120v. Readers should also note the interesting passage in Durán's *Historia de las indias de Nueva España*, 1:13:130, where he describes a ceremony to increase the number of men killed for the goddess Cihuacoatl. This ceremony involved taking the cradle of a child and placing a stone knife in it and delivering it, first, to *"la más principal joyera,"* who then took it to the market to *"la más principal mercadera."* This passage suggests that these women held official positions and may have been hierarchically ranked.

33. Sahagún, *Florentine Codex*, 8:18:43; Durán, *Historia de las indias de Nueva España*, 190. Also see Edward Calnek, "The Calmecac and Telpochcalli in Pre-Conquest Tenochtitlán," in *The Work of Bernardino de Sahagún: Pioneer Ethnographer of Sixteenth-Century Aztec Mexico*, ed. J. Jorge Klor de Alva, H. B. Nicholson, and Eloise Quiñones Keber (Albany: State University of New York, Institute for Mesoamerican Studies, 1988), 171.

34. "aoqujc no teoa cujcoianoz, aoqujc no tenaoaz, ic qujcennaoatia, qujcenmacaoa, yn ichpuchtlaicanquj." Sahagún, *Florentine Codex*, 2:27:97.

35. Durán, *Historia de las indias de Nueva España*, 1:21:189.

36. Cline, *Colonial Culhuacan*, 54; and AGNT 59–3, 1595:fol. 18r. These women's titles were sometimes attached to women who witnessed wills, as in, for example, Marina Tiacapan's will, written in 1561, in AGNT 2729–20, 1562:fol. 3v, or in the Spanish translation of Francisca Tecuchu's will, dated 1560, in AGNT 42-5, 1579:fol. 3r.

37. Nicholson, "Religion in Pre-Hispanic Central Mexico," 414–24.

38. In the edition of Durán's *Historia* edited by Father Garibay (2:Glossary:584), he provided a glossary of Nahuatl terms. Garibay made the following comments about the term "cihuacoatl": "Es el representante del 'principio feminino.' De ahí su nombre, que puede traducirse, 'Mujer serpiente' o mejor 'Comparte feminino.' Es el que sustituye al rey, como la mujer al marido en casa."

39. The concept of the tlatoani as "father and mother" of his people is discussed in Susan Kellogg, "The Social Organization of Households among the Tenochca Mexica Before and After Conquest," in *Prehispanic Domestic Units in Western Mesoamerica: Studies of the Household, Compound, and Residence*, ed. Robert S. Santley and Kenneth G. Hirth (Boca Raton: CRC Press, 1993), 207–24. Also see Robert Haskett, *Indigenous Rulers: An Ethnohistory of Town Government in Colonial Cuernavaca* (Albuquerque: University of New Mexico Press, 1991), 100, 199; and Clendinnen, *Aztecs*, 160.

40. On female deities, see Hellbom, *La participación cultural de las mujeres*, 36–42, 44–47; Betty Ann Brown, "Seen but Not Heard: Women in Aztec Ritual—The Sahagún Texts," in *Text and Image in Pre-Columbian Art:*

Essays on the Interrelationship of the Verbal and Visual Arts, ed. Janet Catherine Berlo (Oxford: British Archaeological Reports Press, 1983), 121–22; Kellogg, "Cognatic Kinship and Religion," 672–73; Cecelia F. Klein, "Rethinking Cihuacoatl: Aztec Political Imagery of the Conquered Woman," in *Smoke and Mist,* ed. J. Kathryn Josserand and Karen Dakin, 237–77; Thelma D. Sullivan, "Tlazolteotl-Ixcuina: The Great Spinner and Weaver," in *The Art and Iconography of Late Post-Classic Central Mexico,* ed. Elizabeth H. Boone (Washington, D.C.: Dumbarton Oaks, 1982), 7–35.

41. Sahagún, *Florentine Codex,* 2:app.:215–16.

42. Francisco Javier Clavijero, *Historia antigua de México* (México: Editorial Porrúa, [1780] 1976), bk. 7:206.

43. On the priestly hierarchy, see Nicholson, "Religion in Pre-Hispanic Central Mexico," 436–37; on the exclusion of female priests from sacrificing victims, see Clavijero, *Historia antigua de México,* 168. On women helping to prepare sacrificial victims, see, e.g., Sahagún, *Florentine Codex,* 4:7:25.

44. Brown, "Seen but Not Heard," 127.

45. "Yoan in aqujn vmpa monetoltiaia, iehoatl conilhujaia in cihoaquacujlli iztac cihoatl, muchi iehoatl quitzontequja in tlein vncan muchivaia atenchicalca." While *quitzontequja* is better understood as "sentencing" or "passing judgment" (as defined by Molina, *Vocabulario,* pt. 2, fol. 153v), which suggests more precisely the role of this priestess, this passage of Sahagún, *Florentine Codex,* clearly shows that there was a hierarchy of priestesses; 2:app.:198.

46. Ibid., 6:39:210.

47. Ibid., 6:30–33:167–82; 37–38:201–07.

48. Ibid., 6:31:171–72.

49. Ibid., 6:31:173.

50. Ibid., 6:23:128. Also see James Cooper Clark, ed., *Codex Mendoza,* (London: Waterlow & Sons, [ca. 1540s, 1938), 3:fol. 61.

51. "Qujmonteca in cioatiticitci"; *Florentine Codex,* 6:23:132. Note the use of the term *ticitl* in the matchmaking context.

52. Susan D. Gillespie, *The Aztec Kings: The Construction of Rulership in Mexica History* (Tucson: University of Arizona Press, 1989), chaps. 1–4.

53. See, e.g., Durán, *Historia de las indias de Nueva España,* 2:10:92; also see Nash, "The Aztecs," 356.

54. See, e.g., Cecelia Klein's discussion of the symbolism of the Mexica goddess Cihuacoatl in her article "Rethinking Cihuacoatl," esp. pp. 237–46.

55. Clendinnen, *Aztecs,* 171–73.

56. Ibid., 164–67, 206.

57. On the imbalance in sex ratios, with more women than men, see Charles Gibson, *The Aztecs under Spanish Rule: A History of the Indians of the*

Valley of Mexico, 1519–1810 (Stanford: Stanford University Press, 1964), 141. Women's access to household headship—in the absence of males—appears to have been a significant cause of litigation among colonial Mexica during the sixteenth century. The relationships among gender, kinship, and litigation during the early colonial period are discussed in Susan Kellogg, *Law and the Transformation of Aztec Culture, 1500–1700* (Norman: University of Oklahoma Press, 1995), chap. 3.

58. Spanish law as it related to women is discussed in great detail by Silvia Arrom, *The Women of Mexico City, 1790–1857* (Stanford: Stanford University Press, 1985), chap. 2. For a useful discussion of women's property rights under Spanish law, see Asunción Lavrin and Edith Couturier, "Dowries and Wills: A View of Women's Socioeconomic Role in Colonial Guadalajara and Puebla, 1640–1790," *Hispanic American Historical Review* 59:2 (May 1979): 280–304. Also see Edith Couturier, "Women and the Family in Eighteenth-Century Mexico: Law and Practice," *Journal of Family History* 10:3 (Fall 1985): 294–304; and Silvia Arrom, "Changes in Mexican Family Law in the Nineteenth Century: The Civil Codes of 1870 and 1884," *Journal of Family History* 10:3 (Fall 1985): 305–17. On women in early modern Spain, see Ann Pescatello, *Power and Pawn: The Female in Iberian Families, Societies, and Cultures* (Westport, Conn.: Greenwood Press, 1976); Jodi Bilinkoff, *The Avila of Santa Teresa: Religious Reform in a Sixteenth-Century City* (Ithaca: Cornell University Press, 1989); and Mary Elizabeth Perry, *Gender and Disorder in Early Modern Spain* (Princeton: Princeton University Press, 1990).

59. Arrom, *The Women of Mexico City*, 67; Lavrin and Couturier, "Dowries and Wills," 282.

60. Arrom, *The Women of Mexico City*, 67–68.

61. The *Leyes de Toro* and *Siete Partidas* are collected in Marcel Martínez Alcubilla, *Códigos antiguos de España* (Madrid: Administración [J. López Camacho], 1885), vol. 1. On inheritance laws, see especially laws seven to ten of the *Leyes de Toro*. Inheritance law is also treated in the *Siete Partidas*, especially in *Partida* 6, also in vol. 1. Also see Arrom, *The Women of Mexico City*, 63; and Lavrin and Couturier, "Dowries and Wills," 286.

62. Lavrin and Couturier, "Dowries and Wills," 287.

63. Arrom, *The Women of Mexico City*, 58–62.

64. Ibid., 61.

65. Ibid., 56–57, 69.

66. Lavrin and Couturier, "Dowries and Wills," 287; Arrom, *The Women of Mexico City*, 66. Also see Beatríz Bernal de Bugeda, "Situación jurídica de la mujer en las Indias Occidentales," in *Condición jurídica de la mujer en México*, ed. Sara Bialostosky de Chazán (México: Universidad Nacional Autónoma de México, Facultad de Derecho, 1975), 21–41.

67. Gibson, *The Aztecs under Spanish Rule*, 355, 569 n. 144; Ross Hassig, *Trade, Tribute and Transportation: The Sixteenth-Century Political Economy of the Valley of Mexico* (Norman: University of Oklahoma Press, 1985), 229.

68. Gonzalo Gómez de Cervantes, *La vida económica y social de la Nueva España al finalizar del siglo XVI* (México: Antigua Librería Robredo de J. Porrúa e Hijos, [1599] 1944), 135. Gómez de Cervantes had been an *alcalde mayor* (chief magistrate) in several towns in the Valley of Mexico including Tlaxcala where he also served as *gobernador* (governor). The observations he makes throughout his text suggest a man especially knowledgeable about law and economic conditions in the central portions of New Spain. Also see J. Benedict Warren, "An Introductory Survey of Secular Writings in the European Tradition on Colonial Middle America, 1503–1818," in *Handbook of Middle American Indians*, vol. 13: *Guide to Ethnohistorical Sources*, ed. Howard F. Cline (Austin: University of Texas Press, 1973), 2:82.

69. Kellogg, "Aztec Women in Early Colonial Courts," 28–29.

70. The description of Indian women's roles in property litigation that follows is based on analysis of seventy-three cases heard by the Real Audiencia during the years 1537 through 1700. The principle behind the choice of cases was that one or more parties to the suit consisted of Indians resident in Mexico City during this time. (Note that 1537 signifies the date of the earliest case I could find.) The documents are housed primarily in the Archivo General de la Nación (hereafter, AGN) in Mexico City in ramos Tierras (hereafter, AGNT) and Vínculos y Mayorazgos. A smaller number are to be found in the Archivo General de Indias in Seville in the sections Justicia and México. A few scattered cases are to be found in other collections, such as the Bibliothèque Nationale de Paris (hereafter, BNP) and the Latin American Library at Tulane University. Thirty-two of just over 700 witnesses were women during the period 1537–85 (5%). Twenty-six of 225 witnesses were women during the period 1585–1700 (11%).

71. For examples of women acting as legal guardians for children, see AGNT 30-1, 1570, or 49-5, 1585. Cases of men claiming property based on dowry include one in which a male litigant claimed his mother brought property as dowry to his father (AGNT 20-1-2, 1572) and another in which a male litigant claimed property ownership based on his wife's dowry (AGNT 20-1-3, 1573). Many male litigants claimed property through *mercedes* (grants). Examples would include AGNT 55-5, 1564; 55-2, 1589; and BNP 112, 1593. Examples of rental include AGNT 24-1, 1568, and 54-2, 1587.

72. The submission of wills was itself a gendered strategy. During the sixteenth century, twenty-five of thirty-three wills were presented as part of litigations. Sixteen were presented by women (six female plaintiffs, ten female defendants) and nine by men (five male plaintiffs, four male de-

fendants). But note that while more sixteenth-century women's wills survive for Tenochtitlan, more men's wills survive for Culhuacan, as Cline describes in *Colonial Culhuacan*, 9.

73. Gibson, *Aztecs*, 350.

74. Ibid., 198. The question of whether and at what rates Indian women paid tribute is complex. Juan de Solórzano y Pereyra suggests that Indian women in New Spain generally did pay tribute. See *Política indiana* (Madrid: Imprenta Real de la Gazeta, 1776), 1:161–62. Also see Arrom, *The Women of Mexico City*, 308 n. 81. Gibson suggests that at the same time that tribute was being extended to the native population of Mexico City and tribute payments were being monetarized, widows and unmarried women were increasingly being pressed to make payments. See *Aztecs*, 203. Gibson also states that widows and unmarried women were not formally exempted from tribute payments until 1758, and by the nineteenth century all women were made exempt; Ibid., 207, 394.

75. Ibid., 198. See AGN Indios 4–194, 1590:fol. 60v for a reference to women receiving assigned places in the city's major markets.

76. Silvio Zavala, *El servicio personal de los indios en la Nueva España* (México: El Colegio de México, Centro de Estudios Históricos, 1984–87), 2:230–33. The *Códice Osuna*, ed. Luis Chávez Orozco (México: Ediciones del Instituto Indigenista Interamericano, 1947 [ca. 1560s]), 339, refers to men and women performing parallel kinds of labor at Viceroy Velasco's *tecpan* (palace).

77. Lyman Johnson, "Artisans," in *Cities and Society in Colonial Latin America*, ed. Louisa S. Hoberman and Susan Migden Socolow (Albuquerque: University of New Mexico Press, 1986), 243–44; Gibson, *Aztecs*, 394.

78. Arrom, *The Women of Mexico City*, 158–59.

79. See, e.g., discussions of the goddess Tlazolteotl by Sullivan, "Tlazolteotl-Ixcuina," 15–19; and Burkhart, *The Slippery Earth*, 92–93.

80. Burkhart suggests that there was some continuity between Eve and Cihuacoatl, i.e., "the woman who first sinned, and who like Cihuacoatl had serpent associations"; *The Slippery Earth*, 93. How frequently Eve was discussed or depicted in the early colonial period is not clear.

81. Burkhart, *The Slippery Earth*, 128–29. Ann Miriam Gallagher also points out how young Mexica women attended "patio schools" to learn Christian doctrine through which notions of "Christian womanhood" were instilled. See "The Indian Nuns of Mexico City's *Monasterio* of Corpus Christi, 1724–1821," in *Latin American Women*, ed. Asunción Lavrin, 150.

82. Burkhart, *The Slippery Earth*, 154–56.

83. Fray Juan de la Anunciación, *Sermonio en lengva mexicana* (México: Antonio Ricardo, 1577), fol. 165r, cited and translated by Burkhart, *The Slippery Earth*, 137 [my emphasis].

84. Fray Bernardino de Sahagún, *Psalmodia christiana y sermonio de los santos del año en lengua mexicana* (México: Pedro Ocharte, 1583), fols. 146v–147v, cited and translated by Burkhart, *The Slippery Earth*, 139 [my emphasis].

85. See AGNT 163-5, 1699. In this suit Nicolasa Teresa and her nephew, Lucas de Santa María, sued over a house site they claimed to have inherited from Nicolasa's husband.

86. See AGNT 183-4, 1607.

87. Silvia Arrom discusses the use of Spanish law as a means to enforce women's sexual propriety in *The Women of Mexico City*, 63–78. Changing concepts of honor in the Hispanic sector of colonial Latin American society are discussed by Patricia Seed, *To Love, Honor, and Obey in Colonial Mexico: Conflicts over Marriage Choice, 1574–1821* (Stanford: Stanford University Press, 1988), chaps. 4, 6. Also see Ramón A. Gutiérrez, *When Jesus Came, the Corn Mothers Went Away: Marriage, Sexuality, and Power in New Mexico, 1500–1846* (Stanford: Stanford University Press, 1991), chaps. 5–7.

88. See Ruth Behar, "Sexual Witchcraft, Colonialism, and Women's Powers: Views from the Mexican Inquisition," in *Sexuality and Marriage in Colonial Latin America*, ed. Asunción Lavrin (Lincoln: University of Nebraska Press, 1989), 192.

89. Ibid., 201.

90. Examples and discussion can be found in Hernando Ruiz de Alarcón, *Treatise on the Heathen Superstitions that Today Live Among the Indians Native to this New Spain, 1629*, ed. and trans. J. Richard Andrews and Ross Hassig (Norman: University of Oklahoma Press, 1984), 65–66, 131–39.

91. Serge Gruzinski, "Individualization and Acculturation: Confession among the Nahuas from the Sixteenth to the Eighteenth Century," in *Sexuality and Marriage in Colonial Latin America*, ed. Asunción Lavrin (Lincoln: University of Nebraska Press, 1989), 109.

92. Behar, "Sexual Witchcraft," 199–200.

93. William B. Taylor, *Drinking, Homicide, and Rebellion in Colonial Mexican Villages* (Stanford: Stanford University Press, 1979), 116. Also see John Tutino, "Power, Class, and Family: Men and Women in the Mexican Elite, 1750–1810," *The Americas* 39:3 (January 1983): 380–81; and Haskett, *Indigenous Rulers*, 39, 84, 199, along with his essay in this volume.

94. Letters by don Carlos Sigüenza y Góngora and others are cited and quoted by Luis Gonzáles Obregón in *Rebeliones indígenas y precursores de la independencia mexicana en los siglos XVI, XVII, XVIII* (México: Ediciones Fuente Cultural, [1906–08] 1952), 408–10. Also see Chester Guthrie, "Riots in Seventeenth-Century Mexico City: A Study of Social and Economic Conditions," in *Greater America: Essays in Honor of Herbert Eugene Bolton*, ed.

Adele Ogden and Engel Sluiter (Berkeley: University of California Press, 1945), 247–48; also see Gibson, *Aztecs*, 384.

95. See Silverblatt, *Moon, Sun, and Witches*, 132–33, 155–58, for a discussion of the influence of colonial rule on Andean gender parallelism.

Chapter 6. Activist or Adulteress?

1. The receptor was usually a trained notary attached to the Audiencia who, according to Woodrow Borah, "heard and recorded testimony, usually in the form of answers to a set questionnaire." This official usually "traveled to the witnesses' location, asked the questions formally set forth in the interrogation, and recorded the qualifications and answers of the witnesses." See Woodrow Borah, *Justice by Insurance: The General Indian Court of Colonial Mexico and the Legal Aides of the Half-Real* (Berkeley: University of California Press, 1983), 236.

2. Archivo General de la Nación, México (AGN) Civil, vol. 1118, exp. 5, fols. 48r–49r (report of the arrest of Josefa María and Miguel Francisco, 1712).

3. Susan Kellogg, *Law and the Transformation of Aztec Culture, 1500–1700* (Norman: University of Oklahoma Press, 1995), 107–13, 117–19; the author adds that women's activities in *cofradías* (lay religious sodalities), as midwives or matchmakers, and in localized rioting may have had a political dimension. Alvis Dunn, "A Cry at Daybreak: Death, Disease, and Defense of Community in a Highland Ixil-Maya Village," and Irene Silverblatt, "Lessons of Gender and Ethnohistory in Mesoamerica," both in *Ethnohistory* 42:4 (Fall 1995): 595–606 and 639–50, respectively. Steve J. Stern, *The Secret History of Gender: Women, Men, and Power in Late Colonial Mexico* (Chapel Hill: University of North Carolina Press, 1995), 204. See also Louise S. Hoberman, "Hispanic American Women as Portrayed in the Historical Literature: Type or Archetypes?" *Revista Interamericana/Interamerican Review* 4:2 (Summer 1974): 138; and June Nash, "Aztec Women: The Transition from Status to Class in Empire and Colony," in *Women and Colonization: Anthropological Perspectives*, eds. Mona Etienne and Eleanor Leacock (New York: Praeger, 1980), 137. Nash sees a "constant" diminution of the power of Aztec women from the time of their migration to the Valley of Mexico through the colonial era.

4. See Hoberman, "Hispanic American Women," 137; June E. Hahner, "Researching the History of Latin American Women: Past and Future Directions," *Revista Interamericana de Bibliografía/Inter-American Review of Bibliography* 33:4 (1983):545–52; and Susan Kellogg, "Aztec Women in Early Colonial Courts: Structure and Strategy in a Legal Context," in *Five Centuries of Law and Politics in Central Mexico*, eds. Ronald Spores and Ross Hassig, Vanderbilt Uni-

382 Notes to Pages 147–51

versity Publications in Anthropology, no. 30 (Nashville: 1984), 25–38. See chapter 14 in this volume for an excellent new interpretation of La Malinche.

5. Kellogg, *Law*, 115; despite her belief that indigenous women did preserve at least a remnant of political activism, she identifies as well the fading of precontact gender parallelism in the Valley of Mexico during the seventeenth century. See also Deborah Kanter, "Native Female Land Tenure and Its Decline in Mexico, 1750–1900," *Ethnohistory* 42:4 (Fall 1995): 607–16, who believes that the position of women as landholders in the Valley of Toluca was on the decline in the later eighteenth century.

6. AGN Tierras vol. 1935, exp. 4 (*hacienda de labor* of doña Inés Cortés of Yecapixtla, 1632).

7. For a full description, see Robert Haskett, "Living in Two Worlds: Cultural Continuity and Change among Cuernavaca's Colonial Indigenous Ruling Elite," *Ethnohistory* 35:1 (Winter 1988): 34–59.

8. AGN Hospital de Jesús (HJ) leg. 210, exp. 71 ("Here is made manifest all the criminals who are arrested and jailed," Cuernavacan Nahuatl record, 1607).

9. See Robert Haskett, "'Not a Pastor, but a Wolf': Indigenous-Clergy Relations in Early Cuernavaca and Taxco," *The Americas* 50:3 (January 1994): 293–336. For discussions of rape and indigenous women, see Matthew Restall, " 'He wished It in Vain': Subordination and Resistance among Maya Women in Post-Conquest Yucatan," *Ethnohistory* 42:4 (Fall 1995): 577–94; and Stephanie Wood, "Rape as a Tool of Conquest in Early Latin America," *CSWS Review* (1992): 18–20.

10. William Clements Library Cuernavaca Papers (Nahuatl primordial titles of Cuernavaca, late seventeenth or early eighteenth century); AGN HJ, leg. 387, exp. 37 (political activities of doña María Cortés of Cuernavaca, 1568); AGN HJ, leg. 96, libro 1 (doña Magdalena Sánchez and doña Magdalena Tellez act in the confirmation of corporate land ownership, Xiuhtepec, 1650); AGN HJ, leg. 208, exp. 218 (widow of an alcalde of Achichipico and others vs. a corrupt former governor, 1720); and AGN Indios, vol. 36, exp. 211 (a *gobernadora*, "woman governor," and widow of Toluca attempts to finish out her husband's term, 1704).

11. AGN HJ, leg. 59, exp. 3, fols. 15r–v, 17r–18v (Cuernavaca, 1631). For a similar case, see AGN HJ, leg. 115, exp. 3 (five Indian women of San Gaspar Coatlan issue a petition complaining of a corrupt governor in cooperation with a political faction seeking his removal, 1720).

12. AGN Civil, vol. 2175, exp. 5, fol. 53r (election dispute in Tepoztlan, 1720).

13. AGN HJ, vol. 86, exp. 50, fols. 15r–20v, 23r–25r (factional dispute in Tepoztlan, 1705).

14. AGN HJ, vol. 85, exp. 21, and vol. 86, exp. 44 (Tepoztlan, 1711); AGN Civil, vol. 1118, exp. 5 (Tepoztlan, 1712).

15. Such women could also be placed in the homes of "respectable families"; see Asunción Lavrin, "In Search of the Colonial Woman in Mexico in the Seventeenth and Eighteenth Centuries," in *Latin American Women: Historical Perspectives*, ed. Asunción Lavrin (Westport, Conn.: Greenwood Press, 1978), 35–36.

16. AGN Civil, vol. 2175, exp. 5 (Tepoztlan, 1720); AGN Civil, vol. 1823, exp. 13 (Tepoztlan, 1724).

17. The following information is taken from AGN Civil, vol. 1608, exp. 10, fols. 84r–223v (conflict and rioting in Tepoztlan, May 1725 through September 1726).

18. William B. Taylor, *Drinking, Homicide, and Rebellion in Colonial Mexican Villages* (Stanford: Stanford University Press, 1979), 116–127, discusses the prominent and aggressive role of women in tumultos. See also Dunn, "A Cry at Daybreak."

19. Taylor, *Drinking, Homicide and Rebellion*, 115.

20. Churches, along with municipal buildings and other structures and people identified with authority, were common targets of rioters; see Taylor, *Drinking, Homicide, and Rebellion*, 119.

21. See a quote from the sixteenth-century judicial official Gómez de Cervantes in Kellogg, "Aztec Women in Early Colonial Courts," 28.

22. Heath Dillard, *Daughters of the Reconquest: Women in Castillian Town Society, 1100–1300* (London: Cambridge University Press, 1984), 148–149. See also Ruth Behar, *Santa María del Monte: The Presence of the Past in a Spanish Village* (Princeton: Princeton University Press, 1986), 126.

23. AGN Civil, vol. 1118, exp. 5 (election dispute and adultery investigation in Tepoztlan, 1712).

24. AGN Civil, vol. 1608, exp. 10 (election dispute and rioting in Tepoztlan, 1725).

25. Ibid.

26. AGN Civil, vol. 1118, exp. 5 (investigation of the affair of doña Josefa and don Miguel, 1712); AGN Civil, vol. 1118, exp. 5 (election dispute and adultery investigation, Tepoztlan, 1725); AGN Civil, vol. 2175, exp. 5 (Tepoztecan election dispute, 1720); AGN Civil, vol. 1608, exp. 10 (election dispute and repartimiento litigation in Tepoztlan, 1725).

27. The quote is from Martha Few, "Women, Religion, and Power: Gender and Resistance in Daily Life in Late-Seventeenth-Century Santiago de Guatemala," *Ethnohistory* 42:4 (Fall 1995): 631; for Spain, see Dillard, *Daughters of the Reconquest*, 170.

28. Lavrin, "In Search of the Colonial Woman," 35.

29. See a charge of this sort in AGN Civil, vol. 2175, exp. 5 (election dispute in Tepoztlan, 1720).

30. AGN Civil, vol. 1608, exp. 10 (rioting in Tepoztlan, 1725).

31. Lavrin, "In Search of the Colonial Woman," 25–26, 41. See also Hoberman, "Hispanic American Women," 137; Asunción Lavrin and Edith Couturier, "Las mujeres tienen la palabra. Otras voces en la historia colonial de México," *Historia Mexicana* 31:2 (October-December 1981): 303; and Edith Couturier, "Women and the Family in Eighteenth-Century Mexico: Law and Practice," *Journal of Family History* 10:3 (Fall 1985): 305–17, who provides a succinct discussion of the scope of action available to both Spanish and indigenous widows.

32. Fray Bernardino de Sahagún, *Florentine Codex: General History of the Things of New Spain*, trans. and ed. Arthur J. O. Anderson (Santa Fe and Salt Lake City: School of American Research and University of Utah Press, 1961), 10:45–50.

33. Ibid.

34. Ibid., 55.

35. AGN Civil, vol. 1118, exp. 5 (petition from a member of doña Josefa's faction, June 28, 1712).

36. Sahagún, *Florentine Codex*, 8:49.

37. Frances Karttunen and James Lockhart, trans. and ed., *The Art of Nahuatl Speech: The Bancroft Dialogues*, Nahuatl Studies Series, no. 2 (Los Angeles: UCLA Latin American Center, 1987), 153; see also, 109. See also Juan Bautista Pomar, *Relación de Tezcoco*, ed. Joaquín García Icazbalceta (México: Biblioteca Enciclopédica del Estado de México, [1582] 1975), 30; José de Acosta, *The Natural and Moral History of the Indies* (New York: Burt Franklin, 1963), 2:333; fray Toribio de Benavente o Motolinia, *Motolinia's History of the Indians of New Spain*, trans. and ed. Elizabeth Andros Foster (Westport, Conn.: Greenwood Press, 1973), 254; Francisco Javier Clavijero, *Historia antigua de México*, ed. Mariano Cuevas (México: Editorial Porrúa, [1780] 1971), 205–06.

38. For example, see María de Jesús Rodríguez, "La mujer y la familia en la sociedad Mexica," in *Presencia y transparencia: La mujer en la historia de México* ed. Carmen Ramos Escandón (México: El Colegio de México, 1987), 16–18.

39. Miguel León-Portilla, *Siete ensayos sobre la cultura náhuatl* (México: Universidad Nacional Autónoma de México, 1958), 103–07.

40. See France V. Scholes and Ralph L. Roys, *The Maya Chontal Indians of Acalan-Tixchel: A Contribution to the History and Ethnography of the Yucatan Peninsula* (Norman: University of Oklahoma Press, 1968), 35–36.

Scholes and Roys believe that women in Mexica colonies were more likely to enjoy some sort of political role than their fully Maya contemporaries.

41. Susan D. Gillespie, *The Aztec Kings: The Construction of Rulership in Mexica History* (Tucson: University of Arizona Press, 1989), 3–120. Silvia Garza Tarazona de González, *La mujer mesoamericana* (México: Editorial Planeta Mexicana, 1991), 42–46.

42. Pedro Carrasco, "Royal Marriages in Ancient Mexico," in *Explorations in Ethnohistory: Indians of Central Mexico in the Sixteenth Century*, ed. H.R. Harvey and Hanns J. Prem (Albuquerque: University of New Mexico Press, 1984), 44 and on p. 43 he states, "a man's rights to rank and office were clearly influenced by his mother's or wife's status." James A. Fox and John S. Justeson, "Classic Maya Dynastic Alliance and Succession," in *Ethnohistory*, vol. 4 of *Supplement to the Handbook of Middle American Indians*, ed. Ronald Spores (Austin: University of Texas Press, 1986), 30, suggest that because women are commonly featured on the essentially political monumental record, they must have had some important political significance, and state that lowland Maya rulers were probably "husbands of a ruling matriline."

43. See Susan Kellogg, chapter 5 in this volume; her article "The Woman's Room: Some Aspects of Gender Relations in Tenochtitlan in the Late Pre-Hispanic Period," *Ethnohistory* 42:4 (Fall 1995): 565–67 (quote on p. 567); and her "Aztec Women in Early Colonial Courts," 33. See also Robert Haskett, *Indigenous Rulers: A Social History of Town Government in Colonial Cuernavaca* (Albuquerque: University of New Mexico Press, 1991), 99–104.

44. *Bancroft Dialogues*, 119–21.

45. Sahagún, *Florentine Codex*, 10:45–49.

46. I am indebted to Ruth Behar, who finds that one reason an old Guachichil woman was able to achieve a good deal of influence among her people in the late sixteenth century turned on the loss of cultural legitimacy of traditional male chiefs, who were seen as having bought too avidly into Spanish culture. The applicability of this insight is striking in the Tepoztlan case, where a powerful faction of local ruling elites actively supported Spanish goals to the detriment of Tepoztecan well-being. Behar's conclusions were first enunciated in "The Visions of a Guachichil Witch in 1599: A Window on the Subjugation of Mexico's Hunter-Gatherers," *Ethnohistory* 34:2 (Spring 1987): 133. Writing after this chapter had been completed, Dunn, "A Cry at Daybreak," also found a pattern of female participation in rioting taking place in what he describes as a "power vacuum." Silverblatt, "Lessons of Gender," 646, discusses the possibility that conflicting gender ideologies could have given indigenous women some space to resist or challenge Spanish ideals.

Chapter 7. Matters of Life at Death

This essay is a revised version of a presentation given at a meeting of the Pacific Coast branch of the American Historical Association in Portland, Oregon, in the summer of 1989, which appeared in *Mesoamerican and Chicano Art, Culture, and Identity/El arte, la cultura, y la identidad mesoamericana y chicana*, ed. Robert C. Dash (Salem, Ore.: Willamette Journal of the Liberal Arts, Willamette University, 1994), 78–103. I would like to acknowledge the helpful suggestions of Susan Kellogg, Dawn Keremitsis, and my coeditors. Any errors that remain are my own.

1. Archivo General de la Nación (hereafter, AGN), México, Civil, vol. 664, exp. 2, fol. 31r (January 5, 1759).

2. S. L. Cline, *Colonial Culhuacan, 1580–1600: A Social History of an Aztec Town* (Albuquerque: University of New Mexico Press, 1986). Cline, together with Miguel León-Portilla, published *The Testaments of Culhuacan*, Nahuatl Studies Series, no. 1 (Los Angeles: UCLA Latin American Center, 1984). Additional testaments are found in Arthur J. O. Anderson, Frances Berdan, and James Lockhart, eds. and trans., *Beyond the Codices* (Berkeley: University of California Press, 1976). Susan Kellogg, "Social Organization in Early Colonial Tenochtitlan-Tlatelolco: An Ethnohistorical Study" (Ph.D. diss., University of Rochester, 1980), and in subsequent publications cited below, also employs sixteenth-century testaments in Nahuatl, among other records.

3. Cline, *Colonial Culhuacan*, 107–23; quote is from pp. 122–123. Susan Kellogg, "Kinship and Social Organization in Early Colonial Tenochtitlan: An Essay in Ethnohistorical Analysis and Methodology," in *Ethnohistory*, vol. 4 of *Supplement to the Handbook of Middle American Indians*, ed. Ronald Spores (Austin: University of Texas Press, 1986), 103–21, says that "men and women received equal rights to urban houses and house sites and often to land, though women's abilities to activate their rights to land were limited," (pp. 105–06).

4. These testaments represent all of the women's wills I have found so far for this region but only about half of the men's wills. Translation of the remainder continues apace. Since the bulk of the testaments studied here date from the eighteenth century, I have not yet analyzed the data for change within my own time period, only in comparison to information available for the sixteenth century. The sample for later colonial times should be expanded (which could be done more easily than for earlier times) before we attempt to discern change within this time frame.

5. These rural women are very different from urban indigenous women of Quito and Arequipa whose testaments are no longer a surprise

and whose lifestyles are difficult to compare here; see Frank Salomon, "Indian Women of Early Quito as Seen through Their Testaments," *The Americas* 44:3 (January 1988): 325–41; and Elinor C. Burkett, "Indian Women and White Society: The Case of Sixteenth-Century Peru," in *Latin American Women: Historical Perspectives*, ed. Asunción Lavrin (Westport, Conn.: Greenwood Press, 1978), 101–28. Closer in experience, yet still different, are the lives of urban indigenous women of seventeenth-century Mexico City, as described by Susan Kellogg in chapter 5 in this volume (based on 18 cases), and those of the tobacco laborers and domestics described by Juan Javier Pescador in "Vanishing Woman: Female Migration and Ethic Identity in Late-Colonial Mexico City," *Ethonohistory* 42:4 (Fall 1995): 617–26. For some communities, surprisingly, we have more testaments for women than for men (see chapter 11).

6. While "doña" was a term more liberally applied to Spanish women than "don" was to Spanish men, the application of titles seems to have worked in the reverse with indigenous men and women. One indicator of this is the higher proportion of dons among the male testators, nine of forty-nine, compared to six doñas out of fifty-nine females.

7. AGN Tierras, vol. 2298, exp. 3, fols. 7r–9r (La Transfiguración, Tenango del Valle, September 13, 1762). The testaments of both Ignacia Cristina and Francisca María contrast notably with those of Hispanic women. See, e.g., Asunción Lavrin, "*Lo femenino*: Women in Colonial Historical Sources," in *Coded Encounters: Writing, Gender and Ethnicity in Colonial Latin America*, ed. Francisco Javier Cevallos-Candau et al. (Amherst: University of Massachusetts Press, 1994), 153–76.

8. Cline, *Colonial Culhuacan*, 79.

9. Ibid., 165.

10. Resource-related uprisings and land litigation, in general, became heated at this time and continued all through the eighteenth century; see Stephanie Wood, "Corporate Adjustments in Colonial Mexican Indian Towns: Toluca Region, 1550–1810." (Ph.D. diss., University of California, Los Angeles, 1984). Over half of the testaments in this study date from the 1750s or later, although the epidemic of 1759–62 is partly responsible for this late surge.

11. The wills illustrating inheritance patterns are too numerous to list individually here, but all come from the same litigation records cited elsewhere in this study.

12. Susan Kellogg, "Aztec Inheritance in Sixteenth-Century Mexico City: Colonial Patterns, Prehispanic Influences," *Ethnohistory* 33:3 (Summer 1986): 313–30 (quote from 318–19). Evidence drawn from twenty-nine Aztec wills from Mexico City may or may not speak for traditions in indigenous

communities in the Toluca Valley, where various ethnic groups coexisted, Matlatzinca, Mazahua, Otomí, and Ocuilteca having been conquered in 1474 by the Aztecs. Cline, in *Colonial Culhuacan*, 302, did not find gender affecting bequest patterns as Kellogg found. Future studies of more indigenous testaments may settle the question.

13. Kellog, "Aztec Inheritance," 319. Edith Couturier provides figures on the use of entail in colonial Mexico in "Women and the Family in Eighteenth-Century Mexico: Law and Practice," *Journal of Family History* 10:3 (Fall 1985): 294–304 (see her note 5).

14. See, e.g., AGN Tierras vol. 1859, exp. 3, fols. 4r-7r (will of Miguel Agustín of Malinalco, October 30, 1695); AGN Tierras, vol. 2538, exp. 6, fols. 1r-2r (will of don Miguel de Santiago of Texcaliacac, June 7, 1737); AGN Civil, vol. 1072, exp. 13, fols. 1r-3v (will of don Tomás de Santiago of Metepec, April 18, 1786); AGN Tierras, vol. 2538, exp. 6 (will of Mateo Martín, former fiscal of Texcaliacac, March 1, 1775); AGN Tierras, vol. 2538, exp. 4, fols. 4r–5r (will of Ventura Ramos of Cuaxustenco, May 1, 1761); and AGN Tierras, vol. 2546, exp. 16, fols. 8r–10v (will of Gaspar Melchor of Xonacatlan, June 13, 1720).

Deborah Kanter ("Native Female Land Tenure and Its Decline in Mexico, 1750–1900," *Ethnohistory* 42 [Fall 1995]: 607–16) finds that the colonial courts in the Toluca region "firmly upheld the principle of partible inheritance" (611) with equal parts intended for all legitimate offspring.

15. These six examples are AGN Tierras, vol. 2391, exp. 1, fols. 26r–26v (will of Jacinto Reyes of Atengo, September 12, 1694); AGN Tierras, vol. 1859, exp. 3, fols. 4r–7r (will of Miguel Agustín of Malinalco, October 30, 1695); AGN Tierras, vol. 2544, exp. 12, cuad. 2, fols. 1r–4v (will of Marcelino de la Cruz of Tenango del Valle, April 14, 1736); AGN Tierras, vol. 2541, exp. 11, fols. 8r–9v (will of Dominga Magdalena of Tepemaxalco, February 13, 1701); AGN Civil, vol. 664, exp. 2, fols. 46r–47v (will of Felix Juan of Tepemaxalco, August 14, 1762); and AGN Tierras, vol. 1501, exp. 3, fols. 13r–16v (will of don Pedro de la Cruz of Tepemaxalco, March 18, 1667).

Susan Kellogg, "Aztec Inheritance," 318, reports that men of early colonial Tenochtitlan usually "left houses to wives, siblings, and children," while "women left houses primarily to their daughters and granddaughters."

16. AGN Tierras, vol. 1501, exp. 3, fols. 15r–16v (will of Jacinto de la Cruz of Tepemaxalco, November 1, 1693).

17. See AGN Tierras, vol. 2298, exp. 5, fols. 21r–22v (will of Agustín de la Cruz of Calimaya, October 22, 1755); AGN Civil, vol. 1120, exp. 7, fols. 7r–8v (will of Juan Andrés of Tepemaxalco, August 21, 1737); AGN Tierras, vol. 2538, exp. 8, fols. 8r–9v (will of Vicente Torres of Tepemaxalco, August 2, 1762); and AGN Tierras, vol. 2301, exp. 10, fols. 10r–v (will of Pascual Nicolás of Tenango del Valle, March 21, 1772).

18. AGN Tierras, vol. 2538, exp. 6, fols. 1r–2r (will of don Miguel de Santiago of Texcaliacac, June 7, 1737); and AGN Civil, vol. 664, exp. 2, fols. 67r–67bis.v (will of Pablo Marcial of Santa María Asunción, September 27, 1762).

19. See, e.g., AGN Civil, vol. 1003, exp. 4, fols. 30r–32v (will of María de la Concepción, Tianguistengo, October 9, 1761); and AGN Civil, vol. 664, exp. 2, fol. 61bis.r (will of Pascuala María of Santa María Asunción, April 24, 1762).

20. Kellogg, "Aztec Inheritance," 320.

21. See Cline, *Colonial Culhuacan,* 116, and Asunción Lavrin and Edith Couturier, "Dowries and Wills: A View of Women's Socioeconomic Role in Colonial Guadalajara and Puebla, 1640–1790," *Hispanic American Historical Review* 59:2 (May 1979): 280–304. We do see indigenous women with dowries in chapter 11; several, at least, were married to Spaniards. See also Carrasco's discussion of "bridewealth" in chapter 3.

22. Many of these women lost their lives in the epidemic of 1759–62, and their wills are found in a cache in AGN Civil, vol. 664. These testaments stand out as somewhat unusual. It may be that ambitious *fiscales* (indigenous assistants to the priests) of the church in Calimaya made a special effort to record these wills, whereas they would normally have gone unrecorded. Or, it may be that poor people's wills and married women's wills were very common but have remained in parish archives.

23. AGN Tierras, vol. 2615, exp. 7, fols. 3r–4v (will of Nicolasa María of Techuchulco, February 27, 1727); and fols. 5r–6r (will of Salvador Miguel of Techuchulco, January 5, 1727).

24. AGN Civil, vol. 997, exp. 2, fols. 6r–7v (will of María de la Cruz of Tenango del Valle, August 22, 1736); AGN Tierras, vol. 2391, exp. 1, fols. 3r–v (will of Juana Rosa of Atengo, June 4, 1736); AGN Civil, vol. 664, exp. 2, fols. 32r–v (will of Marcela María of Tepemaxalco, July 22, 1759; AGN Tierras, vol. 1501, exp. 3, fols. 8r–v (will of Polonia de la Cruz of Tepemaxalco, October 13, 1672); and AGN Tierras, vol. 2541, exp. 9, fols. 8r–v (will of Feliciana María of Tepemaxalco, April 20, 1779). One wonders if cihuatlalli, possibly women's land, is behind any of these examples. Kellogg, "Aztec Inheritance," 320, notes the way testators maintained a distinction between what was their own property and what was that of a parent. She also notes the important distinction in indigenous tradition between purchased land and inherited land, affecting the way it would be disposed—something I have not yet discerned in the Toluca wills.

25. Incidentally, the indigenous version and probable antecedent to surco, *cuemitl,* appears in only one of these testaments: AGN Civil, vol. 664, exp. 2, fols. 66r–66bis.r (will of don Juan Alonso of Santa María Asunción,

November 14, 1692). Fray Alonso de Molina translated *cuemitl* as being equivalent to the Spanish *camellón*, a ridge turned up by a plow or spade. Confusing matters, the Spaniards also translated *chinamitl* or *chinampas* (strips of farmland extending into lakes) as camellones, but I have not seen the term *chinamitl* in Nahuatl records from the Toluca region.

26. This adoption may still disguise native forerunners, however, for one testator used *tlaxelolli* (Nahuatl: part, share, or division) in a way very similar to that in which most used almud. He even counted three tlaxelolli, the most frequently recurring number of almudes. AGN Civil, vol. 1108, exp. 7, fols. 16r–17v (will of Luis Diego of Metepec, March 2, 1767).

27. AGN Civil, vol. 1108, exp. 7, fols. 1r–2v (will of Sebastián de San Juan of Metepec, October 25, 1768); AGN Civil, vol. 1003, exp. 4, fols. 30r–32v (will of María de la Concepción of Santiago Tianguistengo, October 9, 1761); and AGN Tierras, vol. 2616, exp. 4, fols. 6r–7v (will of Pascuala María of Atizapan, April 10, 1760).

28. The use of loanwords versus indigenous terms could be the result of notarial influence, but these patterns do hold across many times and places and among quite a number of different notaries.

29. Burkett, "Indian Women and White Society," 114–19.

30. Rural indigenous women who frequented the regional markets, particularly as vendors, or who worked as domestics on Spanish estates, more like their male counterparts, may have had a wider European vocabulary than the testatrices of this study. Additionally, when men became permanent laborers, or *gañanes*, on estates they usually had families in residence with them. A large estate, such as the Hacienda del Salitre, for example, had 39 resident couples, 8 widows, and 2 widowers in 1754, while a smaller one, the Hacienda de la Asunción (Malacatepec), had only 4 couples. See AGN Clero Regular y Secular, vol. 29, exp. 11, fols. 391v–399v. Such women typically worked as domestics in the estate house or worked, for example, grinding maize or making cheese. See AGN Civil, vol. 109, exp. 6 (San Juan de los Jarros, 1776), and vol. 246, exp. 6 (Ixtlahuaca, 1767–70). Their experiences, in the minority for rural women, are not discussed in this study but would be extremely worthwhile to pursue if records could be found. See chapter 11 of this volume for a different picture of humble, rural, indigenous women who were much more mobile and played a significant role in tribute labor.

31. Men's access to capital and dominant role in agriculture may also relate to their greater likelihood to mention indigenous silos, or *cuexcomatl*, on their land, as noted in table 7.1.

32. See, e.g., a reference to the tending of an *haba* bean field in Tepemaxalco, 1737: AGN Tierras, vol. 2303, exp. 1, fols. 44r–45r.

33. AGN Tierras, vol. 2300, exp. 18, fols. 17r–18v (will of Maria Salomé

of Tepemaxalco, November 19, 1654); AGN Tierras, vol. 1501, exp. 3, fols. 8r–v (will of Polonia de la Cruz, Tepemaxalco, October 13, 1672); and AGN Tierras, vol. 2303, exp. 1, fols. 44r–45r (will of Gertrudis de la Encarnación de Setina of Tepemaxalco, August 17, 1737). While indigenous men were using large European looms in the mass production of cloth by this period, indigenous women probably continued to dominate the production of yarn, cloth, and clothing for use in their own homes. In the Toluca Valley they were not normally producing such items for tribute, as we see in chapters 9 and 11.

34. AGN Tierras, vol. 2547, exp. 14, fols. 2r–4r (will of Salvadora Josefa of Pilpa, August 2, 1732); and AGN Tierras, vol. 2303, exp. 1, fols. 44r–45r (will of Gertrudis de la Encarnación de Setina of Tepemaxalco, August 17, 1737).

35. Some women also tended magueyes on other people's solares. See, e.g., AGN Tierras, vol. 2300, exp. 18, fols. 17r–18r (will of Maria Salomé of Tepemaxalco, November 19, 1654). I suspect that historians have slighted economic production that was associated with the solar and, by extension, women's productivity (see also chapter 11).

36. See, e.g., AGN Tierras, vol. 2540, exp. 9, fols. 17r–22r (will of María Juana of Tilapa, August 18, 1773); AGN Tierras, vol. 2300, exp. 18, fols. 17r–18v (will of María Salomé of Tepemaxalco, November 19, 1654); AGN Civil, vol. 664, exp. 2, fols. 34r–35r (will of María Clara of Calimaya, July 2, 1763); and AGN Hospital de Jesús, leg. 326, exp. 1, fols. 1r–3v (will of Pascuala Melchora of Toluca, August 9, 1717). Men, far from being excluded from this activity, often bequeathed small numbers of maguey plants, and one had 120 plants. See AGN Civil, vol. 1072, exp. 13, fols. 1r–3v (will of don Tomás de Santiago of Metepec, April 18, 1786). Vigesimal numbers associated with properties and goods, incidentally, appear with about equal frequency between the genders, with 28% of the women's testaments and 31% of the men's reporting such figures.

37. See William B. Taylor, *Drinking, Homicide and Rebellion in Colonial Mexican Villages* (Stanford: Stanford University Press, 1979), 45–57, on women's prevalent role in the pulque trade. The table on page 46 of his book shows the importance of the state of Mexico in the trade, listing many Toluca Valley towns. For this region I have also seen criminal records relating to women's illegal making and selling of alcoholic beverages, including one called *tepache*. See AGN Criminal, vol. 207, exp. 1 (Tenango del Valle, 1765), and vol. 124, exp. 6 (Santiago Tianguistengo, 1777). James Lockhart ("Españoles entre indios. Toluca a fines del siglo XVI," *Revista de Indias* 131–38 [1974]: 435–91) also mentions a widow who made pulque in Toluca in the sixteenth century, and Pescador, "Vanishing Woman," 618, references an indigenous woman pulque vendor from late colonial Tenango del Valle.

38. See Stephanie Wood, "Adopted Saints: Christian Images in Nahua Testaments of Late Colonial Toluca," *The Americas* 47:3 (January 1991): 259–93. Because religious objects were much fewer in sixteenth-century indigenous testaments, having not yet been taken into the home on such as massive scale as they would be in later times, Cline does not quantify their presence with regard to issues of gender as I do here. Seeking more evidence of change over time would therefore demand further research.

39. AGN Tierras, vol. 2546, exp. 16, fols. 9r–10v (will of Gaspar Melchor of Xonacatlan, June 13, 1720); AGN Tierras, vol. 1501, exp. 3, fols. 15r–16v (will of Jacinto de la Cruz of Tepemaxalco, November 1, 1693); AGN Tierras, vol. 2616, exp. 7, fols. 25r–26r (will of Jerónimo Francisco of Huitzitzilapan, March 15, 1695); AGN Tierras, vol. 2541, exp. 9, fols. 8r–v (will of Feliciana María of Tepemaxalco, April 20, 1779); AGN Tierras, vol. 2547, exp. 14, fols. 2r–4r (will of Salvadora Josefa of Pilpa, August 2, 1732); and AGN Civil, vol. 1003, exp. 4, fols. 30r–32v (will of María de la Concepción of Tianguistengo, October 9, 1761).

40. See Wood, "Adopted Saints," 280.

41. Cline, *Colonial Culhuacan*, 166, mentions men's tendency to adopt Spanish dress before women did.

42. Charles Gibson, *The Aztecs under Spanish Rule: A History of the Indians of the Valley of Mexico, 1519–1810* (Stanford: Stanford University Press, 1964), 111.

43. As Cline points out in *Colonial Culhuacan*, 34, what we have in wills are "only *outward* expressions of belief," but we can glimpse private feelings in occasional remarks that stand out from the formulaic passages, such as repeated remonstrations to remind heirs about their duties to sweep around altars.

44. Quoted by Robert Ricard, *The Spiritual Conquest of Mexico*, trans. Lesley Byrd Simpson (Berkeley: University of California Press, 1966), 269.

45. Fray Diego Durán, *Book of the Gods and Rites and the Ancient Calendar*, ed. and trans. Doris Heyden and Fernando Horcasitas (Norman: University of Oklahoma Press, 1971), 235.

46. See Kellogg, "Aztec Women in Early Colonial Courts," 33, for a quote by Francisco Javier Clavijero on this subject. See also chapter 1, where Louise Burkhart finds women were the primary sweepers.

47. Wood, "Adopted Saints," 278.

48. Cline, *Colonial Culhuacan*, 120, saw the use of two given names as representing higher status than the use of birth-order names in sixteenth-century Culhuacan.

49. María was still very popular as a second name, with twenty-three occurrences. For some enlightening statistics comparing the use of María by

Indian and Spanish families in colonial Mexico, see William B. Taylor, "The Virgin of Guadalupe in New Spain: An Inquiry into the Social History of Marian Devotion," *American Ethnologist* 14:2 (February 1987): 9–33.

50. For examples of de la Cruz, see AGN Tierras, vol. 1501, exp. 3, fols. 8r–v (will of Polonia de la Cruz of Tepemaxalco, October 13, 1672); AGN Civil, vol. 997, exp. 2, fols. 6r–7v (will of María de la Cruz of Tenango del Valle, August 22, 1736); AGN Civil, vol. 664, exp. 2, fol. 54r (will of Fabiana de la Cruz of Calimaya, September 21, 1758); AGN Civil, vol. 664, exp. 2, fols. 55r–55bis.v (will of Juana de la Cruz of Calimaya, November 7, 1758); and Newberry Library, Ayer MS. 1477B (2) (will of Pascuala de la Cruz of Calimaya, May 19, 1739). The examples of Spanish surnames are: AGN Civil, vol. 664, exp. 3, fols. 52r–v (will of Lorensa de Subersa of Calimaya, October 25, 1759); AGN Tierras, vol. 2303, exp. 1, fols. 44r–45r (will of Gertrudis de la Encarnación de Setina of Tepemaxalco, August 17, 1737); and AGN Hospital de Jesús vol. 15, exp. 1, fols. 143r–144r (will of doña Ana Cortés Acaxochi of Toluca, November 1589).

51. AGN Hospital de Jesús, leg. 380, contains information on the indigenous Cortés family of Toluca.

52. Cline, *Colonial Culhuacan*, 117, found that "the naming of females was conservative and also not very important."

53. Kanter, "Native Female Land Tenure," 612. See also her "Hijos del pueblo: Family, Community, and Gender in Rural Mexico, the Toluca Region, 1730–1830" (Ph.D. diss., University of Virginia, 1993).

54. Kanter, "Native Female Land Tenure," 613.

55. See, e.g., Wood, "Corporate Adjustments," 124, 177. In chapter 10 of this volume, Gosner suggests that evolving gender divisions of labor in rural communities may account for women's greater participation in rebellion in Oaxaca and central Mexico, a hypothesis that brings greater interest to studies such as this one and Kanter's "Native Female Land Tenure."

56. Such AGN collections as Tierras and Civil contain many of these records. They are also abundant in judicial and parish repositories.

Chapter 8. Mixteca *Cacicas*

1. Ronald Spores, *The Mixtec Kings and Their People* (Norman: University of Oklahoma Press, 1967), 64–88; Spores, *The Mixtecs in Ancient and Colonial Times* (Norman: University of Oklahoma Press, 1984), 64–96.

2. Spores, *The Mixtec Kings*, 90–188, and *The Mixtecs*.

3. Spores, *The Mixtec Kings*, 110–54.

4. Archivo General de la Nación (hereafter, AGN) Civil 516; AGN Tierras 24, exp. 6; AGN Tierras 34, exp. 1; AGN Tierras 44, exp. 1; AGN Tie-

rras 59, exp. 2; AGN General de Parte 1, exps. 832, 1047; AGN Tierras 2948, exp. 28; AGN Tierras 3030, exp. 6; AGN Indios 1, exp. 53; AGN Indios 1, exp. 157; Archivo del Poder Judicial del Estado de Oaxaca (hereafter, APJO) Teposcolula, Ramo Civil (hereafter, Tep Civ) 1, exp. 13; APJO, Tep Civ 654; Ronald Spores, "The Genealogy of Tlazultepec: A Sixteenth-Century Mixtec Manuscript," *Southwestern Journal of Anthropology* 2 (1964): 15–31; *The Mixtec Kings*, 131–54; and *Colección de documentos del Archivo General de la Nación para la étnohistoria de la mixteca de Oaxaca en el siglo XVI*, Vanderbilt University Publications in Anthropology, no. 41 (Nashville, 1992); Ronald Spores and Miguel Saldaña, *Documentos para la étnohistoria del estado de Oaxaca. Indice del Ramo de Mercedes del Archivo General de la Nación, México*, Vanderbilt University Publications in Anthropology, no. 5 (Nashville, 1973); Ronald Spores and Miguel Saldaña, *Documentos para la étnohistoria del Estado de Oaxaca. Indice del Ramo de Indios del Archivo General de la Nación, México*, Vanderbilt University Publications in Anthropology, no. 13, (Nashville, 1975).

5. APJO Tep Civ 121.

6. APJO Huajuapan, Ramo Civil (hereafter, Hua Civ), *Cajas* 1–2, Provisionales.

7. Ronald Spores, "Tututepec: A Postclassic-Period Mixtec Conquest State," *Ancient Mesoamerica* 4:1 (1993): 167–74.

8. AGN Tierras 29, exp. 1; AGN Vínculos 272.

9. AGN Tierras 29, exp. 1.

10. AGN Tierras 24, exp. 6.

11. Ibid., exp. 4.

12. APJO, Tep Civ, Administrativa; María de los Angeles Romero Frizzi and Ronald Spores, *Indice del Archivo del Juzgado de Teposcolula, Oaxaca. Época Colonial* (México: Instituto Nacional de Antropología e Historia, 1978).

13. AGN Tierras 3030, exp. 6; AGN Tierras 2948, exp. 28; AGN Indios 1, exp. 157; Spores, *The Mixtec Kings*, 222–23.

14. Archivo del Juzgado, Teposcolula (hereafter, AJT) 7, exp. 2.

15. Archivo Regional de la Mixteca, Tlaxiaco (hereafter, ARMT), Inventario de expedientes, 1843.

16. Spores, *The Mixtec Kings*, 135.

17. Romero Frizzi and Spores, *Indice:* AJT 7, exp. 2; APJO, Tep Civ, *no clasificado.*

18. Ibid.

19. APJO Tep Civ 674.

20. AGN Tierras 59, exp. 2; Spores, "The Genealogy of Tlazultepec," 15–31.

21. APJO Tep Civ 1064, fols. 22–27 [1771]; 1305 [1789]; 1344 [1793].

22. Ronald Spores, "Differential Response to Colonial Control

Among the Mixtecs and Zapotecs of Oaxaca," in *The 'Pax Colonial' and Native Resistance in New Spain*, ed. Susan Schroeder (forthcoming).

23. APJO Tep Civ passim; APJO Teposcolula Ramo Criminal, passim; Spores, *The Mixtecs*, 187–208.

Chapter 9. Women and Crime in Colonial Oaxaca

I would like to thank Ruth Bloch and James Lockhart in the Department of History at the University of California, Los Angeles, who read and commented on earlier versions of this paper. I also gratefully acknowledge the contribution of Kevin Terraciano, who generously shared many of his findings on Mixtec women. I express my gratitude to Sr. Gonzalo Rojo Guerrero, director of the Archivo de Poder Judicial da Oaxaca, for providing access to these documents.

1. Archivo de Poder Judicial, Oaxaca, Ramo Archivo Judicial de Teposcolula (hereafter, AJT) Criminal 3, 375, Teposcolula, 1630.

2. For an example of a study of a modern Zapotec justice system and dispute resolution, see Laura Nader, *Harmony Ideology: Justice and Control in a Zapotec Mountain Village* (Stanford: Stanford University Press, 1990). She uses Villa Alta criminal records from the period 1957–69.

3. "Equality" is an anachronistic term reflecting Western values. It is unreasonable to expect to find equality in social relations in native societies, such as the Nahua, Mixtec, or Zapotec, that were characterized by social differentiation along many axes, including noble/commoner status, age, and gender. I use the term in this chapter only to qualify "complementarity," which can easily be idealized.

Patriarchy has many manifestations in different cultural and historical contexts. For the purposes of this discussion, I define a patriarchal system as one in which (1) authority is invested in the eldest male; (2) a woman has no individual legal status and, therefore, cannot order testaments, witness legal documents, or legally represent herself in court; (3) a woman has no individual economic status and, therefore, cannot own property or carry out economic transactions without approval of her legal guardian (usually, either her father or her husband); and (4) a woman's identity is derived from her association with the family patriarch (either her husband or her father).

4. John Desmond Monaghan, "'We are people who eat tortillas': Household and Community in the Mixteca" (Ph.D. diss., University of Pennsylvania, 1987), and "Sacrifice, Death, and the Origins of Agriculture in the Codex Vienna," *American Antiquity* 55:3 (1990): 559–69; and Mark B. King, "Poetics and Metaphor in Mixtec Writing," *Ancient Mesoamerica* 1 (1990): 142 n. 1.

396   Notes to Pages 201–204

5. Kevin Terraciano has identified the yuhuitayu as the largest and most complex sociopolitical unit in the Mixtec region. *Yuhui* (reed mat) and *tayu* (pair or throne) denote a Mixtec rulerdom. For a detailed discussion of Mixtec sociopolitical organization, see Kevin Terraciano, "Ñudzahui History: Mixtec Writing and Culture in Colonial Oaxaca" (Ph.D. diss., University of California, Los Angeles, 1994); and Ronald Spores, *The Mixtec Kings and Their People* (Norman: University of Oklahoma Press, 1967), and *The Mixtecs in Ancient and Colonial Times* (Norman: University of Oklahoma Press, 1984). See also Kevin Terraciano and Lisa Mary Sousa, "The 'Original Conquest' of Oaxaca: Mixtec and Nahuatl History and Myth," *Indigenous Writing in the Spanish Indies: Special Issue, UCLA Historical Journal* 12 (1992): 29–90.

6. Spores, *The Mixtec Kings*, 131–54.

7. See Terraciano, "Ñudzahui History"; and Spores, chap. 8, this volume.

8. AJT Criminal 1:23, Coixtlahuaca, 1577.

9. James Lockhart, "Some Nahua Concepts in Postconquest Guise," *History of European Ideas* 6 (1985): 465–82.

10. AJT Criminal 5:581, Yanhuitlan, 1684. For a discussion of Mixtec concepts of crime and sin based on a translation and analysis of the murder note left by Pedro de Caravantes, see Kevin Terraciano, "Quachi Ñudzahui: Murder in the Mixteca," *UCLA Historical Journal* 11 (1991): 93–113.

11. AJT Criminal 1:13, Teposcolula, 1573.

12. AJT Criminal 1:61, Teposcolula, 1593.

13. AJT Criminal 1:62, Teposcolula, 1593.

14. Identity in colonial Mesoamerica, as anywhere else, was multidimensional. In addition to community membership, sex, and marital status, other factors such as age and language group were important. See Terraciano, "Ñudzahui History," for a detailed discussion of Mixtec (i.e., Ñudzahui) identity.

15. See, e.g., AJT Criminal 4:412, Tlaxiaco, 1633.

16. AJT Criminal 4:38, Achiutla, 1632. María López explains that Agustín de Barros "la comenzo a ablar para que tubiese que ver con ella y a decirle algunas palabras y que ella como muger flaca y de poco saver luego le dixo que si y con esto se fueron xuntos a una milpa."

17. Archivo de Poder Judicial, Oaxaca, Ramo Archivo Judicial de Villa Alta (hereafter, AJVA) Criminal 4:179, Lachirio, 1716.

18. AJT Criminal 1:88, Tilantongo, 1596. Gerónimo de Arevalo characterized Magdalena as "una buena india y cristiana y que sirve a su marido."

19. AJT Criminal 4:419, Teposcolula, 1639. Juana de Mendoza's and Magdalena Alvarado's Spanish lawyer, Bernabel de Aguilar, states, "Como mugeres flacas y de poco saber se dixaron engañar de Lorenzo de la Cruz."

20. William B. Taylor, *Drinking, Homicide, and Rebellion in Colonial Mexican Villages* (Stanford: Stanford University Press, 1979), 82–83.

21. AJT Criminal 3:276, Teposcolula, 1613.

22. Taylor, *Drinking, Homicide, and Rebellion,* 85, finds the numerous complaints of physical abuse by women "particularly remarkable because husband-wife assaults are routinely underrepresented in the criminal records of societies in which wife-beating is socially acceptable." I would argue that the many cases indicate that wife beating was *not* socially acceptable in these societies.

23. AJT Criminal 1:61 and 1:62, Teposcolula, 1593.

24. AJT Criminal 3:366, Teposcolula, 1630.

25. AJT Criminal 5:527, Nuuyoo, 1675.

26. AJT Criminal 2:188, Coixtlahuaca, 1603.

27. The case records never mention Catalina's marital status. She may have had a husband who could have brought the charges. In any case, she would certainly have had some older male relative who could have spoken on her behalf if it had been considered necessary.

28. AJT Criminal 1:88, Tilantongo, 1596.

29. AJVA Criminal 4:211, Solaga, 1729. The women mention that they first went to the priest, who made several announcements about the crime, but that it did not help them recover the stolen money. This is just one of many suggestions in the criminal records that a great deal of conflict resolution took place outside of formal channels.

30. AJVA Criminal 2:125, Yalalag, 1704.

31. AJVA Criminal 4:241, Camotlan, 1746.

32. In her study of indigenous women's participation in litigation over land in Tlatelolco, Susan Kellogg notes that women rarely appeared as witnesses. She explains that "while women did occasionally serve as witnesses, they did so less often than men. Female witnesses tended to be widows, although there are rare examples of married women providing testimony." See Susan Kellogg, "Aztec Women in Early Colonial Courts: Structure and Strategy in a Legal Context," in *Five Centuries of Law and Politics in Central Mexico,* ed. Ronald Spores and Ross Hassig, Vanderbilt University Publications in Anthropology, no. 30 (Nashville, 1984), 29. There is no obvious correlation between marital status and participation as witnesses in the criminal records from Oaxaca. Whether these differences can be attributed to variations by region or within civil and criminal legal genres remains to be seen.

33. The ratio of three male witnesses to two female witnesses is based on a very rough count of seventeenth-century criminal records contained in AJT. Incomplete records for many cases makes precise calculation impossible.

34. The earliest Villa Alta criminal records contained in the AJVA date from 1650; my sample includes records from 1650 to 1750.

35. The Mixteca Alta experienced greater penetration of Hispanic culture and society and, therefore, the alcalde mayor, priests, and other Spaniards resided in most of the major Mixtec towns, including Teposcolula, Yanhuitlan, Nochistlan, Achiutla, and Chalcatongo. Such was not the case in the Zapotec Sierra.

36. AJT Criminal 1:88, Tilantongo, 1596.

37. AJT Criminal 1:62, Teposcolula, 1593. As in colonial New Spain, "juries of matrons or midwives" in colonial New England examined women and provided expert testimony regarding miscarriages, stillbirths, infant deaths, infanticide, and pregnancy. See N. E. H. Hull, *Female Felons: Women and Crime in Colonial Massachusetts* (Urbana: University of Illinois Press, 1987), 77, 113.

38. AJT Criminal 4:417, Teposcolula, 1633; AJT Criminal 4:419, Teposcolula, 1633; AJT Criminal 4:465, Teposcolula, 1639.

39. These accusations are standard rhetoric of local officials when they cannot meet their tribute obligations. They typically complain that once all of the people were obedient and humble, but now they are restless and disrespectful.

40. Mesoamerican *mantas*, or indigenous capes, were woven in four pieces and then sewn together. In the traditional arrangement, each woman would have produced one piece. By demanding one manta from three women, one of the group would have had to weave two parts. James Lockhart, pers. com.

41. Taylor, *Drinking, Homicide, and Rebellion*, 116.

42. Ibid.

43. AJVA Criminal 4:179, Lachirio, 1716.

44. María Catalina states: "en el pueblo lo hazen por costumbre todos los naturales hombres y mujeres para todos sus fiestas."

45. Juana María explains: "lo hasen todos los naturales en diferentes trapiches que para ella tienen en sus barrancas que es costumbre mui antigua al haserlo en su pueblo en todos los días de fiestas."

46. Spores notes, "Formal lineages were not a feature of Mixtec life. When caciques in colonial times referred to *linaje*, they were referring to 'lines' of ancestors, males and/or females, and not to formal patri- or matri-lineages. No evidence can be found in the kinship system, kin terms, or the language to indicate that lineage or clan organization or 'corporateness' existed among commoners"; *The Mixtecs*, 70.

47. Both Alvarado and Cordova qualify the entry for family with "gente de mi casa" in their Mixtec and Zapotec dictionaries, respectively. See

fray Francisco de Alvarado, *Vocabulario en lengua mixteca,* ed. Wigberto Jiménez Moreno (México: Instituto Nacional de Antropología e Historia, [1593] 1962), 109v; and fray Juan de Córdova, *Vocabulario en lengua çapoteca* (México: Ediciones Toledo, Instituto Nacional de Antropología e Historia, [1578] 1987), 194v.

The lack of a ready equivalent for "family" may be a feature of Meso-american social organization. James Lockhart explains, "Not only do any lineages tend to remain unnamed and undiscussed in Nahuatl sources; no word appears that would have approximately the same scope as English 'family'. Looking in Molina's dictionary under *familia,* one finds the following collection of terms: *cenyeliztli,* 'being together'; *cencalli,* 'one house'; *cencaltin,* 'those in one house'; *cemithualtin,* 'those in one patio'; and *techan tlaca,* 'people who live together in a house'. All the words, then, emphasize the setting in which a joint life takes place, not the origin of the relationships between those living together; as a set, the terms converge on something akin to the English notion of 'household'." James Lockhart, *The Nahuas after the Conquest: A Social and Cultural History of the Indians of Central Mexico, Sixteenth through Eighteenth Centuries* (Stanford: Stanford University Press, 1992), 59. Ibid., for a detailed discussion of Nahua kinship in colonial times.

48. Several scholars seem to equate the gendered division of labor with an ideology of separate spheres. As it developed among the white middle class in the early nineteenth-century United States, separate spheres ideology sanctioned men to operate in the public arena and relegated women to the private sphere. Thus it was considered appropriate for men to work outside the home, hold public offices, and represent the family in the public sphere. Women were isolated within the home as housewives and mothers and unable to participate in public life without their husbands' consent. Separate spheres ideology also assigned distinct physical and personality traits to each sex. Men were characterized as aggressive, strong, and confident; women, as passive, loving, nurturing, and morally superior. For examples of various uses of separate spheres and patriarchy as analytical categories, see Taylor, *Drinking, Homicide, and Rebellion,* 108; Ferdinand Antón, *La mujer en América antigua* (México: Editorial Extemporáneos, 1975), 20; and Fernando Díaz Infante, *La educación de los aztecas* (México: Panorama Editorial, 1982), 139.

49. AJT Criminal 4:469, Teposcolula, 1643.

50. AJVA Criminal 4:179, Lachirio, 1716. The records state that Juana María "dijo que es una pobre viuda y que como sola no tiene caña ni forma de sembrarla que su pobreza le hizo cortar unos platanos para hazer un poco de vivida para selebrar la Pasqua." Bartolomé Manzano reportedly said, "En dicho su pueblo sembrar cañas a los que pueden y estos venden sus mugeres algunas en la plaza desta villa."

51. John Desmond Monaghan, "'We are people who eat tortillas,'" and "Sacrifice, Death, and the Origins of Agriculture in the Codex Vienna."

52. AJT Criminal 1:23, Coixtlahuaca, 1577.

53. AJVA Criminal 4:211, Solaga, 1729.

54. For a discussion of changing gender ideology in Nahua Mexico particularly, see Susan Kellogg, chapter 5 in this volume.

55. AJVA Criminal 2:140, Yasona, 1707.

56. Taylor, *Drinking, Homicide, and Rebellion*, 84.

57. Ronald Spores cites six cases between 1560 and 1699, *The Mixtecs*, 197. I have only seen a few cases of rape in the documents. In some adultery cases, however, the actual sexual act described is rape. I believe that closer examination of the records may bring more cases to light.

58. The degree to which complementarity characterized gender relations in the Mesoamerican political sphere awaits careful and comprehensive consideration. Terraciano has produced evidence that Mixtec cacicas, like caciques, were legitimate rulers and that the Mixtec system of joint rulership should be considered a "rulerdom" rather than a "kingdom." For a discussion of Mixtec sociopolitical organization and principles of dynastic succession, see "Ñudzahui History," 234–325, 361–87, 427–40, and passim; and Spores, *The Mixtec Kings*, 131–54, and *The Mixtecs*, 68–72. Spores was the first to show that the Mixtecs traced their ruling lineage through direct descent and, therefore, to suggest that Mixtec women had very high status.

59. The questions raised in this paper are addressed in greater detail in my current research on Mesoamerican gender and culture.

Chapter 10. Women, Rebellion, and the
Moral Economy of Maya Peasants in Colonial Mexico

For a more expansive treatment of many of the issues discussed in this essay, see Kevin Gosner, *Soldiers of the Virgin: The Moral Economy of a Colonial Maya Rebellion* (Tucson: University of Arizona Press, 1992). Other secondary works on the Tzeltal Revolt include Victoria Reifler Bricker, *The Indian Christ, the Indian King: The Historical Substrate of Maya Myth and Ritual* (Austin: University of Texas Press, 1981), chap. 5; Herbert S. Klein, "Peasant Communities in Revolt: The Tzeltal Republic of 1712," *Pacific Historical Review* 35 (1966): 247–63; Severo Martínez Peláez, *La sublevación de los zendales* (Tuxtla Gutiérrez: Publicación Cultural de la Universidad Autónoma de Chiapas, 1977); Andrés Saint-Lu, "El poder colonial y las iglesia frente a la sublevación de los indígenas zendales de Chiapas en 1712," *Mesoamérica* 11 (1986): 23–34; Donald E. Thompson, *Maya Paganism and Christianity: A History of the Fusion of Two Religions*, Middle American Research Institute, Pub. 19, (New Orleans, 1954); Juan Pedro Viqueira Albán, "¿Qué había detrás del petate de la ermita de Cancuc?" in *Catolicismo y extirpación de idolatrías. Siglos XVI–XVII*, ed. Gabriela Ramos and Henrique Urbano (Cusco: Centro de Estudios Regionales Andinos "Bartolomé de las Casas," 1993), 389–458, and *María de la Candelaria. India natural de Cancuc* (México: Fondo de Cultura Económica, 1993); and Robert Wasserstrom, "Ethnic Violence and Indigenous Protest: The Tzeltal (Maya) Rebellion of 1712," *Journal of Latin American Studies* 12 (1980): 1–19.

    1. Archivo de las Indias (hereafter, AGI), Audiencia de Guatemala (hereafter, AG), 296: Testimonio de los autos y causas criminales en razón de haber parecido difunta la mala india María de la Candelaria, Testimonio de Agustín de López, fol. 60, 1716.

    2. Fray Francisco Ximénez, *Historia de la provincia de San Vicente de Chiapas y Guatemala* (Guatemala City: Biblioteca Goathemala, 1929–31), 3:271.

    3. Her assumed surname derived from the Virgen de la Candelaria, one of the many incarnations of the Blessed Mother.

    4. For background, see William A. Christian, Jr., *Apparitions in Late Medieval and Renaissance Spain* (Princeton: Princeton University Press, 1981).

    5. Francisco Núñez de la Vega, *Constituciones diocesanas del obispado de Chiapas*, ed. María del Carmen León Cázares and Mario Humberto Ruz (México: Universidad Nacional Autónoma de México, 1988), 309–15.

    6. For a good overview of the literature on nagualism, see Alfredo López Austin, *The Human Body and Ideology: Concepts of the Ancient Nahuas*, vol. 1 (Salt Lake City: University of Utah Press, 1988), 362–75.

    7. Alfredo López Austin, *Hombre-Dios. Religión y política en el mundo náhuatl* (México: Universidad Nacional Autónoma de México, 1989). See Viqueira Albán, "¿Qué había detrás del petate?" 414–24, for an interesting discussion of María López as *mujer diosa* "woman-goddess."

    8. Gosner, *Soldiers of the Virgin*, chap. 1.

    9. E. P. Thompson, "The Moral Economy of the English Crowd in the Eighteenth Century," *Past and Present* 50 (1971): 76–136, and "The Moral Economy Reviewed," in *Customs in Common: Studies in Traditional Popular Culture*, ed. E. P. Thompson (New York: New Press, 1993), 259–351; and James C. Scott, *The Moral Economy of the Peasant: Subsistence and Rebellion in Southeast Asia* (New Haven: Yale University Press, 1976). Useful critiques of moral economy approaches include Michael Adas, "'Moral Economy' or 'Contest State'? Elite Demands and the Origins of Peasant Protest in Southeast Asia," *Journal of Social History* 13 (1980): 521–40; John Bohstedt, "The Moral Economy and the Discipline of Historical Context," *Journal of Social History* 25 (1992): 265–81; and David Hunt, "From the Millennial to the Everyday: James Scott's Search for the Essence of Peasant Politics," *Radical History Re-*

view 42 (1988): 155–72. See also Ward Stavig, "Ethnic Conflict, Moral Econ-
omy, and Population in Rural Cuzco on the Eve of the Thupa Amaro II Rebellion," *Hispanic American Historical Review* 68 (1988): 737–70, and Lotte de
Jong, "Community Discourse: A Family Conflict in Eighteenth-Century
Coyotepec, Oaxaca," in *The Indian Community of Colonial Mexico: Fifteen Essays on Land Tenure, Corporate Organizations, Ideology, and Village Politics*, ed.
Arij Ouweneel and Simon Miller (Amsterdam: Center for Latin American
Research and Documentation [CEDLA], 1990), 250–69, for other examples of
moral economy approaches in colonial Latin American history. Critics of
moral economy models argue (among other points) that they understate the
coercive dimension of state power and exaggerate the degree of consensus
within local communities. More recent debates about culture, resistance,
and political process have tended to be reconceptualized around "hegemony," a theoretical framework that reasserts the primacy of the state. Yet
"hegemony" and "moral economy" share some important premises. As Antonio Gramsci wrote, "the fact of hegemony presupposes that account be
taken of the interests and tendencies of the groups over which hegemony is
to be exercised, and that a certain compromise equilibrium should be
formed"; Antonio Gramsci, *Selections from Political Writings, 1921–26* (New
York: International Publishers, 1978), 161. The process of negotiating this
"compromise equilibrium" is what the construction of a moral economy is
all about. For an important essay by a Mexicanist that revisits moral economy premises in light of new theory on hegemony, see Alan Knight,
"Weapons and Arches in the Mexican Revolutionary Landscape," in *Everyday Forms of State Formation: Revolution and Negotiation of Rule in Modern Mexico*, ed. Gilbert M. Joseph and Daniel Nugent (Durham: Duke University
Press, 1994), 24–66.

    10. Scott, *The Moral Economy of the Peasant*, 167.

    11. See, for example, John Desmond Monaghan, *The Covenants with
Earth and Rain: Exchange, Sacrifice, and Revelation in Mixtec Sociality* (Norman:
University of Oklahoma Press, 1995), esp. chaps. 1, 3, 10.

    12. For a useful overview of the theoretical debates on the concept
of social reproduction, see Jane Fishburne Collier and Sylvia Junko Yanagisako, "Toward a Unified Analysis of Gender and Kinship," in *Gender and
Kinship: Essays Toward a Unified Analysis*, ed. Jane Fishburne Collier and
Sylvia Junko Yanagisako (Stanford: Stanford University Press, 1987), 20–25.

    13. See especially Christine Ward Gailey, *From Kinship to Kingship:
Gender Hierarchy and State Formation in the Tongan Islands* (Austin: University
of Texas Press, 1987); Eleanor Leacock, "Introduction," in *Origins of the Family, Private Property, and the State*, ed. Frederick Engels (New York: International Publishers, 1972), 7–67; Sherry B. Ortner, "Is Female to Male as Nature

Is to Culture?" in *Woman, Culture, and Society*, eds. Michelle Z. Rosaldo and Louise Lamphere (Stanford: Stanford University Press, 1974), 67–87; Michelle Z. Rosaldo, "Woman, Culture, and Society: A Theoretical Overview," in *Woman, Culture, and Society*, ed. Michelle Z. Rosaldo and Louise Lamphere, 17–42; and Karen Sacks, "Engels Revisited: Women, the Organization of Production, and Private Property," in *Woman, Culture, and Society*, ed. Michelle Z. Rosaldo and Louise Lamphere, 207–27. For an excellent introduction to this literature, see Irene Silverblatt, "Interpreting Women in States: New Feminist Ethnohistories," in *Gender at the Crossroads of Knowledge: Feminist Anthropology in the Postmodern Era*, ed. Micaela di Leonardo (Berkeley: University of California Press, 1991), 140–71.

14. Irene Silverblatt, *Moon, Sun, and Witches: Gender Ideologies and Class in Inca and Colonial Peru* (Princeton: Princeton University Press, 1987); and Susan Kellogg, "Cognatic Kinship and Religion: Women in Aztec Society," in *Smoke and Mist: Mesoamerican Studies in Memory of Thelma D. Sullivan*, ed. J. Kathryn Josserand and Karen Dakin (Oxford: British Archaeological Reports Press, 1988), 666–81. For alternative interpretations of the status of women in Tenochtitlan, see June Nash, "Aztec Women: The Transition from Status to Class in Empire and Colony," in *Women and Colonization: Anthropological Perspectives*, ed. Mona Etienne and Eleanor Leacock (New York: Praeger, 1980), 134–48; and Inga Clendinnen, *Aztecs: An Interpretation* (Cambridge: Cambridge University Press, 1991), esp. chap. 6.

15. Or, as Collier and Yanagisako have put it, "Domestic/public and nature/culture, like the reproduction/production distinction . . . are variations of an analytical dichotomy that takes for granted what we think should be explained"; "Toward a Unified Analysis," 20.

16. John L. Comaroff, "*Sui genderis*: Feminism, Kinship Theory, and Structural 'Domains,'" in *Gender and Kinship*, ed. Jane Fishburne Collier and Sylvia Junko Yanagisako, 64.

17. Steve J. Stern, *The Secret History of Gender: Women, Men, and Power in Late Colonial Mexico* (Chapel Hill: University of North Carolina Press, 1995), 20. The autobiography of Rigoberta Menchú, the Quiché Maya woman who won the Nobel Peace Prize in 1992, also informs this issue. See Elisabeth Burgos-Debray, *I . . . Rigoberta Menchú: An Indian Woman in Guatemala* (London: Verso, 1984). Much of Menchú's story focuses on her mother, whose hard, inexpressibly tragic history served as a model for her daughter. Menchú represents her mother's civic activism as an extension of the responsibilities and sacrifices that women shoulder on behalf of their children, of the lessons that parents teach their children about mutual obligation, and of the ethnic sensibilities that Maya girls and boys develop through family religious observances that accompany births and marriages.

18. For a fuller treatment of community political structures in colonial Chiapas, see Gosner, *Soldiers of the Virgin*, chap. 4.

19. Clendinnen makes a similar point about female curers among the Mexica; see *Aztecs*, 171.

20. These records can be found in the Archivo Histórico Diocesano (hereafter, AHDSC), San Cristóbal de las Casas, Chiapas.

21. AHDSC, Libro de la cofradía de Santa María Rosario, Yajalón, 1713–16.

22. AHDSC, Libro de la cofradía de Jesús Nazareno, Yajalón, 1713–99. See James Lockhart, *The Nahuas after the Conquest: A Social and Cultural History of the Indians of Central Mexico, Sixteenth through Eighteenth Centuries* (Stanford: Stanford University Press, 1992), 226–67, on female deputies in the Cofradía del Santíssimo Sacramento in seventeenth-century Tula.

23. Lynn Stephen, *Zapotec Women* (Austin: University of Texas Press, 1991), chap. 7.

24. Fray Francisco Núñez de la Vega, IXa Carta Pastoral, in *Constituciones diocesanas*, 752–60; AGI, AG, 295, quad. 3: Testimonio de Sebastiana González, fol. 149, January 1713.

25. In Chiapas, the *visitador* (inspector) don Joseph de Escals condemned the expense of these feasts in the ninth of seventeen *ordenanzas* (ordinances) issued in 1689 to reform both civil and ecclesiastical governments in the province; see Ordenanzas que se han de observar u guardar en toda la provincia de Chiapas, Apéndice no. 7, in Núñez de la Vega, *Constituciones diocesanas*, 219–25. See Lockhart, *Nahuas after the Conquest*, 168–70; Serge Gruzinski, "Indian Confraternities, Brotherhoods, and *Mayordomías* in Central New Spain," in *The Indian Community of Colonial Mexico*, ed. Arij Ouweneel and Simon Miller, 214–15; and Nancy M. Farriss, *Maya Society under Colonial Rule: The Collective Enterprise of Survival* (Princeton: Princeton University Press, 1984), 321–23 and 343–51, on ritual feasting in central Mexico and Yucatan.

26. See Louise M. Burkhart, "Mujeres mexicas en 'el frente' del hogar. Trabajo doméstico y religión en el México azteca," *Mesoamérica Antigua* 12:23 (1992): 23–54; and Evon Z. Vogt, *Tortillas for the Gods: A Symbolic Analysis of Zinacanteco Rituals* (Cambridge, Mass.: Harvard University Press, 1976), for comparative works on this idea.

27. Joseph de Escals, Ordenanzas que se han de observar y guardar en toda la provincia de Chiapas, in Núñez de la Vega, *Constituciones diocesanas* 219–25.

28. AHDSC, Libros de cofradías, 1677–1827.

29. For a more comprehensive treatment of the political economy of seventeenth- and eighteenth-century Chiapas, see Gosner, *Soldiers of the Virgin*, chap. 3.

30. This practice was condemned by don Joseph de Escals in his 1689 ordenanzas: Ordenanzas que se han de observar y guardar en toda la provincia de Chiapas, in Núñez de la Vega, *Constituciones diocesanas*, 220; and again by don Toribio de Cosío after the rebellion, AGI, AG, 195, Las ordenanzas de Toribio de Cosío, March 15, 1713.

31. AGI, AG, 35: Testimonio y autos contra el alcalde mayor don Manuel de Maisterra y Atocha, 1690; AGI, AG, 221: Testimonio del escrito presentado por don Clemente de Ochoa y Velasco y don Manuel de Morales, 1708; AGI, AG, 312: Expediente sobre la averiguación de los fraudes por los alcaldes mayores, 1718–1729; Murdo J. MacLeod, *Spanish Central America: A Socioeconomic History, 1520–1720* (Berkeley: University of California Press, 1973), 316; and Brooke Larson and Robert Wasserstrom, "Coerced Consumption in Colonial Bolivia and Guatemala," *Radical History Review* 27 (1983): 49–78.

32. In 1708, two Spanish citizens in the provincial capital complained that Mayas were no longer bringing corn, cloth, and other goods to market in Ciudad Real because of the repartimientos. As a result, the provincial governor had created a monopoly for himself in these products and was charging exorbitant prices. AGI, AG, 221: Testimonio del escrito presentado por don Clemente de Ochoa y Velasco y don Manuel de Morales, 1708.

33. AGI, AG, 296: Testimonio de Agustín López, fol. 64, 1716.

34. AGI, AG, 293: Testimonios de los autos fechos contra diferentes indios de diversos pueblos por haber administrado los santos sacramentos durante el tiempo de la sublevación de los zendales por do[n] fray Juan Bautista Alvarez de Toledo, February 1713; includes testimony from ladina women who survived. Their testimony is reprinted in *Boletín del Archivo General de la Nación* 19 (1948): 503–35.

35. AGI, AG, 326, Autos por Toledo, Testimonio de Juana Bárbara Gutiérrez, April 1713.

36. AGI, AG, 295, Las ordenanzas de Toribio de Cosío, March 15, 1713.

37. Brian R. Hamnett, *Politics and Trade in Southern Mexico, 1750–1821* (Cambridge: Cambridge University Press, 1971), 12–13.

38. William B. Taylor, *Drinking, Homicide, and Rebellion in Colonial Mexican Villages* (Stanford: Stanford University Press, 1979), 116; Margaret A. Villanueva, "From Calpixqui to Corregidor: Appropriation of Women's Cotton Textile Production in Early Colonial Mexico," *Latin American Perspectives* 44 (1985): 32.

39. Taylor, *Drinking, Homicide, and Rebellion*, 116.

40. Archivo General de Centroamérica, AI.15 559 49: Autos sobre la motín habido en Tuxtla fue asesinado el alcalde mayor, 1693.

41. AGI, AG, 369: Relación de méritos de fray Joseph Monroy, cartas de don Toribio de Cosío, December 17, 1712, and March 12, 1713.
42. AGI, AG, 295, quad. 3, Testimonio de Sebastiana González, January 1713; AGI, AG, 294, Memoria de los brujos y cabesillas del Bachajón, 1713.
43. Taylor, *Drinking, Homicide, and Rebellion*, 116.

Chapter 11. Work, Marriage, and Status

1. For a reconstruction of Maya society at the time of the conquest, see Ralph L. Roys, *The Indian Background of Colonial Yucatan* (Norman: University of Oklahoma Press, [1943] 1972), chap. 7 and 8; on the conquest of Yucatan, see Robert S. Chamberlain, *The Conquest and Colonization of Yucatan: 1517–1550* (Washington, D.C.: Carnegie Institute, Pub. 582, 1948), and Inga Clendinnen, *Ambivalent Conquests: Maya and Spaniard in Yucatan, 1517–1570* (Cambridge: Cambridge University Press, 1987); for more detail on the cah, see Matthew Restall, *The Maya World: Yucatec Culture and Society, 1550–1850* (Stanford: Stanford University Press, 1997); and on the altepetl, see James Lockhart, *The Nahuas after the Conquest: A Social and Cultural History of the Indians of Central Mexico, Sixteenth through Eighteenth Centuries* (Stanford: Stanford University Press, 1992).
2. Personal tribute was a fact of life in Yucatan throughout most of the colonial period. The crown abolished it for all of New Spain in 1635, but many an official was censured for continuing the custom in Yucatan. For Yucatan, see J. F. Molina Solís, *Historia de Yucatán* (Mérida, 1896–1927), 2:223; Chamberlain, *Conquest*, 283–87; Marta Espejo-Ponce Hunt, "Colonial Yucatan: Town and Region in the Seventeenth Century" (Ph.D. diss., University of California, Los Angeles, 1974), 104–105; Nancy M. Farriss, *Maya Society under Colonial Rule: The Collective Enterprise of Survival* (Princeton: Princeton University Press, 1984), 39–56; and Robert Patch, *Maya and Spaniard in Yucatan, 1648–1812* (Stanford: Stanford University Press, 1993). For New Spain, see Sherbourne F. Cook and Woodrow Borah, *Essays in Population History: Mexico and the Caribbean* (Berkeley: University of California Press, 1974), 2:8–14.
3. The encomienda was a grant of indigenous tribute and labor made by the Spanish crown to prominent settlers; see James Lockhart and Stuart B. Schwartz, *Early Latin America: A History of Colonial Spanish America and Brazil*, Latin American Studies, no. 46 (Cambridge: Cambridge University Press, 1983), 92–96. The encomienda lasted two centuries longer in Yucatan than it did in central Mexico; Farriss, *Maya Society*, 370.
4. Archivo General de la Nación (hereafter, AGN), Inquisición, 69, 5, 275.
5. The number of male testators outnumbers female ones in Maya

wills (detailed and cited below) by 1.33:1 in Cacalcheń, Ebtun, and Ixil, whereas women outnumber men by 1.1:1 in Tekanto. Restall, *The Maya World*, chap. 18, argues that the gender bias of most corpora of Maya testaments is a symptom of wealth bias between the sexes. Note that the former statistic coincides with the male-favored gender balance of 1.33:1 in Nahua wills from Culhuacan (S.L. Cline and Miguel León-Portilla, *The Testaments of Culhuacan*, Nahuatl Studies Series, no. 1 [Los Angeles: UCLA Latin American Center, 1984]), although Nahua wills from Tenochtitlan-Tlatelolco favored women by 1.36:1 (Susan Kellogg, "Social Organization in Early Colonial Tenochtitlan-Tlatelolco: An Ethnohistorical Study" [Ph.D. diss., University of Rochester, 1980]).

6. See, e.g., Farriss, *Maya Society*, 132–33.

7. Petition for permission to alienate ancestral property; Homun, AGN, Tierras, 1359, 5.

8. During the colonial centuries a growing number of Spaniards in Mérida and the towns and cabeceras were reared in a bilingual environment, ate native foods in their homes, and were nursed by Maya women. Many were surely of mixed blood. The people of Campeche mentioned this reality as one of their reasons to support their desire for separation after the mid-nineteenth century. See Manuel A. Lanz, *Compendio de historia de Campeche* (Campeche: El Fénix, 1905).

9. For an estimate of the population of Yucatan in the 1810–20 period, see Cook and Borah, *Essays*, 2:114, 120–23.

10. Local and notarial sources make up the documentary base found in Mérida's various archives, including the testaments, bills of [land] sale, petitions, election records, and assorted legal documents written in Yucatec Maya between ca. 1550 and ca. 1850. For a discussion of these Maya sources, see Restall, *The Maya World*, chaps. 18–22.

11. Existing studies of postconquest Maya society are either based primarily on Spanish-language sources (Patch, *Maya and Spaniard*; Farriss, *Maya Society*) or are concerned with specific aspects of that society in a given location (Philip C. Thompson, "Tekanto in the Eighteenth Century" [Ph.D. diss., Tulane University, 1978]); and none focuses specifically on women. For a deeper understanding of seventeenth-century Maya-Spanish contact, see Hunt, "Colonial Yucatan"; and for a detailed analysis of the Maya documents that form the basis of our remarks below on community women, see Restall, *The Maya World*, esp. chap. 10, and " 'He Wished It in Vain': Subordination and Resistance Among Maya Women in Colonial Yucatan," *Ethnohistory* 42:4 (1995): 577–94.

12. See Roys, *Indian Background*, 134–66, and Restall, *The Maya World*, chaps. 6 and 7, for some differing arguments on the governing classes and use of terms such as "cacique."

13. Molina Solís, *Historia de Yucatán*, 2:271–72. Three Francisco de Montejos, father, son, and nephew, attempted to conquer Yucatan, the last succeeding in the 1540s; Chamberlain, *Conquest*. Montejo Sr., the *adelantado* (provincial governor) of Yucatan, was also the encomendero of Azcapotzalco after the conquest of central Mexico. Among the Nahuas who followed him from his original encomienda were some nobles and their children, relations of Moteucçoma; fray Diego López de Cogolludo, *Historia de Yucatán* (Campeche: Talleres Gráficos del Gobierno Constitucional del Estado, [1688] 1954), 3:231–33.

14. The five founding nuns of the Concepcionistas arrived from Mexico City in 1598. Just as in Mexico City, the convent accepted women of noble native birth, although we know only of doña Leonor de la Encarnación. Women of mixed indigenous and Spanish birth also found their way into the convent, since it was a likely place for the illegitimate children of encomenderos or senior officials. In the convent's first fifty years most of the postulants were young Spanish women of good birth whose marriage prospects were not good due to a shortage of suitable men. Entry into the convent was restricted only to women who had a dowry or inheritance. The nunnery was aided by private and crown pensions, but it was not a charitable organization as far as the admittance of postulants was concerned; see López de Cogolludo, *Historia*, 3:233 ff.; Hunt, "Colonial Yucatan," 117–18. For the practices in Mexican convents, see the work of Asunción Lavrin; e.g., Lavrin, "Ecclesiastical Reform of Nunneries in New Spain in the Eighteenth Century," *The Americas* 22:2(1965): 182–203.

15. López de Cogolludo, *Historia*, 3:231–33, which also contains the story of Bérrio's wife, doña Leonor de la Encarnación. Bérrio was one of the original conquerors of the province.

16. AGN, Inquisición, 275, 8; Archivo Parroquial de la Catedral de Mérida (hereafter, APM), book 2, Bautizos y Matrimonios. Doña Isabel Lucero, daughter of Cristóbal and Mencia, married Juan de Aranda. Their daughter, doña María de Aranda, married Captain Ambrosio de Arguelles, a *familiar* (police officer) of the Inquisition.

17. Archivo de Notarías de Mérida (hereafter, ANM), Juan Alonso Baeza, October 3, 1689. The Briceño family births and marriages are found in books 1 to 3 of the APM, Bautizos y Matrimonios.

18. The merchant group in Yucatan was next to that of the encomenderos in social prestige. As the encomiendas diminished in income, commerce became the primary economic activity in the colony, and the *mercaderes* (merchants) rivaled encomenderos for position and wealth. Since the encomienda had a hereditary element, merchants aspired to marry into the old settler families to improve their social status; Hunt, "Colonial Yucatan," 54–74.

19. López de Cogolludo, *Historia*, 3:417. See also J. Ignacio Rubio

Mañé, *Alcaldes de Mérida de Yucatán*. 1542–1941 (México: Editorial Cultura, 1941), 66–67; ANM, Baeza, June 13, 1689, July 14, 1690, April 11, 1691, June 23, November 6, 23, 1692; Títulos de Tetzic, papeles de Don Manuel Zapata, 28.

20. Archivo del Registros de la Propriedad, Mérida, book 1, April 3, 1706. See also APM, Matrimonios, 3, June 21, 1668; ANM, Baeza, September 21, 1689, March 14, 1691, June 11, August 13, 1692.

21. Molina Solís, *Historia de Yucatán*, 2:271–72. See also ANM, Baeza, May 28 and 29, October 22, December 31, 1689; March 15, 1690; May 7, June 20, 1691; April 22, 1692.

22. The Maya had no term of ethnic self-reference, although *macehual* (originally Nahuatl, probably a preconquest loan; see Frances Karttunen, *Nahuatl and Maya in Contact with Spanish*, Linguistic Forum, no. 26, [Austin: University of Texas, 1985], 8), came close to such an expression in the colonial period. Closer still were the phrases *ah cahnal* and *ah otochnal* to denote residents of a particular cah, terms that were only used for Maya inhabitants, Spaniards being *vecinos;* Restall, *The Maya World*, chap. 2.

23. ANM, Baeza, November 9, 1689, March 3, 14, 1691.

24. ANM, Baeza, September 25, 1690, March 14, April 20, September 21, 1691, January 7, February 26, June 10, 1692.

25. The evolution of non-Maya barrios and the process of change and incorporation of the barrios into the capital city is discussed in Hunt, "Colonial Yucatan," 206–44. For the sources in Maya, see Archivo Notarial del Estado de Yucatán (hereafter, ANE-Y), 86 examples in volumes dating 1748–1838, documents dating 1725–1813; Restall, *The Maya World*, chap. 3.

26. ANE-Y, 1815–17, 87; 1828, 7; and 1810ii, 91.

27. ANM, Baeza, December 27, 1692.

28. Ibid., November 29, 1691.

29. Ibid., September 23, 1689.

30. On Maya naming patterns, see Ralph Beals, "Unilateral Organizations in Mexico," *American Anthropologist* 34 (1932): 467–75; Ralph Roys, "Personal Names of the Maya of Yucatan," *Contributions to American Anthropology and History* 6 (1940): 31–48; and Restall, *The Maya World*, chap. 4. On hieroglyphic evidence of the gender status of Maya noblewomen, see Linda Schele and David Freidel, *A Forest of Kings* (New York: William Morrow, 1990), 363–66.

31. William F. Hanks, *Referential Practice: Language and Lived Space among the Maya* (Chicago: University of Chicago Press, 1990).

32. Testaments of Ixil (hereafter, TI), Colección Carrillo y Ancona (hereafter, CCA): will 54. For a more detailed analysis of these testaments, see Restall, *The Maya World*, and *Life and Death in a Maya Community: The Ixil Testaments of the 1760s* (Lancaster, Calif.: Labyrinthos, 1995).

33. The potential paradox of women as landowners not recognized as such under certain circumstances was closely paralleled in postconquest central Mexico; as Kellogg, "Social Organization," 85, 99, remarked in a study based on Nahuatl wills, "the descriptive evidence shows women less frequently used as links to whom a claim was traced," yet women "had rights to alienate property in the most general sense, i.e., buying, selling and leaving it as inheritable."

34. As yet little evidence has surfaced of female involvement in Maya *cofradías* (sodalities) and other religious organizations; Farriss, *Maya Society*, 265, has argued that cofradías in Yucatan were communitywide, but she offers no direct information on female participation. Nor, of course, is there any evidence that Maya women did *not* play a role in religious activities. However, see Kevin Gosner's discussion of women in cofradías in Chiapas in chapter 10, this volume.

35. TI: will 29.

36. Ixil's top twelve families in the 1760s: Cante, Canul, Chan, Cob, Coba, Ku, Matu, Mis, Pech, Poot, Tec, and Yam (TI). Their patronyms were of great importance to the Maya, as indicated by the fact that they hold on to them after the conquest and the fact that women do not adopt their husbands' patronym either in addition to or in place of their own. Patronym groups, termed *chibalob* by the Maya, were exogamous; see Restall, *The Maya World*, chaps. 3, 4, 7.

37. The area was called Ceh Pech after its dominant patronym group; Roys, *Indian Background*, 11–12, 135.

38. A will-based study by Restall, *The Maya World*, chap. 7, details the prominence of the Pech in one cah, Ixil, in the 1760s and also establishes who were the other ruling families; Thompson, "Tekanto," chap. 6, demonstrates that eighteenth-century Tekanto was similarly ruled by an élite affinal group of families.

39. *Libro de Cacalchen* (hereafter, *LC*); see Restall, "The Testaments of Cacalchen (1646–78)" (unpublished transliteration and translation of 33 Maya wills from photostat in Tulane University's Latin American Library).

40. Ebtun wills reproduced in Ralph L. Roys, *The Titles of Ebtun* (Washington, D.C.: Carnegie Institute, 1939); hereafter, *TE* when used and cited as primary material. Ixil wills: *TI*. Tekanto wills in ANE-Y and analysis of them in Thompson, "Tekanto."

41. This pattern is paralleled by inheritance practices in late sixteenth-century indigenous Mexico City, where Nahua men left more agricultural land than did women whereas women bequeathed more urban property; Kellogg, "Social Organization," chap. 3.

42. Thompson, "Tekanto," 176.

43. *TI:* will 42.
44. *TI:* will 29. The terms used are *camissa* [*sic*] (shirt), *ex* (trousers), *ypil* (*huipil*, or dress), and *pic* (slip, or petticoat). *TE:* document (will) 242.
45. *TI:* will 24.
46. S. L. Cline, *Colonial Culhuacan, 1580–1600: A Social History of an Aztec Town* (Albuquerque: University of New Mexico Press, 1986), 114. Sixteenth-century wills in Nahuatl reveal that Nahua women, like their Yucatec counterparts, in general owned more movable goods associated with the solar than did men; Kellogg, "Social Organization," chap. 3, and Cline, *Colonial Culhuacan*, 103–04, 113.
47. Thompson, "Tekanto," 154–76.
48. *LC:* will 11.
49. Data from *LC* (Cacalchen, 1646–78, 25 testators, 2.0 average surviving children mentioned per testator), *TI* (Ixil, 1765–69, 46 testators, 3.0 average), and *TE* (1785–1813, 9 testators, 4.2 average).
50. *LC:* will 33.
51. *TI:* wills 30 and 36.
52. *TE:* document 284. There are other instances of violence against women in the Maya-language record, but the case circumstances tend to be complex. For example, a Maya resident of Tabi complained ca.1580 that the batab had beaten the man's wife for not surrendering to the batab's adulterous advances, but this accusation was thrown in among many others in a larger feud between the two men (Tulane University, Latin American Library, Tabi MSS, 33; see also Restall, "Subordination and Resistance"); the 1812 cabildo of Bolompoyche accused the local priest of beating a Maya noblewoman, but this was one of a series of alleged acts of violence otherwise committed against men (AGN, Bienes Nacionales, 21, 20, 2–4).
53. AGN, Inquisición, 69, 5, 277.
54. TE: document 275.
55. ANE-Y, 1819(iv), 19r.
56. Cline, *Colonial Culhuacan*, 165.
57. All comparisons to Nahuas of central Mexico in this and the previous paragraphs are based on Cline, *Colonial Culhuacan*, 167–68.

Chapter 12. Double Jeopardy

I am indebted to William L. Merrill as well as the following for their critical comments on this manuscript: Karen Powers, Irene Matthews, Susan Kellogg, Sonya Lipsett-Rivera, Donna J. Guy, and Jennifer Brown.
1. Causa criminal seguida del oficio . . . a María Gertrudis Ysidora de Medina, india del pueblo de la Joya, por haber dado muerte, dormido a

Mariano Burero su marido con una peña que le echó en la cabeza, 1806–1812, Biblioteca Pública del Estado de Jalisco, Archivo Judicial de la Audiencia de Nueva Galicia, Criminal, caja 18, exp. 14 (417). I took extensive notes on this document in 1993, but the detailed analysis in this chapter was enabled by William L. Merrill who provided me with a complete photocopy.

2. The "crisis of representation," some consequences, and some antidotes are outlined in Sherry B. Ortner, "Resistance and the Problem of Ethnographic Refusal," *Comparative Studies in Society and History* 37:1 (1995): 173–93.

3. Susan Deeds, "Rural Work in Nueva Vizcaya: Forms of Labor Coercion on the Periphery," *Hispanic American Historical Review* 69:3 (August 1989): 425–49; and "Mission Villages and Agrarian Patterns in a Nueva Vizcayan Heartland, 1600–1750," *Journal of the Southwest* 33:3 (Autumn 1991): 345–65.

4. Susan Deeds, "Las rebeliones de los tepehuanes y tarahumaras durante el siglo XVII en la Nueva Vizcaya," in *El contacto entre los españoles e indígenas en el norte de la Nueva España*, vol. 4: *Colección conmemorativa quinto centenario del encuentro de dos mundos*, ed. Ysla Campbell (Ciudad Juárez: Universidad Autónoma de Ciudad Juárez, 1992), 9–40; and Susan Deeds, "Indigenous Responses to Mission Settlement in Nueva Vizcaya," in *The New Latin American Mission History*, ed. Erick Langer and Robert H. Jackson (Lincoln: University of Nebraska Press, 1995), 77–108.

5. The general tendency among colonial scholars has been to privilege resistance and to conflate empowerment with cultural retention. In following that trend, I draw on James C. Scott, *Weapons of the Weak: Everyday Forms of Peasant Resistance* (New Haven: Yale University Press, 1985), as well as elaborations or critiques of Antonio Gramsci's explanations of hegemony: e.g., Ranajit Guha, *Elementary Aspects of Peasant Insurgency in Colonial India* (Delhi: Oxford University Press, 1983); and James C. Scott, *Domination and the Arts of Resistance: Hidden Transcripts* (New Haven: Yale University Press, 1990).

6. See Susan Deeds, "Legacies of Resistance, Adaptation and Tenacity: History of the Native Peoples of Northwest Mexico," in *Cambridge History of the Native Peoples of the Americas*, ed. Murdo J. MacLeod (Cambridge: Cambridge University Press, forthcoming).

7. See Joan W. Scott, "Gender: A Useful Category of Historical Analysis," in *Gender and the Politics of History*, ed. Joan W. Scott (New York: Columbia University Press, 1988), 28–50.

8. Edward H. Spicer, *Cycles of Conquest: The Impact of Spain, Mexico, and the United States on the Indians of the Southwest, 1533–1960* (Tucson: University of Arizona Press, 1962). For summaries of revisionist views, see

Daniel T. Reff, *Disease, Depopulation and Culture Change in Northwestern New Spain, 1518–1764* (Salt Lake City: University of Utah Press, 1991); and David H. Thomas, ed., *Columbian Consequences*, vol. 1: *Archaeological and Historical Perspectives on the Spanish Borderlands West* (Washington, D.C.: Smithsonian Institution Press, 1989).

9. Deeds, "Environment and Culture at Contact," chap. 1 of "Defiance and Deference in Mexico's Colonial North: Indians under Spanish Rule in Nueva Vizcaya" (unpublished MS).

10. Jesuits commented on the frequency with which married couples changed partners: Andrés Pérez de Ribas, *Historia de los triunfos de nuestra santa fe entre gentes las más bárbaras y fieras del nuevo orbe* is one of the best contemporary ethnographic sources if read critically. The most recent edition is a facsimile reprint (México: Siglo Veintiuno Editores, [1645] 1992); see bk. 10, chap. 7. See also Carta ánua de Padre Juan Font, 1607, in *Crónicas de la Sierra Tarahumara*, ed. Luis González Rodríguez (México: Secretaría de Educación Pública, 1984), 156–60; and report of P. Juan María Ratkay, Caríchic, March 20, 1683, translated from the Latin in the Bolton Collection, Bancroft Library, Mexicana 17.

11. Carta ánua de 1623, P. Pier Gian Castini, Chínipas, in González Rodríguez, *Crónicas*, 51.

12. Relación de la entrada que hizo el gobernador de la Nueva Vizcaya Francisco de Urdiñola a la conquista, castigo y pacificación de los indios llamados xiximes, 1610, University of Texas, Nettie Lee Benson Library, Joaquín García Icazbalceta Collection, Varias Relaciones, I-l.

13. Report of Padres José Tardá and Tomás de Guadalajara to P. Francisco Ximénez, August 15, 1676. There are several versions of this report; I have used a copy transcribed by William L. Merrill and Luis González Rodríguez from a copy in Rome (Archivum Romanum Societatis Jesu, Mexicana 17, 355–92) soon to be published. See also Thomas Sheridan and Thomas Naylor, eds., *Rarámuri: A Tarahumara Colonial Chronicle, 1607–1791* (Flagstaff: Northland Press, 1979), 32–34.

14. Relación de la entrada . . . xiximes, 1610.

15. William L. Merrill and Robert J. Hard, "Mobile Agriculturalists and the Emergence of Sedentism: Perspectives from Northern Mexico," *American Anthropologist* 94:3 (1992): 601–20.

16. Deeds, "Rural Work in Nueva Vizcaya," 441.

17. José Rafael Rodríguez Gallardo to Juan Antonio Balthasar, August 18, 1750, Archivo General de la Nación, Mexico [hereafter cited as AGN], Provincias Internas, vol. 176, exp. 6.

18. Susan Deeds, "Algunos aspectos de la historia demográfica de las misiones de los jesuitas en Topia, Tepehuana y Tarahumara Baja," paper

presented at the IV Congreso de Historia Regional Comparada, Ciudad Juárez, October 1994.

19. Testimony from interrogations regarding the Tarahumara revolts of the 1690s, declaration of Tadeo, Papigochic, May 25, 1697, Archivo General de Indias, Sevilla (hereafter, AGI), Audiencia de Guadalajara, leg. 156, fol. 206.

20. Pérez de Ribas, *Historia de los triunfos*, bk. 9, chaps. 1–4.

21. Tardá y Guadalajara, 1676; for similar practices among the Rarámuri today, see William L. Merrill, *Rarámuri Souls: Knowledge and Social Process in Northern Mexico* (Washington, D.C.: Smithsonian Institution Press, 1988), 63, 101; John G. Kennedy, *Tarahumara of the Sierra Madre: Beer, Ecology and Social Organization* (Arlington Heights, Ill.: AHM, 1978), 194–206.

22. See the related comments of Inga Clendinnen in "Yucatec Maya Women and the Spanish Conquest: Role and Ritual in Historical Reconstruction," *Journal of Social History* 15 (1982): 427–42.

23. Deeds, "Las rebeliones de los tepehuanes y tarahumaras."

24. William B. Taylor, *Drinking, Homicide, and Rebellion in Colonial Mexican Villages* (Stanford: Stanford University Press, 1979), 116.

25. Deeds, "Ethnicity and Identity in Nueva Vizcaya," paper presented at the IX Reunión de Historiadores Mexicanos y Norteamericanos, Mexico City, October 1994.

26. Scott, *Weapons of the Weak*; Deeds, "Indigenous Responses."

27. Sonya Lipsett-Rivera, "Space, Solidarity, and Sexual Danger in Mexico, 1750–1856," paper presented at the IX Conference of Mexican and U.S. Historians, Mexico City, October 1994; Merrill, *Rarámuri Souls*, 27.

28. Carta ánua, 1608, P. Juan Font, in González Rodríguez, *Crónicas*, 160–65; Ratkay report, 1683; report of P. Gerónimo Figueroa, June 8, 1662, AGN, Historia, vol. 19, exp. 16; visita report of P. Juan de Guendulaín, May 18, 1724, Chihuahua, AGN, Archivo Histórico de Hacienda (hereafter, AHH), Temporalidades, leg. 2009, exp. 20.

29. Merrill discusses Tarahumara resistance to Catholicism in his "Conversion and Colonialism in Northern Mexico: The Tarahumara Response to the Jesuit Mission Program, 1602–1767," in *Conversion to Christianity: Historical and Anthropological Perspectives on a Great Transformation*, ed. Robert W. Hefner (Berkeley: University of California Press, 1993), 129–63; for a discussion of confession in central Mexico, see Serge Gruzinksi, "Individualization and Acculturation: Confession among the Nahuas of Mexico from the Sixteenth to the Eighteenth Century," in *Sexuality and Marriage in Colonial Latin America*, ed. Asunción Lavrin (Lincoln: University of Nebraska, 1989), 101–04.

30. Descriptions of these ceremonies, which the Jesuits did not un-

derstand either in religious or in social terms, are interspersed throughout the early chronicles and reports, for example, in Pérez de Ribas, *Historia de los triunfos*, and Tardá and Guadalajara, 1676.

31. Ann Laura Stoler, "Carnal Knowledge and Imperial Power: Gender, Race and Morality in Colonial Asia," in *Gender at the Crossroads of Knowledge: Feminist Anthropology in the Postmodern Era*, ed. Micaela di Leonardo (Berkeley: University of California Press, 1991), 51–101; and Anne McClintock, *Imperial Leather: Race, Gender, and Sexuality in the Colonial Contest* (New York: Routledge, 1995), 21–74.

32. Patricia Seed, *To Love, Honor, and Obey in Colonial Mexico: Conflicts over Marriage Choice, 1574–1821* (Stanford: Stanford University Press, 1988). Of course, deviations from the ideal were rife, as many of the essays in Lavrin, *Sexuality and Marriage*, attest. See also the discussion in Ana María Alonso, *Thread of Blood: Colonialism, Revolution, and Gender on Mexico's Northern Frontier* (Tucson: University of Arizona Press, 1995), 73–103.

33. Testimonies in AGI, Guadalajara 156, fols. 664–670.

34. Reff, *Disease, Depopulation and Culture Change*, 240.

35. Richard Boyer, "Women, La Mala Vida, and the Politics of Marriage," in *Sexuality and Marriage*, ed. Asunción Lavrin, 252–86; and *Lives of the Bigamists: Marriage, Family, and Community in Colonial Mexico* (Albuquerque: University of New Mexico Press, 1995), 129–37. See also Lipsett-Rivera, "La violencia dentro de la familia formal e informal" (forthcoming); Deborah Kanter, "Hijos del Pueblo: Family, Community and Gender in Rural Mexico, the Toluca Region, 1730–1830" (Ph.D. diss., University of Virginia, 1993), esp. chap. 4, "Women, Men and Married Life"; and Sylvia Arrom, *The Women of Mexico City, 1790–1857* (Stanford: Stanford University Press, 1985), 232–38.

36. Quoted in Marcela Tostado Gutiérrez, *El álbum de la mujer. Antología ilustrada de las mexicanas*, vol. 2: *Época colonial* (México: Instituto Nacional de Antropología e Historia, 1991), 144–45.

37. Solange Alberro, *Inquisición y sociedad en México, 1571–1700* (México: Fondo de Cultura Económica, 1988), 183–86, 300–04; Thomas Calvo, *Poder, religión y sociedad en la Guadalajara del siglo XVII* (México: CEMCA/Ayuntamiento de Guadalajara, 1992), 210–25; Ruth Behar, "Sex and Sin: Witchcraft and the Devil in Late Colonial Mexico," *American Ethnologist* 14:1 (1987): 34–54.

38. See, e.g., in the AGN: Inquisición, vol. 516, exp. 7; vol. 791, exp. 31.

39. Taylor, *Drinking, Homicide, and Rebellion*, 85–87; Lipsett-Rivera, "La violencia." It should be noted that the case studied in this chapter contains a reference to another instance of husband murder in the Valle de San Bartolomé (Valle de Allende).

40. The following summary and analysis is based on the lengthy document cited in note 1.

41. In trying to contextualize and interpret this case, I have benefited from the analysis by Ranajit Guha, "Chandra's Death," *Subaltern Studies* 5 (1986): 135–65.

42. Report of P. Domingo de Lizarralde, Satebó, December 26, 1690, AGN, AHH, Temporalidades, leg. 279, exp. 67.

43. The case is found in Archivo de Hidalgo del Parral (hereafter, AHP), microfilm reel 1667, fr. 738–43.

44. Deeds, "Rural Work in Nueva Vizcaya," 440–41.

45. Deeds, "Mission Villages," 359–61; P. Pedro de Estrada to P. Rector Francisco Xavier de la Paz, Satevó, February 19, 1743, AGN, AHH, Temp., leg. 316, exp. 5; various land cases in AGI, Guadalajara 113, and Archivo de Instrumentos Públicos, Guadalajara, Tierras y Aguas, lib. 28, exp. 141, lib. 22, exp. 2; juicio de residencia del gobernador Belaunzarán, AGI, Escribanía de Cámara, 394.

46. Report of P. Juan de Guenduláin, Satebó, 1725, AGN, AHH, Temp., leg. 2009, exp. 99.

47. Report of P. Juan Antonio Núñez to Bishop, Satebó, July 19, 1749, Archivo de la Catedral de Durango, Varios 1749; entrega de Satebó, October 8, 1753, AGI, Guadalajara 137, fols. 515–19.

48. Juan Joseph Ochoa y Herive to Miguel Joseph de Arenibar, Santa María de las Cuevas, November 2, 1755, in registros de bautismos, Parroquia de San Lorenzo, microfilm 162584 of the Genealogical Society of Utah.

49. Padrones, 1787, AHP, microfilm reel 1787b, frames 1382–85.

50. Francisco R. Almada, *Resumen de historia del estado de Chihuahua* (Chihuahua: Ediciones del Gobierno del Estado de Chihuahua, 1986), 135.

51. Peter Gerhard, *The North Frontier of New Spain*, rev. ed. (Norman: University of Oklahoma Press, 1993), 200; Salvador Alvarez, "Tendencias regionales de la propiedad territorial en el norte de la Nueva España. Siglos XVII y XVIII," in *Actas del Segundo Congreso de Historia Regional Comparada* (Ciudad Juárez: Universidad Autónoma de Ciudad Juárez, 1990), 141–79.

52. The leasing of Indian lands by outsiders in the environs of Chihuahua escalated in the late eighteenth century; Cheryl Martin, *Governance and Society in Colonial Mexico: Chihuahua in the Eighteenth Century* (Stanford: Stanford University Press, 1995), 42. On geographic mobility, see Testimonio . . . sobre indios vagos y ocios, 1789, AGN, Provincias Internas, vol. 69, exp. 7; report on the Tarahumara region, n.d., ca. 1800, in *Documentos para la historia de México*, ed. F. García Figueroa (México: Imprenta de J. R. Navarro, 1853–57), 4th series, 4: 117; and Jesuit reports, 1757, AGN, Jesuitas, leg. II-7, exps. 14–23.

53. William L. Merrill, "Cultural Creativity and Raiding Bands in

Eighteenth-Century Northern New Spain," in *Violence, Resistance and Survival in the Americas*, ed. William B. Taylor and Franklin Pease (Washington, D.C.: Smithsonian Institution Press, 1994), 124–52; Almada, *Resumen de historia*, 134.

54. Cheryl Martin, "Public Celebrations, Popular Culture, and Labor Discipline in Eighteenth-Century Chihuahua," in *Rituals of Rule, Rituals of Resistance: Public Celebrations and Popular Culture in Mexico*, ed. William H. Beezley, Cheryl English Martin, and William E. French (Wilmington, Del.: Scholarly Resources, 1994), 95–114.

55. It is curious that this is the only mention of children in the entire proceedings.

56. Partida 7, título 8, ley 12, of the *Siete Partidas* refers to parricide. I am still unversed as to the significance of these symbols, but mutilation and other draconian punishments were prescribed by Romano-Visigothic tradition for private crimes; see P. D. King, *Law and Society in the Visigothic Kingdom* (Cambridge: Cambridge University Press, 1972), 89–91. The prosecutor in this case noted that the penalty had been modified in modern times to hanging the victim before placing him or her in a cask with the first three animals, but without the monkey for obvious reasons.

57. See Fernando Cervantes, *The Devil in the New World: The Impact of Diabolism in New Spain* (New Haven: Yale University Press, 1994).

58. Taylor, *Drinking, Homicide, and Rebellion*, 102, comments on the unsanitary conditions of colonial jails and argues that incarceration was mainly a way of detaining the accused before trial rather than a form of punishment.

59. These findings for colonial Mexico are based on different samples analyzed by Taylor, *Drinking, Homicide, and Rebellion*, 97–106; and Colin M. MacLachlan, *La justicia criminal del siglo XVIII. Un estudio sobre el tribunal de la Acordada* (México: Secretaría de Educación Pública, 1976), 113–42.

60. Ibid., and Michael C. Scardaville, "(Habsburg) Law and (Bourbon) Order: State Authority, Popular Unrest, and the Criminal Justice System in Bourbon Mexico City," *The Americas* 50:4 (April 1994): 501–25. Martin, *Governance and Society*, 166–82.

61. See, for a recent discussion, R. Douglas Cope, *The Limits of Racial Domination: Plebeian Society in Colonial Mexico City, 1660–1720* (Madison: University of Wisconsin Press, 1994).

62. For more on this, see Lipsett-Rivera, "Space, Solidarity and Sexual Danger."

Chapter 13. Women's Voices from the Frontier

1. The generic term "Chichimeca" was applied to all northern nonsedentary groups. In the Saltillo region the major group in the sixteenth

and seventeenth centuries seems to have been the Guachichiles. By the late eighteenth century Apaches were ranging as far south as Saltillo, wreaking havoc in particular during the periods of severe drought that characterized the region in the 1780s and 1790s. In most late eighteenth-century documentation the Indian raiders are described merely as "indios bárbaros." The best general treatment of the colonization plan for the northeastern region remains Vito Alessio Robles, *Coahuila y Texas en la época colonial* (México: Editorial Porrúa, [1938] 1978), 123–62.

2. Philip Wayne Powell's *Soldiers, Indians, and Silver: The Northward Advance of New Spain, 1550–1600* (Berkeley: University of California Press, 1956) is the classic treatment of the Spanish efforts to "pacify" the northern frontier. Saltillo's desperate straits are noted in Alessio Robles, *Coahuila y Texas en la época colonial*, 134.

3. See José Cuello's discussion of the founding of San Esteban in "Saltillo in the Seventeenth Century: Local Society on the North Mexican Frontier" (Ph.D. diss., University of California, Berkeley, 1982), 32–33, 76–77, table 2, "The Population of Saltillo and San Esteban, 1577–1700."

4. Privileges were nothing new to the Tlaxcalans, to be sure; over the course of the sixteenth century the municipal council of Tlaxcala had actively sought and had been awarded privileges ranging from exemption from tribute to prohibition of forced labor in Puebla. But these privileges were most often honored in the breach, which explains in part the Tlaxcalans' avid pursuit of crown guarantees of protection in 1591. See Alessio Robles, *Coahuila y Texas en la época colonial*, 124; Charles Gibson, *Tlaxcala in the Sixteenth Century* (Stanford: Stanford University Press, [1952] 1967), 160–81, 183–84, 229–34, Appendix 7, "Royal Privileges Granted to Tlaxcala."

5. Archivo Municipal de Saltillo, Presidencia Municipal (hereafter, AMS, PM), c. 7, exp. 41, 1704; c. 35/1, exp. 51, 1783. For late eighteenth-century and early nineteenth-century individual challenges to lands held by San Esteban residents, see AMS, PM, c. 31, exps. 13, 23, 1777; c. 58, exp. 17, 1808.

6. In 1784 San Esteban residents protested the attempt by the Marqués de San Miguel de Aguayo to force them to labor on his haciendas; the commander of the Provincias Internas responded by barring such actions by the marqués; AMS, PM, c. 36, exps. 29, 32, 1784. See as well the suit filed by several San Esteban residents against the Saltillo merchant don Miguel Lobo Guerrero for his failure to fulfill the terms of the contract by which he arranged for their labor on his rural estate; AMS, PM, c. 59, exp. 39, 1810.

7. See note 5, above, for references to boundary surveys; I have examined the contention over borders in the larger context of the interde-

pendence of the community in "Variants of the 'Colonizing Experience': Indian/Hispanic Contact in the Mexican Northeast, 1600–1800," in *Rediscovering America, 1492–1992: National, Cultural, and Disciplinary Boundaries Re-examined*, ed. Leslie Bary et al. (Baton Rouge: Louisiana State University Press, 1992), 77–85. The continued use of Nahuatl at least through the 1770s in the writing of testaments and the presence of an interpreter in official encounters with Saltillo's cabildo reflect cultural persistence in this Indian enclave.

8. Susan Kellogg, "Aztec Women in Early Colonial Courts: Structure and Strategy in a Legal Context," in *Five Centuries of Law and Politics in Central Mexico*, ed. Ronald Spores and Ross Hassig, Vanderbilt University Publications in Anthropology, no. 30 (Nashville, 1984), 25–38.

9. My research on native women is part of a much larger study of the Saltillo region at the close of the eighteenth century; the temporal confines of the present study are determined by those of the larger project.

10. It was at least unadulterated Indian, if the 1786 census is to be believed. That census revealed 538 households in San Esteban, each one (excepting the household of the Spanish priest) headed by an *indio principal* (Indian noble), clear indication not only of the presumed ethnic homogeneity but also of the maintenance of the privilege of noble status; AMS, PM, c. 42, exp. 1, 1790. In a later and more extensive census, all 2,115 residents of San Esteban enumerated in 1793 appear to be Indian. While this exclusivity may reveal as much about the assumptions of the census takers as it does about the actual ethnic makeup of the town, nonetheless the naming patterns evident in the census (use of first name or saint's name as surname) suggest the Indianness of the town; AMS, PM, c. 43, exp. 1, 1791. For the seventeenth-century absorption of band Indians, specifically Guachichiles, see Cuello, "Saltillo in the Seventeenth Century," 59, 97–98.

11. In the following discussion I am indebted to Verena Martínez Alier's work on elopement and seduction, treated at length in her *Women, Class, and Colour in Nineteenth-Century Cuba* (Cambridge: Cambridge University Press, 1974), passim.

12. AMS, PM, c. 51/1, exp. 95, 1799.

13. "No es de calidad de mi hija . . . no ser igual de mi hija," in Don José's words; see AMS, PM, c. 50, exp. 39, 1798.

14. AMS, PM, c. 50, exp. 39, 1798.

15. On this particular point the Saltillo cabildo had questioned him sharply, suggesting that its officers suspected that the issue of greatest concern to Hernández was his daughter's honor.

16. "Ha de pasar trabajos su hija," as he phrased it in his suit. No mention is made of sexual transgression in this case, but Martínez Alier suggests this was common in cases where marriage choice was opposed by a

parent and the couple resorted to elopement. See Martínez Alier, *Women, Class, and Colour*, 103–19, esp. pp. 106–08. More recently, Patricia Seed has examined the issue of honor in marriage in her *To Love, Honor, and Obey in Colonial Mexico: Conflicts over Marriage Choice, 1574–1821* (Stanford: Stanford University Press, 1988).

17. As they put it, "la mujer ha sido la causa de todo que a informado mal" (the woman has been the cause of all the misinformation); AMS, PM, c. 42, exp. 8, 1790.

18. "Una pobre mujer cargada de familia y de tierna edad."

19. AMS, PM, c. 42, exp. 9, 1790.

20. AMS, PM, c. 51/1, exp. 40, 1799.

21. The relevant passage reads, "por el pribilegio que como hijos de pueblo gosamos por gracia que nuestro natural señor y sus antecesores no tienen conferida entre otras que como tales hijos gosamos como deve constar de sus reales sabias resoluciones en que no quieren no tan solamente de que se nos multe pero ni aunque paguemientos real derecho de alcabala ni menos diesmos y primicias"; see AMS, PM, c. 55, exp. 3, 1804.

22. Ibid.

23. See Asunción Lavrin's "In Search of the Colonial Woman in Mexico: The Seventeenth and Eighteenth Centuries," in *Latin American Women: Historical Perspectives*, ed. Asunción Lavrin (Westport, Conn.: Greenwood Press, 1978), esp. pp. 40–47. Clearly widowhood provided greater opportunities for women of means who could rely on hefty dowries and shares of their deceased spouses' estates for their subsistence; such economic independence was probably beyond the reach of San Esteban women. But the legal independence was a reality nonetheless, and it appears that this gave weight to the complaints of the two women treated here.

Chapter 14. Rethinking Malinche

1. See James Lockhart, Frances Berdan, and Arthur J. O. Anderson, eds. and trans., *The Tlaxcalan Actas: A Compendium of the Records of the Cabildo of Tlaxcala (1545–1647)* (Salt Lake City: University of Utah Press, 1986), 51, for the commission. The original has been lost, but the *Handbook of Middle American Indians*, gen. ed. Robert Wauchope (Austin: University of Texas Press, 1975), 14:214–18, has an inventory of known copies.

2. The document has recently been transferred to the rare books collection of the Benson Latin American Collection at the University of Texas at Austin.

3. See the double-faced Cortés-and-Malinche mask in Donald Cordry, *Mexican Masks* (Austin: University of Texas Press, 1980), 227.

4. Bernal Díaz del Castillo, *Historia verdadera de la conquista de la Nueva España* (México: Editorial Porrúa, 1955), 1:218–19.

5. For more examples of Malinche masks, see Cordry, *Mexican Masks*, 38, 172, 207, 228.

6. Fernando Horcasitas, ed. and trans., *The Aztecs Then and Now* (México: Minutiae Mexicana, 1979), 130.

7. For three stories as told by doña Luz Jiménez in which Malintzin is associated with mountains and protection, see Fernando Horcasitas, ed., *Life and Death in Milpa Alta: A Nahuatl Chronicle of Díaz and Zapata* (Norman: University of Oklahoma Press, 1972), 8–13; and Anita Brenner, *The Boy Who Could Do Anything & Other Mexican Folk Tales* (New York: William R. Scott, 1942), 30–33, 133–35.

8. Díaz del Castillo, *Historia verdadera*, 2:236.

9. Fray Bernardino de Sahagún, *Florentine Codex: General History of the Things of New Spain*, Book 12: *The Conquest of Mexico*, ed. and trans. Arthur J. O. Anderson and Charles E. Dibble (Santa Fe and Salt Lake City: School of American Research and University of Utah Press, 1975), 2. The text is accompanied by an illustration of the weeping woman.

10. A fine example is the story "Malintzin" told by doña Luz Jiménez in Brenner, *The Boy Who Could Do Anything*, 133–35.

11. See the relations of Andrés de Tapia and Francisco de Aguilar in Patricia de Fuentes, ed. and trans., *The Conquistadors: First-Person Accounts of the Conquest of Mexico* (New York: Orion Press, 1963), 24, 138, 141.

12. The Pérez de Arteaga manuscript is in the collection of the Jay I. Kislak Foundation, Miami Lake, Florida. For corroboration of the claim, see Díaz del Castillo, *Historia verdadera*, 1:219.

13. Díaz del Castillo, *Historia verdadera*, 1:123–24.

14. Elizabeth Salas, *Soldaderas in the Mexican Military: Myth and History* (Austin: University of Texas Press, 1990), 14. Salas is right about the beginning of the decline of doña Marina's reputation, but she is mistaken about details of her life. On page 15, for instance, she states that Cortés was separated from doña Marina when he made his expedition to Honduras, but in fact she accompanied him there as his interpreter, and it was at the outset of the expedition that Cortés married her to Jaramillo and endowed the couple with an *encomienda* (a grant of Indians for tribute).

15. For a thorough study of characterizations of doña Marina in postindependence literature, see Sandra Messinger Cypess, *La Malinche in Mexican Literature: From History to Myth* (Austin: University of Texas Press, 1991), chaps. 4–8.

16. Fuentes, *The Conquistadors*, 215; Frans Blom, *The Conquest of Yucatan* (New York: Houghton Mifflin, 1936), 41–42.

17. Hilde Krueger, *Malinche* (New York: Arrowhead Press, 1948), 65.

18. Peter Gerhard, *A Guide to the Historical Geography of New Spain* (Cambridge: Cambridge University Press, 1972), 383.

19. Octavio Paz, *The Labyrinth of Solitude* (New York: Grove Press, 1961), 86.

20. V. Calero, "Aguilar y la Malinche," in *Registro yucateco. Periódico literario* (Mérida, Yucatan: Imprente de Castillo y Compañía, 1845), 210–212.

21. Rius, *La interminable conquista de México* (México: Editorial Grijalbo, 1983), 13.

22. Rius, *500 años. Fregados pero cristianos* (México: Editorial Grijalbo, 1992), 130–31; translation mine.

23. Anthony Pagden, ed. and trans., *Hernán Cortés: Letters from Mexico* (New Haven: Yale University Press, 1986), 73, 376.

24. Lesley Byrd Simpson, ed. and trans., *Cortés: The Life of the Conqueror by His Secretary Francisco López de Gómara* (Berkeley: University of California Press, 1964), 56–57.

25. Díaz del Castillo, *Historia verdadera*, 1:124.

26. Simpson, *Cortés*, 56; Díaz del Castillo, *Historia verdadera*, 1:123.

27. Fuentes, *The Conquistadors*, 24; Simpson, *Cortés*, 57.

28. Díaz del Castillo, *Historia verdadera*, 1:123.

29. For a description of the upbringing of well-bred Nahua girls, see Zorita as quoted below.

30. Pagden, *Hernán Cortés: Letters*, 376.

31. Simpson, *Cortés*, 370.

32. The first rule of Pig Latin applies to English words that begin with consonants. One transports the initial consonant to the end of the word and adds the diphthong [ei]. Different "dialects" of Pig Latin depend on the second rule, namely, how one handles words that begin with vowels.

33. For the conventions of polite Nahuatl speech, see Frances Karttunen, "Conventions of Polite Speech in Nahuatl," *Estudios de Cultura Náhuatl* 20 (1990): 281–96. For this reason, one should not take the speech of Moteucçoma to Cortés as reported in book 12 of the *Florentine Codex*, 42, at face value. What may strike us as hospitable to the point of servility was required by the conventions of tecpillahtolli.

34. Fernando Alva Ixtlilxochitl, *Obras históricas*, ed. Edmundo O'Gorman (México: Universidad Nacional Autónoma de México, 1977), 2:198.

35. Calero, "Aguilar y la Malinche," 27.

36. Manuel Orozco y Berra, *Historia antigua de la conquista de México* (México: Tipografía de Gonzalo A. Esteva, 1880), 4:112.

37. Orozco y Berra attributes the idea that prior to baptism her name had been "Malinalli" to Fernando Ramírez; *Historia antigua*, 116.

38. Fuentes, *The Conquistadors*, 24; Simpson, *Cortés*, 56–58. Not so long after this, Cortés commissioned Puertocarrero to return to Spain where he fell into political webs and tangles and eventually died in prison.

39. Díaz del Castillo, *Historia verdadera*, 1:127; Sahagún, *Florentine Codex, bk. 12*, 27.

40. Díaz del Castillo, *Historia verdadera*, 1:135.

41. Ibid., 238–48; Simpson, *Cortés*, 126–30; Pagden, *Hernán Cortés: Letters*, 72–76.

42. Sahagún, *Florentine Codex, bk. 12*, 44–45.

43. Bernal Díaz agrees: "And it seems to me that Cortés, through doña Marina, offered him his right hand, and Montezuma [*sic*] did not wish to take it, but he did give his hand to Cortés . . . and those great Princes who accompanied Montezuma held back Cortés by the arm so that he should not embrace him, for they considered it an indignity"; Bernal Díaz del Castillo, *The Discovery and Conquest of Mexico* (New York: Farrar, Straus and Giroux, 1956), 193. Cortés himself reports that Moteucçoma's attendants blocked him from touching their ruler; Pagden, *Hernán Cortés: Letters*, 84.

44. Díaz del Castillo, *Historia verdadera*, 1:300–01, 306.

45. Ibid., 302–03.

46. Ibid., 330–32.

47. Ibid., 328.

48. Susan D. Gillespie, *The Aztec Kings: The Construction of Rulership in Mexico History* (Tucson: University of Arizona Press, 1989), 109; Amada López de Meneses, "Tecuichpochtzin, hija de Moteczuma (¿1510?-1550)," *Revista de Indias* 9 (1948): 471–96. This second Marina and a mestizo Marina of the next generation have been confused with "doña Marina la lengua," leading to the belief that Cortés's interpreter lived a long life and held many properties.

49. Simpson, *Cortés*, 408.

50. Díaz del Castillo, *The Discovery and Conquest of Mexico*, 310–11; Simpson, *Cortés*, 212; Sahagún, *Florentine Codex, bk. 12*, 65 n. 1; Cortés, *Letters*, 477 n. 89.

51. Díaz del Castillo, *Historia verdadera*, 1:404.

52. Gillespie, *The Aztec Kings*, 106–09; López de Meneses, "Tecuichpochtzin."

53. Mariano G. Somonte, *Doña Marina, "La Malinche"* (México: Privately published, 1971), 145.

54. *Diccionario Porrúa. Historia, biografía y geografía de México*, 5th ed. (México: Editorial Porrúa, 1964), 1:743; Fernando Benítez, *The Century after Cortés* (Chicago: University of Chicago Press, 1965); Somonte, *Doña Marina*, 169. Somonte's source for this seems to be family history conveyed to him by don Federico Gómez de Orozco, a descendant of don Martín.

55. Simpson, *Cortés*, 346.

56. Somonte, *Doña Marina*, 175–76; France V. Scholes and Ralph L. Roys, *The Maya Chontal Indians of Acalan-Tixchel: A Contribution to the History and Ethnography of the Yucatan Peninsula* (Norman: University of Oklahoma Press, 1968), 391–92; Díaz del Castillo, *Historia verdadera*, 2:204–05; Simpson, *Cortés*, 355; Pagden, *Hernán Cortés: Letters*, 365–66.

57. Díaz del Castillo, *Historia verdadera*, 2:205.

58. Gerhard, *Historical Geography*, 383; Somonte, *Doña Marina*, 144.

59. Richard Elphick, *Kraal and Castle: Khoikhoi and the Founding of White South Africa* (New Haven: Yale University Press, 1977), 107.

60. Díaz del Castillo, *Historia verdadera*, 1:203, 121.

61. Nor were the sixteenth-century Mesoamericans more generous than we toward their ravished women. Bernal Díaz tells of how, after the fall of Tenochtitlan, Cuauhtemoc requested that women who had been taken by the Spanish soldiers be permitted to return to their fathers and husbands. Few could be located, he says, and of those hardly any would go back because so many of them were already pregnant; Díaz del Castillo, *Historia verdadera*, 2:69.

62. Sahagún, *Florentine Codex*, bk. 12, 49.

63. Alonso de Zorita, *Life and Labor in Ancient Mexico: The Brief and Summary Relation of the Lords of New Spain* ed. and trans. Benjamin Keen (New Brunswick: Rutgers University Press, 1963), 136.

Concluding Remarks

1. We are following Latin American usage by employing "indigenous" (in lieu of Indian) as the English-language equivalent of *indígena*.

2. Some of these ideas are explored by Cheryl Johnson-Odim and Margaret Strobel, "Introduction," in *Restoring Women to History: Teaching Packets for Integrating Women's History into Courses on Africa, Asia, Latin America, the Caribbean, and the Middle East* (Bloomington, Ind.: Organization of American Historians, 1988), 1–30. Joan W. Scott has said of gender that it is "a primary way of signifying relationships of power" in "Gender: A Useful Category of Historical Analysis," in *Gender and the Politics of History*, ed. Joan W. Scott (New York: Columbia University Press, 1988), 48. Susan Kellogg, "Cognatic Kinship and Religion: Women in Aztec Society," in *Smoke and Mist: Mesoamerican Studies in Memory of Thelma D. Sullivan*, ed. J. Kathryn Josserand and Karen Dakin (Oxford: British Archaeological Reports Press, 1988), 666, has suggested that the study of women "can fundamentally alter conventional conceptions of human societies." See also Asunción Lavrin and Edith Couturier, "Las mujeres tienen la palabra. Otras voces en la his-

toria colonial de México," *Historia Mexicana* 31:2 (October–December 1981): 278–313.

3. Key works here include two volumes edited by Asunción Lavrin: *Latin American Women: Historical Perspectives* (Westport, Conn.: Greenwood Press, 1978), and *Sexuality and Marriage in Colonial Latin America* (Lincoln: University of Nebraska Press, 1989).

4. Excellent examples include Irene Silverblatt, *Moon, Sun, and Witches: Gender Ideologies and Class in Inca and Colonial Peru* (Princeton: Princeton University Press, 1987); Steve J. Stern, *The Secret History of Gender: Women, Men, and Power in Late Colonial Mexico* (Chapel Hill: University of North Carolina Press, 1995); the entire issue of *Ethnohistory* 42:4 (1995); as well as many of the works cited below.

5. Inga Clendinnen, "Yucatec Maya Women and the Spanish Conquest: Role and Ritual in Historical Reconstruction," *Journal of Social History* 15 (1982): 437.

6. For further reading, see Mona Etienne and Eleanor Leacock, eds., *Women and Colonization: Anthropological Perspectives* (New York: Praeger, 1980).

7. See Johnson-Odim and Strobel, "Introduction."

8. Johnson-Odim and Strobel mention the possibility of creating gender–equal societies in the future; "Introduction," 5.

9. Irene Silverblatt, "Interpreting Women in States: New Feminist Ethnohistories," in *Gender at the Crossroads of Knowledge: Feminist Anthropology in the Postmodern Era*, ed. Micaela di Leonardo (Berkeley: University of California Press, 1991), 140–71, quote on p. 157. See also Susan Kellogg, "The Woman's Room: Some Aspects of Gender Relations in Tenochtitlan in the Late Pre-Hispanic Period," *Ethnohistory* 42:4 (1995): 563; Michelle Z. Rosaldo, "The Use and Abuse of Anthropology: Reflections on Feminism and Cross-Cultural Understanding," *Signs* 5 (1980): 389–417; and Irene Silverblatt, "Lessons of Gender and Ethnohistory in Mesoamerica," *Ethnohistory* 42:4 (1995): 642–43, all of whom reconsider the applicability of the "public vs. private" model.

10. Silverblatt, *Moon, Sun, and Witches;* Kellogg, "Cognatic Kinship and Religion," 676. Kellogg cautions that terms such as "equal" and "subordinate" impose "Western standards or categories onto the Aztec religious realm [and] obscur[e] the complex organization of their religious structure in which, in some respects, men and women had parallel roles." See also Susan Kellogg, "The Woman's Room," 563–71. Elizabeth M. Brumfiel, "Weaving and Cooking: Women's Production in Aztec Mexico," in *Engendering Archaeology: Women and Prehistory*, ed. Joan M. Gero and Margaret W. Conkey (Cambridge, Mass.: Basil Blackwell, 1991), 224–51, takes a similar line, suggesting that the domestic tasks of Mexica women may have been

much more important in the general social scheme of things than older Western-influenced interpretations would have us believe. Sharise D. McCafferty and Geoffrey G. McCafferty, "Powerful Women and the Myth of Male Dominance in Aztec Society," *Archaeological Review from Cambridge* 7 (1988): 47, argue that "Aztec gender relationships were based more on dialectical oppositions than on hierarchy."

11. Susan D. Gillespie, *The Aztec Kings: The Construction of Rulership in Mexica History* (Tucson: University of Arizona Press, 1989). See also Silvia Garza Tarazona de González, *La mujer mesoamericana* (México: Editorial Planeta Mexicana, 1991), 43–46, who discusses possible political roles exercised by precontact Mesoamerican women; Susan Schroeder, "The Noblewomen of Chalco," *Estudios de Cultural Náhuatl* 22 (1992): 45–86, who like Gillespie stresses the importance of noblewomen in interdynastic alliances and the legitimacy of dynastic succession; and Louise M. Burkhart, "Mujeres mexicas en 'el frente' del hogar. Trabajo doméstico y religión en el México azteca," *Mesoamérica Antigua* 12:23 (1992): 23–54. For two other recent and more general studies of precontact women, see María J. Rodríguez-Shadow, *La mujer azteca* (México: Universidad Autónoma del Estado de México, 1991); and Enriqueta Tuñón Pablos, *El álbum de la mujer. Antología ilustrada de las mexicanas*, vol. 1: *Época prehispánica* (México: Instituto Nacional de Antropología e Historia, 1991).

12. Rosemary Joyce, "Images of Gender and Labor Organization in Classic Maya Society," in *Exploring Gender through Archaeology: Selected Papers from the 1991 Boone Conference*, ed. Cheryl Claassen (Madison: Prehistory Press, 1992), 63–70.

13. See Colin M. MacLachlan, "The Eagle and the Serpent: Male over Female in Tenochtitlán," *Proceedings of the Pacific Coast Council of Latin American Studies* 5 (1976): 45–56, who emphasizes inequality and sees the roots of machismo in both Aztec and Spanish culture. For similar contrasting views of gender relations in the precontact Andes, see Monique Alaperrine-Bouyer, "Des femmes dans le Manuscrit de Huarochirí," *Bulletin de l'Institut Français d'Etudes Andines* 16:3–4 (1987): 97–101, which supports symmetrical gender roles; and Gustavo Valcárcel, "La condición de la mujer en el estado incaico," *Socialismo y Participación* (Lima) 29 (1985): 63–70, which emphasizes subordination for women and gender inequality.

14. By the same token, the language used to describe an especially brave daughter of a Purépecha lord declares, "My woman has been a valiant man." See James Krippner-Martínez, "The Politics of Conquest: An Interpretation of the *Relación de Michoacán*," *The Americas* 47:2 (October 1990): 193, 194. Tzvetan Todorov discusses gendered insults among the Nahuas and takes the extreme view that women's "occupations and attitudes do not con-

stitute a second valued pole of the Aztec axiology. . . . [S]uch weakness is never praised. . . . The worst insult, then, that can be addressed to a man is to treat him as a woman"; *The Conquest of America: The Question of the Other* (New York: Harper and Row, 1984), 91.

15. Clendinnen, "Yucatec Maya Women," 430.

16. For another view of these issues, see Anna-Britta Hellbom, "The Life and Role of Women in Aztec Culture," *Cultures* 8:3 (1982): 55–65, which emphasizes men's and women's different functions, with status largely determined by social hierarchy rather than gender. In general, Hellbom finds that Nahua women had stronger economic than political roles and that they were not high priests but had other significant jobs around the temples. See also Arnold J. Bauer, "Millers and Grinders: Technology and Household Economy in Meso-America," *Agricultural History* 64:1 (1990): 1–17, who stresses the rigor of life for women in the home, bent over their grinding stones for long hours at a time, both before and after the conquest.

17. Clendinnen, "Yucatec Maya Women," 428–31.

18. See Ian Hodder, "Gender Representation and Social Reality," in *Archaeology of Gender: Proceedings of the Twenty-second Annual Conference of the Archaeological Association of the University of Calgary*, ed. Dale Walden and Noreen D. Willows (Calgary: University of Calgary Press, 1991), 13, who believes that "cultural representations of gender rarely accurately reflect male-female relations, men's and women's activities, or men's and women's contributions in any given society"; and Nancy Shoemaker, who states in her recent anthology on indigenous women of North America, *Negotiators of Change: Historical Perspectives on Native American Women* (New York: Routledge, 1995), 5, "Gender differences were crucially important in Indian cultures for organizing behavior and activities but gender was also flexible and variable."

19. A succinct discussion of sedentary, semisedentary, and nonsedentary cultures of precontact Mesoamerica and South America can be found in James Lockhart and Stuart B. Schwartz, *Early Latin America: A History of Colonial Spanish America and Brazil*, Latin American Studies, no. 46 (Cambridge: Cambridge University Press, 1983), 31–60.

20. For Mesoamerica, see June Nash, "Aztec Women: The Transition from Status to Class in Empire and Colony," in *Women and Colonization*, ed. Mona Etienne and Eleanor Leacock, 134–48; and Kellogg, "Cognatic Kinship," 676. For the Andes, see Silverblatt, *Moon, Sun, and Witches*, esp. pp. xxvii–xxix, 81–108. In "Interpreting Women in States," 140–71, Silverblatt provides some cautionary remarks about state formation or state activities as a context in which women were passively acted upon.

21. Incidentally, for a working definition of patriarchy for Hispanic

society of colonial Mexico that seems to fit with our contributors' usage, see Stern, *Secret History of Gender,* 21. Sousa also provides a useful definition in her notes; see chapter 9, this volume.

22. Silverblatt, *Moon, Sun, and Witches,* 197–210.

23. Matthew Restall, "'He Wished It in Vain': Subordination and Resistance among Maya Women in Post-Conquest Yucatan," *Ethnohistory* 42:4 (1995): 577–94.

24. Ann Zulawski, "Social Differentiation, Gender, and Ethnicity: Urban Indian Women in Colonial Bolivia, 1640–1725," *Latin American Research Review* 25:2 (1990): 109, concludes that "gender complementarity still prevailed among native peoples in the seventeenth and eighteenth centuries" in the Andes, too. With further research we may come to better understand the relationship between these findings and Steve Stern's recent conclusion that "among poor women and men in late colonial times, gender right was a bitterly contested arena of social power." See Stern, *Secret History of Gender,* 299.

25. William B. Taylor, *Drinking, Homicide, and Rebellion in Colonial Mexican Villages* (Stanford: Stanford University Press, 1979), has written what is still the standard treatment of the subject for central Mexico. For comparison, see Leon G. Campbell, "Women and the Great Rebellion in Peru, 1780–1783," *The Americas* 42:2 (1985): 163–96; and Alvis Dunn, "A Cry at Daybreak: Death, Disease, and Defense of Community in a Highland Ixil-Maya Village," *Ethnohistory* 42:4 (1995): 595–606, for a recent discussion of the political aspects of women's participation in rioting in a highland Maya community in 1798. See also Stern, *Secret History of Gender,* 189–213, especially pp. 204–09, for a discussion of gender, politics, women, and rioting in very late colonial Mexico, including what is now Morelos and the town of Tepoztlan.

26. John Tutino, *From Insurrection to Revolution in Mexico: Social Bases of Agrarian Violence, 1750–1910* (Princeton: Princeton University Press, 1986), offers a useful model to explain a willingness to engage in violent resistance when, among other things, threats to local autonomy and security are perceived. Dunn, "A Cry at Daybreak," argues that Ixil-Maya women may have assumed prominence in rioting as a result of a power vacuum caused by the death and sickness of many town leaders in 1798.

27. Such work echoes the sentiment expressed by Della M. Flusche and Eugene H. Korth in their research on colonial Chile, that the "unnamed . . . Araucanian [women] remembered primarily as ciphers in . . . the report of a government inspector had little in common with an Inca princess-gobernadora"; *Forgotten Females: Women of African and Indian Descent in Colonial Chile, 1535–1800* (Detroit: Blaine Ethridge, 1983), 68. See also Ana Luisa Izquierdo, "Tasación de la cacica de Gueytlalpa," *Estudios de Cultura Maya*

14 (1982): 289–98; Udo Oberem, "Un ejemplo de auto-valoración social entre la alta nobleza indígena de Quito colonial," *Miscelánea Antropológica Ecuatoriana* 2:2 (1982): 125–34, which presents a facsimile letter of an elite Inca woman of 1611; and fray Juan de Betanzos, *Suma y narración de los incas*, ed. María del Carmen Martín Rubio (Madrid: Ediciones Atlas, 1987), an Andean chronicle of 1551 that is based on the testimony of a woman descended from Yanque Yupanqui, a pre-Hispanic Inca king.

28. See also Kellogg, *Law and the Transformation of Aztec Culture*, esp. chaps. 3 and 4.

29. Elinor C. Burkett, "Indian Women and White Society: The Case of Sixteenth-Century Peru," in *Latin American Women*, ed. Asunción Lavrin, 101–28. See also Frank Salomon, "Indian Women of Early Colonial Quito as Seen through Their Testaments," *The Americas* 44:3 (January 1988): 325–41; and Zulawski, "Social Differentiation, Gender, and Ethnicity," 93–113.

30. For instance, Kellogg, *Law and the Transformation of Aztec Culture*, 158–59, has identified a weakening of gender parallelism among Aztec women in seventeenth-century Mexico City. Juan Javier Pescador, "Vanishing Woman: Female Migration and Ethnic Identity in Late-Colonial Mexico City," *Ethnohistory* 42:4 (1995): 617–26; quote on p. 617.

31. Burkett, "Indian Women and White Society," stresses that whereas under the Inca women did not have to provide labor service, the colonial system did require them to work. Widows also encountered new obligations to produce goods and services under the Spanish system in Peru, at least until tribute laws were relaxed. For similar conclusions, see Restall, "'He Wished It in Vain,'" 583.

32. Clendinnen, "Yucatec Maya Women." She also recalls an intriguing economic theory that women's status increases with "nondomestic" production—a theory that seems to have grown out of the "Western" world's experience and has yet to be proven for other cultures (p. 433). See also Beatríz Castilla and Alejandra García, "El Yucatán colonial. Mujeres telares y paties," *Revista de la Universidad de Yucatán* 22 (1981): 146–80.

33. In frontier regions missionaries may have had a greater opportunity to push assimilationist policies in the areas of "education, land ownership, and religion" which "called for aligning Indian gender roles to fit Euro-American expectations and intended to restructure the extended family into a patriarchal, nuclear unit," as Shoemaker, *Negotiators of Change*, 9–10, suggests for populations inhabiting what is now called the United States.

34. In fact, a recent article suggests that over time Tlaxcalan colonies did incorporate indigenous people of different ethnicities and cultural backgrounds. See Andrea Martínez Baracs, "Colonizaciones tlaxcaltecas," *Historia Mexicana* 43:2 (1993): 195–250.

35. Silverblatt raises this kind of challenge in "Lessons of Gender and Ethnohistory."

36. Ruth Behar, "Introduction—Women Writing Culture: Another Telling of the Story of American Anthropology," *Critique of Anthropology* 13:4 (1993): 307–25; see esp. pp. 309–10.

37. For suggestions that it did, see two recent studies of urban indigenous women of the late colonial Andean region: Luis Miguel Glave Testino, "Mujer indígena, trabajo doméstico, y cambio social en el virreinato peruano del siglo XVII. La ciudad de La Paz y el sur andino en 1684," *Bulletin de l'Institut Français d'Etudes Andines* 16:3–4 (1987): 39–69; and Zulawski, "Social Differentiation, Gender, and Ethnicity." Both indict Spanish colonialism and show a heightened awareness of the importance of class differences, along with rural and urban distinctions.

38. For example, see Clara Sue Kidwell, "Indian Women as Cultural Mediators," *Ethnohistory* 39:2 (1992): 97–107, whose primary interest is with the peoples occupying what is now the United States.

39. For suggestive work in this area, see Elinor C. Burkett, "In Dubious Sisterhood: Race and Class in Spanish Colonial America," *Latin American Perspectives* 4:12 (1979): 13–26.

40. Flusche and Korth, *Forgotten Females*, 68.

41. For further reading on the domestic/public spheres, see the early theoretical discussions in Michelle Z. Rosaldo and Louise Lamphere, eds., *Woman, Culture, and Society* (Stanford: Stanford University Press, 1974), and, for an example of more recent revisionism, Holly F. Matthews, "'We Are Mayordomo': A Reinterpretation of Women's Roles in the Mexican Cargo System," *American Ethnologist* 12:2 (1985): 285–301. Matthews writes, for instance, "that a major consequence of *not* using the domestic/public model is the opportunity to move beyond static, oppositional analyses to look, instead, at the ways in which male and female roles interrelate and function in specific contexts" (p. 288). Regarding community and individual, Eleanor Leacock's argument that gender complementarity rested in part on the "basic principle of individual autonomy" that most North American indigenous cultures shared (paraphrased by Shoemaker, *Negotiators of Change*, 7) provides grist for the mill. Sousa's discussion, chapter 9 in this volume, of the Western concept of family points to another area of Mesoamerican social organization worthy of rethinking and one that might have links to a reexamination of individual and community.

42. Clendinnen, "Yucatec Maya Women," 435.

43. Martha Few, "Women, Religion, and Power: Gender and Resistance in Daily Life in Late-Seventeenth-Century Santiago de Guatemala," *Ethnohistory* 42:4 (1995): 627–37; quote on p. 633.

44. Some interesting cultural patterns found in the material possessions of indigenous women and men are discussed in S. L. Cline, *Colonial
Culhuacan, 1580–1600: A Social History of an Aztec Town* (Albuquerque: University of New Mexico Press, 1986); and Robert Haskett, "Living in Two
Worlds: Cultural Continuity and Change among Cuernavaca's Colonial Indigenous Ruling Elite," *Ethnohistory* 35:1 (Winter 1988): 34–59, and *Indigenous Rulers: An Ethnohistory of Town Government in Colonial Cuernavaca* (Albuquerque: University of New Mexico Press, 1991), esp. pp. 161–95.

Bibliography

Acosta, José de. *The Natural and Moral History of the Indies*. Vol. 2. New York: Burt Franklin, 1963.

Adas, Michael. "'Moral Economy' or 'Contest State'? Elite Demands and the Origins of Peasant Protest in Southeast Asia." *Journal of Social History* 13 (1980): 521–40.

Adorno, Rolena. "Reconsidering Colonial Discourse for Sixteenth- and Seventeenth-Century Spanish America." *Latin American Research Review* 28:3 (1993): 135–45.

Alaperrine-Bouyer, Monique. "Des femmes dans le Manuscrit de Huarochirí." *Bulletin de l'Institut Français d'Etudes Andines* 16 (1987): 3–4.

Alberro, Solange. *Inquisición y sociedad en México, 1571–1700*. México: Fondo de Cultura Económica, 1988.

Alessio Robles, Vito. [1938]. *Coahuila y Texas en la época colonial*. México: Editorial Porrúa, 1978.

Allen, Paula Gunn. *The Sacred Hoop: Recovering the Feminine in American Indian Traditions*. Boston: Beacon Press, 1986.

Almada, Francisco R. *Resumen de historia del estado de Chihuahua*. Chihuahua: Ediciones del Gobierno del Estado de Chihuahua, 1986.

Alonso, Ana María. *Thread of Blood: Colonialism, Revolution, and Gender on Mexico's Northern Frontier*. Tucson: University of Arizona Press, 1995.

Altman, Ida, and James Lockhart, eds. *Provinces of Early Mexico: Variants of Spanish American Regional Evolution*. Los Angeles: UCLA Latin American Center, 1976.

Alva Ixtlilxochitl, Fernando de. *Obras históricas*. 2 vols. Edited by Edmundo O'Gorman. México: Universidad Nacional Autónoma de México, 1975–77.

Alvarado, fray Francisco de. [1593]. *Vocabulario en lengua mixteca*. Edited by Wigberto Jiménez Moreno. México: Instituto Nacional de Antropología e Historia, 1962.

Alvarado Tezozomoc, Fernando. [1878]. *Crónica mexicana*. Edited by Manuel Orozco y Berra. México: Editorial Porrúa, 1975.

———. *Crónica mexicáyotl*. Translated by Adrián León. México: Universidad Nacional Autónoma de México, 1949.

Alvarez, Salvador. "Tendencias regionales de la propiedad territorial en el norte de la Nueva España. Siglos XVII y XVIII." In *Actas del Segundo Congreso de Historia Regional Comparada*, 141–79. Ciudad Juárez: Universidad Autónoma de Ciudad Juárez, 1990.

Alvarez, Victor M. *Diccionario de conquistadores*. 2 vols. México: Instituto Nacional de Antropología e Historia, 1975.

Anawalt, Patricia Rieff. *Indian Clothing before Cortés: Mesoamerican Costumes from the Codices*. Norman: University of Oklahoma Press, 1981.

Anderson, Arthur J. O., Frances Berdan, and James Lockhart, eds. and trans. *Beyond the Codices*. Berkeley: University of California Press, 1976.

Anderson, Arthur J. O., and Susan Schroeder, eds. and trans. *Don Domingo de San Antón Muñón Chimalpahin Quauhtlehuanitzin, Society and Politics in Mexico Tenochtitlan, Tlatelolco, Texcoco, Culhuacan, and Other Nahua Altepetl in Central Mexico*. In *Codex Chimalpahin: Collected Works*, vols. 1 and 2, gen. ed. Susan Schroeder. Norman: University of Oklahoma Press, 1997.

Antón, Ferdinand. *La mujer en América antigua*. México: Editorial Extemporáneos, 1975.

Anunciación, fray Juan de la. *Sermonario en lengva mexicana*. México: Antonio Ricardo, 1577.

Arrom, Silvia. "Changes in Mexican Family Law in the Nineteenth Century: The Civil Codes of 1870 and 1884." *Journal of Family History* 10:3 (Fall 1985): 305–17.

———. *The Women of Mexico City, 1790–1857*. Stanford: Stanford University Press, 1985.

Atondo Rodríguez, Ana María. *El amor venal y la condición femenina en el México colonial*. México: Instituto Nacional de Antropología e Historia, 1992.

Aveni, Anthony F., and Gary Urton, eds. *Ethnoastronomy and Archaeoastronomy in the American Tropics*. New York: Annals of the New York Academy of Sciences, vol. 385, 1982.

Bary, Leslie, Janet Gold, Marketta Laurila, Arnulfo Ramírez, Joseph Ricapito, and Jesús Torrecilla, eds. *Rediscovering America, 1492–1992: National, Cultural, and Disciplinary Boundaries Re-examined.* Baton Rouge: Louisiana State University Press, 1992.

Bataille, Gretchen M., and Kathleen M. Sands, eds. *American Indian Women: A Guide to Research.* New York: Garland Press, 1991.

Bauer, Arnold J. "Millers and Grinders: Technology and Household Economy in Meso-America." *Agricultural History* 64:1 (1990): 1–17.

————, ed. *La iglesia en la economía de América latina siglos XVI al XIX.* México: Instituto Nacional de Antropología e Historia, 1986.

Bautista, fray Juan. *Huehuetlatolli.* México, 1600.

————. *Huehuehtlahtolli. Que contiene las pláticas que los padres y madres hicieron a sus hijos, y los Señores a sus uasallos, todas llenas de doctrina moral y política.* Edited by Miguel León-Portilla, translated by Librado Silva Galeana. México: Comisión Nacional Conmemorativa del V Centenario del Encuentro de Dos Mundos, 1988. Facsimile of the original 1600 edition.

Beals, Ralph. "Unilateral Organizations in Mexico," *American Anthropologist* 34 (1932): 467–75.

Beezley, William H., and Judith Ewell, eds. *The Human Tradition in Latin America: The Twentieth Century.* Wilmington, Del.: Scholarly Resources, 1987.

Beezley, William H., Cheryl English Martin, and William E. French, eds. *Rituals of Rule, Rituals of Resistance: Public Celebrations and Popular Culture in Mexico.* Wilmington, Del.: Scholarly Resources, 1994.

Behar, Ruth. "Introduction—Women Writing Culture: Another Telling of the Story of American Anthropology." *Critique of Anthropology* 13:4 (1993): 307–25.

————. *Santa María del Monte: The Presence of the Past in a Spanish Village.* Princeton: Princeton University Press, 1986.

————. "Sex and Sin: Witchcraft and the Devil in Late Colonial Mexico." *American Ethnologist* 14:1 (1987): 34–54.

————. "Sexual Witchcraft, Colonialism, and Women's Powers: Views from the Mexican Inquisition." In *Sexuality and Marriage in Colonial Latin America,* edited by Asunción Lavrin, 178–206. Lincoln: University of Nebraska Press, 1989.

————. "The Visions of a Guachichil Witch in 1599: A Window on the Subjugation of Mexico's Hunter-Gatherers." *Ethnohistory* 34:2 (Spring 1987): 115–38.

Benítez, Fernando. *The Century after Cortés.* Chicago: University of Chicago Press, 1965.

Berdan, Frances F. "Cotton in Aztec Mexico: Production, Distribution, and Uses." *Mexican Studies/Estudios Mexicanos* 3 (1987): 235–62.

Berdan, Frances F., and Patricia Rieff Anawalt, eds. *The Codex Mendoza*. 4 vols. Berkeley: University of California Press, 1992.

Berlo, Janet Catherine, ed. *Text and Image in Pre-Columbian Art: Essays on the Interrelationship of the Verbal and Visual Arts*. Oxford: British Archaeological Reports Press, 1983.

Bernal de Bugeda, Beatríz. "Situación jurídica de la mujer en las Indias Occidentales." In *Condición jurídica de la mujer en México*, edited by Sara Bialostosky de Chazán, 21–40. México: Universidad Nacional Autónoma de México, Facultad de Derecho, 1975.

Betanzos, fray Juan de. *Suma y narración de los incas*. Edited by María del Carmen Martín Rubio. Madrid: Ediciones Atlas, 1987.

Bialostosky de Chazán, Sara, ed. *Condición jurídica de la mujer en México*. México: Universidad Nacional Autónoma de México, Facultad de Derecho, 1975.

Bierhorst, John, trans. *Cantares mexicanos: Songs of the Aztecs*. Stanford: Stanford University Press, 1985.

————, ed. and trans. *History and Mythology of the Aztecs: The Codex Chimalpopoca*. Tucson: University of Arizona Press, 1992.

Bilinkoff, Jodi. *The Avila of Saint Teresa: Religious Reform in a Sixteenth-Century City*. Ithaca: Cornell University Press, 1989.

Blom, Frans. *The Conquest of Yucatan*. New York: Houghton Mifflin, 1936.

Bohstedt, John. "The Moral Economy and the Discipline of Historical Context." *Journal of Social History* 25 (1992): 265–81.

Boone, Elizabeth H., ed. *The Art and Iconography of Late Post-Classic Central Mexico*. Washington, D.C.: Dumbarton Oaks, 1982.

————, ed. *Ritual Human Sacrifice in Mesoamerica*. Washington, D.C.: Dumbarton Oaks, 1984.

Boone, Elizabeth H., and Zelia Nuttall. *The Codex Magliabechiano*. Berkeley: University of California Press, 1983.

Borah, Woodrow. *Justice by Insurance: The General Indian Court of Colonial Mexico and the Legal Aides of the Half-Real*. Berkeley: University of California Press, 1983.

Boyer, Richard. *Lives of the Bigamists: Marriage, Family, and Community in Colonial Mexico*. Albuquerque: University of New Mexico Press, 1995.

————. "Women, *La Mala Vida*, and the Politics of Marriage." In *Sexuality and Marriage in Colonial Latin America*, edited by Asunción Lavrin, 252–86. Lincoln: University of Nebraska Press, 1989.

Brandes, Stanley H. "The Structural and Demographic Implications of Nicknames in Navanogal, Spain." *American Ethnologist*, 2:1 (1975): 139–48.

Brenner, Anita. *The Boy Who Could Do Anything & Other Mexican Folk Tales*. New York: William R. Scott, 1942.

Bricker, Victoria Reifler. *The Indian Christ, the Indian King: The Historical Substrate of Maya Myth and Ritual*. Austin: University of Texas Press, 1981.

Brown, Betty Ann. "Ochpaniztli in Historical Perspective." In *Ritual Human Sacrifice in Mesoamerica*, edited by Elizabeth H. Boone, 195–210. Washington, D.C.: Dumbarton Oaks, 1984.

————. "Seen but Not Heard: Women in Aztec Ritual—The Sahagún Texts." In *Text and Image in Pre-Columbian Art: Essays on the Interrelationship of the Verbal and Visual Arts*, edited by Janet Catherine Berlo, 119–53. Oxford: British Archaeological Reports Press, 1983.

Brumfiel, Elizabeth M. "Weaving and Cooking: Women's Production in Aztec Mexico." In *Engendering Archaeology: Women and Prehistory*, edited by Joan M. Gero and Margaret W. Conkey, 224–51. Cambridge, Mass.: Basil Blackwell, 1991.

Burgos-Debray, Elisabeth. *I . . . Rigoberta Menchú: An Indian Woman in Guatemala*. London: Verso, 1984.

Burkett, Elinor C. "In Dubious Sisterhood: Race and Class in Spanish Colonial America." *Latin American Perspectives* 4:12 (1979): 13–26.

————. "Indian Women and White Society: The Case of Sixteenth-Century Peru." In *Latin American Women: Historical Perspectives*, edited by Asunción Lavrin, 101–28. Westport, Conn.: Greenwood Press, 1978.

Burkhart, Louise M. "The Amanuenses Have Appropriated the Text: Interpreting a Nahuatl Song of Santiago." In *On the Translation of Native American Literatures*, edited by Brian Swann, 339–55. Washington, D.C.: Smithsonian Institution Press, 1992.

————. "Flowery Heaven: The Aesthetic of Paradise in Nahuatl Devotional Literature." *Res: Anthropology and Aesthetics* 21:88–109.

————. *Holy Wednesday: A Nahua Drama from Early Colonial Mexico*. Philadelphia: University of Pennsylvania Press, 1996.

————. "Moral Deviance in Sixteenth-Century Nahua and Christian Thought: The Rabbit and the Deer." *Journal of Latin American Lore* 12 (1986): 107–39.

————. "Mujeres mexicas en 'el frente' del hogar. Trabajo doméstico y religión en el México azteca." *Mesoamérica Antigua* 12:23 (1992): 23–54.

————. *The Slippery Earth: Nahua-Christian Moral Dialogue in Sixteenth-Century Mexico*. Tucson: University of Arizona Press, 1989.

Calero, V. "Aguilar y la Malinche." In *Registro yucateco: Periódico literario*. Mérida, Yucatan: Imprente de Castillo y Compañía, 1845.

Calnek, Edward. "The Calmecac and Telpochcalli in Pre-Conquest Tenochtitlan." In *The Work of Bernardino de Sahagún: Pioneer Ethnographer of Sixteenth-Century Aztec Mexico*, edited by J. Jorge Klor de Alva, H. B. Nicholson, and Eloise Quiñones Keber, 169–77. Albany: State University of New York, Institute for Mesoamerican Studies, 1988.

———. "Kinship, Settlement Patterns, and Domestic Groups in Tenochtitlan." Unpublished manuscript.

———. "The Sahagún Texts as a Source of Sociological Information." In *Sixteenth-Century Mexico: The Work of Sahagún*, edited by Munro S. Edmonson, 189–204. Albuquerque: University of New Mexico Press, 1974.

Calvo, Thomas. *Poder, religión y sociedad en la Guadalajara del siglo XVII.* México: CEMCA/Ayuntamiento de Guadalajara, 1992.

Campbell, Leon G. "Women and the Great Rebellion in Peru, 1780–1783." *The Americas* 42:2 (1985): 163–96.

Campbell, Ysla, ed. *El contacto entre los españoles e indígenas en el norte de la Nueva España.* Vol. 4: *Colección conmemorativa quinto centenario del encuentro de dos mundos.* Ciudad Juárez: Universidad Autónoma de Ciudad Juárez, 1992.

Carochi, Horacio. [1645]. *Arte de la lengua mexicana.* México: Universidad Nacional Autónoma de México, 1983.

Carrasco, Pedro. "Royal Marriages in Ancient Mexico." In *Explorations in Ethnohistory: Indians of Central Mexico in the Sixteenth Century*, edited by H. R. Harvey and Hanns J. Prem, 41–81. Albuquerque: University of New Mexico Press, 1984.

———. "Social Organization of Ancient Mexico." In *Handbook of Middle American Indians*, gen. ed. Robert Wauchope, vol. 10: *Archaeology of Northern Mesoamerica*, pt. 1, edited by Gordon F. Ekholm and Ignacio Bernal, 349–75. Austin: University of Texas Press, 1971.

Carrasco, Pedro, and Jesús Monjarás-Ruiz, eds. *Colección de documentos sobre Coyoacan.* 2 vols. México: Instituto Nacional de Antropología e Historia, 1976–78.

Castilla, Beatríz, and Alejandra García. "El Yucatán colonial. Mujeres telares y paties." *Revista de la Universidad de Yucatán* 22 (1981): 146–80.

Cervantes, Fernando. *The Devil in the New World: The Impact of Diabolism in New Spain.* New Haven: Yale University Press, 1994.

Cevallos-Candau, Francisco Javier, Jeffrey A. Cole, Nina M. Scott, and Nicomedes Suárez-Araúz, eds. *Coded Encounters: Writing, Gender, and Ethnicity in Colonial Latin America.* Amherst: University of Massachusetts, 1994.

Chamberlain, Robert S. *The Conquest and Colonization of Yucatan: 1517–1550.* Pub. 582. Washington, D.C.: Carnegie Institute, 1948.

Chance, John K. "The Urban Indian in Colonial Oaxaca." *American Ethnologist* 3:4 (1976): 603–32.

Chávez Orozco, Luis, ed. *Códice Osuna.* México: Ediciones del Instituto Indigenista Interamericano, 1947.

Chimalpahin Quauhtlehuanitzin, don Domingo de San Antón Muñón. *Annales.* Translated by Rémi Siméon. Paris, 1889.

———. *Society and Politics in Mexico Tenochtitlan, Tlatelolco, Texcoco, Culhuacan, and Other Nahua Altepetl in Central Mexico*, edited and translated by Arthur J. O. Anderson and Susan Schroeder. Vols. 1 and 2 of *Codex Chimalpahin*. 6 vols. General editor Susan Schroeder. Norman: University of Oklahoma Press, 1997.

Christian, William A., Jr. *Apparitions in Late Medieval and Renaissance Spain.* Princeton: Princeton University Press, 1981.

Clark, James Cooper, ed. [ca. 1540s]. *Codex Mendoza.* London: Waterlow & Sons, 1938.

Claassen, Cheryl, ed. *Exploring Gender through Archaeology: Selected Papers from the 1991 Boone Conference.* Madison: Prehistory Press, 1992.

Clavijero, Francisco Javier. [1780]. *Historia antigua de México.* Edited by Mariano Cuevas. México: Editorial Porrúa, 1971.

Clendinnen, Inga. *Ambivalent Conquests: Maya and Spaniard in Yucatan, 1517–1570.* Cambridge: Cambridge University Press, 1987.

———. *Aztecs: An Interpretation.* Cambridge: Cambridge University Press, 1991.

———. "Yucatec Maya Women and the Spanish Conquest: Role and Ritual in Historical Reconstruction." *Journal of Social History* 15 (1982): 427–42.

Clifton, James A. *Being and Becoming Indian: Biographical Studies of North American Frontiers.* Chicago: Dorsey Press, 1989.

Cline, Howard F. "Hernando Cortés and the Aztec Indians in Spain." *Quarterly Journal of the Library of Congress* 26 (1969): 70–90.

———, ed. *Guide to Ethnohistorical Sources.* Vols. 14 and 15 of *Handbook of Middle American Indians*, gen. ed. Robert Wauchope. Austin: University of Texas Press, 1975.

Cline, S. L. *Colonial Culhuacan, 1580–1600: A Social History of an Aztec Town.* Albuquerque: University of New Mexico Press, 1986.

———. "The Spiritual Conquest Reexamined: Baptism and Christian Marriage in Early Sixteenth-Century Mexico." *Hispanic American Historical Review* 73:3 (1993): 453–80.

———, ed. and trans. *The Book of Tributes: Early Sixteenth-Century Nahuatl Censuses from Morelos.* Nahuatl Studies Series, no. 4. Los Angeles: UCLA Latin American Center, 1993.

Cline, S. L., and Miguel León-Portilla. *The Testaments of Culhuacan.* Nahuatl Studies Series, no. 1. Los Angeles: UCLA Latin American Center, 1984.

Codex Borbonicus. Códice Borbónico. Edited by Francisco del Paso y Troncoso. Facsimile of 1898 Florence edition. México: Siglo Veintiuno, 1979.

Códice Osuna. [ca. 1560s]. *Códice Osuna. Reproducción facsimilar de la obra del mismo título, editada en Madrid, 1878.* Edited by Luis Chávez Orozco. México: Ediciones del Instituto Indigenista Interamericano, 1947.

Cody, Cheryll Ann. "Naming, Kinship, and Estate Dispersal: Notes on Slave Family Life on a South Carolina Plantation, 1786 to 1833." *William and Mary Quarterly* 39:1 (1982): 192–211.

Collier, George A., and Victoria R. Bricker. "Nicknames and Social Structure in Zinacantan." *American Anthropologist* 72:2 (1970): 289–302.

Collier, Jane Fishburne, and Sylvia Junko Yanagisako. "Toward a Unified Analysis of Gender and Kinship." In *Gender and Kinship: Essays Toward a Unified Analysis*, edited by Jane Fishburne Collier and Sylvia Junko Yanagisako, 20–25. Stanford: Stanford University Press, 1987.

———, eds. *Gender and Kinship: Essays Toward a Unified Analysis.* Stanford: Stanford University Press, 1987.

Comaroff, John L. "*Sui genderis:* Feminism, Kinship Theory, and Structural 'Domains.'" In *Gender and Kinship: Essays Toward a Unified Analysis*, edited by Jane Fishburne Collier and Sylvia Junko Yanagisako, 53–85. Stanford: Stanford University Press, 1987.

Comaroff, John, and Jean Comaroff. *Ethnography and the Historical Imagination.* Boulder, Colo.: Westview Press, 1992.

Conway, George R. *La noche triste, documentos. Segura de la frontera en Nueva España, año de MDXX.* México: Antigua Librería Robredo, de José Porrúa e Hijos, 1943.

Cook, Sherbourne F., and Woodrow Borah. *Essays in Population History: Mexico and the Caribbean.* 2 vols. Berkeley: University of California Press, 1974.

Cope, R. Douglas. *The Limits of Racial Domination: Plebeian Society in Colonial Mexico City, 1660–1720.* Madison: University of Wisconsin Press, 1994.

Cordova, fray Juan de. [1578]. *Vocabulario en lengua çapoteca.* México: Ediciones Toledo, Instituto Nacional de Antropología e Historia, 1987.

Cordry, Donald. *Mexican Masks.* Austin: University of Texas Press, 1980.

Correas, Gonzalo. *Vocabulario de refranes.* Madrid: Revista de Archivos, Bibliotecas y Museos, 1924.

Cortés, Hernando. [1519–26]. *Cartas de relación de la conquista de Méjico.* 2 vols. Madrid: Espasa-Calpe, 1932.

Couturier, Edith. "Women and the Family in Eighteenth-Century Mexico: Law and Practice." *Journal of Family History* 10:3 (Fall 1985): 305–17.

Cuello, José. "Saltillo in the Seventeenth Century: Local Society on the North Mexican Frontier." Ph.D. dissertation, University of California, Berkeley, 1982.

Cypess, Sandra Messinger. *La Malinche in Mexican Literature: From History to Myth.* Austin: University of Texas Press, 1991.

Darnton, Robert. "Cherchez la Femme," *New York Review of Books* 42:13 (1995): 22–24.

Dash, Robert C., ed. *Mesoamerican and Chicano Art, Culture, and Identity/El arte, la cultura, y la identidad mesoamericana y chicana*. Salem, Ore.: Williamette Journal of the Liberal Arts, supp. series, no. 6 (1994): 78–103.

Davis, Natalie Zemon. "Iroquois Women, European Women." In *Women, "Race," and Writing in the Early Modern Period*, edited by Margo Hendricks and Patricia Parker, 243–58, 350–61. London: Routledge, 1994.

Deeds, Susan. "Algunos aspectos de la historia demográfica de las misiones de los jesuitas en Topia, Tepehuana y Tarahumara Baja." Paper presented at the IV Congreso de Historia Regional Comparada, Ciudad Juárez, 1994.

——— "Defiance and Deference in Mexico's Colonial North: Indians under Spanish Rule in Nueva Vizcaya." Unpublished Manuscript.

———. "Ethnicity and Identity in Nueva Vizcaya." Paper presented at the IX Reunión de Historiadores Mexicanos y Norteamericanos, Mexico City, 1994.

———. "Legacies of Resistance, Adaptation and Tenacity: History of the Native Peoples of Northwest Mexico." In *Cambridge History of the Native Peoples of the Americas*, edited by Murdo J. MacLeod. Cambridge: Cambridge University Press, forthcoming.

——— "Mission Villages and Agrarian Patterns in a Nueva Vizcayan Heartland, 1600–1750." *Journal of the Southwest* 33:3 (Autumn 1991): 345–65.

——— "Las rebeliones de los tepehuanes y tarahumaras durante el siglo XVII en la Nueva Vizcaya." In *El contacto entre los españoles e indígenas en el norte de la Nueva España*. Vol. 4: *Colección conmemorativa quinto centenario del encuentro de dos mundos*, edited by Ysla Campbell, 9–40. Ciudad Juárez: Universidad Autónoma de Ciudad Juárez, 1992.

———. "Rural Work in Nueva Vizcaya: Forms of Labor Coercion on the Periphery." *Hispanic American Historical Review*, 69:3 (August 1989): 425–49.

———. "Indigenous Responses to Mission Settlement in Nueva Vizcaya." In *The New Latin American Mission History*, edited by Erick Langer and Robert H. Jackson, 77–108. Lincoln: University of Nebraska Press, 1995.

de Jong, Lotte. "Community Discourse: A Family Conflict in Eighteenth-Century Coyotepec, Oaxaca." In *The Indian Community of Colonial Mexico: Fifteen Essays on Land Tenure, Corporate Organizations, Ideology, and Village Politics*, edited by Arij Ouweneel and Simon Miller, 250–69. Amsterdam: Center for Latin American Research and Documentation (CEDLA), 1990.

Devens, Carol. *Countering Colonization: Native American Women and Great Lakes Missions, 1630–1900*. Berkeley: University of California Press, 1992.

Díaz del Castillo, Bernal. *The Discovery and Conquest of Mexico*. New York: Farrar, Straus, and Giroux, 1956.

———. *Historia verdadera de la conquista de la Nueva España*, 2 vols. México: Editorial Porrúa, 1955.

Díaz Infante, Fernando. *La educación de los aztecas.* México: Panorama Editorial, 1982.

Dibble, Charles E. "The Nahuatlization of Christianity." In *Sixteenth-Century Mexico: The Work of Sahagún,* edited by Munro S. Edmonson, 225–33. Albuquerque: University of New Mexico Press, 1974.

Diccionario Porrúa: Historia, biografía y geografía de México. 5th ed. México: Editorial Porrúa, 1964.

di Leonardo, Micaela, ed. *Gender at the Crossroads of Knowledge: Feminist Anthropology in the Postmodern Era.* Berkeley: University of California Press, 1991.

Dillard, Heath. *Daughters of the Reconquest: Women in Castilian Town Society, 1100–1300.* London: Cambridge University Press, 1984.

Dumas, David W. "The Naming of Children in New England, 1780–1850." *New England Historical and Genealogical Register* 132 (1978): 196–210.

Dunn, Alvis. "A Cry at Daybreak: Death, Disease, and Defense of Community in a Highland Ixil-Maya Village." *Ethnohistory* 42:4 (1995): 595–606.

Dupaquier, Jacques. "Naming-Practices, Godparenthood, and Kinship in the Vexin, 1540–1900." *Journal of Family History* 6:2 (1981): 135–55.

Durán, fray Diego. *Aztecs: The History of the Indies of New Spain.* Edited and translated by Doris Heyden and Fernando Horcasitas. New York: Orion Press, 1964.

———. *Book of the Gods and Rites and the Ancient Calendar.* Edited and translated by Fernando Horcasitas and Doris Heyden. Norman: University of Oklahoma Press, 1971.

———. [1570–79]. *Historia de las indias de Nueva España e islas de Tierra Firme.* 2 vols. Edited by Angel María Garibay K. México: Editorial Porrúa, 1967.

———. *The History of the Indies of New Spain.* Edited and translated by Doris Heyden. Norman: University of Oklahoma Press, 1994.

Edmonson, Munro S. "Introduction." In *Sixteenth-Century Mexico: The Work of Sahagún,* edited by Munro S. Edmonson, 4–15. Albuquerque: University of New Mexico Press, 1974.

———, ed. *Sixteenth-Century Mexico: The Work of Sahagún.* Albuquerque: University of New Mexico Press, 1974.

Elphick, Richard. *Kraal and Castle: Khoikhoi and the Founding of White South Africa.* New Haven: Yale University Press, 1977.

Engels, Frederick, ed. *Origins of the Family, Private Property, and the State.* New York: International Publishers, 1972.

Etienne, Mona, and Eleanor Leacock. "Introduction." In *Women and Colonization: Anthropological Perspectives,* edited by Mona Etienne and Eleanor Leacock, 1–24. New York: Praeger, 1980.

———, eds. *Women and Colonization: Anthropological Perspectives.* New York: Praeger, 1980.

Farriss, Nancy M. *Maya Society under Colonial Rule: The Collective Enterprise of Survival.* Princeton: Princeton University Press, 1984.

Fernández de Recas, Guillermo S. *Cacicazgos y nobiliario indígena de la Nueva España.* Instituto Bibliográfico Mexicano, no. 5. México: Biblioteca Nacional de México, 1961.

Few, Martha. "Women, Religion, and Power: Gender and Resistance in Daily Life in Late-Seventeenth-Century Santiago de Guatemala," *Ethnohistory* 42:4 (1995): 627–37.

Flusche, Della M., and Eugene H. Korth. *Forgotten Females: Women of African and Indian Descent in Colonial Chile, 1535–1800.* Detroit: Blaine Ethridge, 1983.

Fowler-Salamini, Heather, and Mary Kay Vaughan, eds. *Women in the Mexican Countryside, 1850–1990.* Tucson: University of Arizona Press, 1994.

Fox, James A., and John S. Justeson. "Classic Maya Dynastic Alliance and Succession." In *Supplement to the Handbook of Middle American Indians: Ethnohistory,* edited by Ronald Spores, 7–34. Austin: University of Texas Press, 1986.

Friedlander, Judith. "Doña Zeferina Barreto: Biographical Sketch of an Indian Woman from the State of Morelos." In *Women in the Mexican Countryside, 1850–1990,* edited by Heather Fowler-Salamini and Mary Kay Vaughan, 125–39. Tucson: University of Arizona Press, 1994.

Fuentes, Patricia de, ed. and trans. *The Conquistadors: First-Person Accounts of the Conquest of Mexico.* New York: Orion Press, 1963.

Gailey, Christine Ward. *From Kinship to Kingship: Gender Hierarchy and State Formation in the Tongan Islands.* Austin: University of Texas Press, 1987.

Gallagher, Ann Miriam. "The Indian Nuns of Mexico City's *Monasterio* of Corpus Christi, 1724–1821." In *Latin American Women: Historical Perspectives,* edited by Asunción Lavrin, 150–72. Westport, Conn.: Greenwood Press, 1978.

Gante, fray Pedro de. [1553]. *Doctrina cristiana en lengua mexicana.* México: Centro de Estudios Históricos Fray Bernardino de Sahagún, 1981.

García, Genero, ed. *Bernal Díaz del Castillo: The Discovery and Conquest of Mexico.* Translated by A. P. Maudslay. New York: Farrar, Straus and Giroux, 1970.

García Figueroa, F., ed. *Documentos para la historia de México.* 4th series. México: Imprenta de J. R. Navarro, 1853–57.

García Granados, Rafael. *Diccionario biográfico de la historia antigua de México,* 3 vols. México: Universidad Nacional Autónoma de México, 1952–53.

García Icazbalceta, Joaquín, ed. *Nueva colección de documentos para la historia de México.* México: Imprenta de Francisco Díaz de León, 1891.

Garibay K., Angel María, ed. "Códice carolino. Manuscrito anónimo del siglo XVI." *Estudios de Cultura Náhuatl* 7 (1967): 11–58.

———. *Teogonía e historia de los mexicanos. Tres opúsculos del siglo XVI.* México: Editorial Porrúa, 1979.

Garza Tarazona de González, Silvia. *La mujer mesoamericana*. México: Editorial Planeta Mexicana, 1991.

Gauderman, Kimberly. "Father Fiction: The Construction of Gender in England, Spain, and the Andes." *UCLA Historical Journal, Special Issue: Indigenous Writing in the Spanish Indies* 12 (1992): 122–51.

Geertz, Clifford, "Life on the Edge." *New York Review of Books* 41:7 (April 7, 1995): 3–4.

Gerhard, Peter. *Geografía histórica de la Nueva España, 1519–1821*. México: Universidad Nacional Autónoma de México, 1986.

———. *A Guide to the Historical Geography of New Spain*. Cambridge: Cambridge University Press, 1972.

———. *The North Frontier of New Spain*. Rev. ed. Norman: University of Oklahoma Press, 1993.

Gero, Joan M., and Margaret W. Conkey, eds. *Engendering Archaeology: Women and Prehistory*. Cambridge, Mass.: Basil Blackwell, 1991.

Gibson, Charles. *The Aztecs under Spanish Rule: A History of the Indians of the Valley of Mexico, 1519–1810*. Stanford: Stanford University Press, 1964.

———. [1952]. *Tlaxcala in the Sixteenth Century*. Stanford: Stanford University Press, 1967.

Gillespie, Susan D. *The Aztec Kings: The Construction of Rulership in Mexica History*. Tucson: University of Arizona Press, 1989.

Glave Testino, Luis Miguel. "Mujer indígena, trabajo doméstico, y cambio social en el virreinato peruano del siglo XVII. La ciudad de La Paz y el sur andino en 1684." *Bulletin de l'Institut Français d'Etudes Andines* 16:3–4 (1987): 39–69.

Gómez de Cervantes, Gonzalo. [1599]. *La vida económica y social de la Nueva España al finalizar del siglo XVI*. México: Antigua Librería Robredo de J. Porrúa e Hijos, 1944.

Gonzalbo Aizpuro, Pilar. *Historia de la educación en la época colonial. El mundo indígena*. México: El Colegio de México, 1990.

———. *Las mujeres de la Nueva España: Educación y vida cotidiana*. México: El Colegio de México, 1987.

———, ed. 1991. *Familias novohispanas: Siglos XVI al XIX*. México: El Colegio de México.

Gonzáles Obregón, Luis. *Epoca colonial. México viejo, noticias históricas, tradiciones, leyendas y costumbres*. México: C. Bouret, 1900–03.

———. [1906–08]. *Rebeliones indígenas y precursores de la independencia mexicana en los siglos XVI, XVII, XVIII*. México: Ediciones Fuente Cultural, 1952.

González Rodríguez, Luis, ed. *Crónicas de la Sierra Tarahumara*. México: Secretaría de Educación Pública, 1984.

Gosner, Kevin. *Soldiers of the Virgin: The Moral Economy of a Colonial Maya Rebellion*. Tucson: University of Arizona Press, 1992.

Gosner, Kevin, and Deborah E. Kanter, eds. *Ethnohistory, Special Issue: Women, Power, and Resistance in Colonial Mesoamerica* 42:2 (1995).

Gramsci, Antonio. *Selections from Political Writings, 1921–26*. New York: International Publishers, 1978.

Green, Rayna. "Introduction." In *Native American Women: A Contextual Bibliography*, edited by Rayna Green, 1–17. Bloomington: Indiana University Press, 1983.

Gruzinski, Serge. "Indian Confraternities, Brotherhoods, and *Mayordomías* in Central New Spain." In *The Indian Community of Colonial Mexico: Fifteen Essays on Land Tenure, Corporate Organizations, Ideology, and Village Politics*. edited by Arij Ouweneel and Simon Miller, 205–23. Amsterdam: Center for Latin American Research and Documentation (CEDLA), 1990.

———. "Individualization and Acculturation: Confession among the Nahuas of Mexico from the Sixteenth to the Eighteenth Century." In *Sexuality and Marriage in Colonial Latin America*, edited by Asunción Lavrin, 96–117. Lincoln: University of Nebraska Press, 1989.

Guha, Ranajit. "Chandra's Death." *Subaltern Studies* 5 (1986): 135–65.

———. *Elementary Aspects of Peasant Insurgency in Colonial India*. Delhi: Oxford University Press, 1983.

Guthrie, Chester. "Riots in Seventeenth-Century Mexico City: A Study of Social and Economic Conditions." In *Greater America: Essays in Honor of Herbert Eugene Bolton*, edited by Adele Ogden and Engel Sluiter, 243–58. Berkeley: University of California Press, 1945.

Gutiérrez, Ramon A. "A Gendered History of the Conquest of America: A View from New Mexico." In *Gender Rhetorics: Postures on Dominance and Submission in History*, edited by Richard C. Trexler, 47–63. Binghamton, N.Y.: Medieval and Renaissance Texts and Studies, 1994.

———. *When Jesus Came, the Corn Mothers Went Away: Marriage, Sexuality, and Power in New Mexico, 1500–1846*. Stanford: Stanford University Press, 1991.

Gutman, Herbert G. *The Black Family in Slavery and Freedom, 1750–1925*. New York: Pantheon, 1976.

Hahner, June E. "Researching the History of Latin American Women: Past and Future Directions." *Revista Interamericana de Bibliografía/Inter-American Review of Bibliography* 33:4 (1983): 545–52.

Hamnett, Brian R. *Politics and Trade in Southern Mexico, 1750–1821*. Cambridge: Cambridge University Press, 1971.

Hanks, William F. *Referential Practice: Language and Lived Space among the Maya*. Chicago: University of Chicago Press, 1990.

Harvey, H. R., and Hanns J. Prem, eds. *Explorations in Ethnohistory: Indians of*

Central Mexico in the Sixteenth Century. Albuquerque: University of New Mexico Press, 1984.

Haskett, Robert. *Indigenous Rulers: An Ethnohistory of Town Government in Colonial Cuernavaca.* Albuquerque: University of New Mexico Press, 1991.

————. "Living in Two Worlds: Cultural Continuity and Change among Cuernavaca's Colonial Indigenous Ruling Elite." *Ethnohistory* 35:1 (Winter 1988): 34–59.

————. "'Not a Pastor, but a Wolf': Indigenous-Clergy Relations in Early Cuernavaca and Taxco." *The Americas* 50:3 (1994): 293–336.

————. "'Our Suffering with the Taxco Tribute': Involuntary Mine Labor and Indigenous Society in Central New Spain." *Hispanic American Historical Review* 71:3 (1991): 447–75.

Hassig, Ross. *Aztec Warfare: Imperial Expansion and Political Control.* Norman: University of Oklahoma Press, 1988.

————. *Trade, Tribute and Transportation: The Sixteenth-Century Political Economy of the Valley of Mexico.* Norman: University of Oklahoma Press, 1985.

Hauser, Raymond E. "The *Berdache* and the Illinois Indian Tribe during the Last Half of the Seventeenth Century." *Ethnohistory* 37:1 (1990): 45–65.

Hefner, Robert W., ed. *Conversion to Christianity: Historical and Anthropological Perspectives on a Great Transformation.* Berkeley: University of California Press, 1993.

Hellbom, Anna-Britta. "The Life and Role of Women in Aztec Culture." *Cultures,* 8:3 (1982): 55–65.

————. *La participación cultural de las mujeres indias y mestizas en el México precortesano y postrevolucionario.* Stockholm: Ethnographical Museum, 1967.

Hendricks, Margo, and Patricia Parker, eds. *Women, "Race," and Writing in the Early Modern Period.* London: Routledge, 1994.

Herlihy, David. "Tuscan Names, 1200–1530." *Renaissance Quarterly* 41:4 (1988): 561–82.

Heyden, Doris. "Las escobas y las batallas fingidas de la Fiesta de Ochpaniztli." In *Religión en Mesoamérica,* edited by Jaime Litvak King and Noemí Castillo Tejero, 205–11. México: Sociedad Mexicana de Antropología, 1972.

Historia de la nación mexicana. Códice de 1576. Edited and translated by Charles E. Dibble. Madrid: Ediciones José Porrúa Turanzas, 1963. Facsimile of the *Codex of 1576.*

Hoberman, Louisa S. "Hispanic American Women as Portrayed in the Historical Literature: Type or Archetypes?" *Revista Interamericana/Inter-American Review* 4:2 (Summer 1974): 138–47.

Hoberman, Louisa S., and Susan Migden Socolow, eds. *Cities and Society in Colonial Latin America.* Albuquerque: University of New Mexico Press, 1986.

Hodder, Ian. "Gender Representation and Social Reality." In *Archaeology of Gender: Proceedings of the Twenty-second Annual Conference of the Archaeological Association of the University of Calgary*, edited by Dale Walde and Noreen D. Willows, 11–16. Calgary: University of Calgary Press, 1991.

Horcasitas, Fernando, ed. *Life and Death in Milpa Alta: A Nahuatl Chronicle of Díaz and Zapata*. Norman: University of Oklahoma Press, 1972.

———, ed. and trans. *The Aztecs Then and Now*. México: Minutiae Mexicana, 1979.

Horn, Rebecca. *Postconquest Coyoacan: Nahua-Spanish Relations in Central Mexico, 1519–1650*. Stanford: Stanford University Press, 1997.

Hoxie, Frederick E., ed. *America in 1492: Selected Lectures from the Quincentenary Program*. Chicago: Newberry Library, D'Arcy McNickle Center for the History of the American Indian, no. 15, 1992.

Hull, N. E. H. *Female Felons: Women and Crime in Colonial Massachusetts*. Urbana: University of Illinois Press, 1987.

Human Biology: Special Issue. Surnames as Markers of Inbreeding and Migration. 55:2 (1983).

Hunt, David. "From the Millennial to the Everyday: James Scott's Search for the Essence of Peasant Politics," *Radical History Review* 42 (1988): 155–72.

Hunt, Marta Espejo-Ponce. "Colonial Yucatan: Town and Region in the Seventeenth Century." Ph.D. dissertation, University of California, Los Angeles, 1974.

Icaza, Francisco A. de. *Diccionario autobiográfico de conquistadores y pobladores de Nueva España*. 2 vols. Madrid, 1923.

Izquierdo, Ana Luisa. "Tasación de la cacica de Gueytlalpa." *Estudios de Cultura Maya* 14 (1982): 289–98.

Jochens, Jenny M. "The Politics of Reproduction." *American Historical Review* 92:2 (1987): 327–49.

Joe, Jennie R. "Gender and Culture: American Indian Women in Urban Societies." In *Violence, Resistance, and Survival in the Americas*, edited by William B. Taylor and Franklin Pease G.Y., 249–65. Washington, D.C.: Smithsonian Institution Press, 1994.

Johnson, Lyman. "Artisans." In *Cities and Society in Colonial Latin America*, edited by Louisa S. Hoberman and Susan Migden Socolow, 227–50. Albuquerque: University of New Mexico Press, 1986.

Johnson-Odim, Cheryl, and Margaret Strobel. "Introduction." In *Restoring Women to History: Teaching Packets for Integrating Women's History into Courses on Africa, Asia, Latin America, the Caribbean, and the Middle East*, edited by Cheryl Johnson-Odim and Margaret Strobel, 1–30. Bloomington, Ind.: Organization of American Historians, 1988.

Joseph, Gilbert M., and Daniel Nugent, eds. *Everyday Forms of State Forma-*

tion: Revolution and Negotiation of Rule in Modern Mexico. Durham: Duke University Press, 1994.

Josephy, Alvin M., Jr., ed. *America in 1492: The World of the Indian Peoples Before the Arrival of Columbus.* New York: Alfred A. Knopf, 1992.

Josserand, J. Kathryn, and Karen Dakin, eds. *Smoke and Mist: Mesoamerican Studies in Memory of Thelma D. Sullivan.* 2 vols. Oxford: British Archaeological Reports Press, 1988.

Joyce, Rosemary. "Images of Gender and Labor Organization in Classic Maya Society." In *Exploring Gender through Archaeology: Selected Papers from the 1991 Boone Conference,* edited by Cheryl Claassen, 63–70. Madison: Prehistory Press, 1992.

Kanter, Deborah. "Hijos del Pueblo: Family, Community and Gender in Rural Mexico, the Toluca Region, 1730–1830." Ph.D. dissertation, University of Virginia, 1993.

———. "Native Female Land Tenure and its Decline in Mexico, 1750–1900." *Ethnohistory* 42:4 (1995): 607–16.

Kaplan, Bernice A., and Gabriel W. Lasker. "The Present Distribution of Some English Surnames Derived from Place Names." *Human Biology* 55:2 (1983): 243–50.

Karttunen, Frances. "Conventions of Polite Speech in Nahuatl." *Estudios de Cultura Náhuatl,* 20 (1990): 281–96.

———. *Nahuatl and Maya in Contact with Spanish.* Austin: University of Texas, Linguistic Forum, no. 26, 1985.

Karttunen, Frances, and James Lockhart, eds. and trans. *The Art of Nahuatl Speech: The Bancroft Dialogues.* Nahuatl Studies Series, no. 2. Los Angeles: UCLA Latin American Center, 1987.

Keesing, Roger. *Kin Groups and Social Structure.* New York: Holt, Rinehart, and Winston, 1975.

Kellogg, Susan. "Aztec Inheritance in Sixteenth-Century Mexico City: Colonial Patterns, Prehispanic Influences." *Ethnohistory* 33:3 (Summer 1986): 313–30.

———. "Aztec Women in Early Colonial Courts: Structure and Strategy in a Legal Context." In *Five Centuries of Law and Politics in Central Mexico,* edited by Ronald Spores and Ross Hassig, 25–38. Publications in Anthropology, no. 30. Nashville: Vanderbilt University Press, 1984.

———. "Cognatic Kinship and Religion: Women in Aztec Society." In *Smoke and Mist: Mesoamerican Studies in Memory of Thelma D. Sullivan,* edited by J. Kathryn Josserand and Karen Dakin, 2:666–81. Oxford: British Archaeological Reports Press, 1988.

———. "Hegemony out of Conquest: The First Two Centuries of Spanish Rule in Central Mexico," *Radical History Review* 53:27–46.

———. "Kinship and Social Organization in Early Colonial Tenochtitlan: An Essay in Ethnohistorical Analysis and Methodology." In *Supplement to the Handbook of Middle American Indians, gen. ed. Victoria Reifler Bricker. Vol. 4: Ethnohistory*, edited by Ronald Spores, 103–21. Austin: University of Texas Press, 1986.

———. *Law and the Transformation of Aztec Culture, 1500–1700*. Norman: University of Oklahoma Press, 1995.

———. "Social Organization in Early Colonial Tenochtitlán-Tlatelolco: An Ethnohistorical Study." Ph.D. dissertation, University of Rochester, 1980.

———. "The Social Organization of Households among the Tenochca Mexica Before and After Conquest." In *Prehispanic Domestic Units in Western Mesoamerica: Studies of the Household, Compound, and Residence*, edited by Robert S. Santley and Kenneth G. Hirth, 207–24. Boca Raton: CRC Press, 1993.

———. "The Woman's Room: Some Aspects of Gender Relations in Tenochtitlan in the Late Pre-Hispanic Period." *Ethnohistory* 42:4 (1995): 563–76.

Kelly, Joan. *Women, History, and Theory: The Essays of Joan Kelly*. Chicago: University of Chicago Press, 1984.

Kennedy, John G. *Tarahumara of the Sierra Madre: Beer, Ecology and Social Organization*. Arlington Heights, Ill: AHM, 1978.

Kidwell, Clara Sue. "Indian Women as Cultural Mediators." *Ethnohistory*, 39:2 (1992): 97–107.

King, Jaime Litvak, and Noemí Castillo Tejera, eds. *Religión en Mesoamérica*. México: Sociedad Mexicana de Antropología, 1972.

King, Mark B. "Poetics and Metaphor in Mixtec Writing." *Ancient Mesoamerica* 1 (1990): 141–51.

King, P. D. *Law and Society in the Visigothic Kingdom*. Cambridge: Cambridge University Press, 1972.

Klein, Cecilia F. "Fighting with Femininity: Gender and War in Aztec Mexico." *Estudios de Cultura Náhuatl* 24 (1994): 219–53.

———. "Rethinking Cihuacoatl: Aztec Political Imagery of the Conquered Woman." In *Smoke and Mist: Mesoamerican Studies in Memory of Thelma D. Sullivan*, edited by J. Kathryn Josserand and Karen Dakin, 2:237–77. Oxford: British Archaeological Reports Press, 1988.

———. "Who Was Tlaloc?" *Journal of Latin American Lore* 6:2 (1980): 155–204.

———. "Woven Heaven, Tangled Earth: A Weaver's Paradigm of the Mesoamerican Cosmos." In *Ethnoastronomy and Archaeoastronomy in the American Tropics*, edited by Anthony F. Aveni and Gary Urton, 1–35. New York: Annals of the New York Academy of Sciences, no. 385, 1982.

Klein, Herbert S. "Peasant Communities in Revolt: The Tzeltal Republic of 1712." *Pacific Historical Review* 35 (1966): 247–63.

Klein, Laura F., and Lillian A. Ackerman, eds. *Women and Power in Native North America*. Norman: University of Oklahoma Press, 1995.

Klor de Alva, J. Jorge, H. B. Nicholson, and Eloise Quiñones Keber, eds. *The Work of Bernardino de Sahagún: Pioneer Ethnographer of Sixteenth-Century Aztec Mexico*. Albany: State University of New York, Institute for Mesoamerican Studies, 1988.

Knight, Alan. "Weapons and Arches in the Mexican Revolutionary Landscape." In *Everyday Forms of State Formation: Revolution and Negotiation of Rule in Modern Mexico*. edited by Gilbert M. Joseph and Daniel Nugent, 24–66. Durham: Duke University Press, 1994.

Krippner-Martínez, James. "The Politics of Conquest: An Interpretation of the *Relación de Michoacán*." *The Americas* 47:2 (October 1990): 177–97.

Krueger, Hilde. *Malinche*. New York: Arrowhead Press, 1948.

Kuznesof, Elizabeth. "Raza, clase y matrimonio en la Nueva España. Estado actual del debate." In *Familias novohispanas. Siglos XVI al XIX*, edited by Pilar Gonzalbo Aizpuru, 373–88. México: El Colegio de México, 1991.

LaFrance, David, and G. P. C. Thomson. "Juan Francisco Lucas: Patriarch of the Sierra Norte de Puebla." In *The Human Tradition in Latin America: The Twentieth Century*, edited by William H. Beezley and Judith Ewell, 1–13. Wilmington, Del.: Scholarly Resources, 1987.

Langer, Erick, and Robert H. Jackson, eds. *The New Latin American Mission History*. Lincoln: University of Nebraska Press, 1995.

Lanz, Manuel A. *Compendio de historia de Campeche*. Campeche: El Fénix, 1905.

Larson, Brooke, and Robert Wasserstrom. "Coerced Consumption in Colonial Bolivia and Guatemala." *Radical History Review* 27 (1983): 49–78.

Launey, Michel. "Contribuciones recíprocas entre la lingüística general y la cultura náhuatl." Paper presented at the Instituto de Investigaciones Antropológicas, Universidad Nacional Autónoma de México, August 6, 1984.

Lavrin, Asunción. "Ecclesiastical Reform of Nunneries in New Spain in the Eighteenth Century." *The Americas* 22:2 (1965): 182–203.

―――. "*Lo femenino*: Women in Colonial Historical Sources." In *Coded Encounters: Writing, Gender, and Ethnicity in Colonial Latin America*, edited by Francisco Javier Cevallos-Candau, Jeffrey A. Cole, Nina M. Scott, and Nicomedes Suárez-Araúz, 153–76. Amherst: University of Massachusetts Press, 1994.

―――. "In Search of the Colonial Woman in Mexico in the Seventeenth and Eighteenth Centuries." In *Latin American Women: Historical Perspectives*, edited by Asunción Lavrin, 23–59. Westport, Conn.: Greenwood Press, 1978.

―――. "Introduction." In *Latin American Women: Historical Perspectives*, edited by Asunción Lavrin, 3–22. Westport, Conn.: Greenwood Press, 1978.

———. "Mundo en contraste. Cofradías rurales y urbanas en México a fines del siglo XVIII." In *La iglesia en la economía de América latina siglos XVI al XIX*, edited by A. J. Bauer, 235–76. México: Instituto Nacional de Antropología e Historia, 1986.

———, ed. *Latin American Women: Historical Perspectives*. Westport, Conn.: Greenwood Press, 1978.

———, ed. *Sexuality and Marriage in Colonial Latin America*. Lincoln: University of Nebraska Press, 1989.

Lavrin, Asunción, and Edith Couturier. "Dowries and Wills: A View of Women's Socioeconomic Role in Colonial Guadalajara and Puebla, 1640–1790." *Hispanic American Historical Review* 59:2 (May 1979): 280–304.

———. "Las mujeres tienen la palabra. Otras voces en la historia colonial de México." *Historia Mexicana* 31:2 (October-December 1981): 278–313.

Leacock, Eleanor. "Introduction." In *Origins of the Family, Private Property, and the State*, edited by Frederick Engels, 7–67. New York: International Publishers, 1972.

Leander, Brigitta. *Herencia cultural del mundo náhuatl a través de la lengua*. SepSetentas 35. México: Secretaría de Educación Pública, 1972.

León Cázares, María del, and Mario Humberto Ruz, eds. *Constituciones diocesanas del obispado de Chiapas*. México: Universidad Nacional Autónoma de México, 1988.

Leonardo, Micaela di, ed. *Gender at the Crossroads of Knowledge: Feminist Anthropology in the Postmodern Era*. Berkeley: University of California Press, 1991.

León-Portilla, Miguel. *Aztec Thought and Culture: A Study of the Ancient Nahuatl Mind*. Norman: University of Oklahoma Press, 1963.

———. "Códice de Coyoacan. Nómina de tributos, siglo XVI." *Estudios de Cultura Náhuatl* 9 (1971): 57–74.

———. *Siete ensayos sobre cultura náhuatl*. México: Universidad Nacional Autónoma de México, 1958.

———. *Trece poetas del mundo azteca*. México: Universidad Nacional Autónoma de México, Instituto de Investigaciones Históricas, 1967.

Lewis, Laura A. "The 'Weakness' of Women and the Feminization of the Indian in Colonial Mexico." *Colonial Latin American Review* 5:1 (1996): 73–94.

Lipsett-Rivera, Sonya. "Space, Solidarity, and Sexual Danger in Mexico, 1750–1856." Paper presented at the IX Conference of Mexican and U.S. Historians, Mexico City, October 1994.

———. n.d. "La violencia dentro de la familia formal e informal." Forthcoming.

Lockhart, James. 1974. "Españoles entre indios. Toluca a fines del siglo XVI." *Revista de Indias* 131–138 (1974): 435–91.

──────. "Introduction." In *Provinces of Early Mexico: Variants of Spanish American Regional Evolution*, edited by Ida Altman and James Lockhart, 3–28. Los Angeles: UCLA Latin American Center, 1976.

──────. *The Nahuas after the Conquest: A Social and Cultural History of the Indians of Central Mexico, Sixteenth through Eighteenth Centuries.* Stanford: Stanford University Press, 1992.

──────. *Nahuas and Spaniards: Postconquest Central Mexican History and Philology.* Nahuatl Studies Series, no 3. Stanford and Los Angeles: Stanford University Press and UCLA Latin American Center, 1991.

──────. "Some Nahua Concepts in Postconquest Guise." *History of European Ideas* 6 (1985): 465–82.

──────, ed. and trans. *We People Here: Nahuatl Accounts of the Conquest of Mexico.* Reportorium Columbianum Series, gen. ed. Geoffrey Symcox. Berkeley: University of California Press, 1993.

Lockhart, James, Frances Berdan, and Arthur J. O. Anderson, eds. and trans. *The Tlaxcalan Actas: A Compendium of the Records of the Cabildo of Tlaxcala (1545–1627).* Salt Lake City: University of Utah Press, 1986.

Lockhart, James, and Stuart B. Schwartz. *Early Latin America: A History of Colonial Spanish America and Brazil.* Latin American Studies, no. 46. Cambridge: Cambridge University Press, 1983.

López Austin, Alfredo. *Cuerpo humano e ideología. Las concepciones de los antiguos nahuas.* 2 vols. México: Universidad Nacional Autónoma de México, Instituto de Investigaciones Antropológicas, 1980.

──────. *La educación de los antiguos nahuas.* 2 vols. México: SEP, 1985.

──────. *Hombre-Dios. Religión y política en el mundo náhuatl.* México: Universidad Nacional Autónoma de México. 1989.

──────. *The Human Body and Ideology: Concepts of the Ancient Nahuas.* 2 vols. Salt Lake City: University of Utah Press, 1988.

López de Cogolludo, fray Diego. [1688]. *Historia de Yucatán.* Campeche: Talleres Gráficos del Gobierno Constitucional del Estado, 1954.

López de Meneses, Amada. "Tecuichpochtzin, hija de Moteczuma (¿1510?-1550)." *Revista de Indias* 9 (1948): 471–96.

López Sarrelangue, Delfina E. *La nobleza indígena de Pátzcuaro en la época virreinal.* México: Universidad Nacional Autónoma de México, 1965.

MacLachlan, Colin M. "The Eagle and the Serpent: Male over Female in Tenochtitlán." *Proceedings of the Pacific Coast Council of Latin American Studies* 5 (1976): 45–56.

──────. *La justicia criminal del siglo XVIII. Un estudio sobre el tribunal de la Acordada.* México: Secretaría de Educación Pública, 1976.

MacLeod, Murdo J. *Cambridge History of the Native Peoples of the Americas.* Cambridge: Cambridge University Press, forthcoming.

———. *Spanish Central America: A Socioeconomic History, 1520–1720.* Berkeley: University of California Press, 1973.

Mankiller, Wilma. "One Woman's 'Trail of Tears' Ends, with Honor, Back Home." *New York Times,* November 4, 1994.

Mankiller, Wilma, and Michael Wallis. *Mankiller, a Chief and Her People: An Autobiography by the Principal Chief of the Cherokee Nation.* New York: St. Martin's Press, 1993.

Marcus, Joyce. *Mesoamerican Writing Systems: Propaganda, Myth, and History in Four Ancient Civilizations.* Princeton: Princeton University Press, 1992.

Martin, Cheryl. *Governance and Society in Colonial Mexico: Chihuahua in the Eighteenth Century.* Stanford: Stanford University Press, 1995.

———. "Public Celebrations, Popular Culture, and Labor Discipline in Eighteenth-Century Chihuahua." In *Rituals of Rule, Rituals of Resistance: Public Celebrations and Popular Culture in Mexico,* edited by William H. Beezley, Cheryl English Martin, and William E. French, 95–114. Wilmington, Del.: Scholarly Resources, 1994.

Martínez, Hildeberto. *Colección de documentos coloniales de Tepeaca.* México: Instituto Nacional de Antropología e Historia, 1984.

———. *Tepeaca en el siglo XVI.* México: La Casa Chata, 1984.

Martínez Alcubilla, Marcel. *Códigos antiguos de España.* 2 vols. Madrid: Administración (J. López Camacho), 1885.

Martínez Alier, Verena. *Marriage, Class, and Colour in Nineteenth-Century Cuba.* Cambridge: Cambridge University Press, 1974.

Martínez Baracs, Andrea. "Colonizaciones tlaxcaltecas." *Historia Mexicana* 43:2 (1993): 195–250.

Martínez Peláez, Severo. *La sublevación de los zendales.* Tuxtla Gutiérrez: Publicación Cultural de la Universidad Autónoma de Chiapas, 1977.

Mathes, Valerie Shirer. "A New Look at the Role of Women in Indian Society." *American Indian Quarterly* 2:2 (1975): 131–39.

Matthews, Holly F. "'We Are Mayordomo': A Reinterpretation of Women's Roles in the Mexican Cargo System." *American Ethnologist* 12:2 (1985): 285–301.

McCafferty, Sharisse D., and Geoffrey G. McCafferty. "Engendering Tomb 7 at Monte Albán: Respinning an Old Yarn." *Current Anthropology* 32:2 (1994): 143–66.

———. "Powerful Women and the Myth of Male Dominance in Aztec Society." *Archaeological Review from Cambridge* 7 (1988): 45–59.

———. "Spinning and Weaving as Female Gender Identity in Post-Classic Mexico." In *Textile Traditions of Mesoamerica and the Andes: An Anthology,* edited by Margot Blum Schevill, Janet Catherine Berlo, and Edward B. Dwyer, 19–44. New York: Garland Press, 1991.

McClintock, Anne. *Imperial Leather: Race, Gender, and Sexuality in the Colonial Contest.* New York: Routledge, 1995.

Mead, Margaret. [1932]. *The Changing Culture of an Indian Tribe.* New York: AMS Press, 1969.

Mendieta, fray Gerónimo de. *Historia eclesiástica indiana.* Edited by Joaquín García Icazbalceta. México: Editorial Porrúa, 1980.

Merrill, William L. "Conversion and Colonialism in Northern Mexico: The Tarahumara Response to the Jesuit Mission Program, 1602–1767." In *Conversion to Christianity: Historical and Anthropological Perspectives on a Great Transformation,* edited by Robert W. Hefner, 129–63. Berkeley: University of California Press, 1993.

————. "Cultural Creativity and Raiding Bands in Eighteenth-Century Northern New Spain." In *Violence, Resistance and Survival in the Americas,* edited by William B. Taylor and Franklin Pease, 124–52. Washington, D.C.: Smithsonian Institution Press, 1994.

————. *Rarámuri Souls: Knowledge and Social Process in Northern Mexico.* Washington, D.C.: Smithsonian Institution Press, 1988.

Merrill, William L., and Robert J. Hard. "Mobile Agriculturalists and the Emergence of Sedentism: Perspectives from Northern Mexico." *American Anthropologist* 94:3 (1992): 601–20.

Miller, Jay. "A Kinship of Spirit." In *America in 1492: The World of the Indian Peoples Before the Arrival of Columbus,* edited by Alvin M. Josephy, Jr., 305–37. New York: Alfred A. Knopf, 1992.

————. "Society in 1492." In *America in 1492: Selected Lectures from the Quincentenary Program,* edited by Frederick E. Hoxie, 151–69. Chicago: D'Arcy McNickle Center for the History of the American Indian, Newberry Library, no. 15, 1992.

Miller, Virginia E., ed. *The Role of Gender in Precolumbian Art and Architecture.* Boston: University Press of America, 1988.

Molina, fray Alonso de. [1569]. *Confesionario mayor en la lengua mexicana y castellana.* México: Universidad Nacional Autónoma de México, 1984.

————. [1571]. *Vocabulario en lengua castellana y mexicana y mexicana y castellana.* Edited and with an introduction by Miguel León-Portilla. México: Editorial Porrúa, 1970.

Molina Solís, J. F. *Historia de Yucatán.* 4 vols. Mérida, 1896–1927.

Monaghan, John Desmond. *The Covenants with Earth and Rain: Exchange, Sacrifice, and Revelation in Mixtec Sociality.* Norman: University of Oklahoma Press, 1995.

————. "Sacrifice, Death, and the Origins of Agriculture in the Codex Vienna." *American Antiquity* 55:3 (1990): 559–69.

———. "'We are people who eat tortillas': Household and Community in the Mixteca." Ph.D. dissertation, University of Pennsylvania, 1987.

Moore, Henrietta. *Feminism and Anthropology.* Minneapolis: University of Minnesota Press, 1988.

Mörner, Magnus. *La corona española y los foraneos en los pueblos de indios de América.* Stockholm: Almquist and Wiksell, 1970.

———. *Race Mixture in the History of Latin America.* Boston: Little, Brown, 1967.

Motolinia, fray Toribio de Benavente. *Historia de los indios de la Nueva España.* Edited by Edmundo O'Gorman. México: Editorial Porrúa, 1979.

———. *Historia de los indios de la Nueva España.* Madrid: Historia 16, 1985.

———. *Memoriales o libro de las cosas de la Nueva España y los naturales de ella.* Edited by Edmundo O'Gorman. México: Universidad Nacional Autónoma de México, 1971.

———. *Motolinia's History of the Indians of New Spain.* Edited and translated by Elizabeth Andros Foster. Westport, Conn.: Greenwood Press, 1973.

Münch G., Guido. *El cacicazgo de San Juan Teotihuacan durante la colonia.* México: Instituto Nacional de Antropología e Historia, 1976.

Muñoz Camargo, Diego. "Descripción de la ciudad y provincia de Tlaxcala." In *Relaciones geográficas del siglo XVI. Tlaxcala,* edited by René Acuña, 1:23–286. México: Universidad Nacional Autónoma de México, 1984.

Murdock, George. "Cognatic Forms of Social Organization." In *Social Structure in Southeast Asia,* edited by George Murdock, 1–14. New York: Viking Fund Publications in Anthropology and Wenner-Gren Foundation for Anthropological Research, 1960.

———, ed. *Social Structure in Southeast Asia.* New York: Viking Fund Publications in Anthropology and Wenner-Gren Foundation for Anthropological Research, 1960.

Muriel, Josefina. *Cultura femenina novohispana.* México: Universidad Nacional Autónoma de México, 1994.

———. *Los recogimientos de las mujeres.* México: Universidad Nacional Autónoma de México, 1974.

———. *La sociedad novohispana y sus colegios de niñas.* Vol. 1. México: Universidad Nacional Autónoma de México, 1995.

Nader, Laura. *Harmony Ideology: Justice and Control in a Zapotec Mountain Village.* Stanford: Stanford University Press, 1990.

Nash, June. "The Aztecs and the Ideology of Male Dominance." *Signs* 4:2 (Winter 1978): 349–62.

———. "Aztec Women: The Transition from Status to Class in Empire and Colony." In *Women and Colonization: Anthropological Perspectives,* edited by Mona Etienne and Eleanor Leacock, 134–48. New York: Praeger, 1980.

Nicholson, H. B. "Religion in Pre-Hispanic Central Mexico." In *Handbook of*

Middle American Indians, gen. ed. Robert Wauchope. Vol. 10: *Archaeology of Northern Mesoamerica*, pt. 1, edited by Gordon F. Ekholm and Ignacio Bernal, 395–446. Austin: University of Texas Press, 1971.

Núñez de la Vega, Francisco. "IXa Carta Pastoral." In *Constituciones diocesanas del obispado de Chiapas*, edited by María del Carmen León Cázarea and Mario Humberto Ruz, 752–60. México: Universidad Nacional Autónoma de México, 1988.

Oberem, Udo. "Un ejemplo de auto-valoración social entre la alta nobleza indígena de Quito colonial." *Miscelánea Antropológica Ecuatoriana* 2:2 (1982): 125–34.

Offner, Jerome. *Law and Politics in Aztec Texcoco*. Cambridge: Cambridge University Press, 1983.

Offutt, Leslie S. "Variants of the 'Colonizing Experience': Indian/Hispanic Contact in the Mexican Northeast, 1600–1800." In *Rediscovering America, 1492–1992: National, Cultural, and Disciplinary Boundaries Re-examined*, edited by Leslie Bary, Janet Gold, Marketta Laurila, Arnulfo Ramírez, Joseph Ricapito, and Jesús Torrecilla, 77–85. Baton Rouge: Louisiana State University Press, 1992.

Ogden, Adele, and Engle Sluiter, eds. *Greater America: Essays in Honor of Herbert Eugene Bolton*. Berkeley: University of California Press, 1945.

Olmos, fray Andrés de. *Grammaire de la langue nahuatl ou mexicaine*. Edited by Rémi Siméon. Paris: Imprimerie Nationale, 1875.

———. [1553]. *Tratado de hechicerías y sortilegios, 1553*. Edited by Georges Baudot. México: Universidad Nacional Autónoma de México, 1990.

Orozco y Berra, Manuel. *Los conquistadores de México*. México: Pedro Robredo, 1938.

———. *Historia antigua de la conquista de México*. vol. 4. México: Tipografía de Gonzalo A. Esteva, 1880.

Ortner, Sherry B. "Is Female to Male as Nature Is to Culture?" In *Woman, Culture, and Society*, edited by Michelle Z. Rosaldo and Louise Lamphere, 67–87. Stanford: Stanford University Press, 1974.

———. "Resistance and the Problem of Ethnographic Refusal." *Comparative Studies in Society and History* 37:1 (1995): 173–93.

Ouweneel, Arij, and Simon Miller, eds. *The Indian Community of Colonial Mexico: Fifteen Essays on Land Tenure, Corporate Organizations, Ideology, and Village Politics*. Amsterdam: Center for Latin American Research and Documentation (CEDLA), 1990.

Pagden, Anthony, ed. and trans. *Hernán Cortés: Letters from Mexico*. New Haven: Yale University Press, 1986.

Paso y Troncoso, Francisco del. *Epistolario de Nueva España*. 16 vols. México: Editorial Porrúa, 1939–42.

Patch, Robert. *Maya and Spaniard in Yucatan, 1648–1812.* Stanford: Stanford University Press, 1993.

Paz, Octavio. *The Labyrinth of Solitude.* New York: Grove Press, 1961.

Pérez de Ribas, Andrés. [1645]. *Historia de los triunfos de nuestra santa fe entre gentes las más bárbaras y fieras del nuevo orbe.* México: Siglo Veintiuno Editores, 1992.

Perry, Mary Elizabeth. *Gender and Disorder in Early Modern Spain.* Princeton: Princeton University Press, 1990.

Pescador, Juan Javier. "Vanishing Woman: Female Migration and Ethnic Identity in Late-Colonial Mexico City." *Ethnohistory* 42:4 (1995): 617–26.

Pescatello, Ann. *Power and Pawn: The Female in Iberian Families, Societies, and Cultures.* Westport, Conn.: Greenwood Press, 1976.

Pomar, Juan Bautista. [1582]. "Relacion de Tezcoco." In *Nueva colección de documentos para la historia de México,* edited by J. García Icazbalceta, 3:1–69. México: Imprenta de Francisco Díaz de León, 1891.

———. [1582]. *Relación de Tezcoco.* Edited by Joaquín García Icazbalceta. México: Biblioteca Enciclopédica del Estado de México, 1975.

Powell, Philip Wayne. *Soldiers, Indians, and Silver: The Northward Advance of New Spain, 1550–1600.* Berkeley: University of California Press, 1956.

Powers, Karen Vieira. *Andean Journeys: Migration, Ethnogenesis, and the State in Colonial Quito.* Albuquerque: University of New Mexico Press, 1995.

Price, Richard, and Sally Price. "Saramaka Onomastics: An Afro-American Naming System." *Ethnology* 11:4 (1972): 341–67.

Ramos, Gabriela, and Henrique Urbano, eds. *Catolicismo y extirpación de idolatrías. Siglos XVI-XVII.* Cuzco: Centro de Estudios Regionales Andinos "Bartolomé de Las Casas," 1993.

Ramos-Escandón, Carmen, et al., eds. *Presencia y transparencia. La mujer en la historia de México.* México: El Colegio de México, 1987.

Recinos, Adrián. *Pedro de Alvarado. Conquistador de México y Guatemala.* México: Fondo de Cultura Económica, 1952.

Reff, Daniel T. *Disease, Depopulation and Culture Change in Northwestern New Spain, 1518–1764.* Salt Lake City: University of Utah Press, 1991.

———. "'He Wished It in Vain': Subordination and Resistance among Maya Women in Post-Conquest Yucatan." *Ethnohistory* 42:4 (1995): 577–94.

———. *Life and Death in a Maya Community: The Ixil Testaments of the 1760s.* Lancaster, Calif.: Labyrinthos, 1995.

———. *The Maya World: Yucatec Culture and Society, 1550–1850.* Stanford: Stanford University Press, 1997.

———. n.d. "The Testaments of Cacalchen (1646–78)." Unpublished transliteration and translation of 33 Maya wills from photostat in Tulane University's Latin American Library (1991).

Ricard, Robert. *The Spiritual Conquest of Mexico*. Translated by Lesley Byrd Simpson. Berkeley: University of California Press, 1966.

Ruis. *500 años. Fregados pero cristianos*. México: Editorial Grijalbo, 1992.

———. *La interminable conquista de México*. México: Editorial Grijalbo, 1983.

Robinson, David J. *Research Inventory of the Mexican Collection of Colonial Parish Registers*. Edited by Roger M. Haigh. No. 6 of Finding Aids to the Microfilmed Manuscript Collection of the Genealogical Society of Utah. Salt Lake City: University of Utah Press, 1980.

Rodríguez, María de Jesus. "Enfoque y perspectivas de los estudios sobre la condición femenina en el México antiguo." *Mesoamérica* 19 (June 1990): 1–11.

———. "La mujer y la familia en la sociedad mexica." In *Presencia y transparencia. La mujer en la historia de México*, ed. Carmen Ramos Escandón, 13–31. México: El Colegio de México, 1987.

Rodríguez-Shadow, María J. *La mujer azteca*. México: Universidad Autónoma del Estado de México, 1991.

Rodríguez-Shadow, María J., and Robert Shadow. "Las mujeres aztecas y las españolas en los siglos XVI y XVII. Análisis comparativo de la literatura social." *Colonial Latin American Historical Review* 5:1 (1996): 21–46.

Rogers, Edward S., and Mary Black Rogers. "Method for Reconstructing Patterns of Change: Surname Adoption by the Weagamow Ojibwa, 1870–1950." *Ethnohistory* 25:4 (1978): 319–45.

Romero Frizzi, María de los Angeles, and Ronald Spores, eds. *Indice del Archivo del Juzgado de Teposcolula, Oaxaca. Epoca colonial*. México: Instituto Nacional de Antropología e Historia, 1978.

Rosaldo, Michelle Z. "The Use and Abuse of Anthropology: Reflections on Feminism and Cross-Cultural Understanding." *Signs* 5 (1980): 389–417.

———. "Woman, Culture, and Society: A Theoretical Overview." In *Woman, Culture, and Society*, edited by Michelle Z. Rosaldo and Louise Lamphere, 17–24. Stanford: Stanford University Press, 1974.

Rosaldo, Michelle Z., and Louise Lamphere, eds. *Woman, Culture and Society*. Stanford: Stanford University Press, 1974.

Rosaldo, Renato. "Ilongot Naming: The Play of Associations." In *Naming Systems*, edited by Elisabeth Tooker. *Proceedings of the American Ethnological Society* (1980) (1984):11–24.

Rose, Mary Beth. "Introduction." In *Women in the Middle Ages and the Renaissance: Literary and Historical Perspectives*, edited by Mary Beth Rose, xiii–xxviii. New York: Syracuse University Press, 1986.

Rose, Mary Beth, ed. *Women in the Middle Ages and the Renaissance: Literary and Historical Perspectives*. New York: Syracuse University Press, 1986.

Rothenberg, Diane. "The Mothers of the Nation: Seneca Resistance to

Quaker Intervention." In *Women and Colonization: Anthropological Perspectives*, edited by Mona Etienne and Eleanor Leacock, 63–87. New York: Praeger, 1980.

Roys, Ralph L. [1943]. *The Indian Background of Colonial Yucatan*. Norman: University of Oklahoma Press, 1972.

————. "Personal Names of the Maya of Yucatan." *Contributions to American Anthropology and History* 6 (1940): 31–48.

————. *The Titles of Ebtun*. Washington, D.C.: Carnegie Institute, 1939.

Rubio Mañé, J. Ignacio. *Alcaldes de Mérida de Yucatán. 1542–1941*. México: Editorial Cultura, 1941.

Ruiz de Alarcón, Hernando. *Aztec Sorcerers in Seventeenth-Century Mexico: The Treatise on Superstitions by Hernando Ruiz de Alarcón*, Edited and translated by Michael D. Coe and Gordon Whittaker. Albany: State University of New York, Institute for Mesoamerican Studies, 1982.

————. [1629]. *Treatise on the Heathen Superstitions that Today Live among the Indians Native to this New Spain, 1629*. Edited and translated by J. Richard Andrews and Ross Hassig. Norman: University of Oklahoma Press, 1984.

Sacks, Karen. "Engels Revisited: Women, the Organization of Production, and Private Property." In *Woman, Culture, and Society*, edited by Michelle Z. Rosaldo and Louise Lamphere, 207–27. Stanford: Stanford University Press, 1974.

Sahagún, fray Bernardino de. *Adiciones, apéndice a la postilla y ejercicio cotidiano*. Translated by Arthur J. O. Anderson. México: Universidad Nacional Autónoma de México, 1993.

————. *Apendiz de la postilla [1579]*. MS. 1486, Ayer Collection, Newberry Library, Chicago.

————. *Códice florentino*. [12 Books in] 3 vols. México: Secretaría de Gobernación, 1979.

————. *Coloquios y doctrina cristiana*. Edited and translated by Miguel León-Portilla. México: Universidad Nacional Autónoma de México, 1986.

————. *Florentine Codex: General History of the Things of New Spain*. 12 vols. Edited and translated by Arthur J. O. Anderson and Charles E. Dibble. Santa Fe and Salt Lake City: School of American Research and University of Utah Press, 1950–82.

————. *Manual del christiano [1578]*. MS. Mexicaine 402, Bibliothèque Nationale, Paris.

————. *Primeros memoriales*. Norman: University of Oklahoma Press, 1993.

————. *The Primeros memoriales of fray Bernardino de Sahagún*. Translated by Thelma D. Sullivan, edited by H. B. Nicholson, Arthur J. O. Anderson, Charles E. Dibble, Eloise Quiñones Keber, and Wayne Ruwet. Norman: University of Oklahoma Press, 1997.

——. *Psalmodia Christiana (Christian Psalmody)*. Translated by Arthur J. O. Anderson. Salt Lake City: University of Utah Press, 1993.

——. *Psalmodia christiana y sermonario de los sanctos del año en lengua mexicana*. México: Pedro Ocharte, 1583.

——. *Sermones en mexicano [1588]*. Vol. 2. MS. 1482, Biblioteca Nacional de México, México.

Saint-Lu, André. "El poder colonial y la iglesia frente a la sublevación de los indígenas zendales de Chiapas en 1712." *Mesoamérica* 11 (1986): 23–24.

Salas, Elizabeth. *Soldaderas in the Mexican Military: Myth and History*. Austin: University of Texas Press, 1990.

Salomon, Frank. "Indian Women of Early Colonial Quito as Seen through Their Testaments." *The Americas* 44:3 (January 1988): 325–41.

Sanders, William T., Jeffrey R. Parsons, and Robert S. Santley. *The Basin of Mexico: Ecological Process in the Evolution of a Civilization*. New York: Academic Press, 1979.

Santley, Robert S., and Kenneth G. Hirth, eds. *Prehispanic Domestic Units in Western Mesoamerica: Studies of the Household, Compound, and Residence*. Boca Raton: CRC Press, 1993.

Scardaville, Michael C. 1994. "(Hapsburg) Law and (Bourbon) Order: State Authority, Popular Unrest, and the Criminal Justice System in Bourbon Mexico City." *The Americas* 50:4 (April 1994): 501–25.

Schele, Linda, and David Freidel. *A Forest of Kings*. New York: William Morrow, 1990.

Schevill, Margot Blum, Janet Catherine Berlo, and Edward B. Dwyer, eds. *Textile Traditions of Mesoamerica and the Andes*. New York: Garland Press, 1991.

Scholes, France V., and Ralph L. Roys. *The Maya Chontal Indians of Acalan-Tixchel: A Contribution to the History and Ethnography of the Yucatan Peninsula*. Norman: University of Oklahoma Press, 1968.

Schroeder, Susan. *Chimalpahin and the Kingdoms of Chalco*. Tucson: University of Arizona Press, 1991.

——. "Nahuas and the *Bona Mors* at the Colegio de San Gregorio." Paper presented at the XVII International Congress of the History of Religions. Mexico City, August 1995.

——. "The Noblewomen of Chalco." *Estudios de Cultura Náhuatl* 22 (1992): 45–86.

——, ed. *The 'Pax Colonial' and Native Resistance in New Spain*. Lincoln: University of Nebraska Press, 1998.

——, gen. ed. *Codex Chimalpahin*. 6 vols. Norman: University of Oklahoma Press, 1997.

Scott, James C. *Domination and the Arts of Resistance: Hidden Transcripts*. New Haven: Yale University Press, 1990.

———. *The Moral Economy of the Peasant: Subsistence and Rebellion in Southeast Asia.* New Haven: Yale University Press, 1976.

———. *Weapons of the Weak: Everyday Forms of Peasant Resistance.* New Haven: Yale University Press, 1985.

Scott, Joan W. "Gender: A Useful Category of Historical Analysis." In *Gender and the Politics of History,* edited by Joan W. Scott, 28–50. New York: Columbia University Press, 1988.

———, ed. *Gender and the Politics of History.* New York: Columbia University Press, 1988.

Seed, Patricia. Book review. *Hispanic American Historical Review* 70:4 (1990): 688–89.

———. *To Love, Honor, and Obey in Colonial Mexico: Conflicts over Marriage Choice, 1574–1821.* Stanford: Stanford University Press, 1988.

Serna, Jacinto de la. "Manual de ministros para conocer y extirpar las idolatrías de los indios." In *Tratado de las idolatrías, supersticiones, dioses, ritos, hechicerías y otras costumbres gentílicas de las razas aborígenes de México,* edited by Francisco del Paso y Troncoso, 1:40–368. México: Librería Navarro, 1953.

Sheridan, Thomas, and Thomas Naylor, eds. *Rarámuri: A Tarahumara Colonial Chronicle, 1607–1791.* Flagstaff: Northland Press, 1979.

Shoemaker, Nancy, ed. *Negotiators of Change: Historical Perspectives on Native American Women.* New York: Routledge, 1995.

Silverblatt, Irene. "Interpreting Women in States: New Feminist Ethnohistories." In *Gender at the Crossroads of Knowledge: Feminist Anthropology in the Postmodern Era,* edited by Micaela di Leonardo, 140–71. Berkeley: University of California Press, 1991.

———. "Lessons of Gender and Ethnohistory in Mesoamerica." *Ethnohistory* 42:4 (1995): 639–50.

———. *Moon, Sun, and Witches: Gender Ideologies and Class in Inca and Colonial Peru.* Princeton: Princeton University Press, 1987.

Simons, Bente Bittman. "Documents Pertaining to the Area of Cholula." *Tlalocan* 4 (1964): 289–310.

Simpson, Lesley Byrd, ed. and trans. *Cortés: The Life of the Conqueror by His Secretary, Francisco López de Gómara.* Berkeley: University of California Press, 1964.

Smith, Daniel Scott. "Child-Naming Practices as Cultural and Familial Indicators." *Local Population Studies* 32 (Spring 1984): 17–27.

———. "Child-Naming Practices, Kinship Ties, and Change in Family Attitudes in Hingham, Massachusetts, 1641 to 1880." *Journal of Family History* 18 (1985): 541–66.

Smith, Michael E. *Archaeological Research at Aztec-Period Rural Sites in More-*

los, Mexico. Vol. 1: *Excavations and Architecture.* University of Pittsburgh Memoirs in Latin American Archaeology, no. 4. Pittsburgh, 1992.

Solórzano y Pereyra, Juan de. *Política indiana.* 2 vols. Madrid: Imprenta Real de la Gazeta, 1776.

Somonte, Mariano G. *Doña Marina, "La Malinche".* México: Privately published, 1971.

Spicer, Edward H. *Cycles of Conquest: The Impact of Spain, Mexico, and the United States on the Indians of the Southwest, 1533–1960.* Tucson: University of Arizona Press, 1962.

Spores, Ronald. *Colección de documentos del Archivo General de la Nación para la étnohistoria de la Mixteca de Oaxaca en el siglo XVI.* Nashville: Vanderbilt University Publications in Anthropology, no. 41.

———. "Differential Response to Colonial Control Among the Mixtecs and Zapotecs of Oaxaca." In *The 'Pax Colonial' and Native Resistance in New Spain,* edited by Susan Schroeder. Lincoln: University of Nebraska Press, 1998.

———. *Documentos para la étnohistoria del estado de Oaxaca. Indice del Ramo de Indios del Archivo General de la Nación, México.* Vanderbilt University Publications in Anthropology, no. 13. Nashville, 1975.

———, ed. *Ethnohistory. Vol. 4 of Supplement to the Handbook of Middle American Indians.* Austin: University of Texas Press, 1986.

———. "The Genealogy of Tlazultepec: A Sixteenth-Century Mixtec Manuscript." *Southwestern Journal of Anthropology* 2 (1964): 15–31.

———. *The Mixtec Kings and Their People.* Norman: University of Oklahoma Press, 1967.

———. *The Mixtecs in Ancient and Colonial Times.* Norman: University of Oklahoma Press, 1984.

———. "Tututepec: A Postclassic-Period Mixtec Conquest State." *Ancient Mesoamerica* 4:1 (1993): 167–74.

Spores, Ronald, and Ross Hassig, eds. *Five Centuries of Law and Politics in Central Mexico.* Vanderbilt University Publications in Anthropology, no. 30. Nashville, 1984.

Spores, Ronald, and Miguel Saldaña. *Documentos para la étnohistoria del estado de Oaxaca. Indice del Ramo de Mercedes del Archivo General de la Nación, México.* Vanderbilt University Publications in Anthropology, no. 5. Nashville, 1973.

Stavig, Ward. "Ethnic Conflict, Moral Economy, and Population in Rural Cuzco on the Eve of the Thupa Amaro II Rebellion." *Hispanic American Historical Review* 68:4 (1988): 737–70.

Stephen, Lynn. *Zapotec Women.* Austin: University of Texas Press, 1991.

Stern, Steve J. *The Secret History of Gender: Women, Men, and Power in Late Colonial Mexico.* Chapel Hill: University of North Carolina Press, 1995.

Stoler, Ann Laura. "Carnal Knowledge and Imperial Power: Gender, Race and Morality in Colonial Asia." In *Gender at the Crossroads of Knowledge: Feminist Anthropology in the Postmodern Era*, edited by Micaela de Leonardo, 51–101. Berkeley: University of California Press, 1991.

Sullivan, Thelma D. "'O Precious Necklace, O Quetzal Feather!' Aztec Pregnancy and Childbirth Orations." *Alcheringa/Ethnopoetics* 4 (1980): 38–56.

———. "Pregnancy, Childbirth, and the Deification of the Women Who Died in Childbirth." *Estudios de Cultura Náhuatl* 6 (1966): 63–95.

———. "Tlazolteotl-Ixcuina: The Great Spinner and Weaver." In *The Art and Iconography of Late Post-Classic Central Mexico*, edited by Elizabeth H. Boone, 7–35. Washington, D.C.: Dumbarton Oaks, 1982.

Swann, Brian, ed. *On the Translation of Native American Literatures*. Washington, D.C.: Smithsonian Institution Press, 1992.

Taylor, William B. *Drinking, Homicide, and Rebellion in Colonial Mexican Villages*. Stanford: Stanford University Press, 1979.

———. "The Virgin of Guadalupe in New Spain: An Inquiry into the Social History of Marian Devotion." *American Ethnologist* 14:1 (February 1987): 9–33.

Taylor, William B., and Franklin Pease, eds. *Violence, Resistance and Survival in the Americas*. Washington, D.C.: Smithsonian Institution Press, 1994.

Tebbenhoff, Edward H. "Tacit Rules and Hidden Family Structures: Naming Practices and Godparentage in Schenectady, New York, 1680–1800." *Journal of Social History* 18 (1985): 567–85.

Tedlock, Barbara, and Dennis Tedlock. "Text and Textile: Language and Technology in the Arts of the Quiché Maya." *Journal of Anthropological Research* 41 (1985): 121–46.

Tedlock, Dennis. Paper, "Re-creating the New World Contact: Indigenous Languages and Literatures of Latin America," NEH Summer Institute, University of Texas at Austin, July 10, 1989.

———, ed. and trans. *Popol Vuh*. New York: Simon and Schuster, 1985.

Terraciano, Kevin. "Ñudzahui History: Mixtec Writing and Culture in Colonial Oaxaca." Ph.D. dissertation, University of California, Los Angeles, 1994.

———. "Quachi Ñudzahui: Murder in the Mixteca." *UCLA Historical Journal* 11 (1991): 93–113.

Terraciano, Kevin, and Lisa Mary Sousa. "The 'Original Conquest' of Oaxaca: Mixtec and Nahuatl History and Myth." *Indigenous Writing in the Spanish Indies: Special Issue of the UCLA Historical Journal* 12 (1992): 29–90.

Thomas, David H., ed. *Columbian Consequences*. Vol. 1: *Archaeological and Historical Perspectives on the Spanish Borderlands West*. Washington, D.C.: Smithsonian Institution Press, 1989.

Thompson, Donald E. *Maya Paganism and Christianity: A History of the Fusion of Two Religions*. New Orleans: Tulane University, Middle American Research Institute Publication, no. 19, 1954.

Thompson, E. P. "The Moral Economy of the English Crowd in the Eighteenth Century." *Past and Present* 50 (1971): 76–136.

————. "The Moral Economy Reviewed." In *Customs in Common: Studies in Traditional Popular Culture*, edited by E. P. Thompson, 259–351. New York: New Press, 1993.

Thompson, Philip C. "Tekanto in the Eighteenth Century." Ph.D. dissertation, Tulane University, 1978.

Todorov, Tzvetan. *The Conquest of America: The Question of the Other*. New York: Harper and Row, 1984.

Tooker, Elisabeth, ed. *Naming Systems*. Proceedings of the American Ethnological Society (1980). Washington, D.C., 1984.

Tostado Gutiérrez, Marcela. *El álbum de la mujer. Antología ilustrada de las mexicanas*. Vol. 2: *Época colonial*. México: Instituto Nacional de Antropología e Historia, 1991.

Trexler, Richard C. *Sex and Conquest: Gendered Violence, Political Order, and the European Conquest of the Americas*. Ithaca: Cornell University Press, 1995.

————, ed. *Gender Rhetorics: Postures on Dominance and Submission in History*. Binghamton, N.Y.: Medieval and Renaissance Texts and Studies, 1994.

Tuñón Pablos, Enriqueta. *El álbum de la mujer. Antología ilustrada de las mexicanas*. Vol. 1: *Época prehispánica*. México: Instituto Nacional de Antropología e Historia, 1991.

Turner, Christina Bolke, and Brian Turner. "The Role of Mestizaje of Surnames in Paraguay in the Creation of a Distinct New World Ethnicity." *Ethnohistory* 41:1 (1993): 139–65.

Tutino, John. *From Insurrection to Revolution in Mexico: Social Bases of Agrarian Violence, 1750–1910*. Princeton: Princeton University Press, 1986.

————. "Power, Class, and Family: Men and Women in the Mexican Elite, 1750–1810." *The Americas* 39:3 (January 1983): 359–82.

Valcárcel, Gustavo. "La condición de la mujer en el estado incaico." *Socialismo y participación* (Lima) 29 (1985): 63–70.

Van Kirk, Sylvia. *Many Tender Ties: Women in Fur-Trade Society, 1670–1870*. Norman: University of Oklahoma Press, 1983.

Vargas G., Luis Alberto, and Eduardo Matos M. "El embarazo y el parto en el México prehispánico." *Anales de Antropología* 10 (1973): 297–310.

Velázquez, Primo Feliciano, ed. and trans. *Códice Chimalpopoca: Anales de Cuauhtitlan y Leyenda de los Soles*. México: Universidad Nacional Autónoma de México, 1975.

Villanueva, Margaret A. "From Calpixqui to Corregidor: Appropriation of

Women's Cotton Textile Production in Early Colonial Mexico." *Latin American Perspectives* 44 (1985): 17–40.

Viqueira Albán, Juan Pedro. *María de la Candelaria. India natural de Cancuc.* México: Fondo de Cultura Económica, 1993.

———. "¿Qué había detrás del petate de la ermita de Cancuc?" In *Catolicismo y extirpación de idolatrías. Siglos XVI-XVII,* edited by Garbiela Ramos and Henrique Urbano, 389–458. Cusco: Centro de Estudios Regionales Andinos "Bartolomé de Las Casas," 1993.

Vogt, Evon Z. *Tortillas for the Gods: A Symbolic Analysis of Zinacanteco Rituals.* Cambridge, Mass.: Harvard University Press, 1976.

Walde, Dale, and Noreen D. Willows, eds. *Archaeology of Gender: Proceedings of the Twenty-second Annual Conference of the Archaeological Association of the University of Calgary.* Calgary: University of Calgary Press, 1991.

Wallace, Anthony. *The Death and Rebirth of the Seneca.* New York: Knopf, 1969.

Warren, J. Benedict. "An Introductory Survey of Secular Writings in the European Tradition on Colonial Middle America, 1503–1818." In *Guide to Ethnohistorical Sources,* edited by Howard F. Cline, vol. 13, pt. 2, of *Handbook of Middle American Indians,* gen. ed. Robert Wauchope, 42–137. Austin: University of Texas Press, 1973.

Wasserstrom, Robert. "Ethnic Violence and Indigenous Protest: The Tzeltal (Maya) Rebellion of 1712." *Journal of Latin American Studies* 12 (1980): 1–19.

Watson, Rubie S. "The Named and the Nameless: Gender and Person in Chinese Society." *American Ethnologist* 13:4 (1986): 619–31.

Wauchope, Robert, gen. ed. *Handbook of Middle American Indians.* 15 vols. Austin: University of Texas Press, 1965–75.

Weaver, Elissa. "Spiritual Fun: A Study of Sixteenth-Century Tuscan Convent Theater." In *Women in the Middle Ages and the Renaissance: Literary and Historical Perspectives,* edited by Mary Beth Rose, 173–205. New York: Syracuse University Press, 1986.

Wood, Robert D. *"Teach Them Good Customs."* Culver City, Calif.: Labyrinthos, 1986.

Wood, Stephanie. "Adopted Saints: Christian Images in Nahua Testaments of Late Colonial Toluca." *The Americas* 47:3 (January 1991): 259–93.

———. "Corporate Adjustments in Colonial Mexican Indian Towns: Toluca Region, 1550–1810." Ph.D. dissertation, University of California, Los Angeles, 1984.

———. "La mujer nahua rural bajo la colonización española. El valle de Toluca durante la época colonial tardía/Rural Nahua Women under Spanish Colonization: The Late-Colonial Toluca Valley." In *Mesoamerican and Chicano Art, Culture, and Identity/El arte, la cultura, y la identidad mesoamer-*

icana y chicana, edited by Robert C. Dash, 78–103. Salem, Ore.: Willamette Journal of the Liberal Arts, supp. series, no. 6 (1994): 78–103.

————. "Rape as a Tool of Conquest in Early Latin America." *CSWS Review* 1992: 18–20.

Ximénez, fray Francisco. *Historia de la provincia de San Vicente de Chiapa y Guatemala.* Vol. 3. Guatemala City: Biblioteca Goathemala, 1929–31.

Zavala, Silvio. *El servicio personal de los indios en la Nueva España.* 3 vols. México: El Colegio de México, Centro de Estudios Históricos, 1984–87.

Zepeda, Tomás. *La educación pública en la Nueva España en el siglo XVI.* México: Editorial Progreso, 1972.

Zorita, Alonso de. *Life and Labor in Ancient Mexico: The Brief and Summary Relation of the Lords of New Spain by Alonso de Zorita.* Edited and translated by Benjamin Keen. New Brunswick: Rutgers University Press, 1963.

Zulawski, Ann. "Social Differentiation, Gender, and Ethnicity: Urban Indian Women in Colonial Bolivia, 1640–1725." *Latin American Research Review* 25:2 (1990): 93–114.

Contributors

Arthur J. O. Anderson died on June 3, 1996, in San Diego, California. The author of a great many works on Nahua society, his greatest contribution to anthropology, ethnohistory, and Nahuatl studies was his collaboration with Charles E. Dibble on the English-language translation of fray Bernardino de Sahagún's 12–volume *Florentine Codex: General History of the Things of New Spain*. In recognition of their achievements Anderson and Dibble were invested with the titles Commander, Order of the Aztec Eagle, by the government of Mexico, and Knight Commander, Order of Isabel la Católica, by the king of Spain.

Louise M. Burkhart is Associate Professor in the Department of Anthropology at the University at Albany, State University of New York. She is the author of *The Slippery Earth: Nahua-Christian Moral Dialogue in Sixteenth-Century Mexico, Holy Wednesday: A Nahua Drama from Early Colonial Mexico*, and numerous other works on colonial Nahua religion.

Pedro Carrasco is Professor of Anthropology and History Emeritus, State University of New York at Stony Brook, and Senior Research Associate, Department of Anthropology, Brandeis University. His major field of specialization is pre-Spanish Mesoamerican society; his most recent book is *Estruc-*

tura politico-territorial del imperio tenochca. La triple alianza de Tenochtitlan, Tetzcoco, y Tlacopan. He currently resides in Framingham, Massachusetts.

Susan Deeds is Associate Professor of History at Northern Arizona University and the author of numerous articles on the ethnohistory of colonial northern Mexico, including "Indigenous Responses to Mission Settlement in Nueva Vizcaya," in the *New Latin American Mission History,* and "Legacies of Resistance, Adaptation, and Tenacity: History of the Native Peoples of Northwest Mexico," *Cambridge History of the Native Peoples of the Americas.* She is completing a book manuscript on the impact of Spanish colonialism among Tarahumara, Tepehuan, Acaxee, Xixime, and Concho Indians in Nueva Vizcaya.

Kevin Gosner, Associate Professor of History at the University of Arizona, is the author of *Soldiers of the Virgin: The Moral Economy of a Colonial Maya Rebellion* and numerous other works relating to Maya populations in the Chiapas region of Mexico.

Robert Haskett, Associate Professor of History at the University of Oregon, is the author of *Indigenous Rulers: An Ethnohistory of Town Government in Colonial Cuernavaca* as well as a number of articles centered on indigenous society and culture in what are now the states of Morelos and Guerrero. He is coeditor of the Mesoamerican Ethnohistory section of the *Handbook of Latin American Studies* and is currently working on two book-length manuscripts.

Rebecca Horn is Associate Professor in the Department of History at the University of Utah. She is Associate Series Editor of the Nahuatl Series, University of California, Los Angeles, the author of *Postconquest Coyoacan: Nahua-Spanish Relations in Central Mexico, 1519–1650,* and is working on a book-length project based on Nahuatl-language texts by peoples of central Mexico.

Marta Espejo-Ponce Hunt is Professor Emerita in the Department of History at El Camino College in Torrance, California. Her research specialty is social change among colonial Spanish and indigenous populations in Yucatan, Mexico, and she is the author of several works on that subject. She currently resides in San Diego, California.

Frances Karttunen is Senior University Research Scientist at the Linguistics Research Center, University of Texas at Austin. Her publications include language contact studies, Nahuatl studies, and, most recently, *Between Worlds: Interpreters, Guides, and Survivors.*

Susan Kellogg, Associate Professor of History, University of Houston, is the author of *Law and the Transformation of Aztec Culture, 1500–1700.* Her interests lie in the area of colonial Latin America, ethnohistory, and women's history.

Leslie S. Offutt, Associate Professor of History and Director of Latin American Studies at Vassar College, is a specialist on colonial Mexican social history and ethnohistory. She is the author of *Una sociedad urbana y rural en el norte de México. Saltillo a fines de la época colonial* and several articles on the Tlaxcalan colony of San Esteban de Nueva Tlaxcala. She recently completed a manuscript on northeastern New Spain.

Matthew Restall is Assistant Professor of Colonial Latin American History at Boston College. He is the author of *The Maya World: Yucatec Culture and Society, 1550–1850* and *Life and Death in a Maya Community: The Ixil Testaments of the 1760s* and coeditor (with Susan Kellogg) of *Dead Giveaways: Indigenous Testaments of Colonial Mesoamerica and the Andes.*

Susan Schroeder is Professor of History at Loyola University Chicago. She is the author of *Chimalpahin and the Kingdoms of Chalco,* general editor of the six-volume *Codex Chimalpahin,* coeditor and cotranslator (with Arthur J. O. Anderson) of volumes 1 and 2 of the *Codex,* and editor of *The "Pax Colonial" and Native Resistance in New Spain.* She has also published in the areas of women, health, indigenous society, and, most recently, Jesuits and Nahuas.

Lisa Mary Sousa is a doctoral candidate at the University of California, Los Angeles, completing her dissertation on native women in central Mexico and Oaxaca during the colonial period. Her research specialties include native concepts of the body, the construction of gender, and Mixtec women's roles in colonial riots. She is the coeditor and cotranslator (with Stafford Poole and James Lockhart) of the original Nahuatl account of the apparition and miracles of the Virgin of Guadalupe (forthcoming).

Ronald Spores is Professor Emeritus in the Department of Anthropology at Vanderbilt University. He is a specialist on the archaeology and ethnohistory of the Mixtecs in Oaxaca and is well known for his many publications on that subject, which include *The Mixtec Kings and Their People* and *The Mixtecs in Ancient and Colonial Times.* He currently resides in Oaxaca.

Stephanie Wood is Assistant Professor of History at the University of Oregon and the author of numerous articles on colonial Mexican history. She is coeditor of the Mesoamerican Ethnohistory section of the *Handbook of Latin American Studies* and has two monographic works nearing completion.

Index

Note: *Although there is considerable overlap in the ethnic designations of Aztecs, Mexicas, and Nahuas, there are also important differences. Contributors' use of these terms has been preserved as much as possible. Readers searching for broad cultural indicators must therefore search all three categories.*

Acaxees, 255, 256, 257. *See also* Sierra Madre peoples
Achiutla, Oaxaca, 190–93
Acosta, José de, 159
Adorno, Rolena, 339n.52
Africans, 328. *See also* Racial and cultural mixtures
Aguilar, Jerónimo de (interpreter), 297, 300, 301, 302, 306, 307
Alcaldes mayores, 136, 155, 202, 225, 378n.68; and *repartimiento de mercancías/efectos*, 225, 226, 228, 229, 405n.32. *See also Corregidores*
Alva Ixtlilxochitl, don Fernando de (Nahua historian), 93, 94, 301
Alvarado, Pedro de (conqueror), 94, 95, 102, 188, 306, 307
Alvarado, Pedro de (indigenous lord), 188
Alvarado Tezozomoc, don Fernando (Nahua historian), 37, 40–41, 44, 49, 321, 348n.94
Amecameca (Amaquemecan), Chalco, 83
Andean societies: gender complimentarity, 428n.24; gender and imperial expansion, 319; gender and militarism, 319; gender and parallelism, 221;

Inca tranformation of gender structures, 142; and naming patterns, 369n.67; postconquest indigenous women and alliances with Spaniards, 325; postconquest labor hardships for women, 326, 429n.31; urban indigenous women and culture change, 175
Anderson, Arthur J. O., 16, 51, 55, 315, 317
Andrada Montezuma, don Juan de (grandson of Moteucçoma), 92
Antilles, 89, 92
Apaches, 265, 417n.1
Arrom, Silvia, 380n.87
Atlixcatl (husband of doña Isabel Montezuma), 92
Atrisco, Puebla, 99
Axayacatl (Aztec ruler), 37, 82
Aztecs: adultery, 74, 80; baptism, 61; calendar, 350n.2; childbirth, 58, 68, 69, 73–74; child rearing, 59–62; coition, 70, 71, 75; deities, 73; harlots, 83–84; healing, 72, 81; herbs, 72, 73; judges, 55–58; kingdoms of the empire, 102; and *machismo*, 426n.13; marriage, 16, 61, 62, 65, 74, 77; men of high rank, 55–58; men's occupations, 59; men-